Karlton E. Hester, Ph.D.
Director of "Jazz" Studies,
University of California at Santa Cruz

Bigotry and the Afrocentric "Jazz" Evolution

Global Academic Publishing 2004
Binghamton University
Binghamton, New York

Third Edition

Areas of Scholarship:
1. Music / Musicology /2. Africana Studies /3. History
4. Sociology /5. Humanities /6. Biography

ISBN 1-58684-228-5

Reprint of the First Edition formerly published as *From Africa to Afrocentric Innovations Some Call "Jazz"* published by Hesteria Records & Publishing Company (2000); with new Preface.

This Global Academic Publishers Edition of *Bigotry and the Afrocentric "Jazz" Evolution* is a republication of the First Edition published in Ithaca, New York by Hesteria Records & Publishing Company. It is reprinted by arrangement with the author.

Co-distributed by:

Global Academic Publishing
State University of New York at Binghamton
Binghamton, New York, 13902-6000, USA
Tel.: (607) 777-4495 or 6104
F ax: (607) 777-6132
E-mail: gporders@binghamton.edu

African American Innovators, LLC
13 Locksley Road
Glen Mills, PA 19342, USA
Tel.: (610) 361-0166
Fax: (610) 361-0165
E-mail: orders@aainnovators.com

Printed in the United States

To the Memory of My Parents,

Clara Briggs and Daniel Webster Hester

Best wishes . . . .

Peace Profound,

Carlton Webster

Forward to the Third Edition

Racism is alive and well in America, it is a growth industry. We need to understand that white world supremacy (racism) is a *given* fact of life in the world and is not vanishing. Therefore, we cannot, if we are intelligent, continue to use racism as an excuse to not execute our worldview. If this is clear, we will save a lot of hearts and minds that think we can change white people with conversation, spiritual sharing, money or astronomy.... I am convinced without doubt or hesitation, that white world supremacy has to be seen as an organized and deliberated attack on all people of color. And an effective defense against it must be incorporated into the teaching of every Black youth in the world.

—Haki R. Madhubuti, 1991

The term "African American" is witness to the continued exclusion of people of phenotypical African ancestry from an unchallenged claim to call themselves American after over 400 years in this land. I never hear objections to the terms Latin jazz, Japanese jazz, Polish jazz, Brazilian jazz, and now even Chinese jazz, but African-American jazz seems to rub people the wrong way. Why is that? I submit that such objections are under the aegis of a paucity of available history written from the African-American perspective ... one of the greatest stories never told. This sad state of affairs effects students of all hues. What is tragic in all of this is that scientists have recently concluded that the total variance in the human gene pool is at the .001 level. Yet, most of the wars on Earth center on racial or ethnic themes. These are facts that cannot be mitigated by cultural blindness but by raising ourselves to a level where we can identify primarily with the common denominators while still appreciating the idiosyncrasies.

The great battle in any cultural war is for the primacy of symbol.

—Jamal Ali, 1990

It follows that African-American culture and arts can only be properly taught or transmitted in the context of an African worldview, the oldest known worldview on the planet. Otherwise it will become extinct with the next generation of its elders who pass away. Absent this requirement and not even a reasonable facsimile of the cultural tradition results. We are steadfastly approaching a time when no one will be around that knows the difference. A read of history from the African-American or African perspective enables one to see a quite different point of view. What is needed is an examination of African-American culture from the perspective of the African worldview. Dr. Karlton E. Hester's treatise addresses and thoroughly challenges the reader to confront both the overt and vestigial expressions of bigotry that continue to plague the evolution of Afrocentric Jazz.

Some would argue that the jazz world is a shining example of democracy at work. They expound examples that fail to notice the subtleties that characterize modern bigotry. Bigotry is evident where it is claimed that the origins of jazz came from Europe, a claim that was anathema before the advent of The US Congressional designation of Jazz as a National Treasure in 1987 (HCR 57). We hear no disputes with the idea that the Chinese invented gun powder or the Europeans invented symphonic music or opera as we know it. As soon as the Black man claims to be the source of positive value, especially at a time when the value is officially declared to be such, there is a dispute over the label. This is the same music that was during my lifetime not considered to be an art form at all by many music schools that today claim it to be "American" as opposed to African-American. Bigotry is expressed in programs that train artists into the European tradition on the assumption that they will be able to transfer their skills into any other tradition in the Western world. This is no more thoughtful than to believe you can teach Latin and expect the student to be able to speak Chinese. Bigotry is expressed whenever an African-American jazz musician is performing without sheet music and is automatically questioned whether they know how to read music. Those who persist in representing the reading of notation as the most valuable skill a musician can acquire are suggesting that the map is more important than familiarity with the territory, another form of bigotry. ASCAP still has a division on its songwriter submittal form headed "for serious music only" (meaning, of course, European symphonic music) clearly indicating that bigotry is still acceptable where it remains unchallenged. When an organization or school uses the term Afro- or African-American in its name, curiously white people generally tend to avoid the school and the community it is in because of the label. The question is why the label Afro- or African-American music almost always is interpreted by white people as meaning "for" African Americans instead of "by" African Americans or "about" African Americans. The answer is it is just another form of bigotry, ample reason to justify building more organizations dedicated to the preservation of the accurate history and development of jazz, the invention of African Americans under oppression now shared and claimed by the world.

Dr. Hester writes, "James Reese Europe (1881–1919), like Antonin Dvorak (1893), realized that African-American music was a powerful source for the development of an innovative twentieth-century American art form. His critics, though strongly influenced by his music, insisted that his music should model itself after European 'serious' composers to be validated by mainstream America."

You see, we colored people have our own music that is part of us. It's the product of our souls; it's been created by the sufferings and miseries of our race.

—James Reese Europe

Cultural bigotry, however, persists in many forms and is evident in the writings of those who disparage jazz openly and even in the writings of some who portend to recognize its higher value and champion its cause. We are all victims of schooling that taught the history of Europe and its conquests as "world" history. This bias has not been eradicated from the minds of *scholars* by the passing of time. Western traditions of scholarship tend to examine phenomena in terms of structure in order to pinpoint characteristics that can be classified, through analysis and correlation of derived facts. The premise is that of separation or distinction as a value that leads to greater understanding, a cultural bias in itself. This approach is evident in the analysis of the renowned ethnomusicologist, Alan Lomax who wrote:

> Early jazz is probably America's most important cultural contribution. No music had ever been so complex ... *these people* were doing counter point in polyrhythm, and all the parts were being improvised jointly. With virtuosic control of the tone, and with everybody singing through the instrument rather then playing notes from music—singing their own song which was contra to the other song. It was polyrhythmically organized, and improvised at the same time, using the concert instruments of Europe. *There had never been anything like this...* Europeans have a whole different approach to music, and to conversation, and to organizing human interaction, than Africans have. We forget that Africans have a musical culture that goes back 50,000 years! It's the first musical culture.... And they have come over here: they're missionaries in our continent. We're learning from them, step by painful step.... There's no European orchestra that plays that way ... they studied European counter point, and they had the whole African tradition available to them. They put it together, and out of it came the most complicated music that the human species has ever produced. Africa plus Europe: the African love, and the European subtleties and gentleness ...the positive together with the positive.
>
> —Alan Lomax

Even today music education systems are teaching Eurocentric music philosophy and methodology and labeling it "multicultural." African-American students extremely scarce in student jazz classes. For example in my own city the annually sponsored Student Jazz Spectacular in 2001 had only two Black jazz students out of 50 in the performing groups. There was also a dramatic difference in the performance levels of the two student groups based on the conductor's style. The first conductor used the African-American style and they played much better than the second group conducted in the European style. Tragically the African-American students along with the other students are receiving no mentoring from the African-American living masters of the music who are available but are not formally trained licensed teachers. Some of them were in the audience wishing they had more access to the students. Traditionally such access was part and parcel of the Black community, however, since music and art education has been turned over to the schools, non-academic living masters of jazz little or no access to the students. Has our schooling indeed interfered with our education?

Afrocentric Jazz Evolution remains America's greatest cultural export yet is largely unappreciated and widely neglected by both audiences and educators at home. An examination of Western models of the human species will reveal the favoring the rational intellectual sense on the assumption that the best qualities of the life experience are to be found in technology, numbers and material pursuits. Dramatic breakthroughs in consciousness research and theory now warn that our neglect of the creative sense has placed us in the position of training our youth in quantitative skills to become poor computers while ignoring the qualitative potential of the creative mind which the computer will never accomplish. If we don't soon re-awaken the creative genius within us from which culture derives its meaning, we will inherit a world where computers make the decisions, robots do the work and androids police the people to keep them from killing each other. We will have forgotten how to think or have fun and will have never learned to get along with each other. It is only the creative sense and the imagination that are capable of new ideas, examining frames of reference, and establishing scales of value by correlating variables in the context of one's world-view, traditional history, identity, self-image and cultural practices.

The present skewed emphasis in favor of math and science as opposed to the arts extant throughout American's educational establishment, fueled by myopic hindsight, can be held responsible for a tremendous imbalance in the quality of life experience by students whose literacy rates have been plummeting. A cursory history of any artistic modality would illustrate that the vision of the artist has always been the beacon of vision into the unknown future upon which great civilizations have been built. Conversely, the suppression or neglect of the artistic sensibilities is historically the harbinger of societal decay. The eradication of a people's vision and hope can be held responsible for the decline of many great civilizations and is the covert aim of white world supremacy (racism) and cultural bigotry.

Dr. Hester's provocative treatise, *Bigotry and the Afrocentric Jazz Evolution*, posits the gauntlet and sets the stage for the redirection of perspective concerning Afrocentric music in areas of scholarship and general understanding.

Nelson E. Harrison, Ph.D., December 2003
Adjunct Professor
Africana & Ethnic Studies, Community College of Allegheny County (CCAC)
Psychologist, Musician, Composer, Lyricist, and Author

Forward to the First Edition

Periodically, a book arrives that transforms the way we see ourselves and the world around us. *From Africa to Afrocentric Innovations Some Call "Jazz"* does just that. You are about to be taken on a journey through time and ideas. You will be surprised, enlightened, outraged, proud, uneasy, defensive, and most of all challenged; challenged to tie the present with the past, and the past with the future.

We live in a complex world that demands we play many roles. As we struggle for acceptance, it is often easier to look the other way when we know society won't hold us accountable. This selective blindness allows extreme injustices to exist in the world.

As much as "jazz" is a celebration of the human spirit, it is steeped in a darkness which we have been reluctant to face; a darkness of racism, sexism, lies, and exploitation to which we have conveniently turned away. It is that very darkness that has fueled so much of the "jazz" we now exalt, but without the full history, the full story, we can never go beyond the past, only repeat it. To be sure, there will be variations, different faces, different cities, but the result will be the same . . . stagnation and decline.

Dr. Hester has shone a light on the darkness, not with vengeance, but with integrity and discipline. And while *From Africa to Afrocentric Innovations Some Call "Jazz"* goes far to explain and link the integral forces in the development of "jazz," it is not complete. It can never be complete. As "jazz" evolves, so must the dialogue concerning the social, creative, and historical forces behind it. To this, *Juba,* a periodical done in the spirit of this book, is dedicated.

You hold in your hands a book that will liberate all who read it with an open mind, and most importantly, open heart. Dr. Hester's commitment to creativity, truth, and justice are evident on every page. With humility, he has visited the place from which this wonderful tradition we call "jazz" comes. His path illuminates the darkness and points the way to the future. Gratefully, he has given us the map of his journey, and all that is left to do is turn the page. . . .

Bill Johnson
January 2000
Philadelphia, Pennsylvania

Table of Contents

Prologue - An Introduction to Afrocentric Music..xxi

Afrocentric Origins of "Jazz"...xxi

Eurocentric Documentation and Control of African-American Music........................xxx

The Impact of Racism and Sexism xxxv

Summary xxxix

I - Traditional African Music..1

Formulating an Approach to Understanding African Music 1

Africa Before the European Slave Trade..3

Early African Contact with Europe 5

Women, Music, and Religion in Africa 7

Stylistic Regions of African Music..14
    I. Northern Africa...16
    ancient egyptian music...16
    ancient nubian written music 18
    moroccan music 19
    north african women musicians 20

Stylistic Regions of Sub-Saharan African Music..22
    II. Eastern Cattle Area 22
    III. Congo Area 23
    central african republic 24
    cameroon 25
    republic of the congo 25
    the pygmy..26
    IV. Guinea Coast Area 27
    liberia 28
    nigeria...28
    V. Khoisan Area 31
    VI. Sudan..32
    northern sudan..32
    western sudan..32

The Function of African Music in African Culture..33

An Overview of Musical Style..36

Characteristics of African Music...38
    Musical Instruments..40
    Structures of African Rhythms..43
    Classes of African Musicians 44

European Methods of Examining African Culture 46

Summary 49

A Survey of African Kingdoms 49
    Kush (Nubia) 49
    Ancient Ghana 50
    Mali (not the Republic of Mali) 51
    Songhay 51
    Kanem—Bornu 52
    Benin 53

II - The Sociocultural Context in Which African-American Music Emerged 57

The Natives of America 58

Africans' Limited Access to Musical Instruments and
    Performance Venues in America 59

Slave Era Music and Cultural Cross-Fertilization 61

African-American Music Convergence Affected by Sex and Marriage 67

Sociocultural Influences on Seventeenth Century African-American Music 70

Eighteenth-Century Sociocultural Changes 72

Witch Craze 77

III - Traditional African-American Music 81

Music Evolves During the Struggle for Independence and Equal Rights 81

American Folksongs and the Blues: Pre-Civil War 86
    Juba 87
    The Cakewalk and Children's Game Songs 89

American Folksongs and the Blues: Post–Civil War 91

Marches 98

Minstrel Shows 98

The Dawn of Ragtime 102

The Term "Jazz" 103

Musical Influence on Religion, Racism, and Revolution 105
    Voodoo 111

Jim Crow Segregation Perpetuates Segregated Musical Styles 115

Summary 118

IV - Innovators Emerging Between 1900 and 1910 121

Ecumenical Music Retention 121

The Continuation of Double Entendre and Other Modes of Communication 124

Afrocentric Dance and Musical Cross-Fertilization 126

Early Blues 129
    Gertrude "Ma" Rainey—"Mother of the Blues" 130

William Christopher Handy—"Father of the Blues" 134

From Vaudeville to Ragtime 137
    Scott Joplin.. 138
    James Scott.. 141
    Thomas Million Turpin.. 141
    James Reese Europe 142

New Orleans—Dixieland "Jazz" ("Traditional Jazz") 146
    "Buddy" Bolden 148
    William Gary "Bunk" Johnson.. 149
    "Jelly Roll" Morton 149
    "Papa" Celestin, "King" Oliver, and Freddie Keppard 152
    Other New Orleans Instrumentalists 153

Turn-of-the-Century Women Musicians 153

New York—Tin Pan Alley 154

African Musical Influences in the Americas 156
    The Evolution of the Drum Set.. 157
    The Double Bass Evolution 158

V - Innovators Emerging Between 1910 and 1920 167

The Blues Continues to Evolve 168
    Two Influential Rural Blues Musicians 169
    Classic Blues 170
    Bessie Smith... 171

Ida Cox and Migrations to Northern Cities 172
    Mamie Smith 177
    Other Women Instrumentalists... 178

Sidney Bechet and the Early Transition from Clarinet to Saxophone 179

Evolution of the Early Piano 181

Politics and the Twentieth-Century African-American Church on
    the Eve of the Harlem Renaissance.. 192

VI - Innovators Emerging between 1920 and 1930 197

Snapshots of American Society 197

The Effects of Changing American Demographics on Music 198

New Orleans and the Movement East... 199

Swing and Its Precursors... 204
    Fats Waller... 205
    New York During the Harlem Renaissance 207

Chicago Dixieland.. 213

The Jelly Roll Morton Documentary 214

Louis "Satchmo" Armstrong and His Associates 214
    Joe "King" Oliver 220
    Lil Hardin Armstrong.. 221

Bix Beiderbecke 222

Big Bands and the Approaching Swing Era 222
    African-American "Jazz" Bands 223
    Commercial and Middle-of-the-Road Bands 224
    Big Bands Swing 224
    Fletcher Henderson 227
    Duke Ellington 229
    Jimmie Lunceford 233
    Bennie Moten 234
    Count Basie 234
    Glenn Miller 236
    Paul Whiteman 237

The Media Continues to Burgeon 237

VII - Innovators Emerging Between 1930 and 1940 243

The New "Swing" Bands 244

Women's Bands during the Early Twentieth Century 245
    Ina Ray Hutton and Her Melodears 247
    International Sweethearts of Rhythm 249
    Other Women's Bands 252

Emma Barrett 253

Other Women Artists 253

Toward Greater Individual Expression 254
    Art Tatum 254
    Mary Lou Williams 257

The "Age of the Sax Masters" Coleman Hawkins and Lester Young 259
    Coleman Hawkins 259
    Lester Young 261
    Ben Webster and the Influence of Hawkins and Young 262

The Voice Continues to Be a Strong Influence 263
    Billie Holiday 264
    Ella Fitzgerald 267

Ellington's Afrocentricity and the European "Mirage" 269

The European Image of "Jazz" 272
    European "Mirage" and "Jazz" Politics 276
    Benny Goodman 281

Other African-American Dance Bands 282

A Glance at the Development of the Guitar in Early "Jazz" 283

VIII - Innovators Emerging Between 1940 and 1950 291

Basic Blues and Early Precursors of Modern "Jazz" 291

Bebop Ties to Past and Present Cultures 293

Bebop Begins to Evolve 297
    Progenitors of the Bebop Revolution 298

Charlie "Bird" Parker and "Black" Music Downtown 306
Misfortune, Drugs, and Alcohol Enter the Bop Scene 320

Bop Brass Instrumentalists 325
Dizzy Gillespie 325
Melba Doretta Liston 329
Howard McGee and Others 330

Bebop Pianists 332
Earl "Bud" Powell 332
Thelonious Monk 333
Women Bop Pianists 334

Other Bop Era Pianists 335
Dorothy Donegan 335
Lennie Tristano 337

Women Vocalists and Instrumentalists during the 1940s 338
Sarah Vaughan 338
Carmen McRae 339
Pauline Braddy (Williams) 340
Mary Osborne 341

"Progressive Jazz" 343

Summary 344

IX - Innovators Emerging Between 1950 and 1960 349

Continued Resistance to African-American Freedom 349

Changes 350

Miles Davis and "Cool Jazz" 353

Louis Jordan and Sonny Rollins 358

John Coltrane and Other New Approaches to Spontaneous Composition 362

Ornette Coleman 367

Cecil Taylor 369

Sun Ra 372

Charles Mingus 377

Two "Jazz" Harpists in the 1950s 382
Dorothy Ashby 382
Corky Hale 383

Art Blakey 384

Phineas Newborn 385

Summary 386

X - Innovators Emerging Between 1960 and 1970 391

Evolution of Innovative Music for 1960s Audiences 391

Restructuring Musical Approaches 397

Artistic Expression or Entertainment? 400

Betty Carter 403

Alice Coltrane 404

Eric Dolphy and the "Jazz" Critics 404

Albert Ayler 410

The Association for the Advancement of Creative Musicians.................. 411

The Emergence of the Art Ensemble of Chicago 412

Dewey Redman, Art Davis, and the New York Scene 414

Amina Claudine Myers 417

Pharaoh Sanders 418

Archie Shepp 421

Joanne Brackeen 425

Charles Tolliver 426

Toshiko Akiyoshi 427

"Traditional Jazz" Continues 429

1960s Music Outside African-American Culture 429

Summary: The American Society That 1960s Music Reflected 430

XI - Innovators Emerging Between 1970 and 1980 437

Changes Around the World 437

Spiritual "Jazz" and New Musical Settings 438
      Changing Attitudes in Europe 439

Connecting Fusion, Miles Davis, and Jimi Hendrix................................ 440
      Jazz-Funk Fusion.. 444
      Jazz-Rock Fusion.. 445
      Donald Byrd 446

The Crossroads of Stylistic Evolution... 449

More Conceptual Expansion 451
      Charles Mingus Reemerges during the 1970s 451
      Anthony Braxton 452
      The World Saxophone Quartet 455
      Joe Henderson.. 455
      McCoy Tyner... 457

Instrumental Style Continues to Evolve 458
      The Evolution of the Flute 460
      Classical-"Jazz" Fusion and Other New Approaches 465
      Santeria and Musical Freedom 467

A Historical Summary... 471

XII - Innovators Emerging Between 1980 and 2000 477

African-American Music in American Marketplace 477
Emphasis Moves from Innovations to Youthful Image 480

Families of Musicians 483
The Age of the Freelance Musician 487

Snapshot: Bay Area "Jazz" in the Early 1980s 490

The Contemporary Midwestern "Jazz" Scene 494

Rap and Hip-Hop Culture 498

Contemporary Politics & Labeling African-American Culture 502

Summary: Afrocentric Snapshots of a Shrinking Society 507

Preface to
Global Academic Publishing Edition

There is a huge difference between the origin of a culture's music and the influences that affect it as it moves through space and time. *Bigotry and the Afrocentric "Jazz" Evolution* begins with the origins of "jazz" in traditional African society. The approach to rhythm, pitch fluctuation, timbre, melodic construction, and other musical elements at the foundation of "jazz" are a conesquence of the linguistic and musical characteristics of African traditional music. We will examine the cultivation of the seeds of "jazz" within African-American culture and traditions (and within a segregated American society), then explore the various influences that continuously shape the art form as it evolves. This daunting task cannot be effectively and thoroughly accomplished without acknowledging the complex socio-cultural milieu that impacted strongly upon the progenitors of "jazz" who perpetually propel the music forward.

This study is perhaps intended to be more informative than entertaining. It is certainly not a nationalistic diatribe intended to make any group of people feel uncomfortable, superior, inferior, guilty or angry. On the contrary, knowledge should be liberating. If we look at history holistically, and with open minds, we will learn much about the path along which "jazz" and other African American music has evolved on an array of stratified levels.

There are no objective histories, although it is important to try to view history from a "Martian's perspective." Nonetheless, this history, like others, is told from the author's perspective. We reveal as much about our personal perspectives by the thing that we don't say (or don't include) as we do with the things we choose to say or include. Throughout the twentieth century books on American music, written by objective scholars, included only European-American composers. Although this history of an African-derived music is told from an Afrocentric perspective, it has to include the contributions of men and women from a variety of cultures. Many of the countless musicians who are not discussed in the body of the text are included in the biographies and discography on the companion resource CD that supplements this book.

I have learned a great deal about European, Asian and other world music when the study of music history was placed within a framework that illuminated the world in which the music developed. African Americans have endured much suffering that is paradoxically reflected in the beautiful musical contribution to world culture some call "jazz." If we can look at the entire story of this powerful music together, its art and its social context, we may all grow in our understanding of the music and musicians involved.

Music is a healing force in our universe. It is not necessary to filter out all elements of history that make us uncomfortable in order to enjoy learning about art we love and respect. The musicians who poured their love, genius, and sincerity into the music we now enjoy and admire deserve our sincere respect. If they could manage to suffer through the painful and oppressive circumstances that engulfed a large portion of American history, then perhaps it is appropriate to look close enough to understand the environment that shaped their lives and artistic expression. Music, and its social history, is for all to share freely.

Because music reflects life in a uniquely vivid way and does not unfold in neat little self-contained chapters, the structure of this book is at times rhapsodic. For instance, racism and sexism effects all generations of African-American musicians. The element that most often impacts upon the lives and careers of African-American musicians is the socio-cultural environment in which they live and create their expressive art. Likewise, some artists continue to evolve throughout their career. The most dynamic artists cannot be contained within a single stylistic era because their music and range of influence traverses broader terrain. Consequently a few innovators are mentioned in more than one chapter when their stylistic evolution warrants positioning them into a broader chronological span of time.

Karlton E. Hester
June 2003
Santa Cruz, California

Prologue

An Introduction to Afrocentric Music

The spirits of truth and falsehood
Struggle within the heart of man;
Truth born out of the spring of Light.
Falsehood from the well of darkness.
And according as a [hu]man inherits truth
So will [s/he] avoid darkness.

—*Manual of Discipline of the Dead Sea Scrolls*

Afrocentric Origins of "Jazz"

Music, dance, and visual arts remain reliable means through which Africans communicate with God, perpetuate their sociocultural history, and harmonize with nature. In America, music inherited a dominant role in nurturing spiritual, intellectual, and philosophical aspects of African culture for displaced people in a hostile environment. Throughout the history of America, the impact of African-American music has gradually affected all who managed to shed their cultural biases long enough to witness the evolution of its innovative beauty, grandeur, and cultural significance. It is small wonder, therefore, that so many people in the world now want to claim African-American music as their own.

It is important to examine the African past carefully if we are to recognize the elements of African tradition that lie at the foundation of African-American music and culture. Avoiding Afrocentric perspectives in discussions of the development of American culture only postpones the inevitable serious study of the music some call "jazz." Just as we examine European music from European antiquity to the present, we must study the complete history of African-American music. Since African culture is much older, and more obscure to Western readers, the task of surveying the history of the vast African continent is formidable. In this study we can only manage to scratch the surface.

The Afrocentric innovations that some call "jazz" are now recognized as Classic American Music and as an American treasure. This music, the invention of Africans in America under the pressures and limitations of an oppressive society, is America's premier indigenous art form. Tracing the history of African-American music carefully from African roots to the present leads to the discovery of the point at which "jazz" evolved from the categories of "Nigger music" and "race records" to the more lofty status of an American art form. It also forces the question, can "jazz" be referred to as "American" music when the people who created were not recognized unconditionally as American (as opposed to African-American)?

The diversity of languages, sociocultural customs, religious practices, political structures, and metaphysical systems among the numerous African nations served to undermine possibilities of unification among those who later became captive "New World" slaves, especially within the regions that eventually became the United States of America. An extremely eclectic culture was apparent even within the small radius of the Gulf of Guinea, the region from which most slaves were obtained by means of bargaining or larceny. Some areas of Africa remained untouched by slave traders. Other northern countries (particularly desert areas such as Egypt) contributed only a few slaves. The difficulties in communicating between fellow Africans, as well as the weak communication between Africans and Europeans, made it difficult for Africans to appreciate and anticipate the severe consequences of the malfeasance that fell upon their continent. To the foreign European slave traders, the social and cultural diversity within African society was interpreted as uncivilized, disorganized, and backward.

Communal presentations of traditional African music and dance are far removed from more passive Eurocentric performances, where the audience remains still and quiet until "appropriate" times to respond. African music was intense enough to lead those involved in spiritual ritual towards ecstasy. Many African American participants in church services in America "get the Holy Ghost" or become filled with the Holy Spirit in ways similar to the possession that comes during the sustained momentum of the rhythmic, dynamic and melodic intensity of African music and dance ritual.

Gospel music was born from spirituals sung by Africans in America during the slave era. Sacred African American music (force-filtered through Eurocentric Protestant religions) emerged from African roots and served dual purposes that included communication and catharsis. Thomas Dorsey of Georgia coined the term "gospel" at the time of the National Baptist Convention in 1921. Dorsey wrote "Precious Lord" and other popular church songs and became known as "the father of gospel music." Spirituals were songs of hope (prior to the Emancipation Proclamation), while blues developed later, after it was clear that the Civil War (and movement to urban areas) did not bring freedom, equality and prosperity to Africans in America. Gospel music eventually provided Africans in America a music source lighter in character than the heavier lyrics of music emerging during the quest for freedom from slavery. Gospels directed African Americans towards their inner selves allowing them to commune with the Creator on personal levels. Afrocentric music most often involves purposes that include sacred worship, communication, and social commentary.

In 1990, CBS Records released an album by the controversial, and highly popular, rap artists Public Enemy entitled *Fear of a Black Planet*. The media reprimanded the group for its "explicit lyrics," perhaps because the clarity, precision, and unreserved nature of the artists' Afrocentric perspective is exactly the thing that America labored arduously to suppress for centuries. Clearly the Public Enemy artists, like many other African-American citizens, wonder to which "good old days" in the incessant history of slavery and oppression European Americans often refer when attempting to thwart social progress in America.

The development of the notion of European supremacy and the perpetuation of a slave culture required the destruction of the history of African people. Oppression required an attempt at the total repression of the minds, bodies, and spirits of not only those captives imported from Africa as hard laborers, but also those forced to live under the countless lies, delusions, and psychological baggage that also enslaved European-American society. The slave era mentality remained a dominant force in American culture while "jazz" and other African-American music evolved. African-American music becomes distorted or obscured if divorced of its African heritage. The melodies, harmonies, timbres, textures, and formal construction of traditional African music are all elements that African-American music has retained in various form of the music labeled "jazz," blues and spirituals.

African Americans, Native Americans, and other victims of colonial conquest were forced to abandon their indigenous religions and adopt Christianity. Paradoxically, African Americans used this same religion—intended to pacify and subdue them—as one of their primary tools for liberation. Similarly, when the drums were taken away from Africans in America (and African music was forbidden) to further annihilate tribal, familial, and sociocultural structure, African polyrhythms were transformed into a new brand of stylistic syncopation unlike any rhythms the world had ever known. Africans forced to sing European hymns did not merely fuse African and European music. European hymns were subjected to an extraordinary fissional process that combined a multiplicity of musical elements and social convergence, experienced by Africans in America, into a socio-nuclear reactor producing billions of musical "electron volts." "Jazz" was the most electrifying result of this experimentation. Not only were the musical elements and concepts novel, but the composers of twentieth-century "jazz" were more fluent in the performance practice of their musical language than most other twentieth-century composers. European twelve-tone and serial composers created exciting new musical concepts and languages, but few could improvise with their new vocabularies the way most baroque, classical, and romantic composers did during their respective eras.

This investigation involves the historical legacy of musical development that evolved from traditional African music and emerged into the African-American innovations labeled "jazz." It's not intended to deny or diminish the participation and contributions of people of European, Hispanic, Asian, Native-American, or other descent in the history of African-American music. All modern art forms are influenced by numerous ancient determinants from the global community. Consequently, as Henry Wadsworth Longfellow said, "Music is the international language of all mankind." Nonetheless, particular art forms evolve from cultural traditions, patterns, and dialects that determine the shapes, colors, and styles of a given artistic manifestation. We cannot confine "jazz," one of the world's most ecumenical and influential musical genres, to a color like black, brown, red, white, or any other hue or ethnicity. It most certainly does have a specific cultural origin, however, and the African-American innovators responsible for its evolutionary development are the focus of this study.

People say that defining "jazz" is a difficult task. Without a doubt, the music some call "jazz" is an African-American invention evolved in the musical world essentially during the twentieth century. Its evolution from traditional African music into an array of related forms involves African-American field hollers, spirituals, blues, ragtime, classic "jazz," swing, rhythm and blues, bebop, cool, hard bop, free "jazz," funk, soul, fusion, neoclassic "jazz," and rap music. Each new African-American musical invention retained elements of traditional African music. It will certainly continue to evolve and retain Afrocentric musical vocabulary in the next millennium.

A clear relationship exists between the African-American use of "blue notes" and similar traditional African stylistic elements in music such as the traditional Fulani song "Nayo" (as sung by Juldeh Camara).[1] Within the context of some African songs we hear emphasis on a pentatonic scale embellished with a flexibility of pitch. These qualities were conspicuous characteristics of early rural blues. Certain Baoulé traditional songs demonstrate a pitch set that has much in common with rural blues tonality. Qualities identifiable with African-American Swing "feel" and "riff" technique, as well as the use of ostinato patterns as grounding structures for polyrhythms and heterophony, have parallels in Malinké and other African music south of the Sahara. A comparison between "All Blues" by Miles Davis with the bass pattern heard in the Malinké "Dance of the Hunters" displays striking resemblance.[2] The blue notes, call-and-response patterns, and other musical elements and devices found in blues and "jazz" are also apparent in various traditional musical forms throughout the African continent. African music is often directly associated with dance and the multidimensional effect in most performance presentations.

The inclinations toward "blue notes" in African music were difficult for Europeans and European Americans to understand before they were exposed to African-American blues. The ability of tonal systems to support both the major and minor third within a single chord of a given key baffled Europeans when they first heard it in Africa. The frequent employment of the unresolved tritone[3] in African music (also a prominent characteristic of African-American "jazz") made African music sound dissonant to the European ear. Likewise, the structuring of musical intonation along flexible lines of tuning aligned with the natural harmonics of vibrating objects (tube, string, wooden or metal bar, etc.) stood in opposition to the even temperament of the European piano. A European-American missionary arrogantly reports:

> But it is surprising that—since our scales are new to them—they at first need a little careful training, or at least the lead of a clear-toned organ reasonably played. Otherwise they are not unlikely to substitute the tones of their own scales. The result is indescribable. Imagine a large congregation singing the doxology with all their might, and about half of them singing G minor instead of G major! But the comparison is inadequate. The singing in some mission congregations is enough to cause a panic.[4]

The blues introduced a harmonic orientation based on an Afrocentric attitude regarding tonal resolution (unstable dominant 7th chords became stable harmonically) and the verticalization associated melodic anomalies. Later, bebop masters heard more involved implications inherent in older blues forms and explored the upper regions of the harmonic series to justify harmonic expansion. Rural blues was not originally the 12–bar standardized type popularized later. The rural blues players invented their own personal forms, refusing to be restricted to standard 4/4 (or any other) meter, choosing instead to treat meter in a flexible manner as well. Listening to Lightnin' Hopkins sing Willie Dixon's song *My Babe* (either live or on studio recordings) is a case in point.

My Baby don't stand no cheating, my Babe.	[circa 4 bars]
My Baby don't stand no cheating, my Babe.	[circa 4 bars]
My Baby don't stand no cheating, no back-talking or midnight creepin',	[circa 4 bars]
My Babe . . . two little children by My Babe . . . don't let me catch you with My Babe. . . . etc.	[circa 5–6 bars]

A connection with sacrosanct or the more ethereal essences of music can be traced through Bantu rain songs, African-American work songs, sea shanties, ring shouts, spirituals, blues, and other Afrocentric musical forms. Relationships between sacred and secular music and art are evident whether observing presentations of the *pokot* witch doctor of Kenya (who draws evil spirits out of patients in the *liakat* ritual) or listening to Lightnin' Hopkins (who reminds us that the "Blues is a Feeling")[5] and other African-American blues singers. The close harmonic, melodic, and rhythmic kinship between blues and spirituals is an indication of the bond that joins these forms.

Recordings of voodoo ceremonies in Haiti are good examples of interdisciplinary Afrocentric celebration and African retention in the "New World" regions where Africans were not completely denied their African heritage.[6] Music for such spiritual occasions resembles traditional African ceremonial sources more closely than any African-American musical style. Nonetheless, the music of "jazz" artists such as Sun Ra, the Art Ensemble of Chicago, and other modern innovators embrace African tradition and are strongly influenced by African music and culture.

A student once asked, "Isn't most of society naturally inclined toward tonal music because it is a natural musical phenomenon to which we grow up listening; and avant-garde music apparently opposes this (sonic) orientation?" This question has some merit, but it reveals what is often a Western indoctrination that presupposes that Eurocentric orientation is pandemic and "natural" for all of world society. An early twentieth-century book (that is a part of the Schomburg collection) containing discussions on musical practices in Central Africa shows elements of the European-American bigotry, fascination, and ambivalence that many people carried with them throughout Africa.

The native songs are elementary but fascinating. Few white men, however, can sing them; for the scales, or tone-systems, upon which most of them are based, are entirely different from our major and minor modes. Their scales have not a distinct tonic, that is, a basal tone from which the others in the system are derived, as, for instance, the first tone, do, of our major scale. It follows that the cadences of their music are not clearly defined; or, as a friend of mine would say, "They don't taper off to an end like ours."[7]

Every analysis Robert Milligan has made regarding African music tends to assume an Eurocentric aesthetic musical model as the supreme standard. Typically, he makes little effort to discover whether African musicians organized their music around an array of fundamental tones that might have evaded Milligan's ear. Yet, he admits, "Although their music is so difficult for the white man, the natives learn our music with astonishing ease, even their oldest men and women, and sing it well—if they have half a chance."[8]

Technically speaking, placing the musical focal point on the lower portion of the harmonic series (musical intervals including the tonic, octave, fifth, fourth, and major and minor third) is no more natural than the modern emphasis on the upper intervals of the same series (namely, major and minor seconds, quarter tones, etc.). African music, and later many African-American counterparts, have preferred to include a wide range of intervalic, timbral and rhythmic possibilities. This too is a very natural inclination, though many Westerners initially perceived of such musical choices as chaotic or dissonant. Understanding the relationship between those stylistic inclinations shared between African and African-American culture is key to developing a knowledgeable appreciation for the Afrocentric innovations labeled "jazz." A thorough and systematic sociocultural journey, from the dawn of African culture through early African-American music, is necessary to expose the Afrocentric roots of "jazz."

Despite Milligan's difficulties in adopting Afrocentricity when analyzing African music, he spent enough time in Africa to gain an awareness of the close relationship between African and African-American music. He eventually realized the importance of African-American music despite his arrogant tone:

So great a musician as Dvorak, when he came to America, was profoundly moved by the original melodies of the American Negro, and became their enthusiastic champion. Indeed, they inspired the most beautiful of all his symphonies, the one entitled, "Aus der Neuen Welt." I do not refer, of course, to the so-called Negro melodies composed by white men. Some of these are beautiful; but they are not Negro melodies. They do not express the Negro's emotional life and he does not care much for them. Those wonderful songs of the Fisk Jubilee Singers are the real thing. Some of the very melodies may have originated in Africa. Others are more developed than any that I heard in Africa; but they are very similar, and they use the same strange scales, which makes them unfamiliar to our ears and difficult to acquire. Among them, I really believe, are occasional motives as capable of development as those of Hungary.

For a long time the music of Africa defied every attempt on my part to reduce it to musical notation. Very few persons have made the attempt; for it is easier to reduce their language to writing than their music. At first it seemed as inarticulate and spontaneous as the sound of the distant surf with which it blended, or the music of the night-wind in the bamboo.[9]

What are other distinguishing features of this music with African roots? In addressing an audience at the African Heritage Studies Association's 30th Annual Conference (March 1998), Dr. Clenora Hudson-Weems (of the University of Missouri–Columbia) suggested that the most conspicuous difference between most Eurocentric and Afrocentric literary approaches is that the former emphasizes form while the latter prefers to focus on content. Regarding Afrocentric literature, Hudson-Weems implies that structure is better determined if extracted from content, and that form itself is not fascinating as an empty package alone.

Transferring that theory to the analysis of music, I find a similar tendency among Eurocentric theorists and musicologists to emphasize the analysis of musical forms and formulas. Central to their investigations, for example, are the examination of music based on the sonata form, the application of Schenkerian and other forms of musical analysis, the tracing of the Golden Section,[10] the cataloguing of materials, or the search for tonal coherence. Afrocentric discussions more often attend to personal styles, musical anomalies, virtuosity, and elusive elements such as spiritual or aesthetic concerns. The two approaches are certainly not mutually exclusive, but the different emphases may reflect aspects of cultural orientation.

Analysis can often help our understanding of a musical subject, but usually only if the system of analysis is derived from the music under investigation. Western analysis generally involves tearing the subject apart without regard for a particular creative goal. At the conclusion of the analysis of music, for instance, there is often little produced other than catalogues of rhythms, scales, chords, and cadential formulas. Once isolated, these elements are like the brushes, paints, canvases, and colors used to produce a beautiful painting: isolated ingredients used in the production of art that tell little of the power and beauty produced from the wellsprings of artistic imagination. Music involves the direct transference of human emotions and thought through sonic images. Musical meaning thus remains beyond the reach of words. Therefore, we often look to the environment upon which artists reflect to find greater appreciation and understanding of their music.

Many African-American "jazz" artists insist that a spiritual orientation is the foundation of their music. As their titles and comments often suggest, some African-American innovators and practitioners insist that their musical expression is inseparable from African-American spirituals, gospel, and other religious music.

Dean C. J. Bartlett and the Reverend John S. Yaryan invited Ellington to present a concert of sacred music in Grace Cathedral (San Francisco).

A review of the September 16, 1965, concert (in the *Saturday Review*) entitled "The Ecumenical Ellington" stated: "These were musicians offering what they did best—better than any others in the world—to the glory of God." Hundreds of newspapers across America carried a UPI report of the concert under the headline "Duke Ellington Talked to the Lord in Grace Cathedral Last Night." Ellington discussed his attempts to "see God" in his autobiography:

> If you can see by seven caroms to the seventh power, then you can see God. If you could see total carom, to total power, you would be thought of as God. And since you can't do either, you are *not* God, and you cannot stand to see God, but if you happen to be the greatest mathematician, you will discover after completing carom that God is here with you.

> So be wise and satisfied with the joy that comes to you through the reflection and miracle of God, such as all the wonders and beauty we live with and are exposed to on earth.

> There have been times when I thought I had a glimpse of God. Sometimes, even when my eyes were closed, I saw. Then when I tried to set my eyes—closed or opened—back to the same focus, I had no success, of course. The unprovable fact is that I believe I have had a glimpse of God many times. I believe because believing is believable, and no one can prove it unbelieveable.[11]

In addition to the bond between sacred and secular dimensions, African-American art forms tend to remain inseparable. Albert Murray considers the sounds contained in music of composers like Ellington onomatopoetic renderings that reflect the dialect, motion, and styles of African-American culture. Ellington was a modernist who developed a rich vernacular African-American compositional language (in collaboration with the creative members of his orchestra) capable of orchestral variety and excitement that remains inimitable. With Ellington and other masters of African-American music in mind, Albert Murray's literature uses "jazz" and blues as a model. The works of visual artist Romare Bearden (1912–1988) were also heavily influenced by "jazz" and blues (*Jazz Village, At the Savoy, Fancy Sticks, In E Sharp,* etc.). Bearden leads the viewer through a prism of his ideas and perspectives with vivid color and textures. His subjects involve collages that create rhythm and form that reflect his childhood in Harlem during the Harlem Renaissance. Fats Waller, Ellington, and other well-known artists visited Bearden's home frequently during their childhood.

Denying Africans in America direct access to past traditions forced them to become the most culturally free people in the world. While American composers continued to express their creative ideas through Eurocentric musical language, they could not expect to achieve a high degree of affinity with an indigenous American musical language. Ellington's musical dedications to Harlem, on the other hand, contain the power, subtlety, elegance, pain, complexity, intensity, and emotion found within that community during the first half of the century. No composer could produce such vivid American imagery without engaging both African-American and European-American culture directly the way Ellington managed. Albert Murray suggests that most Americans preferred attempts at building European edifices, social constructs, and cultural emulation on the American landscape. It is easy to distinguish between music reflecting original cultural patterns created by people of a given cultural milieu from music created through imitation of stylistic innovations from the fringe of a culture, and other such derivative products.

Those musicians and music scholars who refuse to seriously consider the importance of African-American music enter into debates over "where to find a definitive American Music." At a lecture at Cornell University, when composer Lucas Foss mentioned that he abandoned improvisation because he could not master it, a student in the audience asked the appropriate question: "Why didn't [Foss] study with any of the countless number of African-American 'jazz' masters in New York City?" Albert Murray discusses the significance of African-American blues and "jazz":

> And anybody who introduces even the sleeping bag sequence in *For Whom the Bell Tolls* as evidence that Hemingway was out to reduce the world to the gratification of the sex urge would be as intellectually irresponsible as those who describe so-called black Africans as childlike, simple creatures of sensual abandon. An outsider—say, a blonde from the jet set—who comes into a down-home-style hall and pulls off her shoes, lets her hair down, and begins stomping and shaking and jerking and grinding in the spirit of personal release, liberation, and abandon, does not represent freedom; she represents chaos, and only an outsider would do it. Only an outsider could be so irresponsible to the music. Insiders know that the music and dance, like all other artistic expression, require a commitment to form. As is the case with all other artistic expression, they achieve freedom not by giving in to the emotions but through self-control and refinement of technique. Swinging the blues and swinging *to* the blues, however free they may seem to the uninitiated listener and onlooker, are never acts of wild abandon; they are triumphs of technical refinement and are among the most sophisticated things a human being can do.[12]

Many contemporary "Young Lions" and other artists reconstruct musical images from the past, while neglecting the relevance of their own rich contemporary environmental contexts. The best of these Young Lions, performing music that shadows bygone eras, enjoy popularity. African-American innovators, however, remain ostracized from the mainstream music industry. Younger players do not have a thriving music community like Ellington's Harlem from which to absorb and paint as music compositions. "Jazz" programs at most universities in America generally employ European-American faculty, ignoring the potentially rich educational resources that the former members of bands led by Ellington, Count Basie, and other seminal African-American ensembles could provide. Although many African Americans died fighting for their country during two world wars, music innovators such as Charlie Parker, Dizzy Gillespie, Miles Davis, Ornette Coleman, and John Coltrane, were never among those musicians employed by American universities and symphony orchestras. American society lost a great deal, as a consequence, when African-American artists could not share their skills and musical knowledge, and be honored as eminent American composers. Thus young students are denied direct exposure to the process of musical experimentation, innovation, and mentoring enjoyed by earlier developing musicians. Most African-American musicians today learn a significant amount of their music through recordings alone, or within Eurocentric studies at conservatories and university music departments.

Eurocentric Documentation and Control of African-American Music

People on the fringe of the progenitors' culture generally define African-American creative expression. This condition stems from the hegemony of Eurocentric discrimination. The contemporary African-American community is less a victim of slave mentality and oppression than in the past, yet problems related to the exploitation of African-American music continue to intensify. The recent reduction of African-American "jazz" to "neoclassic" imitation by talented African-American musicians is telling. Clearly a movement driven more by business capital than revolutionary artistic motivation, the music of the last two decades stands in striking opposition to the legacy of evolutionary experimentation and innovations of earlier years.

During the era of slave exploitation, language and culture were manipulated to erase African heritage from the minds of Africans in the Americas and to promote negative images of things associated with Africa. Terms such as "jazz," "serious music," "race records," and other politically charged labels perpetuate social notions that foster racial division and economic control.

According to many labeling practices in American society, African Americans produce "popular" music regardless of the actual level of popularity enjoyed by a given style, or despite degrees of musical sophistication and complexity involved. This "popularity," consequently, erodes the music's credibility and deems it unworthy of institutional support or serious study. Only European or certain European-American music are "serious" music. Labels change as needed, however. The increased popularity and prestige of "jazz" finally brings forth the modern phrases "vernacular American music" and "America's classical music." Some innovators in America prefer to find their own labels, such as the Art Ensemble of Chicago's "Great Black Music" or, as Makanda Ken McIntyre puts it, simply "African-American music":

The indigenous music of America is not "jazz," but rather it is music in the African and American tradition since the elements that make up the music come from the African slave and the European. The African Slave brought rhythm, timbre and melody; and integrated them with the European instruments and the twelve tones that make up Western European music. Hence, we have African American music.

Not that the African slave in America did not have instruments, but rather, they were taken away—unlike slavery in the Caribbean, where the slaves were allowed to keep their instruments. Consequently, the connection with Africa is more direct, since the vast majority of musical instruments utilized in the Caribbean are built similar to West African instruments.[13]

Duke Ellington never liked the term "jazz," but acquiesced at times for the sake of clarity. Ellington felt that "jazz is based on the sound of our native heritage. It is an American idiom with African roots—a trunk of soul with limbs reaching in every direction, to the frigid North, the exotic East, the miserable, swampy South, and the Swinging West."[14] When elements of African-American music are freely employed, they are often paradoxically described as too complex, too simplistic, chaotic, or excessive. On the other hand, baroque polyphony is considered ingenious because it conforms to a complex, systematic, Eurocentric musical logic. With each new generation, nonetheless, the understanding of ecumenical musical principles evolves, and a gradual softening of social bigotry takes place. Ellington realized many years ago that this brings an ever increasing number of serious music students and new listeners to study "jazz."

Yet I have reason to be optimistic, for with all those good musicians graduating from the conservatories, the future has got to be bright. Of course, the same people who say they don't like electrically amplified guitar and basses will often add that they "just love a string section." The basic concern should not be the instrumentation, but the taste and skill of the person who plays it. . . . The American listening audience is actually growing more mature every day. I believe the brainwashing will soon subside, because all the brainwashers have become wealthy. Their problem now is that their children, too, have been brainwashed.[15]

Much of the labeling and documentation of "jazz" is done by people with little musical training or understanding of "Black" culture. If those who make decisions regarding the documentation, dissemination, and artistic status of "jazz" were required to pass through Afrocentric musical training, a new governing hierarchy would be established. Those musicians experienced in African-American Culture are best equipped with proper understanding of the aesthetic, intellectual, and spiritual principles involved in the creation of "jazz." The progenitors of innovative African-American music might then be regarded as those best qualified to define and control their art form. Miles Davis' remarks regarding the comment of a woman in the audience at one of his performances is clear and appropriate. The listener complained that she couldn't understand Davis' music. This was Davis' sagacious reply: "It took me twenty years study and practice to work up to what I wanted to play in this performance. How can she expect to listen five minutes and understand it?"[16] Ethnomusicologists stopped referring to African polyrhythms as chaotic cacophony and simplistic only after beginning to transcribe African music. Their transcriptions revealed levels of rhythmic complexity and metrical organization transcending the rhythmic concepts of Eurocentric composers. Andrew White was the first theorist/musician to transcribe all of Coltrane's solos, exposing their richness and complexity (to the embarrassment of those who claimed Coltrane was playing strains of "meaningless notes"). Most of those who transcribe "jazz" extract a single instrument and write out portions of that part in standard Eurocentric notation. More challenging and adventurous performances of African-American masters are rarely subjected to total transcription. Total transcription, of all instrumental or vocal parts involved in a composition, would be the starting point for serious theoretical study of "jazz." Rarely do theorists transcribed entire compositions such as Ornette Coleman's "Free Jazz," John Coltrane's "Ascension," Cecil Taylor's "Unit Structures," or Sun Ra's "Of the Other Tomorrow."

The problems that surround the documentation of African-American music are complex. Anthony Braxton discusses some aspects of the problems rooted in the African-American community in Graham Lock's *Forces in Motion.*

> Here we are, you and I, sitting in this room because you're interested enough in my music to do the book. So OK, that's great. For those African American intellectuals who look at this book and say, "Well Graham Lock is white." . . . Ted Joans, for instance, put down Ross Russell for *Bird Lives*—that was ten years ago, we're still waiting for Mr. Joans' book! I can name—I won't do it, but I could—fifteen African American intellectuals, so-called, who would protest to heights if they see an article or a book on Benny Carter, say, written by a white American intellectual. They would cry out—and rightfully—that a black guy could have written this too. OK, but where are these people? I see only a handful of African Americans at my concerts— well, Braxton's the so-called White Negro, I'm not a good example—but I don't see many at Art Ensemble's concerts, I don't see many at Dexter Gordon's concerts. Are we gonna blame this on white people too?[17]

Braxton later acknowledges, "Dr. Yosef ben-Jochannan: this is an African American intellectual who is like a shining tower in an ocean of despair, an ocean of negligence." Curiously, Braxton fails to mention that African-American authors are less likely to find publishers eager to publish their controversial manuscripts. He also ignores the literary and theoretical contributions of Alain Locke, Amiri Baraka, Bill Cole, Eddie Harris, Wendell Logan, Albert Murray, Andrew White, George Russell, David Baker, and other African-American musicians and scholars. Many musicians would prefer to write about their music themselves. Unfortunately, Louis Armstrong,

Duke Ellington, Charles Mingus, and Miles Davis are among the few African-American master musicians who were able to get their autobiographies published. Nevertheless, Braxton is accurate in pointing out the scarcity of African-American listeners found at "Black jazz" concerts.

European theorists and musicologists write most European music history and theoretical analysis. Social context is often an important element of such studies. Histories of Jewish music during World War II benefit from ample descriptions of the horrible social and political circumstances surrounding the artistic production in Germany under the Nazi regime. Historical research that avoided mentioning the intense brutality and genocide of the time would be poor and insensitive indeed. People may well feel that such histories are better told by qualified Jews than by Aryan Germans. A related set of considerations must be applied to African-American music scholarship and theory.

Jehoash Hirshberg's *Music in the Jewish Community of Palestine 1880–1948* presents a social history that begins with the Jewish immigration to Palestine and ends with the declaration of the State of Israel.[18] Hirshberg discusses the lives of Jewish musicians in the context of two world wars, local skirmishes, and a full-scale national war, then considers the effect that waves of immigrants and refugees had on the development of Jewish music in Palestine. Few would criticize such comprehensive and candid research as polemic. Yet writers often consider frank Afrocentric viewpoints "disturbed and disturbing," as Gene Lees describes *Miles: The Autobiography*. There are those who seem to view any frank Afrocentric position as polemic. The difference in perception is difficult to reconcile.

Although many of the progenitors of the African-American music some call "jazz" have always considered that label for their music derogatory, yet it becomes increasingly clear that artists have little control over the labeling, presentation, documentation, and dissemination of their work. Christopher Harlos feels this is why African-American musicians have wanted to write autobiographies (to define their music themselves).

> One motivation behind the jazz player's move to autobiography, for example, is signaled in the opening of *Treat it Gentle* where Sidney Bechet states flatly, "You know there's people, they got the wrong idea of Jazz," and then a few pages later he asserts it was only "a name white people have given to the music." Likewise, in *Music Is My Mistress*, Duke Ellington makes a point of the fact that he was disinclined to use the term "jazz" as a way of classifying his own musical endeavors.[19]

People did not apply the label "America's Classical Music" to African-American music during the eras in which the music of Scott Joplin, Buddy Bolden, Louis Armstrong, Fats Waller, Jelly Roll Morton, Art Tatum, Fletcher Henderson, Duke Ellington, or Count Basie evolved. Those referred to as "Black," "White," "Asian," "Indians," "Hispanic," "Africans," "Europeans," etc., have composed and performed twentieth-century African-American music. Unfortunately, there are no people referred to as simply Americans in the United States. Is "jazz" becoming a catalyst for the long overdue transformation of this unfortunate social tradition? How has American society come to produce vernacular American music?

If the system used to label citizens is a strong indicator, then there is little chance of creating legitimate vernacular American music in the twentieth century. French composers may compose French music; Japanese composers compose Japanese music; Russian composers compose Russian music. Alexander Pushkin did not produce Afro-Russian literature. But who are the creators of native American music? There are only Native Americans ("Red"), African Americans ("Black"), European Americans ("White"), Hispanic Americans ("Brown"), Asian Americans ("Yellow"), biracial Americans (here we run into problems with colorful labels!), and other such people. There is no category for anyone who is just an "American" on employment or college applications. Since African Americans are the creators of blues, spirituals, "jazz," and other "race" music, why is the music produced by African-American innovators referred to as American music? This does not occur with Latin "jazz" (even when performed by Pamela Wise, an African American), European-American country music (when performed by Charlie Pride, an African American), or Jewish klezmer music (in the hands of Don Byron, an African American) in America.

In a country that has often asserted that African Americans have contributed little to American culture, should labeling "jazz" "American Classical Music" arouse skepticism, suspicion, and trepidation? Will African-American innovators and music scholars finally enjoy appropriate equity and economic benefits commensurate to their European-American musical colleagues? If so, this change should be reflected in a new attitude toward the performance and preservation of African-American music. The conventional terms used by European-American industries to identify African-American music thus remain severely flawed, as McIntyre suggests in the liner notes to his recording *Home:*

> There have been volumes written about "jazz" and the word/term has become synonymous with the music created in America. I have problems with accepting the term "jazz" as the title of the music since the creators of the music did not title the music, but rather it was the writer, F. Scott Fitzgerald who coined the phrase which has become the box for the music created by the African slave in America. Moreover, the term "jazz" was part of the African American vernacular, however, the meaning had nothing to do with music, but it did relate to sex. In fact the definition of the word during the first and second decades of the twentieth century was to copulate.
>
> The term is rather nebulous regarding its heritage. Moreover, it raises questions. For example: What is "jazz"? Are there "jazz" people? Where do they come from? Where did it originate? Who were the creators? What caused it to happen? Is it racial or is it national? Unquestionably, the questions can never be answered by someone who has the ability to manip-

ulate the language. But when one is seeking logical answers, the questions become unanswerable.[20]

The music once sold on "race records" is now a slightly more cherished commodity locally and abroad, and recognized as America's only indigenous art form. One of the consequences of the small measure of success "jazz" and other African-American music now enjoys is the fight over whether the "jazz" art form is community property.

The function and purpose of many general labels used to identify cultural components, social artifacts, and other aspects of our environment, remain fairly unchanged. Such terms are often geared toward justifying actions, maintaining control, and perpetuating prevailing political agenda. It could be argued, for example, that under the cloak of the terms "war," "religion," and "slavery," "New World" men have killed and raped more people, stolen more property ("from sea to shining sea"), and altered or suppressed more information than any other people since antiquity. Propaganda disseminated by black-faced minstrels of the nineteenth century, who promoted racial stereotypes and hatred, seem now converted into media portrayals of criminal African-American men or Hispanic-American men, and unwed African-American or Hispanic-American women. Although African-American citizens represent around 15 percent of the population in the United States, this statistic is not reflected in any positive way in American society. However, well over half of the prison population is composed of African Americans and other "minorities."[21]

Many Americans still refer to Native Americans as "Indians" although none of the numerous tribes labeled as such ever had anything to do with India. Just as many African-American musicians resigned themselves to accept the term "jazz," some Native Americans eventually began to refer to themselves as "Indians." Other labels invented by Europeans, such as Negro, Nigger, Colored, Mulatto, etc., share similar histories, political purposes and social patterns. Labels (for music or anything else) can serve political agendas, therefore, and are not always simply for the purpose of organization and clarity.

The Impact of Racism and Sexism

It is often difficult to approach modern issues involving residual racism, sexism, and other social malfeasance stemming from European colonization. The theory that "might makes right" has enabled conquering armies to dictate the gods that people worship, the history that they believe, the marriages that are socially appropriate, and the art that is aesthetically significant. While a dominant culture may shape fragile and temporary historical records, it in no way changes the course of historical actuality. Nonetheless, those who suffered the limitations and hardships of slave era brutality and oppression could expect punishment if they complain about social conditions or attempted to assert perspectives that contradicted prevailing notions.

Racism is one of the primary factors that thwarts an understanding and appreciation of African-American music. Racism has been a topic of numerous debates and articles in "jazz" publications over the years. It is a complex topic that cannot be investigated meaningfully when Europeans or European-Americans are the sole authors and participants in such discussions.

Given the history and nature of American society, one cannot assume that non-African Americans have documented and evaluated African-American music in an objective, knowledgeable, and equitable fashion. Systematically institutionalized racism and sexism remain a prominent feature of contemporary American society and a constant reminder of even more offensive conditions in the not-so-remote past. Just three decades ago it was highly unusual to find European-American males prosecuted for raping African-American women or for lynching African-American men in many regions of America. Although less overt today, such conditions have not been eradicated. Bigotry is evident statistically among the students and faculties of American colleges, among gainfully employed professionals, and among citizens enjoying economic prosperity. A few years of limited Affirmative Action policies have hardly eliminated the attitudes that perpetuate racism and sexism in America.

Some people feel that "serious" art is a mirror of the conditions within which it resides. A glance at the history of "jazz" in America reveals few integrated bands that remained together for a number of years. Even when musicians were willing to integrate, socioeconomic factors often prevented anything more than tokenism of various kinds. Consequently, musicologists can write two separate histories of American "jazz," each revealing tangible differences reflective of our general American society. There will be distinct African-American and European-American "jazz" forms as long as American socioculture is strongly segregated along racial and ethnic lines.

Today there are many debates over the ownership of the music some call "jazz." While there is agreement that the roots of African-American music are in Africa, some have always claimed that "jazz" evolved from a mixture of almost equal proportions of African and European influences. Regardless of the inaccuracy of the claim, this is a step up from earlier times when Nick LaRocca claimed that "jazz" was a European-American invention with which African Americans had nothing to do. LaRocca claimed that his Original Dixieland Jass Band invented "jazz" and insisted that he and his musical colleagues were completely unaware of (and therefore escaped the possible influence of) the music of African Americans in his native New Orleans.

It is not entirely surprising that LaRocca could gain support for his assertion from at least one individual, the German researcher Horst Lange.[22] It is not clear how much time (if any) Lange spent in America listening to African-American music. Nevertheless, the effects of LaRocca's exposure to African-American stylistic influences (ranging from "front-line" funeral band music, ragtime, and jig bands to other forms extant within the musical community of the day) are obvious in the derivative style of the ODJB's music. It is also obvious that LaRocca and his colleagues were not enclosed within a cultural void as they suggested. If nothing else, the ODJB members received distorted or diluted exposure to African-American music through the media.

If we are to believe the historical documentation of European-American writers, then Paul Whiteman was the "King of Jazz" and Benny Goodman the "King of Swing," and George Gershwin made "jazz a lady."[23] Each musician brings something special to "jazz." Nonetheless, when the various stylistic forms of African-American music are carefully and thoroughly examined from a more objective position, none of the above claims to royalty can be justified in musical terms. European-American musicians have the economic and social advantage over their African-American counterparts (as well as a greater percentage of musicians), yet the evolution of "jazz" innovations has remained entrenched among African-American musicians. If we extract the major innovators from the various sectors of "jazz" history, then it is undeniable that "jazz" is a musical style invented and evolved primarily by African-American progenitors.

Because Eurocentric and Afrocentric musical worlds are most often segregated in America, Eurocentric American "jazz" understandably exhibits different characteristics than the Afrocentric music of Scott Joplin, Jelly Roll Morton, Louis Armstrong, Mary Lou Williams, Basie, Ellington, Bird, Monk, Coltrane, Miles, Sun Ra, Ornette, and Cecil Taylor. This is a question not of musicianship or creativity but, rather, of style and authenticity. Origins and originality itself cannot be fabricated or duplicated.

The economic and political factors that impinge upon the development of African-American music make the question of racism significant. William Julius Wilson is a noted author and professor of sociological and public policy at the University of Chicago. On November 13, 1995, Wilson spoke on the topic "Power, Racism and Privilege" before a packed auditorium in Goldwin Smith Hall on the Cornell University campus. He acknowledged that the problems of the poor and under-served sectors of the American population (especially in inner cities) are exacerbated by racism, but he felt that the roots of the issue lie within the unequal and discriminatory economic class structures: "It's not just simply a matter of race or racism. I assume the race factor. Besides the fact that these places are segregated based on a history of racial discrimination, something else is happening here. We need to go beyond race to explain the impact of these economic and political factors."[24]

Once "Black" music migrated away from the economic infrastructure of segregated African-American neighborhoods, the European-American music industry influenced the definition, the success, and the audience acceptance of "jazz" and other African-American music to a much greater degree. Additionally, as a result of American socioeconomic constructs, European-American "cover" bands that performed music based upon African-American prototypes received much wider acceptance and economic returns than African-American innovators.

Books written by Eurocentric authors have claimed that women were inferior, that Native Americans were savages, that Columbus "discovered" America, and that Africans were only three-fifths human. Sun Ra said, "History is 'his'-story. . . . You have not heard my story. . . . My story is a mystery [*my-story*]. . . . Because my story is not his-story." Self-proclaimed Eurocentric "jazz" authorities frequently display arrogance and lack humility, regardless of their level of knowledge or inexperience, because these men (traditionally, they rarely are women) are seldom challenged. Writer Gene Lees, for example, insists that Bill Evans is the most significant force in "jazz" and in the history of music. He never feels the need to support his claim with any evidence beyond his personal opinion, which he apparently feels is sufficient:

> Given the musical character of the two lands of origin, the question "What would an American jazz pianist of mixed Welsh and Russian background sound like?" deserves the answer: Bill Evans. Yet Bill had explored every aspect of jazz. One night late at the Village Vanguard, when the audience was almost gone, he began to play blues. His gorgeous golden tone was abandoned. He was playing hard and funky, dark Southern blues. After that final set, he said to me with a grin, "I can really play that stuff when I want to." And so he could.

> But why should he? It wasn't him. He had assimilated many influences, but the result was what we think of as Bill Evans, one of the most distinctive, original, and finally influential forces in the history of jazz, and one of the most original in the history of music.[25]

While such a statement would never be taken seriously among African-American innovators, that is irrelevant to Lees. There is no need to ask a blues musician whether they feel Evans can "really play that stuff." Lees implies that Evans is more important to the evolution of "jazz" tradition than Armstrong, Tatum, Ellington, Parker, Coltrane, Coleman, Miles, and other African-American innovators. He somehow concluded from hearing Evans play the blues that he could also play ragtime, stride, bebop, free "jazz," and all other "jazz" styles. His bigoted comments also imply that Evans was required to abandon "his gorgeous golden tone" to play blues.

Likewise, the systematic exclusion of women, children, and people of color from historical records renders subjectively grounded reporting negligible. Sexism minimized the roles women musicians have enjoyed in music throughout the Western world. Although women managed to play a significant role in the development of African-American music, sexism exists to varying degrees in "jazz" as well. The cycles of exploitation and development that women have witnessed tell us something significant about the attitudes and conditions surrounding their musical creations and the music of their male counterparts.

In the minds of marginalized musicians, social insularity, inequality, and institutional malfeasance consequently relegate Eurocentric critics, club owners, or record company executives to positions of "plantation store" parasites. The music industry, therefore, appears bent on destroying "Black" artists who fail to conform to Eurocentric authority. This condition continues virtually unchallenged in America. Labels, catch words, and cryptic signals are assigned by tacit (if subliminal) agreement by an entertainment industry controlled by a social "majority" that benefits economically and egotistically from the exploitation of "minority" artists. The manipulation of seemingly innocuous terms like "jazz" obfuscates the origins of African-American music while facilitating the commercial goals and interests of a music industry born out of a slavery-era mentality. Thus the acknowledgment that "jazz" is America's only indigenous art form has rarely been coupled with the recognition that it is an African-American manifestation.

If reasonably objective music scholarship is a desirable goal, then the elimination of racism should be of mutual concern. Irrational and bigoted propaganda leads to confusion. Many champions of the music of Elvis Presley, for instance, attempt to defend his recordings against attacks from listeners who asserted that Elvis stole music from African-American musicians. Ironically, a few broadcasters have presented programs where they played original versions of numerous African-American blues songs followed by Elvis's versions of those songs. While seeking to prove Elvis's ownership of the music by claiming that Elvis "refined" the original African-American songs to the point of creating a brand new music, these broadcasters inadvertently substantiated the accusations and claims of those they sought to disarm.

Rhythm and blues artists such as Louis Jordan, Fats Domino, Little Richard, and others derived their singing and instrumental style from the Afrocentric speech patterns, dance movements, and other sociocultural nurturing on which they were reared. Rock and roll merely became a "distilled" derivative of rhythm and blues. Since Elvis and other European-American artists had limited direct contact with African-American culture, it is understandable that they could only create parodies of African-American styles. Elvis even adopted the style, clothing, and fake "processed" hairdo of rhythm and blues artists of the 1950s. Despite individual aesthetic preferences, the original creators of the songs Elvis "covered" were indeed African-American.

During the 1960s some European performers who used African-American music or stylistic elements in creating their own music (such as the Beatles) acknowledged their debt to original artists. Why do many Americans find it hard to admit they love, learn from, and borrow African-American music?

Summary

Most American children know more about Bach, Mozart, Beethoven, Picasso, Michelangelo, and Rembrandt than about Ellington, Bird, Miles, Coltrane, Bearden, Sargent Johnson, and Augusta Savage. Perhaps this is because an embarrassingly disproportionate number of the people who teach, compose, perform, document, theorize, criticize, sell, and distribute innovative African-American music are non-African-American. Braxton again discusses some possible reasons for the unfortunate and often absurd notions and attitudes that many Americans hold regarding music.

The fact that we have not had a real understanding of the great African Masters, the great Asian masters, or that many of the great European white masters too have not been understood ... is to do with the way everything is defined in this time period. The notion that the Europeans are the superior races and that every philosophical and scientific idea which has helped the cause of human evolution is related only to the European male is a profound misuse of thinking. Yet this is what young children have to grow up under—the weight of misdefinition, the weight of gradualism, of racism, of sexism.[26]

Gradualism, according to Braxton, refers to redefining of information in the interest of those engaged in the redefinition. He uses as an example "the way Egypt has been written out of classical Greek history, and the white 'takeovers' of both big band swing and rock n' roll."[27] Traditionally, the question of ownership takes on a more prominent role in European cultures than it did in many traditional African societies. European culture traditionally proposes that whoever has possession of an official European document granting the bearer ownership to a property is the "legal" owner. It makes little difference whether the property owned is in Africa, South America, the moon, or just happens to be a particular style of music.

I propose, therefore, that "jazz" have several subdivisions. There are distinct approaches involving African-American, Latin, European-American, Asian-American, Asian, African, and European styles, for instance. Each variation shares basic roots based on evolving American music transplanted from African tradition. Of course, African music has been influenced by local environmental elements everywhere it landed. Nevertheless, each subdivision of music is largely a factor of the specific sociocultural values, attitudes, history, and styles of the various segregated units in which music practitioners find themselves. As we grow closer socially, so too will we begin to produce music that is clearly (unhyphenated) American.

People say that music is potentially a universal healing force capable of bringing peace, understanding, and harmony to the inhabitants of our world. We just entered a new century. How much of the slave era bigotry, selfishness, and ignorance that has retarded the progress of humanity will we take as baggage into the present millennium? Can we find a few answers to relevant questions concerning solutions to our contemporary social problems and strife within a careful study of Afrocentric innovation some call "jazz"? "Jazz" has managed to bring people together from all backgrounds, occupations, and places on earth. Even those who despise and discriminate against African-American people have not escaped their alluring music. In time, given the opportunity, perhaps Afrocentric music might demonstrate even greater positive potential. Reflected in the patterns retained in African-American music, sermons, quilting, painting, dance, and nutritional arts are the oral histories, motivic patterns, and cultural nuances inherent within the songs of the African griots. The psychological, educational, economic, and spiritual benefit of this rich heritage enabled the Africans in America to endure severely debilitating slavery-era conditions.

The mentalities that slavery produced are extremely difficult to overcome. If the African-American music some call "jazz" suffers today under adverse economic and social conditions worldwide, this is more a consequence of its progenitors' African-American identity than of any reasonable aesthetic criteria. The introduction of dodecaphonic music,[28] aleatory music,[29] musique concrète,[30] and minimalism into European and certain American academic musical circles has received far less resistance and condescension than the disrespectful and exploitative tendencies directed toward the influential art forms created by African Americans.

Racism and sexism, like other ridiculous notions, manifest in ludicrous ways that make it clear that only quest for power, sociopolitical privilege, and economic advantage could motivate people to accept weak justifications for their insensitivity and greed. The absurdity of such delusions is clear when society presumes that a woman of African heritage cannot have a "White" child, yet a woman of European ancestry can have a "Black" baby. How did a "White race" evolve so rapidly during the slave era? It took time for Italians and Jews to become "White" in America and parts of Europe. The socioeconomic and psychopolitical frameworks that support such conditioning weigh heavily upon the development of African-American music.

Bishop Desmond Tutu heads the Truth Council in South Africa. This transitional organization grants amnesty to those who confess of atrocities committed under apartheid. Tutu feels that, as painful and inadequate as this process may be, it is necessary to expose facts of history and to arrive at some measure of truth that can aid in the promotion of healing throughout his country. Perhaps by looking squarely and sincerely into the American mirror some call "jazz" we can achieve similar ends.

> Prejudice, intolerance, and discrimination are vain and hollow luxuries in which none but the ignorant, the idle, and the indolent can indulge. Courage, competence, and comradeship come in many colors, and these characteristics have meaning to men who stand together in the face of adversity.[31]

Notes

[1] *Mandinka and Fulani Music of the Gambia: Ancient Heart.* Axiom 314–510 148–42. 1990. CD. Mandinka group: Sukakata Suso, Karnnka Suso, Bolong Suso, Manjako Suso, Jewuru Kanuteh (kora); Mahamadou Suso, Mawudo Suso, Salun Kuyateh (balafon); Saiko Suso, Lamin Suso (batakonkon); Dembo Kanuteh, Mahamadou Suso (dundungo); Bobo Suso, Mahame Camara (voice); Fulani group: Juldeh Camara, Korreh Jallow (nyanyer, voice); Alieu Touray (flute); Amajou Bah, Karimu Bah (calabash); Amadou Jallow (lala); Ousman Jallow (jimbeh); *"Hamaba" "Nayo" "Dangoma" "Sanjon Bilama" "Kumbusora" "Nyanyer Song" "Julajekereh" "Galoyabeh" "Lanbango" "Borasabana" "China Product."*

[2] *African Tribal Music & Dances.* Legacy International CD 328. No year listed. CD. No personnel listed. Music of the Malinké: *"Festival Music" "Solo for the Seron" "Hymn of Praise" "Percussion Instruments" "Festival of the Circumcision" "Dance of the Hunters" "Dance of the Women"* Music of the Baoulé and others: *"Invocation, Entrance and Dance of the Glaou" "Duet for Flutes" "Solo for Musical Bow" "Xylophone Solo" "Male Chorus and Harp" "Dance of the Witch Doctor" "Sicco" "Toffi" "Ibonga" "Gnounba Gnibi" "Dianka Bi" "Sibi Saba" "Sindhio" "Didrenquo" "Bonomiollo."*

[3] Interval composed of 3 whole-steps.

[4] *Fetish Folk of West Africa,* p. 78.

[5] See *Mojo Hand: The Lightnin Hopkins Anthology,* 1993 Rhino Records (R2 71226).

[6] *Voodoo Ceremony in Haiti: Recorded Live on Location.* Olympic Records 6113, 1974. LP. No personnel listed. *"Voodoo Drums" "Nibo Rhythms" "Prayer to Shango" "Petro Rhythms" "Nago Rhythms" "Invocation to Papa Legba" "Dahomey Rhythms: 'The Paul'l'" "Maize Rhythm" "Diouba Rhythm: 'Cousin Zaca'."*

[7] Robert Milligan, *Fetish Folk of West Africa* (New York: Fleming H. Revel, 1912), p. 78.

[8] Ibid.

[9] Ibid., p. 79.

[10] A way of dividing a fixed length in two sections expressed in mathematical terms as b/a = a/a+b (also known as Golden Mean, Golden Ratio).

[11] *Music is My Mistress*, p. 260.

[12] Albert Murray, *The Blue Devils of Nada: A Contemporary Approach to Aesthetic Statement* (New York: Pantheon, 1996), p. 206.

[13] Liner notes from McIntyre's album *Home*. Steeple Chase SCS-1039, 1975. McIntyre plays alto sax, flute, oboe, bassoon, and bass clarinet on this recording.

[14] Duke Ellington, *Music Is My Mistress* (Garden City, N.Y.: Doubleday, 1973), p. 436.

[15] *Music Is My Mistress*, p. 412.

[16] Ibid., p. 244.

[17] Lock, *Forces in Motion: The Music and Thoughts of Anthony Braxton* (New York: Da Capo, 1988), pp. 276–77.

[18] Oxford University Press, 1996.

[19] Christopher Harlos, "Jazz Autobiography," in *Representing Jazz*, ed. Krin Gabbard (Durham: Duke University, 1995), p. 134.

[20] Steeple Chase SCS-1039, 1975. McIntyre plays alto sax, flute, oboe, bassoon, and bass clarinet on this recording.

[21] The number of people referred to as minorities in America collectively compose over 50 percent of the population.

[22] James Lincoln Collier, *Jazz: The American Theme Song* (New York: Oxford University Press, 1993), p. 200.

[23] The latter idea was Leonard Bernstein's.

[24] *Cornell Chronicle*, November 30, 1995, p. 6.

[25] Gene Lees, *Cats of Any Color: Jazz Black and White* (New York: Oxford University Press, 1994), p. 238.

[26] Ibid.

[27] Ibid., p. 313.

[28] Pertaining to twelve-tone musical technique or compositions.

[29] Music involving the introduction of chance or unpredictability into the process of performance or composition.

[30] A conceptual term first coined by Pierre Schaeffer in Paris around 1948, musique concrète involves the recording of any number of sounds (voice, street noises, musical instruments, sounds of nature, etc.) that undergo electronic manipulation, modulation, and enhancement in the recording studio.

[31] Phillip T. Drotning. *Black Heroes In Our Nation's History* (New York, Washington Square Press, 1970). p. ix.

I
Traditional African Music

Brothers and sisters, the white man has brainwashed us black
people to fasten our gaze upon a blond-haired, blue-eyed Jesus!

—Malcolm X

European and European-American art galleries display African art, but
they usually fail to name the artists. They credit tribes or regions with the production of works of art, but rarely did more than one person create these artifacts. Similarly, they pay scant attention to the history of the regions from which
African art emerges. This suggests that museums, like zoos, are interested primarily with the ownership of African art (and the profit that can be made) and
hold less concern for the African people who produced the art.

Although we know the names of a significant number of modern African-American innovators, the music business remains conspicuously more
concerned with profit than with the welfare of their artists. The legacy of exploitation and bigotry that the slave era ushered forth left indelible imprints
on the entire history of Global African music. Relatively few readers interested in "jazz" have a general knowledge of African history. So it is important
to shed at least a bit of light on what Europeans long considered the "Dark
Continent." Exploring the complex history of a continent as large and diverse
as Africa within a few introductory pages is an impossible task. But it is possible to explore the origins of African people and to raise relevant questions
regarding the contexts and circumstances within which "jazz" emerged and
evolved.

Formulating an Approach to Understanding African Music

African Studies in the United States today have moved beyond
dispassionate inquiry, and the history of Africa's music is
evolving beyond the antiquated perspective that considered it
largely a subject fit only for speculation by idle minds traveling
through strange exotic lands. Sweeping assertions of this kind
can be made at the end of the twentieth century. This is because, for Westerners, Africa no longer seems remote; that is, if
distance can be measured by levels of scholarly inquiry or the
intensity of emotional involvement. For millions of Americans
an African heritage exists to be acknowledged and claimed, and
this is true of numerous other cultures too, wherever the African Diaspora has reached.[1]

Considering the vast nature of African cultures, with its tremendous diversity of topography, people, dialects, and traditions, the music of Africa is scarcely known abroad. Whereas the uninitiated might tend to regard African music as homogeneous, it is essential that any such notion be rejected.

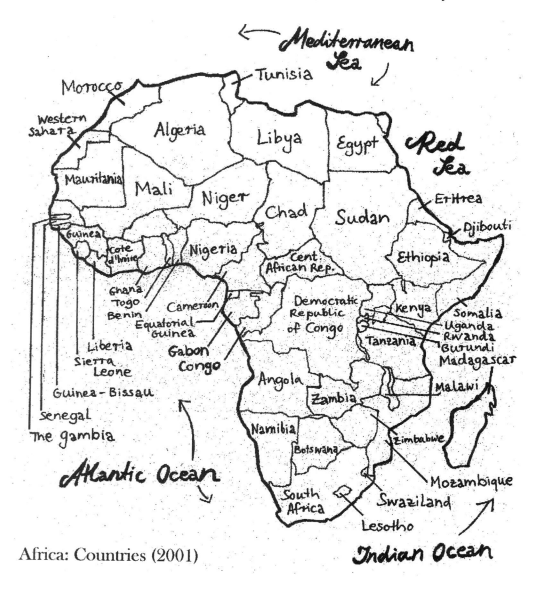

Africa: Countries (2001)

Since a large portion of African music has been transmitted from one generation to another through an oral tradition, the composers and performers of African music evolved in a fashion that places much less emphasis upon written traditions than European "art music" composers. Many non-African musicologists have attempted to notate, classify, analyze, and document African melodies and rhythms, but the methods and procedures employed remains a matter of experimentation and controversy. A study of African structures must pay direct attention to a broad range of components (including dance, instrumentation, history, metaphysics, etc.) if a meaningful perspective is to be maintained. Therefore, it is necessary to develop a perspective that keeps indigenous African music within proximity of appropriate sociocultural contexts.

Traditional societies that were eventually established in time throughout regions of Africa favored a mutual dependence between the social and physical universe. It was felt, within many such societies, that disharmony in one realm of existence would definitely affect the other. The duty of the king or chief was to preside over the assembly, drawn from the community on the basis of individual experience and merit, and to maintain equilibrium between the two realms. Likewise, the monarch would serve as the link and mediator between the living and the dead, would encourage members of the community to voice their grievances without fear of retribution, and would preside over the political and ritual functions.

Traditional African cultures did not fragment the components of daily life from one another. Music accompanies all aspects of an individual's life, and the community participates freely in almost all musical celebrations. Such events generally involve kinetic and visual arts as equal multimedia partners in performances. Traditionally, there was no separate notion of art from spiritual celebration or social entertainment in Africa. Music has always been a mixture of sacred and secular ingredients. While one person may be enjoying music, dance, and colorful masks from an aesthetic perspective, another may become filled with the "holy spirit," while yet a third might experience the event purely as a festive occasion.

In tribal Africa, regional differences were often a result of differences in languages and customs. Limited travel and restricted modes of communication could serve to exasperate tense or highly volatile relationships between strangers or perhaps even distant relatives. In ancient Africa, therefore, both Africans and foreigners often found fertile soil for misinformation, mistrust, and fabrication in situations involving both local and foreign affairs. These vast traditional differences make the African convergence that took place within the "New World" all the more remarkable.

Throughout world cultures, the more secretive, insular and closed a society has remained, the more conflicts and feuds have resulted between families, tribes, fiefdoms, religious sects, etc. Likewise, the abundance of mystery schools, secret codes, and cryptic symbols we find during the Dark Ages in Europe is indicative of the limitations placed upon people's expression and education during that era, despite the presence of a relatively homogeneous and uniform culture. Similar trends can be found in other parts of the world of antiquity as well as within the modern era. The Africans would later develop codes of secrecy that would enable traditional customs and ideas to be perpetuated in the "New World" during the slave era. The path from traditional African music to the various forms of Diasporic African music reflects a cultural struggle in the Western Hemisphere.

Africa Before the European Slave Trade

Who were the ancestors of the African people who created "jazz" in America? What was the nature of African society before the slave trade disrupted African culture? How did the relationship between Europeans and Africans develop into the adversarial condition that created racism and slave mentality? How much effect did this tense relationship have on the African people who eventually created and developed modern African-American music?

As African contributions to the evolution of humanity gradually became undeniable, European scholars began denying that Egyptians and Ethiopians were "black" African people. The parallel between this controversy and arguments over whether "jazz" is an African-American invention is intriguing. Yet, in addition to evidence contained within the Mosaic records, the Ethiopians[2] are always referred to as "black" people in the annals of all the great early nations of Asia Minor.[3] Today, some scholars who insist upon maintaining theories of "European" supremacy find themselves refuting evidence presented by early historians they previously supported. Molefi Kete Asante discusses this contemporary dilemma:

> Lefkowitz and others who once considered Herodotus to be the "Father of History" now find fault with Herodotus because, as Afrocentrists read Book II of *The History of Herodotus*, we find that Herodotus glorifies the achievements of Egypt in relationship to Greece. But Herodotus is not the only ancient Greek writer to be dismissed by classicists who accept what Bernal rightly calls an Aryan interpretation of the ancient world.
>
> Aristotle reported that the Egyptians gave the world the study of geometry and mathematics, and the Aryanists argue that Aristotle made mistakes in what he observed. Lefkowitz carries the denial of the Greeks to a new level, saying essentially that you cannot trust Homer, Diogenes, Laertius, Plutarch or Strabo. Her position is that Strabo, like Herodotus, depended too much on what the Egyptian priests told him. Greeks who wrote on the overwhelming impact of Egypt (Africa) on Greece (Europe) are discredited or set up to be discredited by the Aryanists. The idea to abandon the Greek authors rests on the belief that these ancient Greek writers cannot be counted upon to support the theories of White supremacy.
>
> . . . Lefkowitz could have admitted that Egypt during the times of the Pharaohs—whatever interpretation you have of that ancient society, for example, as ornamented with mystery schools or simply filled with keepers of mysteries at the temples of Ipet sut, Edfu, Kom Ombo, Philae, Esna, Abydos, and other cities— was the source of much of Greek knowledge.[4]

Why is it important to glance at the achievements of an ancient African music and its sociocultural past to understand the evolution of African-American music? We are left with perplexing historical inconsistencies if we fail to provide some historical background to offset the racist propaganda that perpetuates the politics and mentality of the slavery era. Understanding that important ancient kingdoms existed throughout Africa, not only in Egypt and Nubia, but also in Ghana, Mali, Songhay, Kanem-Bornu, Benin, and other regions of the African continent, challenges the stereotypical notions depicting Africans as "savages"—a notion that fails to explain how "socially inferior" African Americans invented one of the world's most sophisticated, intriguing, and beautiful genres of twentieth-century music.

Early African Contact with Europe

The music of Africa must have had some effect on ancient and medieval European music. Donald Jay Grout, claiming that music was an inseparable aspect of European religious ceremonies, traced the early origins of Western art music back to ancient Greek heritage. The cult of Apollo used the lyre as its characteristic instrument, while the aulos (a double-piped reed instrument) was associated with the cult of Dionysus. Grout proposed that both instruments entered Greece from Asia Minor. Greek drama presumably developed from these ancient rituals.[5] Grout fails to factor any Moorish influence into his evaluation of European music history. Just as the influence of European music must enter into any discussion of the development of African-American music, African influence, due to the dominant presence of the Moors in Spain, had some impact on the cultural evolution in Europe until the middle of the fifteenth century.

The Moors are one of the Moslem people of mixed Arab and Berber descent who lived in northern Africa. In Europe, Tarik the Moor expanded the Moorish empire to include the Visigoths' kingdoms subdued by the Moslems twelve hundred years ago. Spain prospered in art, literature, and science for nearly eight centuries under Mohammedan rulers from Northern Africa, at a level and in a fashion not reflected elsewhere in Europe. The knowledge and influence of Moorish conquerors led to advancements in industry and engineering. New cities flourished in the rich valleys of the Guadelquivir and the Guadiana, whose names still commemorate the vanished glories of the past.[6] European fear and hatred of the Moors lasted many years beyond their European conquest. Mozart's two-act opera *The Magic Flute* is an example of the negative perception of Moors in the late 18th century. *The Magic Flute*, a work filled with Freemason symbolism and other archetypes, makes the Moorish character Monostatos the most insensitive and despicable character in the story.

French, German, and English students came to study in the schools and libraries established by the Moors in Spain. Moorish theoretical tendencies perhaps influenced the gradual abandoning of quartal harmony (used in Medieval harmony) in favor of North African tertian harmony (harmony in thirds), eventually contributing to the development of French fauxbourdon and English gymell styles in later periods of European music.

The ancient histories of Egypt and Nubia reveal continual cultural exchange between northern regions of the African continent and Africa south of the Sahara. Within the complex network of African and European cultural exchange in the region of the Mediterranean and elsewhere, therefore, it is unlikely that the music of the Moors escaped the influence of music from their southern African neighbors. Traditional African music preserved by its contemporary practitioners display shared characteristics. For example, a remarkable comparison can be noticed between the "whispered singing" of numerous regions of Burundi (where a male singer accompanies himself on the *inanga*, a type of trough-zither) and the singing of *bägänna* performers in Ethiopia. According to legend, the *bägänna* (a very large ten-string lyre) is the descendant of one Ethiopia's oldest instruments, the harp, "which the future King David played 3000 years ago."[7]

Heavy European intervention began in the mid-fifteenth century when European merchants, possessing charters from their monarchs, raided the African coastal areas for slaves, ivory, gold, and hides. The technical advantage they held over the Africans (in weapons of destruction) changed the Africans' relationship from trade to dependency, which became the pattern for all future contacts.[8] Some reports from European explorations and raiding expeditions make bewildered mention of African music and dance.

From the middle of the seventeenth century, a new factor entered the African societies south of the Sahara. European traders interested in the raw materials came to bargain with African people, but apparently took little interest in African music and culture. European expansion exploited African resources and societies to such an extent that many of these societies finally collapsed. Complete transformation of human relations resulted, though traditional African society offered tremendous sustained resistance. Territorial annexation and forced acculturation were accomplished through merciless military aggression and intimidation.

European colonization led to inevitable conflict between the colonizers and the indigenous people. Colonists usually attempted to confiscate lands used for grazing and cultivation. Efforts were also directed toward turning aborigines into servants and dependents. In southern Africa, as the influx of European settlements accelerated and spread outward from the Cape, the indigenous Khoisans were displaced, dispersed, or integrated into the colonial economy. In time, trade (in the form of skins or ivory) was established with the Bantu-speaking peoples further inland. At that point Europeans began attempting to establish a trade monopoly both internally and with the outside world. Colonists wanted ivory, cattle, hides, and servants. The Africans wanted metal, beads, horses, and, later, manufactured goods such as blankets, knives, guns, and brandy. Trade was difficult to maintain, however, due to the tremendous distance between the administrative capital and the colonies. Due to increasing hostilities, European and African societies remained relatively separate despite active trading, and this mutual detachment prevented cultural understanding.

Economic concerns are generally the prime motivators for the development of slavery in any region. When a project requires a quantity of labor that exceeds the human resources available in a given region, either slave labor must be imported to augment the labor force or new labor-saving devices must be invented. Both Africans (who sold their prisoners of war) and Europeans made profits on the Western slave trade.

Slavery of the particular types found later in Greece and Italy was practiced in ancient Africa. Even in Egypt, where pharaohs such as Khufu and others are often erroneously depicted as despots exploiting slave labor to erect colossal pyramids and other labor-intensive structures, the serfs were never permanently placed in an underclass; nor were they systematically oppressed spiritually, physically, and psychologically, as they were under most European slave systems. Although exploitation certainly existed, the construction of the pyramids was highly organized and did not require the debilitating circumstances similar to those found on southern plantations in America.[9]

In the early days of European colonization, Christian missionaries became an important factor in encouraging interaction between the colonists and the African peoples. Their influence tended to favor settler communities at the expense of traditional African society. Africans often mistook the preachers for seers, rainmakers, diviners, or other bearers of positive information, identifying them with their counterparts within African society. Once invited and established in the African communities, missionaries would proceed to "win the souls"[10] of African people through attempting to teach the gospels and the values of European society (hard work, thrift, temperance, and respect for authority).[11]

Being accustomed to only usufructuary[12] right to the environment, Africans knew nothing of "legal" boundaries, fences, and symbols of private ownership. Consequently, clashes occurred over the interpretation of boundary agreements, taxation of the land, and the use of resources. White settlers, displaying arrogant authority, became notorious among African people as "a people who lacked common humanity, who were opposed to peace, and who were extremely quarrelsome (*makgowa*) and always ready to despoil their neighbors' flocks (*amadlagusha*)."[13] Clashes escalated into wars, and following each war the settlers annexed new land. Again adaptation, at the expense of traditional society, often became the only real alternative.

Women, Music, and Religion in Africa

People often look to natural forces surrounding them for clues to aid in their understanding of the universe. Perhaps the most persuasive aspects of the world our early ancestors encountered were the dynamic and rhythmic sounds of nature. The roll of thunder, the rare explosion of a volcano, the song of a bird, the murmur of a stream, the roar of a lion—all these aural elements of daily life must have been alternately terrifying, soothing, and inspiring.

Since rhythm is formed when any series of sounds occur in nature, the patterns formed by such movement over time must have been compared to the lunar cycles, the human heartbeat, falling raindrops, and other sounds that can be grouped into logical patterns. One basic meaning of religion is "to bind together." The history of humanity's spiritual development demonstrates a primordial inclination toward organizing various rhythms of life cycles into some form of logical order. Totem poles, calendars, sundials, signs of the zodiac, and other tools of measurement that humankind has developed all measure the rhythms we encounter in daily life.

Africans were generally not inclined to separate rhythm, spiritual dimensions, and the order of the universe into compartments. Traditional African societies acknowledged that the drum had a spirit and character that was clearly observable. The gift of the voices of the Great Ancestors had been hidden inside the wood of trees so they could be accessed whenever men and women needed them. Stories associated with African history were maintained through an oral tradition. African vehicles for the transmission of history and knowledge have a value equivalent to that of the written word in European tradition. One traditional African story tells how the bullroarer was created:

> One day an old woman was out cutting firewood when suddenly the splinters from the tree she was felling began to fly around her in the air, crying "Bigu-bigu-bigu-bigu." It frightened the old woman very much. When she told her husband what had happened he said that whatever the thing was it would come to her that night in a dream. And sure enough, it did. That night, as the old woman slept, one of the wood chips came to her and said: "Mother, listen to me. Bigu is my name. That's my name, Bigu! Now I want you to go into the bush and cut a long skin from a tree and make a rope. Then I want you to make a hole close to my nose, and fasten the rope there. Then, mother, plant yams. Then I want you to sling me over your head. The noise will make your garden grow. It will make the wind and rain come. It will wake up the ground."

> Well, the old woman did as Bigu commanded. She found a tree, she made a rope, she hitched it to the splinter, she planted yams, and then she began to swing Bigu over her head. It sounded like a great monster had come to eat them all up. The people first ran and hid under the bushes, screaming, "Dhuramoolan has come to eat us." The old woman called to the people, "Come back! You feel the rain fall? This water is for us to drink. You see the yams grow? Now we have food!"

> The people gathered around her, their eyes wide with fear and wonder. Everywhere the yams were growing and the rain was falling. Oh, the people were happy.
> But not the husband of the woman. Angrily he snatched the bullroarer from his wife and killed her. Then he painted himself with white clay as if he were about to kill a strong enemy. He picked up his spear and called the men to him and said, "All you men, this Bigu gives us power. No longer will women and children be allowed to see it. Only men. Not boys, not girls, not women. This magic is too strong, If any man tells the women and children about this, I will kill him."[14]

Bullroarer (Photo by Alissa Roedig).

The bullroarer story provides insight on several levels. Natural and spiritual forces manifesting through the medium of sound, the story seems to say, provide solutions to problems associated with daily life. This example also shows that once these forces have been harnessed, the power of musical instruments has the capacity to unleash them, a capacity similar to that of virulent nature. Similar folktales also typically demonstrate early society's tendency to be extremely sexist, insecure, and paranoid—in a manner still existent throughout the world. Because of fear, jealousy, and avarice for power, men cordoned off the most potent musical force in the village.

Generalizing about sexism or anything else in African society is no simple matter. Over a thousand languages and cultures can be isolated within the distinct social organizations and diverse kinship systems on the African continent. Nevertheless, common threads can be found within the overwhelming variability of this huge, rich continent. Despite the chauvinist inferences of the bullroarer fable, for example, a consistent factor throughout African cultures has been the prominent role of women.

Throughout the world women have been denied access to many instruments, especially those considered instruments associated with power or assertiveness. In Europe, even within the vocal arena, a tradition that is generally more acceptable as an outlet for female musicianship, the *castrati* (men who were castrated to artificially preserve their high voices) substituted for the female soprano in seventeenth- and eighteenth-century Italian liturgical music. Women were banned from participation in such musical genres.[15]

It is often erroneously reported that African women, while well represented as vocalists, are denied the privilege of playing musical instruments.

Because some "jazz" scholars have apparently not found reason to visit Africa, and because they tend to forget the size of the continent, we often find misinformation generated such as this comment in Frank Tirro's *Jazz: A History*: "African women sing and dance, but only African men play the instruments."[16] A quick glance at the cover of Francis Bebey's well-known book *African Music: A People's Art* [17] should have caused curious scholars to investigate the matter further. This is not to deny that women are severely restricted in music making in certain parts of Africa in ways similar to the sexist limitations they have encountered as musicians in Western society. Nevertheless, in evaluating African music many scholars have relied almost entirely on European reporters rather than on direct contacts with African musicians and historians. If our European musical and cultural values are not tempered by an informed knowledge of the culture under examination, we risk politicizing and polarizing our perspective. The dominant role of the woman in African-American culture is often discussed in American social studies, but rarely is a parallel drawn between this role and related social positions in African culture.

In Africa, with its vast array of cultures and tribes, women have a long history as players of diverse musical instruments. Obviously any discussion of this topic presents a formidable challenge; even today there is an estimated fifteen hundred to two thousand different African tribal groups, and much research remains to be done.

Throughout Africa we find a wide variety of music for the events of everyday life. The music repertoire of a single village generally includes over a hundred songs for various occasions. Secular dance songs and songs of entertainment, like popular music in other cultures, decline in popularity within a relatively short period. Popular songs usually enjoy a longer life span in rural areas than in urban communities. Music for entertainment usually ranges from highly informal performances to more theatrical presentations, such as the *chikona* of the Venda of South Africa. A circle of men playing vertical flutes perform music in hocket while dancing counterclockwise around drummers, who are mostly women. This custom challenges the claim made in some Western sources that women do not play drums in Africa.

Musicologist John Rublowsky did a detailed study of music making in the highly organized and stratified West African kingdom of Dahomey, which by the eighteenth century had become one of the principal suppliers of the flourishing slave trade.[18] The obscurity of African women musicians in historical documents written by European men can be misleading, however. Undoubtedly there were many professional music guilds in many highly stratified West African kingdoms that excluded women. Nevertheless, Linda Dahl challenges some of Rublowsky's conclusions regarding the participation of women in the early guilds in Dahomey society. In her book *Stormy Weather: The Music and Lives of a Century of Jazzwomen* she writes:

> The Dahomans had established guilds to train professional musicians as well as other craftsmen. Such guilds tended to be family affairs that apprenticed the aspiring player in preparation for a series of tough examinations on a variety of instruments, including flutes, trumpets, stringed instruments, xylo-

phones and drums. Just possibly there were women musicians in these musical guilds, for eighteenth-century Dahoman women, unlike their European and American counterparts, were chiefly responsible for conducting the central economic affairs of the society, and they could vote, own property, serve as priestesses and fight as warriors. More probably, though, women were excluded from the music guilds as well as from the craft guilds. "Sculpture and music were arts open to anyone," Rublowsky observes, but his evidence suggests that "anyone" was a male child. The probability of patrilineal musical instruction is supported by African musicologist J. H. Kwabena Nketia: "The transmission of roles from father to son is quite common . . . specialization in musical instruments tends to run through families or households."

However, female musicianship seems to have flourished in the large number of less stratified, more egalitarian African societies. According to Nketia, women in these simpler societies historically formed their own permanent associations specifically to make music. In many places they still do so; a recent documentary on Moslem women in Morocco, made by an all-woman crew, included footage of religious and social gatherings attended only by women and featuring all-female musical groups. Women's dance bands and clubs usually performed for specific occasions such as female puberty rites, the healing of the sick, funerals and wakes, and sometimes court entertainments. Indeed, in most of rural Africa, music making was and is part of the fabric of everyday life rather than a specialized activity.

Though we can cite examples of women instrumentalists in various African societies—professional harp virtuosi in Uganda, fiddlers in Mali, the friction drummers of the Tuareg tribe, water drummers in East Africa, idiophone players in Ghana and Nigeria—it is not clear whether they constitute exceptions to the rule. It may be that in Africa, as in Europe, women musicians were more culturally acceptable as vocalists than as instrumentalists, but on the basis of existing research it is impossible to be sure.[19]

The inherently musical and rhythmic nature of most traditional African cooperative and individual work may account for the link between music and economic life. A smith's pounding hammer or bellows are used to create musical effects. Women sharing a mortar (for pounding) touch pestles between strokes to create syncopation and complex cross rhythms; or fishermen may take the natural rhythm of their paddles and develop rhythmic and tonal variety by tapping the sides of their canoes to accompany their songs. Every available material is used (ivory, bamboo, wood, skin, metal, gourds, horn, vines, grass, stone, etc.) to make a variety of beautiful music. The most primary instrument, the human body (dancing, stamping, clapping, and sing-ing), is frequently exploited. Stamping with feet serves to supply dance rhythms when drums are not used.

The distortion we find in the history of women musicians is common throughout the modern world. Women have always made music (instrumen-tal and vocal) and formed their own guilds when no other opportunities were available. During the days of the American minstrelsy, African-American and European-American women, restricted from the main stage, formed their own independent guilds. Women troubadors had done likewise in medieval Eu-rope. They composed their own verses and often accompanied themselves on the lute. Dahl adds: "The most richly inventive period of female music-mak-ing in Europe began during the Renaissance, when, particularly in Italy, women in convents and orphanages established and directed their own en-sembles (the convent provided a safe and intellectually enriching haven for women during these centuries). Eighteenth century Venice boasted a number of fine women orchestras, with players drawn from the city's four music con-servatories for orphaned girls."[20]

The history of African and African-American women musicians bears evidence of both racism and sexism. The roles of women musicians in all soci-eties reflect a history of sexism. Although music often reflects society, the complex messages contained within art forms are not easily deciphered. Yet it is possible that the roles and status of women musicians declined as women were forced into patriarchal rule. The interconnections between ancient tribal music, social customs, economics, religious ideas, and other traditions may hold clues to the historical and culture place of women in African society.

Today the majority culture often separates "jazz" from its African ori-gins through a number of systematic sociopolitical means, including control over the dissemination, documentation, and definition of the art form. Once redefined, it becomes difficult to reverse the resulting misinformation. Artists are affected by such conditions. Likewise, the classification of musical instru-ments along sexual lines has sociocultural implications. Thus, the diminish-ing of social status and power associated with women through the years has a related history.

According to the Old Testament, the first human group was a married couple, Adam and Eve. This family and their children formed a patriarchal family. From this supposition the idea of the primacy of the patriarchy, with its male leader and subordinate females, has been established by most West-ern cultures to be the very foundation of human society. Today many people assert that the first type of family was likely to have been matriarchal, since the role of the father in procreation was uncertain to ancient people. Al-though, I am told, the whole concept of a matriarchy preceding patriarchy is considered outdated and largely a fantasy of feminists and Marxists by many anthropologists, other professional researchers support such a theory. Ac-cording to proponents of the matriarchal theory, women, with their power to give birth, would have been naturally worshipped as possessors of the extra-ordinary power of creating life. In most cases, however, evidence suggests that most often early societies were matrilineal where men remained in con-trol. Communities organized in a matrilineal fashion (where descent was traced through women, but men remained in charge) can still be found among tribes in Central Australia and the inhabitants of the Trobriand Islands.

Attitudes adopted regarding the music people produce within a region and period of time reflect other social dynamics. Establishing dominance over sectors of a population to facilitate economic supremacy is likewise one of the basic premises upon which sexism and racism are grounded. When European warriors began to claim southern lands for themselves, both sex and skin color became factors belying "religious" concerns. In her book *When God Was a Woman*, Merlin Stone writes:

> Mythological and archeological evidence suggests that it was these northern people [Indo-Europeans bearing the name *maryannu*] who brought with them the concept of light as good and dark as evil (very possibly the symbolism of their racial attitudes toward the darker people of the southern areas) and of a supreme male deity. The emergence of the male deity in their subsequent literature, which repeatedly described and explained his supremacy, and the extremely high position of their priestly caste may perhaps allow these invasions to be viewed as religious crusade wars as much as territorial conquests.[21]

The suppression of Goddess worship that followed as a consequence of the arrival of Indo-Aryan tribes, therefore, began with the emergence of a new mythology that included blending two sets of theological concepts (male and female; dark and light). Ultimately the female deity was completely supplanted.[22] The suppression of religion, music, tribal continuity, and other essential sociocultural dimensions during the European slave trade was engineered for related reasons. Total domination requires that subjects become totally disoriented, docile, and reprogrammed. The early Christian attached the label "pagan" to all African, Oriental, and non-European religions, regardless of its history or contents. Most religions condemned as such paid earnest and dutiful homage to a God of the universe.

It's more difficult to establish dominance over women or other conquered people when, to strengthen their resolve, these oppressed people start to construct deities in their own image. The conqueror's primary goals must ultimately include forcing the enslaved people to adopt his gods, languages, and traditions. Denying Africans their families, traditions, instruments, and religions was designed to strip them of all vestiges of personal power. Wherever prominent elements of African tradition survived, the music of that region retained stronger African characteristics.

When religious zealots spoke of destroying "false idols" in many ancient places of worship, many of those idols were female. Archeologists have discovered some of these female deities with musical instruments. Sheila Collins proposes that "theology is ultimately political. The way human communities deify the transcendent and determine the categories of good and evil have more to do with the power dynamics of social systems which create the theologies than with the spontaneous revelation of truth from another quarter."[23]

Stylistic Regions of African Music

   To facilitate our examination, musical cultures of Africa are classified as that of North Africa (which is essentially Islamic) and Sub-Saharan Africa (alternately referred to as Africa south of the Sahara). Both North Africa and Sub-Saharan Africa contain music that has undergone constant evolution as performers modify traditional elements of musical performance to keep their own presentations unique and contemporary. Since most of the Africans who came to America during the European slave era were from Sub-Saharan Africa, the music from that region will serve as the focal point of our examination. Although most of African music was initially exposed only to regional influences, eventually other outside cultures also contributed to the overall development of the music. It is, however, the elements of traditional African music that will be our concern as we establish the basis of African-American music.

   The North Africa stylistic region includes Algeria, Egypt, Libya, Mauritania (which overlaps the Sudan region), Morocco, Tunisia, and Western Sahara. The area of Northern Africa extends over many miles. In addition to native cultures, the music produced by musicians from the regions are influenced by three outside musical cultures, the Persian, Arab, and Turkish. Islam is a prominent language spoken. Arab-Andalusian music from Morocco is based on heptatonic scales, and does not contain micro-intervals. Much North African music has many elemental properties in common with Middle-Eastern style. During the19th century, military orchestras adapted to prevailing musical styles and offered traditional influence in exchange. This musical stylistic cross-fertilization extends from the borders of the Himalayas to the Atlantic Ocean. A prominent segment of the population of musicians within Northern Africa consists of the Berbers, and the Kurds. Due to a high circulation of migrant people in the region, musical practices in the area are quite diverse and dynamic.

   Cultural areas of Sub-Saharan Africa are grouped into geographical regions (e.g., Khoisan, Guinea Coast, Congo, Sudan, Eastern Cattle areas, and the Pygmy areas) to provide a basic framework for observation of musical style. As a variety of regional and tribal terms are found for closely related musical instruments throughout Sub-Saharan Africa (e.g., the thumb piano is alternately referred to as a *kalimba, mbira, likembe, limba, sanza*, etc.) traditional African terms occur profusely throughout this chapter to facilitate positive identification.

   As we become familiarized with African culture and music the degree of influence that African retentions have on "jazz" and other African-American music becomes increasingly clear. Throughout the history of the African's experience in America, interdisciplinary dynamics, performance styles, and cultural attitudes are found within the music of many African-American church services (although coerced conformity to European musical value systems caused many African-based elements to become more diluted or subdued in most Protestant churches).

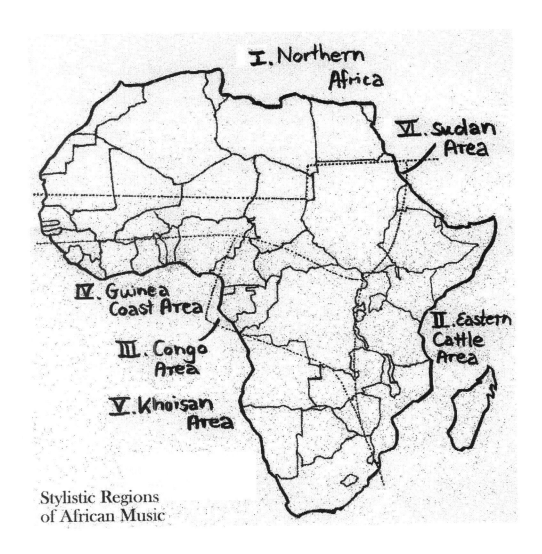

Stylistic Regions
of African Music

Colorful Sunday attire and uninhibited body language observed at Southern Baptist church services in African-American communities throughout America suggest certain characteristics of traditional African traditions. This is particularly evident in the lyrical presentation of the sermon delivered in most churches. The songlike delivery of the pastor, the spontaneous actions of congregation members moved emotionally by the music and sermon, typical call-and-response patterning that permeates all aspects of the service, and other aspects of African-American religious worship are decidedly African in origin.

The element of collective participation is generally characteristic of African music and arts. Without such participation, particularly as related to music and dance, African cultural transmissions to America would have been seriously attenuated under the oppression of the slave era. By engaging oral, aural, and kinetic social tools, the seeds of culture germinated, developed, and prospered, allowing the Africans to sustain traditional elements despite efforts to counter such progress on the part of the oppressors.

Communal African-American musical performance thus functioned as an educational and political sociocultural means of preserving art and heritage while concurrently boosting morale. The role of the African-American church and its music is particularly noteworthy in this regard, since it has been the most stable pillar in the African-American community from its beginning. Children in most African-American church environments received early musical training as participants in (rather than passive consumers of) the musical process.[24] This had also been the case with the younger citizens in traditional African societies.

I. Northern Africa

ANCIENT EGYPTIAN MUSIC

Anthropologists generally agree that the early Nubians and Egyptians share cultural features. Genetic studies of early human remains from both Egypt and Nubia suggest that little physical variation could be detected among the inhabitants of these regions. Karl Butzer has noted that over time, however, physical distinctions became more pronounced. This was perhaps due to an infusion of a new population into Upper Egypt in the Neolithic era (after 7,000 B.C.). Butzer asserts that the Upper Egyptians of the Neolithic and Predynastic eras were not the descendants of the earlier palaeolithic inhabitants, but were immigrants to Upper Egypt. The more recent inhabitants may have arrived probably from the northern Libyan Desert and its oases, which were in a slow process of desiccation at that time.

Egypt dominated parts of Nubia from about 1950 to 1000 B.C. Egyptian colonization resulted in the disappearance of a particular Nubian C-Group, including the Nubian elite who adopted both the worship of Egyptian gods and the Egyptian hieroglyphic writing system. During the reign of Tutankhamen (who was the son of a Nubian woman) colonization was especially bitter. Nubia's gold, ebony, and ivory contributed to the material wealth of Egypt. Nubian products were used in the creation of a significant number of the famed treasures of the Egyptian kings. Forts, pyramids, trading posts, and Egyptian-style temples were built in Kush.

Old Kingdom Egyptian Music has been classified as secular, sacred, and military, though the categories clearly overlap. Surprisingly, the history of Egyptian music presents little evidence of the use of drums prior to 2000 B.C.[25] Egyptian music was apparently melodically driven during early periods. There are exceptions, however. Curt Sachs points out that "a fragment from Ne-user-re's temple of the Sun (about 2700 B.C.) near Abusir, now in the Munich museum, shows the top of a large drum . . . supposed to be identical with the instrument a-lal. As the instrument is unique in the Old Kingdom of Egypt, we suppose its existence is due to an importation from Sumer."[26]

Later, the most common iconography and descriptions depict military trumpets and drums with the processions of the gods. Cylindrical and barrel drums appear prominently during the Middle and New Kingdoms. Sachs continues: "The Cairo museum owns a cylindrical drum which probably was made during the twelfth dynasty, 2000–1788 B.C; it is seventy-five centimeters long and twenty-nine centimeters wide, and has a network of thongs with a tightening tourniquet to stretch the leather skins. A similar drum is still in use on the Congo."[27]

Drums and trumpets were played together and separately. Although drums were often omitted from representations of military campaigns, at the Temple at Kawa (25th Dynasty) the drummer Emhab is shown following his king to war.[28] Trumpeters and drummers would join other instrumentalists at various musical functions during times of peace.

Religious rituals and (occasionally) funerals involved priestesses shaking the cult rattles called sistra. The sound of the sistrum was at times accompanied by the rattling of a heavy necklace made of rows of faience beads (*menat*). Menats were usually carried by women in their free hand rather than worn. Some ensembles, such as the "the musicians of the funeral estate," had specific names that matched their functions. Feasts and other secular social functions involved instrumental music, song, and dance.[29]

The instrumental core of Old Kingdom ensembles, according to ancient paintings, included the harp, an end-blown flute, and a simple clarinet. Although it was common to have more than one harp in an ensemble, only a single flute and a clarinet were generally involved. Nonetheless, the ensemble apparently was far from standardized:

> One provincial tomb shows seven harps; in another a second flute and clarinet have been added, and in a third we have four flutes, while one scene has no clarinets but two flutes. The recently discovered 5th Dynasty tomb of Niankhknum and Khnumhotep at Saqqara near the ancient capital of Memphis has an eleven-man ensemble, consisting of two harpists, two flautists, a man playing an unusually long clarinet, and six chironomists [instructors]. . . . A wooden model of an ensemble dating from the Middle Kingdom has a harpist sitting on either side of the tomb owner and his wife, while three girls sit facing one another at his feet clapping and singing.[30]

Men and women apparently played most instruments. Arched, angular harps were played by both sexes in Ancient Egypt. The tomb of the Middle Kingdom vizier Antefoker contains four excellent representations in which a man and woman are shown performing side by side. Although male musicians generally played the flute, a 12th Dynasty female flautist and chironomist are also depicted in a Theban tomb of Antefoker. Another later scene from the Graeco-Roman temple at Medamud (just north of Thebes) shows three women playing the angular harp, a minute barrel-shaped drum, and a lute, while a fourth woman sings.[31]

Egyptian women of the Nile Valley from mortal women, such as Queen Hatshepsut (who wore men's clothes and ruled as king), to the goddess (Sekhmet) held leading roles in family life, religion, and government. In earlier times, Egyptian women owned and managed property, made business contracts, represented themselves in litigation, ran businesses, and could divorce their husbands. Married women were held in higher regard in domestic life than those who were single and mothers were respected most of all.

Although marriages were usually arranged, ancient love songs suggest that women and men also married for love. Queens Merneith, Nitokret, Sobekne-fru, and Tausret were among the female sole rulers. Other women more often reigned Egypt as regent.

Vocal music was important in Egypt. The variety of forms referred to as the "Harper's Song" is a genre in Egyptian literature. In *Music and Musicians in Ancient Egypt*, Lise Manniche says, "One of its two main themes concerns reflection on life on earth as opposed to life in the hereafter. . . . These songs invite us to spend a happy day, don our best garments, perfume our bodies, and enjoy music and dance with our nearest and dearest at our side."

ANCIENT NUBIAN WRITTEN MUSIC

The Late Palaeolithic Age in Lower Nubia produced the Qada Culture, which thrived ca. 15,000–10,500 B.C. The Qada inhabited numerous sites in an area sprawling from the Second Cataract northward to Toshka. The earliest extant evidence of human remains in the entire Nile Valley has been discovered within this region.

During periods perhaps even earlier than that of the first pharaohs of Egypt, a line of kings lived in Qustul in northern "Kush" (as Nubia was then called). The people of these early cultures buried their dead in stone-lined pit graves, accompanied by pottery and cosmetic articles. The Egyptians referred to these Nubian people as "Ta Sety" (the "Land of the Bow") because of the fame of Nubian archers. By 1550 B.C kings at Kerma were ruling Nubia during a time of increased contact between Egypt and "Kush." People of the Kerma culture were accomplished metalworkers and also turned thin-walled pottery on a wheel.

Most people who think of traditional African music assume that oral and aural traditions were used exclusively throughout the African continent. A sixth-century Ethiopian composer evolved a sophisticated music writing system and was so highly revered that he became a Catholic saint. Saint Yaréd, the son of a wealthy Christian family who lived between the reigns of Emperor Kaleb and his son Emperor Gabre Masqual, was originally a professor of theology. He composed all the Old Testament oriented music for the Ethiopian church's chants. Yaréd acquired his knowledge of theology, natural history, and music from his uncle, Gedewon. Gedewon introduced Yaréd to songs used for praying and singing by Ethiopian churchmen inherited from the creative works of the ancient Nubian Empire.

In later years numerous works accredited to Saint Yaréd were found throughout Ethiopia. Ayele Bekerie explains this incredible number of compositions by saying that Ethiopian epics create "fragments for historiography" that are transformed "to insure perpetual dynamism."[32] Thus, when it is implied that St. Yaréd wrote all the traditional Ethiopian classical music compositions, Ethiopian tradition must be factored into the statement. Early Ethiopian composers (especially Yaréd's students), as a gesture of humility, considered all their inspiration a result of St. Yaréd's influence. Thus, many credited St. Yaréd with their compositions. Music, nonetheless, was not Nubia's oldest writing system.

According to the Ethiopian tradition, poetry composition pre-dates St. Yaréd's musical composition. According to Ato Ale-mayehu Moges, the musical composition of *Digguwa* by St. Yaréd would not have been possible, if it did not rely on the al-ready existing tradition of writing or composing poetry. Poetry is believed to have started around 1500 B.C.E. The originator of *Qiné* is identified as Tewanay, who used to live on the island of Deqe Estefa, which is located in Lake Tana, the source of the river Abbay or Blue Nile.[33]

MOROCCAN MUSIC

In the markets of Morocco's traditional cities, between the afternoon and sunset prayers, food vendors, dentists, fortunetellers, and storytellers con-gregate with musicians and singers. Street cries and songs combine to create a constant evolution of cultural expression. At times, performances by some of Morocco's greatest musician are heard featured on traditional instruments including the *oud, derbouka, tarija, bendir* and *tar* drums.

At times rhapsodic music is expressed around daily life or work. Moroc-can songs can relate the joys and pains of either carnal or spiritual love. The musical culture of the Houara women (Houariyat) is closely tied to the eco-nomic and social role played by Moroccan women. Women are fundamental to the culture and economy, so they do a fair share of the community's work. During breaks in fieldwork the women traditionally sit in a circle and sing, accompanying themselves with hand clapping and percussion instruments. The textile industry (producing rugs and blankets) is the second largest indus-try in the region and workers are exclusively women. This working environ-ment is once again ideal for practicing music within the Moroccan oral tradi-tion.

The Houari musical style reflects the influence of Sub-Saharan and an-cient Northern African music. Polyrhythms (overlapping of different rhythmic cycles mixed with the colorful application of cross accents), use of call and re-sponse patterns, embellished pentatonic scales and the typically cyclical struc-ture of Moroccan music (based on repetition and thematic micro-variation) are features that mirror those of Sub-Saharan Africa. The persistence of hemiola (the superimposition of binary and ternary rhythmic figures) is also a shared feature of Sub-Saharan and Moroccan music. The *ferda* (fire arms) is an "ex-plosion" of drums that incorporates polyrhythms often composed of overlap-ping complex meters (7/8 and 5/4, 5/8 and 3/4, etc.) creating rhythmic ambigu-ity.

A closer look at Moroccan music reveals a compositional construction based on constantly varying permutations of a relatively limited set of rhyth-mic motives that are connected in a variety of ways reminiscent of African textile weaving patterns. The musical form is enhanced and highlighted by dynamics and fluctuations in tempo that suggest organic expansion.

Percussion is the only set musical instruments played in Houara mu-sic. Traditional instruments typically include several types of membrano-phones and one idiophone. The *tara* is a large, single-membrane drum on a round wooden frame (with gut snares inside the frame of the drum). It marks the bass pattern that conducts the dancers and the other percussion in performances. The *tara* is played vertically and held between the thumb and first finger. The other fingers strike the membrane head or, alternately, stop its vibrations. The other hand beats either in the center of the drum, producing a deep muted sound, or strikes the edge for a higher pitch that makes the snares vibrate.

The second drum is the *bendir*; a smaller version of the tara that is often fitted with a skinhead. The *bendir* is played horizontally during the ferda. By resting the instrument on her knees, the musician can play rapid drum rolls with both hands. The *tarija* is a small pot drum with a single membrane head fitted with a snare, stretched over a goblet shaped clay frame. Two or more tar drums are tuned at intervals that allow musicians to play a single rhythmic phrase by alternating notes (in hocket).

The *derbouka* is a goblet shaped lead drum (now fairly common in the West). This single-headed drum produces a piercing sound suitable for solo drum figures that form the upper strata of some percussion ensembles. The *dâwdâw*, a medium-sized drum similar to the *derbouka*, has snares affixed to its head and produces a rhythmic counterpoint to the low frequency tones of the *tara* and *tarija*. Contrapuntal lines emerge through producing two types of sound; *ticka* (high pitch, articulated on the edge) and *dununa* (deep note, articulated at the center). The latter tone is modulated in the *ferda* by placing the hand and part of the arm inside the clay chassis.

The *naqqus* (bell) is typical of the Houara: a tin basin (often replaced by a hubcap today) is struck with two metal sticks, each shaped differently. The very fast beat of the *naqqus* marks the sub-division of metrical time.

One of the dominant traits of all Moroccan music is its complete integration of religion and entertainment. Music is considered a spiritual essence in Morocco, so each concert, whether in a traditional or modern context, begins by calling on the divine spirit, by soliciting the help of the *marabout* (those who belongs to the cult of initiated musician), and praising the Prophet.[34]

NORTH AFRICAN WOMEN MUSICIANS

A socio-historical observation of women musicians in Northern Africa reveals some of the attitudes and practices that shaped the cultural perspectives in the world. The Maghreb of North Africa was a region where the plight of female African musicians can be studied historically. It is a geographical region composed of modern Tunisia, Algeria and Morocco. These countries also developed notable civilizations during ancient times and established links with their African neighbors to the south. It is a rich cultural mosaic that witnessed dominant Mediterranean and western Asian civilizations that date back two millennia to the founding of Carthage. Inhabitants of the region retained Arabic as the predominant language and Islam as the official religion. The population is comprised of an interesting mixture of Black Africans, Berbers, and Arabs.

Tracing the history of professional women musicians in the Maghreb is difficult because of the paucity of documentation. The *qayna* (pl. *qiyan*), however, is one variety of female musicians from Tunisia's earlier centuries that has been discussed more readily. The *qiyan* or, as more frequently designated in Tunisian sources, *jariya* (pl. *jawari*), are terms that can be loosely translated "slave girl" or "singing slave girl." The term *qayna* could be related to the image of "Cain" of northern Semitic religious tradition and early mideastern associations of music with slavery. Consequently, these images could also lead to a number of diverse prejudices.[35]

Qiyan of Tunisia and other Arab kingdoms were imported female slaves from both southern African and non-Arab centers of musical culture. These Arab women were also trained (usually by famous men musicians) for the express purpose of singing and playing the *'ud* (traditional Arab lute). Slave women musicians served as gifts between the wealthy and powerful, or were sold for high prices. *Qiyan* could also be found in taverns and other public houses of amusement. Subjected to such vulnerable circumstances, they suffered more than their share of abuse.

Qiyan were kept in the households of the sultan, his high officials, the nobility, and the wealthy people in Kairouan, Mahdia, Damascus, Baghdad, and other places in the region. Like the African griots, who resided further south on the continent, they served an important function in transmitting musical traditions across the expanse of the Arab empire. Some were "promoted" to the legal status of concubine in the houses of their "masters." The steady importation of women musicians provided a steady influx of new musical materials from outside the Islamic world. Shopping expeditions were frequently sent to Baghdad to purchase "singing girls" and other cultural artifacts by early Tunisian rulers.

Historical documents show that, on one occasion, a mission returned to Kairouan in A.D. 905 with 30,000 dinars worth of *jawari* for the sultan's pleasure-town of ar-Raqqada.[36] 'Abd al-Wahhab concludes that the jawari who went to Spain after the fall of the Aghlabide sultanate (of Kairouan) made significant contributions to the cultural development and brilliance of Cordoba in the tenth century.[37] Therefore, North African rhythms, melodies, and other musical elements clearly left their imprint on the music of Spain more than several hundred years ago. Musically trained slave women and girls later became a lucrative export in Seville where prices up to 10,000 gold dinars were paid for the most accomplished female musicians.[38] However illfated the lives of the *qiyan* may seem, it is important to realize the status of free women in the Islamic countries at this time. The so-called "free" women were confined to quarters, and shielded from the outside world:

> . . . and spared the burdens of literacy and education except later in life, if they sought spiritual edification. The slaves, on the other hand, were frequently women of exotic race or religion, educated and acculturated in their native climes, who brought cultural treasures from the older Asian, African, and European civilizations into the empire of Islam. Much effort was lavished on their education, for their purpose was to provide aesthetic and intellectual entertainment, as well, perhaps, as more basic pleasures. Being bought and sold, presented as gifts, and called upon to perform before their owners' guests, they enjoyed a freedom unthinkable for legitimate wives and daughters. Thus, Bouhdiba maintains, these slave girls were

the true vanguards of female liberation in the Arab world, and it is their prototype that is waiting, ready-made, for the modern Tunisian women to step into as she leaves the sequestration of the traditional family and assumes her role in public life.[39]

The records that remain of the *quiyan* who performed in taverns and public houses survived generally due to the "anathema hurled at them by orthodox moralists."[40] In Fatimid times there seems to have been self-employed female singers as well, who lived more independent lives in respectable districts. These women sang at private parties and weddings, and reportedly kept the neighbors up at night.[41]

Stylistic Regions of Sub-Saharan African Music

Beyond the African continent, astonishingly little is known about the origins of African people in spite of skilled and persistent investigations during the last few decades. The diverse stylistic regions of Sub-Sahara Africa are therefore as difficult to study thoroughly as the various African dialects. Nevertheless, an abridged examination of stylistic traits of representative sections of the Guinea Coast, the Khoisan area, Sudan, the Congo, the Eastern Cattle area, and the Pygmies will indicate some of the similarities and differences among the cultures of the communities within this vast zone. A conscientious historical study of African music should not be restricted to the development of forms and style, as this music is very much a part of social and cultural life. Thus, factors that link African society with the outside world are included to widen the investigation of the stylistic regions.

II. Eastern Cattle Area

Documentary history for much of this region begins in the early second century with *The Circumnavigation of the Indian Ocean*, a commercial handbook written in Greek. Early sailors along the shores of what is now Somalia, Kenya, and Tanzania describe the markets as part of the efficient network of Indian Ocean trade.[42] The majority of ships entering the area were from Egypt and western India. Fragments of these early cultures have been found along the East African coastline, where trade routes from the interior meet the Indian Ocean traffic.

Uganda, Kenya, and Tanzania (the latter formed by the union of Tanganyika and Zanzibar in 1964),[43] form the 618,934-square-mile area of East Africa. The music, customs, creeds, languages, and general ways of living are so diverse that it is difficult to draw general conclusions regarding style. It is clear, though, that the music is extremely rich in rhythm. Rhythms serve a vital function in all dancing and as a means of communication in daily life.

Tribes of East Africa (e.g., Sogo, Ganda, and Acholi) prefer quick and "hot" rhythms in dancing. Slow and graceful rhythms are popular among the

Tusi (Watusi), Kiga, and Karamojang dancers. These rhythms are rich enough to sustain dancing without instrumental or vocal accompaniment.

The chief dancing instrument is the drum. In addition to tuned drums of the Ganda people, large drum ensembles are common but never comprise more than four to six drums. The drumming among the Ganda in Nankasa involves the use of such drums of varying sizes. Expanded ensembles would merely double these standard instruments. Each dancer in Bwola dances of the Acholi carries a small drum in the left hand and a beating stick in the right hand (each dancer playing the same unison rhythms).

In nearly all areas of East Africa clapping is very common, though it is not always used to accompany dances. In the *bwola, dingi-dingi*, and *laraka oraka* dances of the Achoi, clapping is not used at all. Possibly because of the highly organized nature of Agwara dances (which leaves little room for improvisation), clapping is likewise omitted from the *bwola* and *dingi-dingi* dance styles. In various other dances, however, clapping helps singers and drummers to keep steady time. This also enables musicologists to determine accents when transcribing traditional African rhythms.

In Bugunda, drums are sounded to call people to do communal work, such as the building of village roads or footbridges across swamps (*bulungi bwansi*). Drums warn people of approaching danger and call them to defend their village. The use of drums for calling people to worship came with the introduction of Christianity. Shouting while beating the lips rhythmically is also used to signal villagers of approaching individuals.

III. Congo Area

The Old Kingdom of Congo had extended as far as today's Stanley Pool along the banks of the Zaire and Congo Rivers. The king of Congo lost his authority in the area to the north of the Congo River when the Portuguese discovered it in 1482. A new capital was established at Mbanza Congo, situated approximately in the center of the region, creating new geographical boundaries. The king continued to rule the Bantu-speaking tribes, who were skilled in various arts and crafts such as metal works (including iron and copper) and weaving. These people had little or no contact with the more advanced people of the Niger area, where, as early as the fifteenth century, a flourishing university was established at Timbuktu.[44] The Congolese, nonetheless, were later enthusiastic about adopting some of the ways of Western civilization.

Ugandan musician Samite Mulondo.

CENTRAL AFRICAN REPUBLIC

In the center of the African continent lies the region known as the Central African Republic. This area, bordered by Oubangui in the south and Chari in the north, is comprised of numerous ethnic groups that are unevenly distributed throughout the 280,454 square miles of landmass.

Bagandou music of the M'baika region of the Central African Republic employs a thirteen-keyed *sanza, manza,* and other xylophones of various sizes. Linda music (Bambari region), uses nose whistles and *ingoma* drums in some situations, as well as *kalangha* xylophones and wicker rattles to accompany songs and dances. The *ingoma* drums are considered among the most traditional African instruments and were used solely at the king's court in the past.

CAMEROON

Immediately west of the Central African Republic is Cameroon and the music of the Bakweri, Bamileke, Bamoun and Beti. A diverse representation of musical forms and instruments are found within this area. Dance music for youth (e.g., *mendou* and *mbgwana*) and ritual music for the passage of youths into adult society are types of Bamoun music (*nekian*, performed every two years is an example).

The Bamoun court has been noted for the invention of new dances, and for its general artistic vitality. Nboemboe (called the "Giant-King") removed the cloak of secrecy from the *banzie* dance in order to win a war against the Fula.[45] From that point on dance has expanded and developed to a point where today as many as thirty or more dancers may be used for a dance formerly danced in private by two or three members of the court. The *mvet* (imported from Southern Cameroun) is popular at the Bamoun court. The *fok* horn (made from bamboo) is also popular in Bamoun and is generally played by women.

The *kufo*, a secret funeral dance of the Bamileke performed for a princess and other distinguished persons, is danced once a year at the most. The instrumental ensemble for this occasion includes three double bells with external clappers, scapulary bells carried on the shoulders of three men, large tubular drums, and a large funnel-shaped skin drum. Another dance, *lali* (a secret war dance), is performed with the musicians concealed while playing. This dance is reserved exclusively for members of the secret society.

REPUBLIC OF THE CONGO

Most of the inhabitants of the Congo Republic (formerly the Belgian Congo) have lived for many centuries in a manner that still exists today. Though most of its inhabitants have never united themselves in states, there has been some degree of social exchange (particularly in more current times) between the various peoples.

In the northeast lies the Ituri Rain Forest, inhabited by Pygmy tribes as well as tribes driven from the east by stronger warring tribes and slave traders. From the north came the Bangbetu, from the east the BaLese, and from the south the BaBira and BaNdaka. These migrations brought Sudanic, Bantu, and Arabic influences to the region, which combined with indigenous Pygmoid traditions.

The music of the non-Pygmy tribes is highly instrumental and includes harps, lyres, zithers, the musical bow, sacred makata sticks, gongs, and numerous other instruments. The music of the Pygmy tribes, on the other hand, is vocal in emphasis. A harp, thumb piano (*sanza*), or a stick-zither often accompanies non-Pygmy vocal songs. A vocal music tradition is strong among the Balese (of Sudanic origin) who settled near the Pygmies after being driven into the forest and who adopted many Pygmy traditions and customs. The BaBira and several other tribes settled in the narrow strip of eastern grassland. Consequently, their music is freer of Pygmy influence and relies heavily on instrumental accompaniment.

Double bell (*gankogui*) and other metal bells (*dodompe* and *toke*) (Photo by Alissa Roedig).

THE PYGMY

Though many aspects of their lives are inaccessible (knowledge of religious practices, for example), it is known that the forest is the source of all good and for spiritual and practical manifestations for the Pygmy. Other communities consider it a place filled with danger. Music is essential to their culture and traditions and can be roughly divided into at least three categories: *molimo* and *elima* are religious songs; hunting and gathering songs are recreational music; and play songs are the only secular. Because of the extremely high regard the Pygmies hold for the forest, all other songs, which deal with daily life, are considered sacred. The *Nkumbi* initiation, a circumcision rite brought to the region by non-Pygmies, is the only formal ceremony in their tradition for which music has been imported from another tribe.

Much exchange and intermarriage has transpired recently between the Mbuti Pygmies and the neighboring tribes living on the edge of the forest. The Balese relied heavily upon the nomadic Mbuti for help and exchange of forest products for farm products. The BaBenzele and Babinga Pygmies in the Central Congo engage in limited exchange with neighboring tribes at the edge of the forest, causing some Pygmies to settle near their neighbors. This contact has unfortunately resulted in a state of semi-slavery, a condition under which "patrons" take Babinga wives and force other Pygmies to convert to their own customs. On the other hand, the BaBenzele live in the dense forest of the Sangha watershed (a tributary of the Congo), where non-Pygmy tribes are reluctant to enter. They spend most of the year hunting buffalo, gorilla, warthog, gazelle, elephant, and other wild game. For a few weeks during the dry season the BaBenzele barter with the villagers, when they may adopt some of the villagers' customs and language (Sango), only to abandon them completely once entering the forest.

BaBenzele possessions are often made from plants and animals so as not to hamper their nomadism and freedom. Their sense of independence is contained in their music, as is true of other Pygmy traditions. The themes are often centered around the pursuit of game, with drums and clapping often accompanying the music and dancing.

Vocal music is generally polyphonic, so that Pygmy group singing predominates while unison singing is rare. Songs are often binary and symmetrical, providing a basic structure for soloists to respond with a chorus or to improvise (always in a coherent fashion). Polyphonic devices include parallel fifth movement, improvised melismas, melodic imitation, decorated pedalnotes, persistent motifs, and contrapuntal variations.[46] Words are not of significance in BaBenzele and other Pygmy music. Vocal articulation is often limited to a few syllables and onomatopoetic repetition.[47]

Again, due to the nomadic tendencies of the Pygmy, the music utilizes few musical instruments to accompany the vocal songs. Besides the *hindewhu* (whistle), only percussion instruments are used. Three drums are of primary importance: the *motopae* (symbolizing male energy), the *maitu* (symbolizing female energy), and the *mona* (symbolizing the energy of the male child).[48] Ovoid rattles (*awoka*) and dry seeds strung on a vegetable fiber fitted around dancers' ankles (*mangaze*) are among the few other instruments used to accompany Pygmy songs and dances.

IV. Guinea Coast Area

The stretch of land from Senegal to Lake Chad is referred to as West Africa. It includes the countries (from west to east) Mauretania, Senegal, Gambia, Mali, Guinea, Sierra Leone, Liberia, Ivory Coast, Ghana, Burkina Faso, Niger, Togo, Dahomey, Nigeria, and Cameroun. The coastal belt of this area is often referred to as the Guinea Coast. Two points are significant in regard to the Guinea Coast area. First, the majority of slaves were taken from this area during the period of the trans-Atlantic slave trade. It is generally believed that fifteen to twenty million Africans were transported to America alone during the period from circa 1640 onward.[49] Second, during this same period, somewhat paradoxically, Guinea Black kingdoms flourished (in a fashion similar to the earlier great empires of western Sudan) in spite of the fact that a great portion of the young and healthy population was subjugated. Slaves sent to the southern part of the Western Hemisphere, unlike those sent to North America, were able to maintain much of their culture through *batouques* (displays of tribal dancing and drumming). These displays were encouraged by Portuguese slave traders in an effort to create divisiveness and animosity among the slaves.[50] The numerous tribal rivalries that existed prior to the coming of the Europeans to Africa facilitated the efforts of foreigners to divide and conquer Africans throughout the continent. Liberia and Nigeria, located on opposite ends of the Guinea Coast area, will serve as representative regions for the examination of this cultural area of Sub-Saharan Africa.

LIBERIA

Liberia has three distinct regions: a coastal belt, a highland belt of dense unexplored forest, and an inland belt of rich farmland and numerous towns and villages. Over twenty distinct tribes speak many different languages including Bassa, Kru, Lowa, Grebo, Kpelle, Vai, Der, and Kralin. Each tribe tends to maintain its own unique customs and traditions.

Music holds a prominent position in tribal life, serving in marriage ceremonies, funerals, rituals, and other tribal traditions. Traditional folk songs are usually performed by large ensembles and include a variety of drums; these are distinguished according to tone, rhythm, or by their pairing with an assortment of idiophones. The most common of these instruments are the *tanga* drums (pressure drums) and the wooden *zlet*-drums.

NIGERIA

The Federal Republic of Nigeria, Africa's largest country, is divided into twelve regions with the south eastern region covering an area of 13,166 miles and has a population of over three and a half million. The Efik, Ibibio, and Annang to the south, and the Ejagham, Ekoi, Hausa and Yoruba in the remainder of the country, are among the major ethnic groups.

It is difficult to separate the vocal and instrumental music of the Ibibios. Their dialect is inflectionary in character, producing speech rhythms that have influenced both the drumming and dancing styles. Since they were cut off from the effects of colonialism for a long period, their culture has remained much more intact than that of other Nigerian peoples. The *ekpo* masquerade, therefore, is quite different than any other musical tradition of Nigeria. It is interesting to observe that parallels exist between traditional music of the Ibibios and certain modern Western music, such as the harmonies found in Bartok string quartets that are the result of the individual movement of the independent parts. Likewise, a use of vocal patterns analogous to *Sprechstimme* commonly associated with Schoenberg and other Western classical composers, is also characteristic of Ibibio style.

Nigerian artist and musician Prince Twins Seven-Seven.

"Untitled" (left) and "The Spirit of Percussion" (right) – artwork by Nigerian artist Twins Seven-Seven.

The Yoruba and the Hausa are two other societies found within Nigeria. The Yoruba hunter's association (*ijala*) uses a form of chanting characterized by a large variety of texts or verses which are performed at rituals and ceremonial occasions. The Hausa live in a stratified society. Consequently, their music making is left to the lower class while the upper class is content with being entertained.

Kora-player and *jeli* Mamadou Diabate from Mali performing with Hesterian Musicism at Cornell University in October 1999 (Photo by Nicola Kountoupes).

Ghanaian master-drummer Obo Addy.

V. Khoisan Area

Before Portuguese sailors landed in this southern region of Africa in the late fifteenth century, little was known about the Khoisan area. In fact, European settlers in its extreme southwestern corner did not encounter the Bantu-speaking tribesmen until 1702 in an area west of Port Elizabeth. Although most of this area (which includes the Kalahari Desert) is comprised of arid regions with sparse populations, many South African historians claim that the areas inhabited by indigenous tribes have the most favorable natural conditions.

Bushmen may be the oldest inhabitants of the African continent, but their prehistory is obscure. Their anatomy, language, and culture are unique among indigenous African peoples. The characteristic clicks gurgles and guttural sounds of their language have influenced the Bantu and other tribes in the Khoisan area.

Bushmen are divided into three main tribes: the Kaikoum, the Auen and the !Kung. The Auen live in the southern Kalahari; a few Kaikoum live in eastern Ovamboland (South-West Africa); and the largest group, the !Kung, live in the north, west, and central Kalahari.

The !Kung make music on all occasions all day long. The *sanza,* the most common instrument, is used to accompany dancing and singing and is played only by men. The one-stringed fiddle, however, is played by both sexes. The fiddle is made from bamboo with animal sinew for the vibrating string, and a dried calabash, ostrich egg shell, or the mouth provides the resonating chamber. Though the music of the Bushmen has not been studied extensively by musicologists, they have a reputation as being Southern Africa's most proficient musicians.

Other traditional music can be found in all regions of Southern Africa. Much of the music in other portions of the region has assumed a more contemporary form. In Angola, in particular, freedom songs have continued to evolve since the rebellion against Portuguese rule began in March 1961. These songs are concerned with the many villages destroyed by Portuguese bombs, the inhumane living situations to which aboriginal people have been subjected, and other injustices.

VI. Sudan

To the south of the Sahara and the Libyan Desert (one of the hottest and driest desert areas in the world) lies a belt of vegetation that is economically rich and which provides a favorable route for travelers across the continent. Across from the southern Egyptian border was the channel through which Egyptian influence passed southwards to the rest of Africa. Its inhabitants, Cushite tribesmen, ruled northern Sudan for the best part of a thousand years.

Many world cultures have influenced other portions of Sudan as well. During earlier times, the dominant cultures (Kingdoms of Nubia, Merewetiks, etc.) were located in the north. Sudan, touching on nine other countries, has seen the migrations of many small independent ethnic groups bringing such instruments as the Arab *rebec* (a pear-shaped two-or three-stringed instrument) and the *alkaita* (a reed instrument found in Central Africa and northern Nigeria).

NORTHERN SUDAN

Northern Sudan is comprised of four main cultures: the Nubians (the most ancient), the Mahass, the Galien, and the Shaigai, all living on the Nile River. The Nubians use the lyre and the duff (a single-headed drum) to accompany songs and dances. The music is sometimes melancholy with a single melody being performed in a variety of social situations. The tradition of the Mahass is similar.

The rich musical culture of the Shaigai is cheerful and often satirical. The melodies are brief love songs; exotic dances accompanied by the lyre or two *daluka* drums (a clay sounding-box covered with goatskin).

Galien people are noted for having a wealth of songs including *dobeit*, which was introduced by Arabian nomads. *Dobeit* is an elegy which nomads sang at night during early journeys.

WESTERN SUDAN

Western Sudan is divided into the provinces of Kordufan and Darfur. Cattle-breeding nomadic people form a large portion of the population. These people exchange cultural traditions continuously. Songs are closely related to dances, and the names of their presentations (*hassies, garuri, agako*, etc.) are applicable to both songs and dances.

A wide assortment of traditional dance styles exist in western Sudan. *Akako* is a lively dance in compound triple time (also referred to as *mardom*) in which, traditionally, boys stamp their feet while girls clap their hands to accompany the singing. Dance is also a vital part of the musical traditions of the Funy tribe, other Biji people, and the Gumuz tribe. The Gumuz practice the *moshembe da*, where three dancers, including the *kujur* (witch doctor), perform to the rhythms of the *bangia* (lyre) and four *penah* (wind instruments). Many of the numerous dances of the Shilluka in southern Sudan also utilize the lyre.

The Function of African Music in African Culture

Music plays an integral part in rituals of birth and puberty, at marriage and death, in secret-society initiations, and in rituals of livelihood (e.g., hunting, farming, gathering, etc.). Parties often set out singing and dancing their way from one village to another, or a dance may be held to cement good relations with a neighboring village. Costumes, masks, and musical instruments usually attain an "aura of sacredness" in ceremonies and rituals.[51] The Watusi royal drums, for example, are thought to represent a soul (symbolized by a pebble inside) that can do away with evil spirits.

Audience participation, a type of communal sharing, has greater importance in African music than in most Western music. Interaction is closely related to ceremony and ritual. In the West, a symphonic concert is a one-way process where an ensemble performs while the audience waits quietly and patiently for the prescribed moments where it is permissible to applaud. This too is a ritual, but the behavior is generally restricted to a stylized expression of appreciation at the conclusion of a performance, and a spontaneous response at other times is prohibited by tacit agreement. The collective participation characteristic of African music is retained in African-American music when it is performed in African or African-American communities. This emotional freedom attracts listeners from all over the world. Hand clapping, finger popping, vocal prompting, and foot tapping during performances are not considered offensive but are viewed as signs of ardent approval that help to motivate the performing artist.

Music is learned as part of one's cultural and practical education, the birthright of all African children, which provides not only musical education but also a comprehensive preparation for all of life. Young children are often merely listeners at first, but as they get older they soon take an active part in the musical functions of the community. It is not uncommon for three- or four-year-old children to make their own musical instruments such as the frame drum (made from a window frame and animal hide) and then immediately begin to imitate their elders. Musical games have an extremely important educational function among the young.

African children acquire the fundamental principles of music at an early age because musical training is an intrinsic part of their mutual aesthetic and linguistic education. The seminal influence that music exerts on African people is a result of such early stimulation and instruction. The shared knowledge of music explains the communal nature of African (and subsequently African-American) art forms, where high degrees of participation provide outlets for individual musical expression.

Musical sensibilities are actuated, developed, and reinforced through the widespread use of tonal languages, where a single word can have several meanings depending on the pitch or inflection applied. In many areas of Africa, children thus learn to distinguish differences in musical pitch through language. African languages acquire an inherent musicality as pitch acuity and melodic differentials are combined with the rhythmic accents inherent in all languages. Words spoken for reasons of communication take on a musical aesthetic; a conversation between two individuals easily develops the rhythmic pacing and pattern of a quasi-musical performance. One Nigerian musicologist reports that "Yoruba folksongs are, without exception, sung to the tonal inflection of words. . . . So much is this the case that when they listened to simple melodies like the bugle call, the Alberti Bass, or 'La Paloma,' they readily found words to them. . . . Yoruba music is entirely governed by the tonal inflection of words."[52]

The blending of African tonal language, eidetic knowledge, and music education with rhythmic pitch value (associated with lyrics governed by the tonal inflection of words) results in heightened musical sensibility. This vocally grounded process transfers readily to African instrumental music. The "talking" drums found in Ghana, Nigeria, and other African countries provide clear examples of such transference.

The West African *dundun* is perhaps the best known of African talking drums. This hourglass-shaped drum is fashioned with heads that are capable of modulating melodically through a wide range of pitches when the leather cords connecting the top and bottom heads receive pressure from squeezing and relaxing them with arm motion. The sound produced is capable of closely representing the tones and subtle inflections of the languages. With the forced inculcation of Western languages and methods of education, the drum script has been grossly diminished. Some master drummers still pass this tradition on to their children. Official drummers were considered sacred and were chosen carefully for their work in African communities. European missionaries and other invaders later discouraged practitioners of such ilk from practicing their art. Many European youth learn to connect optical phonetic signs with their symbolic musical meanings during their course of training, just as young Africans formerly learned the art of understanding the acoustical phonetic signs of the drums in Africa.[53]

Elements of texture, rhythms, melody as well as linguistic influences were preserved in both African and African-American music despite efforts to destroy African culture in the West. Europeans knew the power of such spiritually based aesthetic forces and, consequently, drums (in particular) and other traditional African instruments were forbidden in America during the slave era.

Adult status within many African cultures began when the adolescent was initiated into adult society, and a variety of music was used to accompany the celebration of this transition. Similar traditions still survive in many regions on the African continent. Among the Adiuku of the Guinea Coast Area (Ivory Coast) tom-toms are ascribed attributes of human beings and are thought to converse with the young initiates. During these graduation ceremonies (*Iohu*) adolescents dance from one age class to another. The young men allowed their hair to grow and dressed as women until the end of the rite of passage, when their hair was cut and they were allowed to dress in men's clothes. The new members then proceeded to career wildly around the village until the ceremony ended (with music and dancing).

Talking drum (Photo by Alissa Roedig).

Music also serves a functional purpose in legal, political, and historical capacities. In some areas it played a prominent role in the maintenance of law and order in earlier times. Traditionally, a plaintiff would often sing his or her case and was judged in terms of the quality of his performance, without referring to guilt or innocence. The most important ideas were to maintain order or, perhaps, to reprimand the wrongdoer without branding him a criminal (particularly for a first offense). Being judged a poor singer could usually be sufficient punishment, and, since the hearing was public, the ridicule was immediate and the offender knew to watch his or her step in the future. Far more important than punishment was prevention in traditional African society, and music was used (particularly in royal courts) as a way of perpetuating the traditional guidelines and ways of the ancestors by singing of those ways. Minstrels wandering the countryside still sing the news of the day and sing of the things pleasing to the ancestors (the good life that all people are expected to lead).[54]

As with most traditional, preliterate societies, the music was socially controlled. Traditional musical activities occurred in private and recreational spheres. The traditional roles were often rigidly prescribed regarding the general framework, responsibilities, and performance of the music. Spontaneous instrumental and vocal songs, on the other hand, continue to enjoy great freedom of expression.

The primary function of music in Africa is communication. It enables participants to "speak with God." In such communication, words are inadequate and without power. When combined with performance and various instruments, music contains the power to convey feelings or emotions rather than naked words.[55] In traditional African society, with its emphasis on community experience and involvement, music has remained essential to institutional life.

An Overview of Musical Style

Music traditions may be observed in every community within the African continent. In most cases, these traditions are both long-standing and complex. Anthropologists and linguists have been able to map the important culture and language areas, although there is much overlapping: the Bantu language, for example, is spoken in both the pastoral and agricultural areas of the region. A similar delineation of musical style, however, has not proven quite as practical thus far. Though earlier observations revealed the predominance of polyphony in parallel fourths and fifths in eastern and southern regions and parallel thirds in central and western regions, further investigations found much more intermingling of intervals than previously suspected.[56] It is interesting that the interval of the tritone (augmented fourth or diminished fifth) is a salient feature in both vocal and instrumental music throughout Africa. It is also an important interval in African-American blues and "jazz" music.

Africans have developed systems of classification of songs. The Bahutu of Ruanda (Burundi) have at least twenty-four different types of social songs. There are songs played by professional musicians for entertainment, songs for harvesting and other work songs, war songs, beer drinking songs, songs commemorating the birth of children, songs admonishing erring members of the society, songs deriding Europeans, vulgar songs, etc. Social songs are separated from ceremonial or religious songs. The Bahutus have other songs associated with paddling against a strong current, paddling with the current, etc.

Examples of music for political purposes include the elaborate fanfares of the Hausa of Nigeria and the elaborate classification of musical genres (according to levels of political leadership) among the Venda of South Africa. Songs are likewise used to spread information on current events of interest, to diffuse gossip, and to perpetuate knowledge. The accompanying rhythms of work songs coordinate tedious group work, making the task easier. The Watusi, also of Ruanda (Burundi), whose lives are centered on their cattle, have songs for herding cattle home in the evening, songs of praise of cows, songs for drawing water for cattle, etc.

A vivid cultural dichotomy has resulted from the intermingling of Sub-Saharan Africans with Western and Eastern civilizations. The result has been, on the one hand, a vanishing of traditional music and, on the other, the appearance of a nucleus of art and "city" music. Notated examples and recorded evidence of traditional music collected before 1950 are relatively sparse, which greatly limits any historical overview of African music. Some interpretive evidence begins with recorded examples such as those supplied by the Czekanowski Central African Expedition of 1907–8. Other historical portraits may be reconstructed through the early musical legacies supplied by the highly biased records of early contacts with other musical cultures. Such evidence mentions several instruments of Malagasy, including an idio-chordic tube zither tuned in thirds (*valiha*) and a free-log thigh-supported xylophone of Malayan origin, dated from the Malayo-Polynesian migrations (circa 2000 B.C. to circa A.D. 500) to Malagasy and the African mainland. Central African xylophone tuning strongly resembles (but is not necessarily derived from) some "ideal" isotonic tuning of the Far East (e.g., the five-step Indonesian *slendro* and the seven-step isotonic scale of Thailand).[57]

In particular, African rhythmic ties with the Middle East and India may be even stronger than those with the Far East. Such ties may have eventually been defined through early migrations and invasions of ancient Egypt south of the Sudan, through the South Indian trade on the East African coast during the third and second centuries B.C., and through the spread of Islam in Africa. A great deal of exchange occurred between the North Africans and the inhabitants of Sub-Saharan Africa. Both musical instruments and formal types of certain techniques are held in common (harps, drums and responsorial singing are examples).

Prior to the advent of contemporary musicological documentation and Western appreciation of African music, African music may not have seemed "pleasing to the ear" of the non-African listener. Nevertheless, the aim of African musicians has been to express life through the medium of sound; not in a fashion that imitates nature, but one that takes natural sounds and incorporates them into music. To those unaccustomed to hearing and understanding this particular aesthetic perspective, the result may seem cacophonous. Nevertheless, each sound has a particular meaning that renders emotions and desires as naturally and directly as possible.[58]

It is difficult to catalogue the many uses of music in Sub-Saharan Africa. In ways the music runs parallel to the uses of folk music in both the African-American and the European tradition. Religious and ceremonial music remains an important category, and a vast amount of music exists for entertainment (such as the performances of musicians at the marketplaces). There is also a larger category of social songs in Africa than is typical of music relegated to folk culture and nonliterate societies.

Characteristics of African Music

By Western standards, African music is characteristically complex; it is often polyrhythmic, heterophonic, and polyphonic. African musicians do not actively conceptualize the abstract principles of their music, however. It is apparent from the unhesitating participation of all members of the African community in musical performance that there are complex yet unverbalized principles underlying music making.[59] One of the characteristics that gives African music its distinctiveness is the large number of colorful instruments used both individually (as accompaniment to singing) and in large and small ensembles. Two or more events tend to occur simultaneously within a musical context. Even players of simple solo instruments (such as the musical bow or the flute) manage to manipulate the instrument in such a way to produce simultaneous sounds by playing overtones with the bow, by humming while bowing, and the like. A percussive quality of sound is always desirable (even on wind instruments). This particular preference is evident from the predominance of plucked string instruments (as opposed to bowed strings).

Melodies often consist of two balanced phrases. There is often a leader/chorus relationship in performance, and polyphonic performances are generally structured so that two parts or two groups of vocalists or instrumentalists often perform in antiphony. This binary musical form often occurs with variations or improvisations on short melodic motifs. Much of traditional African music is associated with dance, which adds to the multidimensional effect of the presentation.

Density and motion are broad characteristics of performance style in Sub-Saharan Africa. Dense orchestral timbres combine with staccato articulation and high degrees of amplitude. High degrees of amplitude may be due to the fact that African music is generally performed outdoors. Musical and kinetic motion is constant, hurried, and complex; dancers and musicians attempt to create as much action as possible in a short time. Of course, there are exceptions; an evening story-singer in a performance on the musical bow, for instance, may be quite different. The range of musical approaches in Africa has always been extremely broad.

Overlapping choral antiphony and responsorial singing are principal types of African polyphony. Various combinations of ostinato and drone-ostinato, polymelody (mainly two-part), and parallel intervals are additional polyphonic techniques frequently employed. Several types may intermingle within one vocal or instrumental piece, with the resulting choral or orchestral tendency being the stacking of parts or voices. Consequently three- or four-part density is not an uncommon African musical feature. Such densities are constantly fluctuating so that continuous triads throughout an entire piece are uncommon. Canonic imitation may occur in responsorial or antiphonal sections of African music as a result of the repetition of the first phrase or the introduction of new melodic material in the form of a refrain. The latter may involve a contrasting section or a completion of the original melody. African ostinato is generally restricted to a relatively small pitch range and is usually short in length. It can occur intermittently or form a continuous pattern situated either above or below the principle melodic line.

Hocket is an important instrumental and vocal device, and is frequently paired with multi-ostinato. Several horns or flutes, each producing a single pitch, may execute both melodic and harmonic hocket derived from two or more ostinato lines. Accompanying dance styles can often include long, broad, outflowing (often convulsive) motion usually presented within an abstract or symbolic context.[60]

Chordal relationships in African music that result from polyphonic combinations are not consonant with the major-minor Western harmonic system. Though these vertical concepts cannot be gauged precisely with Western musical tools, their functions include tension-release, dissonance-consonance, formal balance, varieties of chord combinations and clusters, as well as levels of harmonic patterning.[61]

There is no one African scale that is more common throughout the continent than others among the tremendous variety of scale forms. Certain elements that were retained in the African-American blues have obvious models in the musical variety of numerous African regions. Scales and melodies encompass a narrow range, and tetrachordal and pentachordal spans are common (though larger spans can certainly be found in abundance). The embellishment of these basic scales with an infinite number of graduated pitches of both tempered and non-tempered microtonal varieties are related to the development that occurred with the evolution of the blues melody. The unique micro-tonic pitch system makes African melody subtle and can be disorienting to those accustomed to hearing performances of tempered scales that are fixed and standardized. Both conjunct and disjunct scale patterns are utilized, as are scales composed of equal intervalic relationships (isotonic). It must be noted that these African scales, pitch sets, etc., should not be hastily linked with similar European theoretical notions.

We find, therefore, that traditional African scales involve a diverse set of horizontal arrangements, varying in range and in number of units. Certain musical elements and styles are unique to a given district or village. Hugh Tracey in his study *Chopi Musicians* delineates five such scales corresponding to four villages within the Zavala district of Kenya: Chisiko, Mavila, Banguza, and Zandemela.[62] Of course, Africans developed many of these scales, patterns, and traditions long before the Greek era. Dr. A. N. Tucker remarked that his work was complicated "by the Nilotic intervals not being quite the same as those of our pentatonic."[63] While making recordings of music of the Nilo-Hamitic people, he realized that "the scale intervals of the native's singing voice should be truer than those on the piano."[64] This implies that Nilo-Hamitic tuning may involve just-intonation (in accordance with the natural overtone series) rather than based upon even temperament (originally a Western concept of tuning).

Form, in some varieties of African music, is often based on the immediate repetition of a musical phrase sustained throughout a piece (litany type) or on strophic forms (such as the verse forms found in Ghana). Two or more melodies may be combined to form larger sectional formations, with formal contrast being achieved through a series of musical movements or "acts," each consisting of a section repeated several times.[65]

Musical Instruments

African instruments may be classified as chordophones (stringed instruments), idiophones (instruments that are struck or shaken), membranophones (instruments covered with skin), aerophones (wind instruments), and electrophones (electrical instruments). The latter category includes amplified instruments (such as the electric guitar) found in urban cafes, night clubs, ballrooms, and other places or entertainment where the "highlife" of West Africa, the *kwella* of South Africa, and the popular music of the Congo use Western musical concepts and instrumentation to create new forms of art music. Musical instruments can also be classified as instruments with melodic functions and instruments with rhythmic functions.

Chordophones are used both as a melodic and an accompanying instrument. The musical bow often appears with a resonator attached either in the middle or at the end of the bow; the mouth is often used as a resonator as well. The multiple bow lute, an instrument related to the musical bow, is a five- to eight-bowed instrument (each bow having a single string) found in Central Africa; the bows are attached to a resonator at one end. Zithers in stick, board, raft, trough, and frame form (e.g., the six-stringed triangular-frame zither of the Bassa of Liberia and the *inanga* or trough zither of Rwanda) are found in various areas of Sub-Saharan Africa. Harps and lyres (after Egyptian models) are rarely found south of the equator, and one-stringed fiddles found in many regions are often based on Arabian models.

Balafon (Photo by Alissa Roedig).

African idiophones are found throughout Sub-Sahara Africa, and the *kalimbas* or thumb pianos are a popular brand of these indigenous instruments. The *sanza* (Central Africa, Mozambique, etc.) *mbira* (Southeast Africa), *kembe* (Central Africa), and *limba* (East Central and Southeast Africa) are other variations of thumb pianos found in the region. These instruments are small plucked idiophones consisting of flexible iron or bamboo tongues fixed across a board or box. Additionally, a calabash resonator may be attached to or may house the board. The thumbs (and occasionally the index fingers) are used to pluck the instrument, producing a delicate pizzicato sound.

The mbira is a unique Africa musical invention. Zimbabwe's musicians are among Africa's finest mbira players. Complex polyphonic melodies and polyrhythms frame mbira compositions that are often performed in large mbira ensembles. Such ensembles may include the unifying rhythm of the *hosho* (gourd rattle), low-pitched ostinati performed by the mahon'era, and perhaps drums. Singing is integrated into the composed parts and variations. A high-pitched yodeling style called *huro* intensifies the music. *Kudeketera*, a rapidly executed declamatory style, introduces poetry reflecting various aspects of Shona life and history.

Thumb pianos (kalimba and mbira) (Photo by Alissa Roedig).

Vertical wooden or bamboo flutes, whistles, mirlitons (a kazoo-like instrument), transverse trumpets and horns of ivory (frequently with raised embouchures), and ocarinas are included in the aerophone category of African instruments. In Sub-Saharan Africa ensembles of five or more flutes or horns are typically found performing music in hocket. Wind instruments also include nose flutes, end-blown trumpets, transverse flutes, panpipes, and the bullroarer (an instrument which is often associated with circumcision rites and whose intermittent roaring sound is produced by whirling a slat of wood tied to the end of a leather thong). While the one- or two-pitched flutes and whistles are purely rhythmic in function, the five-stop flute used by the Hausa people of Northern Nigeria (along with various other multi-pitched flutes) serve melodic functions in African music.

Besides the numerous drums, African percussion instruments can be divided into two broad categories: instruments with rhythmic functions and instruments with melodic functions. Large gongs, twin gongs, and ritual gongs; rattles and foot rattle; woodblocks and bells are examples of instruments with rhythmic functions. Instruments with melodic functions include the various wooden and drum xylophones found throughout the region.

The *nyungu* (empty water jar) is an important percussion instrument commonly found in Ankole, Bugisu, Sebei, and Kitosi areas; the rhythms produced are used to accompany singing and dancing. Performers in both Kija and Nkole prefer to use two jars of different sizes simultaneously. Dry plantain fibers, which must be very crisp, are folded to form a beating pad that must cover the mouth of the jar completely with each stroke. The resulting sound is a gentle percussive effect. Using the two jars at the same time produces interesting cross-rhythms.

Djembe (Photo by Alissa Roedig).

Membranophone drums are also utilized as both melodic and rhythmic instruments and come in a variety of shapes and sizes. Some of these drums are beaten with the hand, while other are beaten with a stick or rubbed. They are either single or double-headed and are played in ensembles of varying sizes. Kettledrums (the *ngoma* of South Africa), the West African hourglass "pressure" drum, clay pot drums (*bompili*) usually played by women, frame drums, and countless other drums are played throughout Africa.

Structures of African Rhythms

Rhythm is the most important factor in African music. Even melodic patterns generally serve rhythmic functions as well. An inclination toward ensemble playing lends itself to a wide assortment of vertical rhythmic relationships with Black African music. This results in a stylistic predisposition to the use of hemiola and polyrhythms. At least two independent rhythms are maintained even in solo performances (as previously noted in regard to performers on the musical bow, flutes, etc.). Additionally, each line may contain its own beat pattern, which may not coincide with the pattern of the other complimentary lines. The resulting effect should not be confused with syncopation, where lines are also offset to form a regular (single) underlying pulse. Polyrhythms have rhythmic points of reference, which mark broader rhythmic phrases for each independent pattern. Hand clapping or other percussive accompaniment might accentuate the underlying basic pulse.

Through the shifting of accents, the changing of orchestral timbre and density, and various other techniques, a wide spectrum of orchestral color is achieved. Master drummers and conductors often indicate the tempo, style, dance steps, and other factors, which vary within the course of a single piece of music.

Although there is a predominance of duple motifs, triple and alternating duple and triple motifs are utilized frequently. Similar patterns are found in different African societies, but certain patterns are typical of particular geographic areas (such as the bell patterns of the Niger and Congo regions).[66] Some instrumental rhythms (on melodic instruments) may be metrically free and abstract. Others are lyrical. Melodic instruments of one or two pitches can be effective in creating impressive rhythmic patterns.

Certain rhythmic characteristics link African music with "Black" music of other world cultures. Both metronism[67] (the presence of a strict metronomic pulse) and the importance of percussion are aspects of music that have been retained in the sacred and secular styles of "Black" music outside the African continent. Africanisms came to North America principally via West African sources (more specifically, from the Slave Coast in the vicinity of the Guinea Coast area). With the cessation of slavery, "Black" Americans maintained some of the African musical traditions through activities such as the drumming and dancing in Congo Square, the popularity of street parades, and the tradition of music at funerals.[68]

African rhythmic characteristics have been retained in certain African-American music. The unique rhythmic elements contained in "jazz," operating within various tonal and formal structures, represent one of the music's main characteristics. In addition to the use of polyrhythms, hemiola, the shifting of accents, the application of syncopated patterns, and other devices, the interesting placement of accentuated notes and their relation to the basic pulse provides a source for additional rhythmic color and contrast. "Jazz" interpretation allows the performer the freedom to play consistently behind, ahead, on top of, or right on the underlying beat. These and other "jazz" concepts evolved from an early phase where the emphasis was on collective improvisation, where all instruments tended to play rhythmically. Polyrhythmic innovators, such as Elvin Jones, Max Roach, and Art Blakey, later developed revolutionary styles of "jazz" drumming that conveyed a sense of collective percussion improvisation on a single set of trap drums.

Classes of African Musicians

African musicians might be arbitrarily divided into three main categories: the nonprofessionals, the semiprofessionals, and the professionals. These musicians serve numerous functions for a variety of occasions in traditional African society.

Since all members of the community participate in music making, all Africans are musicians in the broadest sense. Music other than that of professional musicians, teachers, etc., is learned primarily through social experience and communal participation.

Many semiprofessional musicians earn a living through a portion of the year and rely on other occupations for the remainder of the year. Bambara farmers in Burkina Faso (Upper Volta) perform at festivals, during the dry seasons, at which villagers pay the musicians for their efforts. The Senufo orchestras are composed of ten musicians who are also blacksmiths. Many harp and lute players in other areas of Africa are also soothsayers or healers.

Numerous other African musicians earn their living solely through their musical offerings. Trained instrumentalists, master instrument builders, tuning specialists and other professionals are found throughout Sub-Saharan Africa. Musicians may be attached to the court of a ruler, who serves as their patron. Others are paid as they travel from village to village. Training generally takes the form of informal apprenticeships under the tutorial supervision of a relative. Mnemonic aids, such as the singing of nonsense syllables, serve as a basis for basic rote learning. The methods are similar to those used in teaching Hindu drumming and Japanese *gagaku*.

The Basongye of the Congo have five classes of musicians: the professional instrumentalists; performers of slit drums; the rattle and double bell players; the song leader; and members of vocal ensembles. Most Basongye tend to have a low regard for musicians and discourage their children from becoming musicians. Ironically, musicians are still a vital part of the community.

In some societies the privilege of playing particular musical instruments is governed by strict rules. In Ruanda, for example, the privilege of playing the six royal drums was reserved for one particular musician. Only a few young musicians of exceptional virtuosity can aspire to be one of the official drummers. Drumming styles are based on multiple polyrhythms, syncopation, polymetrical stratification, and dense textures.

Slit drums (*ogoro*) (Photo by Alissa Roedig).

The structure of Mandinka society involves three levels of stratification. The privileged class of nobles (*foroolu*) at the upper strata is followed by the artisans called the amaaloolu. Blacksmiths (*numoolu*), leather workers (*karankeolu*), and *jalis* (or *jelis*) are the professionals who make up this class. The *jalis* proper and the *finas* are the two subclasses formed by the subdivision of *jalis* class. The subclass of *jalis* proper consists of musicians who inherit the profession from their fathers. The poet–praise singers who do not play a musical instrument form the subgroup *finas*. The *jalis* subgroup serves as the patron group for the *finas* in a relationship similar to that where the nobles in the village serve as patrons to the *jalis* proper.[69]

Jalis are entertainers who sing and play music to provide music for listening pleasure. They perform numerous other functions including mediating between disputants, serving as marriage brokers, and often functioning as intermediaries between suitors and the parents of the young women considering marriage. Although means of travel is changing in modern times, *Jalis* traditionally visited their patrons and lodged in each of their homes for a few days, bringing their entire family with them. Currently, however, the state of *jaliyaa* practice involves several male *jalis* combining their resources to hire a taxi, not only to circulate between the homes of their patrons, but to make visits to the homes of other wealthy people as well.[70]

Jalis enjoy a special level of privilege enabling them to infringe upon the customs of society, ignore social restraint, and break social taboos without fear of reprisal. The *foroolu* do not enjoy such privileges. A *jali* could, for example, "insult someone's mother or run naked down the street without any serious consequences."[71]

The two main instruments on which the *jali* perform are the kooraa (a twenty-one-stringed harp-lute) and baloo (a nineteen- to twenty-one-keyed xylophone). Although people think of *jali* in terms of their instrumental capabilities, "a good instrumentalist does not feel complete unless he has at least one wife who is a good vocalist."[72]

One of the best-known classes of African musicians of professional caliber is the group of griots. Griots are more esoteric musicians who may be recognized by their characteristic surnames: Keita, Munadi, Diubate, Dibate, Kuyate, and Sory.[73] They are recognized as professional musicians throughout Africa and feared for their dabbling in witchcraft. This caste of people transmit their musical legacies from one generation to another and serve to invoke supernatural beings, singing praises to ensure their satisfaction. The role of the griot in some African societies, in regard to praise singing and historical chants, is extremely important.

Griots, being much more concerned with past events than future ones, are familiar with the history, the philosophies, ethics, and most other aspects of their societies and can relate detailed information to their listeners from memory. This may be accomplished through riddles and proverbs that recall events no longer within the realm of contemporary memory.

Acquiring their virtuosity from years of study under a tutor, griots are comparable in many ways to the troubadour of medieval Europe. In addition to telling old stories, they are constantly collecting new ones for their audiences. Their repertoire includes music for special occasions as well as improvised songs for benevolent patrons. Griots are quick to slander those who are not so generous.

In Equatorial Africa, the players of the *mvet* (harp zither) are the equivalent of the West African griots. They serve the multiple functions of musician, dancer, sibyl, and keeper of the oral tradition. Unlike the griot, the mvet is not treated with scorn since his repertoire does not include songs improvised to praise the rich. Within the music, though, there is ample space for musicians to display their improvisational skills. All African musicians serve to benefit the community at large.

European Methods of Examining African Culture

In her article "Sub-Saharan Africa" Barbara Reeder Lundquist concludes that three historical events affected the Sub-Saharan Africans: the slave trade, European dominance, and the imposition of national cultures. For many Sub-Saharan cultures, music is a means of "power gathering," a method of demonstrating membership within a community. The music leaders have an elevated position in their society because of the high value placed upon music. Sub-Saharan music generally de-emphasizes terraced and other varieties of contrasting dynamics in favor of sustained intensity.

John G. Jackson discusses both the deliberate destruction of African culture and the misunderstanding of African history by students whose knowledge comes from the largely Eurocentric documentation. In the chapter "The Destruction of African Culture" (in his *Introduction to African Civilizations*) Jackson reminds the reader that often African history is presented in such a manner as to claim the best aspects of its culture for Europe or Asia. The ancient Egyptians' knowledge of mathematics and astronomy was much more extensive than we are generally led to believe by most historical documents written by early European historians. It follows, therefore, that this must have also been the case in other African kingdoms where, as in Egypt, pyramids were constructed and where other evidence of advanced technical knowledge is encountered.

Kofi Agawu sets three problems for ethnomusicology: the location of disciplinary borders, the problem of translation, and "a network of political and ideological matters." Agawu asks, "What sort of ethical issues constrain the practical effort to understand another culture? What is the relationship between empire and ethnomusicological representation? Can we—that is, is it a good thing to—study any music without taking note of the social, economic, political, and technological circumstances of its producers?"[74]

Agawu posits that judgmental comments to describe music should be encouraged whether the critic is ignorant about the background of the music, or not. He suggests that flawed judgment can give us information about the beholder. Compared to earlier periods of ethnographic research, critics of today may be "less confident about what their ears tell them,"[75] because they are perhaps a bit more humble and, consequently, less ignorant about the subjects they investigate. Being less quick to judge African and other world music without researching its ethnological background may create a more reliable body of historical information.

Ethnomusicologists, like most "jazz" critics, usually present credentials that have little meaning within certain performance mediums. From an Afrocentric musical perspective, where individuals have studied, how many performances they have attended, or how large their record collections are have far less validity than their level of performance proficiency on a musical instrument, or how well they dance in the cultural style they are reviewing. Credentials may produce a sense of empowerment within a closed social group, but "a collective 'us,' whether a reference to Westerners, white males, or ethnomusicologists, is no more valid than a collective 'them,' which lumps people with different abilities and levels of knowledge about tradition and culture."[76]

Of course, if we fail to give proper attention to the environment in which any subject is found, then our investigation can hardly be deemed empirical. If this practice occurs as a systematic attempt to distort history, it is unfortunate, to say the least. The first spoken words were recorded in pictures etched on rocks in caves to preserve a moment of the history of humankind. As we have evolved to more precise and sophisticated tools of communication (eventually entrusting scholars with the responsibility of keepers of knowledge) racism, sexism, and other bigotry have often thwarted honest and objective reporting. Although this may in itself be instructive, revealing sustained insecurity and tendencies toward malfeasance, it is a dangerous practice when the preservation of knowledge is regarded as a somewhat sacrosanct domain.

The sincere foreign student of African music (or any other music that is unfamiliar) must also attempt to leave cultural baggage behind. It is an extremely difficult task for any of us to accomplish. Biases, cultural and otherwise, are made apparent in the choice of words a listener may choose to describe a musical performance with which she or he may be unfamiliar. We must remember, after all, that words such as unpleasant, discordant, disorganized, etc. are frequently socially conditioned responses subjectively described in politically charged terms. Complete objectivity is a near impossible position or state of existence. We must strive to check provincial orientation and subjective opinions, nevertheless, when attempting to understand African music. "The notorious distinction between what 'we' as Westerners and what 'they' as Africans hear must be replaced by distinctions between what any two individuals hear. . . . Such democratization is only conceivable in a world in which representer and represented inhabit the same sociological and political spheres."[77]

Careful consideration and study of the process of artistic creation can unveil key aspects of sociocultural expression and behavior that can lead to new levels of appreciation and understanding. In making a comparison between a timeless African folk tradition and two centuries of functional harmony, W. E. F. Ward proposes that African harmony may be "as far developed as European harmony in the sixteenth century." He continues: "Africans have not merely cultivated their sense of rhythm far beyond ours, but must have started with a superior sense of rhythm from the beginning."[78] We must ask the question, however: How do we benefit from "contests" involving comparisons of music of a particular culture with that of another?

In the chapters that follow we will begin to reveal the African origins of "jazz." Although the influences of European colonization affected both the Americas and West Africa dramatically, many Africans feel that music is an area where tradition remained relatively stable in many regions of Africa. If the similarities between the traditional music of West Africa and music from African areas where slave traders had minimal impact is an indication, then this is apparently true. Therefore, some West African music from 1600 (the time marking the arrival of West African slaves to the New World) would have probably been perpetuated along an unbroken line of oral tradition with a level of stability that would have maintained traits until the 1950s (when ethnomusicologists began intensive field research in West Africa).

David Such warns "comparisons between early forms of African-American and West African music have to be made under the assumption that the latter remained relatively stable over this period. Hence, West African societies would have had to remain relatively free of outside pressures that might have significantly altered their music."[79] Nonetheless, it is safe to assume that, if African Americans were able to retain significant traits of African music while being deprived of all traditional instruments and tribal connections, Africans on their own continent are most likely to have retained infinitely more sociocultural stability. Although elements of society were modified to a degree, clearly many African languages, dance, visual arts, manners of dress, religious practices, and other significant cultural components remain intact and provide a level of evidence to substantiate this theory.

Summary

African vocal and instrumental slurs and vibratos have counterparts in African-American music in America. Because these elements of music evade some Western musical analysis, they are given little emphasis in most "jazz" research and criticism. Those trying to record early African music during the slave era often became frustrated. ("It is difficult to express the entire character of these Negro ballads by mere musical notes and signs. The odd turns made in the throat . . . seem almost as impossible to place on the score as the singing of birds."[80]) Styles incorporating these decorative and fundamental devices are still heard in traditional African vocal music throughout the continent, where a much greater spectrum of expressive devices are employed. African vocals often include manipulation of timbre, glissando, yodels, trills, vibrato, syllabic, and mellismatic singing, use of falsetto break, and stylized cries. As W. E. B. Du Bois once said, "Africa is at once the most romantic and the most tragic of continents. Its very names reveal its mystery and wide-reaching influence. It is the 'Ethiopia' of the Greek, the 'Kush' and 'Punt' of the Egyptian, and the Arabian 'Land of the Blacks.' To modern Europe it is the 'Dark Continent' and 'land of Contrasts'; in literature it is the seat of the Sphinx, gnomes, and pixies, and the refuge of the gods; in commerce it is the slave mart and the source of ivory, ebony, rubber, gold, and diamonds. What other continent can rival in interest this Ancient of Days? There are those, nevertheless, who would write universal history and leave out Africa"[81]

A Survey of African Kingdoms

The story of humanity may be richer than that we know,
We must examine all of it to know that this is so.
Ham and Noah's other sons created all Hamitic and Semitic cultural levels,
These sons led African and Asian Canaanite tribes from the Tower of Babel,
These tribes were called Phoenicians by Greeks -who adored their strange
      tall palm trees,
Were tribes like the Egyptian Phoenix bird from whose ashes the younger he
      or she leaves?
Some settled in the land of Canaan, named after the youngest son of Ham in
      fact,
Today it is called Israel but biblical leprosy laws confirm these people were
      Black.

Kush (Nubia)

The Kushite kingdom lasted over a thousand years.
They used elephants in combat evoking all kinds of fears.
King Piankhy was the first Kushite king to rule Egypt we see,
He ruled these people fairly during the twenty-fifth Dynasty.
They conquered the Egyptians in 730 B.C. remaining for a century,

They were then defeated by Assyrians with superior iron weaponry.
The Kushites fled to Nubia moving their capital to Meroe in the south,
Soon it was the iron capital of Ancient Africa and strong once again.
It was King Natashien who reigned from 328 B.C. and he was no slouch;
With his firm rule, Nubian hieroglyphics, alphabet and script began.
Trade exploits to Arabia, India and China caused their fame to expand.
After the crucifixion, many Kushites became Christians as times changed;
And by 320 A.D. King Malequereliar became the last king that reigned.
The Axum Empire was eventually the new trade center, and after 1200 years,
Christian Nubia fell to Moslem rule despite all the struggling and tears.

Goddesses became gods when the pagan temples were destroyed,
Her story became his-story as sacerdotal egos became annoyed.
Time can erase the memory of a soul,
Then the mind becomes tired and old.

Ancient Ghana

Ancient Ghana should not be confused with contemporary Ghana at all.
It was the gold capital of the world, then to the Arabs it did fall.
Koumbi, its famous capital was divided into two great and powerful African
    cities,
Where miners found nuggets for the king while keeping the gold dust for
    their own kitties,
The king and Soninke tribe lived in one area, Moslems and foreigners in the
    other,
The latter group taxed all goods entering into or passing through the city.
A strong army kept the Trans-Saharan trade routes open and under cover,
Until 1054, when Almoravids invaded the region for 14 years, finally con-
    quering it, what a pity.

How many mothers, sisters and daughters achieved their arcane aspirations,
Yet it's the names of sons, brothers and fathers that remain preserved within
the nation.
I know destructive force yield an easy way to be,
Yet the universe remains creative if you have the eyes to see.

We know the Sumerians and Hamurabi's Babylonian kingdom of circa 2150
    B.C.,
It takes much more than racist canals to change a history from sea to shining
    sea.
Mesopotamia was inhabited by Ethiopians and some Canaanites were Car-
    thaginians,
Africans were certainly always African from North to South and so were In-
    dia's Druvidians,
Just as all Mayas, Aztecs, Incas, Choctaw, Sioux, Apache, and Eskimos are
    all misnamed "Indian."

Mali (not the Republic of Mali)

Out of the ruins of the Moslem state of Ancient Ghana around 1230 A.D.
Grew Niani, the capital of the Mandingo Empire, and strong it was to be.
Sundiata captured rich salt and gold mining areas then sent his men away,
So his generals became his governors and counsel was held with local chiefs
    each day.
By 1312 King Mansa Musa kept desert raiders away with his 90,000 men,
His infantry was supported by 10,000 more warriors on camels and Arabian
    horses.
Soon peace came and warriors became farmers; they did not have to fight
    again,
Their fair king became known as a lover of music, poetry and created new
    resources.
Mali's empire spread to Tazhaza and the gold areas Galam and Bure to the
    South,
Numeruos gold, copper, silver and leather craftsmen put food in every mouth.
Timbuktu and Djenne became centers knowledge, commerce and culture we
    hear,
But in 1324 Mali's economy became inflated and remained so for 25 years.
A devout Moslems that led a pilgrimage to Mecca took 60,000 men and such,
The victors forced no one to convert, but the gold they left there proved too
    much
Good king Mansa Musa died in 1337, but his empire evolved until its time
    was through;
Many Greek, Roman and Indian scholars came to study there in Sankore at
    University in Timbuktu.

So the great queen Isis is dethroned from the trinity,
And once great folk become indentured for eternity.
The weak, not the meek then inherit the earth . . . for a while,
But insecurity and insanity can be measured in the absence of a smile.

Songhay

It is the largest Ancient African kingdoms we've examined thus far,
Its people came from the region of Dendi on the Niger River bar.
This occurred before the 9th century and by the 11th century or so,
Songhay expanded quickly well beyond the bend (at Niger) to Gao.
Before long this capital city became the Moslem center of learning and trade,
So when Sunni Ali came to power prosperity had already been made.
That was 1464, then beginning in 1468, this warrior king attacked Timbuktu,
Defeating the Tuaregs and Djenne (in the south), subjugating the whole slew.
The war took 7 years, later King Askia Mohammed continued the prolifera-
    tion of this plight . . .
The empire now created farmers, merchants and miners (who were tradition-
    ally out of sight).
Soon every member of the community held roles such as keepers of cattle,
    miners, & fishmen.

Until the Portugese took over the rich African trade and brought things
to a bitter end.

But how does the Queen of Sheba fit into his-story?
Can Queen Nefertiti find her place in all this masculine glory?
Time can erase the memory of a soul,
Then the mind becomes tired, the mind becomes old,
So the great queen Isis is dethroned from the trinity,
And once great folk become indentured for eternity.

Then came invasions, Indo-Germanic and Germanic invasions of Asia,
Greek invasions of the Middle East; Roman invasions of the Middle East and
Northern Africa; Jews and Arabs became involved in the "white" slave
trade . . .
The world was becoming more complex and so were its complexions.

Although these earlier societies had ample prejudices,
They weren't stratified strictly by color—Reading Herodotus makes clear that
         point—yet we are still astonished to find that Socrates was a brother.
Before truth of Moses, Abraham, Cleopatra, Aesop, Hannibal and others was
         told,
Our Western history separated the land from its people; was that absurdity
         dumb or bold?

An Egyptian was an Egyptian; a Greek a Greek; a Hottentot was a Hottentot
The Land of the Free; Home of the Brave—are we moving backwards or
what?

Kanem-Bornu

These twin kingdoms lasted over a thousand years; Idris Alomia was its
         greatest king.
The dominions were located on either side of Lake Chad; its mighty military
         controlled everything.
It traded nuts, leather, ivory, and ostrich feathers for salt and European
         goods.
Their warriors were famed for horsemanship so the Lake Chad Region was
         free of robbing hoods.
Thus the trade and commerce was usually not impeded; consequently, its
         economy could not help but flourish.
To sustain both Kanem and Bornu for so many centuries most certainly took
         strength, wisdom and courage.

How many mothers, sisters and daughters achieved their arcane aspirations,
Yet it's the names of sons, brothers and fathers that remain preserved within
the nation.
I know destructive force yield an easy way to be,
Yet the universe remains creative if you have the eyes to see.

Benin

The trading center for large sections of West Africa, and a culture rich in
communal commitment from people harboring pride within every
heart . . .

Was the forest kingdom of Benin in what is now Southern Nigeria from
whence wood and bronze artifacts sprang forth as African art.

These dignified people used Manillas (or metal rings) and cowrie shells as
money, while making daily shopping and bartering a casual affair;

The Oba or chiefs allowed various officials to manage the kingdom, while a
few miles away the "Queen Mother" groomed the king's heir.

Ewuare the Great (who ruled from 1440 to 1473), a somewhat eccentric chief,
was known as a magician, doctor, warrior and wise man;

The city had long, broad, and straight streets with many houses, complex
temples, and law-abiding citizens—you must understand.

At first the Portugese tried to steal Benin's many riches, but they changed
their approach after being forcefully and repeatedly driven away.

Then they and other Europeans trade partners learned that dealing with
shrewd African merchants took 8 to 10 entire days.

Before making important decisions the custom was to eat, drink and be festive for a significant period of time.

After all, the people of Benin reserved a day each month for celebrating—as
diametrically opposed to plotting crime.

This map shows many of the different languages spoken on the African
continent. The diversity of the languages reflects the length of time Africa
has been settled.

The longer areas of earth have been settled, the more languages are found in that region.

Africa: Languages

Notes

[1] Klaus Wachaman, *Essays Music and History in Africa,* p. 9.

[2] The name "Ethiopian" is Greek in origin. It combines the Greek terms *Ethios* (burnt) with *ops* (face) reflecting the belief that the Ethiopian complexion was a result of their exposure to the intensified rays of the African sun. Rosicrucians, Freemasons, and other worldwide mystical orders acknowledge Egypt as the source of the wisdom and knowledge studied and guarded by their organizations for many centuries. The descriptions of Africa written by early Greek historians were probably not as racially motivated as their modern counterparts.

[3] Lady Lugard, *A Tropical Dependency*, p. 221. (See E. A. Wallis Budge, *A History of Ethiopia*, 1:1–2.)

[4] Malefi Kete Asante, *The Afrocentric Idea* (Philadelphia: Temple University Press, 1989).

[5] Donald Jay Grout, *A History of Western Music*, rev. ed. (New York: Norton, 1973).

[6] Stanley Lane-Poole, *The Story of the Moors in Spain* (Baltimore: Black Classic, 1990), pp. vii–viii.

[7] Notes from the CD recording *Alemu Aga: Bägänna of Ethiopia: The Harp of King David*, Long-Distance Music #7142009.

[8] A. C. Jordan, *Tales from Southern Africa* (Berkeley: University of California Press, 1973), p. xii. Hereafter cited as *Tales*.

[9] W. M. Flinders Petrie, *Social Life in Ancient Egypt* (Boston: Houghton Mifflin, 1923), p. 25.

[10] Ibid., p. xiii.

[11] Ibid.

[12] All inhabitants enjoyed the use and enjoyment of the land.

[13] *Tales*, p. xiv.

[14] Mickey Hart, *Planet Drum* (San Francisco: Harper Collins, 1991), pp. 17–26.

[15] Linda Dahl, *Stormy Weather* (New York: Limelight, 1989), pp. 41–42.

[16] Frank Tirro, *Jazz A History* (New York: Norton, 1977), p. 38.

[17] Francis Bebey, *African Music: A People's Art* (Westport, CT: Lawrence Hill, 1980).

[18] Handy, *Black Women,* pp. 121–24.

[19] Dahl, *Stormy Weather,* pp. 41–42.

[20] Ibid. p. 40.

[21] Merlin Stone, *When God Was a Woman* (New York: Harcourt Brace Jovanovich, 1978), p. 66.

[22] Ibid.

[23] Ibid.

[24] Ortiz M. Walton, *Music: Black, White and Blue* (New York: William Morrow, 1972), pp. 1–5.

[25] Curt Sachs, *The History of Musical Instruments* (New York: Norton, 1940), p. 96.

[26] Ibid.

[27] Ibid.

[28] Lise Manniche, *Music and Musicians in Ancient Egypt* (London: British Museum Press, 1991), p. 80.

[29] Ibid., pp. 24, 64.

[30] Ibid., p. 25.

[31] Ibid., pp. 35, 60.

[32] Ayele Bekerie, *Ethiopic: An African Writing System* (Lawrenceville, N.J.: Red Sea Press, 1997), pp. 132–33.

[33] Ibid., p. 128.

[34] From the liner notes of the CD *Bnet Houariya—Voix des femmes Marrakech,* 1997: "Al Sur." Distributed by Media 7—France.

[35] Koskoff, Ellen, *Women and Music in Cross-Cultural Perspective* (Chicago: University of Chicago Press, 1989), p. 71.

[36] Abd al-Wahhab, Hasan Husni, "Taqaddum al-musiqa fi-sh-sharq wa-l-andalus wa-tunis," *Waraqat,* vol. 2. (Tunis: Maktabat al-Manar, 1966), pp. 196–97.

[37] *Ibid.,* pp. 199–200.

[38] *Ibid.,* pp. 231–32.

[39] *Women and Music in Cross-Cultural Perspective,* p. 71.

[40] *Ibid.,* p. 72.

[41] Abd al-Wahhab, Hasan Husni, "Taqaddum al-musiqa fi-sh-sharq wa-l-andalus wa-tunis," *Waraqat,* vol. 2. (Tunis: Maktabat al-Manar, 1966), p. 202.

[42] Roland Oliver, *The Dawn of African History* (New York: Oxford University Press, 1968), p. 45.

[43] Webster's New Collegiate Dictionary, 9th ed. (Springfield: G. and C. Merriam Co., 1977), p. 1491.

[44] Oliver, *Dawn of African History,* p. 77.

[45] Unesco, *African Music,* p. 74.

[46] John Phillipson, *The Music of !Kung Bushmen of the Kalahari Desert, Africa* (New York: Folkways Records and Service, 1962).

[47] Ibid.

[48] Egyptian symbolism involving the female, male, and their offspring (Isis, Osiris, and Horus) may serve as archetypes for families of musical instruments—such as the three sizes of talking drums found in Nigeria, etc.

[49] Oliver, *Dawn of African History,* p. 68.

[50] Turnbull, *Man in Africa,* p. 244.

[51] *Harvard Dictionary of Music,* Ed. Willi Appel (Cambridge: Harvard University Press, 1969), p. 17.

[52] Ekundayo Phillips, *Yoruba Music (African)* (Johannesburg: African Music Society, 1933), p. 4.

[53] *Language and Music,* pp. 1–5.

[54] Colin M. Turnbull, *Man in Africa* (Garden City: Anchor, 1976), p. 159.

[55] Thomas Monro, *The New Encyclopedia Britannica, Macropaedia,* Benton, William, ed. (Chicago: Encyclopedia Britanica, 19 74), 1:161. Hereafter cited as *NEB.*

[56] *Harvard,* p. 17.

[57] Ibid.

[58] Francis Bebey, *African Music: A People's Art* (New York: Lawrence Hill, 1975), p. 3.

[59] Monro, Thomas, *NEB,* p. 242.

[60] *Harvard,* p. 21.

[61] Ibid., p. 20.

[62] Walton, *Music: Black, White and Blue,* pp. 8–13.

[63] A. N. Tucker, *Tribal Music and Dancing in the Southern Sudan (Africa) at Social and Ceremonial Gatherings* (London: William Reeves), p. 55.

[64] Ibid. Pianos have been "compromised" (tempered) to facilitate playing in different keys.

[65] Ibid., p. 21.

[66] Unesco, *African Music* (Paris: La Revue Musicale, 1970), p. 17.

[67] Paul Oliver, *Savannah Syncopators: African Retentions in the Blues* (New York: Stein and Day, 1974), p. 16.

[68] Ibid., p. 17.

[69] Geoffrey Haydon and Dennis Marks, eds., *Repercussions: A Celebration of African American Music* (London: Century, 1985), pp. 16–17.

[70] Ibid. p. 17.

[71] Ibid. p. 18.

[72] Ibid. p. 25.

[73] Bebey, *African Music*, p. 22.

[74] Agawu, Kofi, "Representing African Music," *Critical Inquiry* 18 (1992): 245–46.

[75] Ibid.

[75] Ibid. p. 260.

[77] Ibid. pp. 249–50.

[78] W. E. F. Ward, "Music in the Gold Coast," *Gold Coast Review* 3 (July–December 1927): 222, 223.

[79] David G. Such, *Avant-Garde Jazz Musicians: Performing 'Out There'* (Iowa City: University of Iowa Press, 1993), p. 33.

[80] Quoted in William Francis Allen et al., *Slave Songs of the United States* (New York: Peter Smith, 1951), p. vi.

[81] W. E. B. Du Bois, as cited in Walton, *Music: Black, White and Blue*, p. 1.

II

The Sociocultural Context
in Which African-American Music Emerged

A single bracelet does not jingle.

—Congo proverb

When it comes to discussing the historical context in which African-American music evolved, denial and avoidance have become trademarks of American history. Most histories of African-American music avoid investigations of the social conditions within which the music evolved. Perhaps, for some historians, there is a need to avoid exposing the disgusting and barbaric nature of American slavery. This is especially true with regards to the historical study of African-American music.

It is impossible to understand the development of African-American music, therefore, without first exploring the unique sociopolitical circumstances imposed by the nefarious European slave era. Certainly it is clear that music making was severely affected by the demands and limitations of daily life: families, tribes, and villages were abruptly separated, and people suffered from physical, psychological, and sociocultural trauma. African instruments were no longer available, so music was expressed through new makeshift mediums.

Undoubtedly, hostility, exploitation, and an unbelievably oppressive environment dominated the creative expression of Africans in America during the first three hundred years of European slave trading. Paradoxically it limited and motivated their daily struggle for survival. Add sexism to such conditions and clearly the lives of women musicians were usually in double jeopardy. The music of Africans and their struggle as slaves (and as free Africans in America) are inseparable. Afrocentric patterns of religious worship, labor, play, celebration, marriage, and social conflict were forced to undergo extreme modifications in America. Still, music remained a part of every aspect of African-American life, despite the severe or austere circumstances of daily encounters.

The slave era mentalities extant in the American colonies infected the attitudes and practices that shape the music industry and society in which modern African-American innovators live and create. Examining the history of the first three hundred years of European contact with the Americas thus sets the stage for understanding and appreciating the complexities of contemporary American conditions and dilemmas that impact upon African-American music.

The Natives of America

Africans alone were not the only victims of severe oppression and genocide in America. The nadir of American civilization was perhaps the long and egregious genocide of Native American people and culture at the hands of European explorers and settlers. With a new basis for racist behavior, the Spanish could now project their long-standing hatred of Jews and Moors upon the Native Americans. The Spanish conquerors now easily labeled them pagans. In the deluded mind of Cortes, the great Aztec temples were *mezquitas* (mosques). Bernal Diaz convinced himself that traces of Jewish influence were extant in Aztec statues and temples and speculated that Jews brought them there during the first-century Diaspora.[1] One Spaniard during this period observed that so many Native Americans were enslaved that they "no longer approach their wives, in order not to beget slaves."[2]

European-American colonists took no more interest in Native American music than European explorers did in African music. Alaine Locke suggests that, had the Native Americans and their traditions been absorbed rather than exterminated, Native American music may have been the folk music of North America: "It could have been, for it was a music very noble and simple, full of the spirit of the wind, woods and water; as serious American musicians have discovered too late to preserve it in any great way. It fell to the lot of the Negro, whom slavery domesticated, to furnish our most original and influential folk music, and because of its contagious spread and popularity, to lay the foundation for Native American music."[3]

Demographics, economic factors, and military power often determine the degree to which a given population is exploited and oppressed. In America it was much more difficult to dominate and enslave indigenous people when all three conditions were not in the Europeans' favor. The occupation colony was a region where the conquest of the indigenous population would be more difficult and costly, and where little land was readily available for white settlement. Traditional Native American music remained intact when tribes remained intact. The Africans on American plantation colonies had no land, organized communities, economy, or military power to defend themselves. They were forced to create new forms of music and dance. Africans did have a greater immunity to European diseases than Native Americans. This physical and psychological stamina ironically served to present African people as perfect candidates for oppressive slave labor in the "New World."

Africans on their own continent, like the Native Americans who succeeded in keeping portions of their communities intact, were able to retain many traditional musical and cultural traits after Europeans invaded their regions. Within the traditions of many Native Americans, traditional music, languages, religious practices, and other cultural characteristics can still be witnessed today. In each case where indigenous culture has survived, the aims of the colonizers were diminished because oppressors could expect limited success in creating new extensions of European civilization within the societies they invaded. Those Native American cultures that lost the ways of the elders (as they merged with Europeans) were not as fortunate.

Africans' Limited Access to Musical Instruments and Performance Venues in America

Some slaves who brought African instruments with them (an Ashanti drum and other African instruments were found in Virginia, for instance) managed to play them despite legislation. A decree issued in Georgia in 1775 stated that "whatsoever master or overseer shall permit his slaves, at any-time hereafter, to beat drums, blow horns, or other loud instruments, shall forfeit 30 shillings sterling for every such offense."[4] However, the difficulty involved in enforcing this particular legislation was clear even in 1811 when lawmakers complained, "It is absolutely necessary to the safety of this province that all due care be taken to restrain Negroes from using or keeping drums."[5] People were well aware of the communicative powers of the drum; they had aided in the development of several slave revolts.

> A little over a century after the first Africans were sent into American slavery, a plot to revolt was uncovered in Saint John's Parish, outside of Charlestown, South Carolina. Slaves from Charlestown and the surrounding countryside assembled, under the guise of a "dancing" bout, planning to seize the armory, get arms, and take over the city. When the drums "signaled" for the "bout" to begin, the militia, hiding in ambush, attacked, killing most of the slaves. Nine years later in Stono, South Carolina, the results were different.[6]

The slaves in the latter case left a dismal twelve-mile trail, destroying all the plantations they encountered.

The mandate that African drumming and other traditions be abandoned caused the Africans in America to exercise extreme caution in their public displays of musical expression. Due to such trepidation, from the moment the first abducted slaves arrived in America musical styles of a subtle nature began to evolve. This subtlety can be highly evasive and deceptive. Eurocentric musicologists have assumed that forced acculturation was entirely successful in persuading Africans in America to adopt European chords and scales. This is not an accurate assessment. Africans in America still maintained fundamental principles of traditional African melodic and harmonic construction through clever ways of exploiting European models. European instruments, forms, melodies, and harmonies were the tools with which musicians were forced to create, but Africans never completely abandoned their own unique methods.

The performance of African polyrhythms was difficult to maintain under conditions imposed by American slavery, so Africans in America were forced to succumb to dramatic rhythmic modifications. African polyrhythms—a metaphorical indication of both the diversity of nature and the unity and harmony upon which life depends—are most effective when individual levels of stratification can be clearly distinguished by range, timbre, and other musical factors. Denied traditional percussive instruments, the African often had only his or her body with which to create music. Drum patterns were transferred to hand clapping, patting "juba" (body slapping), foot stamping, etc. The differentiation of such body sounds was limited and communal performance was less reliable than the communal polyrhythmic ensembles to which Africans had been accustomed in their native land.

Families and tribes had been divided, which limited the shared knowledge of cultural patterns that could have been transmitted communally under more favorable circumstances. As a result of the dissolution of the communal units that accommodated the multilayered African rhythms, elements of modified polyrhythmic African tendencies were modified (and sometimes homogenized) and eventually adapted by the voice and transferred to European instruments as they became available. Limitations were turned into advantages as performers began to conceive of formerly collective rhythmic performance in more horizontal, soloistic terms. African-American musicians began to explore syncopation more vigorously, as a substitute for the vitality of African cross-rhythms and polyrhythms in solo musical performances.

The retention of drums and other indigenous African instruments in Haiti, Trinidad, or Jamaica (and most other "New World" slave societies) resulted in the creation of musical styles with clear African percussive ties and orientation. The forced transference of the functions of the drum to human body and voice transformed the African-American church into a default cultural institution that fostered the development of these new music-making skills. The spirituals that were nurtured during the slave era, in turn, would set the stage for the African-American instrumental music that would find its greatest degree of maturation after the Civil War—in the music some would call "jazz." Legislation forbidding the use of drums during the slave era thus accounts for some of the most important developments in the evolution of African-American music.

Polyphony and antiphony, both widely practiced in African music, were more easily maintained within work songs and subsequently became the basis for African-American music forms and harmonic development. Polyphony takes place when two or more independent musical phrases or melodies are performed simultaneously. Vibrant and rich vertical harmonics are also formed as a result of linear developments. When syncopated body rhythms, hand clapping, and foot stomping are added to singing, another layer of rhythmic intensity, cumulative force, and musical excitement leads to climatic energy that presents the African-American polyrhythm in a new guise, no less powerful than its parent continental African form. Europeans, accustomed only to simple mathematical subdivision of the beat, were somewhat baffled at first by the African-American music they encountered. Yet, some found the music intriguing from the beginning.

Much of the time that Africans in America devoted to music making was in conjunction with labor or religion. When the singing voices of African Americans were directed to the Christian divinity, little resistance was met since conversion to Christianity was one of the slave owners' primary goals. If an oppressed people then begin to worship the oppressors' deity, it becomes easier for them to fall under the spell of the conqueror's political agenda and indoctrination. In "New World" African slave societies where the drum was played, religious practices tended to maintain more clearly defined aspects of the African Orisha and other sacred cults.[7] During the first thirty-five or forty years of slavery in America, most of the slaves came from Africa by way of the West Indies. The influence of vodun in the United States is due to the fact that a considerable number were brought to the American colonies from Haiti and the Dominican Republic (Hispaniola). Most slaves from Dahomey and Togo went to Hispaniola, where they began to practice vodun.

The singing of Christian hymns was one way whereby African slaves could transfer aspects of African religious structures into European forms and then turn these forms to their own advantage. African elements were re-shaped, enhanced, expanded, and strengthened in secluded realms where repressive adversity and humiliation were converted into strength, courage, perseverance, and creative self-expression.

> Christianity alone, adulterated, otherworldly, and disengaged from its most authentic implications—as it was usually presented to the slaves—could not have provided the slaves with all the resources they needed for the kind of resistance they expressed. It had to be enriched with the volatile ingredients of the African religious past and, most important of all, with the human yearning for freedom that found a channel for expression in the early black churches of the South.[8]

Many African-American folk songs and blues compositions had their origins as field hollers, work songs, and other vocal idioms. Later, field hollers were often used to convey cryptic messages such as information about the Underground Railroad. The cries of street vendors at the turn of the present century retained many of the features of this vocal style. The religious music that evolved into the African-American spiritual style was heavily influenced by the cross-fertilization of this nascent African-American music and the congregational psalmody and hymnody that was practiced in European-American Sabbath services. In European-American churches, African Americans were forced to sit in segregated pews marked "BM" (Black men) and "BW" (Black women), even in communities in New England. A presenter would teach songs to all members of the congregation by rote. "Lining out" involved teaching psalms in a fashion where each line would be chanted loudly and clearly by the lead voice then imitated by the congregation until the entire tune was memorized.

Slave Era Music and Cultural Cross-Fertilization

Africans in America were forced to abandon a plethora of languages, religions, metaphysics, and other sociocultural traditions. They were required to modify their customs, music, rituals, family units, and behavioral patterns in ways that forcibly merged European musical and cultural elements with their own. This steady, gradual process produced an African-American music that retained features of both cultures, a music with functional, spiritual, and expressive styles and qualities that existed nowhere else. Africans were resourceful and tenacious. The diverse musical legacy they evolved in America reflects both tenacity and inventiveness.

> [African] music and dance have a quite different and incomparably greater significance than with us. . . . They serve neither as mere pastimes nor recreations. They are not meant to edify the mind aesthetically; nor can they be regarded as a brilliant decoration on festive occasions, or as a means of effectively staging ceremonies. . . . Music is neither reproduction (of a "piece of music" as an existing object) nor production (of a new object): it is the life of a living spirit working within those who dance and sing.[9]

When two peoples interact long enough, each absorbs, inadvertently or not, some of the other's sociocultural patterns and tendencies. It is revealing, therefore, to examine various ways in which people made contact with each other in America to understand why African-American music evolved into an ecumenical art form that eventually transfixed twentieth-century world culture.

Cross-fertilization between the music and cultures of Africans, Europeans, Native Americans, and other people occurred throughout world history. Not all Africans who came to America arrived in bondage. African influence on the "New World" is, therefore, not restricted to the history of European slave trading and colonization. Early African contact with regions throughout the world must have left a measure of influence on world music and culture.

Al-Omari tells us that the brother of Emperor Mansa Musa, prince Abubakari II, sent shipping vessels across the African Sea (Atlantic Ocean) in 1311 and 1312. Abubakari's fishing vessels landed in Mexico, bringing African settlers who influenced the language, myths, rituals, religions, and agriculture of the time. In his book *They Came before Columbus*, Ivan Van Sertima suggests that Africans made other trans-Atlantic voyages to the Americas, navigating by means of the warm ocean currents. Ironically, knowledge of these Atlantic currents apparently later became one of the most important factors in organizing the European slave trade.

There is evidence that Mandingo merchant explorers made over fifty trips to various Caribbean and Central and South American areas between 1310 and 1491. These African sailors visited what is now Panama, Honduras, and Haiti.[10] A successful trade route was already established from the Zambezi River to China when Vasco da Gama and Bartholomew Diaz encountered African influence upon entering the Indian Ocean around 1498. African features can be found on ancient artifacts found in the Americas. Iconographic elements such as the sculpture at La Venta in Mexico and the presence of Africans in the murals in the Temple of Warriors at Chichen Itza are examples that demonstrate an early African presence in the Americas. Bronze objects, ceramic portraiture, mud-brick houses, African plants (such as cotton and the pan-gourd), and other archaeological evidence have been found in the Americas. Books by Moorish scholars also mention the early exploits of these early

African mariners.[11] African music may have left a clear, if more ephemeral, imprint as well. Similarities between a variety of wind, string, and percussion instruments worldwide suggest cultural intermingling dating back thousands of years.

The difference in attitudes of slave era oppressors from various areas of Europe, are reflected in the varying degrees of Afrocentricity in music of the Americas. African traditions remained more intact under Portuguese and Spanish slave owners than under their British counterparts. Portuguese and Spanish slave owners apparently felt they needed primarily to control their slaves' labor, not necessarily their minds. Music produced in regions under Portuguese and Spanish control thus retained more conspicuous degrees of African origin. Slaves under Spanish jurisdiction were generally entitled to one day off each week. Africans often assembled to celebrate with music and dance on these occasions. Many slaves in Brazil and the Caribbean eventually purchased their own freedom. Detailed documentation exists concerning the influence of the Arada and Yoruba tribes on the spread of African culture, worship and traditions in the areas of Brazil, the Caribbean, and New Orleans. *Vodun* (later *voodoo*) and *Santería* (another hybrid "New World" religion of African roots) demonstrate the continuation of African religious ceremonies and traditions in the Americas. In some Portuguese- and Spanish-controlled regions of the "New World," songs and dances for rituals and celebrations were played on gourds, drums, rattles, and other musical instruments that were similar to African prototypes.

Brazil's "Black" population is the second largest in the world (Nigeria has the largest). Bahia, a Brazilian state, has preserved more West African musical elements and traditions than any other place in Latin America or the Caribbean. The Macumban vocal style of Brazil involves the falsetto singing, polymetrical devices, responsorial technique, and polyrhythms that are still heard in western Nigeria. The African slaves who cultivated Brazilian rubber, sugarcane, and cotton blended their music with local styles to produce the Samba ("new dance") and the Bossa Nova ("new touch").[12]

The British had relatively little contact with Africans before the slave era. Therefore, they distanced themselves to a greater degree from the African "savages" and exerted more strident degrees of control over their victims physically, emotionally, and spiritually. Consequently, their particular brand of slavery involved an intensified degree of forced conversion to Protestant faith, stronger deprivation of any elements of African culture, and more strictly enforced laws regarding miscegenation than most Catholic counterparts in the "New World." Thus, Africans retained fewer Africanisms in Protestant church music than in voodoo, Santería, and other Catholic-influenced religious music.

The European slave trade was the largest forced migration in the history of the world (involving 15 to 50 million people between 1482 and 1888). The captured African prisoners undoubtedly experienced despair and trepidation before leaving their native land. They faced the reality that fellow Africans abducted them and often burned villages strictly for the sake of economic gain. The horrific degradation of displaced African people began with suffering at the hands of drunken European sailors, who were prone to violently assaulting their chained victims sexually, psychologically, and physically during the Middle Passage. Half of those abducted died during the devastating five- to eight-week sea voyages under unbearable conditions. Many died of suffocation in slave ship compartments built with only eighteen inches of clearance for its human cargo to assure the placement of as many slaves on board as possible. Amid the most debilitating conditions imaginable, Africans were forced to make music and dance. Fiddles, drums, the voice, and other instruments were used to encourage slaves to exercise to minimize casualties and loss of profits. In the Caribbean, the slave "breakers" attempted to strip the slaves of their African identities and break their spirits through torture, thereby assuring that a docile cargo was prepared for the final destinations.

The economic foundation for European slave trading began when the Spanish found that the indigenous labor in the West Indies was insufficient. The island of Hispaniola received fifty African slaves in 1510 after it became clear that Africans adapted to the heat and workload more readily than indigenous laborers. Rum was sent to West Africa in exchange for slaves brought to the Caribbean. The African slaves were then bartered for molasses, sugar cane, and other goods for the return trip to New England in this trade triangle.

The involvement of the church extended beyond the conversion of souls to Christianity and the singing of psalms during the slave era. Religious leaders in the West did not pass up the opportunity to get their share of the money made on human suffering. The church was paid a fee for the Pope's signature on an *asiento* determining which nation had the church's consent to engage in the brutal institution of slave trading. The Asiento of 1713 between England and Spain is an example of such an agreement. "So profitable was the European slave trade that the Roman Catholic Church entered the business as a grantor of commercial privilege to prevent Christian nations from engaging in fratricidal wars of access to the African coast."[13]

Music played a grand part in early slave revolts in the Americas. Drums and the singing voice were important means of communication during revolts on land. Might music have served similar purposes on board slave-bearing vessels? Africans sang songs, played fiddles, drums, and other instruments during the dreadful Middle Passage to encourage exercise and reduce the number of deaths. Prisoners may have managed some means of communicating. We know Africans organized successful revolts on board slave ships and managed to sail the captured vessels to freedom. Traditional African drumming communicated spoken language quite precisely. In discussing the music of Hausa-speaking Muslims in Nigeria, for instance, Fremont Besmer tells us:

> Certain of the instruments of the court musicians more than others have a specific role in the reciting the *kírári* descriptive epithets or *táké* descriptive drum rhythms of the offices of the court. *Kírári* epithets, for example, are possible in a tonal language system through the exact reduplication of the phonemic tones and syllable-lengths of the phrase to be communicated on the instrument. Given the limited number of lexical items from

which the message can be chosen in addition to the situational context in which *kírári* epithets are heard, there is surprisingly little ambiguity in linguistic meaning.[14]

Europeans considered the maroons "fugitive" African slaves. Some managed to build successful communities in the West Indies in the seventeenth and eighteenth centuries. On rare occasions, others managed to return to Africa. Cinqué, son of an African chief, picked the lock of his shackles with a nail and freed his comrades before defeating the European crew and taking over the *Amistad*. John Adams was eventually persuaded to take the case to the U.S. Supreme Court. Adams spoke for over eight hours in behalf of the *Amistad* Africans. The court ruled that they should be set free.[15]

Drums were crucial in the struggle to resist European slave traders on the African continent. All of Africa was engaged in resistance to foreign invasion on various levels throughout the slave trade era. The European and Arabic traders who sought to exploit the human and natural resources of Africa did not find their task easy. However, two factors made a difference to the advantage of the Europeans: the relatively amiable character of most Africans toward foreigners and their lack of modern military technology. In *The Cultural Unity of Black Africa* the late Senegalese scholar Cheikh Anta Diop concludes that whereas Europeans have been xenophobic in encounters throughout the world, Africans have usually been xenophilic. The African's openness to strangers, rather than fear of them, was usually perceived as a sign of naiveté or weakness. Allowing Arabs and Europeans free passage through their lands conveniently made the unassuming and hospitable African kings and queens seem as though they cared little for their land in the eyes of those who sought to exploit them. By the time Africans became fully aware of nefarious European aspirations, they were unprepared to defend themselves against firmly entrenched European military technology.

A spirit of sociocultural flexibility became a trademark of African-American music. Within the British and European slave systems, each element of cultural circumstance gave birth to countless new forms of African expression that were amplified within the "New World." Each expression thus became a consequence of the environmental soil in which particular traits were sown. Music is a reflection of the degrees of African adaptation in the Americas. The evolution of African-American music was not restricted to plantations or to those Africans abducted directly from the African continent. Just as many people (of an assortment of heritages, including European) labeled "black" by the majority culture were absorbed into the African-American slave community, the music produced by free and enslaved "Black" Americans absorbed and transformed all musical influences it contacted.

Trinidadian dancer Wilfred Mark performing with Hesterian Musicism at the *Global African Music & Arts Festival/Symposium* (Karlton E. Hester, Artistic Director) at UC Santa Cruz in May 2003 (Photo by Sarah Blade/Precious Memories).

Thus an examination of music that emerged in various regions displays characteristics of particular brands of musical and cultural cross-fertilization. The British forced themselves upon the Ashanti in Jamaica, who then adapted to British customs. The Haitian culture involved the influences of both French and Dahoman traditions. Yoruban culture would be combined with Spanish traditions in Cuba, and with British customs in Trinidad. Portuguese language and society would transform Senegalese culture in Brazil. In addition to Native American and Mexican influences, West Africans in the United States adopted all "New World" European cultures.

When we speak of the music of the African people throughout the Americas, we know that their music is influenced by the West African Yoruba,

Ibo, Fanti, Ashanti, Susu, Ewe, and many other African cultural traditions. Africans developed the common elements between their various musical styles (i.e., call-and-response patterns, emotional intensity, complex polyphony, etc.) out of psychological, physical, spiritual, and emotional necessity. Those elements were not merely a fusion of musical styles that formed a collage containing disparate musical ingredients. Instead, they combined to function as an entirely new musical form of communication. The merging of African cultures in the "New World" transformed work songs, songs of praise, and music for various African celebrations into the African-American field songs and spirituals that would later serve as the basis for blues and "jazz."

Ever since the first African slaves were brought to the American colonies in 1619, they continued to bring with them their own traditional music, languages, traditions, and cultural habits. For over two hundred years slaves born in America were constantly reminded of their original homeland and cultural heritage by this constant influx of people from the African continent. Music and dance were the communicative tools through which disparate African traditions were most easily expressed and developed within slave communities. Because of the importance African people gave to music, and because music was often their only viable means of self-expression and communication, music always provided more than mere entertainment. In accordance with African tradition, music became an essential daily necessity of African-American living and a panacea for their suffering. Eileen Southern says, "Ceremonial music composed the largest part of the musical repertory of a village of a people. The Ashanti thought it 'absurd' to worship their god in any way other than with chanting or singing."[16]

African-American Music Convergence Affected by Sex and Marriage

The original inhabitants of America made contact with "New World" Africans in numerous ways. Many free Africans and "fugitive" slaves merged with Native American communities. Since Africans often blended into Native American society without much difficulty in such instances, music and other cultural convergence undoubtedly took place. The merging of Africans and Native Americans continued throughout the history of the United States. Charlie Parker, Sonny Rollins, Julius Hemphill, Oliver Lake, are but a few modern "jazz" innovators with shared African and Native American ancestries.

The assimilation of people and customs into slave society in America was not restricted to people of color. Slavery was not based strictly on race but was motivated by economic concerns. The profit made from American slave labor led to the exploitation of not only Africans and Native Americans but also European Americans. The diverse community of people labeled "Black" by slave traders thus produced a musical synergism ultimately resulting in the creation of Afrocentric music with direct links to all aspects of American society.

Just as Africans retained aspects of their traditions when they arrived in America, children of mixed heritage were affected by aspects of both parents' heritage. Europeans sold into slavery brought European cultural traditions with them into African-American slave quarters. Daughters of slave owners, both illegitimate and otherwise, were occasionally sold into prostitution or to other slave owners.[17]

Because it was impossible to differentiate between "Whites" and some fair mélanges and octoroons, many "White" people were sold as "Negro" slaves. Some brought with them formal European musical training on various instruments. How did such events affect the evolution of "jazz"? African music in America is firmly rooted in the sociocultural configurations fabricated by slave culture in America. The "melting pot" that formed this portion of American society is more complex than history often suggests. Thus, what is claimed to be the birth of "jazz" in New Orleans (actually "jazz" was born in various parts of the United States) involved a somewhat forced musical collaboration between all people considered "Black" in the South near the beginning of the present century (including Creoles and most other people of color).

Since marriages and forced procreation united people of various racial, ethnic, and religious backgrounds, sexual unions were determinants in the cultural exchanges that occurred in early American society. Sexual contact between Americans reveals significant historical information regarding social influences on the development of early African-American music. A law passed in 1681 was designed to prevent white servant women from being reduced to slavery. This law exempted such women from the penalty for marrying an African slave when evidence was presented that the marriage had been contracted at the instigation of the master.

African-American women were raped routinely on southern plantations. African and European-American males were engaged by slaveholders to rape African-American women in order to get them pregnant. "Some white men were paid as high as $20 for each Negro woman they got with child. Robust college students were even invited to spend their vacations on the plantations and turned loose among the slave cabins at night."[18] Because of the wealth that an increase in the population of slaves would automatically yield, this brand of slave breeding was common. European-American male plantation residents of all ages would leave their beds at night to sleep with women in the slave quarters. F. L. Olmstead claimed that "there is not an old plantation in which the grandchildren of the owners are not whipped in the fields by his overseers."[19] In a system similar to that found even today in India, infant slave girls were often betrothed to aged men and were obliged to sleep with them long before they reached puberty. As a result, some American slave owners maintained a fairly close relationship with their mélange offspring. In Alex Haley's film *Roots* one such character was able to develop musical skills on violin due to preferential advantages he received as the illegitimate son of the plantation owner.

While claims of mistaken identity were used to disguise the mercenary foundations for this practice in the beginning, the practice eventually became more overt. One of the leading writers of the times, George Fitzhugh, justified the sale of any color by saying to William Chambers, "Race! Do not speak to us of race—we care nothing of breed or color. What we contend for is, that slavery whether black or white, is a normal, proper institution in society."[20] Nonetheless, the resulting mixture of African-American people imbued African-American music with a depth and quality of cultural diversity rarely witnessed in the history of the world.

Not all Africans that came to America were perpetual slaves. Many were indentured servants, like other Europeans and Native Americans. The terms of such an arrangement allowed the servant to eventually repay the "master" with labor and win their freedom after a designated period of time. Free Africans became exposed to a slightly broader range of European music than African-American slaves restricted to southern plantations. This type of exposure eventually produced European stylistic genres of African influenced music by composers like Frank Johnson and Louis Gottschalk.

Had "white" slavery proven profitable in seventeenth-century England it may have been introduced. A series of judicial decisions were required to establish that slavery was contrary to English common law. There was no general bias against the condition of slavery before such legislation was enacted. International law in the seventeenth century regarded slavery as a legal and proper condition for those who could be defined as captives of war. Africans captured in African wars qualified for the "legal" basis of the participation of Great Britain France, Spain, the Netherlands, and other European countries involved, in the international slave trade. The arbitrary labeling of Africans provided additional support to the justification of slavery as a legitimate commerce. Consequently, when African captives were brought to the American colonies they were conveniently assumed to be prisoners of war.[21]

The interaction between African Americans and European Americans during early colonial times was not as completely laden with virulent prejudice that one might assume. Although many aspects of the relationships between these groups of Americans are in fact ambiguous, it is clear that music making in church services was not the only social contact people from the two cultures had with each other.

Likewise, musical interaction between African Americans and European Americans in the North during colonial times was not restricted to worship in the church. A more intimate exchange of culture in America was the result of interracial marriages. Virginia passed a law prohibiting interracial fornication in 1662, while a fine for interracial marriages was not enacted until 1691. In Maryland, where the attitudes toward African Americans were similar to those in Virginia, a law was passed in 1664 that was described by Winthrop Jordan as having "banned interracial marriages."[22] The latter law was actually limited to a ban on marriages between "Negro slaves" and "freeborn English women." It did not restrict marriages between free Africans and free Europeans. It is apparent that the law was explicitly motivated by a desire "to prevent the offspring of unions between European indentured servant women and African male slaves from following in the footsteps of their mother. The latter condition, as prescribed by law, resulted in offspring inheriting the status of the mother and thus eventually becoming free."[23] From this evidence one may conclude that the cultures and music were blending on many very basic levels during this period.

Most of the evidence of full-throated indignation against miscegenation before the 1690s can largely be explained as a manifestation of the European traditional desire to prevent intermarriage between people of different social stations. This could prove especially inconvenient to owners of slaves and servants. Many African Americans living in the northern United States as free individuals were successful blacksmiths, craftsmen and merchants and, consequently, were attractive potential marriage partners for women of any color. Colonial legislation at the time presents a clear indication that marriage with Negroes, even Negro slaves, was not repugnant to freeborn English women. There would have been no need for such laws had the "problem" of sexual integration not existed in the minds of European officials or society.

Sociocultural Influences on Seventeenth Century African-American Music

There was an amalgamation of a diverse spectrum of sociocultural attributes since little or no regard was given to particular ethnic or cultural origins of subjugated African people in America. Thus, an adaptation of African multilingualism, and the convergence of countless cultural traits, coupled with inevitable memory loss, took place out of necessity within the sociocultural sector of African-American society. As individuals became isolated within their new slave villages, some vestige of their past could be retained and reaffirmed during occasional musical performances or at church. Here, distinctive individual rhythms (from their native villages) could be interjected into the communal polyrhythms.

The music of the European countries involved in the slave trade, was entering the "High Renaissance." The music continued to involve the masses, chansons, and motets that were established in earlier periods, but the chief characteristics of the High Renaissance style were based upon the merging of two vocal techniques, homophony[24] and imitative counterpoint.[25] The Renaissance had followed a period of late-medieval music that ended with some experimentation with meter, polytextuality, and other musical elements. The emphasis on the clarity of the word in the Renaissance could be considered a conservative backlash to counterbalance the "excesses" of older times.[26] The average European American was not aware of the evolution of European music and Renaissance ideals were far removed from Afrocentric music in America during the colonial era.

There is often an assumption that early African-American music consisted exclusively of sad songs. Although many songs did indeed reflect the burdensome situations encountered by slaves, Africans everywhere still managed to express both happiness and sadness through music. Captives on slave ships and on land were frequently forced to sing by fearful slave owners who wanted to thwart plotting that might lead to insurrections. The music made by Africans who became maroons; the songs of those Africans who managed to be absorbed into Native American tribes; the music of those slaves who were treated more humanely than others; and of those who were treated as beasts of burden, all reflect a variety of human experiences. The emotional force poured into each of these early music-making situations culminated in the spirituals, blues, hollers, and work songs that formed the body of African-American music. These types of expressions "echoed emotional despair as well as jubilation and optimistic yearning for a Utopia—a better place without a master, without auction blocks and without conditions of servitude."[27]

Ira Berlin argued that three distinct slave systems evolved in North America during the seventeenth and eighteenth centuries: the northern non-plantation system, the Chesapeake Bay plantation system, and the Carolina and Georgia low-country plantation system. The majority of southern African Americans, however, remained physically and psychologically alienated from the European-American world, leaving them closer to Africa than Euro-America. Berlin claims that the low-country people "incorporated more West African culture—as reflected in their language, religion, work patterns, and much else—into their lives than did other black Americans." Throughout the eighteenth century and into the nineteenth century, low-country Africans in America continued to work the land, name their children, and communicate through word and song in a manner that openly combined African traditions with the unfortunate circumstances of plantation life.[28]

The high concentration of slaves in the South was due to the labor-intensive cotton industry there. As a consequence of this social positioning, the most salient features of early African-American musical evolution took place in this geographical area. According to records dating back to 1688, we find that African-American servants sang with the slave owners on special occasions such as weddings and colonial ceremonies such as the King's Birthday or Election Day. Psalm singing was the common practice of the day, so African Americans adopted the singing of psalms when they began to organize their own assorted religious meetings.[29]

The British soon realized that religious indoctrination was a strong strategy in gaining increased control of the African Americans' minds and spirits. Churches were encouraged to involve slaves at first, and then required in order to teach Christian doctrines to the entire community. A Massachusetts law of 1648 demanded that everyone, "black or white," receive religious instruction once a week. A 1682 teacher's contract demanded that "School shall begin with the Lord's prayer and close by singing a psalm."[30]

During the Pinkster's Mardi Gras-like celebration, slit drums, two-string fiddles, and other African inspired instruments were played. Writers of the period leave no doubt that the flavor of the festival was uniquely African. Pinkster Day, the name given to Pentecost Sunday, became an important celebration for African Americans in parts of the North. It was an occasion when African-American music dominated the day. Although originally a principal holiday for the Dutch in the Netherlands, in America it was initially adopted by the English in New York, parts of Pennsylvania, and Maryland. After the first few days of Pinkster in Manhattan, the Africans would take over, prolonging the festival for days with their Congolese dances. European Americans would come from all parts of the city and from outlying rural areas to witness the "Pinkster Carnival of the Africans." The lead drummer at such affairs was elected King by the community (between c. 1699 and 1824). He was responsible for "leading on the Guinea dance" and also played the banjo, fiddle, fifes, and hollow drums.[31]

That the celebrations came to a sudden halt soon after Nat Turner led his slave revolt in 1831 is probably no coincidence. Following the slave revolt, the gatherings may have been perceived of as threatening; the celebrations were canceled because they suddenly became "too noisy and disruptive" for European Americans in the North.

The sustained intensity that African-based music provided for some religious rituals related to the celebration drove African-American practitioners to a state of religious ecstasy. Perhaps the Pentecostal custom of "speaking in tongues" may have been related to an African-American attempt to converge upon a common language while engaging in spiritual ecstasy during religious services. The Revolutionary War brought the Pinkster slave celebrations to an end in Manhattan.

The eventual return of the dance festivals after the war drew people from Long Island, New Jersey, and other areas. When the war ended, crowds of both African and European-American spectators gathered to watch African dances and hear African songs in Philadelphia, where semiannual jubilees took place in Potter's Field (now Washington Square) until the Revolution. African Americans also congregated in an area referred to as "New Guinea" in Boston on the wharves, where African group dancing occurred. Festivals of this particular type only took place in the North, however.

A stirring blues (or "jazz") performance often contains an emotional propensity related to that experienced in a contemporary African-American Pentecostal service. A similar level of spiritual outpouring occurs at voodoo rituals. Common to each of these inspirational encounters is the gradual buildup of tension through musical repetition, sustained levels of intensity, and liberated emotional and physical states, expressed thorough dance and spontaneous movement. Situations involving the release of emotional tension, alternating with states of relaxation, become an important musical catharsis: they stimulate physical, mental, and spiritual health-giving properties that sustain initiates through difficult conditions.

Eighteenth-Century Sociocultural Changes

America had little music of its own during the eighteenth century. Although European music had a marginal affect on American culture at the time, it was the only music familiar to many European immigrants entering the Americas.

In Europe, near the beginning of the eighteenth century, Antonio Vivaldi was exploring his "Variations on 'La Folia' for Two Violins," Op. 1, no. 12 (1705). The Italian composer Giovanni Battista Pergolesi (questionably of dual African and European ancestry), renowned for his expressive church works, died in 1710. Baroque music of this period attempted to reflect the scientific precision developed in the seventeenth century in the tuning and construction of scales and musical instruments. René Descartes applied new rational methodology to the classification of human emotions and expressions. In turn, music theorists worked to formulate ways to create systems of stylized musical devices that could suggest corresponding emotions and expressions. Professional musicians moved from the patronage of the church to that of the court, joining the court painter and chef. The court musician now enjoyed greater exposure to the developments that took place in music and culture than could be realized within the church, but emphasis was firmly placed on controlling all elements of music. This condition led to regular rhythms, balanced schematic plans, terraced dynamics, and other Baroque formulas. The Baroque fugue exemplifies many of those stylized musical formulas.

American music was little influenced by these European developments. Although Yale Collegiate School was founded at Saybrook, Connecticut, and Yale College at New Haven, America was slow to develop in the artistic realm. European musicians usually toured with itinerant dancing masters and accompanied their dance classes as the instructors made their rounds to various American plantations. African-American slaves played the fiddle regularly at home and for resident dance classes. West African slaves of many regions shared sufficient traditions of music and dance to join together easily in communal celebrations. Some Africans spoke enough different languages to communicate with each other verbally as well.[32] Slaves often participated in community activities with European Americans in addition to holding their own celebrations.

"Lection Day," a colonial holiday which originated in 1750, was celebrated by African folk in New England. Africans elected their own "governors" or "kings" in elaborate ceremonies paralleling European-Americans' Election Day. For this occasion slaves received a holiday generally extending from Wednesday to the following Sunday. It began with a parade of up to a hundred people, on horseback or marching on foot, all dressed in their finest apparel. The music, which was performed by only the best musicians for this event, involved the playing of fiddles, clarinets, fifes, and drums. Games, wrestling, singing, dancing (to the sound of the fiddle, banjo, tambourine, and drums) followed the election ceremony. The festivities undoubtedly stimulated memories of African inaugural celebrations for kings and chiefs in the minds of the slaves.[33] Fiddling, an ancient African tradition practiced in many areas throughout the African continent and transferred to the European violin by African slaves on board slave ships, was later transformed into music of jigs and reels for "Lection Day" and other celebrations.

Undoubtedly, much of the slaves' music was vocal and accompanied only by work tools in the beginning. Only those African-American musicians hired out to perform on a regular basis could expect to have access to a musical instrument.[34] Because music making by most African captives involved singing, most early African-American musical forms were vocal genres, including work songs, play songs, hollers, shouts, street calls, and cries.

The cry involved a wailing sound that could serve as an expression of anguish, anger, joy, sorrow, or dread. The call could express related sentiments, but its original function seemed to be either a loud, high-pitched announcement or signal in the field; or alternately, a more subdued yell or chant. The street vendor's call ushered this style into twentieth-century America. The purpose of the call was to command attention or for "emoting individual expression of relief."[35]

Shouts were generally applied in a religious context such as a spiritual dance in voodoo rituals and by worshippers in some Protestant ceremonies. It was inherited from African religious dances and was applied to a variety of contexts in America. By the Civil War, the shout became a syncopated circle dance that retained elements of African tradition. Work songs and play songs required physical movement and often involved the natural percussive sounds of work or play.

By the beginning of the American Revolutionary War, everyone's circumstances had changed in the United States. Just as Europeans had abandoned many European traditions and manners of thinking to establish new cultural patterns in the "New World," Africans too had formed modified patterns of behavior in America.

> By the eve of the American Revolution, blacks had been living in America for over 150 years. After a century and a half of American captivity, they were not the same people whom John Rolfe had watched march down the gangplank at Jamestown. No longer were the transplanted Africans an alien people whose minds were befogged by the horrors of the Middle Passage, whose tongues were muted by the strange language of their oppressors, and whose senses were confused by the unfamiliar landscape that everywhere surrounded them. By the 1770s, if not earlier, the vast majority of blacks were native Americans with little firsthand knowledge of Africa. Increasingly, second-hand accounts of the "great land across the sea" were losing their meaning to new generations of American-born blacks—just as the fading memories of English life were losing their meaning for new generations of American-born whites. Beyond their master's eyes, many tried to maintain the ways of the old country, difficult though that was. But since adapting to the conditions of the New World was literally a matter of life-and-death, most changed. Slowly, almost imperceptibly, transplanted Africans became a new people. They spoke English, worked with English tools, and ate foods prepared in the English manner. On the eve of the Revolution, many blacks had done so for two or three generations, and sometimes more.[36]

Besides the enormous affect West and Central African traditions had on African-American music and society, Muslim cultural patterns also had a measure of influence. Roughly 10 to 15 percent of the Africans enslaved and brought to North America between 1731 and 1867 were Muslims. These people were the Fula, Serahule, Manding, Songhai, Hausa, Kasonke, and Kanuri who came from sub-Saharan regions between Lake Chad and Senegal. Like other Africans who had been accustomed to proud and dignified stations as political, religious, military, or sociocultural leaders in Africa, their dispositions and bearing made some slave owners apprehensive. Many were healers and musicians. The Muslim minority was particularly conspicuous among the Africans in America because they insisted on covering their bodies and refused to eat pork and to drink alcohol. They read and wrote Arabic and were monotheistic.[37]

Behavioral patterns from the African heritage that survived Middle Passage impacted upon the emerging Anglo-American culture. Both compatible and antagonistic features of African cultures had been randomly united in the barracoons of West Africa, forming a melange that continued to blend under the pressures of New World enslavement. Despite strong resistance to the "postwar manumission fever" that invaded the South after the American Revolution, the population of free African Americans increased rapidly in the Lower South. The Saint-Domingue revolution sent thousands of refugees fleeing toward American shores after 1792. They, of course, brought their eclectic array of music and customs with them. Although the majority was of European descent, many "mélanges" (those of mixed African and European ancestry) and other free people of color who had found themselves on the wrong side of the ever changing lines of battle, were among them. Americans were glad to receive the "white" refugees, with whom they sympathized and even identified, but the influx of brown émigrés was not welcomed.[38]

Voodoo inspired many slave revolts. Haitian nationalists found in vodun a spiritual force that could not be separated from the people's yearning for liberation. The maroons, or fugitive slaves, who held out in the mountains and spurred the slave rebellions of 1758 and 1790, had their priests with them who faithfully practiced vodun rites. About 1758 a prophet or magician named Makandal began to preach the destruction of the whites by poisoning. He was later burned at the stake at Limbe in northern Haiti, but legends about his escape from the fire continued for years.

The spirit of hope was quickened among African Americans when word of the slaves' revolt in Haiti reached the Americas in 1791 and where all the powers of voodoo were invoked.[39] The leaders of the revolution later held that it was the mystical powers of the priests that gave the "Black" soldiers the feeling of invincibility that drove the vanquished English, Spanish, and, finally, the army of Napoleon into the sea. Toussaint L'Ouverture was a highly talented guerrilla, skilled medicine man (or root doctor), and had been a staunch Roman Catholic before the revolution. Upon the arrival of the French expeditionary forces of Leclerc, Toussaint sought divination from a vodun priest who had been a plantation slave at the fort of "Crêt-à-Pierrot. Tradition has it that Dessalines, his successor, knew vodun better than Toussaint and deliberately "incited the Congolese and Guinean slaves to practice it on the eve of battle as a means of obtaining invulnerability."[40] Voodoo, in turn, "played an important part in slave insurrections in the United States and in the music and militancy of a significant sector of the black church down to the twentieth century."[41]

Fearful of slave revolts, Whites wasted little time in barring West Indian free people of color from entering the states of the Lower South. Soon other states made their boundaries off-limits to these immigrants as well.[42] The wake of Toussaint L'Ouverture's revolution caused many others to flock into the nearby ports of Charleston and Savannah. Opposition to their presence prompted a mass meeting in Charleston in 1793 urging the expulsion of "the French negroes," followed by petitions supporting similar demands in South Carolina and throughout the southern United States. In Savannah, ships from Saint-Domingue were barred from entering the harbor. The federal government eventually supported the state officials' postures with a congressional ban on "free-Negro" entry into the United States. The Federal edict was no more successful than those issued by state and municipal authorities in stopping the flow of West Indian coloreds into the South.[43] The population of free African Americans in South Carolina and Georgia suddenly grew large. The effect of this migration on musical evolution in America is clearly reflected in the cauldron of New Orleans music that developed into "jazz."

In addition to the influence that the West Indian culture began to have on the South, the rapid increase of free people of color was encouraging to those remaining in bondage. In the minds of African-American slaves, freedom now seemed attainable. As the number of fugitives grew during the tumultuous war and continued into the post-Revolutionary years, some slaves also saved money to buy their freedom while others began taking their masters to court.[44] Gradually southern African-American music permeated the majority culture as ex-slaves merged field hollers with sea shanties, street cries, and other music not directly associated with plantation life.

Slaves had a difficult time remaining free after escaping from plantations. Freedom had been identified with "whites" in American law and custom; as a consequence, blacks were presumed to be slaves. Physical appearance prevented even the most self-assured "black" fugitive from passing as a member of the light-skinned free "Negro" population. The most successful runaway slaves generally found work as sailors, with the hope of securing freedom in a distant port. It was possible to find work as field hands in free states, and a few men and women chose to take their chances in the woods and live the precarious outlaw's life. The most fortunate ones were adopted by neighboring Native American tribes. The most threatening slaves were those who lived in the woods or swamps and raided nearby plantations. Stringent colonial runaway laws were aimed at these African Americans in particular.[45] Rumors of abolition in the North inspired many to strike out for their liberty.

Despite the South's racial ideology that kept African Americans and European Americans divided, some "whites" occasionally befriended runaway slaves and managed to foster close personal ties. Fugitive slaves who had developed musical skills found friends and work even more readily. In the post-Revolutionary years a large number of Irish apprentices worked alongside slaves, and interracial friendships sometimes developed. Egalitarian ideals that grew out of the revolution also began to challenge racial prejudices. Some European Americans realized that fugitive slaves offered a source of cheap labor and encouraged them to leave their masters. Others found that other forms of interracial cooperation could be profitable.[46] African Americans were sold back into slavery if they were caught and remained unclaimed. Harriet Tubman's Underground Railroad provided an organized plan, provisions, and a relatively safe route for numerous fugitive slaves. The African-American voice replaced the drum as the means through which plans and messages were communicated, encoded in double entendre. Friends (the Quakers, whose religious beliefs held that slavery was wrong) helped with forged papers and certain other aspects of assistance in the journey, but during most of the flight a fugitive was on her own.

The population of free African Americans also grew rapidly in the upper South during this period. When Virginia legalized private manumission in 1782, St. George Tucker estimated the number of those freed from slavery to be about two thousand.[47] The first federal census of 1790 reported that the number had grown to twelve thousand. At the beginning of the nineteenth century there were twenty thousand, and that number doubled by 1810. Between 1790 and 1890 there was nearly a 90 percent increase in the number of free African Americans in the upper South, so that freemen composed more than 10 percent of the region's Negro population. By 1810, the 108,000 free African-American Southerners were the fastest-growing element in the population. States like Georgia and South Carolina, which had sternly refused to enlist blacks in the Revolutionary War and where few masters freed their slaves (and few fugitives found freedom), were now confronted with an overwhelming dilemma.[48] Free African Americans soon outnumbered slaves in states like Delaware, gradually disintegrating the institution of slavery within those regions.

The music of the nineteenth century would continue to express the qualities of African music, but it would begin to codify and pass on a distinct new African-American tradition. As Samuel Floyd concludes, there were many musical tools through which this mission was achieved.

> Meanwhile, the songsters, "musicianers," and "physicianers" of the late nineteenth century kept secular folk music alive in Afro-America, as they performed functions similar to those of the Senegambian *gewel*, singing and playing blues, ballads, and social, comic, and rhyme songs for dances and other functions. The itinerant bluesmen and other folk singers, the rag and barrelhouse pianists, the banjo and mouth-harp players, and the jug- and string-band musicians were giving early shape to African-American secular songs and were playing a large role in determining the directions African American music would take.[49]

Witch Craze

Attitudes that supported oppression during the slave era had corresponding precedents established by the European witch craze. Women throughout American society were rarely seen performing publicly as instrumental soloists in orchestras, bands, or even chamber ensembles. The roles of women musicians in Europe and America were severely restricted. Women most often performed on piano or sang at church or in the home. Women who exercised too much autonomy could expect to be ostracized or, even worse, be branded a witch.

The severe treatment of women who were considered witches demonstrated the inclination in Europe to brutalize defenseless people (women and lower-class people). The witch craze had an effect on all of Europe and America, but certain areas were more brutal than others. Witches were treated as subhuman life forms worthy of torture and humiliation. "Both slaves and witches are human beings who are no longer treated as such; they are humans whose full humanity is sacrificed, and in that process they become guideposts for a confused society."[50] The political and economic incentives that infused the oppressors' motives during the slave era transfer conspicuously to witch craze.

The procedure followed at slave auctions to examine slaves for sale also had historical parallels in Europe. When arrested for witchcraft, women's genitals were routinely searched by men. The humiliation was often a public event in which male magistrates "watched a male searcher strip a 'good-lie' woman, frightening her speechless while feeling her body and applying an irrational 'test' as to her innocence or guilt as a witch." This "established an important point about how women were viewed in early modern society: that women by nature, through their bodies, were susceptible to seduction by the devil, and that they must be controlled and if necessary punished by men."[51] Similar "trials" were also common in Germany, Switzerland, and France.

English colonists brought a brand of this barbaric behavior to New England. Just as slave owners' merciless actions remained unchecked on American plantations, the witch-hunters' deeds went unchallenged because the penalty for a conviction of witchcraft was death.[52] Like situations in African-American slave quarters, men flaunted absolute power over their victims. Regardless of whether she was an accuser in a rape case or the defendant in a trial involving witchcraft, women found it difficult to prove their innocence. In either case the all-male court was operating on a belief in causality and suspected that the accused invited the assault or deserved the punishment.[53] "The execution of the four adult Pappenheimers drew a crowd of thousands from the surrounding countryside. First, they were stripped so that their flesh could be torn off by red-hot pincers. Then Anna's breasts were cut off. The bloody breasts were forced into her mouth and then into the mouths of her two grown sons."[54] Such public humiliation and sadistic torture were tools of slave era brutality. Oppressors in some areas of America brought children to picnics where European-American mobs lynched or burned victims at the stake. Dead bodies of African-American men were often mutilated and body parts (especially genitals) sold as souvenirs. This is the social climate in which African-American music initially evolved.

Notes

[1] Anne Llewellyn Barstow, *Witchcraze* (San Francisco: Pandora, 1994), pp. 147–61

[2] Ibid., p. 147

[3] Alaine Locke, *The Negro and His Music* (Port Washington, N.Y.: 1968), p. 2.

[4] Herbert Aptheker, *American Negro Slave Revolts* (New York: International Publishers, 1969), p. 62.

[5] Ibid.

[6] Ortiz M. Walton, *Music: Black, White and Blue* (New York: William Morrow, 1972), p. 21.

[7] Orishas are personifications of the morality of the ancestors that can be put at the disposal of those who honor those spirits.

[8] Gayraud S. Wilmore, *Black Religion and Black Radicalism* (New York: Orbis, 1986), p. 27.

[9] Erich M. von Hornbostel, "African Negro Music," *Africa* 1 (January 1928): 59.

[10] Molefi K. Asante and Mark T. Mattson, *The Historical and Cultural Atlas of African Americans* (New York: Macmillan, 1992), p. 17.

[11] Ibid., p. 19.

[12] Jack Wheaton, *All That Jazz* (New York: Ardsley House, 1994), pp. 8–14.

[13] *The Historical Atlas of African Americans*, p. 24.

[14] Fremont E. Bermer, "Kídan Dárán Sálla: Music for the Eve of the Muslim Festivals. . . ." (Africana Studies Program: Indiana University, 1974), p. 9.

[15] Steven Spielberg's 1997 film, *Amistad*, resurrects this episode in African-American history. The $35 million production opened amid controversy. Novelist Barbara Chase-Riboud filed a $10 million lawsuit claiming her 1989 novel "Echo of Lions" was plagiarized. Some members of the African-American community felt an African-American director should have produced such a film.

[16] Eileen Southern, *The Music of Black Americans: A History*, 2d ed. (New York: Norton, 1983).

[17] A Civil War heroine said, "One of President Tyler's daughters ran away with a man she loved in order that they might be married but for this they must reach foreign soil. A young lady of the White House could not marry the man of her choice in the United States. The lovers were captured and she was brought back to His Excellency, her father, who sold her to a slave-trader. From that Washington slave-pen she was taken to New Orleans by a man who expected to get $2500 for her on account of her beauty." As cited in J. G. Swisshelm, *Half A Century*, 2d ed., 1880), p. 128.

[18] J. A. Rogers, *Sex and Race* (St. Petersburg, Fla.: Helga M. Rogers, 1989), p. 187.

[19] F. L. Olmstead, *Slave Ships and Slaving* (1927), p. 240.

[20] G. Fitzhugh, *Sociology for the South, or The Failure of a Free Society* (1854), p. 225.

[21] Ibid.

[22] Winthrop D. Jordan, *White over Black* (New York: Norton, 1977) p. 79.

[23] George M. Fredrickson, *The Arrogance of Race* (Middletown, Conn: Wesleyan University Press, 1988), p. 196.

[24] When only one melody of interest exists combined with subsidiary sounds that are often chords.

[25] The same or similar melodies used at staggered intervals.

[26] Interestingly, musical evolution in the West has tended to alternate between periods of artistic experimentation (of medieval motets, Baroque fugues and inventions, and Romantic era chromaticism) and periods of more conservative codification (of Renaissance madrigal, classical symphony, and twentieth-century serialization). The later periods of development of African-American musical styles in the twentieth century reflect a similar tendency. The evolutionary path through ragtime, Dixieland "jazz," swing, bebop, cool, hard bop, "quasi-modal," free "jazz," and fusion, demonstrates movement of stylistic approaches that oscillate between popular and more radical musical experiments.

[27] Hildred Roach, *Black American Music: Past and Present* (Malabar, Fla.: Krieger, 1992), p. 5.

[28] Ira Berlin, "Time, Space, and the Evolution of Afro-American Society on British Mainland North America," *American Historical Review* 85 (February 1980): p. 67.

[29] Southern, *Music of Black Americans*, pp. 32–33.

[30] Ibid., p. 38.

[31] Ibid., pp. 54–57.

[32] *The Life of Olaudah Equiano* (New York, 1791), p. 60. The first edition of the book was published in 1789 under the title: *The Interesting Narrative of the Life of O. Equiano, or G. Vassa, the African*. Paul Edwards published an abridged and edited version in 1967 (New York: Praeger).

[33] Southern, *Music of Black Americans*, p. 54.

[34] Roach, *Black American Music*, p. 19.

[35] Ibid.

[36] Ira Berlin, *Slaves without Masters* (New York: New Press, 1975), p. 10

[37] See Allan D. Austin, ed., *African Muslims in Antebellum America: A Sourcebook* (New York: Garland, 1984).

[38] Ibid., pp. 35–37.

[39] Ibid.

[40] Wilmore, *Black Religion and Black Radicalism*, pp. 19–27.

[41] Ibid.

[42] Jordan, *White Over Black*, pp. 382–84. For a general account of events on Saint-Domingue, see C. L. R. James, *The Black Jacobins: Toussaint L'Ouverture and the San Domingo Revolution*, 2d rev. ed. (New York: Norton, 1963).

[43] Papers Relating to Santo Domingo, 1791–1793; Petition from Charleston 11 December 1797, ? September 1798, SCLP; Grand Jury Presentments, Beaufort, November 1793, Charleston, November 1792, September 1798, SCA; 1793; Proceedings of the Savannah City Council, 5 July 1795, SCH; Lambert, John, *Travels through Lower Canada and the United States of North America*, 3 vols. (London, 1810), 2:404; Fraser, Charles, *Reminiscences of Charleston* (Charleston, 1854), pp. 43–44; *Annals of Congress*, 7th Cong., 2d Sess., pp. 1564–65.

[44] Berlin, *Slaves Without Masters*, pp. 35–37.

[45] Gerald W. Mullin, *Flight and Rebellion* (New York: Oxford University Press), pp. 106–12, 129.

[46] Berlin, *Slaves Without Masters*, pp. 43–44.

[47] Ira Berlin states that "in 1796, St. George Tucker estimated that there were 1,800 free Negroes in the state in 1782," the year Virginia liberalized its manumission code. Seven years later, he apparently revised his estimate to 2,800. Whether this represents an amended estimation of the free African American population or merely a correction of a typographical error is unclear.

[48] Berlin, *Slaves without Masters*, pp. 48–49.

[49] Floyd A. Samuel, *The Power of Black Music: Interpreting Its History from Africa to the United States* (New York: Oxford University Press, 1995), p. 86.

[50] Barstow, *Witchcraze*, pp. 160–61.

[51] Sixteenth-century artists used female nudity to signify the same negative qualities as court officers did. Margaret R. Miles writes that "in the representation of woman as sensual, sinful, or threatening, whether in images of Eve, Susanna, grotesque figures, or witches, the primary pictorial device by which the problem of woman—for all men—is signaled is female nakedness" (Margaret Ruth Miles, *Carnal Knowing: Female Nakedness and Religious Meaning in the Christian West* [Boston: Beacon Press, 1989], p. 120).

[52] Barstow, *Witchcraze*, pp. 130–44.

[53] Gilbert Geis, "Lord Hale, Witches, and Rape." Geis points out that the same man, Matthew Hale, presided over a witch trial that condemned two women to death (at Lowestoft, 1662) and wrote the basic legal strictures on rape that are still followed in English law. The reply to Geis's article by Hugh McLachlan and J. K. Swales, in the same journal, denies, in effect, that the witch hunts were gender-specific and argues that rape is difficult to prove. The latter point may be granted, given the bias against women in sex-related cases, but to claim that witch hunts were not woman hunting is to deny the most obvious facts about them.

[54] Barstow, *Witchcraze*, p. 144.

III
Traditional African-American Music

"Music is the flower of feeling"

—Author unknown

Music Evolves During the Struggle for Independence and Equal Rights

During the Revolutionary War, an African-American revolutionary leader, Crispus Attucks, applied his enthusiasm and fervor in speeches that aroused the colonists and led them to rebellion. He was the first to die in America's struggle for independence in a riot that became known as the Boston Massacre.

Throughout American history, African-American soldiers fought bravely for a society that insisted upon ostracizing them. Some African-American soldiers served as musicians, but at the end of each American war, victory did not bring the liberation promised them. During the War of 1812, for instance, Andrew Jackson promised equality for all his soldiers while the fighting lasted. As the heat of war pursued, the American quartermaster questioned Jackson's policy of equal pay for all soldiers. Jackson ordered payment "without inquiring whether the troops are white, black, or tea."[1] Jackson, however, made no attempt to assure that African-American veterans were able to redeem his pledge to equality after the War of 1812. Consequently, rather than creating a respected group of postwar African-American veterans, a growing slave population remained a victim of a white-supremacist principle.

The talent of women musicians remained largely confined to the piano and voice throughout much of the nineteenth century. While American prosperity increased as a result of the African labor provided by slavery, women gradually revolted against rigid social prescriptions governing their existence. As they began to defy American social conventions, and to educate themselves, women and abolitionism often became closely related within northern European-American socioculture. "Although some causes, like temperance and peace, seemed particularly fitting for women to take up, the cause that attracted many to its side, with compelling force and drastic repercussions, was that of the black slave in America—the most far reaching and potentially disruptive of all reforms. It was through abolitionism that white American women realized their own inequality and began the first organized effort to change their dependence and inferior place in American life."[2]

Despite the gradual disintegration of particular songs and traditional African cultural styles, "New World" Africans invented new musical styles. L. H. Kwabena Nketia said such music was "created in the style of the tradition, using its vocabulary and idiom, or in an alternative style, which combined African and non-African resources." Nketia also suggested that African-American music "must be viewed in terms of creative process which allows for continuity and change."[3] African-American music not only absorbed elements of European styles but also assimilated Mexican and Native American musical elements to which they were introduced as they encountered the various inhabitants of America. As ecumenical elements were absorbed with inevitable assimilation, slaves and other Africans applied free association and imaginative variation techniques to add a measure of freedom to music making that had been unknown in America. Portia K. Maultsby assures us:

> The institution of slavery did not destroy the cultural legacy of slavery nor erase the memories of an African past. The survival of slaves in the New World depended on their ability to retain the ideals fundamental to African cultures. Although Africans were exposed to various European-derived traditions, they resisted cultural imprisonment by the larger society. Slaves adapted to life in the Americas by maintaining a perspective on the past. They survived an oppressive existence by creating new expressive forms out of African traditions, and they brought relevance to European-American customs by reshaping them to conform to African aesthetic ideals.[4]

African retention in African-American vocal music reflects a diverse array of techniques. The rise and fall of vocal inflections often combine with stratified textures to form non-prescribed harmonies. Sometimes, fixed melodies and harmonies set by tribal customs were used. A mixture of African and Asian elements are heard in both the northern and eastern regions of Africa, while a unique African style of ornamentation is frequently found in western and southern Africa. Improvisation on these melodies, in varying degrees, was a characteristic common to all African melodies. Embellishment involved pitch modulation, melodic variation, trills, vibrato, glissandi, microtones, multiphonics, and grace notes, which colored a wide range of syllabic and melismatic melodies.

Music always remained a central force in all traditional and "New World" African communities. The creation of music involves perpetually reinventing art based upon traditional African elements combined with local social circumstances. Because of the inherent degrees of freedom, a fundamental conceptual approach is shared throughout the African Diaspora that requires inventiveness as a prerequisite. Composer Olly Wilson sums up this particular feature by saying that the African dimension of African-American music is not, "a static body of something which can be depleted, but rather a conceptual approach, the manifestations of which are infinite. The common core of this Africanness consists of the way of doing something, not simply something that is done."[5] Those attempting to absorb the essence of the African-American cultural manifestations without engaging the culture directly do not easily duplicate this.

Most Western theorists have been drawn to the rhythmic novelty, complexity, and intensity of African music. The rhythmic sophistication was so far removed from the harmony that dominated European music that rhythm became the most intriguing feature for those encountering elements of African music for the first time. It is the text, however, that seems to have always been the most important element to African people. It was the words of the jali that contained the majority of the power she or he wielded within the village. The tonal African languages require careful attention to pitch and proper articulation of each component of sound attached to the spoken word. The drums in many traditional African cultures imitated the inflections of the voice and transmitted messages locally and over great distances. The percussive sounds produced by African "talking drums" and other hand drums involve a much greater degree of tone flexibility than Western drum music. The significance of the word forms a vortex, which draws all other musical elements (melody, rhythm, harmony, form, timbre, and dynamics) toward its epicenter. This significance of the word is responsible for the rich variety of rhythms and the careful attention to tonal variety that America inherited through African-American music. This predisposition to maximum tonal variety is apparent in the employment of mutes, growls, the nuances of scat singing, and other effects that color African-American music.

In America, where many of the original African languages were eventually lost, the status of the word lost some of its prominence in music as well. Despite this change, lyrics maintained a position of great importance even as African Americans moved from an emphasis on vocal music (prior to the twentieth century) toward a greater degree of emphasis on instrumental music. Many African-American instrumentalists performing during the first half of the twentieth century insisted that musicians be aware of a song's lyrics to render an effective performance. If one listens to the older modulating rhythmic style African-American dialects in the South, it is clear that the tonal features of this so-called "Black English" evolved from stylized approaches to the words of the English language. It embodies tonal inflections, rhythmic emphasis, phrase syncopation, and contains the tendency toward double entendres that are unique African-American features.

Utilization of the double entendre (dual meaning) allowed the slave to communicate more freely while under oppressors' surveillance. Remnants of African language patterns as seen in such cryptic encoding, enabled the African American to cultivate new forms of communication enabling them to survive within a hostile environment.

Through early African-American songs, slaves mastered the art of conveying one meaning to "White" society in general while sending a more genuine meaning to the slaves on the southern plantation. "Swing Low Sweet Chariot," "Steal Away," "Follow the Drinking Gourd" (the North Star of the Big Dipper), and "We Will Stand the Storm" were either fomentations, announcements, or consolations sung to aid escape from bondage or to boost the spirits of apprehensive slaves. The tendency toward double entendre was carried forward in rural blues songs like Lightnin' Hopkins's "Play with your Poodle" and "I'm a Crawling Black Snake," and in later "jazz" compositions such as Billie Holiday's "Strange Fruit" and Rahsaan Roland Kirk's "The Inflated Tear."[6] The "Negro" spiritual embodied both the uplifting quality and the signaling potential of the double entendre. Under the facade of Old Testament stories, many levels of meaning were projected. Many aspects of slavery in Egypt and Babylon could be identified with African Americans' own set of unfortunate circumstances and thirst for freedom. Such songs served as a significant tool for the Underground Railroad as slaves were smuggled to the "Promised Land" out of bondage. Sterling Stucky discusses the protest role of the "Negro" spiritual:

> There seems to be small doubt that Christianity contributed in large measure to a spirit of patience which militated against open rebellion among the bondsmen. Yet to overemphasize this point leads one to obscure a no less important reality: Christianity, after being reinterpreted and recast by slave bards, also contributed to that spirit of endurance which powered generations of bondsmen, bringing them to that decisive moment when for the first time a real choice was available to scores of thousands of them.[7]

Both men and women worked in the fields of the plantations and, consequently, were relegated to the same social position. The harsh working conditions endured on plantation fields were retained in song titles such as "Pick a Bale of Cotton," "Sixteen Tons," "Old Cotton Fields at Home," and other early blues songs. The nineteenth-and twentieth-century lives of disenfranchised African Americans were chronicled in powerful blues songs and sung from front porches and street corners to concert halls throughout the world.

Because most slaves were denied access to musical instruments, both men and women were similarly deprived in that regard. Thus, the voice was most often the primary instrument of music making. As a result, women and men enjoyed fairly equal roles in the development of African-American music throughout a major portion of its early development. The blues evolution, therefore, was heavily influenced by the spirituals, work songs, and folk songs sung by both female and male vocalists. Throughout the line of musical evolution, the female voice would reemerge periodically to reassert an important influence on male-dominated instrumental music. Ronald Davis provides a description of the early blues (sung most often by men).

> Lyrics were harshly realistic and directly related to everyday life. Like the work songs, country blues was almost sung speech. The delta vocal style tended to be hard and unrelenting, producing rough, growling tones, although the falsetto was frequently employed for contrast. Blues singers elsewhere moaned, hollered, murmured or declaimed. "Blue" notes were produced by sliding up to tones. The melodic range in country blues was limited, while accompaniment was simple, initially limited to tonic, subdominant, and dominant chords, used in prescribed arrangement. "Breaks" at the end of each line per-

mitted improvisation on the accompanying instrument and time during which the singer could interject asides, such as "Oh Lawdy!"[8]

Since learning to read or write English was forbidden, the time-tested methods of oral tradition sustained the transplanted African in America. History, legends, music, and other cultural information could be transmitted and retained in this fashion. The improvisational nature of the music of Africans and African Americans is akin to the spontaneous variations that occur when information is transmitted orally. Hildred Roach reminds us that "this practice of variation marked almost each performance and was often suggested at the will of the master drummer or the lead singer. It must be understood that, in African music, this freedom to vary the structure depended upon the basic underlying form and that only specific points within the pieces were used for addition or alterations. Melodic alteration, however, was more liberal, as is seen in African American music."[9]

Early accounts of African-American music suggest that many African instruments were still in use when Africans first arrived in America.[10] As European instruments and singing replaced African musical instruments and stylistic approaches, new tempered scales were also adopted. The Africans' imaginations transformed the new instruments and theories of music, resulting in the emergence of new scales, harmonic formulas and musical forms. The form of the blues as well as its scales and harmonies present clear examples of that transformation. The fixed scale degrees of the Western piano assembled into pitch sets unlike any other existing in the musical world. This revolutionized American music, and eventually the entire world of twentieth-century music.

The messages of the field hollers established a tradition, in both the North and South, that was carried into the cries of street vendors offering their services after the Emancipation Proclamation. "The Hominy Man" of Philadelphia, Henry Anderson (b. 1800), attracted attention initially in 1828 because of his robust tenor voice in the following song:[11]

> Hominy man come out today
> For to sell his hominay. [sic]
>
> The hominy man is on his way
> From de navy yard
> With his harmony.

The cries of women street vendors have not been well documented. There is a clear distinction between the roles of women and men vocalists and instrumentalists in nineteenth-century African-American music. Many early female performers alluded to sexist African attitudes and practices that were apparently existing in the slave churches and the underground fetish religions. Slave narratives, myths, folk tales, songs, and rhymes were forms of cultural transmissions where evidence of sexist attitudes are documented:[12] "The whistling woman, and the crowing hen, / Never comes to no good end." Certain musical domains were for men alone and some exclusively for women. Letters of European and European-American eyewitness travelers who visited the South and observed American slaves performing suggest that African and African-American culture contained fewer musical and dance restrictions along sexual lines than found in most Western cultures. A gathering in Congo Square in New Orleans in 1819 is described by one of those travelers. The square became a famous center for slaves and freedmen to meet and preserve African ritual traditions through music and dance. One of the African-derived instruments mentioned by that writer was "a calabash with a round hole in it, the hole studded with brass nails, which was beaten by a woman with two short sticks."[13]

In situations involving combinations of drums and vocals, the soprano female voice was more capable of penetrating the dynamic intensity of the lower-pitched African drums. Perhaps this accounts in part for the relatively small proportion of female drummers and high number of female vocalists in traditional African society. African women used the tools of labor in their daily work routines in a manner related to the ways African Americans used their picks and shovels in work songs. Throughout the evolution of African music in early America, the female voice remained a guiding force in establishing stylistic features that eventually fostered the development of spirituals, gospel, blues, and "jazz." The expression of emotions through sacred music would develop a uniquely American quality that would register a resounding effect worldwide.

Music is not an isolated art form in African culture. Visual and kinetic arts work together with musical performances to heighten the total effect of the sacrosanct ritual experience. Dress is a very important element as a visual stimulus in both African and African-American performances. The colors and fashions worn by performers charge the atmosphere, and audiences in both environments anticipate being surprised and emotionally stimulated by the imaginative costumes they see on stage. Costumes, therefore, were always important complements to performances when African Americans performed in their own communities. When the music of the African-American culture moved into European-American clubs and concert halls, manners of dress often became more subdued.

American Folksongs and the Blues: Pre-Civil War

The ring shouts and the European-American church phased out other modes of cultural expression, as emphasis was on presenting Africans as a cursed people who offered no religion of value. It was necessary to cast the captive people as such, of course, to justify exploiting them. The "Negro" spiritual was less overtly African than other African-American music, and therefore less threatening to mainstream America. One African-American ensemble, the Fisk Jubilee Singers, popularized the spiritual at home and abroad during the era of Reconstruction in America. Initially motivated by a desire to raise funds for Fisk University, they demonstrated (throughout the Western world) the emotional depth and musical excellence that African Americans brought to sacred, popular, and "classical" music of the period.

Juba

African slaves developed many new songs, games, and folktales on the plantations. When searching for historical details concerning these early forms the term "juba" surfaces frequently. The etymology of the term suggests that it is derived from the African *nguba* or *gingooba*, which means groundnut or goober (peanut) respectively. The African slaves may have applied the term to a feature of their early dietary conditions on southern plantations. Slaves working in plantation houses would often gather leftover food to share with those working in the fields. On the weekends, all of the food gathered from the "big house" was cooked into a stew that was called juba, jibba, or jiba.[14] At times the food was placed on a huge trough where pigs and other animals were fed. African slaves were forced to suffer the humiliation of eating slop under such conditions, but managed to make song and played games to prepare themselves psychologically for these unfortunate meals.

> Juba this and Juba that
> Juba killed a yella' cat
> Get over double trouble, Juba
>
> You sift the meal,
> You give the husk.
> You cook the bread,
> You give me the crust.
> You fry your meat, You give me the skin.
> And that's where mama's trouble begin.
>
> Juba up, Juba down, Juba all around the town.
> Juba for Ma, Juba for Pa.
> Juba for your brother-in-law.

We find here an example of the double entendre that is contained in most African-American lyrics from older times. Beverly Robinson interprets the meaning of the song above roughly as follows: the first stanza means the slaves are eating giblet made out of a little of this and a little of that. This stanza ends with a line that expresses a promise to have better food when the trouble (slavery) has ended; when fresh food could be prepared and served properly. The second stanza represents the mother who would always tell her children that her utmost desire was to give them the food she prepared for the plantation owners, but instead she could only give them the husk, crust, and skin. The trouble began when they were then forced to sing and play to entertain the oppressors, when joy was the last thing they were feeling in their hearts. The final stanza tells us that juba was the meal common to slaves all over the country.[15]

"Patting juba" or "making juba" was a form of rhythmic expression involving syncopated body rhythms as a substitution for (the absence of) the African drum. Groups of slaves (usually men) sat in a circle where each, in turn, would improvise virtuoso rhythm cadences using all parts of the body and any household objects (spoons, cookware, etc.) that were lying around.

Each soloist attempted to outdo the other. Other performers would provide rhythmic accompaniment by stamping their feet on beats one and three, while clapping their hands alternately on beats two and four. Some aspects of this tradition eventually developed into tap dancing.

African-American children would learn many of the traditional folk songs while performing short dramas to accompany story lines. Within the body of African-American songs and ballads are the chronicles of crimes committed against them. Hangings of men, women, and children were common in the United States until the middle of the twentieth century. A ballad entitled "Hangman's Tree" demonstrates the tragic nature of those events and suggests that murder could be converted to extortion if one could afford the price.

> Hangman, hangman, hangman,
> Loosen your rope.
> I think I spy my father coming.
> He has come many a long mile, I know.
>
> Father, have you come?
> And have you come at last?
> And have you brought my gold?
> And will you pay my fee?
> Or is it your intention to see me hung
> Here all under this willow tree?

Another interpretation of the term juba is offered by Dr. John C. Wyeth who asserted that juba was an old African melody in which Juba is an African Ghost. Wyeth assisted Dorothy Scarborough with her 1925 publication, *On the Trail of the Negro Folk Song*. If Scarborough's "intimate and sympathetic knowledge of the American Negro and a surprisingly complete familiarity with the songs that the race has developed" is measured by her evaluation of the blues, then we have yet another example of the ways European Americans often failed to grasp the real meaning and function of African-American music. As a phlegmatic observation from a peripheral position, Scarborough's arrogance and naiveté reflect both the distance that stood between the European-American aesthetic and African-American forms of expression, and demonstrate the levels of delusion extant at the time.

> There are fashions in music as in anything else, and folk-song presents no exception to the rule. For the last several years the most popular, barbaric sort of melody called "blues," with its irregular rhythm, its lagging briskness, its mournful liveliness of tone. It has a jerky tempo, as of a cripple dancing because of some irresistible impulse. A "blues" (or does one say "blue"? . . .) likes to end its stanza abruptly, leaving the listener expectant for more—though, of course, there is no fixed law about it. One could scarcely imagine a convention of any kind in connection with this Negroid free music.[16]

The Cakewalk and Children's Game Songs

Despite the social and economic plight of the enslaved workers, African-American music includes an equally impressive proportion of felicitous music. The cakewalk was originally a cheerful plantation dance where the rhythmic melodies and harmonies of the banjo (an instrument invented by African Americans in the South) played music that motivated the listener to dance. People of all ages celebrated together, generally on Sundays when little work was done. Slaves dressed up in their second-hand finery to do high-stepping prancing struts. The Cake Walk was an opportunity for slaves to ridicule the supercilious manners of the oppressors on the plantations without allowing the European-American spectators to grasp the real point of their antics. The custom of offering a prize began when a "master" awarded a cake to the couple that did the most impressive movement.

It was the popularity of the cakewalk that eventually persuaded circuses to hire African-American dancers, musicians, and acrobats. The earliest African-American acrobats were tumblers, perhaps because somersaults, flips, cartwheels, flips, and spins were performed on the ground and required no props. Anyone could afford to learn to tumble, and the skills acquired were readily transferable to African-American dance. Thus European-American and African-American performers learned from each other when the circus carnivals and minstrelsy merged. The original stomp and other traditional African dances were perpetuated through the African-American dances performed in minstrel shows, while the alliance between music and dance was further fortified. Relationships would eventually extend into the work of Noble Sissle, Eubie Blake, the Nicholas Brothers, Bill Robinson, Ida Forsyne, Whitney's Hopper Maniacs, the Lindy Hoppers at the Savoy Ballroom, and most other African-American dancers in the twentieth century. Cakewalk melodies, rhythms, and harmonies gradually emerged in ragtime music.

While the children were too young to work the fields, since they were not allowed to attend school, their time remained free to play on southern plantations. Consequently, children's game songs were another genre through which Africanisms were perpetuated in America. Before the Civil War, African-American children enslaved on plantations had many of their own ring-game songs. The songs that were preserved show how often the formation of a circle was used in these games. The interval of a minor third is found frequently in these game songs. That same interval occurs rhythmically encircled within the preacher's sermon as intensity gradually grows segueing into a skillfully timed transition to the singing of a spiritual.

Children would join hands and hold them high as they moved to the lyrics of "Ransum Scansum" and other game songs. They were relatively free to run, skip, jump, and move with far less inhibition than enslaved adults. The game songs involved counting, hiding, swinging, and moving freely in a much more robust fashion than work songs could afford. Call and response, movement, and syncopated rhythm are common features of African-American children's game songs. The verses below from two different children's game songs are contrasting, yet they are clearly of a more amicable nature than many other slave songs.

Ransum scansum, through yonder.
Bring me a gourd to drink water.
This way out and the other way in,
In my lady's chamber.
This way out and the other way in,
In my lady's chamber.

Little Sallie Walker,
Sitting in the saucer.
Rise, Sallie, rise, and
Wipe your weeping eyes, and
Fly to the east, and
Fly to the west, and
Fly to the very one that you love the best.
(*Chorus*)
Put you hand on your hip and
Let your backbone slip.
Shake it to the east, and
Shake it to the west, and
Shake it to the very one that you love the best.

The children's game songs, like the songs and dances of the adults in their community, expressed emotions and stories in interpretive movements based upon the dotted rhythms that are reminiscent of African dance. The more amicable rhythmic characteristic is also an inclination stemming from the fact that children's game songs were lighter in nature.

Words and rhythms were digested, processed, and improvised, by child dancers who perpetuated many of the idiosyncrasies and stylistic features of traditional African music. Hildred Roach comments on the ring games and African-American social dances:

In America, dance also occurred at various events, both secular and sacred. Afro-Americans inherited African features of ornamentation or variation upon the basic language of all dances—from complex improvising in walking, running and jumping, to formations of circular, linear or spiraling movements. One dance, the religious shout, was similar to the frenzied dances of fetish chiefs or warriors and was evidently used at both religious and secular outings. The ring games of children and later, the popular dances of the stage also included many effects which were inherited from African recreation. Still others of African background included the calinda, habanera rhythms, mabunda and various voodoo derivatives along with the bamboula.[17]

American Folksongs and the Blues:
Post-Civil War

Before the Civil War, most people in America were interested in folk music of various kinds as a means of recreation. Because there was no radio or television, people often sang and played the piano and other instruments for entertainment. The particular set of popular songs for a given group of people were those that were most closely related to their own particular social domain. The blues is a folk music where songs are adapted, modified, and embellished by many people, who feel their own personal feelings can be expressed through an existing melody. The older blues songs that developed after the Civil War were based primarily upon traditional African-American folk songs.

If spirituals evolved out of antebellum hope for freedom before the Civil War, the blues reflected the postbellum despair within the African-American community after the southern carpetbaggers arrived. They told of the moves from rural southern plantations and communities into city ghettos. Finally, as the realization of their plight set in, they described how African Americans escaped one form of rural institutional slavery only to encounter a more subtle modern form of economic and psychological urban enslavement.

Of course, the Emancipation Proclamation that the Republican president Abraham Lincoln issued was not strictly a document reflecting northern American altruism. Economically driven Republican concerns are designed for the elite, just as the bases of Plato's Republican notions reflected stratified social configurations involving Platonic landlords serviced by the labor of serfs. Many European Americans did abhor slavery. Lincoln made it clear, nonetheless, that he did not consider African Americans equal to "White" Americans. More significantly, the North resented the economic advantage that slavery provided the South.

The poverty and hard times the African-American farm workers, sharecroppers, and urban ghetto dwellers faced were not the first reasons Africans in America had cause to sing the blues. Although the blues became a more dominant musical force after the Civil War years, there were encoded musical messages generated on antebellum plantations in the South that spoke of love, anguish, discomfiture, and the vicissitudes of life. These songs were the early forms of the African-American music later called the blues.

Instruments were fashioned out of any materials at hand both before and after the Emancipation Proclamation. Big Bill Broonzy made his first guitar out of a cigar box, and Buddy Guy made his from tin boxes and window screen wire. Blues musicians found ways of expressing their emotions, ideas, and talent, with whatever they could find around them—just as contemporary rap musicians found ways to create an expressive musical form using common household materials, when the public schools failed to provide young urban students with instruments and music programs. Early street musicians used old bottles, rubber tire tubes, automobile parts, and metal pipes to fabricate the newly invented African-American instruments that performed in consort with accordions, violins, or other European instruments. Washboards became percussion instruments, stoneware jugs became wind instruments, and a washtub and a string could substitute for a standup bass. The heyday of blues occurred in the 1920s and during the years of the Great Depression. As late as 1924 Will Shade formed the Memphis Jug Band. His band included Memphis Minnie, Ben Ramey, Charlie Burse, Furry Lewis, Jab Jones, and Charlie Pierce.

After the Civil War many African Americans remained as workers on plantations. Others moved to towns and other urban areas to earn wages working in stores, restaurants, saloons, hotels, hair parlors, barbershops, or "running on the railroad." They dominated trades from which free Africans were previously barred in the regions. Although specific occupations varied, the demeaning character of "Negro (or nigger) work" was similar throughout the United States. Most were restricted to low-paying service trades dependent on European-American patronage. Although most of the trades continued to be servile in nature, they often required the development of considerable skill.

African-American merchants fortunate enough to own their own businesses were often successful enough to become wealthy. Others discovered favorable economic possibilities as entertainers, performing music using the skills developed on the plantations. Many women continued to work as domestics while others worked as entertainers, seamstresses, educators, or occasionally started their own businesses. African Americans adapted quickly to life in mainstream American society.[18]

Because many freed slaves were left unprepared to cope with urban life in cities like New York, some were forced into lives of crime or idleness. An area in New York City called "Five Points" gained a reputation as one of the worst slums in America. Nevertheless, many African Americans performed there in small ensembles (often featuring violin, trumpet, and drums) in dance halls. They reportedly played a brand of "hot music" long before ragtime or "jazz." Some regard such halls as the antecedents of Harlem's famous "Black and Tan cabarets."

Reportedly, it was at one of these early halls that Charles Dickens encountered William Henry Lane, "Master Juba" (1850–90), dancing the shuffle, double shuffle, and cut and cross cut steps to African drum patterns on a solo tambourine. Dickens wrote about these experiences in his 1842 book, *Notes on America*.[19] Lane, "the greatest dancer known," later set out to reverse the negative African-American stereotypes promoted by European-American minstrels at home and abroad. He became world renowned as a dancer, and was one of the few African-American men allowed to share the stage with European-American men during the period. He served as the link between the stereotypical images of southern "Blacks" (that the "White" minstrels projected) and the authentic African-American cultural reality.

Southern European Americans were equally confused and disoriented when they lost the economic advantage that free labor afforded after African slaves gained their freedom. An African-American folk rhyme entitled "Destitute Former Slave Owner" paints a portrait:

> Missus an' Mosser a-walkin' de street,
> Deir han's in deir pockets an' nothin' to eat.
> She'd better be home a-washin' up de ole man's raggitty britches.

He'd better run 'long an' git out de hoes
An' clear out his own crooked weedy corn rows;
De Kingdom is come, de Niggers is free.
Hain't no Nigger slaves in de Year Jubilee.[20]

African-American work songs were constructed around the natural rhythm of the labor. Music is used similarly in the cadences of soldiers marching in the field and in coordinating the drills of athletes (like the Harlem Globetrotters). Work becomes less burdensome and better coordinated when workers sing together. "Black" workers, like their African ancestors, realized that it is possible to hear and produce music anywhere in nature. The psychological enhancement that rhythm and song brings to work can actually convert arduous labor into energetic play. Employers would sometimes pay higher wages to song leaders, who directed the songs sung by their hard-working colleagues, because they were aware of the difference in productivity and efficiency that singing made within a crew.

African-American work songs were common at tobacco factories in Virginia, at convict camps in South Carolina, on sugar plantations in Louisiana, and almost anywhere a group of African-American laborers was employed. One of the best-known sets of work songs of this type is based on the legend of John Henry, a steel driver on the Chesapeake and Ohio Railroad. This huge and handsome folk-hero resented the intrusion of the modern steam engine. He won a contest in which he out worked the steam-driver with a sledge hammer and hand drill. After his triumphant victory he died.

The work song "Norah," based on the legend of Noah and his ark, is an example of music which incorporates call and response as the main ingredient of its formal structure. Other songs remind us of the fragile hope for freedom held by enslaved African workers, who fully realized that this slim chance was usually dependent entirely upon the will of the oppressive slave-owner.

My old mistress said to me,
"When I die I'm going to set you free."
Teeth fell out and her head got bald,
Clean lost the notion of dying at all!

African-American railroad songs often depict a restless spirit. They also give the train itself a life and personality. Africans romanticizing in songs about trains felt that the vital life force vibrates within all things. The congeniality between people and machines is evident in some songs in this genre.

Jay Gooze said before he died,
Going to fix his trains so
The bums couldn't ride.

Angela Davis discusses the freedom equated with the mobility African-American men enjoyed as musicians and other traveling workers that created a new "Black self-image" following emancipation.

Even as women were compelled to remain at home to care for the children they had borne—and at the same time to earn money by carrying out domestic tasks for white families in the vicinity—men often had no alternative to traveling in search of work. This was the genesis of a historical pattern of male travel within the African American community. This economic catalyst for male travel also set the stage for the evolution of the country blues, an improvised musical form forged by southern black men wandering from town to town and from state to state. They moved—on foot or by freight train—carrying their banjos and guitars in search of work, or simply succumbing to the contagious wanderlust that was a by-product of emancipation.[21]

Railroad songs were also vehicles for love songs. A large proportion of these songs was railroad blues songs or other stories of ill-fated circumstances and broken hearts.

> Got a train in Cairo
> Sixteen coaches long;
> All I want that train to do
> Is to fetch my gal along.[22]

Albert Murray discusses the importance of the railroad motif throughout the evolution of African-American music, from the rural blues musician to the compositions of Duke Ellington, Billy Strayhorn, and others. Murray traces the aspects of this musical theme as metaphors for various dimensions of African-American experience. His description progresses (in reverse) from Harriet Tubman's Underground Railroad to the sound of the whistle on the "A" Train in Harlem.

The actual A train, a subway on the Eighth Avenue Independent Line in New York City, had no such whistle, to be sure. But even so, as Ellington's theme it becomes yet another extension, elaboration, and refinement of the traditional down-home railroad sounds that are so unmistakable in the guitars and harmonicas of the old folk blues musicians. Moreover, in the original recording, Ellington's piano intro rings the departure bell; the calling woodwinds and responding brass shout as if in an all-aboard announcement of destination, as the 4/4 percussion thumps onward, and in this case, homeward.

Most other blue-oriented musicians seem to use the basic railroad onomatopoeia of the folk blues guitar player as unconsciously as they proceed in terms of such idiomatic devices as, say, vamps, riffs, breaks (and pickups), eight-, twelve-, and sixteen-bar choruses and call-and-response patterns, among other things, including the syncopation and special nuances in timbre. To them the stylized sounds of locomotive whistles, bells, pistons, steam, and so on seem long since to have become such natural or conventional elements of their musical grammar, syntax, and vocabulary that they are for the most part as unnoticeable as if they were only so many dead metaphors that go to make up the denotative verbalization of everyday discourse. Ellington almost always proceeds with an awareness of the folk derivative of the blues idiom expression comparable to that of an etymologist, he also had a very special attachment to trains and railroad per se as subject matter. . . . *Happy Go Lucky Local* is no less literal, no less abstract, nor any less symbolic than the trains in traditional folk blues lyrics, in the spiritual and in Afro-American folklore that reaches all the way back to the underground railroad of the antebellum South.[23]

After 1865, the folk songs of European Americans were published far more frequently than any form of African-American music. Ironically, unless a European American confiscated African-American songs, reduced them to diluted written forms, and sold them to publishers as their own, African-American music was generally not considered worthy of publication.

The majority culture had no composers equal to the European master composers involved in the romantic musical period of the day. The most preeminent European-American writer of folk songs was Stephen Collins Foster (c. 1826–64), the son of an army colonel. Foster had spent four years (c. 1846–50) working in Cincinnati for a riverboat agency, where he heard the singing of "Black" boatmen. The songs he wrote amounted to little more than imitations of this music. He was also one of the first European Americans who tried to capture the language and music of African-American people through studying their church music and minstrel shows. Foster's songs, like the popular "Old Folks at Home," were constructed from melodies that were easy to sing and based on simple harmonic schemes. Using an exaggerated slave dialect, his sentimental lyrics were catchy and revealed the influence that African-American ballads, people, and traditions had on him. Foster composed songs for "White" minstrel groups such as Christy's Minstrels.

James Bland (c. 1854–1911), the first composer in the African-American folk tradition to receive popular acclaim, was Foster's counterpart. He composed songs for "Black" minstrel groups and made valuable contributions to the development of ragtime at the end of the nineteenth century. "Carry Me Back to Old Virginny" and "In the Evening by the Moonlight" are among his most enduring songs. Eileen Southern tells us: "At the height of his fame, James Bland was advertised as 'The World's Greatest Minstrel Man' and 'The Idol of the Music Halls.' His songs were sung by all the minstrels, black and white—by college students, and by the American people in their homes and on the streets."[24]

At the end of the nineteenth century the minstrel shows had painted negative images of African-American culture and misrepresented the authentic music from that tradition. Lacking first-hand knowledge of African-American life and culture, many Europeans and European Americans had no choice but to accept that distorted picture. Clearly, the "Black" music and dance presented by European-American "blackface" minstrels and accepted by "Whites" was never quite the same as versions presented by the "Blacks" themselves. Those who had not engaged African-American social domains on any level, and who never heard the original music, were not aware of the degree of distance that existed between the musical styles. Typically, oppressors within a culture do not want to admit that the oppressed people they exploit are capable of making valuable contributions to society. Nonetheless, ragtime music enjoyed by "White" audiences between the late 1890s and the First World War was very different than the ragtime being played in African-American communities.

It was the blues, however, that would be the most enduring African-American prototype for "jazz." The diminished tetrachord, found in so many traditional African songs and instrumental musical styles, became the intervalic structure and core foundation of the blues. W. C. Handy, who is referred to by some as the "Father of the blues," once offered a personal description of blues style:

> But Blues are folk-songs in more ways than that. They are essentially racial, the ones that are genuine,—though since they became the fashion many blues have been written that are not Negro in character,—and they have a basis in older folk songs.

> . . . Each one of my blues is based on some old Negro song of the South, some folk-song that I heard from my mammy when I was a child. Something that sticks in my mind, that I hum to myself when I'm not thinking about it. Some old song that is part of the memories of my childhood and of my race. I can tell you the exact song I used as a basis for any one of my blues. Yes the blues that are genuine are really folk-songs.[25]

Handy learned his folk songs from his parents, who insisted that he sing spirituals rather than "shout songs." The latter religious song style included lively songs that maintained African dance qualities rhythmically—created within an environment in which African Americans were generally forbidden to engage in traditional African dance. Despite the fact that most African-American folk songs were not written down for many years, many of these songs were passed down through an oral tradition. This manner of preserving music proved as efficient as the European-American written method in preserving this cultural genre for respective progeny. Dorothy Scarborough wrote down the lyrics to many "Negro" songs. She conveys some knowledge of oral tradition in her book. Her knowledge is based upon stories she was told while interviewing African-American people for her book.

> By cabin firesides, as before the great hearths in the big house, the old songs would be learned by the little folk as part of their natural heritage, to be handed down to their children and their children's children. Such a survival among the Negroes was remarkable, far more so than song-preservation among the whites, who in many instances kept old ballads by writing down in notebooks, and learning them from old broadsides or

keep volumes; while the Negroes had none of these aids, but had to sing each song as they learned it from hearing others sing it, and must remember it of themselves. And yet they cherished the old songs and had their own versions of them.

African-American music was forced into a secular environment of brothels and honky tonks due to a lack of economic alternatives for most professional African-American musicians at the time. Musicians fell prey to many of the trappings and potentially enervating circumstances found within such environments. Restricted to negative circumstances to earn a living produced predictable results. What remains amazing is that music of such elegance and nobility evolved out of such unfortunate social arrangements.

Musicians and other artists are always exchanging ideas and influencing each other. Out of mutual respect, this influence will generally be acknowledged. Nineteenth-century America did not present social situations where any degree of respect was extended to oppressed people, nor was free and open contact made between all citizens. Musical elements of both Africans and Europeans in America were mutually absorbed and combined when people managed to encounter each other. Due to social restraints imposed by racism, Africans were forced to absorb European customs, but Europeans rarely allowed themselves access to African culture.

The question of musical influence during remote periods of time can be a difficult matter to prove. History is generally written from a subjective perspective that exemplifies political, sociocultural, and personal biases, which tend to conceal facts and obscure objectivity. As African-American music evolved from a time long before it was labeled "race records" to an economically broader (more general) "jazz" category, European Americans have claimed increasingly greater ownership over the music. The evolution of terms reflect American social attitudes, as Makanda Ken McIntyre explains:

> It is, therefore, understandable why the term "jazz" has been given to the music created by African slaves in America, particularly when one considers the fact that the slave was considered sub-human, and for a sub-human, an abstraction such as "jazz" is good enough. We have lived with an abstraction handed to the African slave in America until recently, and the one to which I am referring is the term "Negroe" [*sic*]. . . . To look back and think for a moment and have a map in front of you and ask where Negroe land is, now in hindsight seems totally absurd. We have, however, survived that era and should begin to deal with the reality of music in the African American tradition.[26]

European Americans, and other non-African people, have participated in performing and composing the various musical styles that originated in the African-American community, and are undeniably a part of the history of the music called "jazz." Nonetheless "jazz" remains African-American music, since the origins of the music are African and the progenitors of all forms of African-American music have been African-American musicians. The rhetorical question remains, therefore, why is there so much resistance to calling Afrocentric art forms African-American music?

Marches

Europe's main influence on African-American instrumental music would come from the marches that were heard at outdoor celebrations. Marching bands were especially popular during the latter half of the nineteenth century. This musical genre had an effect on all American listeners. European conductors were usually imported to direct these organizations, and the music retained a "light classical" flavor. Because well-trained musicians were hired to perform with bands, many marching bands were capable of exhibiting virtuosity and precision in their concert performances. Elements of marches composed by Patrick Sarsfield Gilmore, Carl L. King, and John Philip Sousa, made their way into the African-American brass bands, ragtime piano music, and other musical styles. The wind band instrumentation and the musical form of the marches are two conspicuous elements that made their way into African-American music. Although the American symphony orchestras adopted the instrumentation of the Europeans, the marching bands never became completely standardized.

Just as Africans duplicated musical and kinetic gestures during the presentation of plantation skits, European Americans in the northern states saw great opportunity in imitating the "Negro" for profits. When minstrels came to town after the Civil War, parades were formed to welcome these festive events. Brass bands syncopated traditional marches ("ragged a march") for the townspeople on such occasions. The minstrel shows of this era became popular forms of entertainment and were forerunners of the "Black" music reviews that eventually emerged in New York City around 1920.[27]

Minstrel Shows

Thomas Rice, a European-American actor, reportedly noticed an old and decrepit African-American man shuffling along one day in the mid-1820s. He observed the man's jumping, dancing, and skipping, while singing a tune in which the words "Jump Jim Crow" were repeated. Rice considered the man's behavior peculiar and wrote a song which imitated the "Black" man's words and music. He then put together an act in which he exaggerated the man's song and movements, and eventually discovered a way to turn a profit while exploiting racial stereotypes. His racist act was greatly appreciated by a Baltimore audience in 1828. "Negro" impersonators quickly became fashionable. Very soon European-American entertainers were imitating African-American music and dance throughout the country and presenting their racist interpretations of "Black" culture to mainstream American audiences.

Early "blackface" minstrel troupes blackened their faces with burnt cork as they attempted to create stylized "Black" men for European-American and European audiences. Soon bigoted "Negro" caricatures were given stage names. "Mr. Interlocutor" would feed lines for the jokes and slapstick comedy of "Mr. Tambo" and "Mr. Bones." Traditionally, "Mr. Tambo" was tall and thin, and "Mr. Bones" short and fat. The slapstick comedy ended with a grand review of the performers called the "walk around," based upon the African-American cakewalk. "Jim Dandy" soon became another stylized character who strutted in his finery to the banjo music of the cakewalk.

The second part of the minstrel show (or "Olio") consisted of variety acts where performers presented their individual talents. The "afterpiece," a parody of formal stage play mixed with current affairs, ended the presentation. The European-American "blackface" minstrels caricatured the songs, dances, and jokes that had been invented by "Black" plantation slaves, who, in the original African-American cakewalk, had poked fun at the habits and dress of plantation owners. The "blackface" minstrel shows were vicious and cruel and set out to promote racist attitudes that ridiculed slaves.

In another bit of irony, African Americans began to blacken their faces, after 1840, and poke vile "fun" at themselves to earn a living. The economic reality was that African Americans had a slim chance of finding work in the European-American communities unless they behaved as buffoons to please their audiences. Eventually they would supplant the racist minstrels in popularity through promoting the same crude and disparaging stereotypes and negative images about African Americans that "White" performers perpetuated throughout the United States and Europe. It was extremely difficult for freed slaves to find employment. As a few performers gradually gained more autonomy and were able to modify the content of their acts, African-American performers appreciated an opportunity to turn the tables one more time by poking fun at European-American oppressors once again. Nevertheless, the minstrel shows were most popular during times when racial tensions were at their zenith (1850–70). "Coon songs" and "Ethiopian" songs portrayed "Negroes" as childlike, oversexed, and licentious clowns in postures that would haunt African-American artists into the future.

Signor Cornmeali (d. 1842) was a New Orleans street vendor who incorporated musical cries and Ethiopian songs into minstrel music. His appealing voice eventually led him into a career as a popular performer on the professional stage. He was one of a handful of genuine African-American entertainers who avoided the typical derogatory stereotypes of African-American minstrels.

It would not have been possible for people of African and European descent to keep poking fun at each other had their worlds not been distanced so far apart socially, economically, and culturally. Plantation owners were wealthy and able to attend schools to receive a formal education. The slaves who worked for them were economically and educationally deprived members of a highly segregated American society. "Whites" were not interested in the lives of "Blacks" beyond the degree to which their labor could be exploited. Those who did have such an interest could not reveal it. When African-American people poked fun at European-American people in minstrel shows or cakewalks, they did so from a more direct vantage point. African Americans often observed their European-American subjects in their homes, churches, and places of employment. "Whites" saw their underlying meanings as just another example of awkwardness and ignorance. Delusions of superiority deprived them of the ability to consider African Americans clever enough to parody their culture through caricature. Besides, they did not feel slave culture worthy of serious study on any level.

When the cakewalk finally became the craze in European-American society, it was because "White" performers had studied the music and dance, digested it, diluted it, and presented it in minstrel performances. Ragtime became a familiar term within the majority culture as a result of the growing popularity of the cakewalk within the European-American community. Road shows and minstrels introduced the dance steps and music to the mainstream society, which, in turn, learned to imitate the steps and read the published rags at home. By 1897 the cakewalk craze and contests were infiltrating communities throughout the country.

The post-bellum employment base for a sizable sector of the majority culture in America was largely industrial. Greater emphasis was now placed on developing new domestic goods that could be sold at home and abroad. People from rural areas were attracted to urban settings where work could be found in the factories of big cities. Entertainment provided a relief from the toil and monotony of factory work. Some of the European-American musical forms were remakes of European orchestral music and shows put on in British musical theaters. The variety shows were presentations that evolved from the "blackface" minstrels.

As the nineteenth century came to a close, burlesque and vaudeville were two types of popular variety shows frequently produced in the night spots and neighborhoods of European-American culture. Vaudeville was more wholesome family entertainment. Tony Pastor is credited with starting Vaudeville for "White" audiences in 1866 in New York City. Women were also attracted to Pastor's shows because smoking, drinking, and distasteful acts were forbidden. Male audiences were attracted to burlesque shows featuring stripteases, prancing women in leg-shows, and other sexually explicit presentations. The Theater Owners' Booking Agency (TOBA) was the employer for many European-American and African-American artists. "Black" artists did not receive the level of pay that their "White" counterparts received, and, consequently, African Americans renamed the booking firm "Tough On Black Artists" or "Tough On Black Asses."

A number of Africans in America became involved in European music exclusively. Musical experience and formal training of African Americans in various styles of European concert music would later impact upon the growth and development of "jazz" styles. Between 1800 and 1950 many African-American artists performed various forms of European music in America and abroad.

Frank Johnson (c. 1792–1844) was a well-known composer of band and orchestra music. Johnson was renowned as a trumpet player and bandleader in the early nineteenth century. He was the first African-American musician to have his sheet music published (beginning in 1818). His military bands were nationally acclaimed, and his dance orchestras were popular for transforming sentimental ballads into rhythmically and texturally exciting reels. Johnson gave the first formal African-American band concerts and was first to tour the nation widely. His ensembles were the first to present integrated formal performances in America.[28] Johnson was also the first African-American musician to win wide acclaim domestically and in England. He was the first American to produce a concert featuring an integrated group of musicians including African-American and European-American performers. A remarkable musician, Johnson was also the first American musician, "Black" or "White," to take a musical ensemble abroad to perform in Europe.[29] Joseph W. Postelwaite was another African-American composer who published his dances, marches, and piano music between 1850 and 1890.

The Luca Troupe was a touring family consisting of, a father, mother, and three sons, who began performing in 1853. During this time, touring family groups were popular. The family also performed frequently at anti-slavery meetings. In 1859 the Luca Family joined a famous European-American family of performers they met at a meeting for the abolition of slavery. The joint performances raised a few eyebrows within their audiences. The mass culture's reaction to witnessing these two family troupes appear in concert together can be gauged by comments in an article published in Fremont, Ohio, on February 25, 1859:

> The Hutchinsons,—Asa B., Lizzie C., and little Freddie,—accompanied by the Luca family, gave a concert at Birchard Hall on last Wednesday evening. The house was not more than a paying one. When we went to the concert, we anticipated a rare treat; but alas! how woefully we were disappointed! . . . We have, perhaps, a stronger feeling of prejudice than we should have felt under other circumstances, had their abolition proclivities been less startling; but to see respectable white persons (we presume they are such) traveling hand in hand with a party of negroes, and eating at the same table with them, is rather too strong a pill to be gulped down by a democratic community.[30]

Many African-American performers appeared as soloists throughout America and in Europe. Elizabeth T. Greenfield ("The Black Swan") was another world-renowned performer of European concert music. Elizabeth was born in 1809 and remained a slave in Mississippi until she was taken to Philadelphia and adopted by a Quaker woman. Mrs. Greenfield encouraged Elizabeth's singing career from childhood, arranging for the girl to study music despite the Quaker ban on "musical pursuits." She made her debut in 1851 at the Buffalo Musical Association, where she was quickly recognized as an incredible performance artist. Later in 1854, while touring England, she gave a command performance for Queen Victoria.

William Appo and Robert C. Johnson were other African-American musicians especially admired for their performances of sacred music in the antebellum South. Appo was a talented violinist who conducted a small string orchestra in Baltimore beginning in the 1840s. He played in a theater orchestra in Philadelphia, and later played with Frank Johnson's band. Appo was also a violin teacher.

Henry Brown organized a drama troupe that was seen frequently at the African Grove (Bleeker and Mercer, in New York City). As one of New York's four theaters at the time, African Americans managed the African Grove from 1821 to 1828. The African Grove frequently featured a play. Acts were interspersed with comedy scenes and songs. The city soon closed the Grove, and it would be seventy years before African Americans ran an independent theater again in New York City.

The Dawn of Ragtime

Ragtime music did not come into general use in European-American society before a Chicago journalist first put the term "ragtime" into print in 1897, making it famous. This musical style had been familiar to the African-American community for many years. Ragtime grew out of the jig music that "Black" plantation slaves had learned from sailors during the Middle Passage. Both "jig bands" and "jig piano" were nascent forms of the "syncopated songs" that became the basic ragtime form of the late nineteenth and early twentieth century.

African-American musicians who traveled to the towns of the Mississippi plains were sometimes hired by traveling minstrel shows. Many found work in juke joints (illegal social clubs in southern woods that often served bootleg whiskey), honky tonks (saloon bars), or bordellos (brothels). Southern juke joints were designed for working-class African-American men and women and featured blues and other dance music. The walls of these social clubs were of unfinished planks and the roofs were often tin. Entertaining would take place late at night or on weekends (after payday). Small "Negro" areas in many of the burgeoning new communities found across America were eventually referred to as "sporting belts" or red-light districts. Many men of all colors, religions, and economic status visited those areas for the drinking, gambling, and prostitution. The European-American men heard the early rags in such a setting, so it was difficult to discuss their new musical find among the friends at home without disclosing other questionable habits.

As music became an essential component of the "sporting" life, more African-American musicians also began to gain access to the piano. The "hot" syncopated rhythms of the banjo, fiddle, and drum—characteristic musical instruments of jig bands—were consolidated in the syncopated piano rags. The formal layout, melodies, bass leaps, and arpeggiation of European popular songs, dance steps, and marches were also absorbed and transformed into the three-layered stratification of the ragtime piano. The left-hand accompaniment involved a bass line and harmonic patterning that can be found in other nineteenth-century European piano forms. The right hand rhythms, on the other hand, were a syncopated African-American invention. The rhythms provided a sense of tension between the strict, martial left hand and the innovative, dancelike right hand with its African-derived melodic patterns.

The African-American "professors" who "tickled" the piano keys all had their own unique styles, and by the last quarter of the nineteenth century they formed a large community of musicians. The basic structures of songs they played were freely improvised, and changed at each performance. Pianists competed with other pianists and learned each other's songs in ways similar to the communal fashions common in traditional African society. They traveled on an informal performance circuit developing their music both by rote and through writing, and eventually publishing their own songs.

Writing songs down caused ragtime to spread to the majority culture rapidly. European Americans could now learn the music without having to directly engage African-American culture. African-American ragtime pianists were not dependent upon sheet music, but the mass culture generally had little choice but to limit their interpretations of ragtime to the notes marked on the printed page. European Americans were able to market rhythmically diluted forms of ragtime style in written forms that would appeal to "white audiences." Tin Pan Alley was now poised to capitalize on the publication of a style of ragtime that amateurs could play. The majority of amateur pianists were European-American women at the end of the nineteenth century, and American publishers wanted to tap into music capable of initiating a social fad. Thus African-American culture unknowingly gave birth to Tin Pan Alley's first boom. Many styles of music received the label "ragtime" despite their complete lack of authenticity or appropriate musical content. Whether the music was genuine or not, the label sold sheet music.

Scott Joplin was the most prominent figure in the history of notated ragtime. Nobody knew how to write the syncopated rags down on paper. Joplin was the first musician to notate genuine ragtime rhythms, and his published classic ragtime has survived into present times. Scott Joplin experienced much more difficulty getting his own ragtime, operatic works, and other sheet music published than did "White" pianists.

Consequently, it was Ben R. Harney, a European-American musician born in Kentucky, who first got a ragtime composition published in 1895 ("You've Been a Good Old Wagon but You've Done Broke Down"). Harney became fascinated with African-American music in his teens and began performing on piano in bars and dance halls in Louisville. Harney and his wife traveled and performed with African-American entertainers for many years before moving to New York City shortly before the end of the nineteenth century.

The Term "Jazz"

Besides the notion that the term "jazz" was a result of coining the phrase "the Jazz Age," it is clear that the term was used within the African-American socioculture long before "the Jazz Age" began. On his instructional cassette tape "Discovering Jazz," Harold McKinney asks, "How did this African-American contribution to American culture become known as 'jazz'?" He tells us that it has been traced to underworld jargon in England where it has been discovered in the fourteenth-century works of Chaucer and sixteenth-century works of William Shakespeare. Its French origin can be found in the Senegalese French slang version of a term that equates "jazz" with the African-American phrase "stop talking jive." Jive and "jazz" have often had the same meaning. *Jaser* (French; meaning "to chatter"), like the word "jive," is a catch-all word that is often used to describe the conversations in which people engaged when sitting around clubs listening to music. In both instances the word implies toying with someone or something. In the democratic musical environment that "jazz" usually occupies, a type of spontaneous compositional negotiation takes place at swift tempos that often involves toying with musical ideas.

McKinney also suggests that in the mid-nineteenth-century "jazz" was reportedly a sexual term Europeans associated with the voodoo rituals first displayed publicly at Congo Square in New Orleans. To European-American chroniclers of the time, who had no idea of the true essence of traditional African religious rituals, these displays were misinterpreted as orgies. Actually the music and dance were vehicles through which African rhythms propelled the initiates forward in an incessant crescendo culminating in spiritual ecstasy. A similar set of tendencies are found in African-American "jazz," music which is often locked in a "swinging" groove that drives an audience continually forward inexorably to a climax of excitement.[31]

Creoles were originally French and Spanish natives who settled primarily in Haiti to seek their fortunes. They had been lured to North America by the promise of greater economic opportunities. Of those who later settled in New Orleans, many were "Black" and were eventually segregated along with the other African Americans in the region. Many Creoles were trained musicians who taught European classical music for a living in the local community. Creoles are often credited with classifying the term "jazz" as a sexual term (supposedly meaning to copulate). Chicagoans also take credit for the creation of the term "jazz." One of its citizens, trombonist Jasbo Brown, had performed W. C. Handy's "Memphis Blues" and other "hot" music in a Chicago cabaret. He used his derby hat as a mute to make his trombone "talk" and used other innovative devices to produce exciting effects. The audience reportedly became so excited that they began yelling, "More, Jas, more," giving birth to the term "jazz."[32]

"Jazz," a term in use long before 1900 as slang, continued along this path of derogatory connotations as late as 1929. Between 1897 and 1917 the sexual connotations of the term strengthened as economic opportunity drew the music into Storyville, a red-light district in New Orleans where sexual favors were bought and sold. Because this was one of the few places where an African-American musician could find professional employment, "jazz" became known as whorehouse music.[33]

All the complexities of the African-American class and caste structure could be seen in New Orleans. Wealth and skin color were factors that figured prominently in determining social status. Creoles often had close ties to "Whites" by bloodline and business connections. The African-American community began to envy their economic success. Even in regions of the South where the social and economic distance between all "Negroes" was relatively small, some mélangés had condescending attitudes toward other African Americans. For a while, Creoles were able to get better education, jobs, and social status than other "Blacks." In time, however, the arrogant attitudes were checked when "Whites" decided that anyone with even traces of African blood should be discriminated against regardless of prior social standing. A good example of color distinctions among "Blacks" can be found by examining the case of Plessy vs. Ferguson. Plessy was an octoroon who wanted to sit in the "White" section of the public train. When asked to move to the "Colored" section, he took the railroad to court because he felt he was "White" enough to sit in the European compartment. The result was the institution of "separate but equal" legislation in America. Early blues and "jazz" forms benefited from the resulting unification that occurred with the ostracism of formerly affluent (and socially acceptable) people of color.

Once African Americans regained access to the drum, the percussion battery of instruments from the military bands became readily available. The individual percussion instruments alone were not flexible enough to accommodate the polyrhythmic music the African-American drummer was "hearing," so the trap set was soon invented out of artistic necessity. Both hands and feet were employed to coordinate bass drum, high-hat (sock cymbals), snare, and ride cymbal. The tom-toms were adapted to simulate the ceremonial drums of the Congolese. The general sense of this new style of drumming was innovation, never repeating a musical invention. Drummers were seeking to vary a basic rhythmic "feel" indefinitely, a musical characteristic desirable both to Africans in the homeland and to African Americans. Within the music of the innovative drummer, the basic pulse was derived from a series of implied overlaying pulses to form a polyrhythmic network without any single set of predominant beat patterns.

Bandleaders referred to African-American instrumental compositions as syncopated music or ragtime until 1921. When in 1917 Nick LaRoca and the Original Dixieland Jass Band (ODJB) recorded European-American versions of African-American music, the record became a hit and exposed mainstream America to a musical style that would eventually (and subtly) dominate music in America and, gradually, the world at large. That ODJB recording for the RCA record label established the word "Jass" as a European-American market term. African-American bands did not begin to advertise themselves as "jazz" bands until after 1921 when the word was in mainstream use. In 1927 Duke Ellington warned, "If we don't stop calling this music 'jazz' blacks are going to lose control of it."[34]

Musical Influence on Religion, Racism, and Revolution

The only consistently stable institution within which African-American music could develop communally was the church. During colonial times most free Africans and slaves were coerced into adopting Protestant Christianity. During the eighteenth century African musical elements had to be grossly tempered within this European-American religious milieu.

Religion was at low ebb in America and in Europe as a result of liberalism and skepticism. Religious leaders throughout the British American colonies were conscious of this spiritual decline. Under the leadership of Jonathan Edwards, a great revival began in New England, initiating a series of revivals referred to as the Great Awakening. During the "Great Awakening" of the 1730s, the singing of hymns was adopted out of a demand from the European-American community for a livelier sacred song. *Hymns and Spiritual Songs,* by the English minister Dr. Isaac Watts, became a popular source book, especially among African Americans, because of the freshness of the musical approach and the vitality of the words. Despite some protest, the singing of psalms was soon neglected in favor of the new hymns. As the African-American and European-American religions became more closely allied, many African-American worshippers were forced to succumb to Eurocentric musical styles practiced in Protestant European-American churches. Conversely, when African-American churches gained greater independence, the religious services and musical styles again diverged. Since the development of African-American church music is central to the evolution of "jazz," it is important to understand the history of that development.

The Society for the Propagation of the Gospel in Foreign Parts sent clergymen to the colonies to convert slaves to Christianity between 1702 and 1785. The Established Church of England, which became officially recognized in 1701, soon sent missionaries to found schools of religious instruction for African Americans. Schools for similar purposes were established in New York, Williamsburg, Philadelphia, and throughout the colonies. Later, when schools began to become independent of the church, special schools were established to make certain that African Americans continued along these lines of religious indoctrination. Certain schools, such as that ran by Nathaniel Pigott in Boston, advertised "Instruction of Negroes in Reading, Catechizing & Writing" in a local newspaper in 1728. Samuel Keimer's school in Philadelphia had similar objectives in 1723, as advertised in a Philadelphia newspaper.[35]

The African Union Church, incorporated in Wilmington, Delaware, in 1807, was the earliest established "Black" Methodist church. It united with the First Colored Methodist Protestant Church in 1866 to form the African Union First Colored Methodist Protestant Church of America, well before the first general conference of the African Methodist Episcopal Church.[36] By 1787 African Americans had withstood the difficulties involved in opening the floodgates of the independent church movement among African Americans. This movement has been considered the first "Black" freedom movement. Although European-American Methodist ministers were reluctant to allow them to break away and establish independent churches (and presented many obstacles to the realization of this goal), the "Black" ministers stood firmly. The foundation of their position was that the needs of the African-American community could only be met by initiating such a move toward autonomy. At the end of the eighteenth century, numerous African-American churches became aware that they were no longer obliged to suffer the indignities of segregation and the lack of opportunity for advancement previously experienced as ministers and officers in the European-American churches. Now, despite the lack of freedom and equality in secular society, a degree of freedom could be experienced within the church.[37] Baptist churches in the South found less resistance to their independent movement than others, since many southern churches had never been integrated.

The emancipation of churches made the prospect of social freedom a more proactive aspiration within the African-American community. There was quite a movement of ecclesiastical insurrection around Philadelphia in particular. Mother Bethel's African Methodist Episcopal Church began a protest against segregation in St. George's Methodist Episcopal church in that city. Although it ended with the "Black" adoption of "White" Methodism with few changes, a movement was established that began to force the African-American community away from the legal trappings and socially fashionable oppression experienced under the direct influence of European-American church.[38]

The Society of Friends (Quakers) promoted the earliest development of "Black" religious independence in Philadelphia. Although the Quakers of Pennsylvania were highly supportive of the African-American independent church movement, some of the movement's leading ministers were not comfortable with their subdued style of worship, or with some aspects of the individualism of the Society of Friends. Most African Americans wanted congregational, spirited preaching, singing, and the freedom of "Black" worship based upon an African background. Although the Free African Society (the organization at the forefront of the movement) generally followed the pattern of the Methodist class meetings, its broader purpose included secular and sociopolitical, as well as religious goals. The closing words of its preamble indicate the problems that were uppermost in the minds of its leaders, Richard Allen and Absalom Jones. "I established prayer meetings; I raised a society in 1786 of forty-two members. I saw the necessity of erecting a place of worship for the colored people."[39] These two men were highly influential in the movement for free African-American churches.

When itinerant African-American preachers were allowed on plantations to attend to the spiritual needs of slaves, African Americans began to find much greater freedom. They began to organize their own independent church services and express themselves more genuinely. The preachers conducted the emotional pacing of the services in a manner that would serve as a prototype for minstrel performers, interlocutors, and other entertainers in later periods of American musical history. Just as the European hymn and other religious musical forms contributed to the development of African-American spirituals, the more vibrant and exuberant African-American church music would have a reciprocal influence on the European-American singing style at camp meetings. The inventive rhythm, emotional intensity, and sheer tenacity of the "Negro" spiritual would leave many foreign visitors in awe.

"Rapping" at the beginning of a blues, "jazz," or soul song is related to the African griot's storytelling, and establishes rapport with an audience. Many contemporary African-American musicians begin their performances with "sermonettes" that are related to the preaching styles of the "Black" church. The preacher delivers an inspirational message that precedes the singing of the spirituals. Likewise, participation from the audience motivates both the sacred sermon and secular performance.

Early African-American churches scorned adulterers and insisted that religious pastors confirm marriages. They occasionally functioned to reunite separated couples, thus strengthening the moral fabric of the community. Churches were both centers of education and a retreat where "Blacks" might relax and organize community functions and entertainment. Self-governing within the African-American church bolstered people's confidence and aided the development of a community of leaders. It bred a sense of group identity and solidarity, which in turn fostered pride and self-respect and nurtured the ripening belief that free Negroes could control their own destiny.[40] Music thrived in that setting.

The tradition of the camp meeting, or retreat, evolved in America from 1780 to 1830 during the "Second Awakening." The Second Awakening (1797-1805) swept the nation and was particularly spectacular in the west. At outdoor meetings the intensity of emotions caused some of those attending to become affected by "jerks" and "falling exercise." This movement added tens of thousands to the frontier churches and, as a consequence, revivals became the accepted method of work adopted by Baptists, Methodists, Congregationalists, Presbyterians, and later the Disciples.

For both African-American and European-American Protestant people, the Second Awakening involved continuous religious services extending over a period from between several days to an entire week. A rope (that was not to be crossed) separated African-American campsites from those of European-American worshippers. The "Negro" spirituals would find both its champions and severe critics among those who had never heard music of this type; but it could not go unnoticed. Frederika Bremer was a contemporary writer who made the following observation: "Their shouts and singing were so boisterous that the singing of the white congregation was often completely drowned in the echoes and reverberations of the colored people's tumultuous strains. . . . On the black side . . . the tents were still full of religious exaltation, each separate tent presenting some new phases. . . . In one . . . a song of the spiritual Canaan was being sung excellently. . . . At half-past five [the following morning] . . . the hymns of the Negroes . . . were still being sung."[41]

Some African-American spirituals were sung during religious services, whereas others were sung in casual settings. "Ring shouts," "shout spirituals," "ring spirituals," and "running spirituals" are all terms for the music sung with the retention of African traditions of worship that emerged into the African-American "shout." Some spirituals were slow and somber while others were highly syncopated and zestful. Features of African-American music from these early times were appreciated by some of the European-American listeners who heard them, as a letter from colonist Samuel Davies confirms: "I can hardly express the pleasure it affords me to turn to that part of the Gallery where they [the slaves] sit, and see so many of them with their Psalm or Hymn books, turning to the part then sung, and assisting their fellows who are beginners, to find the place; and then all breaking out in a torrent of sacred harmony, enough to bear away the whole congregation to heaven."[42]

Methodist historians document the segregated nature of such religious events, but by 1818 African Americans were presenting their own camp meetings led by the African Methodist and Episcopalian (AME) churches. Thousands of worshippers, including many European-American people, observed or participated in these events on a circuit that included New York, Philadelphia, and Baltimore. The most impressive and influential aspects of the African-American presentations and performances at such meetings were the singing ensembles and soloists. Not all of the European-American worshippers appreciated these musical exhibitions, however. According to Eileen Southern (in The Music of Black Americans, p. 84), a complaint from one of the church fathers of the time is revealing. Discussing the "errors" made by Methodists, he says:

Here ought to be considered too, a most exceptional error, which has the tolerance at least of the rulers of the camp meetings. In the *blacks' quarter*, the coloured people get together, and sing for hours together, short scraps of disjointed affirmations, pledges, or prayers, lengthened out with long repetition *choruses*. These are all sung in the merry chorus-manner of the southern harvest field, or husking-frolic method, of the slave blacks. . . .

. . . the example has already visibly affected the religious manners of some whites. From this cause, I have known in some camp meetings, from 50 to 60 people crowd into one tent, after the public devotion had closed, and there continue the whole night, singing tune after tune, (though with occasional episodes of prayer) scarce one of which were in our hymn books.

This document suggests that African-American congregations soon broke away from the influence of the European hymnal and compiled a new set of songs for their own purposes. The European-American clergy did not generally appreciate the growing independence among African-American churches. Some independent African-American churches in the North continued to develop despite repeated attempts to take their land by European Americans who felt these institutions provided too much social stability and too free a political structure within the "Black" communities they served. In 1808 Ethiopian merchants visiting New York ports provided financial support for a Baptist church which was under threat of such a foreclosure. Some researchers suggest that the church's gratitude for such a generous gesture on the part of the Ethiopians account for the change of the name to the Abyssinian Methodist Church (Abyssinia is the original name for Ethiopia).

The thoughts, history, and suffering of Africans in America were preserved in the "Negro" spiritual. Although many spirituals are based on the major mode, they also include the minor and other modal pitch sets. The harmonization of spiritual songs is also broad. Unlike the disjunct feature of many African melodies, spiritual melodies are typically conjunct lines supported by consonant tonal harmonies. The exploration of the range of spiritual melodies made by H. E. Krehbiel revealed that certain spirituals were more instrumental in their stylistic approach, however. Songs such as "Man Can Hinder Me" and "O'er the Crossing" depart from diatonic construction to explore more disjunct phrase construction. Many spirituals focused on Egypt (where northern Africans once held Jews captive) and Ethiopia (where the "Black" Queen of Sheba gave birth to Solomon's son).[43] The Jews' quest for freedom was similar to the deliverance sought by African slaves. "When Israel Was in Egypt" and "Joshua Fit the Battle" are songs that display the African Americans' identification and affinity with Jewish captivity and suffering. In modifying the subjects metaphorically and subconsciously, thus identifying with the Old Testament point of reference, some African Americans may have seen themselves as a chosen few in America.

African Americans continued to use religion as a means to escape the oppression of their daily lives and to compensate for their stifled ambitions.[44]

The emotional gospel preached in African churches was a defense mechanism for many of its members, and European Americans in both the North and South tried to use the church as an instrument for controlling "Negroes." Robert Ryland, the "White" minister of the First African Church of Richmond and other "Whites" preached that they were divinely instructed to exploit African Americans. "God has given this country to the white people," Ryland bluntly told the African-American congregation, ignoring the fact that Native Americans were the original inhabitants. He continues: "They are the lawmakers—the masters—the superiors. The people of color are the subjects—the servants—and even when not in bondage, the inferiors. In this state of things, God enjoins you to your submission." Although not all "White" clergymen were as obtuse, most deluded themselves into believing "slaves" should be subordinate to their "masters" just as a Christian is subordinate and obedient to God.

The urging of African-American ministers to expect rewards and happiness only in the afterlife facilitated the racist themes the oppressors expounded. Andrew Marshall of the First African Church of Savannah admonished his "Negro" congregation with "some good practical maxims of morality, and told them they were to look to a future state of rewards and punishments in which God would deal impartially with 'the poor and the rich, the black man and the white.'"[45] Frederick Douglass was disappointed that African-American ministers (like Marshall) put their congregations "under the delusion that God required them to submit to slavery and to wear their chains with meekness and humility."

Plantation owners soon became threatened by the political and rebellious potential of the African-American church. Efforts were soon made to suppress church meetings as the number of slave revolts began to rise. Suspicion surrounding African-American religious activity in the South was noticeable in both northern and southern areas, and it led to more direct action. A complaint by Holt Richardson of King William County, dated September 5, 1789, appears in the archives of Virginia *Executive Papers*, describing certain insurrectionary activities in that vicinity:

> I have appointed Patrolers to Keep our Negroes in order & to search all Disorderly houses after night & unlawful Meetings & where they find a large quantity of Negroes assembled at night to take them up & carry them before a justice which has been done, but we have a sett of disorderly People who call themselves Methodists and are joined by some of those who call themselves Baptist, who make it a rule two or three times each week to meet after dark & call in all the Negroes they can gather & a few whites & free mulatoes [*sic*] who pretend under the clock [*sic*] of Religion to meet at a School house where no one lives & there they pretend to preach & pray with a set of the greatest Roges of Negroes in this County & they never break up till about two or three o'clock in the morning & those Negroes who stays with them goes through the neighborhood & steele [*sic*] everything threat they can lay their hands on & our Negroes are not to be found when we are in want of them, but

are at some such meetings and I have ordered the Paterrolers [*sic*] to go to such unlawful meetings & to take up all Negroes that they should find at such places.[46]

The kind of subversive talk and clandestine organizing planters suspected was indeed going on within slave communities under the guise of clandestine church meetings, feasts, and burials. There was enough of a break in the security of the meetinghouses and field worship services for plantation owners to get wind of information that caused a tightening of security by the middle of the eighteenth century. Church services held out of sight and earshot of "Whites" were interrupted by night patrols on plantations in the Carolinas and Virginia. If caught attending such meetings, slaves were usually taken to the authorities and/or had their Bibles confiscated. "Black" preachers could expect to be punished severely for instigating such activities regardless of the harmlessness involved.[47]

Although not nearly as much music was taught to African-American children in schools as in the church, those fortunate enough to attend school learned a variety of European-American songs. The importance of the African-American school was second only to the church in the free "Negro" community. From the time that books were smuggled into slave quarters, Africans in America were always anxious to take advantage of educational opportunities. Because "Whites" knew they could not control slaves if they were educated, early African schools were condemned and thwarted by many of the same agents that the independent churches and benevolent societies encountered. In 1802 Baltimore Quakers reported teaching several "mixed schools," and a few Alexandria teachers taught both "White" and "Black" pupils around the same time. Although the wake of the American Revolution made some European Americans consider extending the concepts of freedom to Africans, the ideals that united poor "Whites" and "Blacks" in evangelical churches did not make their way into the founding of schools. Class distinctions alone excluded most Negro freemen from education. The decrease in funding, the increasing inevitability of the Revolutionary War, and the general hostility of poor European Americans over school integration caused the remaining integrated academies to close their doors or segregate their classrooms by the turn of the nineteenth century.[48] Thus the integration of African-American and European-American music was again thwarted and limited. The schools that succeeded in opening were small, open infrequently, and had limited enrollment.

Voodoo

The conspicuous presence of voodoo in New Orleans may account for reasons people claim the birth of "jazz" in that region. Voodoo kept the rhythms of Africa alive at Congo Square in New Orleans and elsewhere. Consequently, African-American musicians in New Orleans maintained firm Afrocentric roots while exploring the wide range of other influences that life in the cosmopolitan Crescent City provided.

Music making became an experimental enterprise by default: the musicians had been removed from their indigenous communities and placed within an environment where each member might well have represented the traditional values of a particular African village. Yet, the common plight of Africans forced to endure these unfortunate circumstances made it clear that sociocultural similarities had to be discovered quickly. While performing heavy labor and engaging the oppressors' culture, the absorption, transformation, and refinement of these new cultural bonds were a matter of physical, mental, and spiritual survival.

Music was the primary catalyst in preserving and perpetuating various elements of the indigenous traditions left behind. An enormous and unique body of spirituals and secular folk songs grew out of constricted opportunities. Varying degrees of improvisational freedom are found in many forms of traditional African music and, consequently, improvisation became a feature of all African-American musical forms. Singing involved much latitude in pitch and timbre, enhanced through altering the sound of sustained tones, making abrupt changes in dynamic levels, and toying with the rhythms of phrases and melodies. Pitch-bending, a feature also found in various other world music, eventually led to "blue-note" functions in African-American musical practice. No traditional African music allows the freedom found in African-American "jazz," but many aspects of African vocal technique were later transferred to "jazz" instrumental styles.

Freedom is intrinsic to the very nature of a philosophical and spiritual system.[49] The African attitude created an image of God with the exact measure of power required to shield worshippers from their debilitating circumstances. Music was the vehicle that guided them toward liberation from the negative forces of their objective reality. Men may have captured the African's body, but God alone invoked life and death. Music provided the catalyst that reminded the slave that they existed as noble beings in the eyes of the Creator, despite the decrees of evil men and women.

Just as the study of European medieval music requires an understanding of the Catholic mass, an examination of voodoo is significant to the study of African-American music. Christian hymns were certainly not the only religious music to have influence on African-American music. As bans on European slavery were gradually imposed, African Americans no longer regularly came in direct contact with Africans coming from the African continent. Consequently they eventually lost a direct link with African customs and traditions. Voodoo was one of the few ways in which aspects of West African culture was preserved to a significant degree.

Drums were never outlawed on the African continent or in Haiti. Consequently, Haitian voodoo rituals retained strong elements of African religions, music, and dance, while Orishas from Cuba and the Dominican Republic still bear the names of both African gods and Catholic saints in Santeria. The passion and ecstasy that had been a part of African religious rites remained noticeable features of African-American church services. Although historians often mention the effect Protestant hymns had on the development of the spirituals, few are aware of the significant role that voodoo served in maintaining Afrocentric elements in "New World" music and culture.

In Africa, drumming and singing played a significant role at ceremonies in inducing states of possession and trance. Voodoo ceremonies in some areas of Haiti and the American South involved African-style drums until the drums and finally the ceremonies were banned. Before legislation barred voodoo ceremonies from Congo Square, large groups of African Americans gathered there frequently to celebrate their African heritage. As a result, the festive and spiritual qualities of voodoo ritual survived and—along with other important elements of African tradition—found their way into African-American "jazz." Whenever Africans were free of Eurocentric influence, Africanisms emerged in their music and art. The "free jazz" styles of Ornette Colman, Albert Ayler, John Coltrane, and others reflect the Afrocentric tendencies expressed in voodoo ritual.

Conveniently, voodoo allowed Africans to maintain their reverence for the lesser, personal gods (*Loas*) that surrounded the supreme African deity. Displaced people in Africa identified these lesser gods with the saints of the Roman Catholic Church (in veiled form), which enabled them to base their world and beliefs upon something far more familiar to them than their new environment. They could follow the arcane leadership and direction of their own ministers and healers and shield themselves spiritually from the difficult realities, both objective and subjective, that dominated their existence. Music would later serve a similar function for Africans in America.

Denying Africans in America access to their music, language, and the worship of their gods was particularly devastating to a people for whom these elements had been so vital. Many of the African languages were tonal and closely related to their music. The music was a function of the religious ritual. They venerated their personal gods, and religion was the means through which the gods could be invoked directly. The pantheon of African gods was responsible for all aspects of an individual's life and fate. Viewed from the Afrocentric perspective of the period, the severe, constrained, highly puritanical God of the Judeo-Christian tradition was not approachable in daily life, so one could only hope to get close to "Him" in the afterlife.

> This God also laid specific rules of behavior which went against the entire cultural ethos of Africa. The body and the senses were condemned by Christianity—or at least by Christians—and the ascetic existence was considered the highest form of life. In Africa a close personal tie with certain of the more earthly gods was still possible, but now an intermediary was needed in the form of the preacher, and the rules of decorum forbade, except in a very few cases, any emotional behavior during worship. Nevertheless, the African spiritual attitude was preserved through hoodoo, the Afro-American counterpart of the West Indian voodoo. Instead of the guilt that resulted from Christianity, there was an acceptance of life and a spiritual link with nature among the devotees of hoodoo. A hoodoo ceremony is marked by states of emotional catharsis that often led to trances.[50]

The relatively free expression of emotions in African-based religious ceremonies was transferred into African-American musical styles. The difference between the intense emotional displays common in African-American church services and the much more subdued spiritual expression of their European-American counterparts is noticeable.

In voodoo rituals, the instruments "talk" as they invoke the gods (the *Loas*). The music inspires possession and "becomes effortless, but 'hot,' a West African linguistic survival referring to trance."[51] There is an amazing similarity between the spirit and practice of voodoo rituals and the rites of the black Pentecostal Church service.[52]

Some investigators and writers use the terms "vodun" or "voodooism,"[53] while others use "hoodoo." Vodun is not easily defined, but some Western scholars consider this religion and its rituals to be "vestigial remains of African religions that syncretized with Roman Catholicism in the West Indies and Latin America."[54] Other scholars regard it as a much more active force. It is undeniable, nevertheless, that the traditional mythologies, theologies and cosmologies of Dahomey, Nigeria, and other regions of West Africa are closely affiliated with the voodoo rituals of Haiti and other twentieth-century communities.[55]

Voodooists serve the Iwa and beseech their assistance. The hundreds of Iwa divide into two families. *Rada* include benign spirits from ancestral West Africa, and *Pethro* involve fiery spirits who represent Central African and Creole traditions. Spirits often express themselves as triads. The qualities involved in such triads include ancestors, souls of twins, mysteries, and the divine personification of nature. A priest or priestess "feed" the sacred Rada, Pethro, and Congo drums to strengthen them.[56]

Embedded in the roots of voodoo are African spiritual traditions that survived Middle Passage. The name "voodoo" is inherited from the Fon kingdom of what is now Benin (once Dahomey). Their neighbors to the east, the Nago (a Yoruba-speaking people) also influenced Haitian voodoo. The Fon and Kongo kingdoms of West and Central Africa gave voodoo its basic form and content. Fon names for "temple," "priest," "priestess," and "servitor" (*ounfo, oungan, mam'bo, ounsi*) are among the Rada elements retained in voodoo.

The names of Rada ritual drums associated with voodoo rites (*tambou, tambouasoto,* etc.) are also derived from Fon. The *ogan* is an idiophone resembling a flattened bell that the *ogantier* plays with an iron rod. It is the leader of the "chromatic" instruments, so its rhythms control the ritual orchestra. The triangle is another "chromatic" instrument that aids in "opening the path of air." The *ogan* responds to the esoteric formula which signifies the "chief of the magic circle,"[57] and initiates and controls the magic rhythm of the battery (usually three) of drums. In the Congo rite two drums may be used. The Rada ceremonies generally include three drums, one large (the *manman*), one medium sized (the *grondez*), and one small (the *ka-tha-bou*). The chants of the voodoo chorus are sung by male and female *houn'sihs* who are directed by the *houn'guénicon* (generally a woman). Ritual hand-bells, shakers, and other idiophones are also used in ceremonies. One Pethro chant states:

Ahi, manman, hen!	Ahi, mother, hen!
Tambour moin rélé.	My drum calls.
Jou-m allongé... Ahi!	The day I die... Ahi!
Ahi! Manman.	Ahi! Mother.

Some researchers attribute the term *vodu* to the Ewe tribe (from the area formerly referred to as the Gold Coast). The prefix *vo* ("apart") can be loosely translated as "holy" (sacrosanct). In his description of slave worship, W. E. B. DuBois refers to the use of *obi* or obeah charms (or fetishes) to aid in the bewitching of others or in shielding oneself from dangerous forces. Fetishes of this type are often associated with vodun practice. Slaves brought to Jamaica from the Gold Coast had an obeah that was a derivative of the Twi *obayifo*, which Parrinder translates as "witchcraft."[58] The obeah is frequently associated with snake worship. Melvill Herskovits in his study *Trinidad Village* reports a native as saying "all obiamen keep snakes."[59] J. J. Williams refers to an official document published in London in 1789 that says that obeah (witchcraft or sorcery) derives from the Egyptian *ob* ("serpent"), which applies to "one particular sect, the remnant probably of a very celebrated religious order in remote ages."[60] Those who are sincerely involved in vodun worship, however, believe in a benevolent and supreme God incapable of anger.

Voodoo beliefs and practices also reflect the African's encounter with the aboriginal Taino people in the Americas. Haiti belonged to the Taino long before Columbus landed in America. Voodoo, therefore, involves spiritual recycling or syncretism that absorbed a variety of religious customs. Thus it is closely related to the highly syncretic nature of innovative African-American music. The imploding and exploding sounds associated with an assortment of African languages are incorporated into African music. Elements of traditional languages merged with indigenous and foreign languages in America to eventually produce both voodoo and "jazz." The recycling of European articles associated with voodoo is related to a similar recycling of European musical elements in developing African-American music. In both cases Africans met their Afrocentric objectives while adapting to local conditions and circumstances.

African Americans must have realized the true meaning of the metaphor associated with the serpent as "an all-powerful and supernatural being." After all, they resided within a world where most of their modes of communication had to be encoded. Through eventually identifying with the saints of the Roman Catholic Church, many metaphysical details could be embedded within a personification of a hierarchy of gods closely resembling those of Dahomean mythology.[61]

Jim Crow Segregation Perpetuates Segregated Musical Styles

A segregated society can only produce segregated music and art. America could not (and cannot) develop an American music while still remaining a racist and sexist society. America has Native Americans, African Americans, European Americans, Asian Americans, Latino and Latina Americans, etc., but it has no single type of American to compose American music. W. E. B. Dubois left a description of the effects Jim Crow segregation had on African-American life.

> We colored folk stand at the parting of ways, and we must take counsel. The objection to segregation and "Jim Crowism" was in other days the fact that compelling Negroes to associate only with Negroes meant to exclude them from contact with the best culture of the day. How could we learn manners or get knowledge if the heritage of the past was locked away from us?

> Gradually, however, conditions have changed. Culture is no longer the monopoly of the white nor is poverty and ignorance the sole heritage of the black. Many a colored man in our day called to conference with his own and dreading the contact with uncivilized people even though they were of his own blood has been astonished and deeply gratified at the kind of people he has met—at the evidence of good manners and thoughtfulness among his own.

> . . . On the other hand, if the Negro is to develop his own power and gifts; if he is not only to fight prejudices and oppression successfully, but also to unite for ideals higher than the world has realized in art and industry and social life, then he must unite and work with Negroes and build a new and great Negro ethos.[62]

African-American music originally developed out of a separate African-American culture ostracized from mainstream America. Spirituals, gospel music, ragtime, "jazz," swing, bebop, and other musical forms evolved as a consequence. By the end of the nineteenth century, however, African-American music was homogenized, stylized, and packaged as cheap imitations for quick profits. Samuel A. Floyd, Jr., reminds us:

> Ragtime, for example, became associated in the public mind with the image of a white or black piano player—decked out in a straw hat, a white or striped long sleeve shirt with garters at the elbows, and a bow tie, with a cigar in his mouth or between his fingers—beating out vapid but toe tapping versions of the real thing. The multi-meter of folk and classic ragtime was reduced to simple syncopation, and its polyrhythms, so vital to the genre, disappeared. Spirituals were replaced by pseudo-spirituals and Europeanized versions in which the sincere emotional quality of the former was presented as mere sentimentality. Some of the most vital qualities of black folk music were lost or suppressed, and the real thing remained outside the commercially profitable, far-reaching cultural marketplace.[63]

Women in America were still not allowed to vote at the end of the nineteenth century so their power was also limited socially, politically, and economically. Throughout the period that frames the development of early African-American music, women who exhibited too much independence were "put in their place." Although less victimized than African-American slaves, European-American women were not the equals of men in either law or social practice. To sidestep limitations, women musicians eventually began to organize music guilds where they could assemble bands and orchestras to develop their skills.

Other African-American women's clubs were created during the nineteenth century for political and social reasons. These clubs, dedicated to welfare services within the African-American community, established strong ties between middle-class and poor African-American women. The clubs were also in the forefront of the movement against lynching in America. One of the members, an outspoken and experienced journalist named Ida B. Wells (Barnett), published newspaper articles and pamphlets and delivered speeches inspiring resistance to discrimination and lynching. Wells describes dark aspects of the racist climate in America:

> All this while, although the political cause has been removed, the butcheries of black men at Barnwell, S.C., Carrolton, Miss., Waycross, Ga., and Memphis, Tenn., have gone on; also the flaying alive of a man in Kentucky, the burning of one in Arkansas, the hanging of a fifteen year old girl in Louisiana, a woman in Jackson, Tenn., and one in Hollendale, Miss., until the dark and bloody record of the South shows 728 Afro-Americans lynched during the past 8 years. Not 50 of these were for political causes; the rest were for all manner of accusations from that of rape of white women, to the case of the boy Will Lewis who was hanged at Tullahoma, Tenn., last year for being drunk and "sassy" to white folks.

> These statistics compiled by the Chicago "Tribune" were given the first of this year (1892). Since then, not less than one hundred and fifty have been known to have met violent death at the hands of cruel bloodthirsty mobs during the past nine months.

> To palliate their record (which grows as the Afro-American becomes intelligent) and excuse some of the most heinous crimes that ever stained the history of a country, the South is shielding itself behind the plausible screen of defending the honor of its women. This, too, in the face of the fact that only *one-third* of the 728 victims to mobs have been *charged* with rape, to say nothing of those of that one-third who were innocent of the charge. A white correspondent of the Baltimore Sun declares that the Afro-American who was lynched in Chestertown, Md., in May for assault on a white girl was innocent; that the deed was done by a white man who had since disappeared. The girl

herself maintained that her assailant was a white man. When that poor Afro-American was murdered, the whites excused their refusal of a trial on the grounds that they wished to spare the white girl the mortification of having to testify in court.[64]

The early minstrels, country blues singers, ragtime pianists, and other "Black" musicians performed under the constant threat of lynching and other social injustice. The evolution of the music continued nonetheless. Thus, African-American music is more than a set of art forms created for the admiration, analysis, and entertainment of the listener. It is also a historical record that defines the tenacity, struggles, wisdom, spirituality, and genius of African-American people. Africans had to develop quickly the ability to be resourceful, to form a difficult convergence (regardless of the degree of dissimilarity between subjects), to maintain courage and high spirits in the face of adversity, to develop new forms of social expression, and to make other unprecedented social adaptations. The remarkably positive and powerful music, which stems from centuries of treacherous experiences, is the legacy of African-American music.

Summary

America created no indigenous musical forms of its own before the spiritual, blues, and "jazz" forms grew out of the "Black" experience. Stephen Foster, Dan Emmett, Thomas Rice, George Gershwin, Nick LaRoca, and many other European-American composers drew their musical source material directly from African-American musical legacies. To a degree, Igor Stravinsky, Darius Milhaud, Claude Debussy, Alban Berg, and other European composers did likewise. Dvorak, when asked for suggestions regarding a new American music at the seminars he presented, commented that Americans had a hidden treasure in African-American music, a treasure that America should value. Darius Milhaud asked to visit a "jazz" club in Harlem when he arrived in New York in 1921, and Maurice Ravel wanted to hear Jimmie Noone in Chicago when he visited the United States.

Notes

[1] McConnell, *Negro Troops*, p. 78.

[2] Judith Papachristttou. *Women Together: A History in Documents of the Women's Movement in the United States* (New York: Alfred A. Knopf, 1976), p. 3.

[3] Nketia, *African Roots*, pp. 83–84.

[4] Portia K. Maultsby, "Africanism in African American Music," in *Africanisms in American Culture,* ed. Joseph E. Holloway (Bloomington: Indiana University Press, 1990), p. 185.

[5] Olly Wilson, "Significance," p. 20.

[6] For a small sample of Rahsaan Roland Kirk's music, listen to the albums *Rip, Rig and Panic* (particularly the title cut and "No Tonic Press"—with Jaki Byard, Richard Davis, and Elvin Jones, recorded January 13, 1965); and from the album *The Inflated Tear* listen to "The Inflated Tear"—recorded June 15, 1968, with Ron Burton (p), Steve Novosel (b) Jimmy Hopps (d)—and "Introduction and Melody," recorded May 12, 1970.

7 "Through the Prism of Folklore," in *Black and White in American Culture*, ed. Jules Chametzky and Sidney Kaplan (Amherst: University of Massachusetts Press, 1969), p. 183.

8 Samuel A. Floyd, *The Power of Black Music: Interpreting Its History from Africa to the United States* (New York: Oxford University Press, 1995), pp. 77–78.

9 Hildred Roach, *Black American Music*, 2d ed. (Malabar, Fla.: Kreiger, 1992), pp. 8–9.

10 These accounts are summarized by Epstein in *Sinful Tunes*, pp. 19–99.

11 John Thomas Scharf, *History of Philadelphia* (Philadelphia, 1884), 2:930.

12 Shapiro and Hentoff, *Hear Me Talkin'*, p. 92.

13 Ibid.

14 Beverly J. Robinson, *Africanisms in American Culture*, ed. Joseph E. Holloway (Bloomington: University of Indiana Press, 1990), pp. 214–14.

15 Ibid., pp. 215–16.

16 Dorothy Scarborough, *On the Trail of Negro Folk-Songs* (Cambridge: Harvard University Press, 1925), p. 264.

17 Roach, *Black American Music*, p. 11.

18 See the chart in the Appendix for labor details.

19 Eileen Southern, *The Music of Black Americans: A History*, 2d ed. (New York: Norton, 1983), pp. 123–25.

20 Charles K. Wolfe, ed., *Thomas W. Talley's Negro Folk Rhymes: A New and Expanded Edition, with Music* (Knoxville: University of Tennessee Press, 1991), p. 83.

21 Angela Y. Davis, *Blues Legacies and Black Feminism* (New York: Pantheon, 1998).

22 Ibid., pp. 238–43.

23 Albert Murray, *The Blue Devil of Nada: A Contemporary American Approach to Aesthetic Statement* (New York: Pantheon, 1996), pp. 99–100.

24 Southern, *Music of Black Americans,* p. 234.

25 Ibid., p. 265.

26 Liner notes from McIntyre's album *Home*, Steeple Chase SCS-1039 (1975).

27 Jack Wheaton, *All That Jazz!* (New York: Ardsley House, 1994), p. 61.

28 Southern, *Music of Black Americans,* p. 109.

29 Eileen Southern, *The Music of Black Americans: A History* (New York: Norton, 1983), p. 107.

30 Ibid., p. 107.

31 Harold McKinney, *Discovering Jazz* (Wenha Records), cassette tape no. 1.

32 James Haskins, *Black Music in America: A History through Its People* (New York: Harper Trophy, 1987), p. 64.

33 Ibid.

34 Ibid.

35 Southern, *Music of Black Americans,* pp. 35–39.

36 Valuable new research on the African Union Church of Wilmington has been done by Lewis Baldwin, "'Invisible Strands' in African Methodism: A History of the A.U.M.P. and U.A.M.E. Churches" (Ph.D. diss., Garrett Evangelical Seminary, 1980).

37 Wilmore, *Black Religion and Black Radicalism,* pp. 78–83.

38 Ibid., pp. 80–83

39 Allen, *Life Experiences*, pp. 14–21. See Charles H. Wesley, *Richard Allen, Apostle of Freedom* (Washington, D.C.: Associated Publishers, 1935), p. 81.

40 Berlin, *Slaves without Masters,* pp. 300–303.

41 Frederika Bremer, *The Homes of the New World* (New York, 1853), 1:306–17.

42 Samuel Davies, *Letters from the Rev. Samuel Davies and Others: Shewing the State of Religion in Virginia, S. C., & c., Particularly among the Negroes* (London: J. & W. Oliver, 1761).

43 Roach, *Black American Music*, pp. 24–27.

44 This theme is emphasized in Benjamin E. Mays, *The Negro's God as Reflected in His Literature* (Boston: Chapman & Grimes, 1938), and E. Franklin Frazier, *The Negro Church* (New York: Schocken Books, 1963). Also see Joseph Washington, *Black Religion* (Boston: Beacon Press, 1964.

45 Berlin, *Slaves without Masters,* pp. 300–303.

46 Quoted by James Hugo Johnston, "The Participation of White Men in Virginia Negro Insurrections," *Journal of Negro History* 16 (1931): 159.

[47] Wilmore, *Black Religion and Black Radicalism,* pp. 32–33.

[48] "Constitution of the African School Society," in *Minutes of the African School Society* (Wilmington, 1809–1835), Historical Society of Delaware; William C. Dunlap, *Quaker Education in Baltimore and Virginia Yearly Meetings with an Account of Certain Meetings of Delaware and the Eastern Shore Affiliated With Philadelphia* (Philadelphia, 1936), p. 485. The best survey of early Negro education is Carter G. Woodson, *The Education of the Negro Prior to 1861* (New York, 1915).

[49] Mircea Eliade, *Myths, Dreams and Mysteries* (New York: Harper & Row, 1967), pp. 103–6.

[50] Wilmore, *Black Religion and Black Radicalism,* p. 23.

[51] Rudi Blesh, *Shining Trumpets* (New York: Knopf, 1958), p. 43.

[52] Wilmore, *Black Religion and Black Radicalism,* pp. 20–25.

[53] See Joseph J. Williams, *Voodoos and Obeahs* (New York: Dial, 1933); Alfred Metraux, *Voodoo in Haiti* (New York: Oxford University Press, 1959); Maya Deren, *Divine Horsemen: Voodoo Gods of Haiti* (New York: Dell, 1970).

[54] Wilmore, *Black Religion and Black Radicalism.*

[55] See Metraux, *Voodoo in Haiti,* pp. 30 ff.

[56] Milo Rigaud, *Secrets of Voodoo* (New York: Pocket Books, 1971), p. 105.

[57] Ibid., p. 104.

[58] Parrinder, *West African Religion,* pp. 35 ff.

[59] Melvin J. Herskovits, *Trinidad Village* (New York: Alfred Knopf, 1947).

[60] As cited in Wilmore, *Black Religion and Black Radicalism,* p. 20.

[61] Metraux, *Voodoo in Haiti,* p. 34.

[62] *The Seventh Son: The Thoughts and Writings of W. E. B. Du Bois* (New York: Vintage Books, 1971), 2: 209–10.

[63] Floyd, *Power of Black Music,* p. 86.

[64] Ida B. Wells Barnett. *Southern Horrors* (1892; reprint [in a collection of pamphlets] New York: Arno, 1969), pp. 13–15.

IV
Innovators Emerging Between 1900 and 1910

I love what I do. I hope the music I make will affect people in positive, spiritual ways, and provide enjoyment or some type of direction that inspires them to pursue *their* artistic endeavors.

—Saxophonist Sonny Simmons

Ecumenical Music Retention

Innovative "jazz" has always been an ecumenical music that has drawn from all the musical sources it has encountered. It blended various influences through a fissional process to produce music never heard before.

The vocal approach used by many African singers is closely related to the vocal approach of blues singers. The African griots, who function as improvising troubadours, or town criers, perform in fashions that are forerunners of African-American vocal traditions. This is especially evident with regards to rhythm, flexibility of pitch, and timbre variation. African griots still practice their art today. Konde Kuyate of Guinea and Miriam Makeba of the Xhosa tribe in South Africa are women griots who have become famous worldwide. As Ghanaian music scholar and musician Francis Bebey tells us, "Vocal music is truly the essence of African musical art. . . . [A] prime motive of instrumentalists is to reconstruct spoken or sung language."[1] In turn, vocal blues became the foundation of African-American "jazz."

The brass bands, blues, and ragtime were all a part of the developmental history of "jazz," but they differ from early "jazz" because they involve much less improvisation. The rhythmic grid patterns of ragtime and brass band music involved the subdivision of each beat evenly into three or four parts. Early "jazz" began to break away from the grid divisions of beat that were inherited from both European and certain African music, in favor of a more relaxed rhythmic interpretation that would eventually lead to a "swing" feel.

A more democratic approach to improvisation also distinguished early "jazz" from earlier African-American music. The collective improvisation in early "jazz" styles produced a polyphonic texture that allowed each player an opportunity to improvise their own part. The new musical process also produced a new repertoire of early "jazz" music. Here, a greater range of individual stylistic variety occurred than that found in the more regimented individual musical roles of funeral bands, ragtime pianists, or blues singers.

Early vocal blues had a unique approach to improvisation, and because of emphasis upon clarity of the words, it differed somewhat from early instrumental "jazz" approaches. Blues modes of expression eventually evolved into most all "jazz" forms nonetheless. As it gradually emerged as a definitive vernacular American musical form (whose influence infused all other vernacular American music), it developed a stylistic range extending from early African-American slave music to avant-garde "jazz." Blues was capable of conveying universal emotional messages as well as complex and elegant modern theoretical principals. Thus it gained the attention and respect of the global community. In America, however, recalcitrant African-American music of any kind was relegated to marginal musical positions or considered profane by a racist sector of American society. Roger Pryor Dodge provides an excellent example of the arrogant ignorance often hurled at African-American music:

> The blues have developed from the spirituals, which had their genesis in the simple but powerful four-part harmonies of our ["White"] hymns. They are the result of straining a formal and highly cultivated music through the barbaric and musical mind of the Negro. The spirituals are the Negroes' digestion of our hymn tunes. The blues, in turn, are another step in the development, as Handy's book does not neglect to explain, and it is this material that constitutes the basis of true jazz. Into the Negroes' singing or playing of the spirituals crept the savage rhythms that had shaped or been shaped by the ancestral dances of the tribe and these formed in time a definite playing style; and in recognizing this style we recognize jazz.[2]

Dodge, who was not a musician, must have concluded that American society and the world became bewitched by African savagery when European Americans embrace spirituals, gospel, blues, "jazz," and other African-American music. Since the influence of those forms replaced and rendered Dodge's "highly cultivated music" obsolete, his implication suggests that twentieth-century music has taken a serious turn toward barbarism. Samuel Floyd says,

> In the moans, hollers, hums, falsetto, and elisions that [Ronald] Davis mentions, together with the timbre of the guitar and harp—distorted by bottleneck and hand-muffling, respectively—the heterogeneous sound ideal was realized in the blues, revealing the derivation of the music from spirituals and the ring, even down to the use of "Oh Lawdy" in a musical form that is, from the standpoint of Christianity, unabashedly profane. And the improvisatory potential revealed in Davis's description prefigures jazz and confirms the presence of melodic extemporization in the African-American musical arsenal. Of course he says nothing about sadness or lamentation, traits that have been exaggerated—by well-meaning promoters of the black social cause and by the not-so-well meaning record producers—to such a degree that it is commonly thought that the expressive range of the blues is limited to that one quality.[3]

An enriched range of timbre supplied by vocal blues vocabulary, combined with an increased emphasis on instrumental music, allowed African-American music to move closer to the stylistic qualities of traditional African music. A wide range of timbres was an important element of both instrumental and vocal expression from early spirituals and blues to the music of Jimi Hendrix and Ornette Coleman in the modern era. In looking at the history of American music, it seems that the particular audience for whom African-American music is performed determines the proportions of African or European influence it may contain. Spirituals were songs more often sung in the presence of European-American listeners; thus fewer Africanisms remained in spirituals than in blues, which was created primarily for African-American listener consumption. Nonetheless, spirituals and the blues have remained closely allied with even the most abstract forms of innovative African-American "jazz."

Although it is difficult to pinpoint exactly when early African-American musical genres originated, we know that many of the styles born during colonial times evolved further throughout the nineteenth century. Due to lack of experience with African approaches to music, Europeans and European Americans were incapable of fully comprehending "Black" music. The differences in approach, and the raw conditions in which the music blossomed, caused many members of the majority culture to deride what they heard and deem it unworthy of their time. Others from outside the culture, who took the time to listen to African-American music, were often cavalier about the music they heard. "Ear-witness" accounts left by Europeans and European Americans from early periods in American history are generally unreliable and subjective. The inability to objectively analyze African-American music was amplified by the fact that African Americans usually performed a different brand of music in the presence of "Whites" than styles they performed within the privacy of their own communities. This was true throughout the history of "jazz" prior to the bebop era.

As African-American citizens gradually obtained greater degrees of sociocultural freedom, musicians began to move farther away from the stylistic limitations of both African and European traditions to form more personal styles. Regardless of how far innovators traveled from the confines of African musical traditions, however, they retained a measure of the fundamental aesthetics and spirit of African culture. The tension between the perpetuation of musical tradition and experimentation often results in a personal paradox or social dilemma. No major innovations in "jazz" escaped this quandary completely.

The Continuation of Double Entendre and Other Modes of Communication

The effects of Code Noir or Black Codes on the American socioculture, the establishment of the White League in 1874 and the 1894 Segregation Act (requiring separate facilities for "Blacks" and "Whites") made certain that racism would be well preserved in America. The ominous legacy of slavery and the oppressive racism that emerged after the Emancipation Proclamation compelled Africans to encode African-American modes of communication. The earliest Africans in America naturally resisted forced acculturation by Europeans. Frank Tirro asserts that

> Any suggestion that the black slave was willingly accepting elements of the white culture and integrating them into his own music are certainly not acceptable for first-generation slaves. Although not carefully documented, it is possible, and more likely probable, that the slave in America desired to maintain his African musical heritage and was motivated by a need to preserve his African identity and avoid incorporation into the hated white society. The intensity of these feelings is recorded in the words of a slave song, "Sound of Jubilee!"

> See the poor souls from Africa
> Transported to America;
> We are stolen, and sold in Georgia,
> Will you go along with me?
> We are stolen, and sold in Georgia,
> Come sound the Jubilee!

> See wives and husbands sold apart,
> Their children's screams will break my heart;
> There's a better day a coming,
> Will you go along with me?
> There's a better day a coming,
> Go sound the Jubilee![4]

Encoded communication was sustained within songs and instrumental musical styles throughout the twentieth century. As with field hollers of earlier times, the true meaning of messages moved easily from the transmitter to the intended receiver, while completely escaping the insensitive ears of outsiders. As a by-product of minstrelsy, ragtime was an art form that reflected the forced acculturation of a sector of African-American society. The blues and early "jazz" styles, on the other hand, reasserted a greater degree of the African tenacity to maintain its cultural uniqueness. Ragtime may have produced music that was politically innocuous, but most other forms of African-American musical expression clearly mirrored the experience of a disenfranchised people in American society. David Cayer addresses the paradox that the "jazz" phenomenon creates: "Jazz derives neither from a dominant elite enjoying education and cultural advantages nor from the masses of a numerically dominant majority. Most 'high art' has historically come from the former, most 'folk art' from the latter. But jazz . . . sprang from an enslaved minority, under conditions far less conducive to creativity than those faced by most other oppressed minorities. . . . [This] minority produced a major art form and powerfully shaped the majority's culture."[5]

Despite efforts to segregate all aspects of American society, a blending of African and European styles could not be avoided. Africans heard European folk songs and hymns, and Europeans heard the music of the Africans. African Americans fit their musical ideas to basic European formal structures found in hymns, marches, folk songs and concert music (strophic, binary, tertiary, rondo) using the three primary European chord functions (tonic, subdominant, dominant). European folk music was rooted in Anglo-Saxon tradition, which was transplanted to America during the seventeenth to nineteenth centuries. The strophic ballads and the dance music (jigs and other fast fiddle dances) remained distinctive in isolated regions of the Appalachian Mountains, but most of the music spread west to Missouri, Mississippi, and Texas.[6] Africans in America more easily obtained European violins than were other instruments beginning in the 17th century and, as mentioned earlier, the African fiddling tradition was perpetuated for centuries before Africans were enslaved in America. African-American fiddlers found a variety of musical outlets. Reels and jigs were the two most popular dances during the Antebellum period in the South. The reel was a European social dance, while the jig[7] was an energetic solo dance. Sidney Bechet discussed another avenue through which African-American music became contagious:

> These boats used to have contests for music. One boat would line up alongside another and they'd play at each other. . . . There wasn't anything but white musicians on the boats then, but they'd go along the Mississippi, and they'd hear the singing of the Negroes by the river, and some of it reached them. They'd be the songs of the Negroes working, or maybe just going about their business, maybe just resting . . . there'd be all that kind of music like it was some part of the Mississippi itself, something the river wanted to say. And it had an effect, you know; it just naturally had to have an effect on whoever heard it.
>
> . . . That music was so strong, there was such a want for it that there was no moving away from it. The people on the boat couldn't help listening. Some of them, maybe, were not showing their liking, not all of them. There were some even who didn't want to hear it at all. But it was one of those things that kind of comes in and robs you; it takes something in you without your even knowing it. And that's the way it was. Pretty soon the people wanted to hear more of it; they wanted to know more about it.[8]

Some European-American musicians, scholars, and critics have often contended that both improvisation and syncopation could have been influenced as much by European music as by African music. But if European Americans were equal contributors, then why didn't they develop an equal share of "jazz" innovations? All the physical advantages were (and still remain) in favor of those who have the time, training, and support systems required to produce and perpetuate the creation of music. Yet the progenitors and major innovators of "jazz" have unquestionably been African-American.

While it is true that syncopation and improvisation have always occurred to some degree throughout the modern and ancient world, we find no evidence of traditional European music resembling blues, swing, or ragtime. There are no baroque forms, no styles of French or German keyboard *preluding*,[9] that bear the slightest resemblance to stylistic elements of African-American "jazz." Additionally, it would have been difficult for African slaves to hear these musical genres on plantations where the owners knew little or nothing about these styles of European music. But many blues elements are noticeable in traditional African music.

Afrocentric Dance and Musical Cross-Fertilization

During the nineteenth century, European-American dancers imitated the Congo and other African-American dances. African Americans imitated the dances they saw European-American plantation owners perform at social functions. Eurocentric observers often labeled African dances obscene. Many Afrocentric dances conform to qualities Gilbert Chase describes: "The history of social dancing is full of instances in which a dance existed simultaneously on two levels, assuming a decorous form in polite society and manifesting a licentious character among the populace."[10]

Practical reasons supported the evolution of certain American dance forms. Africans on southern plantations knew that one of the ways to escape the treacherous drudgery of backbreaking fieldwork was to become an exceptionally talented musician or dancer. An African-American woman (whose name was not recorded) explained the way she avoided working in the plantation fields. When Leigh Whipper (a former president of the Negro Acting Guild in New York City) saw his old nurse (then over seventy years old) at a funeral and asked why her back had remained straight despite the hardships of slavery, she offered this explanation: "I was a strut gal ... full of bounce. . . . Us slaves watched white folks' parties, where the guests danced a minuet and then paraded in a grand march, with the ladies and gentlemen going different ways and then meeting again, arm in arm, and marching down the center together. Then we'd do it, too, *but we used to mock 'em,* every step. Sometimes the white folks noticed it, but they seemed to like it; I guess they thought we couldn't dance any better."[11] She eventually entered in dance contests on a number of plantations where owners wagered on the outcome of the competition. "I won a lot of times. Missy gave me a dress and my partner a suit."[12]

The minstrel shows often included the singing of English, Irish, and Scottish ballads sung by African Americans. Elements of these songs found their way into the harmony (involving traditional tonic-I, subdominant-IV, and dominant-V chords) of the blues. The influence of the European ballads, however, became unrecognizable once the early blues singers altered them. In the middle of the nineteenth century, African-American people (usually men) would gather around a fire and listen to individual vocalists sing ballads about legendary "Black" figures and daily life experiences. Songs like the "Saint James Infirmary" began the move toward distinctive blues elements (blue notes, syncopated phrases, pitch bending, . . . etc.) that culminated with the total transformation of the ballad into the style of blues typified in Leadbelly's "House of the Rising Sun."

Of course, not all African-American musicians engaged in the performance of spirituals, blues, and "jazz" forms in the late nineteenth and early twentieth century. A few African Americans were able to study music formally, and there were always those who managed to acquire technical training and excel in European genres of music. Vocalist Marie Selika (1849–1937) and soprano Nelie Brown Mitchell (1845–1924) were critically acclaimed singers of European art music. The virtuoso performances of violinists Joseph (José) White (1833–1920) and Walter Craig (1854–192?) were also well received by audiences at home and abroad. Rachel Washington (an accomplished teacher of piano and organ) and the brilliant pianist Samuel W. Jamison both graduated from the New England Conservatory in Boston during the second half of the nineteenth century and pursued successful careers in European music. The Hyer sisters (Anna Madah [1853–193?] and Emma Louise [1855–9?] were also known throughout much of the Western world as impressive vocalists despite the color barriers they encountered.

Montague Ring (c. 1866–1956), J. W. Postlewaite (c.1837–87), N. Clark Smith (c.1887–1933), and Alton Augustus Adams (c. 1889–1987) composed European dances, marches and concert music. One of the leading musicians of the nineteenth century was Louis Gottschalk (1829–69). His piano performances thrilled audiences all over the world. His compositions, "Negro Dance," "Bamboula," "The Banjo," etc., are reminiscent of his childhood memories of New Orleans. "Bamboula," written while Gottschalk was convalescing from an illness, was built around a "dance of the Louisiana Negro."[13] The Bamboula—along with the Calinda, Chacta, Babouille, Counjaille, Juba, Congo, and Voodoo—were the "New World" African dances known both in New Orleans and in the West Indies during the nineteenth century.

In speaking of the numerous influences on Gottschalk's music, Dr. Dominique René de Lerma feels that Gottschalk absorbed various styles in his music including "European, Caribbean, Cuban, Brazilian. He traveled much. I've always said, with all due respect to John Lewis, whom I admire immensely, if you're going to say who is the founder of a Third Stream in American music, I'd have to say it's Gottschalk. Putting habaneras in a symphony orchestra and things of that kind."[14] Gottschalk was widely acclaimed for both his virtuosity and his compositions in America and Europe. He gave his first European performance in Paris when he was sixteen. Many musicians of his era felt that his compositions and performance style contained a unique charm. His concert reviews (such as in *La France Musicale,* a Parisian paper) mentioned the young virtuoso's admirable behavior and often considered his performances flawless to the finish.

Will M. Cook (1869–1944) and Bob Cole (1868–1916) were both among the first "Black" composers/playwrights who wrote Broadway musicals for

"Black" performers. Cook wrote the first all "Black" musical sketches that appeared on Broadway in 1898, despite protests and prejudices from the European-American public. The opening performance went so well that Cook felt "Negroes were at last on Broadway, and there to stay." Cole wrote the first full-length Broadway musical for African-American performers (which also appeared in 1898). He made it a true musical, breaking away from the minstrel comedy routines by adding a plot and character development. Albert Murray discusses ways Ellington was later influenced by Cook's dedication to vernacular African-American socioculture.

> Not only was Ellington, who had named his son Mercer after Cook's son Will Mercer, very much impressed and personally influenced by [Cook], but he was especially taken by the fact that Cook, with all of his formal training and all his strictness about technical precision, also insisted, as James Weldon Johnson wrote, that the Negro in music and on stage ought to be a Negro, a genuine Negro; he declared that the Negro should eschew "white" patterns, and not employ his efforts in doing what the white artist could always do as well. . . . According to Ellington, Cook's advice was "first you find the logical way, and when you find it, avoid it, and let your inner self break through and guide you. Don't try to be anybody else but yourself."[15]

European Americans absorbed newly invented African-American music and added these stylistic ingredients to their own music. Europeans were accustomed to hearing strong metrical emphasis on beats one and three; African Americans placed the emphasis on beats two and four. African Americans' polyrhythms, syncopation, timbres, swing, call and response, ostinati, improvisation, and the transfer of tonal language to instrumental sounds, involved unique and fascinating ways of perceiving modern music.

The removal of the drum from African-American music making resulted in the percussive qualities being transferred to voice and available instruments. The inventions of the banjo, slap-bass technique, the trap set, and other approaches to music were instruments and approaches that compensated for the lack of access to traditional African instrumental tools of expression. The communal approach to the production of music had to be replicated by solo performers in some cases.

Since stylistic innovations overlap in the evolution of "jazz," a strict chronological presentation cannot always be adhered to—nor is it necessarily the most efficient approach for reviewing this history. Some innovators (like Duke Ellington, John Coltrane, and Miles Davis) modify their styles continually, while others (Louis Armstrong, Dizzy Gillespie, and Doc Cheatham) continue to perform in a particular style long after its initial invention. The evolution of twentieth-century African-American musical innovations is laced with irony, contradictions, and equivocations. Tradition and experimentation are the primary polar opposites that propel innovators forward along the path of discovery. Certain music emphasizes one pole at the expense of the another. "Jazz" defies analysis because it is a living art form that renews itself continually. Its major stylistic periods have progressed within oscillations between opposing poles of sociocultural thought, aesthetics, and behavior.

The intimate connection between speech, song, and instrumental performance in traditional African music extends into the development of African-American music. The maturation of the spiritual in nineteenth-century America created a genre of sacred music in the African-American community where sopranos and altos functioned most frequently as the lead voice. Thus, it was largely the female voice (from spirituals) that served as a stylistic archetype for early blues and "jazz" phrasing. African-American vocalists and instrumentalists managed to wield mutual influence over novel approaches to sound production, tonality, and other aspects of musical style in both sacred and secular music spheres. Following the era of male-dominated country blues singers, female-dominated classic blues style contributed significantly to the development of the early "jazz" vocabulary. Women style-setters would continue to advance the vocal and instrumental vocabularies and general blues traditions during the early twentieth century.

Early Blues

Creating an individual sound involves developing an arsenal of musical techniques uncommon to the history of a particular music. This requirement encourages the vocalist to listen to instrumentalists, and vice versa, in pursuit of unconventional ideas. Afrocentric instrumentalists adapted the cries, growls, moans, slurs, shouts, whispers, and wails commonly associated with vocal practice as they formulated modern vocabularies. Likewise, singers often work to develop improvisational technical prowess by studying master instrumental improvisers. The cycles constantly reverse themselves and overlap during periods of historical development. (For example, Bessie Smith influenced early "jazz" styles, Ella Fitzgerald was later motivated by the experiments of beboppers, and Lester Young and Billie Holiday were involved in a relationship that resulted in mutual musical inspiration.)

"Jazz" evolved out of blues and ragtime. Both forms were developed by Africans in America during the last half of the nineteenth century. European-American musicians composed ragtime soon after hearing African-American progenitors perform, but waited much longer before becoming involved with the blues. The African work songs, hollers, and spirituals led directly into the creation of the blues.

Female blues lyrics frequently focused on traveling to a better environment, lost love, hard times, or the hopelessness of living in a grossly unfair world. Songs about daily life in rural America, impersonal sexual relationships, and humor were sung in the local vernacular. Despite the presence of some highly influential female blues singers throughout the blues evolution, rural blues was usually a male domain. All of these musicians had their own personal styles and idiosyncratic approaches to their songs.

From the second half of the nineteenth century, "rural" or "country" blues[16] was a product of the deep South. The Mississippi delta and East Texas were fertile areas for blues development. Some of the most popular musicians in this genre were Blind Lemon Jefferson, Gertrude "Ma" Rainey,

Blind Roy Fuller, Bertha "Chippie" Hill, Blind Willie Johnson, and Clara Smith. After 1926, Jefferson was one of the most successful blues singers in getting his music disseminated publicly. Blues musicians Charley Patton and Robert Johnson would later continue to move the style forward. Robert Johnson could not read music, but he could memorize and play any music he heard. He was fascinated with Son House's bottleneck slide guitar technique and incorporated that influence into his own style. "Ma" Rainey and other blues musicians often worked with a tub, washboard, and jug. Other musicians worked as solo performers accompanying themselves on guitar. Rainey would eventually evolve from the rural blues style into classic blues, a musical style dominated by the female voice. The instrumentation of blues would also continue to evolve, but the guitar would remain a prominent instrument in rural styles.

Although no rural blues recordings were made until the 1920s, the songs were passed on through an aural tradition. The double entendres, puns, and an array of casual topics describing various aspects of the daily life of African Americans were performed for a variety of audiences. Generally, more lewd sexual imagery and songs of protest against "White" exploitation were intended for African American listeners only. Early twentieth-century segregation assured the perpetuation of an encoded African-American dialect because European Americans were not around "Black" communities enough to decode such messages. When they were around, African Americans switched social gears to create a deceptive facade of stereotypical behavior that was perceived as genuine by the uninitiated. Thus, as Paul Oliver points out in *The Meaning of the Blues*, "Few whites would be familiar with voodoo terms such as 'black cat bone' and 'John the Conqueror root' which are found in many blues tunes. In effect, the language of blues is a cultural code, in the sense that few whites would grasp its sexual levels of meaning."[17] Often Southern bigots labeled those who defy racist stereotypes with the phrase "uppitty niggers." This particular stamp often led to severe persecution on the bearer of that unfortunate title.

Many blues songs seem intrinsically pessimistic because the environment to which early blues was relegated was ripe for melancholia. The expressive range of the genre is not always so limited, however, and blues songs are often some of the most humorous American folk songs.

There is a greater sense of rhythm and formal freedom found in rural blues than in later standardized 12-bar (and 16-bar) forms. Listening to blues singers such as Lightnin' Hopkins and other live rural blues performers makes it clear that early blues performances were not restricted by fixed metrical or rhythmic patterning. Singers often altered their approach to a song each time it was sung. Early blues was performed in ways that allowed musical aspects to be altered naturally according to the whims of the performer.

Gertrude "Ma" Rainey—"Mother of the Blues"

Gertrude "Ma" Rainey (c. 1886–1939) was an early blues innovator, performer, lyricist, and composer. She is the acknowledged "Mother of the Blues." Her monumental musical contributions are documented in part through nearly one hundred songs preserved on record. She was the mentor to the powerful "Empress of the Blues," Bessie Smith, through whom her legacy was perpetuated and extended. Her contemporaries have also recognized Rainey's captivating presence. She was the first female vocalist to perform classic blues songs with a "jazz" combo or piano accompanist.

Born in 1886 to Thomas and Ella Allen Pridgett, Gertrude Pridgett was trained from childhood as a singer and dancer. Her talent and flamboyant flair were her trademark since childhood. At the age of fourteen she made her debut at the local opera house singing and dancing in a local talent show called "The Bunch of Blackberries." Despite the artistic respect and influence she garnered throughout her career, Ma Rainey was virtually unnoticed by the music world when she died in the town of her birth, Rome, Georgia, in 1939. She performed until the final four years of her life, yet her death certificate listed her "usual occupation" as "housekeeper."

In 1902 Gertrude heard a woman singing an unforgettable song about a man who had left her. The young Pridgett was impressed, learned the song immediately, and incorporated it into her act. Pridgett called her rendition "The Blues," and featured it as her closing number. It was always enthusiastically received. She would discover much later that her song strongly resembled the composition considered the first official blues (written by W. C. Handy), entitled "Memphis Blues." Handy's blues was published in 1914.

When Gertrude was eighteen years old she met and fell in love with an older vaudevillian with the famous Rabbit Foot Minstrels, Will Rainey. The couple married on April 22, 1904, and Pridgett became "Madame Gertrude Rainey." Madame ("Ma") Rainey was the featured performer when the couple toured together with the Moses Stokes Show.[18] The minstrel show involved comedy, singing, and dancing. Later, "Ma" and "Pa" Rainey traveled with the Florida Cotton Blossoms, the Smart Set, Tolliver's Circus (where they were billed as "Rainey and Rainey, Assassinators of the Blues"), Silas Green from New Orleans, and several other minstrel troupes. Ma Rainey dissolved the partnership with Pa Rainey in 1917 and began touring the South with her own group, Ma Rainey and her Georgia Smart Set. Author Sally Placksin describes a "Ma" Rainey show:

> A typical Rainey show lasted two hours. These were the days when flash, flamboyance, even freakishness filled the bill, and audiences were vocal and demonstrative one way or the other. One can imagine some of the elements of a Rainey performance: the audience making its pilgrimage from miles around the tent filling, blacks on one side, whites on the other—some demanding to be seated in the black section when the seats designated "white" were filled (most reports attest to the fact that Rainey preferred black audiences); and the great Rainey herself, making up backstage, taking over an hour to apply the greasepaint and light powder to her face—and later, says Bernhardt, taking just as long to remove it. Out front, the audience would be waiting.

The band would open with an instrumental, followed by the chorus line—in the unusual combination of light-skinned men and very dark women—dancing "Strut Miss O'Lizzie," "The Cutout," or maybe "Pickin' Peaches," the women dressed in just below-the-knee-length skirts and high-heel lace up shoes. Then came the comedians with ethnic humor and broad comedy; next the soubrette singing a fast tune like "Ballin' the Jack," joined by the chorus. The comedians would reappear, and finally Ma Rainey herself would come on, joking about her craving for "pig meat" and for "bird liver"— young and tender men. "I'm gonna tell you about my man," she'd say, and then probably with her jazz cats she'd start singing "A Good Man is Hard to Find."[19] (Later on, after she had started to record, she used to make her entrance from a huge Victrola, blowing kisses to the audience.)[20]

Ma Rainey earned her title of "Mother of the Blues" by being the most influential blues singer of the day. The scope of her poetry and lyrics covered the range of human emotions. Some songs retained humorous qualities while others were foreboding. She sang frankly and boldly about homosexuality, lesbianism, sadomasochism, woman battering, vengeance, and prostitution. Her "Hustlin' Blues" portrays a streetwalker who pleads:

> O judge, tell him I'm through
> O judge, tell him I'm through
> I'm tired of this life,
> That's why I brought him to you.

The importance of Ma Rainey, and her protégé Bessie Smith, is summarized by Derrick Stewart-Baxter in his book on classic blues singers:

In 1923, two women, Ma Rainey and Bessie Smith, were responsible for a change of taste among that sector of the black population who were buying blues based records. This change was not produced in an instant, but took place over a number of years . . . until the advent of Rainey and Smith, the accent had been on the smooth, refined sophistication of Lucille Hegemin and Edith Wilson, plus the imitators who cashed in on their popularity, even to the extent of making "covers" of their songs for rival companies.

With Ma Rainey came the sounds of the South, the blues of the field workers (or their later derivatives), the songs of the wandering musicians and the ballads of the tent and minstrel shows. This is what Ma Rainey offered on her records; she and Bessie were responsible for the great change that was to take place. It came slowly at first, but with increasing speed in later years.

Although Bessie Smith preceded her in the studio by a few months, it was the older woman who was the most important at the onset.[21]

After World War I, major record labels sought to capture the African-American market by selling them recordings of "Black" artists. These "race records" were originally never intended for "Whites." The record companies' maneuver was motivated by a realization that a mass migration of African Americans from the rural South to northern urban areas was creating a new market for "Black" music. Mamie Smith (1883–1946) opened the market by selling millions of copies of her recordings "It's Right Here For You" and "Crazy Blues." Smith had substituted for an ill Sophie Tucker (a European-American vocal star) and gained overnight success, much to the surprise of the record companies. Robert Johnson, Blind Lemon Jefferson, and Leadbelly would also register success in the marketplace with the recordings they made between 1920 and 1928. When European-Americans began to consider "race records" more alluring and appealing than "White" recordings made available to European-American society, the market changed abruptly to respond to new public demands.

When the "blues craze" began in 1920, Rainey was thirty-four years old. Her big break as a solo recording artist with Paramount did not arrive until three years later in December 1923. She remained with that label exclusively, and over a period of six years (1923–29) she recorded more than a hundred songs, most of which are currently available. Twenty-four of the songs on these recordings are her compositions. Author Rudi Blesh feels that Rainey was the musician most "responsible for the growth in variety and complexity of the accompaniments from simple guitar and piano to the full instrumental jazz accompaniments which help to give some of these records their timeless depth, breadth, and richness."[22] During her career she would record with such legendary figures as Louis Armstrong, Don Redman, Kid Ory, Tommy Ladnier, and Lovie Austin. Rainey recorded "Southern Blues" with the Austin band, which consisted of violin, clarinet, cornet, and piano. The lyrics to that song reflected southern African-American living conditions during the period.

> If your house catches on fire and there
> ain't no water around,
> If your house catches on fire and there
> ain't no water around,
> Throw your trunk out the window and
> let that shack burn down.[23]

Paramount declined to renew Ma Rainey's contract in 1928 as the blues began to fade in popularity and "her down-home material had gone out of fashion."[24] "Jazz" gradually became the new craze in America. She had toured all her life and continued to travel on the road with her own Arkansas Swift Foot Review until it too terminated. She later joined the Al Gaines Carnival Show working in tents throughout the Southwest. The death of both her mother and her sister led her to retire in 1935. The powerful voice and straightforward execution that characterized her performances had a lasting effect on the same "jazz" styles that drove her blues out of popularity.

William Christopher Handy—"Father of the Blues"

W. C. Handy (c. 1873–1958) left an indelible mark on twentieth century American music. His influence on blues, R & B, "jazz," gospel, and the standards of Tin Pan Alley are clearly reflected. His classic "St. Louis Blues" remains the most recorded song of the first half of the twentieth century. George Gershwin acknowledged Handy's importance when the composer autographed a copy of his own *Rhapsody in Blue* and he said: "To Mr. Handy, whose early blues songs are the forefather of this work."[25]

Handy was a composer, cornetist, and guitarist who traveled, performed, and taught music before starting a publishing company with singer/lyricist Harry Pace. He was born November 16, 1873, in Florence, Alabama. He was the son and grandson of Methodist ministers, neither of who were musicians. He studied with Y. A. Wallace, a teacher from Fisk University who drilled his pupils stringently by the *solfeggio* system (where the syllables do, re, mi, fa sol, la, and ti are assigned scale-tones; it is also referred to as the tonic sol-fa system). Handy recalled his father declaring that "he would sooner follow his son's hearse than see him a professional musician."[26] Since no one in his family approved of his musical ambitions, he listened privately to the songs of laborers, band rehearsals, and barbershop quartets whenever he could get away.

During the depression of the Grover Cleveland presidency, he organized a quartet in Birmingham that traveled to the World's Fair in Chicago in 1893. To raise money, he began singing in southern churches, entertained train passengers and crews, and serenaded in assorted venues along the way. Upon arrival he found the fair was postponed. Stranded and destitute in St. Louis, the composer wrote his famous "St. Louis Blues" in memory of this bleak period. Eventually, Handy refined his musical skills and traveled as bandmaster of the Mahara Minstrels throughout America, Canada, Cuba, and Mexico. He performed as a traditional minstrel traveler from 1896 until 1903, with the exception of a two-year teaching job at the A. and M. College near Huntsville, Alabama.

W. C. Handy was the first American to write down a blues composition and was a major innovator of city blues style. Urban blues has a twelve-bar form and is usually sung to an instrumental accompaniment. This was the primary nature of the work Handy created in New York. By 1903 he began to document some of the music he heard on the streets of the city and took down his first version of "Joe Turner" as a lesson in transcribing the African-American folk idiom. His first effort became the novelty tune for the Pythian Band he organized in Memphis in 1905. Handy would later create other tunes based upon African-American melodies from memory, such as "Mr. Crump" composed in 1909. Edward H. Crump, a mayoral candidate in Memphis, had hired Handy's band to promote the campaign he was running. Crump wanted the votes of the sporting crowd in the barrelhouses and dance halls on Beale Street. Handy's composition, later given the title "Memphis Blues," was the first blues composition ever published. Handy began to seek publication for his other compositions only to find a series of rejections "because there were four bars missing to the stanza."[27] European-American publishers were accustomed to an eight or ten-bar melodic construction. The structure of twelve-bar blues form was an African-American creation.

Handy's "Memphis Blues" influenced the popularity of blues music and earned him the appellation "Father of the Blues." Handy also wrote the famous "St. Louis Blues" in 1914, along with many blues, spirituals, marches, hymns, and other songs about African-American culture. Bessie Smith (the "Empress of the Blues") gave a classic performance of the "St. Louis Blues" in 1925. The recording of that stellar performance is a definitive example of classic blues singing.

In written music tradition, W. C. Handy was the first to attempt to notate precisely the elusive blue note. It was his aspiration to devise a music notation to represent African-American stylistic characteristics, especially those involving the voice slurring that often occurred as an interpolation of the minor third and seventh into the major mode.

Some theories on the blues construction suggest that it is a process involving the placement of African melodic style upon a European harmonic framework. To some degree this is true. As mentioned earlier, African-American music adopted the three typical chord qualities (I, IV, and V) used in European tonal harmony. These chords were completely transformed, however, when fused with the African-American blues scale. Melody cannot be separated from its harmonic context, so the addition of blue notes to a major tonality created new harmonic and melodic configurations. Consequently, the symbol I-dominant 7 was substituted for a symbol indicating the I-major (or i-minor) triad common for the tonic chord in European music practice. The I-dominant 7 chord was not seeking resolution to a major chord a fifth below, as in European music tradition; it was both a point of departure and musical destination point. This African-American sonority, like the polyrhythms and rhythmic syncopation, propels the music forward on a perpetual cycle that lends itself to wide-ranging interpretations, permutations, and levels of expansion.

Blues chords and scales are fluid elements that defy traditional Eurocentric analysis. This becomes increasingly more apparent as the instrumental blues evolved into bebop styles. Blue notes are not merely tempered notes of the Western tonal system. Examination of assorted solos by rural blues musicians and modern "jazz" innovators reveal no single blues formula, structure, or scale. Blues scales can be based upon two identical tetrachords superimposed:

[C Eb F Gb + G Bb C Db]	or	[C D Eb E F + G A Bb B C]
[1 3b 4 5b + 5 7b 8 9b]	or	[1 2 3b 3 4 + 5 6 7b 7 8]
same as (1 3b 4 5b)		same as (1 2 3b 3 4) . . . in G blues

It can also be derived from asymmetrical configurations such as follows:

[C Eb E Gb + G Bb B C]   or   [C E F Gb + G A Bb B]
[1 3b 3 5b + 5 7b 7 8]   or   [1 3 4 5b + 5 6 7b 7]
same as (1 3b 3 4)   same as (1 2 3b 3) . . . in G blues

Blues sonority allows for continuous embellishment and expansion of melody, rhythm, harmony, dynamics, and other elements of music. Early blues suggested, and ultimately evolved into, a totally chromatic and pantonal modern style. It created an elastic form in which almost any properly placed note can be reconciled in terms of the prevailing sonority. A blues chord or mode produces a magnetic center and expansive matrix, just as any fundamental tone contains representatives of all other pitches in its overtone series. (For example, the fundamental tone C contains the notes G, C, E, G, Bb, C, D, E, F#, G#, A#, C, C#, D, D#, E, F, etc., in a strict acoustical arrangement above that root.)

Handy sold his song "Memphis Blues" in 1912 for $100 to T. C. Bennett, a European-American promoter. He was later refused permission to include "Memphis Blues" in his own "Blues Anthology" published in 1926. "Memphis Blues" later sold millions of copies.

Within the African-American community there were numerous individuals whose levels of influence was felt more strongly than Handy's. People were often most affected by the musicians they came across in live situations as they moved through their daily lives. Sheet music and recordings were less prominent in their lives. Both Bunk Johnson and Jelly Roll Morton remembered a pianist named Mamie Desdoumes. Johnson referred to her as "a blues-singing poor gal [who] used to play pretty passable piano around them dance halls on Perdido Street." Morton recalls:

> The one blues I never can forget out of those early days happened to be played by a woman that lived next door to my godmother's in the Garden District. The name of this musician was Mamie Desdoumes. Two middle fingers of her right hand had been cut off, so she played the blues with only three fingers on her right hand. She only knew this one tune and she played it all day long.

> *I stood on the corner, my feet was dripping wet,*
> *I asked every man I met . . .*
> *Can't give me a dollar, give me a lousy dime,*
> *Just to feed that hungry man of mine.*

> Although I had heard them previously I guess it was Mamie first really sold me on the blues.

Bunk Johnson says that he "played, man, a concert with [Mamie] singing those same blues. She was pretty good-looking—quite fair and with a *nice* head of hair. She was a hustlin' woman. . . . When Hattie Rogers or Lulu White [top madames] would put it out that Mamie was going to be singing at their place, the white men would turn out in bunches and them whores would clean up." Other "hustlin' women" also worked as musicians. Pianist and music publisher Spencer Williams mentioned a "house run by Miss Antonia Gonzales, who sang and played the cornet."[28]

From Vaudeville to Ragtime

African-American music cannot be separated meaningfully into the categories that market labels suggest. Alain Locke felt that "jazz was carried in the bosom of ragtime and, as has been said, is only ragtime more fully evolved. The Negro folk idiom in melody and syncopated rhythm gives us 'ragtime,' carried over to harmony and orchestration, it gives us 'jazz.' It is one and the same musical spirit and tradition in two different musical dimensions."[29] And as Writer Isaac Goldberg tells us,

> Handy, the recognized pioneer of the "blues" insists that ragtime, essentially, is nothing more than a pepped-up secular version of the Negro spirituals. He recalls how in the old minstrel days they rendered such haunting exhortations as "Git on Board, Little Chillun." To sing it in the traditional fashion of the earnest if ecstatic spiritual was too tame. So sung faster, to the accompaniment of eccentric hand-clapping and gestures, it becomes the "spiritual" disintegrating, breaking up into ragtime successor.
>
> . . . Today, hearing Handy jazz up the invitation to a ride on the heavenly railroad, one exclaims, "Why, he's simply jazzing it." In Handy's minstrel days, they called it "jubing" from the word "jubilee."[30]

Minstrelsy had its effect on ragtime, "jazz," and other African-American music in the late nineteenth and early twentieth centuries. For the European-American community, it began with the "Jim Crow" caricature of a male plantation slave. By the end of the nineteenth century it was called "Zip Coon" and promoted the offensive stereotype of the urban African-American male. Both the African-American cakewalk and the "Jim Crow" caricature converged in the Comic Sallies. These events presented short sketches that managed to poke fun at all aspects of a segregated society and at specific individuals within both cultures. The traveling variety shows expanded the smaller stage presentations into more elaborate shows featuring dance, songs, and skits. Between 1900 and 1910 vaudeville amplified the concept to include jugglers, mimes, and other variety acts and became one of the most popular entertainment forms in the United States.

Many individual performers received wide exposure traveling along the vaudeville circuit or performing at the World's Fairs. D. H. Lawrence, Charlie Chaplin, Al Jolson, and other famous personalities borrowed from the minstrel show in developing their own styles and presentations. England and North America loved the bigoted skits presented by the "black-face" Christies and other minstrels.

The syncopated dotted rhythm patterns found in West African music made their way into familiar African-American songs such as "Bra' Rabbit" (in *gulla* dialect), "Casey Jones," "Turkey in the Straw," "Old Dan Tucker," and other nineteenth-century African-American folksongs. Ragtime involved the transformation of many such folksongs into a unique modern piano style. Geographical areas involved in presenting the World's Fairs were places where many ragtime musicians gained national reputations even before Tin Pan Alley assigned the label "ragtime" to the music. As early as the 1893 World's Columbian Exposition in Chicago, raggedy music was heard. Jig bands, jig piano, syncopated coon songs, and other vaudeville and minstrel shows presented syncopated African-American rags at the Trans-Missouri Exposition at Omaha, Nebraska, in 1899, the Pan American Exposition in Buffalo, New York, in 1901, and at the Louisiana Purchase Exposition at St. Louis, Missouri, in 1904.

Rags were played in mining camps and were used as music for silent films. Scott Joplin's ragtime introduced a relationship between ragtime and American theater. Piano rolls, sheet music publishers, and major record companies inundated the country with this new sound. European and European-American musicians (like John Philip Sousa) would try their hand at ragtime composition. Ragtime would also serve as the stylistic basis for Dixieland. Although the music would meander in and out of fashion, it would never loose its original vigor, appeal, and gaiety.

Scott Joplin

Scott Joplin (1868–1917), a composer and ragtime pianist remembered as the "King of Ragtime," grew up in a musical family in Texas, and earned his living by playing piano. He worked for many years in St. Louis and traveled with a vocal ensemble. Some of his works were published before the ragtime craze. Once ragtime became popular, his syncopated compositions were sought for publishing, enabling Joplin to devote his time to teaching and composing more pieces.

Joplin was a major innovator of his day. In his experimental rag "Euphonic Sounds," he evolved harmonic and rhythmic relationships not yet explored in American music at the turn of the century. In this composition, Joplin deviates from the characteristic "oompah" pattern of the bass line in the left hand. Unfortunately, most of Joplin's documented style is generally from the period when his playing was in decline due to serious illness. However, even these authenticated piano rolls (from 1915 or 1916) prove that he was a prodigious pianist. Joplin collaborated with Henry Jackson, Louis Armstrong, Arthur Marshall, and Joseph Lamb on rags.

Joplin also wrote a three-act opera and financed its production himself. *Treemonisha* (1911) was a work that contained elements of ragtime piano and songs, sentimental ballads, and a dramatic line appropriate for the portrayal of African-American culture at the turn of the century. His application of stylized speech (similar to European *Sprechstimme*) in this opera had been used previously by only a few composers. *Treemonisha* was a stage drama that was a forerunner for the development of American musical theater.[31] It was virtually impossible for Joplin to have heard Schoenberg's *Pierrot Lunaire* of 1912. Unfortunately, his idea for a Ragtime opera was not well received. Joplin insisted upon having his opera realized on stage. He managed to produce it himself and play all the orchestra parts on his piano, but it ran only one night.

From 1897 onward, the demand for rags in the form of sheet music grew, producing two types of ragtime compositions. The genuine African-American ragtime was developed into a more restrained and polished type of music that could be published as sheet music and set on piano rolls for mainstream America. This was the flashy, brilliant, fast music that Tin Pan Alley labeled "ragtime." This style remained popular until around 1909. Irving Berlin later introduced a much more diluted rag in 1911 called "Alexander's Ragtime Band." This tune took the rag out of the African-American stylistic domain and made it more palatable to "White" consumers. Berlin simplified all musical elements, making it easier for amateur European-American pianists (mostly women) to read at home. Their buying power helped revive ragtime, and it lived on until about 1917.

The distinctions made between the genuine African-American ragtime and the commercial imitations produced for European America by Tin Pan Alley reflect the nature of the ongoing American social hiatus. The production of "race records" by "Black" recording artists for African-American consumption—and a separate brand of records for a "White" audience—clearly demonstrates a continuing effort to maintain a segregated society.

Within oppressive social systems, certain people are denied an opportunity to express themselves. Categorical decisions are often made without consulting an authoritative (native) position.[32] In 1886 James Trotter discussed the benefits of shedding cultural and racist bigotry:

> The inseparable relationship existing between music and its worthy exponents gives, it is believed, full showing of propriety to the course hereinafter pursued, that of mingling the praises of both. But, in truth, there was little need to speak in praise of the music. Its tones of melody and harmony require only to be heard in order to awaken in the breast emotions the most delightful.

> While grouping, as has here been done, the musical celebrities of a single race; while gathering from near and far these many fragments of musical history, and recording them in one book,—the writer yet earnestly disavows all motives of a distinctly clannish nature. But the haze of complexional prejudice has so much obscured the vision of so many persons, they cannot see (at least, there are many who affect not to see) that musical faculties, and power for their *artistic* development, are not in the exclusive possession of the fairer-skinned race, but are like the beneficent gifts of the Creator to all his children. Besides, there are some well-meaning persons who have formed, for lack of information which is here afforded, erroneous and

unfavorable estimates of the art-capabilities of the colored
race.[33]

Comparing Scott Joplin's compositions "Euphonic Sounds," "Maple
Leaf Rag," or "The Entertainer" to Irving Berlin's popular "Alexander's Ragtime Band" provides a clear portrait of the difference between genuine African-American ragtime style and the European-American commercial variety
of the day. Joplin's compositions contain highly syncopated melodies and a
systematic rhythmic conflict between the right and left hands, and their
quasi-rondo form involves a new melody in each new section. "Alexander's
Ragtime Band" introduces only one melody at a fast tempo containing relatively little syncopation. The syncopation and rhythmic complexity characteristic of African-American varieties made the music very hard to play, and
thus of little appeal to the targeted amateur "White" pianists.[34]

Both the genuine and the commercial ragtime gained some degree of
notoriety as early as 1901. In the eyes of many European-American listeners,
however, ragtime was the invention of an oppressed and despised race, stereotyped as ignorant and incapable of contributing anything of value to American culture. Its origins in districts of ill repute made it convenient for respectable (and bigoted) "Whites" to claim that Irving Berlin's music was more
civilized and refined, and thus more acceptable aesthetically. Meanwhile *Musical America* complained in 1913 that ragtime "exalts noise, rush and street
vulgarity." Ragtime music was associated with repulsive dance halls and restaurants. Comparably colorful and vivid qualities yet never appeared so prob-
lematic in Stravinsky's "Rakes's Progress," Carl Orff's "Carmina Burana,"
Kurt Weill's "Three Penny Opera." or in other European composer's music
dealing with the gay street life discovered in their respective communities.
Elements of racism contributed to these ideas.

> Second, ragtime was seen as a threat to classical European mu-
> sic. In 1901, the president of the American Federation of Musi-
> cians ordered his members to stop playing ragtime. "The musi-
> cians know what is good," he said, "and if people don't we will
> have to teach them." In order to put down ragtime, classical
> musicians tried to show that it was not as good as their kind of
> music. The *Musician* of November 1901, for instance, asserted
> that "unusual rhythmic combinations and syncopations have
> been so extensively used by high-class composers that it is not
> possible for coon song composers to invent anything along these
> lines."

> But, as we saw earlier, the syncopation of ragtime *was* differ-
> ent from that used in classical European music. So, in trying to
> put down ragtime, the *Musician* had simply shown that it did
> not fully understand this kind of music. Mistakes of this sort
> were to be repeated many times in the years that followed. In
> 1901, for example, we find *Metronome* magazine assuring white
> Americans that "ragtime's days are numbered." We are sorry to
> think that anyone should imagine that ragtime was of the least

musical importance. It was a popular wave in the wrong direction.[35]

In actuality, nevertheless, many prominent European composers were intrigued by this new American music. Claude Debussy, Alban Berg, Igor Stravinsky, and other musicians tried their hand at writing ragtime. It soon became clear that ragtime and other African-American music offered entirely new perspectives on rhythm, melody, and harmony yet unexplored in Europe or elsewhere in the world. In retrospect, the ragtime written by "serious" European composers sounds naive when compared to authentic African-American syncopated songs.

James Scott

James Scott (1896–1938) was a composer of rags who displayed remarkable craftsmanship and consistency. His compositions were not as adventurous as those of Joplin's, although he did occasionally explore themes in the minor mode in his ragtime introductions (the introduction to "Rag Sentimental," for instance). Born in Neosho, Missouri, he was essentially self taught, and published his first rag at age seventeen. His music is considered closest to that of Joplin's.

He met Scott Joplin in St. Louis in 1914. Joplin's influence undoubtedly enabled him to have his compositions published soon after that meeting. Scott worked as an itinerant teacher before accepting a job as organist and arranger for the Panama Theater. Shortly after moving to Kansas City in 1919, his "Broadway Rag" and other new music publications were overshadowed by the ascension of traditional "jazz." He formed his own eight-piece band and continued teaching into the 1930s. One of his favorite melodic devices was a rocking pattern, where the right hand produces both the usual ragtime syncopation and the alternations of chords with single notes.[36]

Thomas Million Turpin

Thomas Turpin (c. 1873–1922), a self-taught pianist, had been the first African American to publish a rag ("Harlem Rag" in 1897). He and his brother opened a saloon called "The Rosebud" (at 2220 Market Street in the Tenderloin of St. Louis), which eventually became a ragtime center. Joseph Lamb (c. 1887–1960), Scott Hayden (c. 1882–1915), Louis Chauvin (c. 1883–1908), and Arthur Marshall (c. 1881–1915) were other ragtime pioneers who made important contributions to the repertoire. The spirit of competition among the ragtime musicians was usually friendly and supportive. The older and more experienced musicians were expected to serve as mentors for younger players. Musical ideas were exchanged freely. Even competitive rivals would end up teaching each other new songs. In this fashion, music innovations continued to be conveyed to younger generations of pianists and other musicians. This oral/aural tradition established a subtle and effective informal institution that held little in common with traditional modes of European music education.

The economic depression of the late nineteenth century was largely responsible for the creation of ragtime. As restaurants, dance halls, bordellos, cabarets, cafes, and gambling halls began to close down across the country, those that remained in operation were forced to trim their orchestras until only the pianist remained. Since the clienteles at such establishments were accustomed to hearing Barrelhouse music arrangements for full ensembles, the role of the pianist was forced to expand. Keyboard approach was now obliged to produce the sound of the bass in the lower register, banjo chords in the middle range, and harmonize melody instruments on top. Rhythmic vitality was necessary to maintain interest with the solitary timbre of a lone piano, and forceful delivery allowed the music to be heard over the noise level often found in typical performance venues. Although ragtime is most closely associated with piano music, it has been played on virtually every instrument. Ragtime bands and orchestras consisting of unusual assortments of instruments ragged a variety of songs.[37] Ragtime inspired and evolved abreast of the development of twentieth century American vernacular dance. As Marshall and Jean Stearns suggests, "jazz dance, like other arts, has its rival factions, its heroes and legends, its fashions and trends—in a word, its own unique history. This history is closely linked to the economics of show-business, the changing status of the American Negro, and the evolution of jazz."[38]

James Reese Europe

James Reese Europe (1881–1919) was one of the most influential musicians at the turn of the century. He organized a "Black" musicians' union called the Clef's Club early in the twentieth century, but Reese remains better known for his work as a composer. He was also renowned for conducting huge bands and orchestras with as many as 145 members. His ensembles consisted of mandolins, harps, guitars, banjos, violins, saxophones, tubas, cellos, clarinets, trombones, cornets, timpani, drums, basses, and occasionally as many as ten pianos. This orchestra was featured in an exceptional concert in Carnegie Hall in May 1912. His musicians sang and played in a syncopated style that had a cogent and powerful effect upon the audience in attendance. Still, critical reviews were predictably mixed. James Weldon Johnson wrote about the effect that Europe's "Clef Club March" (the opening composition) had on the patrons at the concert: "New York had not yet become accustomed to jazz; so when the Clef Club opened its concert with a syncopated march, playing it with a biting attack and infectious rhythm, and on the finale bursting into singing, the effect can be imagined. The applause became a tumult."[39]

James Reese Europe was a spokesman for African-American music. He avoided the labels imposed upon African-American music by Eurocentric culture and acknowledged that many European imitators were playing ragtime. The term "ragtime" was fading within the majority culture, but Europe stated firmly:

In my opinion there was never any such music as "ragtime." "Ragtime" is merely a nick-name, or rather a fun name given to Negro rhythm by our Caucasian brother musicians many years ago. The phrase "ragtime" is dying. Why? Because in these days of theme famine, so many eminent Anglo-musicians have become inoculated with that serum—Negro rhythm ("ragtime"), and with their knowledge of musical theory embroider their plaintive ragtime theme with a wealth of contrapuntal ornamentation and a marvelous enrichment of tone coloring and complicated instrumentation, that the primal Negro rhythmical element —"ragtime"—is so disguised that a mere hint of a "motif" of the "ragtime" rhythm is lost to the popular ear. No! "Ragtime" is neither dead nor dying, but is undergoing a vast development, and is more popular now than ten years ago. Mr. [John Philip] Sousa always interpreted Negro music admirably, yet as a composer, he remained immune from its contagion, although he closes a "suite" of his own compositions with a reminiscent Negro theme.[40]

Although he explored diverse compositional styles, Europe was best known as a composer of what might be called symphonic rags. His popular "Castle House Rag" and other compositions were well received when he took his Hellfighter Band (369th Regiment Band) to Europe during World War I.[41] Although few "jazz" musicologists have discussed his significance, James Reese Europe's stylistic approach made his band the most popular of all United States musical ensembles stationed in Europe. Although the Original Dixieland Jass Band is usually credited with producing the first "jazz" recording, Reese recorded improvisational "ragtime" music years before the ODJB was organized. In the liner notes of a recent collection released of some of Reese's early recordings, Bark Berresford states: "James Reese Europe is a name familiar to collectors and enthusiasts of early jazz, mainly for the dramatic circumstances of his death. However, few know more than the basic details of his life and even fewer the records he made between 1913 and 1919, an extremely under-researched area of syncopated music history, falling as it does between the failure of Joplin's opera 'Treemonisha' and the first explosion of jazz popularity, ignited by the recordings of the Original Dixieland Jazz Band."[42]

James Reese Europe enlisted in the Fifteenth Infantry Regiment of the New York National Guard and was asked by Colonel William Hayward to organize a military band of comparable caliber as his Clef Club and Tempo Club groups. He recruited men from all over the United States and Puerto Rico. Noble Sissle was his drum major. The band was marked for distinction from the beginning. The French were particularly fond of his music. The French Garde Républicaine bandsmen were so impressed that they borrowed Europe's scores to attempt to duplicate his band's sound.[43]

His Negro National Orchestra and Negro Symphony Orchestra were influential both in musical and social circles in New York City. Lieutenant Europe played many of W. C. Handy's compositions overseas. The United States was proud of Europe's band insofar as a New York Times' reporter wrote, "all Americans swore, and some Frenchmen admitted, [Europe's] was the best military band in the world."[44] His music would be labeled "jazz" although his men played the music strictly as it was notated with minimal additional improvisation. Nevertheless, Europe did introduce some innovative musical techniques that later found home in "jazz" and other contemporary music:

> With the brass instruments we put in mutes and make a whirling motion with the tongue, at the same time blowing full pressure. With wind instruments we pinch the mouthpiece and blow hard. This produces the peculiar sound, which you all know. To us it is not discordant . . . we accent strongly in this manner the notes which originally would be without accent. It is natural for us to do this; it is, indeed, a racial musical characteristic. I have to call a daily rehearsal of my band to prevent the musicians from adding to the music more than I wish them to. Whenever possible they all embroider their parts in order to produce new, peculiar sounds.[45]

James Reese Europe, like Antonin Dvořák, realized that African-American music was a powerful source for the development of an innovative twentieth-century American art form. His critics, though strongly influenced by his music, insisted that his music should model itself after European "serious" composers to be validated by mainstream America. Europe explained that his instrumentation, which allowed the mandolins to produce the "peculiar steady strumming accompaniment," made his music distinctively African-American. The ten pianos provided the particular style of chord progressions that were "essentially typical of Negro harmony." His mandolins and banjos replaced the violins of a typical European symphony orchestra; two clarinets were used instead of an oboe; and baritone horns and trombone substituted for French horns and bassoons.[46] Europe continued:

> You see, we colored people have our own music that is part of us. It's the product of our souls; it's been created by the sufferings and miseries of our race. Some of the melodies we played Wednesday were made up by slaves of the old days, and others were handed down from the days before we left Africa. . . . [Some] would laugh heartily at the way our Negro Symphony is organized, the distribution of the pieces, and our method of organization.

> We have developed a kind of symphonic music that, no matter what else you think, is different and distinctive, and that lends itself to the playing of the peculiar compositions of our race.[47]

Europe's 369th U.S. Infantry "Hell Fighter" Band experienced intense racial prejudice while undergoing military training in the South. Colonel Hayward managed to have the band transferred to Europe, where French officers treated them appropriately. Upon his return from abroad, Europe reaffirmed his original perspective and position on the new African-American music that he was generating:

> I have come back from France more firmly convinced than ever that Negroes should write Negro music. We have our own racial feeling and if we try to copy whites we will make bad copies. . . . We won France by playing music which was ours and not a pale imitation of others, and if we are to develop in America we must develop along our own lines. . . . Will Marion Cook, William Tires [Tyres], even Harry Burleigh and Coleridge-Taylor are truly themselves [only] in the music which expresses their race. . . . The music of our race springs from the soil, and this is true to-day with no other races, except possibly the Russians.[48]

Europe was the musical director for a European-American dance team, Irene and Vernon Castle. Some jealous European-American musicians did not appreciate the success the bandleader experienced. Eugene de Bueris wrote the Boston *Globe* complaining about society people's preference for "Black" musicians, saying that it "will not be long before the poor white musician will be obliged to blacken his face to make a living or starve." De Bueris asked, "Why should a famous dancing couple prefer a Negro orchestra for their dancing exhibitions?"[49] In fact, when the Castles first heard Europe's music they decided it was exactly what they needed and they wanted to work with no other musicians from that point on. Europe created music for the couple and is credited with inventing the fox-trot, the turkey-trot, the Castle Walk, and other dances that spread across America.[50]

A crazed bandsman during a concert murdered Europe on May 10, 1919, at Mechanic's Hall in Boston.[51] Private Herbert Wright fatally stabbed Europe after the bandleader chastised him for walking rudely across the stage against Europe's orders. The sentiments of those shocked by his death were reflected in a New York Times editorial statement that commented on "the untimely death of a man who was ranked as one of the greatest ragtime conductors, perhaps the greatest, we ever had." Only forty years old at the time of his death, Europe was an innovative musician who enhanced American prestige abroad.[52] At a concert of African-American music on May 1, 1912, Europe said:

> The Negro have given us the only music of our own that is American—national, original, and real. This concert, which is organized for tonight at Carnegie Hall, will be from beginning to end a concert by Negro musicians. The musicians volunteer their services. The proceeds of the concert will be devoted to the Music School Settlement for Colored People. This school is intended to encourage and develop musical talent in Negroes, and there is no doubt that those taught by it will contribute to the pleasure of the public and make valuable additions to the musical works of this country.[53]

New Orleans—Dixieland "Jazz" ("Traditional Jazz")

"Jazz" emerged from the African-American culture in a number of locations including New Orleans, Chicago, New York, Kansas City, Memphis, and St. Louis. All of these places, therefore, have claimed themselves to be the birthplace of "jazz." Nevertheless, all "jazz" recordings made before 1924 were by New Orleans musicians or those influenced by that particular style. Musicians in a variety of places were creating "jazz," but New Orleans had the nurturing environment that enabled it to develop more fully.

In the late nineteenth and early twentieth centuries, New Orleans fostered a great cosmopolitan admixture of French, Spanish, African, and other European music, performed at funeral marches, fancy-dress balls, resort picnics, Mardi Gras, and the opera. It was an active shipping port that attracted people from all over the world. New Orleans opened the first opera house in America and organized one of the first African-American symphony orchestras. New Orleans was unquestionably the first great "jazz" center, and the hub of nightlife activity was the Storyville vice district. Beyond the Storyville section, additional opportunities were available for the development of New Orleans "jazz" in dance halls and theaters throughout the busy city. Street bands outdoors (particularly brass bands) could be heard ragging marches and religious music in highly personalized styles.

Storyville drew its name from an alderman in New Orleans named Sidney Story, who in January 1897 made a detailed study of prostitution and its regulations in European capital cities. He then offered a proposal to permit sectioning off a section of the French Quarter of the city where prostitutes and their madams would be permitted to conduct business. This permission to do business was not legalization, however. In July of that year, Story managed to provide two segregated districts for these purposes. One was located in the French Quarter and the other above Canal Street, which became known as Storyville. Storyville was immune from police and politicians. Legal officials saw that Section I of the Ordinance 13032 (the rules governing Storyville) was enforced nonetheless. Many people stood to profit from this decision, and, soon, printed guides (like the *Blue Book*) were sold as directories to the bawdyhouses of New Orleans's Sporting District.[54]

Thus, New Orleans became a musical center with ample performance opportunities within which a class of modern professional musicians developed. Legally cordoned from the "respectable" citizens to allow for drinking and prostitution, Storyville offered an ample supply of jobs for musicians. During its best days, before finally being shut down, this red-light district supported around two hundred "houses of ill repute" and a plethora of saloons, bars, and dance halls. The lavishly appointed whorehouses were world famous for their elegance, music, and multiracial mix of women. Piano professors, string trios, and small bands provided constant entertainment for the assorted clientele. The Storyville neighborhood had little shacks, or "cribs," where down-and-out whores and streetwalkers (often addicted to drugs and riddled with venereal disease) were also readily available to customers from all walks of life. Men came strictly to drink, gamble, drug, and whore, and music provided a backdrop for their lewd adventures. Associations of nightlife with early ragtime and "jazz" led these art forms to be deemed "the devil's music." The fact remains that early African-American professional "jazz" musicians had little choice but to play where they could be paid for their services.

Most musicians in New Orleans also heard or played mazurkas, quadrilles, polkas, waltzes, and various other types of music. These traditional ingredients were mixed into the emerging musical styles. Pop tunes, quadrilles, and marches were European styles to which African-American musicians also applied their own timbre modifications, pitch alterations, ragged rhythms, and stylistic embellishments. Various types of music were played in Storyville, and ingredients from these musical genres mixed with African elements to contribute to the development of "jazz."

The African tradition of having expensive funerals, merged with the French tradition of presenting community marching bands at local celebrations, produced a New Orleans tradition that still exists today. New Orleans juju-oriented secret societies would employ brass bands to play at social functions to add an air of dignity to their funerals. Typically, slow and somber music was provided as the bands marched behind the deceased on the way to the cemetery. Tunes such as "Amazing Grace" and "Nearer, My God to Thee" were appropriate for this segment of the tribute. On the return trip, a quiet recessional moved the funeral party a suitable distance from the burial site. At that time the band would engage a hot and swinging style of music to the happy tune of "When the Saints Go Marching In," "South Rampart Street Parade," and other familiar upbeat celebration songs. Since both the African-American and European-American communities participated in the marching band tradition, it became an arena for interactions between "Blacks" and "Whites."

New Orleans parades were communal affairs that allowed bands and drill teams to display their talents while entreating the audience. This music compelled the bystanders to become an active part of the celebration. Members of social clubs, dressed in their finest attire, marched in formation, and clubs created floats for certain parades. Children and other passersby joined the procession in the streets to form the traditional "second line." The parade grew in size and intensity as it progressed. When familiar marches were played, the second line increased its dancing, high stepping, leaps, and frolicking. When a march ended, a rudimentary drum cadence filled in. These customs are still maintained in New Orleans parades.

The syncopated rhythms and collective improvisations of these bands were among the fundamental sources of "jazz." Taking conventional marches, the bands "ragged" the rhythms and altered the harmonies until marching music was transformed into dance music heard throughout the streets of New Orleans. The early New Orleans pioneers set many standards for future generations of innovators and performers. Cornets and clarinets were the first solo instruments of choice in bands at the turn of the century. The players manipulated these instruments, enabling them to sing the blues while stretching the conventional range of the instruments. Plungers, drinking glasses, soft drink bottles, and other household items were used as musical devices to enhance the range of colors and "dirty" tones available to performers. Traditional African musicians sought a "living" sound, rich in overtones, musical character, and depth; and African-American instrumentalists shared these musical aspirations.

In New Orleans, the great cornetists of the brass band and Dixieland "jazz" traditions were a legacy of the post–Civil War era. Many of the African-American and European-American musicians from this period played in the community bands that performed all over New Orleans. As the earliest definitive instrumental "jazz" combos style, "traditional jazz" (also New Orleans Style "Jazz" or Dixieland) ensembles were direct descendants of the marching bands. The scaled-down New Orleans Dixieland band usually consisted of clarinet, cornet, trombone, piano, banjo, drums, with sousaphone or double bass on the bottom. Each instrument developed a stylized role in the ensemble. The clarinet played obbligato lines that arpeggiated the harmony on the top layer of the instrumental stratification, and also decorated the melodic function of the cornet in either a heterophonic or contrapuntal style. The trombone typically produced a counter melody and characteristic glissandi, while the remaining instruments provided rhythmic chords and a simple leaping ("oompah") bass pattern.

"Buddy" Bolden

Charles "Buddy" Bolden (1877–1931) is often called "The Father of Jazz" because he was the first great bandleader and was renowned as a legendary improviser on the cornet. Bolden's style was honed through the rich heritage of the brass bands.

Bolden, a barber turned horn player, may have been the first to play the New Orleans style of "jazz." The Buddy Bolden Brass Band was the name used for several brass bands in Uptown New Orleans during the 1890s before Storyville was created. Bolden later performed blues and ragtime music in Funky Butt Hall and Odd Fellows Hall. His band's music embellished melodies, strong rhythms, and powerful instrumental tones.

Because of his cornet's tremendous amplitude, he is said to have drawn an audience from a five-mile radius with his powerful sound. Although he could read music, he and his fellow bandsmen usually preferred to play by ear. He was considered the first musician to improvise on standard blues and ragtime pieces. Folklorist Alan Lomax quoted a man named Paul Dominguez as saying: "See, us [Creoles], we didn't think so much of this ['Black'] jazz until we couldn't make a living otherwise. . . . If I wanted to make a living I had to be rowdy like the other group. I had to jazz it or rag it or any other damn thing. . . . Bolden caused all that. He caused all these younger Creoles . . . to have a different style altogether from the old heads [who played the same standard European music as the 'White' musicians]."[55]

Bolden's bands marched for funerals and Mardi Gras, and played their theme song, "Sensation Rag," as they marched through the red-light district. The Baptist hymn "What a Friend We Have in Jesus" was treated with variations when played at funerals, and "Oh Didn't He Ramble" was the song his band performed as people returned from the grave.

Bolden's last job was with the Allen Brass band in 1907. He contracted syphilis and was committed to a state institution the same year. He remained there until his death in 1931.

William Gary "Bunk" Johnson

"Bunk" Johnson (c. 1879–1949) was another cornet and trumpet player who played second cornet with Buddy Bolden as a teenager (between 1895 and 1899). He was born in New Orleans and died in New Iberia, Louisiana. Johnson was a leading figure of early New Orleans Style "jazz" who was heard on and off in New Orleans until the early 1930s. Yet, his importance in the early history of "jazz" has never been satisfactorily established. Because he developed his own style (as opposed to copying the style of either Bolden or Oliver) he failed to gain popular recognition but gained a reputation as a "musician's musician." Johnson was a chief witness to the history of Bolden. Bolden's bands contained men like clarinetists Frank Lewis and Willie Warner; Frank Keely (valve trombone) and Willie Cornish (trombone); bassists Bob Lyons, Bebey Mitchell, and Albert Glenny; Johnson on cornet and trumpet; and another trombonist, Frankie Dusen, who would eventually follow Bolden as leader of the band. Johnson discussed his early experience with Bolden: "Here is the thing that made King Bolden's Band be the first band that played jazz. It was because it did not read at all. I could fake like 500 myself; so you tell them that Bunk and King Bolden's Band was the first one that started jazz in the City or any place else."[56]

"Jelly Roll" Morton

Ferdinand "Jelly Roll" Morton (born Ferdinand La Manthe in Gulfport, Louisiana, in 1880 and died in Los Angeles in 1941) was a pianist and composer. Morton changed his name to avoid being called "Frenchy," a name biracial people (called "Creoles" in Louisiana) often had to endure. He originally played the guitar (as well as the harmonica, drums, violin, and trombone) but soon switched to piano. His early gigs as a youth involved singing, playing guitar with a string trio, and performing with a strolling quartet that specialized in performing spirituals at funerals and burials.[57]

Jelly Roll Morton's parents, who were from New Orleans, paid for Morton's piano lessons. On his classic Library of Congress recordings (1938) he tells how his original teacher disguised the fact that she couldn't read music by improvising upon the same European style at each lesson. He finally realized that all the music he brought for her to sight-read sounded the same as other music she performed for him. He soon found another teacher.

Many consider Morton one of the essential giants of the evolution of New Orleans "jazz." Morton claimed that he was the originator of "jazz" because he was the progenitor of what came to be known as the "swing" approach to rhythmic phrasing. His boastfulness and his self-proclaimed title as the founder of "jazz" caused some musicians and listeners to dismiss his music unfairly. He did contribute some of America's best-known early "jazz" recording sessions, including recordings of "King Porter Stomp," "Milenburg Joys," "Wild Man Blues," "Shoe Shiner's Drag," and other memorable selections.

There is little argument today that Jelly Roll Morton was an extremely influential artist during the early "jazz" era. He could improvise two or three complimentary melodies simultaneously on piano. His stylistic contributions bridged the gap between ragtime and "jazz" composition by loosening the march-like execution of ragtime's rhythmic approach, moving the resulting music closer to a "swing" feel. He was also responsible for decreasing ragtime's stylized embellishments. Morton was one of the first "jazz" musicians to blend composition and improvisational technique in balanced fashion. His arrangements for his bands were later emulated by many big bands in the swing era.

By the time Morton left New Orleans for Chicago, his reputation enabled him to record with Joe "King" Oliver and the New Orleans Rhythm Kings (a band of European-American musicians who migrated from the Crescent City) virtually as soon as he landed in the Windy City. The Volstead Act (passed by the U.S. Congress in 1919) outlawed the sale, manufacturing, and transportation of alcoholic beverages. Ironically, more Americans than ever then began drinking alcoholic beverages. Speakeasies, where illegal alcohol could be purchased, derived tremendous economic benefit from this era. "Jazz" music provided appropriate entertainment for the Speakeasy atmosphere; as a result, Morton and other "jazz" musicians found ample employment. Morton also composed sheet music for Chicago publishing houses whenever he needed money. The Melrose brothers bought more of Morton's music than any one else, eventually turning a greater profit on their investment than did the composer.

When the "jazz" scene shifted to New York, Morton moved there. The new direction of "jazz" shifted musical emphasis away from the ensemble toward soloists such as Louis Armstrong, Coleman Hawkins, Jabbo Smith, and others. Although Morton's strength was as an ensemble arranger, he continued to record his original compositions (such as "Kansas City Stomp," "Deep Creek," "Georgia Swing," and others) for Victor between 1928 and 1930. Musicians did not make enough money to survive from recording at that time, so Morton attempted to assemble a number of short-lived bands and find performances. Disappointed with the results he was getting in New York, he moved to Washington, D.C., in 1935. Morton opened a small club there but still found little success. Finally, in 1938 Morton ran into good fortune. A folklorist who knew Morton's importance to early "jazz" approached him to do an important set of recordings.

"The Saga of Mr. Jelly Lord," recorded by Alan Lomax for the Library of Congress Archives, is one of the most important American "jazz" documents by an individual artist ever recorded from Morton's era. Morton realized the importance of the event and, despite his failing health, summoned all his powers to present brilliant performances and discussions of his music, supported by an incredible variety of other related music chronicling the history and development of the early New Orleans musical world. He recreated musical pictures of life in the ragtime era and performed examples of all the musical forms that contributed to the development of early "jazz."

Jelly Roll Morton (Photo courtesy of HRP Library).

It is part of genius that Morton had so keen a sense of his period and of belonging to it, and of the creative opportunity—not to mention the challenge—that it offered him. And it is part of genius, too, that sitting down, fifty-three years later, to record his story and that of his music, Morton could, with complete acuity of memory, recapture the pervading mood, the miniature detail, and the wide implications of this period in which an infant music grew to maturity.

. . . Only Morton, characteristically enough, seemed fully conscious of the importance of the music, itself, and hence the occasion. Few, in 1938, thought of jazz as more than a minor folk-music. No one—unless it was Jelly Roll himself—recognized it as a fine art. Although for nearly twenty years previously it had strongly influenced European music, its own pure values and intrinsic greatness were still hidden.[58]

The sixteen albums Jelly Roll Morton and His Red Hot Peppers (the name he and the other musicians who worked with him used) made for Victor records between 1926 and 1928 remain unique and important classics of early small-band "jazz."

"Papa" Celestin, "King" Oliver, and Freddie Keppard

Another cornetist who performed with brass bands and eventually led his own small groups was Oscar "Papa" Celestin, who was born in Lafourche, Louisiana, about 1884 and died in New Orleans in 1954. Some of his ensembles became among the longest lived and best known in New Orleans.

One of the most celebrated and influential bandleaders and cornetists of the day was Joseph "King" Oliver. Born in New Orleans circa 1885, Joe Oliver was one of the most important alumni of New Orleans brass bands. He was also a teacher and the first important mentor for Louis Armstrong, who joined Oliver's band in Chicago in 1922. Oliver was an important innovator who carved out significant portions of the framework of what would later be referred to Dixieland "jazz." As one of the first successful musicians to take the nascent "jazz" forms out of New Orleans, he was perhaps the most important of all bandsmen in promoting the dispersal of "jazz" from New Orleans to the north, east, and west. As musical director of his "Creole Jazz Band," he was reportedly the first cornet player to incorporate mutes, cups, and bottles in professional performances. After turning down a Cotton Club contract in December 1927, for which Duke Ellington filled in, Oliver gradually ceased to play a significant role in "jazz." He was a virtually obscure man by the time of his death in Savannah, Georgia, in 1938. Trumpeter Wynton Marsalis described the New Orleans Dixieland "jazz" style of the type promoted by King Oliver: "The New Orleans style of music (Dixieland) is a classic example of democracy in action. Dixieland is collective improvisation, placing maximum emphasis on personal expression within a voluntary group format. The group encourages and nourishes individual development. That's America!"[59] Oliver's performances of "Sugar Foot Stomp," "Dippermouth Blues," and other recordings reveal the polyphonic density of one of New Orleans's earliest premier "jazz" ensembles. This approach to group improvisation was possible because each performer knew the other members' musical personalities well enough to anticipate and compliment the moves of other musicians instantaneously. Louis Armstrong (cornet), Honoré Dutrey (trombone), Johnny Dodds (clarinet), Lil Hardin (piano), Bill Johnson (banjo), and Baby Dodds (drums), were members of one of Oliver's earlier recording bands after moving east from New Orleans. His bands were known for their expressiveness and sensitive treatment of the blues.

Another legendary cornetist was Freddie Keppard, born in New Orleans around 1889. His style was aggressive, exciting, and powerful, but he never received many recording opportunities. During what should have been his prime, his problem with alcohol led to his death in Chicago in 1933.

Other New Orleans Instrumentalists

A distinctive trombone style developed from cramped seating conditions that left trombonists short on space for their slide movement. To remedy the situation, the trombonists sat on the rear wagons or trucks (the tailgate) that carried the brass bands in parades. Here they had ample room for working their slides. Though not a consistently brilliant soloist, the ensemble playing of Edward "Kid" Ory (c. 1886–1973) is the essence of the New Orleans tailgate trombone style. Born in La Place, Louisiana, Ory was a versatile musician who played trumpet in New Orleans before switching to trombone in California in the twenties. The trombone was the instrument he played with both King Oliver and with Louis Armstrong's recording Hot Five. He was an excellent big band trombonist and became musical director of Edward "Kid" Ory's Original Creole Jazz Band featuring Baby Dodds, "Mutt" Carey, Ed Garland, and Wade Whaley. Notable musicians such as Johnny Dodds, Jimmy Noone, King Oliver, and Louis Armstrong were all occasional sidemen in his band

Turn-of-the-Century Women Musicians

The piano was generally considered the "proper" instrument for women to play at the turn of the century. Women were not commonly seen performing with brass bands and could not salvage their reputations if they were caught performing in New Orleans' red-light districts. Pianos were associated with the home and the church. Consequently, those were the places in which most women instrumentalists developed their musical skills.

General patterns are apparent in the gender associations applied to musical instruments throughout the world. One ridiculous notion that persists is the greater the size of the instrument and the lower its sound, the more masculine is its nature.[60] In a 1929 review of the Boston Women's Symphony Orchestra, under direction of Ethel Leginska, it was stated that "women performers are not likely to attain masculine proficiencies with such un-feminine instruments as the double bass, French horns, trombones and tubas."[61] Whether considering the phallic or sexual symbolism of the flute and drums in preliterate societies, the electric guitar in contemporary American popular music, or the typically assertive nature of "jazz" saxophones and trumpets, the most popular solo instruments in "jazz" have remained largely the domains of male performers.[62] The inconsistencies of chauvinism are transparent and illogical.

At times, modified use of an instrument transforms its association with one sex or another. The flute today is considered a female instrument in spite of its earlier label as a phallic symbol. The early identification of the trumpet with military battlefields can account for its masculine implications. "Retaining this militaristic-masculine significance, trumpets and cornets made perfect lead and 'signifying' horns in the marching bands of early American popular music and in the New Orleans jazz ensembles that played exuberantly after funerals and at parades and fetes."[63] The power of the trumpet seemed almost tangible in some early societies. Some anthropologists report that the mere sight of a trumpet or horn was said to be fatal to women in some Amazon River tribes.[64] Of course such notions were only intended to keep women away from particular instruments.

In 1941, Duke Ellington recorded an album entitled "A Drum is a Woman."[65] Madam Zajj is the main character in Ellington's story. With her coquettish behavior and personal confidence, she "plays" the character Carribee Joe like a drum (opposing the implication of the album's title). Musicologist Francis Bebey says that African drums "are virtually a male prerogative" on their continent of origin. Although drums are often symbolic of the female, in some cultures it is believed that drums must usually be "interpreted" by men.[66] Certain African tribes use drums in their fertility rites and view them as "mouthpieces of the gods, a sacred medium of communication."[67]

In spite of sociocultural obstructions, women have always resisted sexism in musical circles and managed to defy overwhelming odds. A noteworthy example is Isabelle Taliaferro Spiller, who played the saxophone, trumpet and piano. She was born about 1888 in Abington, Virginia, and was a graduate of both the New England Conservatory and the Juilliard School of Music. Spiller later studied voice with Madam Azalia Hackley and theory with organist Melville Charlton. In her youth, Spiller played organ, piano, and mandolin in an orchestra featuring her mother on guitar and family friends playing harp and violin. Around 1906 she joined The Musical Spillers, a vaudeville group organized in Chicago by her husband William Newmeyer Spiller. Her primary instrument was the tenor saxophone, but she also doubled on alto, baritone, and occasionally on trumpet. Isabelle also served as co-director of the group for a time.

Upon leaving The Musical Spillers in 1926, Isabelle organized the Spiller School of Music in New York City. She played with Della Sutton's All Girls' Band during that time. From the late 1920s until her death in New York City in 1974, however, her primary musical focus was teaching and working as a musical director. She supervised the Woodwind, Brass and Percussion Institute of New York City's Federal Music Project (WPA) and supervised the instrumental program for the 1939 New York World's Fair, both on the grounds and on the airwaves.[68]

New York—Tin Pan Alley

During the heyday of European imperialism, colonizing forces stole art, knowledge, and sacred cultural artifacts from around the world. The booty was sold for profit or placed in European museums. Arrogance, of course, precluded acknowledging the creators of the confiscated art. European-American slave culture inherited a similar knack and applied it to the acquisition of African-American music.

New York's Union Square in the summer of 1900 was where professional songwriters sold songs to the public in great numbers, and made huge profits for the publishers who printed them. Many Tin Pan Alley pianists played piano with only one finger, and did not always hit the right note, and most pianos were often out of tune. With dozens of them working during the summer with windows open, there was an amazing mixture of noise. For this reason the area became known as "Tin Pan Alley." It was the beginning of the "pop" music industry, as we know it today.[69]

A Tin Pan Alley song was written in a fashionable musical style. Songs had to be sentimental, nostalgic, or about something currently held in the mind of the public. The sentimental ballad became popular with Americans during the nineteenth century and, consequently, became the mainstay of the Alley's output. Tin Pan Alley remained quick to take over and change different musical styles for its own ends, if there was a profit to be made. The most important of these styles came from the music of "Black" Americans. The first successful Tin Pan Alley style was ragtime.

Songwriters sometimes got their titles and stories directly from the public. Lyricists would occasionally sit all night in a New York restaurant listening to other people's conversations and would write down phrases or ideas in notebooks for future use as a title. The title for the 1923 hit song "Yes, We Have No Bananas" supposedly came from a New York fruit vendor who spoke little English. Such contacts reassured writers that they were attuned to the public mind.

Tin Pan Alley was a tightly knit community with numerous offices located in buildings within the same small general area of New York. Everyone seemed to know each other. Tin Pan Alley produced an enormous number of songs quickly, and, as a consequence, one song tended to sound much like another.

> A song-writer would hear a new song by someone else, and the melodies would sink into his head. Sometime later, when writing one of his own songs, these melodies would come out in a slightly altered version. Alternatively, the song-writer might use bits of older music that he had heard. A good example of this can be heard in "Yes, We Have No Bananas." If the song is listened to carefully it is possible to detect parts of "The Hallelujah Chorus" in some places, and parts of "My Bonnie Lies Over the Ocean" in others.

In order to get the public to buy their songs music publishers tried to get as much public exposure for them as possible. The best way of doing this was to get a well-known artist to sing the song in a vaudeville show. So, in the early days of Tin Pan Alley, the publishers themselves used to travel round the vaudeville theatres in New York trying to persuade artists to sing their songs.[70]

Presenting new songs to name artists was an important part of the process of publisher persuasion. Publishers would buy drinks for artists and their bands, and would sometimes take performers out for meals to convince the artist that a song was a potential hit. The artists who agreed to push songs were frequently given royalties.

African Musical Influences in the Americas

African rhythms went underground in the Americas after ancestral worship was forbidden. Voodoo dances, secret rituals, and work songs preserved some African rhythms. Slave regions outside America retained traditional African music and culture in greater detail. Cuney-Hare observes:

> The earliest traces of music in Africa are found in connection with dances of worship. Regardless of the particular practices of various religious cults or sects, dances were essential parts of their rituals. Some of the most interesting of the worship dances connected to mythological gods were the fire dances accompanied by the *Batta* drum. The Tshi-speaking people of the Gold Coast, between the Volta and the Assini river, present these dances in connection with the worship of the tutelary deities. Some dances, such as the sacred Dako Boea Dance of the Nupe tribe invoking the Great Spirit, were eventually forbidden by European missionaries.[71]

Capoeira, a Brazilian martial art, dance, and spiritual ritual, uses the Batta drum and *berimbau* (a bow used to produce music as well as for hunting), to accompany choreographed movement and mock battles. Originally, capoeira was a disguised form of military maneuvers engineered by African slaves to keep mentally and physically fit. Africans in Brazil maintained many aspects of African traditional culture and self-defense patterns through this poetic martial arts movement. The berimbau is closely related to the one-stringed fiddle played in Africa (by the Kaikoum, the Auen, and the !Kung). It is played by both sexes in the Khoisan Area (particularly the southern, northern, western, and central Kalahari). The music of the berimbau lead dancers from one set of movements to the others. The bow player was also the lookout and changed the pattern (to warn martial artists/dancers) when he saw plantation guards approaching.[72]

Typical *merengue* from Santa Domingo involves the *tambora* and *guira*, Dominican instruments of African origins. The *bomba* and *plena* used in Puerto Rico's *salsa* and other musical styles have related sources. African rhythms motivated the development of Cuban *clave* patterns. Beginning in the 1930s, the Latin feel crept into "jazz" in the United States and became particularly widespread after Dizzy Gillespie hired Chano Pozo in 1947. Candido was featured on conga drums in the music of Charlie Parker and others. Babatunde Olatunji and other master drummers brought African patterns directly to "jazz." Mongo Santamaria, Willie Bobo, Flora Purim, Airto Moreira, Hermeto Pascoal, Machito, and other musicians helped to develop and popularize Latin "jazz" in the United States, allowing it to flourish during the 1960s. The music of all these styles merged with African-American music easily due to mutual African qualities within each global African tradition.

Unlike slave areas in North America, the patterns of cross-fertilization among enslaved Africans in other regions contained clear lines of distinction. In Dutch Guiana, in the northern part of South America, Bushmen came as slaves. Marshall Stearns discussed the degree to which they managed to maintain African musical traditions in the Western world: "A wide sampling of the music of Dutch Guiana has been recorded by Herskovits and analyzed by Kolinski, who found: 'With the exception of a few songs, the music of the Bush-Negroes displays traits that are essentially African.' In fact, since African music has been influenced by ours in recent times, Bush-Negro music, it has been suggested, is more African than African music today."[73]

The islands of the West Indies exhibit varying degrees of African and European influence. In Haiti, the influence was a combination of French and Dahomean cultures; in Cuba it was Spanish and Yoruba; in Trinidad, Ashanti and British; in Brazil, Portuguese and Senegalese; and in Jamaica, Ashanti and British. Unexpected things often happened as a result of cultural cross-fertilization. In 1797, England forced Protestantism upon Trinidad's African and Catholic tradition, for instance. As a consequence, Trinidad Shouters created a powerful music akin to that evolved in America.

The Evolution of the Drum Set

Although the trap set was invented in the United States, the particular components of the American drum set were imported from various parts of the world. Bass and snare drums came from England and Germany; Tom-toms were originally Chinese instruments; and cymbals were originally from China and Turkey. Nevertheless, the bass drum and hi-hat pedals, the throne, various drum and cymbal stands, and other unifying elements of the set reflect the needs of "jazz" players and were invented in the United States. Eventually, paraphernalia augmenting the basic drum set expanded to include cowbells, wood block, triangles, gongs, etc. The use of added percussion began with musical accompaniment to silent movies, and reached a peak during the Swing era.

One of the legendary pioneers of "jazz" drumming was Edward "Ed Dee Dee" Chandler (c. 1870–1925). The nascence of "jazz" drumming from a newly assembled battery of percussion would evolve throughout the twentieth century. Chandler is credited with the invention of the bass drum foot pedal (1894). He attached a wooden pedal for his right foot to articulate the bass drum so his hands were free to play other drums with his sticks. This eventually led to a similar pedal being attached to the cymbals of the hi-hat. Thus, Chandler invented a trend that evolved into the modern drums set (or drum kit).

A long line of American drummers contributed to the evolution of the trap set. "Papa" Jack Laine (1873–1966) was another early New Orleans "jazz" drummer. Laine organized a variety of brass bands and small groups. He sponsored dozens of distinguished European-American "jazz" musicians in New Orleans from his late teens until shortly after World War I. While a member of the Fate Marable and King Oliver bands, he was recognized for his creativity, and for a reduction of exhibitionism. Warren "Baby" Dodds (1898–1959), became the first musician to demonstrate the drum set's full potential. Baby Dodds evolved his musical conceptions in early "jazz," yet his approach is related to modern "jazz" styles. As a continuation of Dodds's contribution, Chick Webb modernized drumming in the 1930s, with an experimental style combining rudimentary drumming with swinging "jazz," anticipating future innovations.

Chick Webb (1909–39) was the first to explore patterns for the drums that were removed from the rudimentary or military drumming commonly employed during the early years of "jazz" evolution. Gene Krupa (1909–73), who was heavily influenced by Webb, brought the drums front and center as a showcase instrument, giving the drums a higher degree of respectability as a solo instrument. Kenny "Clook" Clark (1914–85) took drums to yet another level by placing less emphasis on the bass drum, and using it only for punctuation. This shifted rhythmic focus to the snare, high-hat, and cymbals. Clark moved completely away from the rigidity of the military (rudimentary) approach. Instead, he provided bebop style a more fluid rhythmic approach, allowing the double bass to provide the bulk of the punctuation, freeing up the drums to apply color through a more liberated type of thematic drumming and coordinated independence. During the 1940s and 1950s, Max Roach (b. 1924) introduced a new emphasis on polyrhythms to the trap set, akin to that applied to traditional forms of African drumming. Roach combined these elements with a carefully orchestrated approach to the drums.

Elvin Jones (b. 1927) made the new emphasis on polyrhythms much more complex, unpredictable, and fluid. The earlier styles were amalgamated, in turn, by the powerful and more mercurial musical temperament that distinguished Jones's drumming, particularly during the sixties. Anthony Williams (1945–97) carried the power and astute sensitivity displayed by Jones into a new direction when he joined Miles Davis during the 1960s. His incorporation of electronics into percussion performance and composition expanded the realm of musical possibilities beyond those previously envisioned.

The Double Bass Evolution

The bass was usually eliminated during early recordings because of its lack of projection. It was often bowed during ragtime (beginning in the 1890s). Early in the twentieth century tubas were preferred to the gentler sound of the bass in recording sessions. Later the bass fashioned its accompaniment function after the tuba, and left-handed "oompah" patterns of the piano. In time, however, the bass violin served as the backbone and heartbeat of "jazz." Its importance evolved continually from its early appearances in string ensembles and ragtime orchestras (beginning around the late nineteenth century) to its current status as an instrument with a broad technical and expressive musical vocabulary.

Bass players who played ragtime often played the tuba as well. With the introduction of electrical recordings in 1925, the stringed bass was used in rhythm sections (at first primarily in larger ensembles). Tuba players such as John Kirby and Robert Ysaguirre began to switch to the stringed bass during that period.

Until the 1920s the bass was bowed (arco) rather than plucked (pizzicato) in New Orleans orchestras and combos. The man who introduced the style involving pizzicato articulation on the "jazz" bass was Bill Johnson (1872–1972). He played with power, used triplets, and his bass lines were steeped in syncopation. Johnson began as a guitarist, but by the 1900s was active in many New Orleans ragtime bands as a bassist. In 1908 he brought the New Orleans sound out west and then in 1922 went to Chicago and worked with King Oliver. After a year of playing with Oliver, Johnson decided to freelance in Chicago before retiring in 1950. He played a significant role in introducing new and distinguished characteristics into New Orleans bass playing.

Bill Johnson was known for using double repeating notes in a rudimentary style either at the unison or the octave (in a fashion related to the left-hand octave pattern employed by the stronger boogie woogie pianists). Johnson's style was originally derived from a modified marching band style with emphasis placed on metrical beats one and four in common time. Johnson's solo on a tune called "Bull Fiddle Blues" marks the first recorded pizzicato solo on double bass. In that historical recording his five two-bar ("stop-time") breaks employ syncopated arpeggiations of the harmony in a slap-bass fashion.

In the hands of the early African-American bassist, the double bass was a percussive instrument capable of adding a complimentary rhythmic dimension to drum patterns. The technique later employed by New Orleans bass players involved a slap-bass style of articulation. This technique involved pulling strings away from the neck of the instrument allowing the string to slap the wood and produce a percussive effect. Because double basses were rarer than tubas (and usually more expensive), bassists were not readily available and could demand a fairly high price for their work. Due to this scarcity, the washtub bass and tuba were more common in earlier days. In the usual musical settings, where a brass instrument was the most dominant voice, the less audible double bass was also unable to compete in amplitude. This slap-bass technique allowed the bassist to project more volume than with conventional pizzicato articulation.

Projection remained an ongoing problem with the double bass. The limitations of early recording equipment made the lower frequencies and diffused sound of the double bass virtually inaudible. Even with today's amplification for lyrical bassists, metal strings (instead of gut strings) are used for greater projection and to create a more percussive tone. Bridges are raised to allow the performer to pluck harder without getting slap tones while still obtaining a bigger sound.

In the early days, bassists were usually confined to executing either straight quarter-note pulse-keeping roles (playing on beats one and three, or on all four beats of the measure) or imitating the earlier tuba players' "oom-pah" bass lines. Besides enhancing the texture in this fashion, the bassists during early "jazz" would often double the lines of the trombone or cellos during transitional passages. Bassist Steve Brown contributed to the development of a double bass approach that involved mixed rhythms (a half-note followed by a pair of dotted eighths and sixteenth-notes, for example).

Jelly Roll Morton's bassist John Lindsay (1894–1950) broke away from the traditions of his day during the peak of the "classic jazz" era (1924–29). Lindsay was born in New Orleans and started playing bass during his teens.

During most of his professional career he played trombone, a skill acquired while a member of the Army band. In New Orleans he worked with John Robichaux, then later became a member of Dewey Jackson's band on the riverboat Capitol. In 1925 Lindsay moved to Chicago while still playing and recording on trombone, but began increasing his familiarity with the double bass. In 1930 he played bass with Louis Armstrong. He continued his career in Chicago playing with various artists from the local scene. Henry Kimball and Bill Johnson influenced his style. Technically advanced for his era, Lindsay displayed a flexible approach to meter later adopted by many bass players.

Through a synthesis that fused a descending two-beat rhythm with his muscular four-beat pattern,[74] Lindsay defined a new direction for the bass on Morton's first recording of "Grandpa's Spells." He alternated between bowing and plucking, and introduced the stop-time rhythm (playing on the first beat of the measure). His creativity throughout his career made his performances varied and colorful. Lindsay used the slap-bass sound during the recording era. (Others such as Pops Foster and Wellman Braud used the slap style until the swing era, when it became obsolete.)

Early "jazz" bassists generally played the fundamental and primary notes of the chords, often doubling the left hand of the piano in a highly restricted fashion. The more liberated role of the bassist (particularly as soloist) would come later, following several phases of stylistic and technical evolution. During the 1930s, gut strings were common (limiting sound projection), and high bridges held the strings a great distance from the fingerboard (resulting in reduced flexibility).

The bass players in the 1930s and 1940s concentrated on producing a tone that was smoother than earlier slap-bass style. The prevailing custom among bassists during that period involved a more melodic approach. Ensembles often played in large ballrooms, where people would dance the jitterbug during the swing era. Swing was the genesis of the American popular music craze, where thousands of young people gathered to enjoy concerts of the latest musical creations. As early swing music evolved into more structured arrangements to accommodate expanding ensemble size, it lost some of its ensemble improvisational freedom in the exchange. There were two distinct types of swing bands: "Black" and "White." The "White" bands played more popular songs for the mass culture, while "Black" swing bands maintained greater degrees of improvisation and produced a hard driving beat.

One of the best-known bass players of the swing era was John Kirby (1908–52). Like players before him he also played tuba and trombone. His walking bass lines were strong, and always occurred on all four beats of the measure. Kirby's bass lines would run the entire range of the instrument with precise intonation, clear tone, and striking articulation. His touch was much lighter than that of his peers.

Walter Page (1900–57) advanced a pioneer style of walking bass during the swing era. Page was a member of the Count Basie Orchestra. In the large ensembles of that era bass solos were extremely rare, but Page created melodic and rhythmically intricate lines that swung.

Ellington's bassist Wellman Braud (1891–1966) played a distinctive, syncopated style (listen to Ellington's "Freeze and Melt") and introduced features that would influence subsequent bass players. Moving away from the straight quarter-note pattern, Braud often introduced eighth notes on the second half of the first beat that propelled the remaining quarter notes in the measure forward. Braud was instrumental in reshaping the sound and function of the bass during the swing era. His strong and rhythmic slap-bass style became quite refined and his intonation remained impeccable. His new approach, involving freer bass lines, helped pave the way to the modern swing feel.

Jimmy Blanton (1918–42) and Pops Foster (1892–1969) were respected for their exemplary bass playing. It was Jimmy Blanton, however, who introduced the bass as a solo instrument. Blanton, considered the Father of Modern Bass, was a very popular performer during the swing era but remained closer to tradition than some of his peers. Blanton liked his string action high and used little amplification. Duke Ellington heard him playing on riverboats in 1939 and immediately enlisted him in his band. The incorporation of Blanton's bass transformed the Ellington sound, stabilizing the orchestra's rhythm section and enhancing its swing. Blanton's theoretical sophistication involved a frequent use of non-harmonic passing tones in his walking bass lines. Blanton lived a very short life, but left over 130 recordings from Duke Ellington's band as well as other small group performances. Blanton's innovations lead directly into the evolution of bebop bass style.

The bass made further advances during the early 1940s, as bebop demanded a quicker and more expressive style of execution. The bassist reverted to the earlier bass function as timekeeper, to allow other members of the new combos and modern big bands greater freedom of movement. This freedom was extended to the piano and drums as their former time-keeping responsibilities evolved into more fluid and less predictable roles. As bebop emerged, it evolved into a style that only certain virtuosos could understand, perfect, and perform. Performed after hours in small bars, usually with crowds typically containing an ample number of fellow musicians, the new music intensified harmonic pacing and introduced unprecedented speed and demanding melodies. Musicians who were looking for improvisational freedom were attracted to bop.

Slam Stewart (1914–87) began his professional career during the swing era, but his style was flexible enough to adapt easily to the demands of sessions with Red Norvo and others in the bebop era. Moving away from the strict time-keeping role, Stewart hummed (scatted) his melodic bass solos an octave higher. He abandoned the limitations of the arpeggiated bass lines and joined the other bebop instrumentalists in extending and enriching the harmonies of both traditional and newly composed melodies. The chromatic passages Stewart introduced in his solos contain harmonic alterations that incorporated flatted fifths and ninths. His innovative approach to melodic improvisation influenced later generations of double bass players. Slam Stewart worked with Slim Gaillard, Benny Goodman, Dizzy Gillespie, and, most notably, Art Tatum.

Major Holley (1924–90) followed in the simultaneous singing-while-playing tradition established through Stewart's legacy by setting his own trademark bowing of the bass while humming his melodies in unison. Holley began his career as a violinist, switched to tuba, and eventually began formal bass studies at Groth School of Music. He later worked throughout the United States and abroad with Dexter Gordon, Wardell Gray, Charlie Parker, Ella Fitgerald, Oscar Peterson, Duke Ellington, and many others.

As amplification became possible for the bass, more legato and more pure sound replaced the slap-bass approach. Ray Brown's (b. 1926) bass lines, along with the beautiful work of bassist Oscar Pettiford (1922–60) and inventive four-to-the-bar walking bass lines of Leroy Vinnegar (b. 1928), also advanced the melodic capabilities of the bass as a solo instrument. This approach added to the sense of freedom being developed within the bebop rhythm section. His bass had lower action and used more sophisticated amplification than his contemporaries. (He was the first bassist to use amplification.) Brown was one of the most eminent bassists to work with the Dizzy Gillespie ensembles.

The microphone was eventually replaced by the electronic pickup, which received a more direct sound from the bass. This new setup was more efficient and enabled modern bassists to extend their melodic capabilities during solos. Projection was now maintained even while providing support for the unyielding breakneck pulse during adventurous bebop forays. The prominence brought to the bass by the combination of improved amplification, lowered bridge, and steel strings encouraged musicians to experiment with other technical aspects. Cello tuning in fifths (an octave lower), as employed by Red Mitchell (1927–92), introduced different tuning systems. Mitchell (also a pianist) worked with a diverse spectrum of musicians ranging from Woody Herman and Billie Holiday to Ornette Coleman. He also recorded film and television soundtracks. When Mitchell introduced a style of tuning his instrument in fifths (C-G-D-A), this left him with an open sound, expanded range, and enhanced ability to use double stops in effective ways.

Another tendency involved using an increased number of fingers (two or three) on the right hand for greater power and speed. This technique facilitated the new flexible approach, increased speed, and the more liberated left hand of the modern bassists.

Charles Mingus (1922–79) extended the emerging freedom of bebop bass style. He tapped all preceding styles of "jazz" bass techniques and incorporated this amalgamation into the development of his own style. Mingus developed a unique approach by avoiding conventional bass emphasis on beats 1-2-3 and 4, and through playing more syncopated patterns (on the off-beats). This produced an expanded bass foundation for the modern "jazz" combo and became the cornerstone of many of Mingus's own original compositions, his accompaniment style, and his beautiful bass solos.

Steel strings provided the capability of a bigger sound from his instrument, and Mingus maintained traditional blues, gospel, and funk influences elements in his bass style. Those elements also served as the lifeblood for his innovative approach to composition. His technical facility enabled him to engage in a speech-like style, heard in musical conversations with Eric Dolphy on "Hope So Eric" and other Mingus compositions. This approach required techniques for which written notation proved inadequate, so Mingus (like Sun Ra, Cecil Taylor, and other artists finding themselves in similar situations) often sang parts to members of his ensembles. He was one of the first bassists to maintain customary background functions, while exploring the middle-ground harmonies, and providing foreground counterpoint simultaneously. This created a colorful rhythmic accompaniment that was always fresh and unpredictable.

Third stream music represents a merger of classical European music and "jazz." Mingus became involved in experimenting with this mixture. At times his music was constructed from atonal structures. At other times he experimented with using few chords, giving the soloist a greater range of freedom.

Paul Chambers (1935–69) was Miles Davis's longest serving sideman. He began playing the double bass in 1949 and developed his stylistic voice during bebop alongside such players as Bennie Green, Sonny Stitt, and Joe Roland. He was considered a more conservative player than some of his more adventurous colleagues, but Chambers mastered the walking bass in tonal and modal settings. Paul Chambers maintained the solid harmonic foundation that allowed other members of the ensembles to explore freely above his clear rhythmic and harmonic outlines. He later worked with John Coltrane on some of his classic recordings. Jimmy Garrison (1934–76) was the bassist that fit Coltrane's more adventurous demands, however. His counterpoint, firm ostinati, double- and triple-stop pedal points, and other musical devices, added elements of drama and surprise that rounded off his style and provided an ideal compliment to John Coltrane's innovative explorations.

The power, firmness, and precision of both Mingus and Chambers were taken to greater heights in the music of Ron Carter (b. 1937). Carter's rich tone and solid rhythmic sense were evident from his early period with Miles Davis, Herbie Hancock, Wayne Shorter, and Tony Williams. Along with the drone, ostinati, and counter-melodies he inherited from senior bass players, his solid playing and ability to construct strong bass solos made him the most sought after bassist of his time. He later moved the melodic capabilities of bass playing into a new realm as he introduced the piccolo bass (like the cello, sounding an octave higher than the double bass).

Ron Carter started playing the double bass in 1954. He performed in the Philharmonia Orchestra of the Eastman School. After his graduation in 1959, he moved to New York to play with Chico Hamilton's quintet (with Eric Dolphy) and enrolled at the Manhattan School of Music. In 1960, Carter made recordings with Dolphy and Don Ellis (later famed as "the quarter-tone trumpeter"). In 1963 Carter began one of the most important jobs of his career. He began performing with the Miles Davis Quintet. He remained with Davis until 1968. By this time he had developed a distinguished reputation. Carter has recorded more than a thousand albums. He has mastered bass technique, and his presence in rhythm sections assures stability, creativity, and flexibility.

As a result of Leo Fender's development of the electric bass guitar in 1952, the late 1960s and early 1970s witnessed the emergence of a revolutionary electric style of bass playing. The new electronic instrument was less demanding, due to its measured frets (which virtually eliminates intonation difficulties), miniature dimensions, and total electronic sound (a built-in remedy to the problem of projection). The instrument is incapable of producing the rich overtones of the double bass sound, because of the decreased dimensions of the resonating body and length of strings.

Fender bassist Monk Montgomery toured with the Lionel Hampton Orchestra during the early 1950s helping to legitimize the role of the electric bass guitar in "jazz." Montgomery was also one of the first musicians to place the bass on the melody lines as a lead voice, while leading his own bands during the 1970s.[75] The popularity of the electric bass attracted musicians like Stanley Clark (b. 1951), who also experimented with piccolo bass, and Paul Jackson (b. 1947). Explorations continued with five- and six-string basses, electric upright basses, and various other basses in assorted shapes and sizes. Nevertheless, the electronic bass is essentially a bass guitar and can not reproduce the rich sound of the double bass.

As the term implies, "Jazz"-rock fusion, which came about in the late 1960s, is the progeny of both "jazz" and rock music. Fusion style produced Jaco Pastorius (1951–87), a devout electric bass player. Pastorius started out playing the drums, but a football accident caused him to switch to the bass. Like other virtuoso bass players, he took advantage of the easier fingerings possible on the electric bass guitar to increase the speed of the modern bass line.

Notes

[1] Bebey, *African Music*, p. 115.

[2] Roger Pryor Dodge, *Hot Jazz and Jazz Dance: Collected Writings 1929–1964* (New York: Oxford University Press, 1995), p. 4.

[3] Samuel Floyd, *The Power of Black Music: Interpreting Its History from Africa to the United States* (New York: Oxford University Press, 1995), p. 78.

[4] Frank Tirro, *Jazz: A History* (New York: Norton, 1977), p. 45.

[5] David Cayer, "Black and Blue and Black Again: Three Stages of Racial Imagery in Jazz Lyrics," *Journal of Jazz Studies* I (1974): p. 39.

[6] Ibid., p. 14.

[7] The name "jig" originated from the French dance called the *gigue*.

[8] Sidney Bechet, *Reading Jazz: A Gathering of Autobiography, Reportage, and Criticism from 1919 to Now*, ed. Robert Gottlieb (New York: Pantheon, 1996), pp. 9–10.

[9] See Mark Gridley, *Jazz Styles: History and Analysis*, 3d ed. (Englewood Cliffs, N.J.: Prentice Hall, 1988), p. 45.

[10] John Martin, *The Dance* (New York: Tudor, 1963), p. 179.

[11] Marshall Stearns and Jean Stearns, *Jazz Dance: The Story of American Vernacular Dance* (New York: Da Capo, 1994), p. 22.

[12] Ibid.

[13] Raymond Martinez, ed., *Portraits of New Orleans Jazz: Its People and Places* (Jefferson, La.: Hope, 1971), p. 3.

[14] Gene Lees, *Cats of Any Color: Jazz Black and White* (New York: Oxford University Press, 1994), p. 30.

[15] Albert Murray, *The Blue Devil of Nada: A Contemporary American Approach to Aesthetic Statement* (New York: Pantheon Books, 1996), p. 92.

[16] Also "southern" or "folk" blues.

[17] Paul Oliver, *The Meaning of the Blues* (New York: Collier, 1963), p. 58f.

[18] Where Bessie Smith later landed her first job.

[19] Sandra Robin Leib, *The Message of Ma Rainey's Blues: A Biographical and Critical Study of America's First Woman Blues Singer* (Ann Arbor, Mich.: University Microfilms, 1979), pp. 28–29.

[20] Sally Placksin, *Jazzwomen: 1900 to the Present* (London: Pluto, 1985), p. 14.

[21] Derrick Stewart-Baxter, *Ma Rainey and the Classic Blues Singers*, ed. Paul Oliver (New York: Stein and Day, 1970), p. 35.

[22] Liner notes in Barbara Caplin and Arnold Caplin, *Gertrude "Ma" Rainey, Queen of the Blues*, vol. 3, Biograph Records, 1923–1924.

[23] Paramount Records 12083.

[24] Ibid., p. 16.

[25] *Playback*: ASCAP Member Magazine, December 1998, p. 14.

[26] Liner notes by Abbe Niles on the album, *W. C. Handy: Father of the Blues*, DRG Records, 1980.

[27] Alain Locke, *The Negro and His Music* (Port Washington, N.Y.: Kennikat, 1968), pp. 75–76.

[28] Bunk Johnson and Jelly Roll Morton, quoted in Lomax, *Mister Jelly Roll*, pp. 20–21; Spencer Williams, quoted in Shapiro and Hentoff, *Hear Me Talkin' to Ya*, p. 7.

[29] Ibid., p. 70.

[30] Goldberg, *Tin Pan Alley*, p. 141. Jubing is a derivitive of juba.

[31] Joplin could not have known that, in 1907, Charles Ives introduced a related musical approach in his "Soliloquy," because it was not published until 1933.

[32] Ted Gioia, *The Imperfect Art: Reflections on Jazz and Modern Culture* (New York: Oxford University Press, 1988). This book is an example of how contemporary writers can place European art and values in a superior position while relegating African-American music to a second-class status strictly in terms of European criteria. Gioia seems to feel, nevertheless, that he is a defender of "jazz" in this process. He calls Bach's work "perfect." This alone is enough to prove his position an arrogant and a subjective one.

[33] James M. Trotter, preface to *Music and Some Highly Musical People* (Boston: Lee and Shepard, 1886), p. 3.

[34] Ibid.

[35] Ibid., pp. 36–37.

[36] Tirro, *Jazz: A History*, p. 101.

[37] Goldberg, *Tin Pan Alley*, pp. 36–37.

[38] Stearns and Stearns, *Jazz Dance*, p. xvii.

[39] James Weldon Johnson, *Black Manhattan* (New York, 1930), pp. 123–24.

[40] Reid Badger, *A Life in Ragtime: A Biography of James Reese Europe* (New York: Oxford University Press, 1995), p. 51.

[41] Will Dixon, another African-American musician, band director, and "dancing conductor," also led a successful and enchanting group called the Nashville Students. His musicians were neither from Nashville nor students, but played at Hammerstein's Victoria (a vaudeville theater) in New York and on the Roof Gardens for evenings of dancing. Those referred to as "Black Bohemians" attending these social affairs heard an orchestra composed of mandolins, banjos, guitars, saxophones, drums, a violin, a pair of brasses, and a double bass.

[42] "James Reese Europe: Featuring Noble Sissle," IAJRC, 1996. Reese recorded his 369th U.S. Infantry "Hell Fighter" Band between March 3 and May 7, 1919.

[43] Southern, *Music of Black Americans*, p. 352.

[44] Editorial in *New York Times*, May 12, 1919.

[45] Europe, "A Negro Explains Jazz," p. 226.

[46] Southern, *Music of Black Americans*, p. 288.

[47] Europe, James Reese, "Negro's Place in Music," *New York Evening Post*, March 13, 1914; reprinted in Robert Kimball and William Bolcom, *Reminiscing with Sissle and Blake* (New York: Viking Press, 1973), p. 61.

[48] *Literary Digest*, April 26, 1919; cited in Southern, *Music of Black Americans*, p. 289.

[49] Badger, *A Life in Ragtime*, p. 122.

[50] Liner notes in "Black Music: The Written Tradition," Center for Black Music Research, Columbia College, Chicago. Recorded live in 1989.

[51] Southern, *Music of Black Americans*, p. 354.

[52] *New York Sun*, March 17, 1919; cited in ibid.

[53] Badger, *A Life in Ragtime*, p. 66.

[54] Raymond Martinez, ed., *Portraits of New Orleans Jazz: Its People and Places* (Jefferson, La.: Hope, 1971).

[55] Haskins, *Black Music in America* (New York: Harper Trophy, 1987), p. 61.

[56] Quoted in Harris, *Jazz*, p. 82.

[57] Haskins, *Black Music in America,* p. 61.

[58] Liner notes from "The Saga of Mr. Jelly Lord," recorded by Alan Lomax for the Library of Congress Archives, L14002.

[59] George Varga, *San Diego Union*, February 11, 1991.

[60] Quoted in Shapiro and Hentoff, *Hear Me Talkin' to Ya*, p. 30.

[61] Quoted in Barker, *Bourbon Street Black*, p. 69.

[62] Linda Dahl, *Stormy Weather* (New York: Pantheon), pp. 35–38.

[63] *Ibid.*

[64] Discussed in Williams, *Jazz Masters*, pp. 89–90.

[65] On Columbia Records CL-951.

[66] Hadlock, *Jazz Masters of the Twenties*, p. 10.

[67] *Stormy Weather*, pp. 35–38.

[68] Antoinnette Handy, *Black Women in American Bands and Orchestras* (Lanham, MD: Scarecrow Press, 1998), pp. 129–31.

[69] Goldberg, *Tin Pan Alley*, pp. 1–3.

[70] Ibid., pp. 5–10.

[71] Ibid., p. 91

[72] Mickey Hart and Fredric Lieberman, *Planet Drum* (San Francisco, Harper, 1991), p. 98.

[73] Marshall W. Stearns, *The Story of Jazz* (New York: Oxford University Press, 1958), p. 23.

[74] He introduced the playing of bass notes on every beat of the measure, or, in other words, beats 1 2 3 4 in a common time passage.

[75] Listen to *Monk Montgomery: Bass Odyssey*, Chisa Records CS 806, or *Monk Montgomery: Reality*, Philadelphia International Records KZ 33153.

V
Innovators Emerging Between 1910 and 1920

Mercury [with whom Adderley was under contract] was promoting me as the new Bird and all that foolishness—against
my wishes; I had nothing to do with that. I talked to Bob Shad
[a Mercury a&r man at the time] and he said, "Our business is
to sell records, and we feel this is the best way. That's all."

—Cannonball Adderley

The Fourteenth Amendment was ratified in July 1868, giving African-
American men (but not Asian men) the right to vote but depriving all women
that privilege. Suffrage remained a national issue as women continued the
fight to prevent the states from denying the right to vote to any citizen on the
basis of sex or race. The American women's movement was gaining momentum. Despite defeats for the suffrage movement in New York, Massachusetts,
Ohio, Michigan, Pennsylvania, Nebraska, Wisconsin, New Jersey, and the
Dakotas, important victories occurred in Washington (1910) and California
(1911).
    Perhaps imitation is indeed the highest form of flattery. In any case,
many European American musicians and listeners exposed to African-American music appreciated the value and importance of "jazz" immediately. Consequently, the ownership of "jazz" became a political, economic, and sociocultural issue early in the twentieth century. The legacy of slavery instilled
the notion that African Americans were entitled to nothing of real value.
Plantation mentality dictated that all things produced by the slave belonged
to the master. Such racist and sexist attitudes were profitable, and they became the basis for a new cycle of exploitation in twentieth-century African-
American music. It was important for European Americans, who enjoyed
large profits from the exploitation of African-American music, to insist upon
using the term "jazz" to facilitate claiming ownership of African-American
music. Ken McIntyre suggests:

By using the term "jazz," there are implications—one is that
the music came into being around 1916 with the Original Dixieland Jazz Band, and for a vast majority of European (and
perhaps African) Americans, that is probably true since the literary writers of books and newspaper columnists began writing
about "jazz" at that time. The music, however, existed long before the writers decided to write about it. In fact, the music has
a history for as long as man has been on the continent of Africa. The rhythm was transplanted in America via the Africans

who were deposited on these shores during the seventeenth and eighteenth centuries as slaves. Consequently, the chants, shouts, cries and hollers—all forms of communication—preceded spiritual, blues, ragtime which preceded jazz, swing, gospel, which preceded boogie woogie, rhythm n' blues, be-bop, which preceded soul, funky, rock n' roll, which preceded new thing, avant-garde jazz, black music and contemporary music in the African American tradition. Moreover, the titles given to the different eras/styles act as dividers rather than a link, which is what should be implied, since there are links that tie together all of the eras/styles, and they are: (1) feeling, (2) rhythm, (3) energy, and (4) creativity.[1]

There were now a wide variety of places for a musician to find professional work. Although not all musicians found full-time employment performing on their instruments, other daytime work was found to pay the rent, allowing musicians to pursue music after hours. Pianist, composer, and maverick historian Willie "The Lion" Smith claims that various forms of the blues were born in the brickyards of Haverstraw, New York. According to guitarist Danny Barker at the turn of the century, "There were countless places of enjoyment that employed musicians . . . as well as private affairs, balls, soirees, banquets, marriages, deaths, christenings, Catholic communions, confirmations, picnics at the lake front, country hay rides and advertisements of business concerns." Zutty Singleton, one of the first great "jazz" drummers, remembers that many musicians had a wide assortment of day jobs. He says, "they were bricklayers and carpenters and cigar makers and plasterers. Some had little businesses of their own—coal and wood and vegetable stores. Some worked on the cotton exchange and some were porters."[2]

African-American culture and society flourished between 1910 and 1920, a period W. E. B. DuBois called the "mystic years." Independent businesses were established, farms were developed, and individuals found work in a variety of areas. This progressive period prevailed until the Ku Klux Klan ushered in their clandestine and cowardly acts of violence, intimidation, and murder throughout America. The combined acts of the carpetbagger and the Klan would establish a pattern of economic disfranchisement for the African-American community that remained virtually unchanged throughout the twentieth century.

The Blues Continues to Evolve

Many regions were involved in the development of the rural blues. The Delta—an agricultural region between the Mississippi and Yazoo Rivers in the states of Mississippi and Alabama—contains a dense "Black" population, with "Blacks" outnumbering "Whites" by more than 2:1 shortly after the turn of the twentieth century. This area had a strong oral tradition and produced a great number of country blues singers. The rural blues were also popular in the Territories (Texas, Louisiana, Arkansas, Oklahoma, and Missouri) and in the region of the southeastern seaboard (Georgia and Florida). Rural blues, a folk expression originating among African Americans in the South, were usually sung by men accompanying themselves with a fiddle, guitar, or banjo. The phrase structure generally consisted of singing for two measures of verse then playing instrumental responses during the break.

Two Influential Rural Blues Musicians

Blind Lemon Jefferson and Huddie Ledbetter (Leadbelly) were two of the first male rural (or country) blues musicians to record during the 1920s and 1930s. Jefferson was born on a farm near Wortham, Texas, in 1897. Like many other African Americans born blind in the United States, Jefferson turned to music to make a living during adolescence, working casual dances and parties. As a young adult he moved to Dallas, where he continued to perform in barrooms and brothels. Eventually he began to travel and was discovered in the South by Paramount Record Company. The more than eighty records he made for that label between 1926 and 1929 were extremely popular within the African-American community. Around 1930 he died suddenly of undetermined causes.

Leadbelly (born in the early 1880s), the only son of Sallie and Wes Ledbetter, was a Jefferson protégé who began performing publicly at age fifteen. He was married for the first time a year later. His mother doted on him as a child. He in turn protected her from his father's temper and took her into his home after she became a widow. After moving to Dallas he worked with Jefferson. Between the ages of twenty-five and fifty, Leadbelly, a man of short temper, spent a total of thirteen years in prison, often for crimes some claim were in self-defense. African-American inmates (like Buddy Moses and others) on chain gangs contributed as much to the development of the blues as did street singers, mill workers, and rural field hands.

Leadbelly's musical break came while serving time for attempted homicide in Louisiana State Penitentiary. It was there that Alan A. Lomax, Sr., first recorded Leadbelly in 1933. Upon his release, the blues musician became a celebrity of sorts, playing nightclub engagements and concerts that eventually took him to Paris to perform in 1949. He died in December, 1949, just as his career was beginning to take off.

If the titles of his songs are reliable indications, Leadbelly was fond of women. The most important woman in his life was his wife, Martha Promise, whom he married in 1935. His songs were often personal or autobiographical. "Mary and Martha" recalls his highly supportive wife and her twin sister. Recordings of songs like "Goodnight Irene," "Roberta," and "Old Hannah" were performed as straightforward blues tunes, or began with long personal narratives that explained the story behind the song. He wanted to educate his audiences about his life and music; the two aspects seemed inseparable.

Leadbelly played a finely tuned twelve-string guitar. Although he was a self-taught musician, his original approach to the guitar defied imitation. He lived and performed in New York City, and traveled to Pennsylvania, Kentucky, Washington, and California for other engagements. Later in his life he also enjoyed playing college engagements. The way Leadbelly spoke—as a Sarah Lawrence student recalls from a concert in the summer of 1946—

"showed he had a strong awareness of his important place in music (sometimes referring to himself in the third person, a mark of people who see themselves in history already)."[3] His contribution to the rural blues tradition is undeniable.

Classic Blues

Classic blues expressed the problems surrounding ghetto life in the cities and were usually sung by women at the piano or with ensemble accompaniment. The vocalists added improvisation to their melody lines to imbue it with freedom and originality. Innovators of this style included Ma Rainey, Bessie Smith, and Billie Holiday. Classic blues had centers in Chicago, Kansas City, and Memphis. Classic blues singing is closely related to country blues rhythmic, melodic and harmonic vocabulary, but was more successful at introducing rural African-American folk music to a broader entertainment world.

Classic blues mixed swing and boogie-woogie elements to eventually produce rhythm and blues during the 1940s. Blackface caricatures were usually used in advertisements for "race records" made by African-American artists through the end of the 1930s. The race records that Ma Rainey recorded for Paramount Records were in high demand during the 1920s. Until the Great Depression, even some African-American owned companies felt it necessary to adopt the wide-eyed, grinning images to sell their music. The title "race records" was still applied to records made by Louis Jordan (the progenitor of rhythm and blues) and other jump bands.

Other blues and rhythm and blues stars included Arthur "Big Boy" Crudup, Blind Willie McTell, Memphis Slim, Big Bill Broonsy, Will Shade, Chuck Berry, Otis Redding, and B. B. King. The features of various forms of blues blend, transcending the market labels used to describe them, much as the distinction between African-American blues and "jazz" can easily become indistinguishable.

Mary Straine was the first African-American woman to make a record when her legendary vaudeville routine (with celebrity Bert Williams) was produced in 1919. It was not until 1920 that the struggle to convince the European-American music establishment to record another African-American female blues singer was successful. Okeh Records[4] recorded Mamie Smith's "The Crazy Blues" and realized a success so great that the label became a rival to the larger Paramount and Columbia record industries. Thus the doors of the music industry opened for African-American blues artists in the 1920s.

As European American producers cashed in on the new "race records," artists were paid only for the recording date. They received no royalties (or other revenue) from sales regardless of the number of records sold. Despite the exploitation that took place, the effect the music had on American culture was undeniable. Just as the voodoo queens had encouraged interracial interaction among women in New Orleans earlier, the powerful singing of Ma Rainey, Bessie Smith, Ida Cox, Sippie Wallace, and other African-American blues women affected female European-American singers like Sophie Tucker and Connie Boswell.[5]

Bessie Smith

Blues vocalist Bessie Smith was born in Chattanooga, Tennessee, around 1895 and died in Clarksdale, Mississippi, in 1937. She went on the road while still in her teens as an apprentice to Ma Rainey on the Theater Owners' Booking Association (TOBA) circuit. By 1915 Bessie had moved from the song and dance of the chorus to singing and evolving her own solo blues style. Clarence Williams, who also worked the TOBA circuit as a comic and piano player, was Bessie Smith's pianist at the time. He later became the key man in arranging Smith's recording sessions for Columbia, after the pair came to New York during the early 1920s. Later, Smith would almost single-handedly save Columbia records from virtual bankruptcy through the strength and popularity of her musical style.

Frank Walker from Columbia records heard Smith sing in Selma, Alabama, while she was traveling the honky-tonk, carnival, and tent-show circuit. At two hundred ten pounds and five feet, nine inches tall, the Empress of the Blues was an imposing figure with a voice and personality to match. Her astonishing variety of rhythmic attacks, striking timbre variations, and expressive vocal phrasing influenced future vocalists and instrumentalists for generations. During the post–World War I era, Smith was the most popular African-American recording artist in the world.

"Downhearted Blues" was the song selected for Bessie Smith's recording debut in February 1923. By the time she recorded "Jailhouse Blues" in September of the same year, it was clear that she was moving from a rudimentary style toward a more spontaneous, freer, and sophisticated "jazz" style of song interpretation. By 1925 Bessie had become a mature performing and recording artist. Her work with Louis Armstrong on their classic "St. Louis Blues" recording became a definitive symbol of classic blues style; moreover, the similarities of phrasing styles and melodic vocabularies of their musical reciprocity clearly illustrate the intrinsic connection between "jazz" and blues innovators. The song was recorded a few years later on a movie short where Smith was supported by James P. Johnson on piano, members of the Fletcher Henderson Orchestra, and the Hall Johnson Choir.

The twelve-bar blues began to replace the freer (less standardized) country blues forms during the 1920s and 1930s. Generally, classic blues form consisted of a short statement in the first two measures of the piece with the accompaniment filling in the next two bars of this four-measure phrase (essentially on a tonic seventh chord [I-7]). The next four bars (measures 5–8), basically in the subdominant seventh region (IV-7), repeat the phrase structure of the beginning (perhaps with slight variation). The final four bars, beginning in the dominant region (V-7), provide new lyrics that respond to the earlier statements (in bars 9 and 10) before the harmony returns to the home key in the final two bars of the form (11 and 12). Some blues songs in this period interpose a bridge between repetitions of the twelve-bar structure, and variants on the form persisted despite efforts by record producers directed at the standardization of blues form.

Smith's recordings represent the epitome of the classic blues style, and she too experimented with modifying formal elements. Her 1931 Columbia recording of "Blue Blue" opens with an ABB repetition pattern (rather than the AAB phrase structure described above), followed by a sixteen-measure bridge which entails four repetitions of the same phrase (CCCC). Other subtle modifications of phrase and formal structures can be heard on other Smith recordings. Within such structures she combined the flexibility and elegance of "jazz" with the "down home" appeal of country blues. This convincing, durable, and natural formula made Smith a favorite in the African-American community.

All aspects of her professional career—her voice, powerful bearing, timing, and her ability to work with the finest "jazz" musicians of her day—entitled Bessie Smith to the title "Empress of the Blues." Her career and personal life contained peaks and valleys, but never in the memory of any of those who heard her, and on none of the records she made, did she fall below the highest level of blues singing. Highly evocative phrasing and a distinctly crisp diction also characterize Smith's style. In addition to her own recordings and movie shorts, she performed with Louis Armstrong, Joe Smith, Jack Teagarden, Benny Goodman, and other notable "jazz" musicians.

Smith's personal and professional life went into decline in the late 1920s. Because her popularity had saved Columbia records from bankruptcy, John Hammond (Smith's producer) continued to record her until 1933. She was on tour when her tragic death occurred. She died of "shock" and "possible internal injuries" at G. T. Thomas Hospital for "Blacks" on September 26, 1937. Hammond claimed she was refused admission to a segregated hospital after an automobile crash. She reportedly died from loss of blood while being sped to a hospital that admitted "Negroes."[6] Elaine Feinstein, a Smith biographer, claims no one asked Richard Morgan (who was in the car with Smith when the accident occurred) for his version of the story. According to Bessie's son, Jack Gee, Jr., Morgan said that a Dr. Smith (who happened to pass the scene of the accident and stopped to attend to Bessie Smith) was asked by a spectator why he would not take Bessie to the hospital himself. The doctor reportedly replied "that it would make his car too bloody."[7] Morgan had to set out on foot to get an ambulance. A second minor accident occurred when a European-American couple rear-ended Dr. Smith's parked vehicle. Morgan also told Jack Gee, Jr., that once he returned with the ambulance, someone said, "Let's see what's the matter with the white couple first."[8] In any case, Bessie Smith received no treatment for seven hours.

Miles Davis once said Bessie Smith's music affected him as much as Lead Belly's blues, or as strongly as the poetry of Paul.

Ida Cox and Migrations to Northern Cities

Many African-American women came to urban areas from southern rural environments, seeking the glamour and excitement of Harlem and other vibrant urban areas. Thus, the messages carried by blues singers were not always about societal victimization. Many young women left home when they were only fifteen or sixteen years old. Like Ida Cox and other successful musicians from this era, they chose to escape the religious and social sanctions imposed upon them within African-American communities of the time.[9]

Cox's lyrics to "Wild Women Don't Get the Blues" provide insight into her particular perspective on a new caliber of women in urban America.

> Now, when you've got a man don't ever be on the square,
> If you do, he'll have a woman everywhere.
> I never was known to treat one man right,
> I keep them working hard both day and night,
> Because wild women don't worry,
> Wild women don't have the blues.

The women to whom Ida Cox refers were tenacious because they possessed extraordinary drive and perseverance, enabling them to become financially and emotionally independent within a world of immense exploitation. At times their cynicism stems from the fact that they often escaped the oppression of the church only to experience sexual abuse and abandonment in secular circles. They witnessed the economic injustice of being denied jobs when European-American women refused to work with them.[10] Some adapted to these situations by developing talents and personalities that empowered them despite an American society that constantly denied them their rights as individuals. Others were not so tenacious and less fortunate.

Not all of the African-American women who moved to urban areas developed the survival skills needed to cope with big-city environments. Many accepted unfavorable living conditions while dazzled by potential opportunities for freedom, fame, and fortune that a performing career on stage offered. A number of women found work in raunchy whiskey joints and other unsavory employment venues. Limited job opportunities made the attractive salaries of cheap dance halls, cabarets, and brothels appealing. It also left them vulnerable to dishonest and unscrupulous employers. Young African-American women were frequently sought after by European-American men, who vehemently disapproved of cozy relationships that often developed between "White" prostitutes and "Black" male piano players,[11] a hypocritical disposition that remained an American social trademark.

Streetwalkers in Chicago, in Norfolk, Virginia, and in other cities became the targets of concern for African-American communities between 1916 and 1922. When the living situations of young women engaged as streetwalkers eventually became critical, and their families failed to persuade them to return home, the African-American community demurred and expressed deep concern. In one instance the Chicago Commission on Race Relations reported objections to these activities that were directed at the Pekin Café by the African-American community. Citizens were dismayed "because it offered jazz, vulgar dances and mixed couples, all considered immoral enticements for the young black women who performed there."[12]

Not all serious-minded musicians moved to urban areas in the North. Many female vocalists and instrumentalists continued to work and develop in New Orleans. Not all were "wild women." Women instrumentalists in New Orleans often performed in ensembles with their husbands. Although the most significant flood of women instrumentalists would not occur until the 1930s, many female musicians were developing their skills.

One of the pioneers who paved the way for younger female musicians was boogie-woogie pianist Sadie Goodson. Goodson was born in Pensacola, Florida, around 1900. She was well known for her association with Buddy Petit's band, especially during their steady engagement on the S.S. Madison. Her husband Chinee Foster also played in the band. Later, during the 1930s, she played cabaret jobs with Kid Rena and Alec Bigard. Her younger sister, Billie Pierce, was also a boogie-woogie pianist and blues shouter who worked with her husband, De De Pierce.

Pianist Emma Barrett (born c. 1900) led her own popular group under the name "Sweet Emma the Bell Gal." Although she could not read music, she was a successful professional musician who worked with John Robichaux, Sidney Desvigne, and Armand J. Piron (ironically, all considered New Orleans's top "reading" bands). She started working with Papa Celestin in 1923 and was widely recorded.

Lizzie Miles (born March 31, 1895 in New Orleans) was a popular vocalist who recorded in the 1920s. She worked mainly at Davila's Mardi Gras lounge and eventually moved to Los Angeles with Bob Scobey. Vocalist Esther Bigeou was also born in New Orleans around 1895 (she died around 1936). Bigeou toured on the Theater Owner's Booking Association's vaudeville circuit and worked with Peter Bocage. She sang and recorded with the A. J. Piron Orchestra in the 1930s under the stage name "The Creole Songbird."[13]

Some women made successful livings performing primarily with all women bands and orchestras. Although trumpeter and saxophonist Leora Meoux is remembered primarily as the wife of pianist, arranger, and orchestra leader Fletcher Henderson, she was also a strong performer in her own right. Born in the late 1890s in Louisville, Kentucky, Meoux never suffered from a lack of musical employment. Much of her time was spent in New York, where she met Fletcher while both musicians were playing on a Hudson River boat. The couple married in 1924, after she divorced trumpeter Russell Smith, a member of Fletcher's extraordinary band. Because she was a "schooled" player, her early years were confined to performing European classics. Leora credits her husband Fletcher with teaching her to play "jazz" and to "go beyond the printed page." It was Louis Armstrong, however, who taught her to play "hot trumpet."[14]

Although Leora Meoux occasionally substituted with the Henderson band, her steady professional affiliations were with women's bands. Meoux performed with The Musical Spillers, the Negro Women's Orchestral and Civic Association, Lil Armstrong's All-Girl Band, and The Vampires, her own small combo. In 1919 she was a member of the orchestra that played for a show entitled *The Blue Pearl* at the Lafayette Theater, under the direction of Hallie Anderson. Later she performed in an orchestra under the direction of Mildred Franklin Gassaway at the same theater.

During the late 1920s and early 1930s, the Henderson house on 139th Street served as the meeting place for many of the world's "jazz" luminaries, including Bessie Smith, Clara Smith, Cab Calloway, Bix Beiderbecke, and Joe Venuti. Some musicians came for rehearsals or fellowship, while others were regular boarders. According to Calloway, "Usually Lee [Leora] cooked.... All ate together before going their separate way to gigs.... That included Lee, because Mrs. Henderson was a fine trumpet player in the pit orchestra at the Lafayette Theater."[15] Mrs. Henderson was affiliated with the Lafayette Theater House Orchestras for nine years. She died around 1958 in New York City.

Although female instrumentalists experienced a measure of success during the early "jazz" era, the period between 1910 and 1920 provided the greatest set of opportunities for the female vocalists. Blues singers made the rounds on the vaudeville circuit as early as 1914. African-American communities became familiar with the music of blues artists Gertrude "Ma" Rainey and Lillian Glinn between 1910 and 1920, as they traveled with shows like the Rabbit Foot Minstrels. The potentially lucrative blues market attracted European-American men who knew they could make money exploiting African-American artists: so long as they had no "White" middleman. African-American musicians were denied equitable participation in the mainstream marketplace. Professor Daphne Duval Harrison describes the situation in her book, *Black Pearls: Blues Queens of the 1920s*:

> The market for black stage talent was lucrative enough to attract exploiters; living and performing conditions often bordered on the hazardous; black talent and audiences remained under the financial control of white theater owners and booking agencies; and the quality of some of the acts and shows were sometimes amateurish.

> TOBA had a reputation that ranged from laudable for its regularizing of engagements and management to despicable depending on who was telling it. It was called "Tough on Black Asses" by those who were booked under its auspices. Acts and theater owners bickered constantly about salaries, conditions of theaters and housing, and scheduling of engagements.

> Let us take a closer look at TOBA and its real value to the black entertainment world. The TOBA was organized in 1909 by Anselmo Barrasso in Memphis after he had noted the success that his brother had running a number of southern theaters that catered to blacks. Barrasso noted the potential market for black acts, and created a booking association to supply the demand. The TOBA scheduled acts for the theaters that belonged to its network, much as a movie distribution company might rent films to a favored chain. This became a busy circuit for many black vaudeville shows and acts, reaching from Chicago to Florida, and from Oklahoma to New Orleans, with Memphis, Toledo, Chattanooga, Atlanta, Pittsburgh, and other towns in between. A long string of outstanding headliners appeared on the circuit and indeed a few received good salaries, often working year round. The most notable included Bessie Smith, Rainey, Sara Martin, Butterbeans and Susie, Kid and Coot, S. H. Dudley, the Whitman Sisters, Sweet Mama Stringbean (a.k.a. Ethel Waters), and Hamtree Harrington.[16]

Although the TOBA artists who received top billing received fairly good salaries and treatment (though those wages were inferior to their European-American counterparts), the majority of other African-American artists were subjected to poor conditions on all levels. They were forced to work for racist managers who cheated them. Artists often had to dress beneath the stage and slip onstage through the orchestra pit while the lights were low. Artists on meager salaries were forced to pay all their own traveling expenses. African-American performers usually found it difficult to find accommodations in the towns in which they performed.

Traveling from one Jim Crow town to another was dangerous during the time when some European Americans were enjoying bludgeoning, lynching, and burning the bodies of victimized African Americans. "Black" performers encountered ample experiences upon which to substantiate apprehension about potentially being dragged from a train, theater, or other public places by "White" people who wanted to demonstrate their delusions of superiority. One headline during this period read, "Orchestra Lured from Fashionable Hotel to Distant Forest and First Robbed, Then Clubbed and Stoned—Another Instance of Barbarism of South."[17] Other articles documented harassment by the Ku Klux Klan in New Orleans and in other cities throughout the United States.

The African-American community always realized that it would have to be self-contained and self-sufficient before it could successfully modify the repugnant nature of their plight in America. Entrepreneur Camille Cosby (wife of actor/producer Bill Cosby[18]) said in an interview that the African-American people "are going to have to be more self-sufficient, almost the way black communities were when they were segregated. We need to buy the theaters in our communities; we need to buy television stations. We need to have more money in our own banks if we want to purchase and be competitive on that level."[19]

Just as blackface minstrels maintained their popularity among nineteenth-century European Americans, Camille Cosby parallels the stereotypical role of the African-American buffoon that most European American exploiters insist upon portraying in the entertainment industry. "When it comes to us," Cosby says, "something like bigotry is always made to be funny. But when it comes to other groups, they don't make that funny; you begin to see very serious films. For example, you don't see anything comedic about Hitler."[20]

The carpetbagger's mentality made its way into all aspects of the entertainment world and still remains ensconced in areas of American society. Duke Ellington's 1927 warning, "If we don't stop calling this music 'jazz' blacks are going to lose control of it,"[21] was based upon observed realities confronting the African-American performer. Perhaps the early "jazz" musicians, who reportedly covered their right hands with handkerchiefs when playing the trumpet, had reasons for being paranoid when performing in European-American clubs. After all, many remembered the times when Tin Pan Alley laid claim to African-American songs because "Black" composers could rarely publish music on their own in a music industry controlled exclusively by the majority culture.

Mamie Smith

Mamie Smith (1883–1946) was born in Cincinnati's "Black Bottom" district and performed on her first professional job early in 1893. "Ma" Rainey was only seven years old when the ten-year old Mamie began touring as a dancer with the Four Dancing Mitchells. Mamie was a show-business veteran of seven years by the time Pridgett made her debut at the Springer Opera House in 1900. Smith was touring with the Smart Set a year before she arrived in Harlem with her husband, William Smith (a tenor also known as "Sweet Singing Smitty") in 1913. She performed in such clubs as Barron's, Leroy's, Edmund's, Percy Brown's, and in a Perry Bradford revue, *Made in Harlem*. Pianist Willie the Lion Smith recalls that she "became one of the most popular singer-entertainers in town."

Perry Bradford, an African-American songwriter and music publisher, was able to arrange for Smith's 1920 record date, despite letters from north-ern and southern groups threatening a boycott of Okeh phonographs and rec-ords if they recorded any African-American performers. The opportunity for Smith's first recording date came when Sophie Tucker, scheduled to record, fell ill at the last minute. Bradford convinced Okeh to let Smith replace her. The two relatively undistinguished numbers she recorded that day were not blues tunes but songs geared for a European-American audience and re-corded with European-American musicians accompanying her. Her musical impact was strong enough, however, to put Smith back in the Okeh studio six months later with an African-American band singing the blues.

The song Smith chose for the second session was an old blues strain that she used in a show called *Maid of Harlem* at the Lincoln Theater (under the title "Harlem Blues"). James P. Johnson claimed he used this strain in his 1916 composition "Mama and Papa's Blues." Other barrelhouse pianists remembered portions of the melody from an old lascivious song played in the sporting houses. Nevertheless, "Crazy Blues" was the first version of that particular blues that was released on record. After touring began, Mamie Smith's frequently shifting personnel included such legendary players as Johnny Dunn, Bubber Miley, Joe Smith, Sidney Bechet, Curtis Mosby, and Coleman Hawkins.[22] Fletcher Henderson recruited members of Mamie Smith's band (like Coleman Hawkins) to improve the sight-reading caliber of his band. Smith employed the top African-American musicians in the United States because, as the highest-paid African-American artist of the day, she could pay her musicians well. Nonetheless, maintaining steady personnel was complicated by the fact that many African-American musicians refused to travel in the South during this period.

Smith received $2,000 per night during this period of popularity and sported an ostrich-plume cape worth $3,000. She reportedly had a piano in every room of her New York apartment. Smith toured and recorded through-out the twenties, and, according to Leonard Kunstadt and Bob Colton, at the peak of her career "her name was synonymous with the word success. Her furs, jewelry, apartment buildings, lover's quarrels, and gun-chasing antics were receiving much notoriety. The advent of a recording session by Mamie was nearly enough to declare a national holiday in the Negro districts of the nation."[23]

Her film appearances during the early forties included *Mystery in Swing* (1940), *Murder on Lenox Avenue* (1941), *Sunday Sinners* (1941), and *Because I Love You* (in 1943 with Lucky Millinder). Despite this success, Smith died penniless in a Harlem hospital, following a long illness, and was buried in an unmarked grave in Frederick Douglass Memorial Park, Staten Island, N.Y., in 1946.

Other Women Instrumentalists

Sexist thinking leads to the assumption that not all instruments are created for women to play. There is evidence, for example, that women were not allowed to play the sacred ritual drums in many world societies. But stringed instruments have long been associated with women musicians. Women have been restricted to these "gentler" instruments, particularly in the Near East and India, where stringed instruments have typically symbolized the passive female. Women played the lute in ancient Egypt, the guitar in Europe, and the musical bow in Mexico. The harp has remained an especially feminine symbol, perhaps because of its association with angelic or pristine qualities. In "jazz," amplified and electrified string instruments have produced more aggressive and percussive roles for these instruments. With the increase in the dynamic potential of strings, the passive stereotypes and connotations are transformed, allowing the instruments to become a generally acceptable vehicle for male players.[24] Thus, women have been less visible performers on modern electric string instruments in "jazz," blues, rhythm-and-blues, and rock settings.

It has often been said that behind every successful man is a good woman. This adage suggests a chronic social problem reflected clearly in the history of "jazz." The phrase openly declares that the man enjoys the bulk of success. Women are considered merely good servants that provide support needed for the man to realize his aspirations. Because the playing field on which this relationship exists is tilted toward the advancement of the male member, the female cannot hope to enjoy the same degree of success, development, or ego gratification as a man. In fact, while the man has been clearly labeled "successful," the woman has not been identified with a progressive social position. Her demeanor alone is characterized (as "good"). She is not evaluated as a producer of tangible manifestations.

The careers of women musicians are often tormented by the complexities of living dual lifestyles and juggling a multitude of social options. Deciding whether to pursue a career in the music industry, to stay at home and raise a family, or to combine the two directions is a dilemma that often confronts women musicians. Male artists are rarely forced to choose between pursuing a career as a musician and having a family.

As female musicians moved into the realm of secular music in increasing numbers, conflict precipitated within African-American communities over whether loyalties should remain with sacred music or whether the singing of one secular style disqualified the musician from participating in sacred forms of expression. Double standards allowed communities to place guilt upon women who traveled on the road (leaving their children at home), while men traditionally were allowed to do so without experiencing similar degrees of social scorn or persecution. If women surmounted these obstacles, they still had to find their way within a male-dominated professional musical culture.

The blues combined elements of the spiritual, field hollers, African music, and other African-American music, molding them into a personal form of expression appropriate for a new world of southern carpetbaggers, disappointments, enjoyment, and new urban realities. As blues innovators were faced with a new kind of victimization after 1865, their music was ripe for expressing the sorrow, pain, wisdom, humor, isolation, mischief, and social commentary that encompassed all aspects of daily life.

Transitions from sacred spirituals to secular African-American blues and "jazz" forms are difficult to understand if we fail to realize that not only were the musical vocabularies of these various genres closely related, but the spirit of the expression was also essentially the same. A related range of emotional dynamics, rhythmic vitality, and modified Africanisms are found in many African-American musical settings. According to Alain Locke, in the jubilation of the camp meeting the dividing line between the spiritual and ragtime became almost completely blurred: "For then we have approximately the same contrast between the stately spiritual chorale and the jubilant spiritual camp meeting shout in the religious music that in the secular music we have between the slow swaying melancholy blues and the skipping rag and fast-rocking jazz."[25]

The sexual associations that were established between "jazz" and "lewd" women—a result of the environments in which early professional African-American musicians were employed—forged unfortunate stereotypes within American culture. It was difficult for musicians to escape those stigmas.

Many African-American women developed their musical skills on piano and voice in the church. Some European-American women formed successful minstrel groups during the nineteenth century, although this usually involved some form of sexual exploitation. Finding professional work as an African-American woman instrumentalist in a minstrel show was difficult until after the Civil War. Despite difficulties they encountered, certain African-American women barnstormed their way through the South, making appearances at carnivals, working in tents, performing at circuses, or displaying their talents in theaters just as did other European-American minstrels of the period.

Many women performed in routines with men. Ma Rainey's mother was a stage performer after Reconstruction. Around 1900 a pianist by the name of Edythe Turnham began to develop a reputation in minstrel shows. By 1902 the "Mother of the Blues" herself (Ma Rainey) was using the stage to create an incipient form of the traditional blues style.

Sidney Bechet and the Early Transition from Clarinet to Saxophone

At the turn of the century the primary "jazz" woodwind was the clarinet. The names Johnny Dodds, Lorenzo Tio, "Big Eye" Louis Nelson, and

Alphonse Picou were among early performers of note in the New Orleans clarinet tradition. Also prominent during the early period of "jazz" development was the great New Orleans cornet/trumpet style as established by Buddy Bolden, Freddie Keppard, and Bunk Johnson (the last of the three would spark a revival in the 1940s). With the emergence of Joe "King" Oliver and especially Louis Armstrong, the trumpet later remained in the vanguard of "jazz" innovation until the late thirties.

Around 1919 a new feature instrument appeared which gradually supplanted both the clarinet as the primary "jazz" woodwind and the trumpet as the centerpiece of innovation. The ascent of the saxophone changed the course of "jazz" forever. Its unique dual nature as both a brass and woodwind instrument allowed it to easily absorb elements of both the clarinet and trumpet tradition.

Adolph Sax, a Belgian instrument maker, invented the saxophone; he patented it on June 22, 1846. Sax won a gold medal at the Paris Industrial Exhibition in 1859 for his invention. After further experimentation and improvements, the saxophone was utilized in European military bands. It was primarily through this tradition that the saxophone made its way to America. The use of the saxophone in concert bands and vaudeville programs included shows such as the famous Brown Brothers, a group that featured six saxophones. But aside from Ibert, Ravel, and Bizet, "serious" European composers virtually ignored the saxophone.

Sidney Bechet (1897–1959) was one of the musicians responsible for the popularity of the saxophone in "jazz" and dance bands. In his recordings, Bechet (originally a New Orleans clarinetist) can be heard contributing to the transition from the prominent New Orleans clarinet style into the evolution of the soprano saxophone. Earlier in his career, until he was twenty, Bechet played cornet. He was attracted to the brass instruments and spent his formative years with New Orleans brass men Freddie Keppard and King Oliver. His musical contemporary, Louis Armstrong, especially influenced him. In examining Bechet's musical contribution, we sense an instrumentalist who apparently became stifled by the limitations of the clarinet. Although Bechet continued to play clarinet throughout his career, his frustration with that instrument led him to acquire his first soprano saxophone in London about 1919.

Sidney Bechet's early musical reputation was gained as a soloist rather than as an ensemble player. In fact, he was often criticized for "stepping on the cornet's lines," prompting author Rudi Blesh to claim that "Sidney was a cornetist without a cornet." With the soprano saxophone, he had the means to satisfy his desire to have a more brass-oriented instrument, capable of confronting the trumpet, yet retaining the supple versatility and fluidity of the clarinet. Bechet's style was characterized by wide vibrato (typical of early New Orleans clarinet style), forceful melodic lines and through a sustained rhythmic equanimity and intensity similar to that employed by Armstrong. A good example of these inclinations can be heard on his performance of "Hindustan," recorded in the late 1930s on the Commodore label. (Bechet's horn practically obfuscates Wild Bill Davison's musical contribution, thus justifying the "stepping on the trumpet line" criticism.)

Bechet's initial assault on the primacy of the trumpet as the original "jazz" centerpiece was continued through the work of saxophonists Johnny Hodges, Willie Smith, and Pete Brown. The culmination of this ascendancy was realized in the saxophone style of Coleman Hawkins and his contemporaries. The soprano saxophone, however, would remain a rarity until the late fifties when Steve Lacy, Pony Poindexter, Lucky Thompson, and, most important, John Coltrane adopted the instrument.

Bechet's most notable influence was largely with the realm of tone quality. Another saxophonist, Frankie Trumbauer, also produced a timbre and approach that found further development with the alto soloing of Benny Carter and, to an extent, Johnny Hodges. Hodges declared, "the only models for developing saxophonists when I was young were Sidney Bechet and Frankie." Later, Lester Young not only influenced the saxophone's timbre conception but revolutionized most of the harmonics and harmonic thinking regarding the capabilities of the instrument. The subtlety of Young's limpid approach was adopted by Miles Davis, Lee Konitz, Stan Getz, Lennie Tristano and the whole West Coast "cool" school of "jazz" in the fifties.

Evolution of the Early Piano

It is impossible to present a complete history of "jazz" piano innovation here. We can only discuss some of the legendary innovators of the first half of the twentieth century who were responsible for the piano's impact on the musical development of America.

Both the blackface minstrelsy and the ragtime phenomenon were important contributors to the rise of "jazz" in New Orleans. Barrelhouse styles found their way into the tenderloin district of the Crescent City. Most of the early performers who traversed the mining camps and lumber camps playing this vivacious music were not documented. Nevertheless, the barrelhouse players anticipated the emergence of ragtime, "jazz," and blues styles in New Orleans. Using elements of the early piano styles, Jelly Roll Morton, Tony Jackson, James White, Buddy Carter, and other musicians transformed late stages of ragtime into early polyphonic "jazz."

Many African Americans did not gain general access to the piano until after Reconstruction. The self-taught composers and players at that time frequently emulated devices currently used by marching bands. The left hand would frequently play octaves (as well as other perfect intervals) and single notes in the bass register (mimicking the tuba, usually on beats one and three). Triads and occasional dominant seventh chords were played alternately on beats two and four. Another device involved the execution of repetitive left-hand chords, which supported linear right-hand syncopation.

During ragtime's formative years, marching bands were some of the most popular ensembles in America. Unlike strophic form (repeated with only the lyrics changing on each repetition), marches were written in sectional forms (a succession of contrasting sections). Rounded sectional forms bring back the initial theme after a contrasting section. This form often divides a march into two main parts. The second half of this type of march is called a trio (ABA—CDC). Other additive sectional marches do not engage in "rounding off" but keep introducing new material in each section (ABCD etc.)

Ragtime pianists borrowed these forms and rondo form (ABACA) for sectional compositions. The phrase structures of both marches and ragtime relied upon blocks of systematic repetition. The beat was most often subdivided into multiples of two. (In other words, the quarter notes in duple meter were subdivided evenly into two, four, or eight parts.) The metronomic tempo of ragtime was generally moderate and most of the left-hand rhythms consisted of two-step "oompah" bass lines (later referred to as "stride piano"). This style also involved syncopated right-hand melodies. There were no stylized "swing" elements, as we know them today. Nevertheless, some listeners found ragtime's exuberant feeling fresh and innovative. Others thought it was degenerate because it was "too syncopated" and often had sexually explicit lyrics. It was also much too African for many people. Ragtime pianist Eubie Blake understood the subtle connection between ragtime and African music. His ragtime album entitled, *The Sounds of Africa*, reflects his attempt to make that connection.

Despite a flirtation with lyrics, ragtime was a notated instrumental style that focused primarily upon the piano. Melodies became syncopated through the use of tied notes, anticipations, and delayed attacks (on the upbeat). As ragtime developed, the use of polyrhythmic effects eventually came into play. For instance, superimposing three against four (a hemiola) created an effect that temporarily obscured the prevailing meter and the common duple rhythmic division of common time. In other rags, two rhythms of different phrase lengths but made up of related or identical melodic ingredients were superimposed over a steady bass line as a metrical experiment. In a group of twelve sixteenth notes, for example, repeating a three-note (as opposed to a four-note) pattern four times in a row could shift the accent. Consequently, each new pattern appeared in a new metric context. Most rags were written in a sixteen-bar form, starting with the tonic and then moving to the dominant after the first set of sixteen bars. Ragtime foreshadowed the emergence of both stride and swing styles.

Listening to Scott Joplin's "Maple Leaf Rag" (as performed on a 1916 piano roll) and comparing his version to Jelly Roll Morton's later interpretation will introduce the listener to some of the subtle changes that separate ragtime from other "jazz" forms. Joplin's performance is a strict and regular interpretation of his own notated sheet music. The form is basically sectional and additive (AABBACCDD), and each section is exactly sixteen measures in length. The form of Jelly Roll Morton's version of "Maple Leaf Rag" is more truncated (ABACCD) and introduces a more elaborate left hand that is not restricted to oompah bass figures. A higher level of syncopation is incorporated into the Morton rendition, and a swing feel is more pronounced than in Joplin's version. Morton feels free to embellish the melody with trills and turns that are influenced by the New Orleans clarinet tradition. He also takes liberties in transposing melodic patterns and modifying rhythmic patterns to provide greater variety. One of the most important aspects of Morton's interpretation is his improvisation on the melody and harmonies of the piece. The sum total of these innovations led Morton to resent the claims of radio personality Robert Ripley and others who suggested that W. C. Handy was the "originator of jazz and the blues." In a letter to *Down Beat* magazine Morton said, "I myself happened to be the creator of jazz in the year of 1902."[26]

The younger "jazz" musicians began to wander across America just as the ragtime pianists before them had done. The high unemployment rate in the South after the First World War sent many African-American workers to Chicago. Musicians were a part of this movement. In the same working-class ghettos that attracted rural instrumentalists and blues singers, the boogie-woogie piano style also found fertile ground. Other "jazz" musicians soon found room to evolve there. Musicians like Louis Armstrong moved the music from a collective style of combo playing to an approach that emphasized individual virtuosity. Jelly Roll Morton imposed a new level of compositional discipline upon the vitality of New Orleans–style combo playing. Both of these trends would alter the direction of "jazz" throughout America.

Morton introduced the ratio of 3:1 between notes for rhythmic patterns (the quasi-12/8 feeling) and developed this rhythmic feel in his ragtime band. A comparison of Morton's original 1923 solo piano recording of "Grandpa's Spells" with his 1926 version of that song with his Red Hot Peppers demonstrates further musical evolution into a new "jazz" style. The earlier piano version retains many ragtime elements. His ensemble version reflects many of the New Orleans Dixieland "jazz" elements that would soon become common. The most notable of these elements lies in the textures of the two versions. The solo piano performance has an accompaniment that is primarily homophonic in nature and the improvisation involved is generally an embellishment of the melody. The Red Hot Peppers' version is orchestrated to allow for a greater degree of textural variety than a pianist could accomplish alone. After the four-measure introduction there is a stop-time break that features guitarist Johnny St. Cyr; this too was a new formal device. Polyphonic texture occurs as several simultaneous melodies are played at once. The musicians also improvise over the basic framework of the tune. There are solo sections and tutti sections (all players performing) providing variety in texture. The trumpet, clarinet, and trombone are stratified in such a way that their independent stylized roles contribute equally to the polyphonic mosaic that unfolds above the rhythm section. This type of structuring would become a hallmark New Orleans Dixieland "jazz" style.

Willie "The Lion" Smith (1897–1973), James P. Johnson (1894–1955), and other musicians developed left-hand innovations which became known as "Harlem piano" or "stride piano" by the 1920s. This technique consists of playing a single note deep in the bass, then "striding" up to a chord in the middle of the keyboard. It differs from the stride of the ragtime pianists in its degree of departure from the I–V tuba patterns. The newer technique enabled the player to use a more sophisticated left-hand harmony, more harmonic inversions, and a more complex chromatic root movement. James P. Johnson was the mentor of both Fats Waller and Willie "The Lion" Smith. Early recordings by Fats Waller are instructive demonstrations representing early stride style. Ellington was also influenced by James P. Johnson and remembered performances involving these innovative pianists:

Later, when I showed up in New York, I found [James P. Johnson] there. . . . He'd written the show *Running Wild*—not the tune but the show—and that's where the "Charleston" was born. So he wasn't hungry. But he never lost contact with his foundations, with the real, wonderful people in Harlem. Harlem had its own rich, special folklore, totally unrelated to the South or anywhere else. It's gone now, but it was tremendous then.

So there in that atmosphere I became one of the close disciples of the James P. Johnson style. Some nights we'd wind up—James, Fats Waller, Sonny Greer, and I—and go down to Mexico's to hear The Lion. I was working and would buy a drink. . . . So we would sit around, and during intermission I would move over to the piano. Then it would be Fats. Perhaps he'd play "Ivie." . . . Afterwards, he'd look over his shoulder jovially at James and call, "Come on, take the next chorus!" Before you knew it, James had played about thirty choruses, each one different, each one with a different theme.

By then The Lion would be stirred up. James had moved into his territory and was challenging. "Get up and I'll show you how it's supposed to be done," he'd say. Then, one after the other, over and over again they'd play, and it seemed as though you never heard the same note twice.[27]

It is not difficult to become confused by the parallels between ragtime, stride, and swing piano. The oompah bass pattern can occur in all three styles, but the degree of dominance and the musical context in which it occurs are altered with each style. Pianists like Mary Lou Williams and Jaki Byard would eventually mix elements of boogie-woogie and walking bass lines with stride patterns. As mentioned, the main innovations of ragtime were the use of syncopation in the right hand, and the emphasis of beats two and four in the left hand, which created a polyrhythmic effect (but failed to produce a legitimate "swing" feel). To a degree this is also true of stride, but now eighth notes were played in a long-short "swing" style.

Duke Ellington was among the seminal modernists (including Earl Hines and Art Tatum) whose influence helped shape contemporary "jazz." Ellington's roots began when the piano was the main source of musical entertainment in American homes. Ellington, like most "ticklers" of his time, developed his own personal style after mastering James P. Johnson's "Carolina Shout" and other compositions he learned from piano rolls.[28] He belonged to the school of "stride" pianists whose function (like that of the early barrelhouse pianist) was to create the illusion that an entire band was represented in their playing. His reputation grew as a composer and arranger whose orchestrations redefined American music in dramatic ways. Although his compositional skill overshadowed his prowess as a pianist, Ellington's performance style on piano is one of the most distinctive and instantly identifiable in "jazz."

One of the most influential innovators of early "jazz" was Earl Hines, whose style upset traditional notions of "jazz" piano in the late twenties. An extraordinary trailblazer, Hines had a significant effect on Art Tatum, Bud Powell, and other influential musicians. The great force with which he played actually broke a few piano strings during some of his performances. Hines was one of the first musicians to employ hornlike piano solo phrasing in his right-hand technique. These characteristics were undoubtedly due in part to his close association with Louis Armstrong. The epic series of records they made together demonstrates Armstrong's soaring trumpet lines (which influenced all subsequent "jazz" performers, vocal and instrumental) and Hines's impressive keyboard counterpoint. It sounded as though Hines was attempting to make his melodies breathe through the piano as they might through a trumpet.

Hines frequently used octave doublings, and his rhythmic approach was more flexible than that of ragtime pianists. He also employed walking tenths and surprising offbeat left-hand patterns that surfaced intermittently to shape his melodies. He was also one of the earliest pianists to diminish the significance of the characteristic oompah left-handed stride pattern and to periodically engage in the complete elimination of the left hand. After the active role of the left hand in the early ragtime and boogie-woogie piano playing, these were dramatic musical departures. His "classical" touch supported futuristic harmonic and rhythmic ideas.

Hines became a living legend during his lifetime. Although elements of his impressive piano style (developed during the late 1920s) remained virtually intact throughout his career, he continually refined and polished his technique. The incisive single-note "trumpet sound" in his right hand was mixed with a dynamic application of octaves, tremolos, and other melodic embellishments. Hines also led some of the best big bands in America during the golden era of coast-to-coast live "jazz" broadcasts.

Other keyboard innovators who began to evolve around this time were the blues-based piano stylists. Of the various forms of blues (rural, classic, folk, southern, urban, etc.), one of the most distinctive is boogie-woogie. The left hand first played repeated simple chords but later took on horizontal driving rhythms. The right hand played its hornlike "leads" based upon the blues scale-tones. Initially a simple walking line in the left hand used a rhythmic style that emphasized the weak beats of the measure. Eventually this emphasis became more emphatic with the use of dotted notes. Other kinds of boogie involved more agitated rhythms. Instead of the typical sixteen-bar rag form, blues frequently used the twelve-bar form developed by the classic blues singers. Boogie's affect on rhythm and blues became apparent beginning with one of the progenitors of that style, saxophonist/vocalist Louis Jordan.

Boogie-woogie is at once a jubilant, passionate, and virtuoso style of piano blues. Some people claim it was derived from the sound of the steam locomotive. Others say it evolved from a quickening and expansion of the blues development in the lower Mississippi River area. Regardless of where it originated, authentic boogie-woogie players were well aware of the value of the art form they were advancing. Playing boogie-woogie required a technical precision, discipline, and endurance that only the finest pianists could sustain. Yet, like other styles of "jazz," the term "boogie" was often used as a euphemism for sex. The lyrics are revealing: "Nobody can boogie like my man [or woman] can" and "I boogied all night, all the night before, / When I woke up this morning I want to boogie some more."

Others claim that boogie-woogie was born in juke joints, honky tonks, barrelhouses, and gutbucket cabarets. Like barrelhouse styles, boogie-woogie was played by itinerant pianists for lumberjacks and levee workers. Consequently, history usually describes the boogie-woogie milieu as a man's domain; yet women were always instrumental contributors throughout its development.

Sippie Wallace (1898–1986) was a Texas blues shouter and pianist who performed boogie-woogie in a brothel (commonly referred to as a "boogie house" early this century). Her first recording was made in 1923 with Eddie Heywood, and she recorded with Clarence Williams the following year. Throughout the 1920s she worked with King Oliver, Louis Armstrong, and Perry Bradford's Jazz Phools. She got her younger brother, Hersal Thomas, a job playing in a boogie house, and he eventually became one of the greatest of the early barrelhouse pianists. Her older brother, George, was a pit pianist in Houston and composed "New Orleans Hop Scop Blues" in 1911. That song, with its boogie-woogie bass line, became one of Bessie Smith's big hits twenty years later. In 1983 Wallace was nominated for a Grammy for her album "Sippie."

Boogie-woogie may be loosely derived from an African style of hocket singing hoisted over vigorous drum patterns. Boogie-woogie involves the right hand improvising melodic, motivic, or rhythmic lines over a continually ascending and descending blues-oriented bass pattern in the left hand. As the musical momentum builds, the right hand often progresses to create cross-rhythms and heavily syncopated chords. Its melodic variations, speed and intensity make it the most colorful and flamboyant blues-based piano style. Blues great T-Bone Walker (guitarist) remembers being exposed to boogie-woogie through listening to women pianists in church when he was young: "The first time I heard a boogie woogie piano was the first time I went to church. That was the Holy Ghost Church of Dallas Texas. That boogie-woogie was a kind of blues, I guess."[29]

Boogie-woogie was formalized on the South Side of Chicago during Prohibition. People who could not afford to go to speakeasies, created private parties in their homes for dancing, drinking, and gambling. These social functions were called "rent parties," "skiffles," "boogies," "shakes," "parlor socials," or "percolators." Lil Hardin Armstrong played boogie-woogie in Chicago before her soon-to-be husband, Louis Armstrong, arrived to join King Oliver's Creole Jazz Band. A well-trained musician, Hardin taught Louis quite a bit about music and life as a professional musician after they were married in 1924. "Miss Lil" loved boogie piano and performed her particular stylistic approach for over forty years.

The lines separating boogie-woogie, blues, and ragtime are not as clearly defined as one might think. African-American barrelhouse pianists were heard performing all three styles. Likewise, New Orleans style and the Dixieland style (alternately referred to as "Chicago-style jazz") do not have absolutely definitive distinctions. Either style was performed with two-beat or four-beat emphasis. The use of clarinet and saxophone, the interchangeable guitar or banjo configuration, in addition to the use of polyphony and related formal ingredients (introduction, coda, section form, etc.), were traits that could be found in either style as well.

The stylistic characteristics of boogie-woogie became clearly defined around 1918 in New Orleans. Jimmy Yancey (the "father of boogie," c. 1894–1951), one of boogie-woogie's most prominent pioneers, began performing his new style in Chicago in 1915. In 1938, other pioneers influenced by Yancey, such as Meade "Lux" Lewis, Albert Ammons, and Pete Johnson, presented a milestone boogie concert in Carnegie Hall in New York City. Yancey performed in the same hall in 1948. Clarence "Pinetop" Smith (1904–29) became another popular performer and a key innovator of the style. Smith worked on the TOBA circuit during the 1920s, but his composition "Pinetop's Boogie-Woogie" became popular only after he was shot to death. Although he missed the boogie-woogie boom by a decade, Smith is credited for the name of his eight-to-the-bar style.

Other influential pianists of the first half of the twentieth century include Count Basie and Art Tatum. Basie started out as a stride pianist who, like other pianists trained in that style, often accompanied silent films. During the 1940s some of his idiosyncratic characteristics had firmly matured, such as his trademark "plink plink" chords on the higher keys suspended over moments of silence and his classic economical piano comping style. While soloing, he emphasized silence to pace his melodic lines while his unusually gentle, but well groomed, rhythm section gained space to be clearly heard. His touch was unpredictable, light, and precise. Unlike some earlier pianists, Basie did not rely on the more assertive qualities of the piano. Because his musical timing was excellent, "less became more" in his approach to the keyboard. He stressed all four beats fairly evenly, and his bands created a "groove" that generated a free-floating feeling. His main innovations, however, included the invention of a novel comping style and the stylistic codification of the modern rhythm section. Basie developed the skill of "feeding chords" to solo performers, elevating the level of intensity and increasing the flexibility of the underlying harmonic structure. His accompaniment for Carl Smith and other early woodwind soloists are among the first examples of comping style on record.

Mary Lou Williams started her professional career in vaudeville when she was fifteen years old. Her career as a performer, leader, and composer spans almost sixty years. She accompanied the minstrel team of Seymour and Jeanette in 1925. Later, after marrying alto saxophonist John Williams, she joined Andy Kirk's Clouds of Joy in 1929 as an arranger. At the time she joined his band, Kirk already had a pianist, but Williams soon won the piano chair in the band nonetheless. She also served as the ensemble's musical director and remained its chief composer/arranger. After divorcing John Williams, she moved to New York to join the new bebop scene in 1941. She married trumpeter Harold "Shorty" Baker and formed a band with him. When the band and marriage failed, she launched her successful solo piano career. When not involved in solo performances, she wrote compositions for Duke Ellington, Benny Goodman, and others.[30] Williams's symphonic composition *The Zodiac Suite* was performed by the New York Philharmonic at Town Hall in 1945, rendering her the first "jazz" musician to be honored by this musical establishment with such a concert.

Williams's eclectic piano style reflects the entire range of "jazz" history from its early days into the avant-garde. In addition to the influences of boogie-woogie, blues, and Earl Hines, she thoroughly absorbed the bebop language. Thelonious Monk, Bud Powell, Tadd Dameron, and other young piano "Turks" often sought her counsel and encouragement. The 1950s proved a major transitional period for Williams. After living in England and Paris for a couple years, she returned to the United States a devout Catholic and firmly converted to religious music. Duke Ellington sums up her contribution to "jazz" evolution: "Mary Lou Williams is a perpetual contemporary. Her music retains a standard of quality that is timeless."

Through the skill and genius of innovative solo pianists, like Earl Hines and Art Tatum, the "jazz" piano emerged as a powerful "orchestral" instrument, placing many distinct sonic layers at their fingertips. Art Tatum (1909–56) consolidated traditional stylistic features into his own fascinating musical system. Pianists from Thelonious Monk to Vladimir Horowitz acknowledge that Tatum is a towering figure on piano ("jazz" or otherwise).[31] He was a harbinger of the musical future. One of Tatum's magnificent contributions to left-hand accompaniment was his use of the scale-tone seventh chord with the third displaced up one octave (C-Bb-E). The harmonic richness of Tatum's left-hand style beautifully supported his dazzling melodic improvisations of his right hand.

Tatum was one of the most amazing pianists in "jazz" history. His style merged Count Basie's stride style with the hornlike soloing of Earl Hines, and his ambidextrous technical mastery of the piano left all his peers spellbound. Tatum's flexibility of tempo and his long, fast, symmetrical runs (that sometimes converged upon each other) supported inventive techniques that remain unsurpassed. He was a master of applying spontaneous alterations and chord substitutions to popular tunes. His method of modulating (changing keys) several times within a phrase, and gradually resolving systematically to the original key, served as a model for the harmonic advances that evolved during the bebop era. Many pianists sought to emulate his cascading right-hand runs and patterns in subsequent eras. Art Tatum remains the standard by which other pianists are judged.

Dorothy Donegan (1929–1998) had Tatum as her pianist mentor, and her ambidextrous virtuoso style reflects his influence. Moreover, her playing displays her own unique "postmodern" approach. Donegan based her style upon the absorption of an enormous scope of songs and musical genres. She was adept at performing both European concert piano repertoire and a wide range of twentieth-century African-American improvisational styles. Elements of Bach's "*Goldberg* Variations" or a phrase from a Rachmaninoff composition were likely to surface cleverly embroidered in one of her performances, amid elements of Fats Waller's or Earl Hines's styles. The fearless verve of her boogie-woogie left hand, matched with flawless execution, rendered Donegan capable of adapting any composer's message to fit her own sensibilities.

Donegan's eclectic performances were always unpredictable. She might have begun with a quiet ballad that suddenly burst into an energetic rendition of a Scott Joplin rag. The ragtime mood might then move skillfully toward rhythms and harmonies that suggest Monk's "outside" approach. This might then slide into a chorus or two of "'Round Midnight" before returning to the ballad with which she began her musical journey. Her stamina and self-confidence allowed her to perform several sets a night all over the world throughout her long and illustrious career. When asked about her high level of energy Donegan stated resolutely: "I do have that incredible stamina and power and great pyrotechnics and technical skill. But I lead a clean life, and I get a lot of rest, and I don't smoke or drink or use narcotics. I've always had that power. When I was eight years old I used to play baseball. I used to bat the ball over the fence on the South Side of Chicago. I think God gave me something a little extra."[32]

Dorothy Donegan was never a "cutesy cooed" female. She has always been independent, assertive and commanding, and was in demand throughout the world. The Embers (a nightclub-restaurant on New York's East 54th Street) offered Donegan an unprecedented contract calling for her services several weeks a year for ten years. She also ran her own "jazz" club in Los Angeles. Her unrestricted genius and eclectic playing has made her style hard to pin down, much to her critics' frustration or chagrin.

Some male musicians seemed intimidated by her music. Oscar Peterson reportedly refused to play on the same bill with her if she used her trio. George Shearing would not allow her to play on a concert stage with him under any conditions. Nevertheless, Count Basie, Dizzy Gillespie, and Duke Ellington played with her and acknowledged her talent and importance to the evolution of music. Phineas Newborn admits that he too greatly admired her.[33]

Donegan, Peterson, and Newborn each retained the sheer brilliance and virtuosity of Tatum's piano playing. These innovators were capable of sustaining musical interest and variety over the course of an entire evening, without the aid of a bassist or drummer. Peterson pursued Tatum's aesthetics and managed to obtain command of a full range of orchestral effects on the piano as a solo performer, thus entering a level of virtuosity that only Tatum himself had enjoyed. Newborn, like Tatum, was also fond of taking standard tunes and drastically re-harmonizing the melodies.

In a 1956 review of Newborn's first album, Ralph Gleason wrote in *Down Beat*: "He is one of the most impressive pianists to emerge in recent years, a gifted technician, a startling improviser, and a musician with well-developed harmonic and rhythmic sense. Newborn will clearly grow in stature. He has a command of the instrument to make other pianists weep, and an ability to say whatever he wishes."

After 1940 the need arose for piano styles that were more conducive to modern ensemble situations. An innovator involved in pioneering this revolutionary new piano style was Bud Powell. Powell reduced Tatum's scale-tone tenths to smaller "shells" of thirds and sevenths. He also placed less emphasis on the elaborate left-handed contributions of Tatum's solo style. This was a necessary adaptation for the bebop ensemble context. As a result, Powell virtually eliminated the stride application and comping chord patterns employed by many swing pianists of the previous generation.

Despite such transformations, Powell retained use of certain Tatum, Hines, and Basie influences in the creation of a modern "jazz" piano style. As an alternative to a steady pattern, Powell's left hand played brief two- or three-note chords at irregular intervals. This sparse comping style was even more exiguous than Basie's swing era piano style. Harmonic emphasis was minimized. This was the antithesis of some earlier piano conceptions, where musicians aspired to create a bigger sound through building broader chords. Sometimes Powell's comping chords were sustained, and sometimes none were played at all. Powell took Basie's notion of supplying chords for the soloist and expanded it a step further. Certain rhythmic and harmonic responsibilities were switched from the left hand to the right-handed improvised line. The left-handed harmonic shells, utilizing the interval of a minor seventh without thirds, left the tonality highly ambiguous. The responsibility of dictating more detailed chord qualities was then assigned to the right hand. This also allowed the modern pianist to keep up with the faster harmonic pacing of the prevailing period more adeptly.

Of all the Bop pianists, composer Thelonious Monk (1917–82), a major contributor to bebop composition and performance style, was the most eccentric. His compositions are among the most challenging and beautiful of the bebop and hard bop eras. Monk's melodies have unique symmetry and are often supported by colorful accentuation at irregular intervals. His composition "Straight, No Chaser" uses a single phrase, based upon a five-note motive that is rhythmically transformed subtly and continuously, giving rise to a series of rhythmic variations on the chromatic phrase. Its incessant accents fall on different parts of the measures to create a wonderful effect. Like Basie, Monk can fashion masterpieces out of musical economy and simplicity. He can keep the listener off balance. Some of his compositions begin on a weak beat and involve subsequent entrances that are rhythmically and melodically unpredictable (especially during his improvisational sections). Other pieces contain harmonic pacing that can use four or more chords in a single measure.

Monk is known for his use of cluster tones. These involve dissonant chords, which do not resolve to the consonant ones anticipated. Combined with his unique rhythmic style, such characteristics surprise the listener's ear in a pleasing manner. His lean and mysterious style often dwell within the lower register of the keyboard for long periods of time. He explored the piano as a percussive, harmonic, and melodic instrument. Monk's contributions to "jazz" would influence the next wave of "jazz" pianists.

"Jazz" gained a reputation as an "outlaw" music because of its unconventional conceptual approaches, fingerings, timbre, harmony, and novel musical elements. Some people (preferring more conventional approaches) failed to appreciate its subtleties, sophistication and artistic significance. Listeners and critics had a particularly difficult time accepting Monk's stylistic approach. Nevertheless, Count Basie, Coleman Hawkins, Charlie Christian, Dizzy Gillespie, and other musicians appreciated Monk's innovative and revolutionary contributions. They recognized the uncompromising Africanisms present in his piano style; qualities that seemed to revolt against the revolutionary rules of Bud Powell and other boppers. Monk's iconoclastic musical behavior was firmly grounded in the stride style of Fats Waller and James P.

Johnson, despite his seemingly neoteric traits. His ear for personal melodies and harmonies led him down a path beyond the limitations of even temperament. Monk set out to discover ways "to play within the cracks" (i.e., between the keyboard's chromatic keys).

Not all pianists during the 1940s were focused upon bebop innovations. Erroll Garner (1921–77) developed a startling piano style that shared Monk's interest in "playing between the cracks" while emphasizing danceable and infectious "grooves." His style was infused with an accessibility that reached beyond esoteric bebop audiences to reach mainstream audiences. Garner's approach formed a link between bebop and a broader "jazz" audience. His beautiful ballad "Misty" is an example of the timelessness and ecumenical quality of his compositions. He worked with Slam Stewart between 1944 and 1945 but otherwise generally performed as a soloist or as a leader of his own trio.

In the mid 1940s Milt Buckner (1916–77), a "jazz" pianist, organist, and arranger, developed a locked-hand position, producing blocked chording and harmonized melodic "planing" that managed to create interesting harmonies with both hands. Buckner would take a four-note chord, play the melody with the right hand on top, and use the left hand to double the melody one octave lower. Buckner's treatment of the melody in the tune "Pick Yourself Up" is illustrative of this technique. This stylistic innovation first developed by Buckner was later popularized by George Shearing (b. 1919) around 1949. The George Shearing Quintet featured not only piano but also guitar and vibes. Both the guitar and vibraphone imitated Shearing's locked-hands style. This blocked style was reminiscent of the scoring for winds used by composers and arrangers during the swing era.

The technical innovations of Horace Silver (b. 1928) in the early 1950s were, for some critics, un-pianistic. His style involved a strong wrist stroke, which emphasized blue notes as strategically positioned rhythmic and melodic accents that suggested a "soulful" and driving piano style, which became appropriately known as "funky" piano. The 1955 recording of "The Preacher" with Art Blakey and The Jazz Messengers was one of the period's first soul hits. Silver's contributions as a "funky" sideman were valuable to Miles Davis and other leaders. Silver's influence on piano giant Oscar Peterson is clear on Peterson's recordings of "Take the 'A' Train" in the late 1950s. Pianist Gene Harris (b. 1933) also used Silver-influenced funky devices in Ellington's "In a Mellow Tone" during the same period.

Pianist Amad Jamal (b. 1930) is a master of developing long lyrical melodic lines. Miles Davis, and other musicians working toward a more lyrical style of playing, appreciated the clarity and economy of his playing. His ability to swing hard and his absolute control of the metrical pulse at all tempos produce an exceptionally free style of phrasing. His attention to layers of musical stratification neutralizes distinctions between musical elements of foreground, middle ground, and background throughout the developmental course of his improvisations. Jamal's musical excursions into exploration of formal devices and compositional structure employ linear development, harmonic expansions and substitution, motivic exploitation, textural and timbre experiments, as well as flirtations with time and tempo. Like all masters of

African-American music, Jamal is a perennial student of the entire evolutionary tradition of "jazz," and one of its finest innovators.

One of the musical contributions of pianist Bill Evans (1929–80) during the 1960s was his subtle left-hand voicing. Evans often omitted certain chord tones, especially the root, and expanded his chord voicing by adding extensions of ninths, elevenths, and thirteenths to provide more transparent textures. His musical style was vaguely reminiscent of Debussy's turn-of-the-century Impressionism. Such harmonic extensions were introduced and exhaustively explored by earlier pianists such as Tatum and some bebop innovators. Yet, Evans's approach reflected a more restrained European sensibility, akin to styles introduced by West Coast "cool" and "progressive jazz" players before him.

Politics and the Twentieth-Century African-American Church on the Eve of the Harlem Renaissance

Little has been written about "Black" Holiness and Pentecostal churches, and their distinctive contributions to the development of "Black" Christianity in America and overseas. Recent studies show that these religious denominations grew rapidly from the end of Reconstruction through the Great Depression, and made a particularly strong impression upon the African-American lower class.[34] Other members of the working-class African-American community did not feel restrained by any particular church. Garveyism was a movement born of certain religious attributes of converging and polarizing aspects of black religion and radicalism.[35]

> It was ripe for the kind of leadership that could transmute the radical impulses of the folk religious tradition, with its attenuated African background, into a way of self-actualization that would bypass the value system of "whites" and erect an alternative style—a way of diminishing the injustices and frustrations of second-class citizenship and poverty through "black" empowerment, consciousness and nationalism. That leadership came, first of all, from Marcus Garvey.[36]

Despite the divisions within the African-American community that slave-era brutality caused, close relations between global African music and social politics remained remarkably intact. Similar struggles produce affinity. It is not surprising, therefore, that ties exist between "jazz," Garvey,[37] and the Harlem Renaissance. Ted Vincent points out:

> Regrettably, the involvement in the jazz revolution on the part of Garvey and his organization has been overlooked, denied and rejected. There are a number of reasons for this neglect.

> From the Westernised view that separates mind from body and seriousness from fun, one would not expect the playfulness and

individuality of the jazz scene to fit in with the intense para-military regimentation associated with the Garvey Movement. The UNIA [Universal Negro Improvement Association] was noted for its uniformed African Legions and their snappy marching steps; for its uniformed Police Force; its uniformed Black Cross Nurses; for its polite but firm uniformed monitors at meetings; and for the seriousness of its purpose—African Liberation.

Recently-arrived West Indian immigrants composed a majority of the Garveyites in the United States during the UNIA's growing years of 1917–21. During this "acculturation" period a test of Garveyite interest in "jazzy" music would have to include a look at their members' relationship to the "hot" music from the islands, such as Trinidadian calypso.

Little research has been done, for example, on Lovey's Trinidad Band and on the West Indian calypso and ragtime musician Lionel Belasco, of Belasco's Latin American Orchestra, two of the groups advertised in the Negro World during its first year.[38] What little is known of Lovey and Belasco suggests they were as innovative as the African-American jazz artists. According to jazz researcher Donald R. Hill, the recording session in New York on 20 June 1912 by Lovey's Trinidad Band marked "the first 'hot' music from any English-speaking country on record." Belasco, a Trinidadian of Black and Sephardic Jewish descent, is said to have produced some of the earliest ragtime recordings by a Black artist and was a popular band-leader in New York throughout the 1920s.[39]

Garvey was born in Jamaica (on August 17, 1887) to parents who were members of the Wesleyan Methodist Church. Roman Catholicism interested Garvey, and his children were baptized in the "High-Church" tradition later in life. Reverend W. H. Sloely and Reverend P. A. Conahan tutored him as a young adult, and he attended church services regularly in Kingston. There he learned the art of elocution and platform decorum from various preachers.[40] When he was eighteen years old, he was employed as the manager of a printing company and tutored young persons in public speaking in his spare time.

Publication of Garvey's periodical the *Negro World* spurred masses of Global Africans caught up in the poverty and despair of the ghetto. They were motivated by the incisiveness of his writing and speeches. His statistics indicated that by June 1919 the UNIA had reached a membership of over two million. Although his claims have not been firmly substantiated, "such a figure may be close to the truth for there is little doubt that he led the largest and most successful mass movement of blacks in the history of the United States."[41] The growing trend toward African-American independence would have a noticeable impact on the music of the "Roaring Twenties." Traditions that had been firmly established during the first decade of the twentieth century would be stretched and challenged in the subsequent decade.

Notes

[1] Liner notes from McIntyre's album *Home*, Steeple Chase SCS-1039 (1975). McIntyre plays alto sax, flute, oboe, bassoon, and bass clarinet on this recording.

[2] Ibid., p. 83.

[3] Joe Papaleo's comments in Sean Killeen, "Lead Belly and Sarah Lawrence," *Lead Belly Letter*, Spring/Summer 1992.

[4] "Okeh" means "it is so" or "so be it" in Chocktaw.

[5] Sally Placksin, *Jazzwomen: Their Words, Lives and Music—1900 to the Present* (London: Pluto, 1985), pp. 4–5.

[6] Recent allegations by a writer in *The Chronicle of Higher Education* claim that this story is another African-American "myth" that has not been properly substantiated. Ironically, the person who made this assertion offered no counter-evidence to substantiate her refutation of the claim. Southern hospitals certainly were not admitting African Americans into "white" hospitals at this time.

[7] Elaine Feinstein, *Bessie Smith: Empress of the Blues* (New York: Penguin Books, 1985), pp. 91–92.

[8] Ibid., p. 92.

[9] Daphne Duval Harrison, *Black Pearls: Blues Queens of the 1920's* (New Brunswick: Rutgers University Press, 1988), pp. 9–10.

[10] Ibid., p. 64.

[11] Ibid., p. 22.

[12] See the *Chicago Defender*, April 8, 1916; *The Afro-American*, May 20, 1916; and Chicago Commission on Race Relations, *The Negro in Chicago: A Study of Race Relations and a Race Riot* (Chicago: University of Chicago Press, 1922), p. 379.

[13] Al Rose and Souchon Edmond, *New Orleans Jazz Album* (Baton Rouge: Louisiana State University Press, 1967).

[14] Shapiro and Hentoff, *Hear Me Talkin' to Ya*, pp. 218–23.

[15] Cab Calloway, *Of Minnie the Moocher and Me*, p. 70.

[16] Harrison, *Black Pearls*, pp. 23–24.

[17] *Chicago Defender*, February 22, 1922.

[18] She tells how her husband approached the NBC network owners to purchase the conglomerate, and the executives at General Electric (the owners) suddenly took the network off the market. The Cosby Show had provided the NBC network with its last period of glory, yet they would not sell to an African-American buyer regardless of who he or she happened to be.

[19] Sharon Fitzgerald, "Catalyst Camille," *American Visions*, December/January 1995, p. 23.

[20] Ibid.

[21] According to pianist Harold McKinney in his audio cassette *Discovering Jazz*, Wenha Records (distributed by Rebirth).

[22] *Jazz Women*, pp. 21–23.

[23] Ibid.

[24] Linda Dahl, *Stormy Weather,* pp. 35–38.

[25] Alain Locke, *The Negro and His Music* (Port Washington, N.Y.: Kennikat Press, 1968), p. 71.

[26] Ian Carr, *Jazz: The Rough Guide,* p. 456.

[27] Duke Ellington, *Music is My Mistress* (Garden City, N.Y.: Doubleday, 1973), p. 94.

[28] Grover Scott, liner notes, *Piano Giants,* vol. 1, Prestige P-24052.

[29] Liner notes, *Boogie Blues: Women Sing and Play Boogie Woogie*, Rosetta Records (1983).

[30] She was not always given credit for these works.

[31] Ibid.

[32] *Dorothy Romps: A Piano Retrospective, 1953–1979,* CD, Rosetta Records, Women's Heritage Series, 1991.

[33] Ibid.

[34] See Nils Bloch-Hoell, *The Pentecostal Movement: Its Origin, Development and Distinctive character* (Oslo: Universitetsforlaget, 1964); Walter J. Hollenweger, *The Pentecostals: The Charismatic Movement in the Churches* (Minneapolis: Augsburg, 1972).

[35] See Walter Rodney, *The Groundings with My Brothers* (London: Bogle-L'Ouverture, 1969), pp. 60–67.

[36] Gayraud S. Wilmore, *Black Religion and Black Radicalism* (Maryknoll, N.Y.: Orbis Books, 1986), p. 145.

[37] Garvey was born to parents who were members of the Wesleyan Methodist Church on August 17, 1887, in Jamaica.

[38] *Negro World*, 6 November 1920, and 28 April 1921.

[39] Ted Vincent, *Keep Cool: The Black Activists Who Built the Jazz Age* (London: Pluto Press, 1995), pp. 127–28.

[40] See Edmund D. Cronon, *Black Moses* (Madison: University of Wisconsin Press, 1962), p. 7. Cronon's reliable and well-known work on Garvey has been superseded by more recent research: see Tony Martin, *Race First: The Ideological and Organizational Struggles of Marcus Garvey and the Universal Negro Improvement Association* (Westport, Conn.: Greenwood, 1976); John Henrick Clarke with Amy Jacques-Garvey, *Marcus Garvey and the Vision of Africa* (New York: Random House, 1974); Elton C. Fax, *Garvey: The Story of a Pioneer Black Nationalist* (New York: Dodd, Mead, 1972); Shawna Maglangbayan, *Garvey, Lumumba, Malcolm* (Chicago: Third World Press, 1972).

[41] Wilmore, *Black Religion and Black Radicalism*, p. 146.

VI
Innovators Emerging between 1920 and 1930

The new music affected the older guys like Coleman Hawkins. Of course, there were the so-called "mouldy figs"—the staunch dixielanders or "two-fours," as we called them. There was a lot of territory between them and the boppers which covered everything I was involved in: swing, jazz . . . whatever you want to call it. In those days bop was considered the raw edge of jazz; they were the radicals. Now the boppers are almost the mouldy figs. If the mouldy figs heard some of the music of today, they'd be in hysterics!

—George Duvivier (bassist)

Snapshots of American Society

As the 1920s began, the Ku Klux Klan activities became more violent throughout the southern United States. Hooded cowards went on racist rampages destroying property, branding people (with cattle tools), and whipping African Americans and European-American sympathizers. In 1921 the New Ku Klux Klan, assuming the name of the Bigoted Post-Civil War Organization, gained political power in the United States.

In 1929 the stock-market crash brought the Roaring Twenties to a halt. The Great Depression began, plaguing almost every aspect of American society and culture. Some record companies were forced to close while others dropped all but their best-selling artists. The "jazz" and popular music industries were almost destroyed. People had little money to buy records, but the movie theaters and ballrooms were still affordable forms of entertainment for most Americans. Dixieland bands gradually disappeared but big bands and swing bands endured.

During this era, organized crime received a big break on January 16, 1920, when Congress enacted the 18th Amendment to the United States Constitution, making the manufacturing, sale, and transportation of intoxicating liquor for beverages illegal.

Female musicians experienced absurd stereotypes and vulnerability throughout the musical world. Perceptions regarding which musical instruments are properly "male" or "female" in a given society tend to shape gender associations in general. They can even shape or color the way music is heard. Unconscious social attitudes affect both instrument assignments and types of careers women can choose in music. In 1938 "the eight hundred women instrumentalists who were members of Local 802 of the New York Musicians

Union charged that the eighteen thousand male members had a virtual monopoly on professional work in New York City, with the result that the only women who could get jobs were the harpists, pianists and organists."[1] In other words, the women who played the traditionally acceptable "female" instruments were the only members "qualified" to get work as professional musicians.

The Effects of Changing American Demographics on Music

The extemporaneous music that African Americans developed in the South, now called "jazz," has been compared with many fast-moving and futuristic concepts in the twentieth century. Futurists applied the term "jazz" to various manifestations ranging from airplanes to skyscrapers. Le Corbusier dubbed the Manhattan skyline "hot jazz in stone and steel."[2] F. Scott Fitzgerald presented his work entitled "Tales of the Jazz Age" in 1922. The "Roaring Twenties" was commonly referred to as the "Jazz Age." In her book *Hole in Our Soul: The Loss of Beauty and Meaning in American Popular Music*, Martha Bayles compares "jazz" to cubism:

> Equally striking is the way in which both jazz and cubism gain or lose audiences depending on how expressive or cerebral they are. As it happens, the first phase of jazz was the more popular: From Armstrong through the 1940s, the music was strongly colored, richly textured, full of bright lights and deep shadows. The material being dissected remained recognizable, with its emotional power enhanced rather than diminished. Thus the *first* phase of jazz resembles the *second* phase of cubism, the so-called "synthetic" phase initiated by Picasso in 1913, which combined brighter color, denser texture (including that of collage), and greater contrast with more attention to the direct representation of the sensuous appeal of subject matter. Not surprisingly, this phase of cubism still attracts a larger audience than its predecessor, the "analytic" phase that, beginning in 1907, limited itself to a muted palette of browns and grays in order to carry out its highly complex, sometimes unrecognizable dissections.[3]

The irony is that former slaves invented the most liberated music in modern history largely due to African-American progenitors' freedom from all Old World traditions. "Jazz" is not an embellished "African" music, and it is conspicuously removed (conceptually) from the European musical styles that developed in Germany, France, and Italy over the past centuries. Few Africans or Europeans have managed to contribute innovations to "jazz" convincingly because it is dependent on direct contact with the American experience. Like any other music, innovative "jazz" music requires an awareness of the primary characteristics of a contemporary culture. Astute recognition of, and direct contact with, a culture creates musical syntax and distinguishing elements of vernacular style. Such elements make a certain type of music universal in its appeal but difficult to imitate in detail. Without such awareness, therefore, musicians can only mimic existing recordings and become journeyman musicians who preserve the past but are not equipped to contribute to the evolution of the "jazz" musical legacy. Over the years "jazz" has grown through a fissionary process that involved isolating and recombining elements of any music in which it came in contact—African, European, Asian, Native-American, Latin—establishing a new musical universe.

> Although jazz is not African music, it is, without question, the creation of American blacks. There have been many great white jazz musicians like Jack Teagarden, Benny Goodman, and Stan Getz, three influential players who have made important contributions to the music. The fact remains that these white players were taking up a music which had been created first by blacks. Furthermore, on any list of, say, the top twenty jazz players, probably fifteen would be blacks. The great innovators in jazz, like Louis Armstrong, Duke Ellington, and Charlie Parker, probably the three most influential of all players, are black.

> I don't mean, however, that jazz is black man's music. It is *American* music and belongs to all of us, white and black both. Even though it was created by blacks, it is now part of our American heritage. To those of us who have grown up with it, it seems as natural as eating. To be sure, there are some extremely good jazz players in other countries, and no doubt as time goes on and jazz becomes more and more widespread, other nations will produce many more good players. But the truth is that although a few non-Americans play jazz well, most simply can't compare with our American players. Jazz is a musical language that Americans understand better than anyone else.[4]

Unfortunately, social disparity continued to thwart the progress of African-American innovators. Listening to the disparity that existed between the studio recording quality of African-American "jazz" masters (such as Fats Waller, Art Tatum, and Coleman Hawkins) as contrasted with European-American "jazz" artists (Benny Goodman, Glen Miller, or Paul Whiteman) gives a clear indication of the racism practiced by the American music industry during this period. It is embarrassingly evident from listening to such recordings that greater attention, time, and significantly more money was invested in the recordings of European-American "jazz" musicians.

New Orleans and the Movement East

The Spanish were the first to encounter Native Americans in what is now New Orleans. Soon the French established a colony there. Both of these Catholic cultures were less restrictive than the Protestant Europeans that settled elsewhere in the "New World." They allowed colonial slaves to retain more of their African traditions. Generally, West-African cultural traits and musical elements survived more readily around Catholics than their Protestant counterparts. The powerfully communicative aspects of African music and traditions caused trepidation among European Americans in the Mississippi Delta areas in time, however. Eventually, fear of African "magic" led to a ban on the importation of Africans from the West Indies throughout the colonies.

Vodun (or voodoo) was the African religious ritual most feared in America at the time. Its pantheistic vodun deities were disguised within the forms of Catholic saints. In this way elements of Catholicism were blended imperceptibly with vodun. The Louisiana Purchase later caused the ban on immigration to be lifted, and many West Indian Africans came to Louisiana. The private practice of vodun suddenly flourished in the region.

In New Orleans and elsewhere in America during the nineteenth century, women used song to convey improvised messages along the "grapevine telegraph" alerting the African-American community of voodoo rituals. Although these religious "cults" were strictly forbidden during earlier times, "a message could be conveyed from one end of the city to another in a single day without one white person being aware of it." An African-American woman working in the kitchen would sing a Creole song,

> which sounded innocuous enough to any white listener, but at the end of the verse she would sing a few words intended as a message. . . . [A] second servant would then go outside and attend to her duties. She would sing the same song and her voice would be heard by servants in the house next door. In this way, by means of a song, news of a meeting of a voodoo society would be carried from one end of the city to another and upon the appointed night Negro men and women would slip from their beds before midnight and would assemble for their ceremonies.[5]

Aside from passing the word about secret meetings, the voodoo queens of New Orleans and other women were central to the process of music making during voodoo rituals. Sanité Dédé, Marie Saloppé, and Marie Laveau (the most famous and long-lived queen) were clever businesswomen and showwomen who were powerful members of their communities after the Louisiana Purchase (1803). At the time, it was less difficult for African-American women to accrue power and stature as religious and spiritual leaders than it was for African-American men. Therefore, vodun became predominantly matriarchal in America, whereas its archetype had both a king and queen in Africa. The queen's function was valued within African-American communities because it was difficult to find spiritual and emotional releases in antebellum America. Women played hand percussion, drums, and led chants during public voodoo ceremonies at Congo Square in New Orleans after 1817. Sally Placksin presents other social aspects of voodoo during the nineteenth century:

Not only were the voodoo queens and women an important force in the black community; at a time when black and white women in America were ruled and manipulated by what Adrienne Rich called a "divide and conquer" strategy devised and sustained largely by southern white men, the secret voodoo cults also provided an early ground on which women of both races mixed, for some of the women who attended the secret rites were white. Newspaper accounts consider it scandalous when white women were discovered at the ceremonies. (One man actually committed suicide the day after his wife was found at a meeting and the news was printed in the morning paper.)

Some women argued (successfully) in court that voodoo was a "religious" practice, and the law "had no justification for its attitude towards them," while in another group, in which "several" white women were present, "the white ladies claimed that they had been unclad only because of excessive heat, and had been present only because they had one and all collapsed simultaneously on the doorsteps of the Voodooienne." (The women were merely fined and dismissed.)[6]

In New Orleans, Africans were permitted to engage in their traditional music and dance regularly on Sunday afternoons at Congo Square. In addition to the profits local businesses hoped to make off these African displays, they also felt that allowing African Americans to exercise some aspects of vodun practice in public would minimize the mystique and secrecy surrounding voodoo meetings and rituals. Exposed, traditional African music eventually blended with the European marching band music of French tradition. New Orleans Africans and mélangés also participated in the music of the French operas, concerts, and balls to a lesser degree. When the Confederate armies disbanded at the end of the Civil War, leaving their military band instruments behind, African-American musicians began to form their own brass bands. These ensembles performed at picnics, church affairs, parades, funerals, and most other community celebrations. The melodies of the music they played were based on the African vocal tradition, which had never been lost during the long years of American slavery.

Ragtime adopted many of the elements that were floating freely in the New Orleans environment. The ragtime style remained popular for about twenty years. Its strong influence was retained however, in the oompah bass and right-handed syncopated melodies that became prominent features of newer styles of African-American music. The first subsequent style was essentially instrumental music performed in small bands or combos, where greater variety of rhythms and counterpoint began to manifest. The new improvised melodies, developed primarily in the Mississippi Delta (and particularly in New Orleans), maintained a close relationship to the blues and other traditional African-American music.

Small "jazz" bands were formed in the early 1900s. They continued to play the social functions that earlier brass bands played, and were later hired to play on riverboats in and around the area. The cornet (or trumpet), clarinet, and trombone formed the nucleus of these bands. The rhythm sections varied, but it could include banjo, guitar, tuba, piano, and drums. Saxophones and the string bass were common later. These bands often traveled around the streets of New Orleans in horse-drawn wagons with the name of the ensembles affixed on advertising strips.

At first, many African-American musicians of the day were self taught and did not read music very well. Those fortunate enough to receive formal training eventually taught their musical colleagues to read. The blues established the basis of the music they improvised and the twelve-bar blues form eventually became the form most often applied. When new musicians came into an ensemble they were expected to "just listen" for a while and "hear" what was happening with the music. Then they would "play what they were feeling." The stylized roles of the traditional instruments in these early groups developed into a polyphonic style that created carefully partitioned improvised layers of counterpoint.

Instrumental blues form was often framed by an introduction, which was usually played by the whole band, followed by at least one chorus of the melody. Each player then took turns improvising over the form before everyone reentered by "jamming" (improvising collectively) until reaching consensus on the ending of the piece. The music of Joseph "King" Oliver, Louis "Satchmo" Armstrong, Lil Hardin Armstrong, Edward "Kid" Ory, Ferdinand "Jelly Roll" Morton, Warren "Baby" Dodds, Johnny Dodds, and other early "jazz" immortals, was often structured on this basic form. Louis Armstrong became the most famous of all "jazz" musicians and eventually earned the title "Ambassador Satch" when the United States Department of the State sponsored his tours to Europe, Africa, and Latin America. Armstrong retained certain aspects of the African vocal sound in his trumpet timbre throughout his career.

As a consequence of the movement north by many key musicians, New Orleans was phasing out as a center of "jazz" music during the 1920s. When word of Joe Oliver's success in the North spread, many other musicians left for New York and Chicago, which became the new centers of the music industry. As the allure of commercial success took away the Crescent City's most loyal members of the African-American musical community, the status and importance of the locally based musicians dwindled. No longer were powerful musical archetypes (like Bolden, Oliver, Ory, and Armstrong) available on the street corners and in neighborhood establishments to serve as a sociocultural catalyst. Now a centralized music industry could gradually step in from outside the African-American community to dictate what music would be packaged and sold to the public.

In this new atmosphere, where music no longer stood before the local community strictly on its own merit, a group of European Americans like the "Original Dixieland Jass Band" succeeded in imitating and selling features of African-American musical style. When the image of a "jazz" musician was no longer restricted to an African-American prototype, a biased European-American industry recorded and promoted the new "White" musical product. Once these enfeebled copies were packaged and sold as the "original," all musicians, "Black" and "White," were again obliged to adopt certain characteristics of the "White" performance model (as with minstrelsy) in order to gain access to the commercial market place. The ownership of the clubs and tonks, in which African-American musicians were accustomed to performing, slowly changed hands, thus destroying an Afrocentric infrastructure and traditional sources of employment. New styles of furtive "carpetbaggers" soon stepped in to exploit these changing conditions.

> Like the present narcotics situation, prohibition meant extra-large profits for the underworld. The majority of night-clubs and honky-tonks had to close down, but a series of clandestine operations called speakeasies quickly arose, which sold liquor illegally and often provided music. Since these were one of the few sources of steady employment, musicians were hardly in a position to refuse the opportunity of working in them. Brothels run by Blacks, another source of employment for black musicians, were closed down in New Orleans and other cities during World War One. Houses like that of Marie Laveau, the New Orleans voodoo queen, catered to the wealthy, including many whites. The houses and honky-tonks were places where relatively large amounts of capital flowed into the black community—that is, until official government decrees allowed take-over of these enterprises by immigrant ethnic gangster groups.[7]

Many European Americans performed New Orleans "jazz" by the time it reached Chicago, but few managed to engage "Black" culture directly. William Kenney asserts that many European-American jazzmen shared a notion of social rebellion through "jazz." He concludes that:

> they all passed through a complex process of personal orientation toward the world of music in general and of black music in particular. The white Chicagoans sought out black cabaret music at an early age, but they generally did not grow up in neighborhoods that were rich in African-American music. Rather, they lived in a separate white world that received its impressions of African-Americans through the media. Because the entertainment and recording industries were tightly segregated, Art Hodes, for example, had reached the age of twenty-three before even hearing a record of a black person playing jazz. Max Kaminsky had played popular dance music professionally for six years before hearing the recordings of the black jazz pioneers.[8]

It is not surprising, therefore, that European-American Chicagoans developed a taste for recordings of the Original Dixieland Jass Band, which contained "a brand of music which they later repudiated as corny and out of date; but at the time they first heard it, the ODJB's sharp ragtime syncopations and sardonic, vulgar animal imitations had an appealing impudence."[9] This style of music was new to mainstream America. Meanwhile, African-American innovators continued to evolve beyond the clowning attitude of the

ODJB, adopting a more serious approach to African-American music. Howland says, "The smoother, more swinging beat of the New Orleans Rhythm Kings, and the King's serious musical attitude made a longer-lasting impression on ["White" audiences], in part because some listened to NORK in person at Friars Inn, as well as on record."[10] Ralph Berton, Bix Beiderbecke's biographer, put it in a way more reflective of mainstream American attitudes of the period: "They [NORK] played not in the zany, tongue-in-cheek spirit of the white bands . . . but *seriously*—mean and low down, pretty or funky, driving or lyrical, but always *for real*. As we said in those days—there was no higher praise—*they played like niggers*."[11]

For the local African-American musicians, the zenith of the volatile, creative, and affluent days of New Orleans had passed. The bureaucratic centralization of the music industry was eroding the formerly communal local scene. As a result of this debasement, the musicians who originally created and developed the New Orleans styles could now only condemn the music scene while watching their music transform into stolid phonograph recordings and radio shows performed by European-American musicians.

The prosperity that enabled musicians to prosper during the Jazz Age in Chicago and other major cities eventually dissolved as the convergence of technology, intensified racial segregation, and political forces forced many musicians to move to New York. Again, the "White" musicians gained the advantages of preferential hiring. As Kenney tells us,

> Many of the white jazz musicians who left Chicago for New York in 1927 quickly succeeded. Beginning in 1928, Ben Pollack took his band from the Venetian Room of Chicago's Southmoor Hotel first to New York's Little Club and then to the Park Central. There, for a year and a half, Jimmy McPartland, Benny Goodman, and Bud Freeman earned some of the best salaries in the business . . . Goodman, moreover, quickly moved into the lucrative studio scene in New York, playing jingles, popular songs, arrangements of all types of dance music, and jazz with all-white groups.[12]

European-American music was influenced by the Africans in America since the singing of spirituals at early camp meetings. Although the minstrels' racism often disguised their genuine interest in African-American music, European-American musicians were intrigued by the music they imitated. They continued to play these styles from the time initial contact was made with slave music on plantations into the more innovative African-American styles that evolved throughout the twentieth century.

Swing and Its Precursors

After ragtime completed its evolutionary journey from its emergence alongside the Mississippi River to its more permanent home in St. Louis, a freer style of music began to solidify. Art does not evolve in simply cumulative or chronological periods. Aggregates of composers and performers of one style overlap and blend forces to create the next style. Blues, ragtime, boogie woogie, and Dixieland shared the same world and time frame. Scott Joplin's "Maple Leaf Rag" and Thomas Million Turpin's "Harlem Rag" were fading in popularity, but Eubie Blake's "Chevy Chase" continued to be played. Louis Armstrong and Sidney Bichet introduced the world to other ways of thinking about music improvisation, musical construction, and self-expression.

Younger innovators were beginning to get recognition on the scene. Duke Ellington and Fletcher Henderson used the twenties to develop the basic structures for the big bands of the thirties, whose popularity boosted the size of the "jazz" listening audience in America. There were also other cultural and pecuniary advances made as "jazz" began to mature. Big bands employed more African-American musicians than ever before. Africans in America had few symphony orchestras. Most of the musical ensembles that took part in the creation of "jazz" had unfurled as brass bands or small ragtime or Dixieland combos. The big band was a substantive employer in the African-American community that provided greater opportunities for professional musicians. Big bands provided an efficient communal setting in which musicians now developed. Such an infrastructure, which employed large numbers of professional musicians, has not been duplicated within the African-American community since the Second World War.

Fats Waller

Thomas (Fats) Waller (1904–43) was still a Harlem pianist during the years after World War I when Harlem was the center of "jazz" piano activity. Waller's father was a clergyman and wanted his son to follow a similar career. Fats played organ in his father's church, studied piano privately, and then became a professional musician at the age of fifteen.

Waller is considered to be one of the links between early and modern "jazz" piano playing, and he was also one of the first to adapt "jazz" styles to the pipe organ. His performances of some of his most famous compositions, including "Honeysuckle Rose" and "Ain't Misbehaving," were heard on the radio and later seen in performances as movie shorts. The panache, inventiveness, and euphonious spirit of Waller's music was, in turn, a reflection of the effect he had on people in his daily life. In his biography, entitled *Ain't Misbehavin*, author Joe Vance describes Waller's influence on those with whom he came in contact: "Waller's entrance into any room betokened joy; he was a year round Santa Claus. Standing five feet ten inches and weighing, in his words, 'two hundred and eighty-five pounds of jam, jive, and *everything*,' he brought instant smiles and affection. There are few people in the world whose talent is to bring instant gladness, and it is that part of Waller's genius that has most sustained the tale of his life. Waller graced the planet by his living; he gave the human race a good reputation."[13]

Waller's initial success was at rent parties uptown in New York City and on the "chitlin' circuit." European-American musicians started hearing about the piano feats of Waller, James P. Johnson, and Willie "the Lion" Smith, and came uptown to listen to and learn from these artists. George Gershwin, who had written an unsuccessful one-act opera (*135th Street*) in an

attempt to emulate African-American life in Harlem,[14] was among this group
of Waller admirers. Gershwin invited Waller's piano trio to several Park
Avenue soirees. Gershwin, an American composer with a talent for writing
memorable melodies, was thrilled by the exemplary caliber of melodic invention and variations he witnessed. He and other musicians purchased songs
from African-American artists (Gershwin reportedly bought the song "Summertime" from Waller for around fifty dollars.[15])

Waller was a good reader and arranger, and he "could play any kind of
a tune, on the organ or the piano."[16] His talents made him one of the busiest
musicians in the country even before his solo career was launched. His experience with publishers was typically opprobrious, as an article published in
the *New World-Telegram* (shortly after Waller composed "Hot Chocolates")
clearly demonstrates:

> The high spot of Waller's career . . . took place at Carnegie Hall
> where he was the soloist at the recital of W. C. Handy's group
> of blues interpreters [April 27, 1928; Waller also performed J.
> P. Johnson's piano rhapsody, "Yamekraw"]. Here he came into
> contact with white composers and publishers. He discovered
> that it was easy to sell tunes to white song-writers, who would
> vary them slightly and re-sell them as their own. The average
> rate for such a song, he says, was $250. Among the songs thus
> disposed of was one which knocked about for three seasons un-
> til it was finally inserted in a musical comedy. Featured in that
> show, it became the best seller of its season and netted $17,500
> to its "composer," who paid Fatts [*sic*] $500 for it.

Waller was not always as amiable as he appears to be in his movie
shorts. While traveling with his bands, he often abandoned the tours when he
was confronted with the incessant obstacles African-American musicians
faced all over the United States. Fats Waller's biographer Joel Vance wrote
that the pianist could often be seen stomping angrily offstage yelling that he
was off to Kansas City to see his good friend Count Basie and to "go get
crooked for spite."

> The incident which made the normally tolerant and whimsical
> Waller explode was the last of a chain of aggravating insults,
> disappointments, and stupidities which characterized all of his
> one-night-stand road tours. The band had just completed a
> road trip of 643 miles from Denver, only to find that the date in
> Kansas City had been canceled because the promoter had not
> paid a deposit on the theater.

> There were other incidents on his road tours that often led,
> sometimes quite justifiably, to Waller's, bolting back to New
> York. On a date in Mississippi, where the band was booked at a
> backwoods affair, local white apes slashed the tires of Waller's
> car and poured sand in the gas tank. Hotel accommodations for
> the band were simply not possible down South, so the musi-

cians had to be put up in private homes. They were denied meals in restaurants, and sometimes gas stations refused to service "Old Methusela," as the bus was nicknamed. During a local tour in Florida, Kirkeby attempted to charter a private railroad car for the band so that the players would not be disturbed, but when they arrived in Jacksonville the railroad management took one look at the sixteen black customers and said that no cars were available. On still another occasion the band arrived at a club in time to see it still being built! Local sheriffs were especially obnoxious and hostile, and usually very quick to demonstrate that they were heavily armed.[17]

Waller was the first "jazz" pianist to give a solo concert at Carnegie Hall. He was well aware of his value as a musician. After becoming embroiled in a minor controversy with the American Society of Composers, Authors, and Publishers, which tangentially involved a question regarding the royalties from John Philip Sousa's estate, Waller reportedly asked, "Do those Congress people feel I am not as good an artist somehow as Mr. Sousa? I have always been an admirer, so to speak, of Mr. Sousa's work too. Of course, it isn't jazz, but it's all right for that kind of stuff. To tell you the truth, I had an idea I would put that tune of his, 'The Stars and Stripes Forever,' to swing. If they mess around with me though, I won't do it. I just won't do it."[18]

Waller made a historic performance and recordings playing the organ in Paris at Notre Dame cathedral. He later recorded his "Jitterbug Waltz" and other compositions on Hammond organ between 1940 and 1942.

New York During the Harlem Renaissance

Marcus Garvey convened an international gathering of Africans in Harlem under the banner of the University Negro Improvement Association and the African Communities League in 1920. This action would pave the way for the Harlem Renaissance that began in 1921.[19]

In New York during the early 1920s, composer Don Redman was one of two pioneer arrangers for the "jazz" orchestra that became famous for establishing the new big band sound. He was a conservatory-trained multi-instrumentalist who moved to New York (from Pittsburgh) with Billy Paige's Broadway Syncopators in 1923. His new approach was the predecessor to the swing band style that began to evolve and merge with traditional "jazz" ensemble approaches. The other pioneer, Fletcher Henderson, provided an alternative version of the "jazz" orchestra that came into existence concurrently with Redman's. As the Harlem Renaissance initiated its cultural explosion of art, music, dance, and literature, Henderson proceeded to make his innovative contributions to the propagation of swing style. In turn, Redman incorporated Henderson's big band style into his own scores. The resulting music was perfect for the dancers at Roseland Ballroom. Coleman Hawkins said, "No matter how musical he arranges today, Don used to make some very good gutbucket arrangements! Rock n' roll with a little music behind it!"[20]

The Spasm Band and the Harlem Piano School developed distinctive local musical styles. The "Black" Music Theater continued in much the same fashion as it had since the beginning of the century, but the African-American community was growing weary of older styles that were derived from music of minstrel days. The blackfaced "Black" entertainer was never a reflection of the African-American community, and the entertainer's nescient persiflage eventually suffered the consequences accordingly. It was difficult to overcome the stereotypes established by the minstrel plots from the past on the eve of the Harlem Renaissance.

> The force of the Harlem Renaissance movement during the years following the war might have produced a major change of direction had it not been for the phenomenal success of the first black musical to reach Broadway in almost a decade. *Shuffle Along*, with book by Miller and Lyles, featuring their popular characters, Peck and Jenkins, and recycling parts of their 1918 show, *Who's Stealing?* probably doomed any effort to advance a more serious concept. Almost all the books for black musicals during the 1920s tried to equal the success of *Shuffle Along* by recycling plot devices that were almost two decades old; most shows were unsuccessful in their attempt to attract a Broadway audience for more than several months. By 1930 James Weldon Johnson had already recognized the problem: although Miller and Lyles "were as funny as ever" in *Rang Tang* (1927), "the thought arose that perhaps the traditional pattern of Negro musical comedy was a bit worn."[21]

The Harlem community became a magnet for African Americans from all over the United States, as well as for other people from the African Diaspora, who moved to New York City. The level of sophistication and the large Pan-African population of working "Blacks" assured most entertainers an enthusiastic audience who could afford to pay for professional entertainment. During the 1920s and 1930s, African Americans aspired to remove racist stereotypes from the minds of the majority culture by fostering the creation of art and literature that would demonstrate the true nature and quality of African and African-American culture. Dispelling racist myths and stereotypes—the product of a long and arduous attempt by "Whites" to characterize Africans as ignorant, lazy, and incapable of equaling or surpassing the technical and intellectual achievements of Europeans—was indeed an enormous and arduous task. The legacy of inexorable harangues that produced and perpetuated negative African images in the "New World" were intended not only to expunge the self-respect of the targeted people but also to guarantee that America would have a permanent underclass. Slavery provided America an economic advantage over the rest of the world, so the importance of an easily exploited labor force was clear to most capitalists in American society.

The economic and social stratification that remains a salient feature of American culture was not simply a race-based phenomenon. Division within the African-American society itself was often tantamount to racial segregation. According to Clare Crane, from the Civil War through the Negro Renaissance, those at the helm of the movement were an esoteric set of African-American elites in relation to the majority of "Blacks" in their community.[22] The members of this movement were separated from the average African-American citizen in the community by virtue of their social circle, education, wealth, and cosmopolitanism.

> Many spent time abroad and their interactions at home were expanded to include a wide-ranging interracial spectrum of people—made up a new class of persons who did not have, to use Nathan words, "a grass roots attachment." This elitism remained an intact principle despite certain philosophical differences among disparate perspectives—for example, devotion to a referential or propaganda theory of art vis-à-vis Locke's espousal of a more absolutist perspective, i.e., art for art's sake.[23]

The African-American intelligentsia sought to transform "Black" folk culture into a formal culture with structures that resembled European culture. According to Huggins, most "aspired to *high* culture as opposed to that of the common man, which they hoped to mine for novels, poems, plays, and symphonies."[24] Huggins also suggests that while people like James Weldon Johnson and Alain Locke respected "jazz" as an example of folk music, poet Langston Hughes was the only Harlem intellectual who took "jazz" seriously. Those who valued "jazz" held expectations for the potential transformation of the "folk-art" form into "serious music of high culture by some race genius in the tradition of a Dvorak or a Smetana."[25]

The movement was financed in part by successful "Black" businessmen and businesswomen who wanted to bring European-American clientele into Harlem. They opened new entertainment centers like the Cotton Club that catered exclusively to "White" audiences. The club enjoyed the benefit of live weekly broadcasts that exposed the entertainers who performed there to a wide American audience. Surrounded by masters of ceremony, beautiful showgirls, comedians, and tap dancers, many "jazz" legends like Duke Ellington, Lena Horne, and Cab Calloway saw their careers skyrocket into superstardom after successful engagements at the Cotton Club.

The work of Eubie Blake also enabled the musical theater to enjoy relatively high levels of success. During the Harlem Renaissance, many members of the African-American community envisioned the "Black" musical as an arena in which "Black" music could rise to the realm of "high art." Most efforts fell short of these expectations. But the success of Eubie Blake's *Shuffle Along* in 1921 could not be denied.

> It almost single-handedly brought black musical theater back to Broadway and provided the impetus during the following decade for a renewed interest among whites in black popular art and artists. Although any intellectual interaction between the movement and the shows of the 1920s would appear to have been minimal, in the public's mind, some linkage was probably perceived. Thus, the Renaissance as a movement

probably benefited from the success of the black musicals on Broadway.[26]

The music performed in the theater during this period produced a somewhat heuristic result within the artistic community. Bob Cole (c. 1868–1911), Will Marion Cook (c. 1869–1944), J. Rosamond Johnson (c. 1873–1954), Chris Smith (c. 1879–1949), James Reese Europe (c. 1881–1919), and Ford Dabney (c. 1883–1958) were composers that helped establish a course at the beginning of the century for other serious composers (like Duke Ellington) who soon followed related stratagems to various extents. Several other composers of the period were ragtime and early "jazz" pianists of note. The introduction of ragtime rhythms and adventurous harmonies to vaudeville and the Broadway scene set a standard for experimentation. By the middle of the second decade, innovations were adopted by the musical mainstream and were vigorously imitated by Tin Pan Alley composers. Broadway musicals reflected this influence through increased use of sophisticated harmonic progressions and the incorporation of major seventh, ninth chords, and other former dissonances into its popular songs. African-American composers during the period continued to provide Tin Pan Alley with music that reflected the unique ethnic qualities of African-American culture.[27] The wide dissemination of the blues contributed a concurrent dimension to this progression.

> By the 1920s another aspect of their culture, the blues, was infusing the form and substance of popular song as it had earlier with piano ragtime. This secular genre was first popularized by Ma Rainey in the early part of the century and was brought to wider public attention through the success of W. C. Handy's "The Memphis Blues" (1913) and more particularly "St. Louis Blues" (1914), which, according to one source, was "the most important piece of popular music published in 1914." Throughout the twenties, novel and innovative harmonic experimentation continued to be in evidence. It is regularly encountered in the music of Eubie Blake (1883–1983), James P. (Jimmy) Johnson (1894–1955), C. Roberts (1895–1968), and Thomas (Fats) Waller (1904–1943), who were active as composers of instrumental rags as well as songs. Their songs often reflect the influence of instrumental writing, especially in the use of more secondary dominant chords and modal borrowing.

> The importance to white society of the orchestras founded by Europe, Dabney, and Cook added another sphere of influence; they played many white engagements and popularized ragtime dances that were black in origin. As early as 1913 the dancing public was introduced to a new step in Jim Burris and Chris Smith's "Ballin' the Jack"; over the next decade, other new dances were introduced. The various trots, the Grizzly Bear, the Charleston and its inevitable imitations, and the Black Bottom, among others, were all well received and became the rage of the period.[28]

Eubie Blake and other African-American composers were not only performers and songwriters in several "Black" stylistic genres, but they often wrote fluently in the prevalent "White" popular styles of the period as well. Blake's *Shuffle Along* contained commercial Tin Pan Alley songs like "I'm Just Wild About Harry" and "African Dip," and African-American comedy numbers such as "If You've Never Been Vamped by a Brownskin, You Haven't Been Vamped at All" all within the same musical. Songs composed for the theater by many African Americans used colorful blue chords and blue notes and interchanged major and minor modes to make their style more variegated than the music of other composers commonly heard on Broadway during the 1920s.

The skillful composers did not merely apply classic blues structures to new lyrics, but used the familiar musical metaphors contained in the blues to create elements of surprise. The composition "Love Bug," which was heard in the successful show *Runnin' Wild* (1923), demonstrates James P. (Jimmy) Johnson's fluent and progressive use of blues idiom. Ragtime rhythms brighten the mood of the music as opening measures of the melody alternates blue notes A with A-flat (3 and b3) and C with C-flat (5 and b5) to create modal ambiguity. This phase of the melody is supported by a tonic chord (F-blues), in measures 1–4. The next four bars do not move to the expected subdominant region (IV) but explore the lowered mediant chord, A-flat major, before resolving to the dominant seventh (C7) in measure 8. The second half of the formal structure begins with a borrowed dominant chord constructed on the flat-VI degree for two measures before resting briefly on the tonic in bars 11–12. The final four measures move through G7, a secondary dominant, setting up the dominant-7 (C7) that brings us back to the home key F blues. The composition proceeds from this point into the chorus. Johnson expands the traditional twelve-bar A A' B blues structure to sixteen measures of harmonic progression and manages to obscure both harmonic and melodic directions.

In Fats Waller's "Rhythm Man" (from *Connie's Hot Chocolates*—1929), a blues vocal melody is supported by blues harmony that cleverly manages to avoid the tonic chord (through the employment of parallel seventh chords most of the time). In "Keep Shufflin'" (1928), the chorus of "Got Myself Another Jockey Now" joins the newer blues idiom with the old two-step march cliché producing a fresh sounding result. Waller also enjoys obscuring the tonality by replacing the blues seventh chord at the beginning of the piece and refusing to resolve it in accordance with the laws of European functional harmony. Waller, unlike the rural blues guitarist, mixes old ingredients with new harmonic, melodic, and formal styles to keep the listener situated between the familiar and the unexpected in an ease of manner that was cohesive and unobtrusive. In fact, Waller's effortless technique, when mixed with his humor and twaddling, could be so completely disarming that listeners could easily fail to appreciate the richness and technical sophistication of his musical offerings.

When the new forms of African-American music began to receive broader airplay, the creators of the music did not receive the kind of royalty payments that composers of "serious" European music received. After music copyrighting came into existence in 1909, there was concern and litigation over song ownership and performance rights in regards to radio airplay. Since most of the music of "serious" European composers played over the air at the time were deceased, European music posed few problems of ownership rights. The American Society of Composers, Authors, and Publishers (ASCAP) was a "nonprofit" organization that granted licenses to play songs under ASCAP rules for a "reasonable fee." In 1923, nevertheless, it was assumed that practically none of the "jazz" selections and popular songs would be aired over radio stations and agreements were made accordingly.[29] By 1928 it was clear that stations would be playing "jazz" and a new agreement was worked out.

Although ASCAP was open to any composer or author of regularly published compositions, African Americans had a difficult time getting published. Since ASCAP mainly benefited musicians with access to music publishing firms, radio broadcasts, and favorable contracts, European-American composers were generally the ones who reaped the benefits of ASCAP membership. Getting published was difficult for anyone, but it was nearly impossible for African Americans during the 1920s.

When African Americans had their own separate musicians unions, they were able to work out better royalty deals than after "Black" and "White" locals "amalgamated." (Until the end of World War II, musicians maintained the two separate unions: one for "Black" musicians and the other for their "White" counterparts. African Americans generally hired "Black" bands for their functions while European Americans hired "White" bands for theirs.) When separate, African-American unions found work for their members on a much more steady basis. Presently, as during the early decades of the twentieth century, European Americans are hired for the vast majority of Union Trust Fund jobs.

There was a fourfold increase in American record production between 1911 and 1921, when 100 million recordings were sold. Most of this prosperity was due to the commercial success of the "jazz" music now played in ballrooms across America. Yet African-American musicians, though the source of this economic success, were excluded from this boom. This was just the beginning of a new era of exploitation for "Black" artists and entertainers.

> The growth of the music-recording industry is historically and parasitically connected with the growth of Jazz. The industry's growth was, and still remains, dependent on the grooming and packaging of white "popular" music models derived from imitations of definitive Afro-American models. It was not until the early Twenties, after the succession of music reproduction inventions and the advent of radio, that the music industry was fully able to capitalize on the use of white imitators![30]

Chicago Dixieland

After 1917 many African-American musicians left the Mississippi Delta for different parts of the United States. Some moved to Memphis, Kansas City, Los Angeles, St. Louis, Chicago, and New York, while others moved abroad to France. King Oliver, Armstrong, and others brought their New Orleans Dixieland style up north. The majority culture's dance music was generally performed by small ensembles who primarily played waltzes, quadrilles, and other European dance music. The people who heard this new African-American music became excited about it, and many European-American musicians (like the Original Dixieland Jass Band) began to learn the Dixieland style.

While Louis Armstrong, Joe Oliver, Freddie Keppard, Lovie Austin, Johnny Dodds, and other prominent artists worked the south side of Chicago, European-American musicians like Eddie Condon, Mezz Mezzrow, and Muggsy Spanier were employed on the north side. At that time, a group of young European-American men called the Austin High Gang began to listen to African-American music and eventually formed their own professional ensemble during the 1920s. The group first got their name from the fact that they had all attended Austin High School in Chicago. The group used the New Orleans Rhythm Kings as their model.

New Orleans Dixieland style reflected the lifestyle and pace of an agricultural environment; Chicago Dixieland was played at a more frantic and faster pace, reflecting the lifestyle of an urban industrial area. Customers in speakeasies wanted to be entertained with dance music. Special dance halls for young adults were created, and dancing to "jazz" became the craze.

African-American musicians working in New Orleans, New York, Chicago, or any other urban area have rarely gained economic or social autonomy. A plantation mentality was merely retooled to fit urban American environments. The urban ghetto replaced the rural slave quarters. Urban businessmen replaced the plantation owners. The majority culture appears to find it difficult to pay homage to African Americans in any profession (except when some measure of respect is shown posthumously). Therefore, from the early New Orleans era to the present day, the sale of liquor and sex has indirectly (and unfortunately) been one of the primary sources of revenue available on a steady basis to subsidize African-American music.

The syndicate has maintained an economic stranglehold on the African-American community and on many "jazz" musicians since the 1920s. In the mid-1920s the Capone headquarters was in Cicero (in the Chicago suburbs), but the Capones and other gangsters enjoyed night life in the city and "jazz" was often their music of choice. The speakeasy was the typical establishment that was owned outright by the mob. Earl Hines mentioned that his good friend Jimmie Noone (in addition to Lucky Millinder, Tiny Parham, and Boyd Atkins) was employed by the Capones at various times.[31]

The Jelly Roll Morton Documentary

Jelly Roll Morton's interview sessions, chronicling the evolution of "jazz" in New Orleans, are the most complete and important oral document of the history of early twentieth-century African-American music on record, despite the embarrassingly poor recording quality. The significance of the content of the recordings will undoubtedly continue to grow in prestige with the passage of time.

Jelly Roll Morton was not only an important progenitor of "jazz," his style involved a synthesis of African-American field hollers, blues, spirituals, ragtime, early African-American and European dance music, Protestant hymns, minstrel show tunes, Caribbean music, and popular songs. He displayed his knowledge of the history of all this music within the colorful sociocultural context of New Orleans. He also performed examples that vividly traced the history and development of African-American music and the personal musical style he managed to create.

When Morton was managing and performing at a small club in Washington, D.C., Alan Lomax approached him and gained Morton's approval to begin recording his oral history. Lomax knew the importance of this event but was apparently unable to obtain approval and financial support to conduct the venture properly. Lomax purchased a Presto portable home disc recorder at his own expense and asked Morton to discuss and perform anything he wanted to present at a series of sessions. The Presto recorder's turntable moved at a consistently slow speed on some occasions, thus producing inferior pitch control and sound quality.

Although he considered himself a Jelly Roll Morton admirer, Lomax's narration exudes typical arrogance, a general lack of sensitivity, and latent impudence. Lomax's nescience is exposed as he continually interrupts Morton's narration and music, purely for the sake of his own personal agenda. His disposition makes one wonder whether he was as interested in getting Morton's message down for posterity as he was in emphasizing his own significance as folklorist and musicologist. Lomax's tendency to treat a composer-pianist of Morton's stature as a "folk" figure did serve to undermine the project's effectiveness to a significant degree. Although Morton was very ill at the time, he seems to have been inspired by an opportunity to produce this document. He created a colorful milestone odyssey through his piano playing, singing, vaunting, reminiscing, and theorizing.

Author Rudi Blesh obtained the rights from the Morton estate to issue these esteemed performances on Circle Records in the late 1940s. The musical documents appeared in twelve 78 rpm and twelve LP volumes. In 1958 Riverside licensed Circle material and reissued the Morton albums with minor alterations.

Louis "Satchmo" Armstrong and His Associates

Louis Armstrong, considered by many musicians to be the definitive "Father of Jazz," was the most influential trumpet player of his day. As a dramatic solo stylist and highly talented improviser, he blazed new musical directions which future generations of "jazz" musicians would follow.

Armstrong was born to Willie and May Ann Armstrong on a little street in New Orleans called James Alley in 1900. As a young child Armstrong attended the Fisk School. Armstrong retained early memories of the sound of the brass bands in his neighborhood. From the first moment he heard the sound of the New Orleans cornet players, he was impressed by the instrument.

> Of course at the age of five I was not playing the trumpet, but there was something about the instrument that caught my ear. When I was in church and when I was "second lining"—that is, following the brass bands in parades—I started to listen carefully to the different instruments, noticing the things they played and how they played them. That is how I learned to distinguish between Buddy Bolden, King Oliver and Bunk Johnson. Of the three Bunk Johnson had the most beautiful tone, the best imagination and the softest sense of phrasing.

> . . . To me Joe Oliver's tone is just as good as Bunk's. And he had such range and such wonderful creations in his soul! He created some of the most famous phrases you hear today, and trends to work from. As I said before, Bolden was a little too rough, and he did not move me at all.[32]

During the exultant period of celebration that takes place in New Orleans between Christmas and New Year's, many people fire their guns or set off Roman candles. As a young boy, Armstrong found his stepfather's .38 caliber pistol in his mother's old trunk. Armstrong fired the gun to impress his young friends and was arrested and taken to Juvenile Court. He ended up at the Colored Waifs' Home for Boys, where he eventually joined the school's brass band and began his study of music. He eventually began to play so well that soon the band director made him student "leader of the band." As the band paraded around the district, the "sporting crowd" appreciated Louis's playing so much that they gave him hats full of money. Armstrong used the money to buy new uniforms and instruments for the band. This made him an even greater asset to his school's ensemble. He left the Home at age fourteen proud of the time he spent there.

At age fifteen Armstrong got a professional job at a honky-tonk joint owned by Henry Ponce in the red-light district. After playing cornet all night he hauled coal all day to help his family. Armstrong began listening to cornetist Freddie Keppard, who had a unique approach to the trumpet. "Whenever he played in a street parade he used to cover his fingers with a pocket handkerchief so that the other cornet players wouldn't catch his stuff."[33] Joe "King" Oliver's band "was the hottest jazz band in New Orleans between 1910 and 1917." Louis recalled that Joe Oliver was "blowing up a storm on his cornet" at Pete Lala's cabaret in Storyville with a band that featured drummer Harry Zeno, Buddy Christian on guitar (doubling on piano), clarinetist Jimmy Noone, double bassist Bob Lyons, and Zue Robertson on trombone.

Louis Armstrong (Photo courtesy of HRP Library).

Storyville provided steady employment for many great musicians that Louis remembered. Jelly Roll Morton made a lot of money playing the piano for Lulu White, "playing in one of her rooms" at Mahogany Hall in Storyville. Wealthy European-American businessmen and planters would come from all over the South to spend large sums of money in her pleasure house. Before the end of the decade the Navy began to crack down on the crime in Storyville. "It sure was a sad scene to watch the law run all those people out of Storyville. They reminded me of a gang of refugees. Some of them had spent the best part of their lives there. Others had never known any other kind of life. I have never seen such weeping and carrying-on. Most of the pimps had to go to work or go to jail, except a privileged few."[34] Jelly Roll Morton, Freddie Keppard, Jimmy Powlow, Bab Frank, Bill Johnson, George Fields, and other musicians left New Orleans before the closing of Storyville.

After his paramount tenure with Oliver in the early 1920s, Armstrong began recording his own records in 1925 as "Louis Armstrong and His Hot Five." Other early recordings included "Big Butter and Egg Man," "Skid-Dat-

De-Dat," "Cornet Chop Suey," and his first big hit, "Muskrat Rumble." His recording with the Hot Five released in 1926 also produced the "jazz" classics "Gut Bucket Blues" and "Heebie Jeebies." The latter composition was the side on which Armstrong introduced his scat singing style. He was very influential as a singer, and many musicians from assorted styles were influenced by his stylistic approach. As the genre's first great soloist, many musicians consider him the single most important figure in "jazz." Duke Ellington said, "If anyone was Mr. Jazz, it was Louis Armstrong."

The Armstrong 32-bar rondo (ABAC) composition "Struttin' with Some Barbecue" demonstrates the level of performance that Louis Armstrong and His Hot Five were capable of in 1927. The quintet features Armstrong's cornet, Johnny Dodds playing clarinet, Lil Hardin on piano, the trombone of Edward "Kid" Ory, and Johnny St. Cyr on banjo. The hot tempo of the performance provided an opportunity for Armstrong to display his pure and articulate command of melodic embellishment, as well as his high register cornet prowess. After a twelve-measure introduction, Armstrong takes the traditional New Orleans stylized cornet (and trumpet) role, staying close to the original melody with his lines and taking on the leadership role within the group polyphony. A two-bar banjo break sets the opening ensemble chorus apart from the first solo section. The next 32-bar chorus is shared, with the clarinet taking the first half (1–16) and the trombone finishing up (17–32). The last two bars of each of these two solos are again marked by breaks; the first in measures 15–16 and the second in 31–32. Armstrong shows an intriguing ability to create complex rhythms effortlessly as he improvises the next thirty-two bars, with breaks in the same locations as before. An ensemble break, reminiscent of Jelly Roll Morton's New Orleans style during this period, fills the last two bars of the form. A final chorus leads to a struttin' coda that provides a blithe and spirited ending.

From 1926 on, Armstrong began to approach the "jazz" solo "in terms not of a pop-tune more or less embellished, but of a chord progression generating a maximum of creative originality."[35] A 1928 recording of "West End Blues" displays the "new jazz" music as even more "abstract, sophisticated, virtuosic, emotionally expressive, [and] structurally perfect" than the earlier forms. Gunther Schuller discusses Armstrong's radically new transformation of King Oliver's standard:

> The block-like polyphonic structures of Oliver's performance, which were broken only by two-bar built-in breaks and revealed no organic development from chorus to chorus, are translated by Armstrong and Hines into an overall new form in which each chorus builds and feeds upon the preceding one. The means are twofold: variation technique combined with gradual dissolution into splinter subdivisions of the original sixteen-bar structures. . . . A necessary corollary to this structural progression was an analogous breakdown of the thematic material.[36]

Armstrong, while being acknowledged by most of his fans and colleagues as the Father of Jazz, did not avoid heavy criticism from the African-

American community for the "Satchmo smile." Nat Hentoff called this mask-like facial expression "the broadest and seemingly most durable grin in the history of Western man."[37] More critical fans considered Satchmo's toothy, squinty-eyed smile to be a grotesque caricature, much as the minstrel blackface had been: "Armstrong's squint was especially effective in hiding his intelligence, and as he grew older, he exaggerated it (and his toothiness) to the point where the contrast between the Satchmo mask and his features in repose was really quite startling. The sophistry of this seemingly jovial gesture was startling and offensive, to some observers, because for many jazz lovers the mask was the symbol of Armstrong's having "sold out.""[38]

After generations worth of racial stereotypes such as "The Frito Bandito," Dick Tracy's cartoon partners "Joe Jitsu" and "Go Go Gomez," and the stereotypical comedians Amos and Andy, it is easy to understand the African-American community's suspicion and trepidation when staring into another "Step 'n Fetchit" grin in public. Yet Armstrong's sincerely amiable personality and his personal conceptions about show business protocol must also be factored into the argument. It is less a matter of a smile of good humor or innocent social persiflage being perceived as inappropriate, than it is a fact that this behavior has been stereotyped by the majority culture to support its own bigoted agenda. The generally good-natured, xenophilic and unassuming Native American, African, and other peoples were considered less intelligent than the xenophobic European explorers who stole their land and labor or massacred them after indigenous people had befriended them. Joy and good cheer has always come naturally in African cultures. Oppression tends to check this high spirit and bring it down to the stoic and repressive demeanor so often associated with many aspects of European civilization.

"Jazz" critic Gary Giddins concludes: "The standard line about Armstrong . . . goes like this: Louis Armstrong was a superb artist in his early years, *the* exemplar of jazz improvisation, until fame forced him to compromise, at which point he became an entertainer, repeating himself and indulging a taste for low humor."[39] Giddins assumes that Armstrong's grin was a two-faced facade that disguised his wisdom and intelligence even though Armstrong never claimed to make such a distinction. He had never been a burnt-cork minstrel, but, as Giddins explains, he never minded making good use of a show-business style.

> [Armstrong]'s ability to balance the emotional gravity of the artist with the communal good cheer of the entertainer helped enable him to demolish the Jim Crow/Zip Coon/Ol' Dan Tucker stereotypes. In their place he installed the liberated black man, the pop performer as world-renowned artist who dressed stylishly, lived high, slapped palms with the pope, and regularly passed through whites-only portals, leaving the doors open behind him. . . . He was as much himself rolling his eyes and mugging as he was playing the trumpet. His fans understood that, but intellectuals found the whole effect too damn complicated.[40]

People often find it difficult to reconcile the comic entertainer's role, which both Fats Waller and Louis Armstrong incorporated into their performance presentations, with the musical genius that allowed both artists to create incredible music. The process of understanding this dilemma is further complicated by the notion that African-American composers and improvisers are "instinctive" and "spontaneous," while European composers are more sophisticated "geniuses." Both sets of musicians deal with the same notes and manipulate them to produce similar aesthetic and cultural results. Armstrong's greatness as an instrumentalist cannot be disputed, but many Europeans and European Americans relegate his creativity to an obscure "magical" process, a supposedly genetic feature with which African Americans are "innately endowed." This delusion is essential in a chronically racist society in which the majority culture has claimed intellectual and social superiority.

A more empirical and pertinent investigation clarifies the matter. Most "serious" musicians understand the profundity of Armstrong's contribution. Miles Davis said, "You know you can't play anything on a horn that Louis hasn't played—I mean even modern."[41] The brass section of the Boston Symphony went backstage after an Armstrong performance on one occasion to ask him to repeat a certain passage. He was glad to oblige, with brilliant variations, and the group of musicians were awestruck. One said, "I watched his fingers and I still don't know how he does it . . . playing there all by himself, he sounded as if a whole orchestra were behind him. I never heard a musician like this, and I thought he was just a colored entertainer."[42] Composer Virgil Thomson said a salient feature of Armstrong's contribution was to "combine the highest reaches of instrumental virtuosity with the most tensely disciplined melodic structure and the most spontaneous emotional expression, all of which in one man you must admit is pretty rare."[43] Albert Murray had this to say:

> The worldwide acclaim for Armstrong's genius and the unsurpassed sense of earthy well-being that his music generated everywhere he went seems to have meant very little if anything to spokespersons in the ever so dicty [sic] circles of the neo-Victorian watchdogs of proper black decorum. To them, apparently, there was no such thing as a genius who sometimes doubled as a court jester. In their view Louis Armstrong was only a very popular "entertainer" anyway. But even so, he owed it to "his people" to project an image of progressive if not militant uplift.

> Ironically, offstage Armstrong in his heyday was not only a preeminent influence in sartorial matters but also a major source of the fashionable speech of the most elegant and sophisticated "men about town" from border to border and coast to coast. Nor at any time after he became a public figure was his offstage presence any less awe-inspiring than that of the sparkling tongue-in-cheek regal bearing of Duke Ellington or the laid-back banker-calm Count Basie. People from the bossman down to the hired help became downright reverential

when they approached him in person. No matter how informal the situation was, this sometime court jester was always given the deference of royalty.[44]

Armstrong is often remembered for both his inventiveness and for allegedly "selling out" to commercial music. His transformation from innovator to entertainer (during the early 1930s) came at a time when it was difficult to survive as a musician—during the Great Depression.

Joe "King" Oliver

Papa Joe Oliver (1885–1938) was Armstrong's mentor; he gave Armstrong an old cornet, which Oliver had played for years. Armstrong said: "I still think that if it had not been for Joe Oliver, jazz would not be what it is today. He was a creator in his own right." Armstrong began to organize his own combos and found work in the red-light district. "A new generation was about to take over in Storyville. My little crowd had begun to look forward to other kicks, like our jazz band, our quartet and other musical activities."[45] Drummer Joe Lindsey, Morris French (trombone), and Louis Prevost were members of the sextet Armstrong formed at this time. Kid Ory and Joe Oliver collaborated to form "one of the hottest jazz bands that ever hit New Orleans." They would advertise for concerts and other musical events by playing in a tail-gate wagon. Armstrong explains (in his autobiography) that:

> When they found themselves on a street corner next to another band in another wagon, Joe and Kid Ory would shoot the works. They would give with all that good mad music they had under their bellies and the crowd would go wild. When the other band decided it was best to cut the competition and start for another corner, Kid Ory played a little tune on his trombone that made the crowd go wild again. But this time they were wild with laughter. If you ever run into Kid Ory, maybe he will tell you the name of that tune. I don't dare write it here. It was a cute tune to celebrate the defeat of the enemy. I thought it was screamingly funny and I think you would too.[46]

When Joe Oliver left the Ory-Oliver "jazz" band to move to Chicago, Louis was recommended for the cornet spot in the best band in town. Armstrong was beginning to establish a reputation for himself. Fate Marable (1890–1947), a redheaded bandleader, liked Armstrong's tone and persuaded him to leave Kid Ory's band to join his band playing on the excursion steamer *Sydney*. Marable was a fine pianist and calliope player who had been performing on moonlight trips up the Mississippi River for over sixteen years. The musicians in Fate's band were equal to the musicians in Ory's Band in their ability to improvise; but, unlike Ory's musicians, they could read music as well. Armstrong became a "feature man" in Marable's orchestra. Armstrong enjoyed both the high level of musicianship and the steady pay. He also learned how to approach the business of being a professional musician.

In the past, even with his own combos, he enjoyed performing so much that he ignored the business end of things. He never cared to be a leader because he did not want to end up quarreling over money. Music was too important to be adulterated by such mundane things for Armstrong. He states in his autobiography that:

> The only advance money we musicians ever got in those days was the deposits on the gigs we used to play. The only person who got that money was the contractor for the job or the leader of our little tail-gate band. I never signed a contract for any of those jobs. That was done by Joe Lindsey, our drummer, who would keep all the deposits. The rest of us did not know enough to pay attention to what was going on. We were so glad to get a chance to blow our horns that nothing else mattered.

Oliver's Creole Jazz Band was the first African-American band to record frequently, and, consequently, it became an influential ensemble. Born in 1885 in Louisiana, Oliver began to perform in New Orleans "jazz" bands when he was about twenty, after studying trombone and cornet. After gaining an impressive reputation as a musician in and around the Crescent City, he moved to Chicago in 1918, where he worked with various bands. In 1920 he took over the leadership of one of the local groups, which he renamed the Creole Jazz Band. Some of the finest New Orleans musicians of the time, including Louis Armstrong, became members of this ensemble. Oliver began to record in 1923, and the King Oliver band reigned supreme until he moved to New York in 1928.

The musicians in the ensemble were expected to improvise within the confines of a stylized New Orleans formula to which Oliver strictly adhered. It was required that musicians remain close to prescribed musical lines and patterns that were worked out in advance. Louis Armstrong, seeking a greater range of freedom, left the Creole Jazz Band in 1924. As Oliver insisted on remaining relatively static artistically with the "authentic" New Orleans Dixieland "Jazz" style, his audience began to seek more progressive musical styles such as Louis Armstrong's. Consequently, Oliver's focus on tradition and logic left him out of step with the next phase of the "jazz" evolution.

The final unfortunate blow came to King Oliver when trouble with his teeth began making it impossible for him to play his cornet. After the band dispersed, Oliver ended up in Savannah, Georgia, where he died in 1938.

Lil Hardin Armstrong

Lil Hardin (1898–1971) had joined "King" Oliver's legendary Creole Jazz Band in 1921. Oliver then sent for Louis Armstrong in 1922. Louis accepted his friend and mentor's offer to play second trumpet. Lil and Louis married in 1924. "Miss Lil," as she was affectionately called, was credited (by friends, the press, and Louis himself) with having tremendous influence on Louis's career. In addition to lessons in music theory, business advice was also provided. As "jazz" journalist John Chilton remarked, "Lil's place in jazz history will not rest solely on her piano playing, which was sturdy rather than spectacular. Her composing skills and the role that she played in Louis' life during his formative years in Chicago were much more important."[47]

All of Hardin's professional life was spent in Chicago, except for a few years in New York City, where she worked as "house pianist" for Decca Records from 1937 to 1940. The superb bands she led from 1920 onward were frequently booked extensively, and she recorded many of her compositions (which numbered over 150) at sessions for the Okeh, Paramount, Gennett, Columbia, Black and White, and Decca labels. She and Armstrong separated in 1931 and finally divorced in 1938.

Bix Beiderbecke

Although Bix Beiderbecke (1903–1931) was almost always performing with high profile "commercial" ensembles, he was one of the first European-American soloists to develop a reputation as an improviser in "jazz." Beiderbecke, was a self-taught musician born in Davenport, Iowa, began piano lessons when he was five years old but never learned to read music adequately. He soon switched to cornet. After listening to the music of Nick La Rocca and the Original Dixieland Jass Band as a teenager, he was finally introduced to the music of Louis Armstrong when the Riverboats brought his music to Davenport. When he began to work in Chicago, he was occasionally able to catch King Oliver or the New Orleans Rhythm Kings in concert.

He joined the Wolverines in 1923 and later worked with Charlie Straight's commercial orchestra. His low reading skills kept him from being a successful ensemble musician. Eventually, it would be his improvisational skills that got him work with Frankie Trumbauer's ensemble, the Paul Whiteman "King of Jazz" Orchestra and other prominent music groups. He was the first "White" musician to gain a measure of respect from African-American musicians for his delicate cornet tone. The fact remains, however, as Wynton Marsalis reminds us in the film *Trumpet Legends*, that Beiderbecke was a good musician who has become a "romantic figure" for many European Americans after his brief career came to an end. Recordings of his performances do not bear out claims that his importance lies in the innovations contained within his music. Perhaps the psychological pressure and pervasiveness of such romanticism among the members of the majority culture, even during his lifetime, led to the drinking that caused his early death. Although Paul Whiteman had been a popular figure since 1920, Beiderbecke was well aware of the difference between music played in the Whiteman band and the innovations that Armstrong, Bechet, Oliver, J. P. Johnson, and others were creating at the time.

Big Bands and the Approaching Swing Era

The traditional New Orleans Dixieland "Jazz" ensembles and the Chicago-style combos were not large enough to fill the large rooms that became typical new dance halls built throughout the United States during the 1920s and 1930s. As the fox-trot and other new dance steps replaced the older ones, Dixieland music was unable to adapt to accommodate new popular demands. Rooms the size of the Roseland Ballroom in New York City could hold more than a thousand dancers at a time. The bands that played for these functions had to increase in size to be heard in response to the dance craze that swept the nation after World War I.

Between the mid-1920s and late 1930s big band and swing music began simultaneous lines of development. Although the labels "swing" and "big band" are often used interchangeably, the big band format generally refers to a specific instrumentation. "Swing" is a stylistic African-American genre of music that gave way to bebop in the 1940s. Big bands, on the other hand, continued to develop in various forms from the mid-twenties to the present. Miles Davis, Don Ellis, Stan Kenton, Gil Evans, Lester Bowie, McCoy Tyner, and other musicians modified both the instrumentation and musical style of big bands that performed modern swing music. Even during the swing era, commercial dance bands (or stage bands) like Guy Lombardo's, the Paul Whiteman Orchestra (which often included thirty or more players), or Art Hickman's ensemble were often confused with swing bands, although many were not "jazz" bands at all. European-American audiences most often preferred the slick ensemble work and predictable efficiency of the commercial "White" big bands, and the "Middle-of-the-Road" bands, to the "Black" swing bands. Most "Black" bands often performed and recorded under relatively poor acoustical conditions. African-American bands were thus criticized by the mainstream for sounding alien and unrefined.

African-American "Jazz" Bands

The Fletcher Henderson and Duke Ellington orchestras were perhaps the most important and influential ensembles in the late 1920s. Henderson and his arranger, Don Redman, created an African-American "jazz" band sound that served as the progenitor of both big band and swing styles. Most African-American bands played for "Black" audiences, and these audiences generally wanted to hear "jazz." This situation continued until mid-century when African-American "jazz" was no longer performed within the "Black" community to the same degree as during the first half of the century. From the 1960s onward, the situation became exacerbated, as most innovative African-American "jazz" was performed in foreign establishments within the American majority population's communities.

The Henderson and Ellington orchestras were soon followed by bands led by Louis Armstrong, Jimmy Lunceford, Earl Hines, and others during the late 1920s. Count Basie moved out of Kansas City to New York in the 1930s and developed one of the greatest swing bands of all times. Bennie Moten, Cab Calloway, and Jay McShann's excellent bands emerged in the 1930s and 1940s and were followed by the bands of Billy Eckstine, Erskine Hawkins, Dizzy Gillespie, and other prominent bands.

During the heyday of Harlem night-life, Connie's Inn (on the corner of 131st and Seventh Avenue) was an active club along with the famous Lafayette Club next door. A third night spot, the Tree of Hope, completed the triad of competitors who drew European-American audiences uptown, and competed with the popular Cotton Club and Smalls's Paradise in that regard.

In 1929 Connie's Inn featured Louis Armstrong and the Hot Chocolates. Connie's hired Fletcher Henderson's Orchestra two years later on the heels of Ellington's success at the Cotton Club and Elmer Snowden's triumphant stay at Smalls's. The decline in popularity of the famous Harlem "jazz" club scene followed the repeal of Prohibition in 1933. Connie's moved downtown the following year. Dancing remained popular, however, and radio broadcasts kept the music of the big bands alive into the final triumphs of the swing era around 1935. Henderson's band was not one of those fortunate enough to reap the benefits of immense popularity during the swing era.

Commercial and Middle-of-the-Road Bands

The European-American bands were not concerned with performing for "Black" audiences and, thus, were not required to play "jazz." The mere sight and sound of saxophones, trumpets, trombones, and a rhythm section was enough to convince most European Americans in the 1920s and 1930s that they were hearing "jazz." Contrary to appearances though, virtually none of the music performed by the commercial dance bands could be considered "jazz." Commercial bands like the Paul Whiteman Orchestra featured a string section, solo vocalists, and vocal ensembles. Bands like those of Glenn Miller, Guy Lombardo, Lawrence Welk, Jan Garber, Eddie Duchin, and others were the most popular ones with "White" audiences from the early 1920s until the 1940s. A propensity toward improvisation or innovation were not features germane to the development of such bands.

The Middle-of-the-Road big bands such as those led by Harry James, Artie Shaw, Tommy Dorsey, Jimmy Dorsey, Claude Thornhill, Les Brown, and others performed both commercial arrangements that appealed to mainstream "White" audiences and "jazz" arrangements that featured outstanding soloists. The record companies called the ensembles MOR big bands in its mediaspeak, to describe bands that catered to both "jazz" fans and those who wanted slick, smooth commercial sounds. The most lucrative employment for musicians required that the bands play a majority of commercial, watered-down arrangements. Eventually, a few brave "White" bandleaders branched out into more adventurous musical territories. Beginning in 1936, one of the earliest bandleaders to lead an authentic European-American "jazz" band along the musical path blazed by African-American Swing bands more than a decade earlier was Benny Goodman. The bands of Stan Kenton, Woody Herman, Gene Krupa, and Charlie Barnet eventually followed along this more experimental path.

Big Bands Swing

The big band is usually divided into three sections: woodwinds, brass, and rhythm. The woodwind and brass form the horn section, basically an expansion of the New Orleans "front line." The woodwind section consists of from three to five saxophone players (one or two altos, one or two tenors, and a baritone) and may be augmented to include flute, soprano sax, clarinet, and bass saxophone doubles. (In most bands the woodwind players double on another instrument to allow for orchestral augmentation.) The brass section is divided into trumpets (three to five players and occasionally a flugelhorn) and trombones (most often two or three players). A tuba can also be included on rare occasions. The evolution from the small combo of four to six players to the big band required highly structured arrangements, since it was often difficult to improvise or "jam" full spontaneous compositions the way some small New Orleans bands were capable of managing. Jelly Roll Morton was one of the few earlier traditional New Orleans style arrangers who wrote individual parts for the musicians in fashions that eventually became the norm during the swing era. The rhythm section was a direct descendant of the New Orleans-style section, with a couple of notable changes. The piano, double bass, guitar, and drums remained while the tuba and banjo gradually faded into obscurity. Each section generally had its featured soloist, and band members were dressed in formal attire and placed on a stage.

The horn sections are usually contrasted in a variety of ways. One basic technique used by arrangers was the "jazz riff." The riff is a short melodic or rhythmic motive that usually occurred over one or two measures. The riffs were often used between sections in a call-and-response fashion where sections might answer each other or respond to the soloist. This style was adapted from African antiphonal and call-and-response patterns. African-American slave work songs and spirituals retained these elements.

African Antiphonal Patterns:

An Old Bornu Song
Give flesh to the hyenas at daybreak,
    Oh, the broad spears!
The spears of the Sultan is the broadest,
    Oh, the broad spears!
I behold thee now—I desire to see none other
    Oh, the broad spears!
My horse is tall as a high wall,
    Oh, the broad spears!
He will fight against ten—he fears nothing,
    Oh, the broad spears! . . .

Early Slave Work Song (call-and-response patterns):

An Old Boat Song

(Lead Singer)	*(Chorus)*
We are going down to Georgia, boys,	Aye, Aye.
To see the pretty girls, boys;	Yoe, Yoe.
We'll give 'em a pint of brandy, boys,	Aye, Aye.
And a hearty kiss, besides, boys.	Yoe, Yoe.

Antiphonal Patterns in Spirituals:

Lay Dis Body Down
I know moonrise, I know star-rise,
    I lay dis body down.
I walk in de moonlight, I walk in de starlight,
    I lay dis body down.
walk in the graveyard, I walk troo de graveyard,
    I lay dis body down.
lie in de graveyard and stretch out my arms,
    I lay dis body down.
go to de jedgement in de evenin' of de day,
    I lay dis body down.
An' my soul an' your soul will meet in de day,
    I lay dis body down.[48]

Sketchy arrangements called "head charts" were comprised of brief melodic and harmonic musical reference materials that were collectively expanded upon improvisationally. The generation and development of the spontaneous motives and harmonization emerged as music was composed on the spot, largely by the members of the ensemble.

Other composers and arrangers worked with varieties of interweaving lines that were not closely related to the contrapuntal New Orleans Dixieland style. When the whole band played together, one section was given the melody while the others outlined the harmony unobtrusively in the background. Other composers and arrangers would eventually adopt a style of writing "across the sections," where sonorities of a saxophone, trumpet, and trombone might be combined to present the lead line. A variety of levels of contrast were achieved by having various sections play together, alone, or in an array of combinations. The rhythm section contained the busiest musicians in the ensembles, since they were required to play virtually all of the time. The way a composer or arranger wrote for the band determined the organization's particular stylistic signature.

Since urban areas were the places where professional musicians could find financial sustenance, big bands were largely a product of urban life during the 1920s and 1930s. The enormous ballrooms and night-clubs provided an appropriate atmosphere for large ensembles to entertain dancers, accompany floor shows, and (later) to host concerts. In vibrant nightlife establishments like the Apollo and the Cotton Club in New York City, people in the 1920s did not want to merely sit and listen passively; they wanted to be entertained with swinging dance music. The ballrooms that people visited were exotically decorated, and the grandiose atmosphere added to the appeal of the exciting new big bands.

Network radio-broadcasts aired bands live from ballrooms and casinos throughout the country, contributing to the musical organization's glamour, popularity, and financial success. Most of the bands that enjoyed this benefit were European-American ensembles like Glenn Miller's band, which was featured on the most popular radio show of the day—the "Chesterfield Hour." There were more than four hundred dance bands traveling across America by

1940. By way of introduction, let us take a glance briefly at some of the pioneer musical organizations that provided America with a variety of big band and swing music.

Fletcher Henderson

Fletcher Henderson (1897 or 1898–1952) was the first important African-American big band leader and arranger. He graduated from Atlanta University in 1920 with a degree in chemistry, then moved to New York for his graduate work. He soon abandoned his academic studies and built an impressive band, making a reputation for himself and his colleagues at the Roseland Ballroom. He led one of the first and most influential "jazz" big bands in New York between 1924 and 1939. His bands were among the first to record the big band sound (beginning in 1924).

Henderson arranged for his own band as well as for other musicians. He played piano on many of the earliest recordings made by Bessie Smith and Ethel Waters. His charts were frequently constructed in a call-and-response and popular song style that became a primary influence on all the bands of the period. Between 1924 and 1925 both Louis Armstrong and tenor saxophonist Coleman Hawkins, two of the greatest soloists in "jazz," joined his orchestra. Louis Armstrong had a tremendous influence on the improvisational style of the Henderson band when he was hired as its featured soloist. The musicians were formerly styled as a reading band, but Armstrong opened up the ensemble's improvisational dimensions. Henderson introduced Armstrong to bandleaders he knew in New York, among them Guy Lombardo.

Fletcher Henderson managed to merge the old syncopated New York "jazz" style with a new Dixieland approach that soon had ears perked in The City. He evolved this merger into what was called a "Creole" style around 1923. Henderson's band arrangements, which were originally based on head arrangements, often alternated solo sections with ensemble playing, and frequently exchanged call-and-response activity between brasses and reeds. When Coleman Hawkins was a featured soloist with the Fletcher Henderson Orchestra, the big band sound that he and his chief arranger Don Redman (in the mid-1920s) formulated became the prototype for that style. Careful balance was maintained between sections, as well as between solo choruses and ensemble passages. Benny Carter said, "Joining the Fletcher Henderson band naturally made a great impression on me. My goodness, that was the band everybody was hoping to play with! It was the acid test. If you could make it with Fletcher, you could make it with anybody. It was the hardest music and the best music around."[49]

Henderson's 1926 recording of "The Stampede" displays these qualities admirably. He did not run his band in the traditional New Orleans style but instead encouraged his band members to express their musical ideas freely. Henderson, still in his early twenties, hired many young musicians, ones who had not allowed themselves to become stuck within the confines of past traditions. Armstrong flourished in such an environment, where his ideas and creativity were tested. During the following decade Henderson would augment his wind sections and the band continued to evolve into a definitive swing band paradigm. Ellington admired Henderson:

> Fletcher was a big inspiration to me. His was the band I always wanted mine to sound like when I got ready to have a big band, and that's what we tried to achieve the first chance we had with that many musicians. Obviously, a lot of other musicians wanted the same thing, and when Benny Goodman was ready for a big band, he sent for Fletcher Henderson to do his arrangements. That was consistent with good taste, and I am always glad to be identified with those who have good taste.[50]

Personnel changes were inevitable in Henderson's band. Henderson often recruited members from the band of Chick Webb (1909–39). Lester Young replaced Coleman Hawkins when Hawkins left for Europe in 1934. Young's tone did not impress musicians who were accustomed to Hawkins' full-bodied sound. Eventually Young was replaced by Ben Webster, who displays Hawkins's influence on recordings such as "Limehouse Blues," "Big John's Special," and "Happy as the Day is Long," recorded September 11, 1934, with Henderson in New York. As Dicky Wells felt, "Fletcher had a way of writing so that the notes just seemed to float along casually. You had to play the notes and the arrangement was swinging. He didn't write too high—there wasn't any screaming—but his music used to make you feel bright inside. Of course, you had to have a drummer with a beat. Fletcher's Walter Johnson used to lay there, and play a simple kind of drums, and let the musicians go for themselves."[51]

For a while Henderson was extremely successful and influential in New York. (He inherited the unfortunate label "The Black Paul Whiteman" on the first recording he made entirely under his own direction.) Later he was unable to keep his band supported financially. After 1939 Benny Goodman and the Dorsey brothers acquired music from Henderson's book and the innovator was reduced to working periodically for Goodman and other leaders as a pianist. Henderson never reached the level of fame or financial stability he deserved considering the influence he had on the development of the big band swing era. The European-American swing bands that imitated his style, on the other hand, were immensely popular and economically successful.

When he left New York and moved to Chicago, composer/pianist/mystic Sun Ra eventually came through the Henderson band. Fletcher Henderson heard Sun Ra (Sonny Blount) on piano rehearsing dancers for one of the floor shows at the Club DeLisa, where Sun Ra was hired to play with the house band that performed opposite the featured ("big name") attractions. He also worked closely with choreographer/producer Sam Dyer. For fifteen months beginning on February 18, 1947, Henderson and his Orchestra was the featured attraction at Club DeLisa—the longest engagement of his career. When Henderson's pianist, Marl Young, left the band to attend law school, Sun Ra was hired to play piano. Henderson conducted the fourteen-piece orchestra, with the exception of the arrangements that featured Henderson on piano ("Stalin' Apples" and "Humoresque," for instance). Sun Ra stayed with Henderson (his childhood idol) until the elder bandleader left town in 1948.

At least two writers, Lincoln Collier (1988) and Gunther Schuller (1968), have made disparaging remarks about Fletcher Henderson's personality. Neither man has ever played with Henderson and chances are they failed to engage him socially either. Sun Ra told Phil Schaap (in an interview in 1989) that "he was a gentleman and he had a sense of humor. . . . I don't see him with any vices or anything like that." In regards to Henderson's musical contributions Sun Ra says:

> Fletcher was really part of an angelic thing. I wouldn't say he was a man. I wouldn't say Coleman Hawkins was a man, because they did things men haven't done, and hadn't done before. And they didn't learn it from any man. They just did it. So therefore it came from somewhere else. A lot of things that some men do come from somewhere else, or they're inspired by something that's not of this planet. And jazz was most definitely inspired, because it wasn't here before. It wasn't here, where did it come from?[52]

When Fletcher Henderson became Benny Goodman's staff arranger in the early thirties, he contributed tremendously to Goodman's huge success. Some of the Henderson arrangements and compositions that became big band classics include "Mandy, Make Up Your Mind," "Wrapping It Up," "Copenhagen," "King Porter Stomp," "Down South Camp Meetin'," and "The Stampede." To Coleman Hawkins' disgust, the unassuming Henderson exchanged many of his fine scores for those of less capable composers with inferior bands.[53] Henderson never recaptured his initial success and influence, largely because his ideas anticipated the enormous success of the big bands by a number of years. Nonetheless, he continued to bring the careers of new star musicians into prominence, including those of Roy Eldridge and Chu Berry.

Duke Ellington

The ensemble of Edward Kennedy "Duke" Ellington (1899–1974) became the most internationally celebrated "jazz" orchestra lead by the most famous American composer/pianist in the world. His musical organization was renowned, not only for the ensemble performances heard around the world, but also for the individual artistry of many of Ellington's innovative performers. Aided by the low level of turnover within Ellington's stable band, the musicians traveled through many developmental transformations. His band members stayed with him for many years, and they produced popular hits repeatedly as a consequence. They eventually moved the "jazz" orchestra into the realm of an American symphonic compositional style based strictly upon the African-American "jazz" tradition.

Ellington was born to a middle-class family in Washington, D.C., and began piano lessons when he was seven years old. Although he considered the visual arts and athletics as possible careers, he was a composer from the time he was a teenager, when he completed his "Soda Fountain Rag," until the end of his distinguished career. His first copyright to a composition was received in 1923 and his first Broadway musical review, *Chocolate Kiddies*, was written in 1924. After moving to New York, Ellington fronted a six-piece band at the Broadway Kentucky Club. His five-year tenure at the Cotton Club began in 1927.

After Ellington's career began to take shape (when he was hired to play in Harlem's Cotton Club) he hired Irving Mills as his manager in 1926. Mills, who had successfully managed the career of Cab Calloway and other African-American performers, was notorious for skimming "off the top more profits than he should have,"[54] and laid unwarranted claim to some of Ellington's compositions. Yet the clever businessman was also known for giving his artists' careers valuable direction. This Ellington appreciated. Mills suggested that the Duke augment his band and concentrate on the new "jungle sound" that was becoming popular with African-American bands. Ellington said,

> If you ask Irving Mills, he will most likely confess that he is the man who (1) insisted that I make and record only my own music; (2) got me into the Cotton Club, the RKO Palace, and *The Black and Tan Fantasy* movie; (3) had big fights with record companies to get the black artists into hitherto all-white catalogues; (4) fought with the Dillingham executives to have us play in concert with Maurice Chevalier; (5) achieved our entry into picture houses, which we pioneered for big bands regardless of race; (6) arranged our interstate tours of the South and Texas in our own Pullman cars; (7) triumphantly secured my entrance into ASCAP; (8) took us to Europe in 1933, where we played the London Palladium and met the British Royal Family on several occasions.[55]

Ellington's "jungle sounds" incorporated the growling trumpet and trombone of Bubber Miley and "Tricky Sam" Nanton, respectively. "Bubber Miley," Ellington said, "was from the body and soul of Soulsville. He was raised on soul and saturated and marinated in soul. Every note he played was soul filled with the pulse of compulsion. *It don't mean a thing if it ain't got that swing* was his credo." And "'Tricky Sam,' Joe Nanton, was a youngster who made it to all the joints around Harlem where you could hear the music people insisted on calling jazz."[56]

Unusual articulations, mutes, and other new instrumental techniques were combined to execute his "jungle" orchestrations. The orchestra would eventually include numerous legendary artists, such as Ben Webster and Jimmy Blanton (both of whom joined Ellington in 1939). The Juan Tizol composition "Caravan" became famous for this distinct Ellington sound. Ellington collaborated often with other composers and arrangers in his band. Other hits composed around this period include "Black and Tan Fantasy" (1927), "Mood Indigo" (1930), "Sophisticated Lady" (1932), "Solitude" (1934), and "In A Sentimental Mood" (1935). The writing responsibilities for the band were also shared with Billy Strayhorn during the period some writers label the "Golden Age of Ellington" (1940–42).

Ellington's music, more than that of any other American composer, reflected the colorful urban American lifestyle in vivid detail. Street life, romance, cosmopolitan mixtures of people, trains, subways, traffic, and conversations from daily life can be heard in Ellington's music. Harlem was a rich source of such images. Albert Murray observes:

> He had written *A Tone Poem to Harlem*, a concert piece commissioned by Arturo Toscanini for the NBC Symphony Orchestra some ten years earlier [before going to Paris]. But long before that there were such standard Ellington dance-hall and nightclub numbers as *Harlem Speaks, Echoes of Harlem, Uptown Downbeat, Harmony in Harmony, I'm Slappin' Seventh Avenue with the Sole of My Shoe,* and *Harlem Airshaft,* that were also unexcelled evocations and celebrations of life in uptown Manhattan. Nor was the cacophonous hustle and bustle of midtown Manhattan, with its urgent horns and motors and neon lights and twinkling skyline, ever more compellingly rendered than in *Mainstem*, his special arrangement of a finger-snapping tone parallel to Broadway.[57]

Eschewing the riff style, Duke set new standards on almost all levels of the big band phenomenon. He wrote in conventional big band style, working one section against another; but, he also expanded the possibilities of the style beyond the explorations of all other big band and swing band composers. He used the wordless vocal to great orchestral advantage on songs like his 1927 "Creole Love Call." His 1930 recording of "Mood Indigo" explored scoring (voicing) across sections before this was a common procedure. Clarinet, muted trumpet, and muted trombone combined as a single voice to create a melodic color that had never been used before in "jazz" or in any other music. Among his many other firsts, Ellington featured the pizzicato double bass in a melodic role on his 1940 recording of "Jack the Bear." Ellington was able to write to suit the musical personalities of specific players based on their ability and style, and his works often depended on collective improvisation and spontaneous composition. A musical passage scored for a particular section might include a written instruction inviting a soloist to improvise over the prescribed parts.

Duke Ellington survived and prospered in a racist America as an unacknowledged but undeniable master of twentieth-century music. After seventy-five years of undisputed leadership in America, it is clear that if anyone deserves the title "king" of the era, Duke Ellington is best qualified. Ellington and his contemporaries came in contact with a "peculiar style of American exploitation when his first group was organized after World War One."[58] Harold Cruse discusses the dilemma they confronted in his book, *The Crisis of the Negro Intellectual*:

> The role of the Negro, as entertainer . . . is still being used, manipulated, and exploited by whites (predominantly Jewish Whites). Negro entertainment talent is more original than that of any other ethnic group, more creative ("soulful" as they say),

spontaneous, colorful, and also more plentiful. It is so plentiful, that in the marketplace of popular culture, white brokers and controllers buy Negro entertainment cheaply (sometimes for nothing) and sell it high—as in the case of Sammy Davis. But there is only one Sammy Davis. In the shadows, a multitude of lesser colored lights are plugging away, hoping against hope to make the Big Time, for the white culture broker only permits a few to break through—thus creating an artificial scarcity of a cultural product. This system was established by the wily Broadway entrepreneurs in the 1920s. Negro entertainment posed such an ominous threat to the white cultural ego, the staid Western standards of art, cultural values and aesthetic integrity, that the entire source had to be stringently controlled.[59]

In Spike Lee's film *Mo' Better Blues*, the director centers a sociocultural artistic statement around the contemporary life of the fictitious African-American "jazz" artist Bleek Gilliam (Denzel Washington). The initial negative criticism of the film often centered around Lee's alleged stereotypes and caricatures involving Jewish agents for African-American clients. Nat Hentoff attacks Spike Lee's "bigotry" and "banal clichés" while admitting that "there were Jews who exploited black musicians" like the stereotypes depicted in *Mo' Better Blues*.[60] Author Alan Vorspan tells us in his book *Black Anti-Semitism and Jewish Racism*, "One of the clichés heard more and more frequently in Jewish gatherings is: 'After all we have done for them, they no longer want us. They hate us.'"[61] Vorspan continues, "Another implication is that black-Jewish [sic] relationships used to be good and now they have turned sour. The truth is, of course, that they never were really good. . . . In the fight for equality for blacks, we were the superior people. This was no relationship of peer to peer, equal to equal, powerful group to powerful group." Finally, he argues that "Jewish-black relations were once equivalent to parent-child relations."

Harold Cruse's reasons for singling out "Jewish Whites" are probably not anti-Semitic. Rather, he is apparently focusing upon the fact that the majority of promoters, agents, and managers who performed the role of liaison between African-American artists and the music industry (dominated by European-American businessmen) were Jewish Americans. Many of the songsmiths who listened to African-American songs, transcribed them, then peddled them on Tin Pan Alley were also Jewish Americans. While many European-American music industry people shunned African-American artists, Jewish Americans took advantage of the opportunity to represent the ostracized "Black" artists in a racist socioculture. This reciprocity did not always result in gross exploitation, but often it did—just as Africans sold their fellow African captives into slavery, Native-American scouts worked with European soldiers in the subjugation of indigenous American people, and Europeans burned their women as witches. Few people in the history of humankind have remained noble enough to refrain from taking advantage of others less fortunate.

In addition to his compositional genius and exemplary skill as a band leader, Duke Ellington was also one of the most creative "jazz" pianists in the history of American music. His constant experimentation kept him on the forefront of "jazz" innovation longer than his contemporaries.

Jimmie Lunceford

Jimmie Lunceford (1902–47) began to construct his first big bands while a music educator. His young musicians were molded into an ensemble whose style emphasized precision and discipline. Lunceford received a music degree from Fisk University in Nashville before engaging in private study with Wilberforce J. Whiteman (bandleader Paul Whiteman's father). The fastidious Lunceford band soon evolved into one of the most creative and exciting "jazz" bands of all times. Ensemble blending, articulation, and unity of phrasing never interfered with the band's ability to swing. Unlike the typical bands of the day, the level of artistic meticulousness within the Lunceford aggregation was sufficient to challenge the professionalism, excellence, and efficiency of renowned European "classical" ensembles of the 1930s, while remaining an unparalleled showband as well.

The Jimmie Lunceford Orchestra was exhilarating to watch. Each section's gestures onstage were carefully choreographed and scrupulously executed, adding powerful theatrical flare to the music. While saxophones would sway, trumpets moved up and down, and trombones flashed their bells from side to side. Glenn Miller and other band leaders soon copied many of the Lunceford band's movements and used the choreography with their own musical ensembles. Lunceford used an augmented big band instrumentation uncommon for the period (temple blocks, timpani, celeste, etc.). His emphasis on melodies with unpredictable phrase lengths, colorful orchestral devices (timbral and dynamic contrasts, etc.), and capable soloists coalesced to create a style that matured into an important stylistic contrast to the music produced by Fletcher Henderson.

The Lunceford reed section was so strong that the leader was forced to break with tradition and place them behind the brass! As section leader, alto saxophonist Dan Grissom rarely took solos, but the rest of his colorful reed section were capable improvisers. Alto saxophonist Willie Smith became the most notable of the group. The Decca recordings of the band contain examples of the lyrical interchange that took place between Smith and tenor saxophonist Joe Thomas on many memorable occasions.

Lunceford carried three exciting arrangers on his payroll. The most gifted musical architect was trumpeter (and vocalist) Melvin "Sy" Oliver, who later contributed arrangements to Tommy Dorsey's big band book. Oliver's contributions were essential to the development of the "Lunceford Sound" that reached its peak between 1933 and 1939. Gerald Wilson, Edwin Wilcox, and Roger Segure also contributed arrangements to the Lunceford band book. The dynamic control and balance between sections, and between sections and soloist, made listening to the Lunceford band an exhilarating experience. Tunes like "Margie," "Hi Spook," and "Life is Fine" were popular arrangements performed and recorded by the orchestra. Jimmy Lunceford's career was cut short by a fatal automobile accident in southern California. His band "was one of the most beautiful vehicles of jazz in the annals of music."[62]

Bennie Moten

Bennie Moten (1894–1935) was bandleader of one of the leading bands in the Midwest during the early swing era. Although New York City was a sort of commercial clearinghouse for big band and swing music during the 1920s, African-American swing also enjoyed popularity and continued development in other cities before being exported to the Big Apple. Moten, Charlie Creath, and other musicians in St. Louis and Kansas City imitated the riverboat "jazz" music in the dives where barrelhouse and ragtime piano was played opposite fine blues singing. Moten was still playing elements of both of these piano styles in his 1928 recording "Get Low-Down Blues."

Moten trained Count Basie in the Kansas Blues and Swing styles that became the foundation for young Basie's development (after taking over Moten's band following the bandleader's death). Moten developed a riff style (after Armstrong's combo riff style) and later established a tradition of trading fours and other terse and economical musical devices. His band, too (like the Fletcher Henderson Orchestra), was often in dire straits even when recording, yet it still managed to establish the swing feel that dominated the big band era. Moten borrowed sophisticated chord structures from popular songs and incorporated them into his arrangements to augment his blues-based harmonic approach. Basie would eventually drop the emphasis on traditional blues and early "jazz" to evolve a more modern "hot" swing–based style.

Count Basie

William "Count" Basie (c. 1904–84), born in Red Bank, New Jersey, is considered by most musicians to be the real King of Swing. In addition to his affiliation with Bennie Moten early in his career, Basie accompanied Bessie Smith, Clara Smith, and played with the Blue Devils before becoming a band leader. He carried the Kansas City style forward within his exemplary musical organizations, which included the most influential and unique instrumental soloists and vocal stylists of the day (Coleman Hawkins, Lester Young, Billie Holiday, etc.). As the bands under his direction continually set the standards for swing band performance, Basie himself established a trademark comping piano style that influenced many generations of pianists.

After inheriting the Moten band, Basie began to explore jump rhythms and the juxtaposition of brass and reed riffs, and he developed the most facile and smoothest sounding rhythm section in swing. In May, 1936, "jazz" entrepreneur John Hammond heard Basie at the Reno Club in Kansas City. Basie came to New York that year to play at the Roseland Ballroom and to record for the Decca record label. Listeners were astonished to hear the hottest of all swing bands achieve its effects through extremely elegant yet unadorned musical means. The "powerhouse" sound of the Basie band was based on hot-riffs and innovative solo improvisations, supported by the pianist's minimal and perfectly timed piano interjections. Basie's prodding from his keyboard was buoyant, flexible, and unpredictable. His style was originally based upon the stride tradition of Fats Waller and James P. Johnson. This style, in its maturity, created a sense of seething tension that would drive an audience wild with anticipation and surprise, but only with the slightest musical gestures.

Count Basie (Image courtesy of HRP Library).

His approach demanded perfect tempo and timing as the element of constancy within the relaxed and subdued quality of Basie's rhythm section. Clarity was achieved as each musician in the rhythm section left rhythmic space for their musical cohorts, and by a careful balance and blending of piano, bass, drums, and guitar. The Kansas City–style arrangements for the horn section were less busy and elaborate than those the New York bands were used to presenting, and Basie avoided the older interwoven counterpoint of the New Orleans Dixieland style. Both the lead lines and background figures (behind soloists) were often driven by riffs. These cogent motives were sometimes written down, but often they would manifest spontaneously during rehearsals or performances. Because the genesis of the spontaneous riffs began off the top of a performer's head, they were called "head charts" (or "head arrangements"). "Moten's Swing," "One O'Clock Jump," and "Lester Leaps In" are well-known examples of the Basie riff band style.

The imposition of gas rationing restricted travel during World War II and the military draft also took its toll. Entertainment taxes and public curfews reduced audience attendance at dances. When the war ended in 1945, bebop had emerged as the new modern style of innovative African-American music, leaving swing sounding somewhat old fashioned. Basie took all the transitions and changes in stride. In 1947 his RCA Victor recording of "Open the Door Richard" became a hit and earned him revenue. Nevertheless, the economic realities of the day made the big band format financially impractical. On several occasions Basie spent his entire bank account to pay his band the wages he felt they deserved. The turnovers within the band eventually left Freddie Green and Jimmy Rushing among the few members from the early Basie Orchestra. On January 8, 1950, Basie decided that the band could no longer survive. "I just made up my mind and then called everyone together and told them," he said.[63]

The Count's sextet debuted at the Brass Rail in Chicago on February 10, 1950. Although the sextet played a modest but sufficient number of performances, Basie was not satisfied musically. In the spring of 1952, saxophonist Marshall Royal (1912–1995) helped Basie organize a new orchestra. The new ensemble used one-night-stands to rehearse the book, and opened at Birdland on July 24, 1952. By March 1954 the band made its first European tour. Vocalist Joe Williams joined the band that year, enabling Basie to reach the top of the popular music charts. Although the constant turnover within the band still kept it from becoming the unified set of innovative improvisers that characterized the swing era Basie Orchestra, Basie had staged an impressive and lasting comeback.

Basie appeared in over a dozen films and recorded numerous records. The roster of musicians who performed with his band contains many of the finest soloists in "jazz." With only a few rare exceptions, Count Basie remained on the road from 1936 until his death in 1984. His band kept people swinging through bebop, cool, funky, rhythm and blues, rock and roll, and many other dance styles and musical periods. Ellington remembered:

> When I first came to New York, Count Basie was playing over on Fifth Avenue between 134th and 135th at a place called Edmond's. . . . I used to go over there every night and stand on the opposite side of Fifth Avenue and listen to Count Basie. It was wonderful except for the fact that I was too young to be allowed into a place like that. One day, I shed my adolescence by putting on long pants. They thought I was a grown man and let me in. I fooled them, and I'm glad, because I finally got to stand alongside the piano and watch the great Count Basie.[64]

Glenn Miller

Glenn Miller (1904–44) led a band that was well disciplined but more commercial than many of the other Middle-of-the-Road big bands. Miller placed less emphasis on the unrestrained improvising of his sidemen and more on arrangement and orchestration. Miller played with the Dorsey brothers and Ray Noble's band before trying to start a string quartet "jazz" combo and another band in 1937 (both of which failed because he could not find a suitable audience). Finally, after two years of experimenting with combinations of instruments, his big break came with a steady gig at the Glen Island Casino in 1939. The casino was the launching pad for the Dorsey brothers, Charlie Barnet, and other European-American bands. The casino also paved the way for Miller's band to become one of the most popular big bands in mainstream America. He enlisted in the Air Corps during World War II and organized a fine service band. Miller, a martinet on the bandstand, was killed in plane crash enroute to Paris in 1944.

Paul Whiteman

Paul Whiteman (1890–1967) was the son of the conductor of the Denver Symphony Orchestra. He was trained in the European tradition and played with the San Francisco Symphony in 1914. Whiteman spent a good deal of his time in the Barbary Coast (San Francisco Bay Area), drinking and womanizing. Nevertheless, he had a genius for self-promotion. In time, he began styling himself as more than just a presenter of dance music. He described himself as a performer of *symphonic jazz*, a "new" art form of which he was king. Paul Whiteman was by no means an innovator or a "jazz" king, but he became an immensely popular figure among European Americans. He paraded popular songsters on stage and featured elaborate "semiclassical" arrangements and compositions for large commercial orchestras. He purposely chose big name "jazz" musicians for his ensembles, not strictly for their improvisational ability, but to increase his popularity. As a result, however, the addition of improvisers rendered the band capable of performing some Middle-of-the-Road big band music.

The International Sweethearts of Rhythm was founded in 1937 at the Piney Woods Country Life School for poor and orphaned African-American children (in Mississippi). The band gained its name because it included Asian-American, Mexican-American, European-American, and African-American women. It was inspired by earlier women swing bands that its school director, Laurence Clifton Jones, had heard. Ray Lee Jones became the leader of the musical organization, and Anna Mae Winburn became its musical director. Many women's bands were able to break into the industry while men were off fighting the war. The Sweethearts soon became the primary fundraisers for the school.

The Media Continues to Burgeon

The world was undergoing rapid change during the first quarter of the century. The emancipation of the slaves in America provided one of the catalysts that prompted the Industrial Revolution. Bereft of the coercive power over persons that slavery provided, the United States developed its industry.

Technology replaced cheap or free (unpaid) labor to sustain the economic acceleration that the country had enjoyed for three centuries. As this new technology came knocking on vaudeville's door, the entertainment world was hurled into a new frontier.

The piano roll emerged along with the creation of the vogue mechanical pianola during the ragtime era. When the phonograph and radio came into general use, the African-American community was no longer the primary spawning ground for African-American musicians. Now a primarily European-American audience became the standard used to determine audience acceptance of musical forms. As race records gradually made their way into both African-American and European-American homes, the phonograph became a major boon to the rapid expanding music industry. Theoretically, a single performer could now be duplicated and reproduced endlessly, providing maximum profits with a minimal financial investment. Leaders and songwriters were the only musicians in a legal position to receive royalty payments from record sales. All other artists ("sidemen") received payment only for the initial performance, although record sales could run into the millions.

The greatest payoff for record companies were the "hits," since they allowed a company to conserve its financial resources by eliminating the need to invest in (or take a chance on) new artists. Radio broadcasting began in the early 1920s, but "jazz" was not performed on that medium until 1928. When "jazz" broadcasts were finally aired, the performers were generally "commercial" European-American bands, such as those led by Paul Whiteman and Rudy Vallee. "Soon what people wanted to hear became synonymous with what was (packaged) selected or programmed for them to hear."[65]

With the recording industry in place, the definitive African-American musical styles could be studied systematically and copied by European-American imitators, who were (and still are) promoted by the new media nationally and internationally much more readily. This process of cultural parasitism did not begin with "Tin Pan Alley." As Eileen Southern reminds us, "Blackface minstrelsy was a form of theatrical performance that emerged during the 1820's and reached its zenith during the years 1850–70. Essentially it consisted of an exploitation of the slave's style of music and dancing by white men, who blackened their faces with burnt cork and went on the stage to sing Negro songs (also called Ethiopian songs), to perform dances derived from those of the slaves, and to tell jokes based on slave life."[66] John Tastes Howard tells how Stephen Foster was engaged in a similar type of exploitation: "It is interesting to compare the refrain of Stephen Foster's 'Camptown Races' with several other songs of the period. It is almost identical melodically with the Negro Spiritual 'Roll Jordan, Roll' and has its counterpart in music and text with the chantey, 'Doo-Dah-Day.'"[67]

The European-American "jazz" band that had most carefully observed the "Black" New Orleans style was billed as the "Original Dixieland Jass Band, the creators of Jazz," and sent quickly off to Europe. The men in the ODJB first performed with "Papa" Jack Laine and other senior African-American band-leaders in New Orleans and listened to (and learned from) King Oliver and other elder musicians ("the LaRocca boys used to hang around and got a lot of ideas from his gang," says Preston Jackson).[68]

They had learned the music of the Negroes in New Orleans, and they brought their "jazz" to Chicago, New York, London, and the world at large. Thus to a vast number of people, for quite a long time, the kind of music the Original Dixieland Jazz Band played represented all of jazz. Actually, the impression that this particular band was, in itself, a starting point is somewhat of an exaggeration. They were far from being the first jazz band, of course; were not even among the very first white bands, not the first to bring the music out of New Orleans and up North. But ... they made the initial jazz recordings, in 1917. And ... like many another group of their time, they went in for cowbells and other dubious "novelty" effects.[69]

The phonograph became available around 1877. Radiotelegraph and the radiotelephone were just around the corner, arriving in 1895 and 1906. The airplane was ready to fly in 1903. By 1915 long distance telephone calls could be made. It was the movie industry, however, that had the most direct effect on prospective stars in the performing world. Talking pictures were the fashion before the swing era was in full bloom. In fact, the movie industry had been developing for almost a full century by the time most swing bands had matured.

African Americans did not gain an equal or comparable opportunity in the film industry. Bessie Smith, Louis Armstrong, Duke Ellington, Lena Horne, Cab Calloway, Fats Waller, Pearl Bailey, and other musicians did receive valuable media exposure. Bessie Smith earned two thousand dollars a week at the beginning of 1929 as a recording artist, and even more money after starring in her low-budget film that year. In the mid-1930s, after the effects of the depression were full blown, her average recording fee for two sides of a record was reduced from three thousand dollars to fifty dollars per side.

The industries began to apply terms and labels such as "refined," "sweet," or "clever" to some of the more inchoate music European Americans learned to imitate by listening to recordings of African-American music. The Woody Allen film *Radio Days* inadvertently illustrates the racial imbalance found in media presentations and promotions of this era, while also capturing the glamour and excitement that was associated with big band broadcasting. In addition to portraying such aspects of American culture, the film displays the magnitude and grandiloquence of early dance band performances as they were heard in large rooms like the Roseland Ballroom and Radio City Music Hall in New York City.

Even the few African-American musicians who were able to partake in the substantive offerings of the new American media found that the quality of their recordings, the length of their movies, or the frequency of their live radio broadcasts did not equal that enjoyed by their European-American colleagues. Listening to recordings by both African-American and European-American artists from around 1915–40 makes this inequity conspicuous and demonstrates the pervasiveness of racist attitudes in America at the time. Movies such as the early Paramount comedy *Gasoline Gus* (1921), with Fatty

Arbuckle, and 20th Century Fox's *Old Kentucky* (1935), with Bill Robinson, continued to present negative African-American stereotypes.

Notes

[1] Linda, Dahl, *Stormy Weather*, pp. 35–38. Interview of October 7, 1959.

[2] As quoted in John A Kouwenhoven, *The Art in Modern American Civilization* (New York, 1967), p. 222.

[3] Martha Bayles, *Hole in Our Soul: The Loss of Beauty and Meaning in American Popular Music* (New York: The Free Press, 1994), p. 89.

[4] Leonard Feather, *Insid e Jazz* (New York: Da Capo Press, 1977), pp. 33–35.

[5] Robert Tallant, *Voodoo in New Orleans* (New York: Collier Books, 1946), p. 74.

[6] Sally Placksin, *Jazzwomen: Their Words, Lives and Music—1900 to the Present* (London: Pluto, 1985), pp. 4–5.

[7] *Music: Black White & Blue,* pp. 60–67.

[8] William Howland Kenney, *Chicago Jazz: A Cultural History, 1904–1930* (New York: Oxford University Press, 1993), pp. 98–99.

[9] Ibid., p. 99.

[10] Ibid.

[11] Ibid.

[12] Ibid., p. 160.

[13] Joel Vance, *Fats Waller: His Life and Times* (New York: Berkley Medallion Books, 1977), p. 55.

[14] This work served as a prototype for "Porgy and Bess."

[15] No one has produced hard evidence to support this claim, however.

[16] According to Mike Lipskin in Vance, *Fats Waller: His Life and Times*, p. 59.

[17] Joel Vance, *Fats Waller: His Life and Times* (London: Robson Books, 1992), pp. 127–28.

[18] From an article appearing in the *World-Telegram* as cited in Vance, *Fats Waller: His Life and Times*, p. 108.

[19] *Historical and Cultural Atlas of African Americans*, pp. 186–87.

[20] Ian Carr, Digby Fairweather, and Brian Priestley, *Jazz: The Rough Guide* (London: Rough Guides, 1995), pp. 529–30.

[21] Henry T. Sampson, *Blacks in Blackface: A Source Book on Early Black Musical Shows* (Metuchen, N.J.: Scarecrow Press, 1980). Also, James Weldon Johnson, *Black Manhattan* (New York: Alfred A Knopf, 1930).

[22] Clare Bloodgood Crane, "Alain Locke and the Negro Renaissance" (Ph.D. diss., University of California–San Diego, 1971), p. 28.

[23] *Black Music in the Harlem Renaissance*, p. 29.

[24] Nathan Irvin Huggins, *Harlem Renaissance* (New York: Oxford University Press, 1971), p. 5.

[25] *Black Music in the Harlem Renaissance*, pp. 29–30.

[26] Ibid., p. 108.

[27] Margaret Just Butcher, *The Negro in American Culture* (New York: Mentor Books, 1956), p. 35.

[28] Sigmund Spaeth, *A History of Popular Music in America* (New York: Random House, 1948); and Alain Locke, *The Negro and His Music* (New York: Arno Press, 1969).

[29] *New York Times*, May 20, 1923, p. 12.

[30] *Music: Black White & Blue*, p. 66.

[31] Dave Dexter, Jr. *The Jazz Story* (Englewood Cliffs, N.J.: Prentice-Hall, 1964), p. 38.

[32] Louis Armstrong, *Satchmo: My Life in New Orleans* (New York: Prentice Hall, 1954), pp. 24–25.

[33] Ibid. p. 53.

[34] Louis Armstrong, *Satchmo: My Life in New Orleans* (Da Capo Press, 1986).

[35] Gunther Schuller, *Early Jazz: Its Roots and Musical Development* (New York: Oxford University Press, 1986), pp. 59, 89, 103.

[36] Ibid., p. 125.

[37] Nat Hentoff, *Jazz Is* (New York: Limelight, 1984), p. 68.

[38] Martha Bayles, *Hole in Our Soul: The Loss of Beauty and Meaning in American Popular Music* (New York: The Free Press, 1994), p. 86.

[39] Gary Giddins, *Satchmo* (New York: Doubleday, 1988), p. 2.

[40] Ibid., p. 34.

[41] As quoted in ibid., p. 32.

[42] As quoted in Hentoff, *Jazz Is*, p. 68.

[43] As quoted in Giddins, *Satchmo*, p. 33.

[44] Albert Murray, *The Blue Devils of Nada: A Contemporary Approach to Aesthetic Statement* (New York: Pantheon Books, 1996), pp. 69–70.

[45] Louis Armstrong, *Satchmo: My Life in New Orleans* (Da Capo Press, 1986).

[46] Louis Armstrong, *Satchmo: My Life in New Orleans* (Da Capo Press, 1986).

[47] "Lil—Louis' Second Lady," *Melody Maker*, September 4, 1971.

[48] Patricia Liggins Hill, ed., *Call and Response: The Riverside Anthology of the African American Literary Tradition* (New York: Houghton Mifflin, 1998), pp. 33, 53–54.

[49] Stanley Dance, liner notes from the album "Fletcher Henderson: 'Swing the Thing'—Volume 2 (1931–1934)," DL79228.

[50] Edward Kennedy (Duke) Ellington, *Music is My Mistress* (Garden City, N.Y.: Doubleday, 1973), p. 49.

[51] Dance, liner notes.

[52] John C. Reid, "It's after the End of the World," *Coda*, no. 231 (April/May 1990): 30.

[53] Dance, liner notes.

[54] James Haskins, *Black Music in America: A History Through Its People* (New York: Harper Trophy, 1987), p. 85.

[55] Ellington, *Music is My Mistress*, p. 77.

[56] Ibid., p. 106.

[57] Murray, *Blue Devils of Nada*, pp. 101–2.

[58] *Music: Black White & Blue*, pp. 60–67.

[59] Harold Cruse, *The Crisis of the Negro* (New York: Morrow Paperback, 1971), p. 109.

[60] In the *Village Voice*, September 4, 1990.

[61] Vorspan, *Black Anti-Semitism and Jewish Racism*, introduction by Nat Hentoff, with James Baldwin, Earl Raab, Rabbi Jay Kaufman, and other contributors (New York: Schocken, 1970), p. 208.

[62] Alain Gerber, liner notes on "Jimmie Lunceford 4: 'Blues in the Night'—1938–1942," MCA-1314 (1980).

[63] Bud Kliment, *Count Basie: Bandleader and Musician* (Los Angeles: Melrose Square, 1994), p. 158.

[64] Ellington, *Music is My Mistress*, p. 102.

[65] *Music: Black White & Blue*, pp. 60–67.

[66] Eileen Southern, *The Music of Black Americans: A History* (New York: Norton, 1983), p. 100.

[67] John Tastes Howard in the *New York Times*, May 30, 1971.

[68] Carr, Fairweather, and Priestley, *Jazz: The Rough Guide*, p. 483.

[69] Orrin Keepnews and Bill Grauer, Jr., *A Pictorial History of Jazz* (New York: Crown, 1955), p. 19.

VII
Innovators Emerging Between 1930 and 1940

WHY WOMEN MUSICIANS ARE INFERIOR

SHOULD BE ABLE TO GET MORE OUT OF HORN THAN A MERE CRY FOR HELP

Women don't seem to be able to develop a lip, which stymies their taking more than one chorus at a time. The mind may be willing but the flesh is weak . . . women are as a whole emotionally unstable which prevents their being consistent performers on musical instruments . . . gals are conscious of the facial contortions so necessary in "blowing it out" and limit their power for fear of appearing silly in the eyes of men.

—Down Beat (during the 1930s)

Many African-American artists, authors and historians had a difficult time getting work published, and this discouraged some of them. It is clear, however, that the early musicians (Bechet, Armstrong, Ellington, Basie, Lunceford, Moten, etc.) were able to keep their bands working together performing primarily in African-American communities. The musical communities still engaged in communal music making during the swing era (polyphonic interplay, big band call and response, close families of musicians, etc.), and the managers and other business associates were generally African American. There seems to have been less chance of being exploited from within African-American communal networks. Problems involving narcotics were less pervasive than during the modern "jazz" period (particularly after the bebop era), when the music moved out of the African-American communities. "Jazz" in the 1930s was dominated by its only truly popular style, big band swing. Small groups were still on the scene, however, as Ellington reminds us:

> The foundation of jazz as we know it today had by now been thoroughly laid. What was built upon it was the work of great innovators. I must emphasize that jazz was and is a highly competitive form of music, and many of the ideas that transformed it were first heard in what we called "cutting contests" or "jam sessions," where the musicians tried to learn from and outdo one another. The rise of the big bands did not mean the end of small groups, for they were always to be heard in the smaller clubs and in those places where musicians played "af-

ter hours," very late at night. There you might find James P. Johnson, Fats Waller, and the Lion competing with one another. Or several trumpet players, or saxophonists, or clarinetists. Ideas were exchanged, and newcomers learned from those with more experience. Certain innovators, like the great virtuoso of the piano, Art Tatum, remained virtually inimitable, but they were a constant source of inspiration.[1]

The New "Swing" Bands

Music was less competitive within the stylized musical roles of early "jazz" until Louis Armstrong and other experimenters set new levels. Until then, although leaders remained the most dominant member of an ensemble, performances were usually based upon more strictly democratic and casual communal approaches. In his book *Swing That Music* (p. 121), Armstrong talks about the new standards required to perform the more progressive style.

> To become a front rank "swing player," a musician must learn to read expertly and be just as able to play to score as any "regular" musician. Then he must never forget for one minute of his life that the true spirit of swing music lies in free playing and that he must always keep his own musical feeling free. He must try to originate and not just imitate. And if he is a well-trained musician in the first place, he will be able to express his own ideas as they come to him with more versatility, more richness and more body. . . . To be a real swing artist, he must be a composer as well as a player.

In addition to responsibilities as a performer, the composer or arranger is often a facilitator who inspires, embellishes, refines, guides, and organizes the improvised experiments of her/his musical collaborators.

The evolution from the early New Orleans style bands into swing was not a simple sequence of events. King Oliver's Creole Jazz Band introduced the New Orleans sound to the greater world.[2] Lil Hardin was the only player in the group not from New Orleans. Oliver's band performed with a greater degree of finesse than Buddy Bolden. In the early days of Jelly Roll Morton's Red Hot Peppers, we see the genesis of a first-generation of "jazz" band orchestrators.[3]

It was Fletcher Henderson, however, who originated the swing band concept of obtaining unity from the tremendous diversity of performance approaches found among the musicians at the beginning of the swing era. Henderson, whose bands set the style for swing, had a great effect on the swing era. Hsio Wen Shih asserts:

> The increasing popularity of swing arrangements on the Henderson model led to a general similarity in style of all the big bands, Negro and [W]hite. Goodman, Shaw, the Dorseys, Bar-

net, Hines, Calloway, Teddy Hill, Webb, were all approaching the same standards of proficiency. There is a terrifying record, an anthology called *The Great Swing Bands* on which most of these bands are represented. If they are played without consulting notes or labels, it is impossible to distinguish one from the other.[4]

Although this critic is no "jazz" expert, it is clear that many styles were indistinguishable to the listening public. He also reminds us of the impact Fletcher Henderson's music had on swing bands during the 1930s. Other essential elements of swing style were launched by the mixture of precision, power, and showmanship of Jimmie Lunceford's Orchestra.[5] Duke Ellington's music involved maximum color, diversity, and personalized scoring that remains unsurpassed.[6] When Count Basie was asked what his "biggest thrill" as a listener had been, he replied:

> My biggest thrill as a listener came one night back in, I think it was, 1951. The so-called progressive jazz was going big then, and here comes Duke Ellington on opening night at Birdland. He had just revamped his band, and no one knew just what he'd have. We all dropped in to catch him—and what we heard! What a thrill that was!
>
> The Duke was swinging. All this "progressive" talk, and the Duke played the old swing. He scared a lot of people that night. Of course the Duke has always had the greatest band at all times. There's never been any other band for me, year in and year out.[7]

When asked if he meant "present company excepted," Basie said firmly, "No. I do not. I mean that Duke Ellington is the greatest of them all." Basie also liked the bands led by Jimmy Lunceford, Benny Goodman, and Fletcher Henderson.

Women's Bands during the Early Twentieth Century

Generally speaking, all musical genres during the 1920s and 1930s were segregated by race, context, and content. Almost all music composed by African-American musicians was heard in clubs or other similar settings. The African-American blues was the domain of those who knew that particular brand of saturnine emotions most intimately (through their firsthand experience), and the strongest, most innovative improvisers evolved within an environment that held spontaneous creation in highest regard. The majority culture made a clear distinction between "Black" music and their own "White" music, and did so without disguise: African-American music bore the ludicrous brand "race records."

The popular song was questionably the only common middle ground of sorts during this early period. The popular song requires lyrics and constant repetition of an easily accessible melody, which often guarantees popularity. A composer of the caliber of Fats Waller was able to transform the structure of the common song into a more flexible form that supported his skills as a composer, satirist, phenomenal pianist, entertainer, and master of humor. He used the lyrics to gain the listener's attention, but also left ample room for improvisation after skillfully disarming his audience. Few improvising artists gained immense popularity the way Waller managed among his fans, while creating impressive and innovative improvisations. Swing composers and arrangers also explored the popular song form, but made rhythmic alterations never heard before. African-American and European-American song (in terms of musical performance) nonetheless remained noticeably separated stylistically throughout the 1930s.

An even longer lasting schism in the world of music, however, has remained the separation between female and male instrumentalists. The formation of all-women bands and orchestras by both African-American and European-American musicians during the early years of "jazz" was a response to difficulties experienced while attempting to gain access to established male-dominated musical ensembles. Although not generally recognized, women did indeed participate in early "jazz" groups, but their numbers were not what they could have been had they not been discriminated against. Women's groups served the practical purpose of giving players both amateur and professional experience, and providing peer encouragement, support, and acceptance.

Women's bands were continually dismissed by promoters, audiences, and fellow musicians as novelty acts. Often women were presented as sex objects in promotional campaigns, or lumped together under the label "all-girl" bands. *Swing* magazine produced an article that testifies to the prevailing skepticism among listeners in America in the 1930s. It described the "hooting" and "scoffing" at the "all-girl gimmick" among "experts who were convinced of the impracticality of women insofar as popular dance music was concerned (in 1938)." Linda Dahl writes:

> For these reasons many women musicians resisted the women's band per se as a professional tactic. For example, clarinetist Ann Dupont, who was compared favorably by some writers to Artie Shaw, declared in 1939 that she was through with women's bands; she went on to lead an all-male band and managed to hold it together for several years. Just as many contemporary women musicians wish to be treated simply as musicians and do not make an issue of their sex, so did many of the women players of earlier eras. But whether they liked it or not, it *was* an issue, and an important reason for the scarcity of women in the established bands. The women players who eschewed the all-woman groups had few options; if their music remained "respectable," their careers quite often remained marginal.[8]

Ina Ray Hutton and Her Melodears

Ina Ray Hutton and Her Melodears was another important band of the era. Ina Ray Hutton was born in Chicago in 1916. She was a tap dancer who performed with the Ziegfield Follies. The "Blond Bombshell" was not the musical leader of the band, but held the baton while reed player Audrey Hall counted things off and served as the actual musical director. Hutton's function was merely to provide sex appeal for the audience.

In 1934 Irving Mills recognized the commercial potential of presenting an all-woman swing band, and put up the financial resources to back one. Backed by Irving Mills, and with Hutton's personal influence, the Melodears got some of the best gigs available during the swing era. The Mills office also managed Duke Ellington and Cab Calloway. Calloway's orchestra alternated top billing with the Duke Ellington Orchestra during the 1930s.

Some of the best European-American women musicians around were collected to form the original Melodears. Ina Ray Hutton was also eventually supported by swing arrangements from the best staff of arrangers in the business—Eddie Durham, Jesse Stone and Alex Hill. Durham and Stone later became arrangers for the International Sweethearts of Rhythm. The Melodears enjoyed high visibility because they were the first all-women's band to record, and their recordings were well distributed and promoted. Ina Ray Hutton and Her Melodears also made films and performed in the best halls and theaters in the country. They shared the bill with Ellington, Basie, and other top musical organizations. With the stability of the powerful Mills organization as their sponsor, Ina Ray Hutton and Her Melodears developed the most popular women's band of the day. Hall (who had been a member of the Fourteen Bricktops and Babe Egan's band), one of the veteran musicians of the ensemble, was a pioneer member of the Melodears. She was responsible for bringing many of the original members into the organization.

> "I had a little notebook that I took names down in," she says, "and when I was traveling, if I heard that there was a good girls' group playing, I'd look them up and listen to them, and if there was somebody I liked very much, I'd take the name and address and enter it in that little book. And I did that all across the United States as I traveled. So, when they got this bug about Ina Ray Hutton—there was really a lot of money back of it when it was first organized—where were they going to get their musicians? I got out my little book, and we got them from all over the United States. Many times they were just small combos and, of course, nobody knew of them." (Hall, like a number of other women who worked on the road, confirms that many talented women who could be heard in small local settings undoubtedly never had the chance to leave their hometowns.) After the band was chosen, Hall remembers, Ina Ray Hutton was selected to be the leader.[9]

The original Ina Ray Hutton and Her Melodears band's roster included such excellent players as trombonist Alyse Wills (who played over

twenty instruments and had toured the world with Tommy Dorsey), pianist
Betty Roudybush, trumpet player Estelle Slavin, and tenor saxophonist Betty
Sattley. Pianist-composer Alex Hill (who had arranged for Fats Waller, Andy
Kirk, and Benny Carter) provided the tightly orchestrated swing arrange-
ments that propelled the Melodears into overnight success.

By 1936, Ina Ray Hutton and Her Melodears had reorganized, and
hired Eddie Durham to manage and arrange for the ensemble. Although
some original members had left, Alyse Wills and other strong performers remained. "She had international perfect pitch," Durham recalls of Wills.
"She'd go down to the dressing room and give everybody a note. They
wouldn't have to tune by no piano. They'd tune by her voice. She was a *great*
musician. She was the first trombone player, then she helped to pick the others."[10]

After several weeks of rehearsal, the band went into the Paramount
Theater in Newark, New Jersey, and eventually moved on to the Paramount
in New York. Durham remembers when the band was in upstate New York
for a preview. "Duke Ellington came. They sent him up and lots of guys like
that come up to see what they think the future of that band was." There was
quite a bit of interest in the organization at the time. By the time the band
hit the Paramount, it had reached the level of excellence at which subsequent
versions of the Melodears continued to play. Ina Ray Hutton and Her Melodears performed a concert that featured twelve bands at Madison Square
Garden. Durham asked Hutton to use her influence (of which she apparently
had plenty) to have the Melodears placed just ahead of the Count Basie band
on the program. At the end of the set, the band played all the Basie numbers
and attempted to duplicate the Basie solos (learned from listening to his
band's recordings). "They played 'One O'Clock Jump,' and I had numbers in
there like 'Jumpin' at the Woodside' and 'Out the Window.'" The success continued. Durham recalls:[11]

> For some reason, the formation of a girl band today is regarded
> by everyone as an unusual achievement. It is true that the for-
> mation of any kind of a successful band is quite a job, but I am
> very happy in the realization that I am a member of one group
> which has played its way into a state of popular approval—and
> with that approval expressed "financially."
>
> Jazz . . . presents a formidable job for anyone to put over cor-
> rectly. But putting it over is well within the capabilities of the
> fairer members of the human tribe and wherever music goes
> when it develops away from swing, the girls will have little
> trouble accompanying it.[12]

After 1939, Hutton was no longer associated with the Mills Agency.
When the all-woman band was no longer successful financially, she disbanded the Melodears. The band broke up that year (1939) when Mills backed out
because in the new era he felt "girls didn't sell." Hutton went on to put all-
male groups together.[13] The press reported that she was "tired" of female musicians. The lack of support from a male-dominated business may have been

one of the stronger reasons the band failed to survive. In his book *The Big Bands,* critic George T. Simon writes the following regarding Ina Ray Hutton: "The early part of her career had been spent fronting an all-girl orchestra, one that most of us have forgotten and that she had been probably trying to forget ever since she gave it up to surround herself with men. For her all girl orchestra was like all all-girl orchestras, 'Only God can make a tree,' I remember having written in a review of some other such outfit, and 'only men can play good jazz.'"

Simon's sententious chauvinism was not atypical. Nevertheless, while most female musicians of the day were unable to record their music, the Irving Mills backing made the Hutton band one that enjoyed careful documentation in the studio. The band developed a solid sound and featured excellent soloists in all its sections. The Melodears' emphasis was on swinging and avoided becoming just another commercial big band (with a novel twist) for most of its existence. Nevertheless, the band broke up in 1939 when Mills backed out. Hutton went on to put all male groups together.[14]

Dropping the women's band did not insulate Hutton completely from arrogant ignorance or guarantee her greater success. Regarding her new all-male band, George Simon now said that it had "several good jazz musicians ... played well, if usually too loudly," maintained a following with "its good dance music."[15] This band lasted until the end of the war, "but she never again reached the prominence she had enjoyed during the 1930s, when she and her famous Melodears were one of the top bands on the circuit."[16]

International Sweethearts of Rhythm

The International Sweethearts of Rhythm followed the era of the Melodears to become the preeminent all-women's band of the 1940s. Its origins trace back to 1910, when Laurence Clifton Jones founded the Piney Woods Country Life School for poor and orphaned African-American children in the Mississippi Delta. The school was established primarily to teach these children a trade. In the tradition of the Fisk Jubilee Singers, Jones toured the country for eighteen months with the children singing and raising thousands of dollars for the school. In 1937 Jones heard Ina Ray Hutton and Her Melodears in Chicago and decided to form an "all-girls" band at his school. The most talented young women at his school were selected and coached in the art of syncopation by an alumni of the school, Consuella Carter.

The International Sweethearts of Rhythm was founded in 1937. "It was apparently the looks of Willie Mae Wong, Chinese Saxophonist; Alma Cortez, Mexican clarinet player; Nina de LaCruz, Indian saxophonist; and Nove Lee McGee, Hawaiian trumpet player, that inspired the label 'International.'"[17] The rest of the members were African-American. This racially integrated ensemble performed for over a decade but remained relatively obscure because the European-American media flagrantly shunned it. It was inspired by earlier women swing bands that its school director, Jones, had heard. Ray Lee Jones became the leader of the musical organization, and Anna Mae Winburn became its musical director. Many women's bands were able to break into the industry while men were off fighting the war. The Sweethearts soon became the primary fund-raisers for the school. When they played the Apollo they got $32 a week (half of the union scale). Some people wanted to go backstage to see what "boys" were playing the music that the women were "faking."

Dr. Billy Taylor at the Cornell University "Jazz" Festival (Karlton E. Hester, Director) in April 1997 (Photo by Nicola Kountoupes).

In 1940 the International Sweethearts of Rhythm performed a successful debut concert at the Howard Theater in Washington, D.C., which was followed by another impressive engagement at the Apollo Theater in New York. Most of the band's performances were in African-American communities, and pianist Dr. Billy Taylor remembers their impact on an audience over forty years ago: "The International Sweethearts of Rhythm created a sensation when they made their debut at Howard Theater in 1940. . . . It was unusual to see women playing all the instruments in the orchestra. The biggest surprise was their sound and the way they swung."[18]

The women disassociated themselves from the school in 1941 after learning that eight of their fellow students, who had been touring and raising money for the school for three years, were not going to graduate at the end of the term. The Sweethearts "took the school bus [they had been touring in] and, pursued by highway police, fled through seven states to Washington D.C. and freedom."[19] They moved into a ten-room house in Arlington, Virginia, and went to work rehearsing.

Eddie Durham was their first music coach. He had performed with, arranged for, and had his compositions played by Bennie Moten, Count Basie, Ina Ray Hutton, Jimmie Lunceford and other world-class artists. He made adjustments in the group and worked the players diligently, teaching them to swing their parts and even choreographed some of their movements. Durham left the job when he learned that their management was cheating the young women. The Sweethearts received thirty-five dollars a week for playing the Apollo (about half of union scale). Durham says he asked the women, "Well, what did they [the management] tell you?" "Well," the Sweethearts replied, "we gotta have money to pay for the bus [they now had a live-in bus with berths, air conditioning, and bathrooms], we gotta pay the mortgage on that home [in Arlington]." Durham continues, "And I didn't tell them they didn't have no home. The man [their backer] owned that home. He gave them that home just to live in, but they didn't buy it."[20]

The Sweethearts lived in the bus, not only because it was cheaper, but because racism in America prevented them from lodging or eating in most "White" establishments in the towns they visited across America. Racist bigotry had other effects on the exposure the band received, as Rosetta Reitz points out:

> The International Sweethearts of Rhythm was the hottest all-women's band of the 1940s. It was the first racially integrated women's band and it lasted for over a decade. Many people have not heard of the Sweethearts because it played primarily for black audiences and was practically ignored by the white media. Middle-aged Afro-Americans remember the thrill of hearing and seeing the group when it first played at the Apollo Theater in Harlem back in September 1941 and many times after that.[21]

The band grew musically when tenor saxophonist Vi Burnside, trumpeter Tiny Davis, and other seasoned professionals joined the ensembles. Davis was an exemplary trumpet soloist, "jazz" vocalist, and band leader. The women had ranged in age from fourteen to nineteen when they left the school. Now they were developing into mature soloists. The response to their return engagement at the Howard Theater in 1941 was so strong that the *New York Age* headlined its report: "Sweethearts of Rhythm Set New Box Office Record." The theater had never held 35,000 patrons in a single week before. In 1943 Dorothy Donegan performed on a bill with the International Sweethearts of Rhythm that also included comedienne Jackie "Moms" Mabley. Following the engagement, Donegan remembered how much the Sweethearts' fans loved them and how they stirred their audience into enthusiastic yelling, clapping, stamping, and warm synergism. The "Sweethearts" also appeared in a short film, *That Man of Mine,* starring Ruby Dee. Marian McPartland summed up their achievements: "At last the Sweethearts had realized some of their earlier dreams. They had played to audiences of thousands in the United States and abroad, recorded overseas broadcasts with big name Hollywood stars, had made records and films. What was left for them?"[22]

The Sweetheart's musical director, Ray Lee Jones fell ill after the bands highly successful USO tour in 1945. This, combined with the poor management that the organization experienced during its final days, caused the group to disband in the late forties. Roz Cron, Tiny Davis, Vi Burnside, Toby Butler, and Roxanna Butler continued with their professional musical careers while other members settled down to raise families and pursue non-musical vocations. Their leader, Anna Mae Winburn, continue to put versions of bands together under the Sweetheart's name for a while.

Other Women's Bands

Few of the numerous sources on "jazz" history written by men include the International Sweethearts of Rhythm. Many other women's bands were organized since the late nineteenth century. Reitz discusses some of the bands and orchestras that African-American women formed:

> The International Sweethearts of Rhythm is not even mentioned in the two books that claim to document the big bands. Yet Afro-American women's bands had existed since 1884 when the ladies Orchestra of Chelsea Massachusetts "played the best halls and parties in and around Boston and in various cities in Connecticut" according to their leader Marian Osgood. That band stayed together for ten years. The Boston Fadettes, led by Cardine D. Nicholas, was also more than a fad. It began in 1888 and lasted for thirty-two years. There is also record in 1889, of a sixteen-piece Colored Female Brass Band in East Saginaw, Michigan led by cornetist Viola Allen. Hallie L. Anderson's women's orchestra was performing for the public at the Hamilton Street Church in Albany, New York in 1906 and in 1919 her Lady Band performed regularly at the Lafayette Theater in Harlem. She was not the first in Harlem. In 1914, Ethel Hill was leading the Astoria Ladies Orchestra at Barron's Astoria Cafe and trombonist Marie Lucas led her Ladies Orchestra at the Lafayette Theater that same year. The first women's black band playing for whites only was advertised in the *New York Times* as The Twelve Vampires—"12 Girls Who Can Play Real Dance Music." It was booked in the Roseland Ballroom early in 1927. Leora Meoux, Fletcher Henderson's wife, was in the trumpet section.
>
> Chicago has always been a good town for women musicians. They played a lot of piano and led male bands. Lovie Austin was the most outstanding. In 1916 Marian Pankey, a drummer, led her Female Orchestra on the South Side with great success. Some old musicians told me that the best women's band was the one Lil Armstrong had in 1932. She led the band from the piano with Dolly Jones and Leora Meoux playing trumpet, Alma Long Scott (Hazel's mother) playing sax and Mae Brady playing a hot violin. Valaida Snow, the trumpet player who had a lotta theatrical flair, had a hot thirteen-piece band in the mid-thirties and all the women except herself, wore blond wigs. Georgia White's twelve-piece women's band of the mid-forties was the blusiest.[23]

Most of the women who did manage to break into the early New Orleans "jazz" scene were piano players who mastered the strong, stomping piano accompaniment often called "gutbucket" style.

Emma Barrett

Emma Barrett was born in 1898 in New Orleans. She drew from her rich local musical atmosphere and, as a young girl, listened to "guys who used to gather on the street corners at night with one or two guitars and sing some of the old tunes."[24] After practicing on her own and working with informal groups in her neighborhood, Barrett soon joined Papa Celestin's Original Tuxedo Orchestra. As the pianist with Celestin's ensemble from 1923 on, she had the distinction of being one of the very first women players to be recorded. Mercedes Garman Fields often played with Oscar "Papa" Celestin's Orchestra during the 1930s and 1940s. Celestin also later introduced New Orleans jazzwoman Jeanette Salvant Kimball (born in 1908 or possibly 1910) to performing and recording activities.

The name "Sweet Emma" allegedly came from Barrett's "artistic" temperament. Nevertheless, she was later nicknamed "The Bell Gal" because of her custom of wearing a red dress, red garters, red cap and jingling knee bells that shook as she played. Barrett was in steady demand throughout the twenties and thirties. She developed her coarse barrelhouse style, which has been described as a "pile-driver attack" through these experiences. She also toured with Percy Humphrey's group. Barrett had been playing professionally for at least forty-five years when she had a stroke in 1967. After recovering, she continued to play throughout the seventies and into the eighties at such New Orleans "jazz" centers as Preservation Hall. Largely unrecorded throughout the thirties and ensuing decades, she was fairly well documented on record during the revival of interest in New Orleans ensemble-style "jazz" in the sixties and seventies. Barrett died in 1982.[25]

Other Women Artists

Despite the fact that many mothers just would not allow their daughters to perform with "jazz" bands, and communities had equally prohibitive attitudes, women still managed to gain local recognition for their skills. Camilla Todd played with The Maple Leaf Orchestra during the early 1920s; Margaret Kimball was heard in John Robichaux's Orchestra (during the same decade); and Wilhelmina Bart was a member of Joe "King" Oliver's Creole Jazz Band, The Willie Pijeaud Band, and The Amos White Orchestra. Lottie Taylor was another woman musician who played occasionally with Oliver's band in the early 1920s. Sadie Goodson was a regular with Buddy Petit and Henry "Kid" Rena's bands well into the 1930s. Pianist Edna Mitchell worked with various groups including an ensemble with young trumpeter Louis Armstrong.[26]

Ethel Minor was a pianist with Estella Harris' Ladies Jazz Band in 1916 and was recognized along with Lil Armstrong and Lovie Austin as nationally renowned early "jazz" band pianists living in Chicago. Ida Mae Maples, Lottie Hightower, and Garvinia Dickerson were other pianists who also functioned as effective bandleaders in the 1920s. Diamond Lil Hardaway played with "King" Oliver at Lincoln Gardens in 1924, and with The Lee Collins Band in 1931 at King Tut's Tomb. Other pianist/leaders on the Chicago jazz scene during the late 1920s and early 1930s were Irene Armstrong (Wilson/Kitchings), Georgia Corham, and Dorothy Scott. Laura Crosby and Dorothy Rogers appeared on the roster of Johnny Long's Roaming Troubadours. Hattie Thomas appeared with Billy Bailey's Rhythm Girls, and Mattie Walker-King's group between performances with various pick-up orchestras.

Mattie Gilmore played keyboard in New York City with Will Marion Cook's New York Syncopated Orchestra. She also accompanied the group on its tour of Europe. At the same time, Helen Ray worked regularly at the City's Crescent Cafe, joined by a male cornet player and a male drummer. Other names that frequently appeared on the New York Cafe band circuit were Cleo Desmond and Cora Cross. Bertha Gonsoulin was Lil Armstrong's replacement with Joe "King" Oliver's band on the West Coast in 1921. When the band returned to Chicago in 1922 to play an engagement at the Royal Garden, Gonsoulin was still the pianist.[27]

Toward Greater Individual Expression

Art Tatum

Tatum was one of the most undeniably original, musical, and exciting piano virtuosos America has produced. He was born in 1910 in Toledo, Ohio, with cataracts on both eyes, but some small degree of vision was restored through surgery. Nevertheless, Tatum was legally blind. He began learning hymns on the piano at age three and began performing at rent parties and in cafes in his early teens. He was eventually hired as staff pianist for the radio station WSPD in Toledo at seventeen years old. His fifteen-minute radio show was so impressive that it was soon selected for national broadcast by the network.

He had ceaseless energy, and combined a variety of innovative techniques to lead swing "jazz" piano to unprecedented heights. Tatum took "show tunes" and transformed them into his styles of choice to chronicle twentieth-century American music. As an inimitable piano virtuoso and master of swing keyboard style, Tatum had both musical perspicuity and a technical control of his instrument that allowed for flawless execution of any musical idea he conceived. This ability not only impressed all "jazz" pianists of his time but also influenced performers of European piano repertoires such as Horowitz and Rubinstein.

Art Tatum and Billie Holiday (Photo courtesy of HRP Library).

Tatum was admired for his incredible ambidexterity and rhythmic inventiveness. These innovations influenced many "jazz" artists, especially Bud Powell and Lennie Tristano. His music was a rich mixture of beautiful melodies, dazzling arpeggios, infectious swing-rhythms, and sagacious counterpoint that alternated equally between both of his hands. His precocious harmonic knowledge allowed him to modulate freely in the middle of a song, moving on a musical journey involving chord substitution and extensions that had never before been explored. His more esoteric musical experimentation stretched swing vocabulary into incipient bebop vocabulary, while anchoring his fanciful voyages with anything from conventional stride piano to beautifully balanced impressionistic or romantic European musical characteristics.

Tatum's music involves pianistic expression incorporating a mastery of early "jazz" styles. This ability allowed Tatum to switch from one style to another effortlessly and instantaneously. His early influences came by way of James P. Johnson, the founder of "stride" piano, where harmonic and rhythmic elements are emphasized at the expense of melody. Art Tatum moved beyond the stylistic perimeters of stride piano to an orchestral approach to the piano. His stylistic eclecticism gave equal emphasis to all primary musical elements (melody, rhythm, harmony, tempo), creating an elastic flow that is at once accessible and highly inventive. Few have been able to accomplish his level of artistry within a spontaneous art form.

Tatum had the ability to maintain interest through melodic, rhythmic, harmonic, and bass functions on a single keyboard instrument. He incorporated styles from a broad range of influences, including barrelhouse, European romanticism, and stride piano. Stride players generally performed in unaccompanied settings without the aid of a rhythm section; so the right hand was obliged to cover melodic and harmonic levels while the left covered the bass, rhythmic, and alternate harmonic functions.

The more lyrical right-hand melodies had been explored by some of Tatum's innovative predecessors. The interplay between Armstrong and Hines on "Weatherbird" and other tunes is a significant departure from J. P. Johnson's influence and the conventions of "jazz" of their time. Hine's and Tatum's piano styles merged with and bridged the gap between swing and the new age of Modernism that came with bebop in the 1940s. Tatum uses the "jazz" tradition to underscore certain musical ideas, but gets away from the stride in the left hand at faster speeds, during rubato passages, and when squeezing in large and unusual groupings of notes that are expressed freely in hypermetric musical operations.

Tatum's harmonic explorations had a great effect on the improvisational styles and vocabularies developed by Coleman Hawkins and other musicians in the decade prior to the 1940s. Bebop musicians took many similar ideas to their natural conclusions during the subsequent era.

In 1932, after accepting a job with then cabaret singer Adelaide Hall,[28] Tatum quickly earned a reputation that made even the best pianists in New York nervous to have him in the house. Fats Waller, once acknowledged Tatum's presence at one of his appearances one night, by stopping to announce, "I play the piano, but God is in the house tonight."[29] Duke Ellington remembered: "[Tatum's] first visit to New York stirred up a storm. In a matter of hours, it got around to all piano players—and musicians who played other instruments, too—that a real Bad Cat had arrived and was threatening the position of The Lion, James P. Johnson, Fats Waller, etc. Though he challenged them, they loved him, and this kind of association with fellow musicians is a big and profound subject that is impossible to explain."[30]

Tatum generally performed as a soloist for the next decade, but would occasionally perform with other musicians. During the heyday of "jazz" on Fifty-Second Street Tatum was immensely popular but rarely recorded. He did record one solo album in 1933 but subsequent recordings were (surprisingly) not immediately forthcoming.

In 1943 he formed a trio with two other well-known musicians, guitarist Tiny Grimes and bassist Slam Stewart. Stewart, himself an important innovator, hummed an octave above the bass solos he created. The Art Tatum Trio, known for its exquisitely sensitive interactions between the musicians, was one of the main attractions of the day until it was temporarily overshadowed by bebop. In the following decade, however, the eleven albums recorded for Norman Granz (between December 1953 and January 1955) contained more than a hundred piano solos that projected Tatum into the limelight once again. Tatum spent much of his time in after-hours clubs, according to musicians of his day, where he often executed his most impressive performances. After the repeal of Prohibition, these types of illegal early-morning establishments were ubiquitous in places like Harlem.

Tatum's harmonic approach remained peripatetic. He would dazzle his audiences by substituting chord changes, executing complex arpeggiated figures, and performing double runs (often in contrary motion) effortlessly and in close succession. In addition to demonstrating the harmonic possibilities of "jazz" better than any other musician of his period, he possessed a technical command of the piano that was unquestionable for all but the most injudicious "jazz critic" or listener of his day.

It is perhaps due to overindulging in eating and drinking for many years, that Tatum became ill around the time of the Granz recordings. Although he stopped drinking completely in 1954, he died in November 1956. He was one of the first modernists in "jazz." His style emphasized a set of controversial musical elements (including free modulation, rubato, and other liberated approaches to meter, and rhythm) at a time when an artist could be criticized harshly for not "swinging." He demonstrated a higher musical understanding of artistic balance and flexibility than his peers, one that realized that the range of elements could be employed to aid in the creation of new musical messages.

Mary Lou Williams

Born in Atlanta, Georgia, Mary Lou Williams (Mary Elfrieda Scruggs) (1910–1981) became known as "The First Lady of Jazz." By the time she was six years old she was making a living playing professionally, known as the little "piano girl" who played at parties for a dollar an hour. By age twelve Williams was working occasional jobs with union bands in Pittsburgh. She toured the TOBA vaudeville circuit in "Hits and Bits," with Buzzin Harris, and the Gus Sun Circuit. She also worked with the B. F. Keith and Orpheum circuits and with Seymour and Jeanette. She continued to perform with Jeanette James after Seymour's death.

Williams "sat in" during these early years with Duke Ellington's Washingtonians, and later with The Syncopators (also known as The Synco Jazzers), a band led by her future husband, alto and baritone saxist John Williams. Williams made her recording debut with The Synco Jazzers. When her husband John went to Oklahoma City to join The Andy Kirk Band in 1929, Mary Lou remained in Memphis for a period of time, continuing as The Syncopators' leader. When she joined her husband she also began a memorable, long-standing affiliation with Kirk's ensemble. Actually, she did not join the Kirk band as a full-time pianist until 1931. During the first two years she was part-time chauffeur, arranger, and pianist. When the group (then based in Kansas City) secured a Brunswick recording contract, the "part-timer" substituted as recording pianist. Before long, "the substitute" became the permanent pianist.[31]

Mary Lou Williams (Photo by William
P. Gottlieb and Posie Randolph).

As a pioneering composer, Mary Lou Williams introduced her brand of
"Symphonic Jazz" and became the first "jazz" musician to have her compositions performed at Carnegie Hall. Williams was also the first woman to be
recognized as an important figure in the swing era. She was a pianist and
composer who could move from stride to swing, to boogie, to bebop, with
power and clarity in each style. Later in her life she became interested in a
personal religious "jazz" movement and composed several pieces for that musical genre. Her "jazz" spiritual works were later performed in St. Patrick's
Cathedral.

Critics unanimously agreed that Williams's addition to the Kirk band
marked the beginning of the group's rise to competitive status. Her billing
with Kirk read, "The Lady Who Swings the Band." She remained with Andy
Kirk and his Twelve Clouds of Joy until 1941. During this period she took on
additional arranging assignments for Benny Goodman, Louis Armstrong, Cab
Calloway, Tommy Dorsey, Glen Gray, Gus Arnheim, and Earl Hines.

Following the Andy Kirk years, Williams began fronting her own combo, which included her second husband Harold "Shorty" Baker on trumpet, and drummer Art Blakey. When Baker joined The Duke Ellington Band, Mary Lou joined as arranger. "Trumpet No End" was the only Williams composition that Ellington recorded, but the two became close friends for life. Williams later performed at Ellington's funeral. In the mid-1940s and early 1950s she worked as a freelance arranger. Williams also performed as a soloist or with a trio, mainly in New York City but also on the West Coast and in Europe.

In the mid-1950s Williams embraced Catholicism and began devoting much of her time and energy to religious activities. For brief periods she disappeared from public performance. The religious works she wrote beginning in the early 1960s set a precedent, which Duke Ellington and other innovators followed.

She completed a residency at The Composer in New York City and appeared with The Dizzy Gillespie Orchestra at the Newport Jazz Festival in 1957. Williams then resumed her regular public performances and throughout the 1960s and 1970s appeared at many "jazz" festivals and completed residences at The Embers, Hickory House, Cafe Carlyle, and The Cookery in New York City and at other clubs in Washington, D.C.; Rochester; New York; San Francisco; Toronto; and London. She made numerous solo, duo, and trio appearances on college campuses. She also enjoyed presenting lecture-concerts at the Smithsonian Institution and Whitney Museum. She initiated and produced the Pittsburgh Jazz Festival in 1964, and her sacred music continued to bring performances. "Mary Lou's Mass," one critic wrote, "turns out to be almost an encyclopedia of black music, richly represented from spirituals to bop and rock. . . . It reflects the self-effacing style of Mary Lou Williams, both as a musician and as a woman, as well as the persuasions of her spiritual convictions."[32]

Williams returned to Kansas City, where a street had been named in her honor (1973), to be featured performer at the International Premiere Concert of the Women's Jazz Festival in March 1978. On the subject of Mary Lou Williams, Ellington says: "Mary Lou Williams is perpetually contemporary. Her writing and performing are and have always been just a little ahead and throughout her career . . . her music retains—and maintains—a standard of quality that is timeless. She is like soul on soul."[33]

The "Age of the Sax Masters"
Coleman Hawkins and Lester Young

Coleman Hawkins

Another important precursor of modern "jazz" during the swing-dominated era is Coleman Hawkins (c. 1904–1969). His virtuosity and originality on the tenor saxophone helped make this one of the most popular instruments in "jazz." Throughout a career as a sideman in some of the consummate big bands of the 1930s and as a leader of several small combos, Hawkins continually demonstrated his talent for improvising memorable and logically constructed solos. In fact, many consider him to be one of the leading soloists in "jazz." Lester Young said, "He's the person who played the tenor saxophone, who woke you up and let you know there was a tenor saxophone."[34]

Hawkins evolved a manner of shaping the melody line to the chord changes using arpeggiated chords and phrases based on intriguing scale patterns. During the first sixteen measures of his solo in the 1940 recording of "Sheik of Araby," Hawkins intersperses three arpeggiated chords of the same construction among scale-like melodic figures. This tendency to frame his beautifully constructed melodies with horizontalized harmonies became the basis for his style. Hawkins was initially the tenor saxophonist who was most influential in the transition from swing to bebop. Hawkins could create a new melody from the harmonic structure of any well-known tune. He digressed from the usual treatment of swing tunes (involving melodic variation and embellishment) and leaned heavily instead upon harmonic structure to create an unprecedented melodic force.

Both Coleman Hawkins and Lester Young ushered in the "Age of the Tenor Saxophone Masters." With the primary elements of the "jazz" saxophone now in place, and the recent displacement of the trumpet as major instrumental force secured, the two major influences on the "jazz" saxophone style from the swing era to the dawn of the bop era come clearly to the fore. The Hawkins style was generally full-toned, resonant, and employed vibrato. Improvising formulaic responses to changing harmonic contexts in "jazz" has sometimes been termed "running the changes." With this approach, because the chord changes mostly determine the shape of the melodic line, coherence among constituent phrases of the melodic line decreases. Some musicians who favored a high degree of coherence in the melodic line sought alternative approaches. Young played for Count Basie's Band, and became known as the founding father of "cool jazz." He was another very influential tenor sax player who introduced a style much lighter than Hawkins' and maintained subtly accented melodic lines.

The Hawkins style can be heard to great advantage on his work starting in the late thirties (most notably, the famous and much copied "Body and Soul," which has become a repertoire piece for saxophones) through the late forties and early fifties ("Half a Step Down," "Bean and the Boys," etc.). Prior to the late thirties, we can see the development of the Hawkins style in his work with Fletcher Henderson ("Hocus Pocus," "Where There's a Will There's a Way") and a famous early solo with the Mound City Blue Blowers ("One Hour"). Hawkins developed a huge burly sound and vibrato, which was influenced by Sidney Bechet. His rhythmic approach seems to have gained something from Louis Armstrong.

Hawkins continued to evolve when bebop introduced a new harmonic vocabulary and stylistic approach. While other swing players felt insecure about making a transition into the modern style, Hawkins was not; he felt challenged by the music Parker, Gillespie, and Monk introduced, and never declined as an innovative soloist.

Lester Young

In the 1930s, while a member of the Count Basie band, tenor saxophonist Lester Young (c. 1909–1959) played "against the changes." While Coleman Hawkins' melodic line adhered more strictly to the chords of the tune, Young emphasized the internal development of the melody over the chord changes. The integrity and direction of the prevailing spontaneous melody became a force that rebelled against the relevance and significance that Hawkins gave to harmonic construction.

Lester Young replaced Coleman Hawkins in the Fletcher Henderson orchestra and rejoined Basie after a fairly unsuccessful stint with Henderson's musical organization. His career also included work with the Blue Devils (1932–33) and Bennie Moten (1933–34). Young's solos are also noted for their unexpected irregularity of rhythm, phrasing, and melodic contour. Furthermore, he often played phrases that extended beyond the turnarounds and bridges of the tune, foreshadowing developments in bebop. Hawkins' phrasing generally conformed to harmonic (and formal) structures to a greater degree. Lester Young's new approach had a great influence on the young saxophonists who emerged in the 1940s and 1950s. Thus, in many ways, he became the tenor sax progenitor of both bebop and "cool jazz" saxophone style.

Although a product of the melodic tendencies of the swing era, Young was comfortable merging with the styles of either, Louis Armstrong and Charlie Parker. His seminal debut recording solo on "Lady Be Good" in 1936 demonstrated his durability and flexibility even at the beginning of his career. His dignified approach to the tenor saxophone avoided musical hyperbole, yet his intensely original style was a vortex containing all the tenor playing that preceded it. His highly personal tone had never been heard before, and it stood in direct opposition to that of Hawkins. His equipoise with the instrument resulted in a musical meditation that explored melody, rhythm, and harmony with unprecedented economy, resulting in a phrasing quality that heightened the potential level of surprise. This approach made it impossible to anticipate his melodious direction. This again distinguished his ethereal improvisations from the much more saturated, assertive, and trenchant harmonic approach that was associated with Coleman Hawkins.

Young's translucent sound contained a rhythmic freedom that reflected the influence of vocal inflection on his melodic style. The majority of his early reputation was made primarily with the Count Basie Orchestra beginning in 1936 and extended into the forties. Some of his most celebrated work with Basie includes "Broadway," "Every Tub," "Jive at Five," and "Jumpin' at the Woodside." His work with smaller groups such as the famous Kansas City Six and Seven (his solo on "Pagin' the Devil" is a good example from this period) and his famous solo on "Sometimes I'm Happy" would become influential examples for "jazz" combos of the forties and fifties.

Lester Young was evolving at a time when racial lines of stylistic musical development were becoming less dramatic. Lester admits being influenced by a host of musicians including European-American musicians such as Frank Trumbauer and Bud Freeman. Yet it is impossible to find direct links to any of these performers. In evaluating styles of other saxophonists, his fascination seems to have been with the mastery of saxophone technique and an effortless approach to tone production, rather than other stylistic concerns. Lester Young's style was innovative and subtle at a time when most players were emulating Coleman Hawkins. Leora Meoux (Fletcher Henderson's wife), Billie Holiday, and other musicians tried unsuccessfully to persuade Young to modify or suppress his style, suggesting instead a tenor sound toward that of Hawkins.

At the height of his career when he was conscripted into the U.S. Army, an event that occurred that left deep psychological scars on Young when he was released in 1945. He had just finished making the short film *Jammin' The Blues* for Warner Brothers.[35] Young remained apprehensive about being in the hands of racist military officers and spent much of his time detained in a military disciplinary center. He said, "It was one mad nightmare. They sent me down to Georgia—that was enough to make me blow my top."[36]

After bebop, though, many saxophonists (most conspicuously Zoot Sims, Stan Getz, and Al Cohn) imitated Lester Young. Young's modern saxophone style, and the monosyllabic dialect he invented, influenced a host of other disciples. Although the introverted innovator was still creative and popular in 1946, many of the younger players were able to cash in on Young's innovations at his expense. Young invented hip nicknames for many of his colleagues including Count Basie ("The Holy Man"), Buddy Tate ("Moon"), and Harry Edison ("Sweets").

Ben Webster and the Influence of Hawkins and Young

Ben Webster (1909–73) began his musical training as a violinist before studying the piano. Later Webster became the tenor saxophone soloist with the Ellington band of the forties and was another strong influence on the development of the tenor saxophone during the swing era. He incorporated aspects of the Hawkins's style (as well as that of Johnny Hodges) to create his own very influential virtuoso tenor saxophone style. Such Ellington classics as "Cottontail" and "Blue Serge" display Webster in his musical prime. Nevertheless, the influence of Young and Hawkins remained the most dominant factors in the development of the "jazz" tenor saxophone through the thirties and forties.

Hawkins' Influence: Don Byas; Hershell Evans; Charlie Ventura (Webster); Lucky Thompson (Webster); Sonny Stitt; Eddie "Lockjaw" Davis; Wardell Gray; Joe Thomas; Harry Carney (baritone); Sonny Rollins; Dick Wilson.

Young's Influence: Paul Quinichette; Zoot Sims; Buddy Collette; Al Cohn; Stan Getz; Serge Chaloff (baritone); Hank Mobley; Budd Johnson; Wardell Gray; Gerry Mulligan (baritone); Lee Konitz (alto); Paul Desmond (alto); James Moody.

Hawkins/Young Combination: Ben Webster; Illinois Jacquet (Webster); Dexter Gordon (Parker); Gene Ammons; John Coltrane; Charlie Parker; Flip Phillips (Webster); Ike Quebec (Webster); Chu Berry; Frank Wess.

The primary influences on the alto saxophone during the swing era were Johnny Hodges, Benny Carter, and Willie Smith. While their effect on the modern saxophone was not as strong as that of the tenor saxophonists listed above, their styles did contribute to the development of styles of many musicians. The lists above and below demonstrate common musical realities among musicians; they all influenced each other and tracing this influence completely and reliably is an impossible task.

Hodges: Earl Bostic; John Coltrane; Tab Smith; Johnny Bothwell; Woody Herman; Hilton Jefferson; Willie Smith; Ben Webster; Eddie Vincent.

Smith: Pete Brown; Earl Bostic; Boots Mussulli; Earl Warren.

Carter: Marshall Royal; Hal MacIntyre; Toots Mondello.

The Voice Continues to Be a Strong Influence

Most blues singers trained in the pre-microphone days of vaudeville, tent shows, and revues, were required to project their voices to fill the performance space, to be quite precise in their stage diction, and to give full value to their song lyrics as musical interpreters. This produced a power, clarity, subtlety and suppleness of style that separated certain blues and "jazz" female vocalists from the pop singers of the era. In regards to the singing style of Ethel Waters, author D. Antoinette Handy states:

> Perhaps the prime example is Ethel Waters, who sang blues material early in her career but developed into a sophisticated singer of popular song with a jazz approach. The style she had perfected by the thirties nicely illustrates the difference between straight and jazz-based pop singing. With a fairly direct reading of the lyric, she manipulated tone, timbre and rhythm to give her delivery a permeating jazz flavor. Another approach was brilliantly advanced by Waters' contemporary Bessie Smith. Though billed as the "Empress of the Blues," Smith has come to be regarded as the first important woman jazz singer. Especially through her mastery of time, so essential to an effective jazz performance, she succeeded in conveying deep intensity of feeling and multiple meanings in her material.[37]

"Bessie's way," wrote bandleader Huphrey Lyttleton, "was to restrict the range of a song to no more than five or six notes and to construct her phrases so economically that a change in direction of just one note could have a startling dramatic or emotive effect."[38] Smith possessed an "unnerving rhythmic instinct based, like Louis Armstrong's, on an underlying rhythm of twelve eighth-notes or four quavers triplets to the bar," and she used "improvisation in its fullest sense on the melody of a song to express a deeper meaning than that of the words on their own."[39] This powerful stylistic influence places Smith among the giants of African-American vocalists performing music during the twenties. Richard Hadlock states, "Like the best instrumentalists, Bessie Smith could fashion a compelling solo from the absolute minimum of musical raw material and, again like most jazzmen, was frequently forced to do just that. . . . In her work, instrumentalists recognized the sort of individuality they tried to express on their own horns and strings."[40]

Billie Holiday

Alice Adams describes Billie Holiday (1915–1959) as the charismatic star riding high on fame in the thirties in her novel *Listening to Billie*: "Then suddenly she is there, and everybody knows, and they crane their heads backward to see her, since she has come in [to the nightclub] by the street entrance like anyone else. Or, not like anyone else at all: she is more beautiful, more shining, holding her face forward like a flower, bright-eyed and smiling, high yellow cheekbones, white teeth and cream-white gardenia at her ear."[41] Maya Angelou met Holiday shortly before her death. In *The Heart of a Woman*, she describes another side of Holiday, an embittered, toughened woman at the end of her career, "a lonely sick woman, with a waterfront mouth."[42] Over a lifetime, American society, perhaps inadvertently, had contributed to the wanton destruction of one of its most uniquely expressive and honorable musical artists.

Billie Holiday (Image courtesy of HRP Library).

The Columbia Records impresario John Hammond, who persuaded clarinetist Benny Goodman to record with her in 1933, mentions Holiday in his autobiography: "She had an uncanny ear, an excellent memory for lyrics, and she sang with an exquisite sense of phrasing."[43] "Your Mother's Son-In-Law" and "Riffin' the Scotch" were debut albums she recorded with the clarinetist. Holiday made seminal recordings with Buck Clayton, Lester Young, and Teddy Wilson in 1935 before signing with Louis Armstrong's manager, Joe Glaser, later that year.

Most of those who knew her felt that her musical inventiveness was well developed from the start, but her need to improvise sometimes cost her jobs during her formative years. Billie Holiday's home, where her mother ran a combination restaurant and social club, became a retreat for many "jazz" musicians and followers, and Billie attended jam sessions and cutting contests there frequently. Her platonic relationship with Lester Young dated from this period. "The romance between Billie and Lester is one of those rare exquisite moments when melodrama and prosaic reality reach out and touch for a while. It is a truism of jazz history that the partnership with Lester Young, personal as well as professional, was the most vital association of Billie Holiday's career. It proved to be a working romance which was usually fruitful, as connoisseurs well know."[44]

Billie Holiday's songs were not of the personal type that grew out of Bessie Smith's world. Holiday's genius resided in her ability to take any song, no matter how insipid, and imbue it with an abundance of life and incredible emotional depth. Louis Armstrong and other musicians had also contributed to restoring life to popular songs; but because she was dealing with words and imbuing them with unadulterated emotional honesty, her message (which was often about love) could be received and understood more intimately even by the most resistant listener. The love between her and Lester Young influenced the music of both.

> It is too tempting to draw the obvious conclusion, to say that the two careers became one and were never the same after the parting. Or that Lester's uncanny knack of completing Billie's vocal phrases was the result not just of musical instinct, but of musical instinct enhanced by the passion of a love affair. There is remarkable parallelism in both the rate and nature of their artistic declines that might be more than coincidence. But then, Lester's oblique instrumental comments on a vocal performance may just as easily be found behind Jimmie Rushing as Billie Holiday. . . . What failure there was in the careers of each of them seems to have been a failure of temperament, not a failure to meet a romantic crisis.[45]

In Billie's words: "For money Lester was the world's greatest. I loved his music, and some of my favorite recordings are the ones with Lester's pretty solos. . . . Lester sings with his horn; you listen to him and can almost hear the words. People think he's so cocky and secure, but you can hurt his feelings in two seconds. I know, because I found out once that I had. We've been hungry together, and I'll always love him and his horn."[46]

By 1937 Billie Holiday was with the Count Basie Orchestra and soon reached national fame. She remained with the Basie band for about a year. She joined Artie Shaw's band in 1938 and began to experience the harsh realities of road conditions for an African-American woman touring with a European-American band. She had originally assumed that the situation was tougher with a "Black" band. She found the working conditions with the ambitious Shaw unbearable, and resented the humiliating treatment the bandleader expected her to endure. In 1939 Holiday embarked on a solo career at a multiracial establishment owned by Barney Josephson named the Café Society.

Her work with pianist Teddy Wilson's orchestra (1935), Basie's band, and Shaw's band brought her great exposure and praise. Linda Dahl highlights a portion of Holiday's career:

> When she was offered a steady job in New York at Cafe Society Downtown starting at seventy-five dollars a week, she consolidated her fame among the sophisticated nightclub set. There was no other singer with the appeal, personal as well as musical, of Lady Day. After staying at Cafe Society for about two years, she went on to star as a featured solo artist at top clubs around the country, recording steadily and upping her salary considerably, to a thousand dollars a week and more. She was glamorous, beautiful, adored; her impeccable musicianship made her an inspiration to other singers.[47]

Holiday's most enduring work was documented on over eighty recordings she made in collaboration with Teddy Wilson between 1936 and 1942. Carmen McRae speaks of her impressions of Holiday during this period: "In her visualization of song, and in her aura, she was to me, then a young hopeful, a combination of idol, alter ego, and mentor."[48] Dahl continues:

> Billie Holiday's immense musicianship stayed with her to the end; as tired as her voice became, the feelings never ceased to flow in song—almost unbearably so at times during those last ravaged years. An intuitive artist who made any tune, pop, blues or standard, her own, she was a musician among musicians, never a "girl singer" fronting the band. She was also a composer and wrote a number of songs that became classics alongside her interpretations of standards. Her "God Bless the Child," with lyrics by Arthur Herzog, is said to have been inspired by her grandmother. It is her most famous song, and one of our most moving musical statements about the "haves" and "have-nots." With Herzog she wrote another moving ballad, "Don't Explain," and the swinging, blues-inspired "Fine and Mellow." Her "Billie's Blues" is a self-portrait of a troubled but proud woman.

The standard Billie Holiday set as a jazz singer was one of implicit, sure and unrelenting swing—the essential sense of time or pulse upon which the jazz interpreter relies to fashion a statement. Her diction and phrasing, underpinned by this often implied rhythmic drive, cast ever-changing light and shadow on the lyrics of a song, revealing ever new layers of meaning.[49]

Holiday's importance as an innovator can be measured not only by her effect on the American vocal tradition, but on the impact she also generated among instrumentalists. Lester Young was certainly not the only master innovator in instrumental "jazz" who reflected aspects of Holiday's style in his own music. Like Bessie Smith, Billie Holiday's substantive musical presence was a seminal experience. Holiday wanted desperately to work in films and, like Smith, she played the standard humiliating African-American role as a maid in New Orleans in her 1947 film debut.

Ella Fitzgerald

Ella Fitzgerald (1981–1994), "The First Lady of Song," remembered her early career:

> The Dean Martin Show was a ball. . . . Then on the Andy Williams Show I did "Sweet Georgia Brown." . . . On each of these shows I did something of a different type; yet each time I probably reached certain people who said, "Now that's the way I dig her; that's the real Ella." On another show I might do a little bopping and someone else will make the same kind of remark. Yet I don't want to feel that everything needs to be in any one of those grooves or that any one is the real Ella.[50]

Born in Newport News, Virginia on April 25, 1918, Fitzgerald said that as a child she never knew her father but experienced a happy childhood in Yonkers, New York. "Everybody in Yonkers thought I was a good dancer; I really wanted to be a dancer. One day, two girl friends and I drew straws to decide which of us would go on the amateur hour. I drew the short straw, and that's how I got started winning all those shows." She soon won the $25 first prize singing "The Object of My Affection" at the Apollo and a contract with the prestigious Arthur Tracy show for a program called "Street Singer." Her mother died during this time and Ella, orphaned and too young to sign a contract, was obliged to return to the amateur hour circuit.

After the Harlem Opera House (the Apollo's rival) hired Fitzgerald, her professional break came when she was heard by master drummer and bandleader Chick Webb (1909–39). Her first gig with Webb was at a Yale University prom. "Well, the Yale boys—they liked me a lot so Chick kept me on," Fitzgerald said. "And I stayed."[51]

Webb's band was one of the most respected ensembles of his era. Through the years the band featured Louis Jordan (1908–75), Wayman Carver (1905–67), Mario Bauzá (1911–93), and other stellar artists. Begin-

ning in 1927, Chick Webb's band remained an institution at the Savoy Ballroom in Harlem for a decade.

For the first year or so after joining Webb's band, however, Fitzgerald
didn't feel she could sing a ballad. Her rise to fame was steady nevertheless
until Webb died in 1939. After his death Ella inherited the band. Norman
Granz wanted to hire the band without her. He did not recognize her genius—"Sure, he used my musicians, but he didn't want me—he didn't dig
me"—until Ray Brown invited her onstage one evening in 1948. From that
time on Granz was her strong advocate and supporter.[52] She made a wise
business move when she hired Granz as her manager. Fitzgerald was later
married to "jazz" bassist Ray Brown (between 1948–1952) after a previous
marriage to Benny Kornegay (between 1941–1943).

Fitzgerald came into scat singing by accident. She recalls: "I did a
show with a disk jockey somewhere, and on a song called 'Simple Melody' I
started doing a do-do-do-doodly-do, and this man said I was scat singing. I
never considered it jazz or bop. I learned how to sing like that from Dizzy Gillespie."[53]

Ella Fitzgerald and Dizzy Gillespie (Photo by William P. Gottlieb).

Ella Fitzgerald won thirteen Grammys and scores of other awards and honors. Her memorable performances with Ellington, Basie, Armstrong, Oscar Peterson, and countless other masters were documented on over 250 albums as she traveled the globe for almost fifty years. Fitzgerald dedicated her timeless "songbook" recording to Harold Arland, Duke Ellington, George Gershwin, Jerome Kern, Johnny Mercer, Cole Porter, and Irving Berlin. As the trombonist Bennie Green has said, her "perfect intonation, natural ear for harmony, vast vocal range, and purity of tone help to make Ella's versions of these beautifully witty, gay, sad, lovingly wrought songs the definitive versions."[54] Fitzgerald's greatness as a singer and innovator remains unmatched.

Ellington's Afrocentricity and the European "Mirage"

Duke Ellington set many standards as an innovative composer, accomplished pianist, and meritorious bandleader throughout his illustrious career. Ellington is indisputably one of the most celebrated composers in the history of American music. He didn't follow the blues-based riff style or other conventions of the day, but developed his own unique approach to composition and orchestration. He freed up the string bass, enabling that instrument to function as a melodic and harmonic voice that was not restricted to fundamental chord tones. His compositional approach matched sanguine subtlety with bold experimentation. He combined his personal broad-based Pan-African cultural awareness and dignity with more ecumenical musical and social concerns.[55]

Duke Ellington's "Creole Rhapsody" is a dramatic extended composition from 1931 that avoids the common swing era formulas. Its construction is based upon five-measure phrases, and opulent permutations maintain continuity throughout its multiple sections. The formal structure and phrase structure alone make the "Creole Rhapsody" one of the most innovative "jazz" compositions to evolve out of swing era repertoire.

Ellington is clearly the preeminent composer of American "vernacular" music. Such music embodies an aesthetic reflection of America's rich, variegated, cosmopolitan, and constantly expanding cultural history. It combines both premeditated and spontaneous compositions that reflect the unique sounds, rhythms, and emotions of American life.

Since African Americans tended to remain less sheltered from the broader American society (which includes a mixture of cultures) than European Americans during the 1940s, "jazz" was able to absorb the style, technique, freedom, and philosophical-mindedness that represented an amalgamation of American influences. For example, African Americans were required to engage in European-American culture more than European Americans in African-American culture.

The attributes that set Ellington apart from other composers in America go beyond the indigenous elements that he drew from metaphors of American socioculture and worked into his compositions. Composers who conduct their own works are able to suggest styles, moods, tempos, dynamics, phrasing, and articulation to the orchestra. Ellington could not only control these elements from his piano, but he could also alter ensemble voicings, spontaneously create new melodies, rhythms, and embellishments, and allow new organic musical growth with each performance. His ingeniously democratic approach to composing for his orchestra benefited from the merging of minds and experience of the entire ensemble. Through this methodical yet musically liberating process, absolute ensemble precision and unity (as well as the individual freedom of expression of each contributing musician) were maintained. Albert Murray summarizes Ellington's compositional technique:

> What he did, of course, was to play each composition into the desired shape and texture during rehearsal. It was not a matter of drilling the musicians on each passage until each section of the orchestra could play its assignment in the new score to his complete satisfaction, as was the case with most other composers. It was rather a way of continuing the process of creation and orchestration that he had begun on the piano some time before. Each musician was provided with a score, to be sure, which each could read and play expertly at sight if necessary. But Ellington, who was always as sensitive to his sidemen's musical personalities as a choreographer is to the special qualities of each dancer's body in motion, always preferred to leave himself free to take advantage of the options that opened up during rehearsal and during the performance itself.[56]

Ellington's influence can be measured by the indelible imprints his music made on the experimental approaches of Charles Mingus, Mary Lou Williams, and Cecil Taylor. In the hands of these and other experimentalists, Ellington's orchestral techniques found their way into either combo formats involving collective improvisation (Williams' "Zodiac Suite" or Taylor's composition "Unit Structures," for instance), or within the levels freedom and craftsmanship explored in orchestrations of later experimentalists (Mingus' album "Let My Children Hear Music" or Anthony Braxton's "Creative Orchestra Music 1976"). Cecil Taylor remarks, "It's Ellington who influenced my concept of the piano as an orchestra, which meant that the horn players and all of the other players other than the piano were in a sense soloists against the background of the piano."[57]

The rare brand of confidence and wisdom that permeates Duke Ellington's music served concomitantly as his guiding force as a democratic bandmaster. Like John Coltrane, Pharoah Sanders, Mary Lou Williams, and other later innovators, Ellington remained concentrated on the evolutionary development of his music, allowing his art to express particular aspects of his spiritual, social, and political views. Richard O. Boyer wrote in "The Hot Bach," his 1944 *New Yorker* profile of Ellington, that the composer thought it "good business to conceal his interest in American Negro history," since Duke doubted it would help "his popularity in Arkansas, say, to have it known that in books he has read about Negro slave revolts he has heavily underlined paragraphs about the exploits of Nat Turner and Denmark Vesey."[58] But, as Mark Tucker understands, creative artists realize that the communicative force of their artistic statements must stand on its artistic merit alone. Consequently, the articulate innovator has a highly effective means of disseminating her or his ideas, emotions, and reactions, and is not reliant upon more limited forms of communication such as written or spoken dialogue. Tucker remarks: "If Ellington kept his reading habits private, his music made public a passion for black history. The year before, in 1943, he had premiered at Carnegie Hall his massive musical parallel to the history of the American Negro, *Black, Brown, and Beige*. Earlier he had celebrated the emancipation of black entertainers from racial stereotypes in *Jump for Joy* (1941), and explored the Afro-American heritage in *Symphony in Black* (1934) and *Creole Rhapsody* (1931)."[59]

Duke Ellington (Image courtesy of HRP Library).

Ellington's awareness of African and African-American culture was not a product of his Harlem Renaissance experience in the 1920s, but inherent qualities instilled as a result of the environment he encountered as a child. Tucker continues:

Yet Ellington's hometown was filled with people equally dedicated to preserving and promoting black culture. In 1915 Howard University professor Carter Woodson founded the Association for the Study of Negro Life and History, which soon began
publishing the *Journal of Negro History*. The Bethel Literary
and Historical Association and the Mus-So-Lit Club provided
forums for discussing black politics, social issues, and literature. And in the schools, Ellington recalled, "Negro history was
crammed into the curriculum, so that we would know our people all the way back."[60]

Another source that focused attention on black history was the
pageants put on by church, school, and civic groups. The most
extravagant one during Ellington's youth was "The Star of
Ethiopia," presented in October 1915 at the American League
Ball Park. In 1913 it had been produced in New York for the
National Emancipation Exposition by W. E. B. DuBois. [61]

The European Image of "Jazz"

People have often said that "jazz" is more appreciated in Europe than
in America. It is true that "jazz" was particularly interesting to many Europeans during periods when they considered African-American music exotic,
but this infatuation was relatively brief. At times Afrocentric "jazz" music
was all but totally rejected in Europe. In more recent times, after Europeans
felt they understood the inner workings of "jazz," African-American musicians have failed to maintain the reputed degree of respect some assume to
be associated with European audiences. Although musicians of Ellington's
caliber were appreciated by an esoteric set of fans, most Europeans did not
immediately embrace "jazz" or fully recognize its artistic value. Some European musicians and fans recognized the complexity and novel beauty of "jazz"
music, but the average audiences developed a taste for African-American music more slowly. Musicians who tried to learn "jazz" were nevertheless in awe
of those who were masters of the art form. They knew that their European
imitations of this music from America were a far cry from the original.
    Neither Ellington nor Armstrong were able to attract large European
audiences or work regularly abroad during the early 1930s. In 1934, the *Melody Maker* reported, "It has been usual, during the London appearances of
celebrated American hot stars, for the fans to cheer themselves hoarse, but
for the majority of the audience to register boredom, if not sheer dislike."[62]
    Sidney Bechet (1897–1959) was in England and France with Peyton's
Six Jazz Kings periodically in the 1920s and did some freelancing there. Initially, despite the powerful endorsement of the great Swiss conductor Ernest
Ansermet as early as 1919, Bechet's influence was initially minimal. He was
deported from England during this period and spent time in a French jail for
several minor offenses. Eventually, however, Bechet came to represent a
unique instance in "jazz" by having his statue in a public square in Antibes, a
city on the French Riviera. Ansermet's comments expose the conflict that Be-

chet and other great African-American artists caused within the European psyche during an age characterized by an uneasy mixture of immense admiration, prophesy, exoticism, presumption, and bigotry.

> There is with the Syncopated Orchestra an extraordinary virtuose [*sic*], the first of his race, I am told, to have composed perfectly elaborated blues on his clarinet. I heard two of them, which he had slowly worked into a definitive form before playing them to his partners so that they could provide an accompaniment. Each very different from the other, they were both admirable for their rich inventiveness, their strong accentuation and their bold, disconcerting freshness. Here, undoubtedly, was a style, and its form was striking—abrupt and rugged, with a brusque, merciless ending, as in Bach's second Brandenburg Concerto. I want to mention the name of this genius among musicians, for, personally, I shall never forget it: Sidney Bechet. Having myself so often searched through the past for one of those figures who gave birth to our art—men of the seventeenth and eighteenth centuries, who developed significant works out of dance-tunes, thus opening the way to Haydn and Mozart—I was deeply moved to discover this big black boy, with his white teeth and narrow forehead, happy to find himself appreciated, but unable to comment on his artistry, except to say that he followed his "own way"; and I thought that, for all we know, this "way" may well be the highway where tomorrow's world traffic will stream.[63]

The appearances of most of these artists in Europe were limited to occasional concerts or short performance runs on variety bills. None of the innovators from America made any significant performance engagements in Europe between the Original Dixieland Jass Band's tour of 1919 and Armstrong's appearance in 1932. After a six-year hiatus, Ellington's second tour in 1939 was the first real effort extended on the part of European promoters to bring him back for a serious concert.[64]

Racist bigotry in Europe was not that far removed from the American variety. Since fewer Africans were encountered in Europe, the level of racially based confrontations was minimal. Racist stereotypes and bigotry still made it difficult for Europeans to approach an art form created by African Americans with objectivity, respect, and humility—regardless of its intrinsic value. Although slightly less threatened by the music than the majority of European-American society, Europeans still found it difficult to acknowledge that an African-American art form—one that had evolved within a few decades under some of the most oppressive social conditions in the modern world—could rise to compete with a similar range of experimental notions and degrees of empiricism as those engaged by "serious" twentieth-century European composers.

Some Europeans on both continents chose to ignore "jazz," while others restricted their reactions to disparagement. Interest in "jazz" on the part of English intellectuals was almost entirely absent. In 1921 Clive Bell, a member of England's most celebrated intellectual avant-garde circle (called the Bloomsbury Group), wrote: "But jazz is dead, or dying at any rate . . . only the riff-raff has been affected. . . . The movement . . . was headed by a band and troupe of niggers, dancing. . . . Jazz art is soon created, soon liked, and soon forgotten. . . . Niggers can be admired artists without any gift more than high spirits."[65]

It was not only Europeans and European Americans who felt that African-American music was less noble and essential than European music. Some African-American champions of the music felt that the full potential of this "Negro" art form could only be obtained through a process that resembled those used to produce European musical models.

Alain Locke considered products of the "jazz" orchestras of Fletcher Henderson, Earl Hines, Luis Russell, Claude Hopkins, "Fats" Waller, Cab Calloway, Louis Armstrong, Don Redman, Jimmie Lunceford, Duke Ellington, and the other notable leaders whose orchestras were emerging in the late 1920s "jazz classics." Locke thought "Negro" musicians had a greater responsibility for the music, but considered the contributions of European-American bandleaders like Jean Goldkette, Paul Whiteman, Ben Pollack, Red Nichols, Ted Lewis, The Casa Loma Orchestra, Jimmy Dorsey, and Benny Goodman meaningful to the development of "classical jazz." He felt that the European American musicians were restricted by a dependence upon having to imitate the African American originators before mastering a "jazz" style. Nonetheless, Locke felt Whiteman, Goodman, and other "White" leaders succeeded in "not only rivaling their Negro competitors musically but rising more and more to commercial dominance of the new industry."[66]

Locke's "classical jazz" and "modern American music" were interchangeable genres of music. He also clearly equated commercial dominance with the highest levels of musical success. In his mind, the most obvious process through which classical "jazz" could experience full maturity was what he refers to as symphonic "jazz" experiments. His conception of what classical "jazz" should be apparently validated the music of Whiteman and Goldkette because of their musical proximity to European symphonic music, and not because of their contributions to the evolutionary tradition that had taken place in America during the twentieth century. He felt this form, derived from dance "jazz" and popular song ballads, involved a level of refinement that ultimately divorced symphonic "jazz" from its more "primitive" source.[67] Locke said that "jazz" is the "spirit child" of the African-American musician and "its artistic vindication rests in its sound development by these musicians."[68] For this reason Locke viewed Ellington with the greatest critical admiration: "In addition to being one of the great exponents of pure jazz, Duke Ellington is the pioneer of super-jazz and one of the persons most likely to create the classical jazz toward which so many are striving. He plans a symphonic suite and an African opera, both of which will prove a test of his ability to carry native jazz through to this higher level."[69]

But Locke was no expert on "jazz." He was the first "Black" Rhodes Scholar at Oxford. He studied under Brentano and Meinong while he was a student of philosophy at the University of Berlin, and under Bergson in Paris. Locke considered Ellington's work especially important because his music placed intuitive music under control, as it restrained and refined the

"Negro's" crude musical materials.[70] "Someone had to devise a technique for harnessing this shooting geyser, taming this wild well," he said. Locke also felt that "classical jazz" successfully transposes the intuitive "jazz" elements of a folk variety into the more sophisticated and traditional big band music forms.[71]

Ellington noted that many of swing's progenitors, who were swinging a decade and a half before, viewed swing in 1954 as an "amusement world" or as a "farce" of which they were either intolerant of or amused. Ellington said that "jazz," which remained "still in the throes of development and formation," had always taken an original and authentic form despite being alienated by its own country. Acknowledging that it had to battle with the poor judgment of "causified critics," "jazz" managed to get its own message across and toiled for acceptance as a legitimate American art form.

Ellington proposed that "Child Jazz" evolved into its "adolescent youth, Swing." He continues: "Ten years ago, when this type of music was flourishing, albeit amidst adverse conditions and surrounded by hearty indifference, there were yet those few enthusiasts in whom the music struck a responsive chord."[72] He also recognized that the swing craze created many beneficial effects. The music required superior musicianship. To perform in the best swing bands required a wide range of specialized skills.

> Greater flexibility, superior tone and range, and intelligence in the use of phrasing and dynamics are all qualities that are far more consistently demanded from the swing musician than they were in the past from the average player. . . . Nevertheless, little progress had been made recently. It is repetition and monotony of the present-day swing arrangements, which bode ill for the future. The mechanics of most of the current "killer-dillers" are similar and of elementary quality.

> Once again, it is proven that when the artistic point of view gains commercial standing, artistry itself bows out, leaving inspiration to die a slow death. The present dearth of creative and original music is not, I'm convinced, due to lack of talent.

Listeners and musicians often claim that music has to swing to be danceable. Ellington realized that this assumption is excessively narrow. He prefers to say that, "Swing is merely one element in good dance music." The stagnation among musicians was partially a consequence of the status of the audience:

> When audience level improves, it will likely inspire our artists to a high level. . . . Without a doubt, progress must await audience development.

> It has thwarted the improvement of many good bands, which for commercial reasons remain in the same uninspired groove and refuse to risk rising above the current public taste.[73]

Ellington was pleased by the growing affinity between the exponents of swing and the exponents of "legitimate" music. However, gaining the approval of European America was clearly not his primary motivation.

> We are not concerned personally with these conditions, because our aim has always been the development of an authentic Negro music, of which swing is only one element. We are not interested primarily in the playing of jazz or swing, but in producing musically a genuine contribution from our race. Our music is always intended to be definitely and purely racial. We try to complete a cycle.

> The boys in our band play in a certain style; the music I write is inspired by those things they play. We write the music for the men in our band, it is inspired by those men, and they play it with the realization and understanding that they are playing their own music.[74]

European "Mirage" and "Jazz" Politics

Locke considered "symphonic" or "classical jazz" "a somewhat unstable and anemic hybrid" that could include Gershwin's *Rhapsody in Blue* and *Porgy and Bess*, William Grant Still's *Afro-American Symphony*, Edmund Jenkins's *Charlestonia: A Negro Rhapsody for Full Orchestra*, and William Dawson's *Negro Folk Symphony*.[75] Locke viewed the work of these composers, combined with the masters of the swing era, as pioneering contributions to the efforts that would result in elevating "jazz" to the level of the classics.[76] The degree of Locke's respect for "classic jazz" is unclear because he speculated that the music to which he referred might be a transitional stage of American musical development that would "eventually . . . be fused in a vital but superior product" of a nature that was left unspecified.[77] Russian, Hungarian, and Bohemian composers are cited as examples. Locke felt these composers "widened the localisms of their native music to a universal speech; they were careful, in breaking the dialect, to reflect the characteristic folk spirit and preserve its unique flavor. What Glinka and his successors did for Russian music, Liszt and Brahms for Hungarian music, and Dvorak and Smetana for Czech music, can and must be done for Negro music."[78]

In Paul Burgett's essay "Vindication as a Thematic Principle in the Writings of Alain Locke on the Music of Black Americans," the author explores the dilemma that Locke and other members of the "Negro" elite faced when attempting to analyze the purpose and value of "jazz" based upon a Eurocentric system of logic. Burgett concludes:

> It is difficult to understand fully what Locke's real motivation was in urging these efforts at vindication. On the one hand, his language suggests a psychological undercurrent of cultural inferiority about Negro music. His statement, "Fortunately, [jazz] is also human enough to be universal in appeal and expres-

siveness," raises serious questions about how Locke really felt about the value of "jazz." His observations about the use of Negro materials in the Dvorak E-minor symphony reveal a pitiable straining for respectability. Locke's reliance on white arbiters of taste is revealing when he cites the following critics of "jazz of the better sort" as names "certainly authoritative enough": Kreisler, Rachmaninoff, Loussevitsky, and Stokowski. Other white critics of "jazz" whom Locke cites as among the most authoritative include Henri Prunieres and Robert Goffin of Paris, Constant Lambert of England, and Hugues Panassie, author of *Le Jazz Hot*.

Locke's aesthetic perspective, to some extent, was affected by a vindication syndrome, which in fact, was dissimilar from the efforts of late nineteenth-century western European Nationalist composers with whom he invites comparison. The disturbing thread of cultural inadequacy implied in Locke's language about the music suggests the inexorable pull on him of western monism, which despite its uncompromisingly racist posture, simply may have been too irresistible in the end.[79]

The realities of Locke's experience as a "Negro" in a racist American society conflicted sharply with the social and educational influences he encountered within the same society. He was twice a graduate of Harvard (magna cum laude and Phi Beta Kappa honors, 1907; Ph.D. in philosophy, 1918), where he "was exposed to the Golden Age of liberalism and, deeply influenced by Barrett Wendell, Copeland, Briggs, and Baker, shed the Tory restraints for urbanity and humanism, and under the spell of Royce, James, Palmer, and Santayana, gave up puritan provincialism for critical-mindedness and cosmopolitanism."[80] Perhaps, due to the weight of his educational influences, Locke's views on "jazz" were less Afrocentric than he may have intended them to be.

While many people argue that "jazz" qualifies as a form of musical modernism, a large proportion of the European music establishment still hesitates. Two forms of twentieth-century experimental music, African-American "jazz" and European modernism, had many related levels of aspiration, developmental phases, and mutual influences. The mutual influence has never ceased to exist. The musical innovations introduced by the language of "jazz" were as significant to the development of a new twentieth-century vocabulary as those introduced by the "Second Viennese" school (or any other "serious" European genre of music). One of the chief reasons for the hesitation in accepting this fact is that "jazz" has failed to gain the acceptance of the European modernist composers. This can never be justified in concrete elemental musical terms; arguments can only be made based upon highly subjective Eurocentric aesthetics. In calculating the quantity, functions, or quality of *notes* on a more objective musical basis, this position cannot be substantiated. The real questions remain: Why should an African-American art form have to justify itself in accordance with European musical values?

Could twentieth-century European music withstand the critical scrutiny of a particular school of African-American aesthetics?

Upon first hearing African-American improvised music, many European composers were intrigued by it and tried their hand at writing ragtime music of their own. Before 1913, Debussy had imitated ragtime in three of his compositions. He was followed by Stravinsky after World War I, and Alban Berg in his opera *LuLu* (an unfinished work, a major portion of which was sent to his publishers in 1935). Similar efforts were made by Ravel and Milhaud in France. The failure of each of these composers to access the "jazz" language convincingly exposed their lack of a metrical, rhythmic, and harmonic understanding of the African-American musical vernacular. That must have registered as a bit unsettling. For the European world's foremost composers to produce naive sounding imitations of African-American music (referred to as simple folk music) exposes the distinctive complexity and sophistication of "jazz."

The realization of the validity and value of "jazz" arrived after claims were made that tonal music had been fully exhausted through the workings of European Romanticism (as "jazz" was concluding its periods of incubation and moving into nascent forms). This must have caused some reconsideration and apprehension on the part of those who engaged this particular quandary. This situation may certainly have warranted further intellectual investigation on the part of the European modernist had racism not been a strong factor attached to this set of musical problems. It was soon clear that "jazz" musicians were equipped with the capability of rendering meaningful interpretations to the neoteric music they composed. It was also doubtful that European symphonic musicians were equipped to approach this new idiom. Hodeir discusses an aspect of this problem:

> Anyone who is acquainted with jazz knows that the best-conceived rhythms remain insignificant unless they are performed with swing. Similarly, jazz sonority cannot be expressed by a stereotyped timbre or series of timbres; it must be created anew with each phrase. It takes a long acquaintance with jazz to assimilate its language; what concert soloist, what chamber music specialist has enough time to bring off such an attempt successfully?[81]

The arrogance that segregated the European composer and the African-American "jazz" composer precluded any meaningful coalescence or further investigation into "jazz" art forms through direct channels. Therefore, the European modernist may have scapegoated their failure in this area on "jazz" music, perhaps anticipating a time when they might have European "jazz" sources to consult and evaluate. Milhaud declared in 1927: "The influence of jazz has already passed by, like a salutary storm after which the sky is purer . . . renascent classicism is replacing the broken throbbings of syncopation."[82] As Hodeir points out, such premature declarations were usually based on limited exposure. Hodeir also says, that "the French composer [Milhaud] was not even curious enough to investigate a certain Louis Armstrong, though people were beginning to talk about him at that time." Milhaud's visit to America during the 1920s was reportedly not extensive enough for him to grasp the differences between Broadway revues and authentic "jazz."

After studying composition in Paris, Aaron Copland returned to New York to create a music of "conscious Americanism." In actuality, this involved three compositions including superficial "jazz effects" that were created between 1925 and 1929.[83] Again, stylistic socialism and naive approaches to African-American musical language was preferred in lieu of the original musical models. Copland then declared that "jazz" was "an easy way to be American in musical terms, but all American music could not possibly be confined to two dominant jazz moods: the blues and the snappy number."[84] Again an arrogant position was taken by a European-American composer who failed to produce either the blues or a snappy number in his attempts at recreating this genre of music. Fortunately, musical and historical records remain that make it clear that many composers who failed to master early African-American "jazz" forms either proceeded to make disparaging remarks about the music or ignored it in the future. Hodeir draws the conclusion: "Stravinsky made history when he wrote *Le Sacre du Printemps*; he placed himself in the margin of history when he wrote *Ragtime*."[85] The inabilities to either access or understand innovative African-American music has caused an assortment of reactions from mainstream America. McIntyre thinks:

> Ethnocentricity by a vast majority of European Americans has a great deal to do with the reluctance of accepting the reality of the African American music tradition in America—since it is outside the European American experience to become included in anything that is not European. The laws, the educational system, and ethics were set up by European Americans and for European Americans. And the experience of thinking of participating in African American music is mind boggling. This is understandable, however, since it was possible for European Americans to reach college age in certain parts of America and not see an African American.[86]

Constant Lambert, who would eventually be hailed as a European intellectual who helped discover "jazz," focused his attention upon European-American composers who were not even involved with the African-American musical genre. Under the guise of "symphonic jazz," Lambert discussed the music of Berlin and Gershwin, demonstrating the limitations of his purview and nugatory knowledge regarding the "jazz" music of which he spoke with bigoted arrogance in 1928: "The point is that jazz has long ago lost the simple gaiety and sadness of the charming savages to whom it owes its birth, and now, for the most part, a reflection of nerves, sex-repressions, inferiority complexes, and general dreariness of the modern world. . . . Jazz, in fact, is just that sort of bastard product of art and life that provides so acceptable a drug to those incapable of really coping with either."[87]

Racism alone was by no means the sole factor that made Europeans hesitant to embrace "jazz" in the beginning. Few Europeans were aware of the Original Dixieland Jass Band records when they began to appear frequently on the American scene in 1917. When they arrived in England in

1919 the press was uniformly disconcerted and befuddled by what they heard, and their articles suggested that English audiences were equally dissatisfied and perplexed. Lew Davis, a reviewer for *The Star* who attended one of the ODJB performances, felt that most listeners were "obviously bewildered by the weird discords, but some, to judge by the cynical smiles, evidently think that it is a musical joke that is hardly worthwhile attempting."[88] The *Melody Maker* was less kind in a later interview and claimed the band "was a complete flop at the Palladium. Nobody understood it."[89] Clearly the band failed to produce any English imitators at that time, and was soon forgotten after it left.[90]

When early swing bands and dance bands were in high demand in Europe, and could command good salaries, local musicians were exceedingly jealous and resentful about this American influx.[91] This animosity eventually resulted in Germany attempting to get rid of American musicians;[92] France ordered American musicians out in 1924,[93] and at least one musician from the United States was deported from England during that period.[94] In 1935 English musicians were eventually able to institute a ban on American bands, which lasted until after World War II. Collier concludes that, "Europeans were thus deliberately closing the doors on the American musicians who could have taught them the new hot music, although some did work sporadically in Europe especially in London and Paris, during the 1920s."[95]

When "jazz" did finally catch on, it was not due to a profound understanding of its underlying musical, spiritual, or aesthetic principals. When American artists finally found work abroad, their European-American managers often worked their clients very hard. Louis Armstrong said: "My chops were beat when I got back from Europe. My manager worked me too hard, and I was so tired when I got back that I didn't even want to see the points of my horn."[96] During the late 1930s, on the eve of the destruction of European Jewish music, there was a growing attraction to African-American music in areas of Germany. Collier concludes that the favorable turn of events was a politically charged reaction to the Nazi influence in Europe. "Jazz became popular in Europe only during the war [World War II]. This was due in considerable measure to the fact that Hitler had anathematized jazz as black and Jewish, and therefore non-Aryan. Going to jazz concerts became, for the people of the captive nations, a political act, and the audience for the music suddenly ballooned. By the end of the war, traditional jazz had become the basic dance music for European students; even bop was finding small audiences."[97]

A writer of the time, who was at the center of European "jazz" activity, said, "Although isolated jazz events had caused a great stir in Paris before the war—notably the Duke Ellington triumph of 1933—typical affairs of the Hot Clubs, even Paris sessions featuring Django Reinhardt and Eddie South, drew only about 400 spectators." James Lincoln Collier claims that Harry Lewis told him that, "in Europe, then, through the 1930s jazz remained the private hobby of a small clique. There were no jazz clubs as such anywhere in Europe. In London, for example, jazz was played at one or two after-hours clubs by a handful of musicians who loved the music and who come in and jam for drinks. There was hardly any jazz on the radio, and jazz records were issued in small editions, mainly by small labels run almost as hobbies."[98]

Successful "jazz" concerts were sporadic in Europe during these times, and conditions for African-American "jazz" musicians did not improve rapidly in Europe. Musicians were often led to believe that Europeans were much more appreciative of their music than their European-American counterparts, and at later times this may have been true for a brief period. Musicians who traveled to Europe found some opportunities to play for small wages, but were often disappointed with what they found abroad. In 1953 the New Orleans pioneer drummer Zutty Singleton and his wife Marge returned discouraged from Paris to the United States. Singleton told a *Down Beat* reporter:

> I saw ["Black" American] musicians around there who'd been fooled by all the talk about how great things were, and now they were living from day to day, working for 2000 francs ($5) a night, just barely getting by. . . . We actually feel freer in America than we did in France. . . . When I think of things like the night a fan told me he saw old Pops Foster trudging through the snow carrying his bass fiddle—because he couldn't afford a taxi—I wonder how people fall for all that stuff about conditions in Europe.[99]

Benny Goodman

In 1938 Benny was considered to be "The King of Swing" by European Americans. None of the leaders of the leading African-American swing bands (Ellington, Basie, Lunceford, Henderson) considered Goodman the king, but this was not important in America when evaluating African-American music. Goodman, however, did become one of the first European-American bandleaders to work consistently with African-American musicians.

Goodman's financial success enabled him to invite some of the best musicians of the day to a concert in Carnegie Hall on June 16, 1938. Count Basie played piano, Johnny Hodges was on alto saxophone, Cootie Williams played trumpet, and Walter Page was on bass. Other musicians on this performance included Lester Young (tenor saxophone), Harry James (trumpet), Ziggy Elman (trumpet), Jess Stacy (piano) and Gene Krupa (drums).

On other occasions, Goodman worked with Billie Holiday and other great vocalists. Goodman initially refused to work with African-American musicians, but after he was finally persuaded to do so, he worked enthusiastically with "jazz" masters such as Lionel Hampton, Teddy Wilson, and Charlie Christian.

Critics and historians of African-American "jazz" often claimed that the European-American "jazz" bands were more refined. Actually, they were merely more closely related to European musical aesthetics and cultural values, nothing more. This is why, in retrospect, to call Paul Whiteman the "King of Jazz" is absurd to the point of embarrassment. Goodman's importance to "jazz" was never assessed by African-American musical standards during his heyday. Listen to Goodman's version of "Body and Soul" (where Teddy Wilson is conspicuously the senior improviser at the recording session and compare his interpretation to Coleman Hawkins's work with the same composition.

A fair assessment of the musical situation in America is difficult to obtain unless sociocultural conditions are factored into the equation. Certain African-American artists were unable to get their bands employed, recorded, and promoted, or their documentary materials distributed. Some African-American innovators (consider the cases of Fletcher Henderson and Mary Lou Williams) were forced to write for or sell their arrangement to artists like Goodman. Their creative output helped to boost Goodman's reputation and make the clarinetist famous among the majority culture.

Other African-American Dance Bands

William McKinney (1910–95) was a drummer and manager of pianist Todd W. Rhodes's "Synco Septet" before changing the name of the group and becoming the leader of "McKinney's Cotton Pickers." The racist implication of that particular appellation suggests that it was the European-American manager of the Arcadia Ballroom in Detroit who favored the name change. Nevertheless, the septet was soon to become a big band.

The group moved into the Greystone Ballroom in Motor City, in 1926. The fame of the band spread rapidly, and in 1928 McKinney signed a contract with Victor Records. After Don Redman (1900-64) joined the band (in 1927), McKinney's Cotton Pickers enjoyed their most enduring period of musical success. McKinney persuaded Redman to leave Fletcher Henderson's band, and hired him for $300 a week to build his band's repertoire. That period of success ended in 1931 when Redman suddenly announced that he was leaving the band. Rex Stewart (1907–67) and Benny Carter (b. 1907) soon joined the band as new members. Carter inherited the position as musical director, but he remained with the band for only one year. The band worked until 1934 before finally deciding to bring the organization's history to a close.

During the Depression years Alphonso E. Trent (1905–59) formed a band that enjoyed success and relatively good exposure. In 1923 Trent was leading a small band at a dance pavilion near Dallas, Texas, when he was heard by the management of the famous Adolphus Hotel in downtown Dallas. Trent augmented the band to ten members and became known as "Trent's Adolphus Hotel Orchestra." Despite the traditional racism of the Southwest at this time, the performance marked the first appearance of an African-American band at a major American hotel. Many outstanding musicians would become members of the band during the 1920s, including Sy Oliver, Harry "Sweets" Edison, Stuff Smith, and Peanuts Holland.

The Al Trent Orchestra was one of the first big bands to perform over the radio (or wireless telephone, as it was referred to by many at the time) at station WFAA, Dallas. His band became the most famous "territory band" in the country.

Trent engaged the Floyd Campbell band in a historic "battle of the bands" in the summer of 1927. The event drew an audience of over five thousand listeners.[100] The Al Trent Orchestra recorded a series of records for Gennett Records of Richmond, Indiana, between 1927 and 1931. In 1932, after the ensemble reached full big band proportions, domestic matters forced Trent to leave his orchestra. He soon reorganized another big band only to disband a final time in 1934—unfortunately, just before the popular age of the big bands. After this period, Trent worked with small combos until his retirement.

Alto saxophonist Louis Jordan, trumpeter "Cootie" Williams, pianist Teddy Wilson, and tenor saxophonist Coleman Hawkins were among many world-renowned instrumentalists who formed short-lived big bands. Other notable big bands include Andy Kirk and His Clouds of Joy, Chick Webb and His Chicks, Ella Fitzgerald and Her Orchestra, Mills Blue Ribbon Band, The Jeter-Pillars Band, Harlan Leonard and His Rockets, Fess Whatley's Vibra Cathedral Band, The Sam Wooding Orchestra, and many others.

A Glance at the Development of the Guitar in Early "Jazz"

The five-stringed African-American banjo was the "New World" version of the African *halam*. Listening to repetition in recordings of older African music reveals itself in many forms in African-American music. American southern blues players like Gus Cannon exhibit a close stylistic tie to traditional African *halam* playing. The quick decay of the banjo's tones requires a technique that must involve rapid execution of repeated rhythmic figures. Once the blues players moved to the guitar, a much more sustained tone was possible and the accompaniment took on a more lyrical quality. A greater integration of voice and guitar began to occur that had not been possible with the banjo.

The banjo was the primary string instrument in the early "jazz" band until 1930. It is a chordal instrument that could supply harmony for early ensembles. The incisive sound quality of the banjo satisfied the needs of the early African-American bands because of its loudness and portability. The banjo was the only portable chordal instrument that could be heard among the particular set of wind instruments typically found in early "jazz." During that time, the guitar was primarily used to accompany solo blues vocalists (Leadbelly, for example).

Banjos were gradually replaced by the guitar after Gibson manufactured the first arched-top guitar (the F-5) with metal strings in 1923. This more resonant modern version of the guitar was capable of projecting sound more efficiently compared to the standard nylon-stringed classical guitar. The guitar now offered two main musical qualities that made it an attractive replacement for the banjo. First, the guitar's rich sound blended well with horns, as opposed to the more strident sound of the banjo. The particular type of blending that became a characteristic quality of the big band sound of swing era required this enhanced capability. Second, the guitar was capable of the more complicated harmonic voicings that "jazz" was beginning to explore.

Even with its arched top, however, the guitar's low amplitude rendered it incapable of playing a major role in "jazz" orchestra during the swing era. The role of the guitar was limited to merely a rhythmic sound effect emphasizing the meter. This musical function became even more obscure and less significant when the drummers started placing more emphasis on the hi-hat around 1927. Some players, notably Freddie Green in the Count Basie Orchestra, tried to improve the function of the guitar in the big band by finding new rhythmic spaces to fill. These efforts became more clearly recognizable with the improvement of the recording technique and the incorporation of the electronic public address system. Players like Green became better recognized as electronic developments in amplification continued to improve, enabling their musical contributions to surface from the within the large ensembles.

When guitar players became frustrated with their strictly supportive positions in orchestras, they had two possible solutions: amplify the sound even more or perform in smaller groups. Examples of the latter solution can be heard in Eddie Lang's duo recording with Joe Venturi (1903–78) or with Lonnie Johnson (1899–1970). Other guitarists began to form smaller groups as well.

Efforts directed toward achieving dynamic contrast with the acoustic guitar in regular "jazz" bands were generally futile, as the softer notes played could not be heard. Consequently, the early "jazz" guitar players performed all the notes with full force. Even in typical small ensemble the audiences were noisy. The only circumstances in which the guitar could usually be approached in a more flexible manner were recording studio settings. Other players had to await the appearance of the electric guitar to compete with the noise levels in live performance situations.

Without the application of dynamic contrast, it is difficult to make distinctive musical phrases. The adaptation that resulted produced a style of guitar solo involving an incessant discharge of notes. This situation was similar to that which occurred during the transition period between European baroque and classic keyboard styles. After the forte piano (which had a broader range of dynamics) was invented and replaced the harpsichord, composers became conscious of more expressive styles of keyboard phrasing, eschewing terraced dynamics.

The direct electric amplification of the guitar, first introduced in the early 1920s, was popularized around 1935 by the Gibson ES150 equipped with the pickup later called "the Charlie Christian pickup." Since the sound of an acoustic guitar decays rather quickly when the string is plucked with full force, guitar players could not phrase in the lyrical style that became popular during the late swing period. With his new amplified hollow-body guitar, Charlie Christian (1916–42) was able to become the first virtuoso guitarist capable of playing with a volatile scope, musical purview, and expressive latitude similar to that of the leading horn players of the time. Benny Moten's guitarist, Eddie Durham, was probably the first to amplify the guitar when he placed a mike inside the sound hole of his guitar around 1929. It was Christian, nonetheless, who secured the preeminence of the electric guitar over the acoustic forerunner. Although he did not live long enough to discover his full potential on guitar (he died of tuberculosis when he was only twenty-six years old), he became a major pre-bop figure with his single-note solo style.

Christian found new ways of playing the guitar like a horn with the smooth legato, a rich tone that was free of distortion, and the clear and relaxed phrasing in his solos. He still used banjo-like strumming figures when he was in the background. He developed swinging riffs, often centered around a single note or unusual accentuation, and demonstrated a remarkable sense of time. His use of augmented and diminished chords, and chordal extensions to the 13th, gave an unconventional and fresh flavor to his approach to the guitar. Christian's innovations were documented on recordings with Benny Goodman's combos and big band. He also performed in informal jam sessions with Thelonious Monk and Dizzy Gillespie that were preserved and released on records. An enthusiast named Jerry Newman recorded important after-hour sessions in 1941 involving Christian at Minton's Playhouse and Monroe's Uptown House, two popular Harlem establishments. His solo performances on "Topsy" and "Stompin' at the Savoy" are two recordings that demonstrate the young guitarist's inimitable style, control, and inventiveness that influenced all subsequent guitarists. With Charlie Christian and the invention of the electric guitar, guitarists began to establish their positions as soloists in the "jazz" band.

The next step for guitar players was to explore the uniqueness of the guitar, beyond its timbre alone, in order to secure their position in the development of "jazz." Some used the special effects like glissando or pitch-bend intensively in their play. However it is very difficult to maintain the listener's attention for a long period of time by merely using such effects. In time, guitar players found their voice somewhere between that of the piano and the horns.

Django Reinhardt (1910–1953) was a Belgian Gypsy guitar virtuoso known for his scintillating phrasing, intriguing grandiloquence, and impressive command of the copious musical notes he usually played. The mercuriality of his piano-like solos contrasts sharply with Christian's hornlike metronomic approach. Reinhardt did not engage in the swing eighth-note style that Christian perfected but incorporated more triplets and sixteenth notes while emphasizing vibrato and pitch bending to color his solos. Although Reinhardt was missing two fingers on his hand, he tried to destroy the stereotypical notion of guitar as strictly a rhythm instrument.

Wes Montgomery (1925–68) would later realize that playing his melodic lines in parallel octaves would not only create a unique guitar timbre, but it had the added advantage of better dynamic projection. By the 1960s, guitarist Jimi Hendrix (1942–70) would embark upon a pioneering journey to fully explore the unique qualities of electric guitar in ways never before imagined. Although his music was labeled rock and roll, it was considered much more than that by Miles Davis and other "jazz" musicians. According to Hendrix's manager, Jim Marron, the guitarist stayed with the less demanding rock-and-roll style because of financial concerns:

> Quite frankly, I don't think Hendrix wanted to take the financial risk that a manager change represented. He would have much preferred to [tinker] with his current situation rather than go broke. [Alan] Douglas's taste in music leaned heavily toward American jazz, and quite honestly, Hendrix could have been a great jazz player, but he had been a starving artist be-

fore and wasn't interested in going that route again. There was
no money in jazz at that time. There still isn't.[101]

George Benson (b. 1943) was influenced by Charlie Christian at an
early age and was ready to join Jack McDuff's organ quartet for four years in
the early 1960s. His virtuosity and clarity firmly established his reputation
by 1966. He also sang, and by the 1970s Benson was singing along with his
improvised guitar lines. Soon he became commercially successful, selling over
a million copies of his album "Breezin'" in 1976. The following year he won a
Grammy. Benson co-produced the albums *Face to Face* (1986) and *The Heat
of the Heat,* which were clearly conceived to gain popular acceptance. Although his commercial success led the guitarist to lean more toward singing,
his use of octaves, harmonics, funk patterns, speed, and precision have remained impressive. His influence is evident in younger guitarists such as
Earl Klugh (b. 1954) and Kevin Eubanks (b. 1957).

Although Kenny Burrell (b. 1931) never achieved the level of popular
appeal that either Wes Montgomery or George Benson, he contributed a great
deal to further the style initiated by Charlie Christian. After making his debut recording with Dizzy Gillespie in 1951, Burrell recorded with a wide
number and variety of "jazz" masters. Burrell gained a reputation for his
ability to consistently supply a reliable accompanying role.

Earl Klugh developed an interesting style on the Gibson Chet Atkins
acoustic guitar (with nylon strings); it retains the facile virtuosity of Benson's
style that Klugh often dovetails into the fusion domain. His melodies,
rhythms, and harmonies display his own personal musical stamp, but the unobtrusive predictability of his music make Klugh popular among "easy-listen-
ing jazz" clientele.

Kevin Eubanks is also an extraordinary guitarist who was eventually
influenced by the lure of popular music. He began touring with Art Blakey in
1979 and later worked with the drummer Roy Haynes' band. His early albums *Guitarist* and *Sundance* were examples of the work Eubanks was doing
in performances at clubs such as Bradley's and Spring Street before taking a
more commercial direction in the 1980s. The initial releases were a mixture
of fusion and hard-bop approaches that used the pickless thumb technique of
Wes Montgomery combined with Charlie Christian–influenced banjo-strum-
ming figures. Eubanks took over as the leader of The Tonight Show house
band when Branford Marsalis gave up the position.

The most provocative innovator to emerge during the 1980s was
Stanley Jordan. Jordan's unorthodox experimental guitar seems well grounded in the African music, African-American "jazz" tradition, the music of Jimi
Hendrix, and electronic music. He began as a pianist and transferred his two-
handed keyboard technique to the guitar after switching instruments. Jordan
listened closely to Charlie Christian as a child and studied electronic music at
Princeton as a music major. His eclectic style is the result of all these influences. He managed to extend the range and conception of the guitar, winning
a Grammy nomination and film roles,[102] and yet remaining innovative while
appealing to a large following throughout the world.

The guitar cannot be as broad harmonically or as effective contrapun-
tally as the piano. It is capable of playing only six or seven notes simultane-

ously, depending on the number of strings. Yet the guitar can add vibrato or bend the pitch in a way pianists cannot. Guitarist George Van Eps may have been one of the first "jazz" guitar players to use a seven-string guitar to play both the bass line and the harmonized melody at the same time. As "jazz" moved toward more elusive musical criteria, mixes of functional advantages and disadvantages contributing to an individual instrumentalist's individuality, the stature of the modern guitar increased.

Notes

[1] Duke Ellington, *Music is My Mistress* (Garden City, N.Y.: Doubleday, 1973), p. 420.

[2] "Alligator Hop" (1923) provides a good example of the band's sound.

[3] Listen to Morton's "Strokin Away" (1930) for a sample of his style at the beginning of the swing era, after his pioneering compositions had contributed to the setting of the stage for the most popular era in "jazz" history.

[4] Hsio Wen Shih, "The Spread of Jazz and the Big Bands," in Hentoff and McCarthy, *Jazz*, p. 72.

[5] "Margie" (1938) is an example.

[6] "Breakfast Dance" (1929—clarinet trio) and "Caravan" (1930s) are just two of countless examples.

[7] Don Freeman, "My Biggest Thrill? When Duke Roared Back: Basie," *Down Beat* 61, no. 2 (February 1994), p. 31; first published May 16, 1956.

[8] Linda Dahl, *Stormy Weather* (New York: Limelight Editions, 1989), pp. 47–48.

[9] Placksin, *Jazz Women,* pp. 95–96.

[10] Ibid., p. 96.

[11] Ibid., p. 97. The Hutton band of this period can be seen in the film *The Big Broadcast of 1937*, and such shorts as *Accent on Girls* (1936) and *Swing, Hutton, Swing* (1937).

[12] "Ina Ray Hutton: 'Blonde Bombshell' Has Hottest Gal Swing Band," *The Orchestra World*, unsigned, undated clipping, LCL-M; as cited in ibid., p. 98.

[13] Ibid., p. 98.

[14] Ibid., p. 98.

[15] George T. Simon, *The Big Bands* (New York: Macmillan, 1967), pp. 260–61.

[16] Placksin, *Jazzwomen,* p. 98.

[17] Liner notes, "The International Sweethearts of Rhythm," Rosetta Records, RR 1312 (1984).

[18] Ibid.

[19] *Afro-American,* May 3, 1941.

[20] Placksin, *Jazzwomen.*

[21] Liner notes, "International Sweethearts of Rhythm."

[22] Robert Gottlieb, ed., *Reading Jazz: A gathering of Autobiography, Reportage, and Criticism from 1919 to Now* (New York: Pantheon Books, 1996), p. 650.

[23] Ibid.

[24] Quoted in Alan C. Weber, liner notes to *Sweet Emma Barrett and Her New Orleans Music*, Southland LP 241, 1963.

[25] Ibid.

[26] Handy, D. Antoinette. *Black Women in American Bands and Orchestras* (London: Scarecrow, 1981), pp. 159–62.

[27] Ibid.

[28] Best known for her wordless vocal on Ellington's "Creole Love Call."

[29] James Lincoln Collier, *The Making of Jazz*, p. 378.

[30] Ellington, *Music is My Mistress*, p. 170.

[31] Antoinette, *Black Women in American Bands*, pp. 176–79.

[32] "The Spirit of Mary Lou," December 20, 1971, p. 67.

[33] Ellington, *Music Is My Mistress*, p. 169.

[34] Ian Carr, Digby Fairweather and Brian Priestley, *Jazz: The Rough Guide* (London: Penguin Books, 1995), p. 281.

[35] The film was nominated for an academy award in 1945.

[36] *Jazz: The Rough Guide*, p. 713.

[37] Linda Dahl, *Stormy Weather*, p. 99.

[38] Ibid., pp. 97–110.

[39] Humphrey Lyttleton, *The Best of Jazz*, pp. 79, 83.

[40] Richard Hadlock, *Jazz Masters of the Twenties*, p. 224.

[41] Alice Adams, *Listening to Billie* (New York: Alfred A. Knopf, 1978), p. 1.

[42] Maya Angelou, *The Heart of a Woman* (New York: Random House, 1981), p. 17.

[43] John Hammon, *John Hammond on Record*, p. 92.

[44] Benny Green, *The Reluctant Art: Five Stories in the Growth of Jazz* (New York: Da Capo, 1990), pp. 144–45

[45] Ibid. p. 144.

[46] Ibid.. pp. 144–45

[47] Linda Dahl, *Stormy Weather*, p. 138.

[48] Quoted in John Chilton's *Billie's Blues*, p. 86.

[49] *Stormy Weather*, p. 139.

[50] Leonard Feather, "Ella Today (And Yesterday Too)," *Down Beat*, March 1994, p. 36.

[51] "Misty Over Ella: Ella Fitzgerald Dies," *New York Post*, June 16, 1996.

[52] Leonard Feather, "Ella Today (And Yesterday Too)," *Down Beat*, March 1994, pp 37–38.

[53] Article on Ella Fitzgerald in *Off the Record*, by Joe Smith, 1988.

[54] *Jazz: The Rough Guide*. p. 211.

[55] For the Pan-African cultural awareness, listen to Duke Ellington's album *My People,* Contact, Mono CM-1 (1963); for the more ecumenical concerns, listen to Ellington's *The Afro-Eurasian Eclipse*, Fantasy F-9498 (recorded in 1971).

[56] Albert Murray, The Blue Devil of Nada: A Contemporary American Approach to Aesthetic Statement (New York: Pantheon Books, 1996), p. 110.

[57] Spellman, *Four Lives*, p. 72.

[58] Peter Gammond, ed., *Duke Ellington: His Life and Music* (1958; New York: Da Capo, 1977), p. 49.

[59] Mark Tucker, "The Renaissance Education of Duke Ellington," in *Black Music in the Harlem Renaissance: A Collection of Essays*, ed. Samuel Floyd, Jr. (Knoxville: University of Tennessee Press, 1993), p. 117.

[60] Ibid. See also Ellington, *Music Is My Mistress*, p.17.

[61] Ibid. See also W. E. B. Du Bois, "The Star of Ethiopia," *Crisis* 11 (December 1915): 90–94.

[62] *Melody Maker*, September 1, 1934, p. 1.

[63] Published in *Revue Romande,* October 1919, as cited in the liner notes on the album "Sidney Bechet: Superb Sidney," CBS 62 636.

[64] *Duke Ellington: His Life and Music*, pp. 42–49.

[65] Clive Bell, "Plus de Jazz," *New Republic*, September 21, 1921, pp. 92–96.

[66] Alain Locke, *The Negro and His Music* (1936; New York: Arno Press and the New York Times, 1969), p. 112.

[67] Ibid., p. 82.

[68] Paul Burgett, "Vindication as a Thematic Principle in the Writings of Alain Locke on the Music of Black Americans," in Floyd, *Black Music in the Harlem Renaissance,* p. 36.

[69] Locke, *The Negro and His Music,* p. 96.

[70] Burgett, "Vindication as a Thematic Principle," p. 36.

[71] Locke, *The Negro and His Music,* p. 96.

[72] Ibid.

[73] Ibid., p. 20.

[74] Ibid.

[75] Ibid., pp. 110–12.

[76] Burgett, "Vindication as a Thematic Principle," p. 36.

[77] Locke, *The Negro and His Music,* p. 130.

[78] Margaret Just Butcher, *The Negro in American Culture*, 2d ed. (New York: Knopf, 1972), p. 91.

[79] Burgett, "Vindication as a Thematic Principle," p. 38.

[80] Stanley J. Kunitz and Howard Haycraft, eds., *Twentieth Century Authors* (New York: H. H. Wilson, 1942), p. 837.

[81] Andre Hodeir, *Jazz: Its Evolution and Essence* (1956; New York: Grove, 1980), pp. 261–62.

[82] As quoted in ibid., p. 249.

[83] Samuel Lipman, *Music after Modernism* (New York: Basic Books, 1979), p. 67.

[84] As quoted in Headington, *History of Western Music*, p. 356.

[85] Hodeir, *Jazz*, p. 263.

[86] Liner notes from McIntyre's album *Home*, Steeple Chase SCS-1039 (1975). McIntyre plays alto sax, flute, oboe, bassoon, and bass clarinet on this recording.

[87] *Life and Letters* 1, no. 2 (July 1928): 125–26.

[88] *Star* (London), April 19, 1919.

[89] *Melody Maker*, June 2, 1919.

[90] Collier, *Reception of Jazz in America*, p. 42.

[91] *Orchestra World,* January 1926, p. 19.

[92] *New York Times*, December 11, 1924, sec. 2, p. 5.

[93] *New York Times,* May 31, 1924, sec. 1, p. 2.

[94] *Orchestra World,* January 1927, p. 7.

[95] Collier. *Reception of Jazz in America*, p. 42.

[96] Louis Armstrong, "My Chops Was Beat—But I'm Dyin' To Swing Again," *Down Beat* 61, no. 2 (February 1994), p. 20; first published June 1935.

[97] Collier. *Reception of Jazz in America: A New View* (Brooklyn, NY: Institute for Studies in American Music, Conservatory of Music (CUNY), 1988), p. 49.

[98] *Down Beat,* August 26, 1946, p. 4. Article by Delaunay.

[99] *Down Beat*, February 5, 1953, pp. 6, 16.

[100] Gene Fernett, *Swing Out: Great Negro Dance Bands* (New York: Da Capo, 1993), pp. 41–42.

[101] John McDermott, *Hendrix: Setting the Record Straight* (New York: Warner Books, 1992), p. 282. Alan Douglas is the current administrator of the Hendrix tape vault.

[102] He appears in *Blind Date* as Bruce Willis's guitar-playing sidekick.

VIII
Innovators Emerging Between 1940 and 1950

He could teach anybody, but me . . . the shit was going
too fast.

—Miles Davis

The 1940s was a decade of change and social progress in the United
States. Richard Wright wrote *Native Son* and Benjamin O. Davis, Sr., became
the first African-American army general in America. The first successful heli-
copter flight in the United States was sponsored by the Vought-Sikorsky Cor-
poration, and an American, Ernest O. Lawrence, won the Nobel Prize for
Physics for the development of the cyclotron.

The Zoot suit was the most fashionable attire among the hepcats in
the United States in 1943, just as the jitterbug replaced the Lindy hop. Eisenhower
announced Italy's unconditional surrender, and the British joined the United
States forces in Africa. In the United States, race riots broke out in cities where
the labor force had grown as a result of a huge influx of African-American
workers from rural areas.

Joe Louis defended his crown successfully for the twenty-third time in
1946, and boxing sensation Jack Johnson died. In 1948 Babe Ruth died and
Joe Louis retired from boxing. In 1949 Wesley Brown became the first African-American cadet to graduate from the U.S. Naval Academy at Annapolis.

Music becomes classic when it is studied and admired long after its
stylistic era has passed. African-American musicians created a number of
classic styles during the twentieth century that have been emulated continually and expansively throughout the world. The 1940s contributed bebop to
modern music. Like blues, ragtime, classic "jazz," and swing before it, bop
quickly became one of the most challenging and pervasive of all American
musical innovations.

Basic Blues and Early Precursors of Modern "Jazz"

The eras of the 1940s and 1960s were not the only revolutionary periods in the history of African-American music. European-American writers
have said that the rebellious nature of bebop is akin to the avant-garde musicians of the "free jazz" era. The styles that evolved from those two periods
may be more conspicuous due to the more radical nature of their departures
from Eurocentric conventions of the day, but all the major periods of twentieth-century African-American music were somewhat extremist.

"Jazz" has always been an innovative and evolutionary art form. As alto saxophonist Bobby Watson said recently, "Jazz has never been about anything conservative!"[1] On the surface, this fact may not always be clearly evident. The contemporary music scene usually promotes the most popular artists rather than the most innovative ones; consequently, conservative forms of "jazz" can appear to dominate the style of a particular period. Less popular forms have nonetheless usually produced the defining music for each epoch.

It was only during the swing era that "jazz" enjoyed wide popularity. Even during that auspicious period, the more conservative and fashionable bands enjoyed greater economic and popular success than the innovative bands. Few if any of the members of that money-making machine the music business represents have mastered the music they evaluate and criticize, but the lack of valid credentials has not mattered traditionally to mainstream America. As a result bands led by such "jazz" greats as Ellington, Lunceford, Basie, Moten, and Henderson were less celebrated during the swing era than some of the less evolved European-American bands. Nevertheless, the depth and beauty of the music of the true "jazz" masters has made their innovative contributions more enduring with the passage of time.

During the 1930s and early 1940s "jazz" was a source of popular entertainment. Americans could dance and marvel at the musical skills and passion of musicians while dancing in large ballrooms. Big band music was presented in elegant (and even lavish) settings in African-American and European-American communities throughout America before World War II. After the war, combos replaced large orchestras. Former lavish communal ballrooms (generally owned by cheap proprietors) gradually became small clubs for esoteric audiences in European American neighborhoods. T. S. Monk (Thelonious Monk's son)[2] comments:

> [Music that best] reflects the American democratic idea [was banished to] dark little, stinky clubs. . . . For many years no one was saying jazz was important except for intellectuals. . . . [Club owners decided to] close their dance floors [because] White restauranteurs wanted to bring the music downtown to a more "civilized audience." . . . If anybody thinks Thelonious Monk or Miles Davis or John Coltrane enjoyed playing in a Five Spot or stinking Village Vanguard all the time, that's mythological b.s.[3]

The element that sets the more radical stylistic departures of bop apart from other evolutionary musical contributions is the enjoyment and incorporation of greater degrees of artistic freedom. Under repressive European and European-American domination, Africans were forced to temper the range of freedom they formerly enjoyed within their traditional cultures. Music, like other aspects of society, is governed by laws. African culture approached the establishment of laws in ways that were often diametrically opposed to European methods of lawmaking. Similarly, the laws of bebop were contrary to many of the laws of European music and aesthetics.

European composers began to eschew tonality in favor of twelve-tone and serial techniques developed by the members of the Second Viennese School (Arnold Schoenberg, Alban Berg, and Anton Webern). A few composers (Debussy, Stravinsky, Bartok, Scriabin, etc.) explored the higher intervals above a given tonic (that is, intervals a 9th, 11th, and 13th above a root), but the majority of composers of "serious" European music abandoned tonality. Many composers of academic American music followed the lead of the Europeans. African-American "jazz" musicians knew that tonality had not been completely exhausted. They felt there were many aspects that had never been explored, and realized that new artistic manifestations can always be created through different fissionary combinations of older and newer traditions. Author Albert Murray's discussion of visual artist Romare Bearden's work is closely related to the modern "jazz" musician's conception of traditional musical elements.

> Bearden, who is nothing if not an exponent of the flat surface, sees no reason why his pictures should not tell a story so long as the narration and depiction do not get in the way of the painting as such. In his view, a painting does not have to say anything either literal or symbolic, but it can if it wishes. Of course, it must always avoid unintentional counter statement or detrimental empathy. On the other hand, there can be no question of any violation of scale, perspective, or non realistic color destroying the illusion in a flat painting, since description is always subordinate to design.[4]

Bebop Ties to Past and Present Cultures

Bebop was not a very popular music during the forties. Dizzy Gillespie and music critic Leonard Feather discussed the social disrespect, racism, and negative stereotypes that surrounded bebop during the 1940s in the documentary film *Celebrating Bird*.[5] Bebop struggled against the tendency of many listeners to insist on extending the reign of swing an additional decade. During the forties attempts were made to create a Dixieland revival that would resuscitate music from the 1920s and 1930s. To a degree such reactions are to be expected. Even today, musicians who perform retrospective "jazz" styles (basically from the 1940s and 1950s) realize far greater degrees of economic and popular success in contemporary American society than experimental "jazz" artists enjoy. Despite social trends that become realities, innovation continues to be the primary prerequisite in all phases of the "jazz" evolution. The lack of financial support means that innovation often takes place underground, away from the critical eyes and ears of general audiences. Unfortunately, listeners in America rarely hear or see much experimental music in the media.

History demonstrates that a balanced formula involving evolution and tradition had always been connected to all African-American music. Listening to the music of the griots and other traditional African musicians makes it clear that significant changes occurred when Africans were transported to America. The fragmentation of African heritage in America is related to the efforts undertaken several centuries ago by the European world to fragment African society. Destabilizing the continent facilitated the exploitation of African resources. Nature and mankind collaborated to divide a portion of the Arab world from the African continent. Professor Ali A. Mazrui calls our attention to the creation of the Suez Canal, which completed the schism.

> The problem goes back several million years when three cracks emerged on the eastern side of Africa. . . . Three cracks had occurred on the African crust—yet only the one which had resulted in a sea was permitted to "dis-Africanise" what lay beyond the sea. The other two cracks resulted in "rift valleys," . . . The eastern and western rifts left the African continent intact but the emergence of a strip of water called the Red Sea had resulted in the physical separation of Africa from Asia.

> The final drama in the separation of the Arabian peninsula from what we now call Africa occurred in the nineteenth century. If the Arabs had been in control of their own destiny they could have been discussing building communications between the two parts of the Arab world. But, in fact, Egypt in the nineteenth century was oriented towards Europe. And so the Suez Canal was built, by a Frenchman, Ferdinand de Lesseps, not in order to facilitate traffic between Africa and Arabia but to make it easier for Europe to trade with the rest of the world. An estimated 120,000 Egyptians lost their lives in the ten years it took to build the Suez Canal (1859–69). A natural cataclysm which had occurred several million years previously and torn off the Arabian peninsula from the rest of Africa was now completed through its canal.[6]

Laws are often proposed to promote order and decency in society. Africans based their fundamental laws upon phenomena observed in nature and attempted to attune themselves with such universal principals. Rules for hunting or planting were designed to align and harmonize with the cycles of creation. Opposing natural cycles was obviously self-defeating since, within the state of humility and respect Africans held for the Creator, no mortal could overwhelm or control nature. Power came as a result of understanding and working in harmony with natural forces. There was no need for numerous complicated laws in Africa because it was clear that disharmony produced its own retribution or karma. The best rulers have understood that those who rule least rule best. The more laws that are created, the more difficult the job of enforcing them becomes. This leads to complicated lifestyles in situations covered by numerous laws. Africans preferred the freedom that came with simplicity and natural order. This manner of thinking lies at the heart of the most liberated approaches to innovative African-American music.

Bebop formed its laws in harmony with the logical extension of the overtone series as applied to evolutionary blues and "jazz" traditions.

Samuel Charters traveled to the mother continent in search of blues elements in traditional African music. He discusses his findings in his book *The Roots of the Blues: An African Search*. In regard to some particular African songs he says,

> It was clear, as I had first realized listening to the griot songs, that they didn't sound much like the blues, but both the griot's music and the music of the southern United States had changed, each of them going in their own directions. The voices themselves had a great deal of similarity in tone and texture. If a griot like Jali Nyama Suso had sung in English the sound of his voice would have been difficult to distinguish from an Afro-American singer's. There was the same kind of tone production, the same forcing of higher notes. In the gruffness of the lower range and the strong expressiveness of the middle voice. I could hear stylistic similarities to singing I had heard in many parts of the South.[7]

European Americans felt it imperative to strip the Africans in America of their past in order to control and inculcate "White" values and a feeling of inferiority. It is clear, therefore, why European Americans would still prefer to insist that they were successful in "breaking" the Africans' spirit and memory of their homeland so a strategic psychological and political victory could be declared. As Charters points out, however, their efforts were not as thorough as they like to vaunt. While pronounced differences separate the songs that Charters discusses from rural blues, the comparison also presents an interesting case for other forms of twentieth-century African-American music. He continues:

> The differences came in the structure of the melodies and the accompaniments that the griots played. . . . Melodically they were built from a long, lyric line that introduced the subject of the text. As the singer went on he half-sang, half-chanted the new verses, sometimes saying a great deal in a short space of a song, and in the new verses he continued to suggest the outline of the original melody he had started with. . . . I could best characterize it for myself by thinking of it as a kind of set of variations on a melody, but the variations were shaped by the words of the text, and not by the melodic embellishment. . . . Some of the songs had an A-B form. There was a kind of refrain that alternated with the narrative verse. . . . The refrains, and the phrases of the songs themselves, were generally clear and simple—they had a form that was easy to remember after a few hearings, and their simplicity helped hold together the "variations" in the melodies that came later.[8]

This description could easily fit variations within the performances of many modern "jazz" and avant-garde African-American spontaneous compositions. The particular treatment of lyric, melody, and form by bebop instrumentalists and scat vocalists is also related. European and European-American researchers have assumed on occasion that African music was amorphous and randomly based. In order to quickly explain the order inherent in "black" American music it was declared that European music provided the basic structure for African-American music. Rather, it is more possibly the case that, like vodun syncretism, African-American musicians selected those musical elements most closely resembling their own as they heard songs sang upon contacting European culture. As African Americans were often obliged to perform publicly for European Americans, certain European characteristics were also forced upon the music they presented.

There are other qualities that were retained by the African in America; some of the most clearly identifiable elements were rhythmic ones. Charters found that

> There was no harmonic change in the accompaniments played on the kora or the balafon. The backgrounds were built of short, repetitive rhythmic units. The units were usually in a duple meter—nothing that I heard was in triple meter. There wasn't a close integration between the sung rhythm and the accompaniment rhythm. They functioned as a kind of complement to each other, but at the same time they were dependent on each other since each song had its own unique accompaniment. It was clear that—as in almost all African music—there was a conscious avoidance of a rhythmic stress that came in both the voice and the accompaniment at the same moment. In all of the songs there was a subtle rhythmic texturing. The accompaniment themselves had a multileveled texture, achieved with the thumb and the fingers setting up different rhythms. This was easier to do with the kora than on the halam, but halam players did it with beats on the skin of the instrument.[9]

The most powerful African retentions found in modern "jazz" styles are subtle influences. The quest for musical freedom instilled the realization within the innovator that laws and commandments from a "superior" human authority had little bearing on the process of creativity. They were concerned primarily with the dictates of the subconscious mind and the expression of their revelations through music. The laws that applied to their styles were based entirely upon self-determination and mutual agreement to follow certain principles. The modern innovators did not consider the laws, criticism, and judgment of those who had not demonstrated tangible expertise in performing modern "jazz" valid.

Ptah-Hotep lived during the time of the Fifth Memphite Dynasty in Egypt. His writings and precepts are considered to constitute the oldest book in the world. The quotation below both reflects the attitude held by Egyptians during his day and summarizes the positions held by many modern innovators:

> If thou hast, as leader, to decide on the conduct of a great number of men seek the most perfect manner of doing so that thy own conduct may be without reproach. Justice is great, invariable, and assured; it has not been disturbed since the age of Osiris. To throw obstacles in the way of the laws is to open the way before violence. Shall that which is below gain the upper hand, if the unjust does not attain to the place of justice? even he who says: I take for myself, of my own free-will; but says not: I take by virtue of my authority. The limitations of justice are invariable.[10]

Like their traditional African counterparts, bebop musicians, and certain other modern innovators who followed, based their harmonic laws upon the harmonic series, and their rhythmic principals were steeped in polyrhythms. The members of the bebop combo placed a greater degree of emphasis on polyrhythm than the swing band performers. Because of their latitude of freedom, polyrhythms suggest a structured rebellion against fixed meter. Nevertheless, the basic approach to most African-American music generally involves rhythmic and structural independence that occurs between melody, harmonic accompaniment, counterpoint, and meter. Premeditated European music generally remains much more integrated metrically. Rhythmic and harmonic modes operate according to more prescribed formulas. Stratification along the multileveled lines is less pronounced in contrapuntal European and European-American compositions (as well as in most European and European American "jazz," rock, blue grass, and symphonic music). Charlie Parker's and Dizzy Gillespie's compositions were, therefore, often perceived as chaotic by some listeners due to their explicit and implied multileveled textures.

K. Welsh-Asante concludes that the African aesthetic comprises seven aspects, which she refers to as "senses": polyrhythm, polycentrism, dimensionality, repetition, curvilinearity, epic memory, and holism.[11] In the artistic presentation of several colors interacting in a painting, or where several isolated movements occur in different parts of a dancers body, we have polycentrism. African lines are most often curved in aural, kinetic, and visual arts. Epic memory allow both artist and audience to empathize with the same pathos or celebration because of a shared historic memory. Adu Shardow Abarry defines holism as "the unity of the collective parts of the art work despite the various unique aspects of the art."[12] If we examine Bebop and other innovative African-American music, with these senses in mind, the artists' perspectives may be better understood.

Bebop Begins to Evolve

One of the fiats that propels the "jazz" evolution forward seems to be, "If you focus too much on the past, you can get lost in it—to such an extent that the present and future may pass you by. On the other hand, if the past is ignored completely your knowledge base will be limited and you run the risk of floundering within the realm of that which has already been explored." This way of thinking has created a set of spontaneous composers in the twentieth century whose thinking is related to the intuitive composers of all ages and regions of the world. The unique difference in the evolution of "jazz" is, however, that it has undergone continual stylistic changes within a period of less than a hundred years, at a pace that exceeds all other music in the history of the Western world.

The evolution into bebop was not the sole invention of the musicians experimenting at Minton's in New York. The progression of African-American music has always been an experimental and evolutionary process, involving both communal and individual efforts, grounded in recollections and retentions.

Progenitors of the Bebop Revolution

When Charlie Parker met Dizzy Gillespie in 1941, the duo became the catalyst for the bop revolution and eventually brought this burgeoning twentieth-century improvisational style to fruition. The new standards that accompanied their approach subtly affected virtually every aspect of twentieth century music (harmony, melody, tonality, rhythm, etc.).

The bebop revolution was more than a nascent musical rebellion marking the beginning of modern "jazz." African-American music was now removed from the supportive (and somewhat insular) environment of its own African-American sociocultural community. It migrated into a performance and social milieu where young experimental artists were required to adapt to (and adopt) more ecumenical principals, form new coteries, and explore new settings. This process involved an arduous and gradual transition that often precipitated inexorable frustration and discontentment for many of the pioneers of the new music. As they came into increased contact with the majority culture, musicians encountered not only the adversities of racism but also rejection by some of their elder musical colleagues.

The presence of women instrumentalists, which culminated during the war years, would find its nadir during the height of bebop. The International Sweethearts of Rhythm was the last women's swing band to gain worldwide acclaim. The most successful women musicians would again be singers.

Through artistic prowess, bebop musicians demonstrated that all people possess similar native intellectual faculties and potential. Their artistic exhibitions presented notions that ran counter to conclusions drawn from traditional Eurocentric stereotypes, the results of biased standardized American IQ testing, and the racist nescience and propaganda expounded by George Fitzhugh and other bigoted nineteenth- and twentieth-century American authors. Fitzhugh wrote a virulent study (after the Civil War) directed at defending his polemic position that not only were "Negroes" incapable of living as free men and women but "that nineteen out of twenty individuals have a 'natural and inalienable right' to be taken care of and protected, to have guardians, trustees, husbands, or masters; in other words, they have a natural and inalienable right to be slaves."[13] This book enjoyed popularity among "white" men who shared this imbecilic viewpoint.

Lucky Thompson, Dizzy Gillespie, Charlie Parker and Billy Eckstine (Photo courtesy of HRP Library).

Bebop musicians were some of the most liberated artists America has produced. Education (formal or otherwise) provides native intelligence with useful tools, structures, and materials. Bebop musicians had found mentors during the swing era who grounded them in the tradition of innovative African-American music. Despite the accomplishments of bebop progenitors, Doris Parker (wife of Charlie Parker) reminded us that it takes more than musical genius to neutralize bigotry and arrogance. When Ms. Parker said that "jazz musicians were a shade below garbage (during the 1940s), and black musicians were a shade below that," her reminder suggests that America did not embrace bebop in the 1940s; a small esoteric group of fans and musicians kept it alive.

Bebop masters were not often commercially successful artists. Parker did not receive television or movie offers. His limited popularity in the United States provided concert appearances primarily in New York City, Philadelphia, Detroit, and a few areas of California. The media used exaggerated images of racial stereotypes to exploit the modern bebop style and to sell products. Relatively few studio recordings were made of Charlie Parker, Bud

Powell, and other bebop progenitors. Many of the recordings of these and other artists, released over the years following the bebop era, were made by fans with their own crude home-recording devices who managed to make bootleg copies of certain performances.

The question of intelligence has often been used by majorities to persecute, marginalize, and exploit minority populations of citizens in various cultures. Perhaps intelligence is the ability to navigate through the vicissitudes of life while continuing to grow in knowledge and wisdom. Individuals capable of advanced creative thinking and equipped to manage adroit adaptations to an infinite array of arduous social circumstances and experiences are highly intelligent. Perhaps they are the survivors to whom Darwin refers.

The founders of bebop developed carefully and systematically through study, practice, and shared musical experiences. Bebop pioneers performed in swing bands to gain their grounding in the "jazz" tradition, and with this firm foundation, they began to explore musical regions that were yet uncharted. The result was an extension of an African-American art form that few members of the majority American musical culture could totally comprehend or execute convincingly. Even the most decorous musicians well educated in the technical aspects of European music found their training inadequate when approaching modern innovative "jazz" forms. "Jazz" musicians who tried to apply antiquated or undeveloped musical knowledge to bebop could not make the new "changes." Dizzy Gillespie recalls: "Cats would show up [at Minton's] who couldn't blow at all but would take six or seven choruses to prove it. So on afternoons before a session, Monk and I began to work out some complex variations on chords, and we'd use them at night to scare away the no-talent guys. After a while, we got interested in what we were doing as music, and as we began to explore more and more, our music evolved."[14]

Bebop progenitors, like other artistic revolutionaries, created new forms of expression fashioned from the particular limitations and prominent elements of their immediate environment. The restrictions that a paucity of financial support afforded an "underground" art form made it difficult for musicians to procure the rights to published songs. Consequently, Parker and Gillespie created new melodies based on "standard" chord changes to overcome that problem. The harmony prescribed by Fats Waller for "Honeysuckle Rose" became Parker's "Scrapple from the Apple"; and old tunes like "Back Home in Indiana" became the harmonic foundation for Bird's new composition "Donna Lee." On the other hand, perhaps to make certain that posterity understood this process, in 1947 Parker took a song like Gershwin's "Embraceable You" and left the title and composing credit in place, although he never played a single phrase from Gershwin's melody. These melodic, harmonic, and other conventional structures were sometimes transmogrified beyond recognition. This ingenious process resulted in the creation of countless new matrixes, forming music that inspired master saxophonist Ben Webster to state (after hearing Parker), "He's playing Tatum on the saxophone!"

Many of the popular big bands were forced to disband during the 1940s as American society witnessed the induction of numerous professional musicians into the armed forces. America also experienced a rancorous wartime economy and high entertainment taxes levied against cabarets during this critical juncture. A recording ban imposed by the government on the National Federation of Musicians from August 1942 until November 1944 caused the Musicians Union to respond by striking against record companies. These conditions occurred during the six-year transition within which the intense period of bebop gestation took place. This development may or may not have taken place under more halcyon conditions had the general economic climate for music been more stable. Yet musical attention may not have been so sharply focused upon individual development if the communal setting of the swing band had remained undisturbed. Bebop became the new style, but the big bands never completely disappeared, and the stylistic vocabulary that was codified during the swing era has remained unparalleled throughout the remainder of the twentieth century.

The exploration that matured in the 1940s began in the big band configuration. Many of the elder (conventional) "jazz" players did not always appreciate what the new innovators had to say musically, as bassist Milt Hinton recalls: "Diz was a kid when he joined Cab's [Cab Calloway's] band in the late '30s. Many guys in the band laughed at his playing, but a few of us who listened recognized that he was ahead of his time. He was always willing to share his knowledge. Sometimes when we worked the Cotton Club and the weather was warm, the two of us would take our instruments up to the roof during intermissions. He'd show me some of his chord inventions and get me to try new ways of playing."[15]

Essentially the timbre alone of the modern big band continued to evolve after the swing era. The addition of electronic instruments, string sections, and other augmentations took place, but the rehearsal bands, dance bands, concert and recording bands, etc., all continued to draw from swing, bebop, cool, modal, and hard bop vocabularies. In other words, the melodic, rhythmic, and harmonic resources never expanded beyond the swing styles developed during the 1930s and 1940s. The most significant evolutions in "jazz" would begin to take place in smaller configurations. A small number of "jazz" musicians began to meet regularly at Minton's Playhouse in Harlem to jam and experiment with new musical concepts during the early days of bebop. From these sessions, where new melodic explorations were launched over expanded approaches to harmonic structure, the foundation and inspiration for modern "jazz" was born.

The word "bebop" reportedly originated from the African-American "jazz" musician's practice of scatting instrumental melodic lines with nonsense vocal syllables. Bebop phrases frequently had a characteristic long-short stylistic pattern with the staccato endings producing a sound phonetically akin to the word "bebop." The name seems to have appeared first in print as the title of a tune recorded by the Dizzy Gillespie Sextet in New York in 1945. "Jazz" musicians soon shortened the term to "bop." Bop musicians ushered in not only a music style, a manner of dress, and a hipster's dialect but also a new trumpet—Dizzy's: "I decided I liked the horn bent because I can hear a note the minute I hit it. This way I can hear my mistakes faster."[16]

Although there were a few bop big bands, the common bebop tendency was to return to a format similar in size to that of early New Orleans "jazz" (from the 1920s). The small group managed to remain somewhat popular even during the swing era. Most big bands and swing bands of the thirties relied on outside arrangers for their musical repertoire. Charlie Parker's composition "Chasin' the Bird" is an example often referred to by "jazz" musicologists and theorists to illustrate the degree of deviation from swing stylistic practices. There was an entirely novel approach to the traditional "standards." "Chasin' the Bird" is based upon the chord changes of the popular tune "I Got Rhythm," which is a typical pattern Gershwin borrowed from early American musical theater harmonic clichés. Parker and other bop musician adapted this type of framework to suit the formal needs of the new "jazz" experimentations. In the hands of bop innovators, none of the original ingredients escaped transformation.

The rift between the popular music of the Tin Pan Alley variety and innovative "jazz" began to widen significantly during the dawn of modern "jazz." The Second World War and the union strikes were forces that served to free many "jazz" instrumentalists from the grip of an American music industry. The industry, of course, made no attempt to understand or keep pace with the nature of the musical evolution that was continually taking place in "jazz." Beginning in the 1940s there were two distinct paths to be taken: a commercially oriented road, which involved conforming to the dictates of the producers, and a path that allowed the artist to listen to her or his own inner voice as a means to discover new musical directions.

Bop rhythms became more complex and varied. A greater range of rhythmic dynamics was executed with increasing degrees of subtlety. Melodies became more angular and were generally played once (perhaps twice in certain twelve-bar blues). It was now the improvisational solo that preempted the significance of melody as the primary focus of a composition. Spontaneous bebop melodies formed the most interesting portions of the musical presentations, while tunes merely began and ended with the fixed melody serving functional roles. Formal structure remained simple and unpretentious.

Some writers reporting on the bebop era are eager to claim some bebop advances for Europe and suggest that the progenitors of modern "jazz" were becoming more "Europeanized" in their manner of dress, styles of speaking, and general social and musical behavior. Collier makes such astonishing claims:

> Indeed, the extent to which the boppers Europeanized themselves, not merely in music, but in their presentation, is astonishing. The new scales and harmonies were far more similar to those of Stravinsky and the modernists than to the old scales of black folk music; and while the new rhythms did relate back in the sense that there was a good deal of metric by-play in them, there at so far a remove that they were incomprehensible not only to jazz fans of both races, but to the older musicians, as well.

> But it was not just the music: Gillespie, Parker, Coltrane, and others eschewed the gaudy show-business costumes of Calloway and Ellington, and dressed like Westchester County

stockbrokers. Their horn-rimmed glasses were the classic symbol of the overbred bookworm, and the berets they affected
were standard with the Bohemian artists and intellectuals of
the period, who in turn had adopted the style from the French
painters and intellectuals of the generation before. Furthermore, both Parker and Gillespie would at times affect a sort of
British accent, and on the stand refer to each other as "my colleague" in a formal manner.

A good deal of this of course, was parody—a put on. But some
of it was not; and the net affect was to give the boppers a Europeanized appearance, which was markedly different from the
vaudeville-derived tradition of the black entertainer most
blacks were used to.[17]

The author fails to identify the particular "European scales and harmonies" because no such scales existed in European music. When listening to
the variety of tritonal pentatonic scales, the abundance of embellishments
involving "quasi-blue note" ornamentation, and other harmonic and melodic
features of African music, the musical relationship of these features to African-American music is quantifiable. The music Gillespie, Parker, Coltrane,
and other innovators produced in the 1940s continued to be blues-based evolutions. Collier does finally realize that much of the bebop facade "was parody," but he is hardly familiar enough with bebop culture to determine how
much "was not." With only twelve notes to deal with, there are bound to be
remote pitch commonalities between pitch sets around the world. There are,
however, no sets of scales that can be named that bop shared with any European scalar patterns of the day. "Jazz" musicians realize that bebop is
grounded in the blues and merely extends the system of matrixes that were
always inherent in instrumental blues practice. Anyone would be hard
pressed to present or demonstrate an example of any Debussy, Stravinsky, or
Bartok composition that employs such a blues system. The minds of twentieth-century innovative artists have converged on mutual conclusions and
pondered related aesthetic conceptions. By the end of the century the distance between the vocabularies of both spontaneous and premeditative composers would be greatly diminished. It is perhaps the compositional process,
and not the indigenous stylistic characteristics of the musical product, that
accounts for the majority of perceivable differences as we approach the
twenty-first century.

Bebop musicians were basically outcasts in popular and academic society. They developed a number of characteristics that set them apart from the
rest of the world. Bebop musicians knew that they did not look like French
painters or Bohemian artists. Goatees, berets, wing-collar shirts, and drape-
shape suits were the norm for beboppers. When they went to work they wore
semiformal attire that demonstrated their respect for the music tradition to
which they were honored to contribute. The new language they developed
strengthened their sense of community, confidence, and unity. While it is
true that bebop musicians no longer felt the need to wear zoot suits, tuxedos,

or other costumes to work, the suits they wore were not removed from typical apparel worn to African-American church services at the time. Unfortunately, many of those involved in the media—that is, those who paid any attention at all to the bop era—expended quite a bit more effort on deriding the modern "jazz" created by African-American musicians than they spent on promoting it.

Many Americans who listened to bebop in the forties claimed that the musicians had no engaging connection with the audiences for which they performed. They would often walk offstage immediately after their individual solos and demonstrated no interest in entertaining the listeners (in the vaudeville sense) as their musical elders had. Bebop developed a new and unique musical elite based on an individual musician's knowledge and ability to negotiate the newly evolved musical vernacular; musicians who didn't fit that musical criteria, were excluded. For most bop musicians, their attitudes were no longer influenced by the prospect of remunerative rewards or employment.

"Jazz" musicians were no longer tolerant of being held suspect by laypeople unfamiliar with their work. African-American musicians were now performing within a Eurocentric society in which they were often discriminated against or resented. Many in that society lacked the musical discernment to understand the modern approaches to "jazz." The resentment and racism African-American musicians continued to encounter throughout the bebop era (and beyond) was reflected in the artists' impersonal concert presentations. Musicians now received their greatest thrills in communicating among themselves. Beneath the social surface, modern "jazz" was also beginning to be perceived as threatening to the specter of an elevated European art music. Its accelerated artistic evolution and intimidating virtuosity was elevating it to an engaging, introspective, and challenging "art" music. While some viewed this movement as a movement toward European values, others (by virtue of the same criteria) considered bebop a unique Afrocentric artistic revolution.

Summarily, bebop became an "art" music in the sense that it was not simply a music for dancing. Its primary emphasis was on highly sophisticated technical skills, and it was appreciated by a relatively small elite who took satisfaction in being challenged as listeners. It follows as a corollary then that bop did not intend to enjoy popularity equal to that of swing in America, despite its musical efficacy. This can be explained in several different ways. American listeners have historically preferred relatively uncomplicated, predictable dance music. Bop was strongly unpredictable and complicated. The reserved visual aspects of bop also detracted from its popularity; bop did not have the entertaining visual appeal of swing; it involved few singers and was not primarily intended to be "danceable." Dancers who could maintain the speed, prodigious youthfulness, and intensity of bop had no problem relating to the music, however.

Instrumental virtuosity engendered a natural adaptation within the rhythm section involving stratification: comping (accompanying) became more prevalent than stride style and on-the-beat chord patterning. Drummers played time-keeping rhythms primarily on suspended cymbals, rather than emphasizing the snare drum, high-hat, or bass drum, which created more musical space for soloists. The emphasis on the blues seventh chords, diminished scales, and other tritone based harmonies in bop tunes caused chord progressions to project a more unresolved, volatile, and ambivalent quality. The general mood of bop was more agitated stylistically than swing. One of the features that made bop improvisation more complex was the employment of thematic material, often with less conspicuous relationships existing between individual themes. As in the music of Art Tatum, excursions outside the tune's original key, and a greater scope of rhythmic permutations and development, became desirable. The element of surprise was highly valued in bop.

Bop's harmonic pacing was intensified and more complex than most other music in the tonal tradition. Since many modern "jazz" theorists fail to engage in total transcription (involving all instrumental parts on a recording) to illustrate their theories, the extent of this complexity has been oversimplified. The structural layers of bebop harmony are most effectively realized when one analyzes all the parts: the lead, piano, bass, and drum. The clever use of dissonances is heightened by chord extensions and substitutions. New scale formations are applied to a transfigured traditional harmonic framework. Bop texture and rhythm moved beyond the polyrhythmic and modified heterophonic musical mannerisms of earlier "jazz" combo styles. In bop, unlike Dixieland, performers did not develop propensities for high levels of communal polyphony and counterpoint.

Bebop musicians often relied upon twelve-bar or thirty-two bar formal structures, just as the early New Orleans "jazz" bands and big bands had done. Typically, thirty-two measure forms are divided into four eight-measure sections that can be labeled AABA. The A-melody is stated and repeated in the first two sections. A key change (or new pitch level), as well as a new fixed or improvised melody, forms the B section (or bridge). The A-melody is repeated again at the end. The soloist then improvises within the same harmonic framework of the thirty-two measure formal cycle. The melody of the initial thirty-two-measure AABA chorus is repeated again at the end of the improvisational process.

Bebop, therefore, did not just burst on the "jazz" scene suddenly; it developed gradually through blues traditions and expanded upon the rhythmic, harmonic, and melodic contributions made by swing era innovators. The players extended the evolutionary vocabulary to include new approaches to musical phrasing and emerged with a style involving more advanced methods of negotiating and pacing harmonic progressions. Players often created their own compositions rather than relying solely upon reworking existing melodies. The primary innovators—Charlie Parker (1920–55), Dizzy Gillespie (1917–92), Ella Fitzgerald (1918–94), Thelonious Monk (1917–82), Bud Powell (1924–66), and others helped establish a language that still persists as the primary language of many "jazz" musicians performing in the present era.

Stylistic differences from swing include bop players' tendencies to leave phrases suspended or unresolved. The tone color of the typical combo changed because instruments like the clarinet, banjo, and guitar were left aside after the 1930s, and the ride cymbal and pizzicato bass were commonly emphasized for time keeping. "Bombs," or syncopated off-beat accents, re-placed the previous steady quarter-note beat of the bass drum, making room for increased spontaneous musical feedback and making the musical structure more elastic. Now the rhythm section was able to provide a greater degree of inspiration and engage in more fluent conversations with the soloists within a flexible musical universe filled with a wider range of musical options.

Saxophonists or trumpet players were the most common lead soloists, and the group was usually organized around these instruments during bebop. The typical bop groups didn't cater to the audiences with lavish shows, stereotypical antics, or pretty women onstage as visual objects. Now that many musicians were removed from more comfortable African-American neighborhoods and transported to a more hostile environment "downtown," many bop musicians became more introverted and introspective. Some withdrew into lifestyles involving increased contact with drugs.

A few earlier transitional pioneers and innovators became harbingers of the new (1940s) era. Art Tatum's revolutionary and dominating presence was one such manifestation. Tatum's impact on "jazz" history helped enormously to provide the mitigating circumstances that made the gradual evolution into bebop possible. The fast melodies, improvised lines, and substitute chords of Tatum's inventive solos were absorbed by Charlie Parker and other progenitors of bebop. Bud Powell became one of the first modern pianists to systematically expand the comping technique introduced by Count Basie.

Comping ("accompanying") involves playing brief and carefully spaced intermittent chords either against or in response to the lead player's melodic line and rhythms for the purpose of complementing what has been played. The technique also involves suggesting a different harmonic direction for the soloist to follow. Powell was also one of the first modern "jazz" pianists to development significantly the stylistic direction that Earl Hines initiated with his right-hand technique (which emulates the phrasing styles of solo wind instruments).

Charlie "Bird" Parker and "Black" Music Downtown

Resistance to bop was so great that an attempt was made during the 1940s to revive New Orleans Dixieland "jazz" as the "authentic jazz" music. It was essentially European-American musicians and their supporters who formed the vanguard of the Dixieland resurrection, but some African-American music veterans were also enlisted. This attempt to revitalize early "jazz" accommodated a general and common tendency in America aimed toward the perpetuation of the tried and proven (thus artistically less demanding) musical formats. Such "products" were safer and easier to market. Since people have more time to absorb them, preexisting genres are easier to analyze and more accessible to a broader range of musical ability. Musicians whose music had gone out of fashion before the advent of swing, moreover, were anxious to derive personal benefit from this revival; and players who wanted to avoid competition with the technical demands of bebop virtuosity preferred creating less formidable musical styles—like the West Coast Cool that developed later. It was also difficult for the majority culture to claim ownership of, or effectively criticize, music they failed to learn or imitate.

This unity of "black" and "white" Dixieland musicians had not always been so amiable. Conspicuous friction between the two largely segregated musical communities existed from the early days of "jazz" Dixieland. Musicians realized that James Reese Europe's orchestra was the only African-American ensemble recorded before the Original Dixieland Jass Band's recording debut, despite an abundance of veteran African-American Dixieland ensembles. The social inequity this fact suggested created a rift between many African-American and European American Dixielanders.

Aware of the true origins of their music, African-American pioneers knew clearly those musicians responsible for making significant contributions to the invention of New Orleans "black jazz" music. The most improbable assertion—that the ODJB single-handedly created "jazz" without any traditional cultural reference whatsoever (since the stylistic basis for "jazz" didn't exist in European or European-American musical culture at the turn of the twentieth century)—raises the question: Given their privileged status, why didn't the most formidable performers, innovators, and progenitors of "jazz" evolve out of European American culture? The obvious advantages that superior economic support, mass popularity, institutional training, privilege, and greater degrees of leisure time afford majority culture musicians in America create a quandary as to why "jazz" was invented and dominated by "Black" musicians.

During the 1940s, "jazz" and the visual arts reflected the acute alterations in the American society that World War II provoked. The big bands were forced out of the large ballrooms and many musicians were recruited into the armed forces. There some found opportunities to practice and continue their musical progress within the boundaries and restrictions of military life. Others, like Lester Young, were permanently damaged psychologically by their experiences in the American armed services. A few of those not suited for military indoctrination managed to avoid contact with the military entirely. The young musical revolutionaries (who would only later be considered natural artistic evolutionaries) that began to hold jam sessions and experiment together during the period of worldwide turmoil that was World War II, eventually created some of the most influential music heard in the twentieth century.

Alto saxophonist and composer Charlie "Bird" Parker (1920–55) contributed greatly to the development of bebop. Parker did not care for the terms "jazz" or bebop to describe his new invention. He said, "Let's not call it bebop. Let's just call it music." Parker rejected the bebop-hipster jive associated with the popular market labels, while Dizzy Gillespie found it easier to capitalize upon the popularity of such faddish trappings. The innovative and comprehensive system he built with Dizzy Gillespie and other bop artists created an expressive vehicle for his improvisations and compositions. These musical inventions served as pivotal archetypes for future generations of musicians.

Parker began to absorb the blues and swing traditions on the band-stand with the big bands of Jay McShann (b. 1909), Earl Hines (1903–83), and Billy Eckstine (1914–1993). McShann's band toured the country and played at the Savoy Ballroom in New York City in 1941 (while Parker was a member). Earl Hines' all-star lineup of musicians included Dizzy Gillespie (trumpet), Sarah Vaughan (piano), Benny Green (trombone), Shadow Wilson (drums), Julie Gardner (accordion), and Billy Eckstine on vocals when the orchestra played at the Apollo Theater in New York City on April 23, 1943 (with Parker on alto). Joining Hines' band provided an opportunity for Bird to avoid the negative effects of the Petrillo recording ban. The eight-month period with Hines also provided an opportunity for Bird to work closely with Dizzy. When Billy Eckstine asked him to take charge of his reed section, Bird hired Gene Ammons on tenor and Leo Parker on baritone saxophone. Miles Davis (1926–91) also played in the band. Bird's first wife, Rebecca Parker, remembered that Duke Ellington offered Bird a position in his orchestra. Parker felt that he wasn't ready at the time for the regimen of the Ellington organization, or for a life of one-nighters.[18]

Bird has been called the most important saxophonists in "jazz" history as well as one of the most brilliant musical figures in the twentieth century. Parker's musical imagination astonished other musicians in terms of his unprecedented mastery of the saxophone, the speed at which his spontaneous musical ideas unfolded, and for the strength and beauty of his melodic inventions. Gillespie said that many musicians were experimenting with musical concepts at the dawn of bebop, but Bird provided the "pyrotechnics" needed to focus and advance those ideas.[19] Drawing upon the traditions set and advanced by "jazz" masters such as Lester Young, Mary Lou Williams, Coleman Hawkins, and Art Tatum during the 1930s, Parker and his musical bebop colleagues brought the new musical ideas introduced during swing to some of their logical conclusions.

Parker was born in Kansas City, one of the most significant musical communities in America during the 1930s and 1940s. He grew up during a time when Jim Crow racism and sociocultural ignorance were rampant in the United States. The distinguishing qualities of African-American music were often stultified by the majority culture, a number of whom preferred to champion the imitations of European-American "jazz" players rather than celebrate the original inventions of "Black" musicians. There were two music conservatories in Kansas City when Parker received his first used alto saxophone, but, for an African-American music student, attending either one to study any form of music was definitely out of the question.

Bird's career was intense. At age sixteen he was humiliated and laughed off the bandstand when drummer Jo Jones threw his cymbal at Parker's feet because the young saxophonist was playing "outside the changes" at a Kansas City jam session. A year later he was playing with Jay McShann after a focused and relentless period with his alto saxophone in the "woodshed." Parker was the acknowledged leader of a new movement by his contemporaries by the time he was twenty-five years old. At twenty-nine his fame was of such an elevated stature that the club Birdland in New York City was named in his honor. He remained a nonconformist, despite his fame, and helped establish a language that our present generation (including the "Young Lions," neoclassical bop players, etc.) is still attempting to digest and explore.

Few of Bird's recordings were authorized. Many unauthorized tapes of radio programs or live performances were recorded by amateur fans who were well aware of Bird's artistic value. Some of these fans, like Dean Benedetti, followed Parker religiously with his tape recorder always in tow. Although Benedetti lacked the musical awareness to record the entire band (he usually shut off his tape recorder after the horn solos), he still managed to later cash in his tapes. Parker received little money (royalties, etc.) for the fruits of his labor, even on authorized recording sessions. He received scant compensation for the publication of his original compositions. The general response to his music was not always supportive or enthusiastic. Author and "jazz" musician Benny Green (1923–77) talks about some of the various responses to Parker's music.

> During a career short even by jazz standards, he wrecked the canons of criticism and severed the music forever from the dilettante followers to whom an affection of jazz enthusiasm was a social asset or a personal vanity. After Parker you had to be something of a musician to follow the best jazz of the day. If you were sentimental about the good old days, if you clutched at the fading recollections of your own adolescence, if you thought your opinions were valid just because you possessed the recordings, Parker exposed you for a charlatan.

> . . . The extent to which he was passed over by professed experts is truly extraordinary. What of the earless ones who said he was playing wrong notes? What of those brilliant analysts that announced that the whole thing was a practical joke? What of those who denied his music the descriptive adjective "jazz"? There was one priceless philistine who took his tape recorder to Minton's sessions and switched off whenever Parker started to play, because his jazz was not as decorous as that of Herbie Fields, a musician whom the owner of the machine worshipped to such an insane degree that he compiled tape after tape.[20]

In 1939 Parker, bored of orthodox changes, discovered a new way to approach music by reworking "Cherokee" rhythmically, harmonically and melodically. His comments about his new discoveries, and other interesting perspectives on bebop, were documented in a *Down Beat* interview in 1949.[21] Bird says, "I kept thinking there's bound to be something else. I could hear it sometimes, but I couldn't play it." He felt that "music is your own experience, your thoughts, your wisdom. If you don't live it, it won't come out your horn." Green concludes that, "the advent of Charlie Parker caused more violent eruptions, more bitterness, more sheer apoplectic rage than that of any jazz musician before him."[22] As Gary Giddins realizes in his book, *Celebrating*

Bird: The Triumph of Charlie Parker, Bird knew early on in life what music meant to him and was well aware of his position within the evolution of a new art form. "The fledgling, who many years later would answer a query about his religious affiliation by declaring himself 'a devout musician,' was too conscious of his genius, too possessed of pride, too much the product of racial repression and maternal sanction not to suspect that a larger world awaited him—a world he could recast in his own image."[23]

Parker created new scales, interjected unusual passing tones, toyed with motivic interpolations, and introduced chord extensions containing pitches that were seemingly unrelated to the basic chord changes of the tune serving as the basis of his melodic improvisations. His musical experimentation prefigured future evolutionary developments that stretch the rules of functional harmony systematically to the breaking point. Parker's rhythmic approach is inseparable from his melodies and harmonies. An examination of his composition "Relaxin' at Camarillo," and other rhythmically challenging compositions, demonstrates the effect that metric displacement has on his melodic and harmonic unfolding.

Coleman Hawkins created solos in which arpeggiated chords were mixed with more conjunct phrases based on scale patterns. Charlie Parker expanded this approach to include a grand array of his own personal motives and melodic phrases that served as a basic set of improvisational axioms. Within a seemingly straightforward harmonic context, these motivic and melodic seeds were interwoven into complex series of musical extensions that always maintained an air of familiarity. Parker's style was successful in avoiding imitation of the prevailing formulas that earlier musicians such as Louis Armstrong and his contemporaries had established and applied ingeniously.

Part of the magnetism of a beautiful composition from any genre of music is often the organic growth suggested by its musical elements. Within such compositions a small seed can generate into a full-blown work. Such a process, at first glance, may appear evasive, seemingly defying or transcending analysis. This is clear within of the subjects of Bach fugues, the principal melodies of Mozart, and the primary motives employed as the motivating essences of Beethoven's works. It is also true of the music of Charlie Parker, John Coltrane, Duke Ellington, or Cecil Taylor. By the time the basic ingredients that such works are based upon are catalogued, the experimental musical world has often evolved to new styles and moved on to explore other sets of artistic concepts. Theorists generally want to make their latest findings ("discoveries") clear, relevant and meaningful at the moment their conclusions happen to surface. Research on innovative music is valuable to those wanting to know the inner workings of the music of the past generations, but it generally holds little relevance for innovative creators of the music examined.

Many listeners, critics and musicians during the 1940s and 50s considered bebop music chaotic. It comes as little surprise, therefore, that some investigators were later astonished to discover tonal coherence, superbly balanced melodies, or formulaic construction in the music of Parker, Coltrane, Taylor, or other innovative artists. Classic art forms that endure for long periods of time are generally ingeniously constructed, whether or not listeners discover their "secret" formula while the music is still in common practice. In music and other art forms, intuitive inspiration, emotional sincerity, and logical construction may be difficult (or impossible) to isolate empirically. Discovering the exact nature of certain elements of music, such as "soul" or "feeling," is as evasive as defining the spirit energy that imbues organisms with life force. The patient, serious listener, investigator, or artist knows when "living" elements reside within artistic manifestations. Cataloging Parker's (or Beethoven's) motives, pet phrases, or stylistic aspects of a particular melodic vernacular does not define, change, or diminish the beauty, spiritual content, and efficacy of the music.

Terms to describe music can be politically charged in the Western world. Adjectives used to describe the classic music of European composers (riveting, organic, ingenious, powerful, moving, etc.) become diluted when applied to the music of African Americans in America (moving = entertaining; organic = formulaic; ingenious = clever; powerful = intense; aleatory = chaotic, etc.). Many serious artists take cues from the natural environment and apply them to their artistic manifestations. The term "formulaic" implies a crutch is used when applied to African-American music. "Organic," on the other hand, suggests a conscious and controlled desire to achieve coherent and natural musical ends. Author Thomas Owens reached the following conclusion regarding Bird's music almost half a century after the music was created:[24]

> Parker, like all important improvisers, developed a personal repertory of melodic formulas that he used in the course of improvising. He found many ways to reshape, combine, and phrase these formulas, so that no two choruses were just alike. But his "spontaneous" performances were actually precomposed in part. This preparation was absolutely necessary, for no one can create fluent, coherent melodies in real time without having a well-rehearsed bag of melodic tricks ready. His well-practiced melodic patterns are essential identifiers of his style.[25]

This description has some merit, yet is concomitantly misleading and contains language often associated with African-American music analyzed by European-American theorists. Parker *was* indeed composing spontaneously. He used a personal vocabulary that he developed through intense practicing. Just as we build verbal vocabularies, full of jargon, pet words, and quotations (of our own or borrowed) to enable us to express our individual ideas clearly, spontaneous composition does likewise. Composers of premeditated European music have always emphasized cadential formulas, economy of means, and repetition. Because elements of certain vocabularies are somewhat fixed does not imply that they are meager or inhibit the ability to speak spontaneously when we engage in sincere conversation.

Few European musicologists would tolerate the verbal reduction of Bach's music to phrases such as "music limited to formulaic exercises on major and minor triads and their variations (with the rare exception of occasional dominant seventh chords), where motor rhythms are supported and disguised by terraced dynamics, orchestration, and a fixed set of other predictable devices." Is it reasonable to describe the numerous stylistic signatures found in Mozart's compositions as formulaic material derived from a "well-rehearsed familiar bag of melodic tricks?" Even if this was the case indeed, would the fact that a fixed vocabulary is used render any powerful music less potent or effective?

Instead theorists and historians infer that the "perfect art" that Bach achieved through an infinite variety of ideas evolved through a limited set of tonal musical means to produce masterpieces. Beethoven's famous Fifth Symphony would not be attenuated because the chief motive in that work was used an "unbearable" number of times.[26] Yet when an economy of means is discovered in African-American music, a set of values and quality of analysis are applied. Owens continues:

> Because Parker's recorded legacy is extensive it is possible not only to compile a list of Parker's favorite figures but to see how he used these figures in different contexts. A study of his hundreds of choruses of the blues in B♭, F, and C and dozens of choruses of *I Got Rhythm*, *What Is This Thing Called Love?*, *How High the Moon*, and others shows that his improvising was highly formulaic. The specifics of the themes were rarely significant in shaping his solo; instead, he favored a certain repertory of formulas for the blues in B♭, a slightly different repertory for the blues in F, a much different one for *A Night in Tunisia* in D minor, and so on. Some phrases in his vocabulary came from swing, either unchanged or modified; others he created. But whether using borrowed or original melodic formulas, his way of combining and organizing them was his own.

Many elements of Mozart's Flute Concerto in G Major are certainly found in his Flute Concerto in D Major and many of his other compositions. We find the major scale in unembellished ascending runs frequently in both works, for instance. If Owens examines a Parker performance of a tune like George Gershwin's "Embraceable You," we find that the specific features of the principle themes were extremely significant in shaping his solo, yet no two phrases are exactly alike and the contexts in which they occur are different each time.

One of Parker's most provocative revolts against musical conventions was his composition "Koko." "Koko" is a piece based on a bebop melody that contains the characteristics of a typical bop improvised solo. Related approaches to compositional coherence and unity is found in Bird's approach to the standard "Summertime," Gillespie's "Night in Tunisia," his own "Relaxin at Camarillo," and many of his other performances. On some occasions the development of the themes involves rhapsodic flashbacks involving the original pitch-sets. Other times variations on thematic rhythms are maintained while pitches of particular motives and harmonic directions are interpolated or infrapolated.

Regardless of the ways critics, historians, and theorists analyze or criticize Bird's music, his music had an impact on the twentieth-century musical world in a way that extremely few other artists of the period were able to manage. The range of Parker's basic vocabulary mixes a wide range of different blues "formulas" with popular songs from the swing era, with the Latin/quasi-modal approach of "Night in Tunisia," and with his own. Gillespie was also very interested in Latin music: "I've always been a Latin freak. Very early in my career, I realized that our music and that of our brothers in Latin America had a common source. The Latin musician was fortunate in one sense. They didn't take the drum away from him, so he was more polyrhythmic."

Owens is attempting to analyze elements of Bird's solos outside the context of the ensembles within which Parker constructed his musical ideas. Each phrase Parker played was affected by the musical ambiance and the specific context of notes supplied by the rhythm section, string ensemble, and other wind players performing with him. Once the musical context is taken into account the description of any particular "formulaic" gesture must be severely modified. Performers and spontaneous composers of Parker's caliber are continually responding to music created by their fellow improvisers. A theorist must, therefore, think in terms of the overall impromptu dialogue and democratic compositional environment. Performers are not approaching the construction of a solo on the bandstand in the same fashion as they might use in constructing solos while rehearsing or performing alone. Improvising blindly with an ensemble, without becoming sensitively aware of the music other musicians involved were performing, would be self-centered, ineffective, and unmusical. Still, Parker's music is often isolated and dissected in a clinical fashion that suggests the music made by the other members of the ensemble is irrelevant and has little bearing on Parker's alto saxophone solos.

A related situation arises when examining the use of polyrhythms in modern African-American music. An analysis of ragtime rhythms reveals that syncopated rhythmic patterns were substituted for African polyrhythms once ensemble playing became less possible. The shifting of accents in ragtime syncopation often implies metrical shifts or "changes." Meter places stress on certain beats to establish a sense of periodicity or time organization. When an opposing meter is superimposed on the existing meter, the result is a shift of metrical orientation or polyrhythm. Syncopation, on the other hand, can cause a sense of rhythmic modulation akin to some of the aural illusions created by composite polyrhythms. Shifting the stress to the "weak" beats does not change the nature of the aural illusion. It is still possible to hear areas of accented syncopation as points that articulate new meters. If syncopation becomes irregular or unpredictable, then the metrical perception may be "tricked" into hearing an array of unconventional or opposing meters. If these "multiple meters" are above a prevailing 4/4 metrical organization (and appear to oppose the duple metrical time), then a ragtime rhythmic structure is capable of retaining both the polyrhythmic and polymetrical arrangement. This situation can be misinterpreted if analysts attempt to impose Western

notions of rhythmic organization on African-based music. The following comment by author Hayden Carruth serves as an interesting example:

> The slaves brought their music with them, a complex, distinc-
> tive, and very expressive music; but like all radically displaced
> people in history, they lost touch with their cultural origins,
> partly through "normal" dissociation, partly because their
> whole heritage, religious and cultural, was intentionally sup-
> pressed by the slave owners. (Drumming, for instance, was for-
> bidden on the grounds, not entirely unlikely, that it was used
> by blacks to communicate from one plantation to another and
> therefore was a means to foment rebellion.) Thus although we
> can hear polyrhythmic elements in spirituals, hollers, and
> other black music deriving from slavery, as heard in the field
> recordings made by Alan Lomax in the 1930s, and although a
> polyrhythmic tendency is discernible in the recorded instru-
> mental work of early blues musicians, especially guitarists, this
> important aspect of black musical consciousness is greatly sim-
> plified in comparison to the extraordinary recorded perform-
> ances of West African drumming. As the years passed, Afro-
> American music, including the blues, became more and more
> fixed on a plain 4/4 measure, no matter how the beats were ac-
> cented. The polyrhythmic tradition, the feeling, was gone, or at
> least much weakened. In fact very talented drummers in recent
> decades, like Max Roach and Shelly Manne, have had to re-
> learn the concepts of polyrhythmic figuration partly by listen-
> ing to "ethnological" recordings from Africa.
>
> By polyrhythm I mean the imposition of different meters upon
> one another in a controlled, significant, and apprehensible pat-
> tern. A kind of layering that reaches almost inconceivable com-
> plexity—at least to some senses—among the multi-percussive
> ensembles of Africa.

Although this is a good description of the willful dissociation of African-Americans and their African heritage during hundreds of years, this did
not actually occur to the same degree in the development of African-American
music. We can trace African retentions throughout antebellum America and
into the twentieth century. Just as the recurring theme "Jazz is dead!" has
continually asserted itself (seemingly in attempt to become a self-fulfilling
prophesy in America), those who wanted to dominate virtually all aspects of
African-American existence during and following slavery wanted to feel that
their mission was successful and thorough. Parker's music, and that of numerous other African-American innovators, intensified and advanced some
traditional African musical elements. Whereas Max Roach (b. 1924) may
have listened to traditional African music to consciously incorporate those
elements into his own style, few African drummers could listen to Roach and
Elvin Jones (b. 1927) and reproduce their music. If "jazz" drumming was a

distillation or simplification of African music, then African master drummers would have little problem reproducing the music played by "jazz" musicians.

In America an individual drummer learned to create modified poly-rhythms that previously required a percussion ensemble in traditional Africa. Stylistic components had to be modified to accommodate African-American musical evolution. However, if an ensemble including Max Roach, Elvin Jones, Rashied Ali (b. 1935), and a few other American master drummers was formed, the resultant music might involve hyper-imposition of meters.

A simple way of understanding ways syncopation functions as metrical modulations and polymetrical figurations can be understood by considering the following example:

```
1     2    3|   1         2    3|   1    2 |   A
1& 2  & 3  & 4  &|    1    & 2  & 3  & 4  &|   B
```

If B is a basic 4/4 meter and A forms a mixed 3/4 to 2/4 combination superimposed on the weak beat of B, then we have a simple polymetrical setting. Most "jazz" is much more rhythmically (and therefore metrically) complex than this. It may involve mixtures of duple and triple divisions of the beats, hemiolas, and other musical devices that add to the polyrhythmic structures described above.

Syncopation and a "swing" feel replaced the African rhythmic devices in America. As far as the absence of African polyrhythmic feeling is concerned, if this was true then the music involving both "jazz" and African rhythmic conceptions and marriages would not have been so highly successful throughout the African Diaspora. Recordings of groups led by Willie Bobo, Mongo Santamaria, Olatunje Babatunde, and many other great musicians (who fused related styles into new musical phenomena) reveal the success of cross-cultural collaborations in modern "jazz." Both Parker and Gillespie worked with African- and Latin-based rhythms during bebop. In 1951, after his experiments with strings, Bird looked to the rhythms from South of the border and used Latin percussionists in his music (such as in the composition "Tiko Tiko").

With the arrival of Charlie Parker in the mid-forties the sounds of not only the saxophone but of all instruments were changed. The alto took its place next to the tenor as a major "jazz" vehicle, and the tenor itself received a new approach based largely upon the influence of the higher pitched saxophone. New harmonic possibilities were added: a new rhythmic subdivision placed primary emphasis on the sixteenth note (as opposed to eighth notes) as the generating melodic force; and a new manner of ensemble stratification and timbre was required to keep up with the pace that bop set. These and other innovations can be heard on Parker's recordings of "Just Friends" (with strings) and "Bird of Paradise." A short list of his stylistic influence on alto saxophonists of note include Cannonball Adderley, Sonny Stitt, Lou Donaldson, Art Pepper, Phil Woods, Charles McPherson, Jackie McLean, Ernie Henry, Sonny Criss, and Bud Shank.

According to Parker, Dizzie Gillespie wasn't aware of bop structures until 1942, after Parker had finally worked out his own personal harmonic system. "Bop is no love-child of jazz," Parker says, "bop is something entirely separate and apart" (from older "jazz"). Bird believed the music had to be played in a small band context. "It's just music. . . . It's trying to play clean and looking for the pretty notes." These remarks may have been made slightly understated. Gary Giddins reminds us that "he jousted with the critics—celebrating the traditions of 'jazz' in one interview (*Down Beat* 1948) and dismissing those traditions in another (*Down Beat* 1949)."[27] Parker's justification for separating bebop from "jazz" was that "the beat in a bop band is with the music, against it, behind it. It pushes it. It helps it. Help is the big thing. It has no continuity of beat, no steady chug-chug. Jazz has, and that is why bop is more flexible."

After Parker heard Stravinsky's "The Firebird" he became interested in the possibility of composing for the symphony orchestra. His thinking in this direction was expressed in the same *Down Beat* 1949 interview: "This has more chance than the standard jazz instrumentation. You can pull away some of the harshness with the strings and get a variety of coloration." Parker wanted to move toward a freer style of performance. He continued, "They teach you there's a boundary line to music, but, man, there's no boundary line to art." In an interview with Paul Desmond (1924–77) and Dave Brubeck (b. 1920) during the early 1950s, Parker said that he had spoken with Edgard Varèse, and the composer had expressed interest in writing for Bird. Gillespie also realized the broad dimensions that modern "jazz" encompassed: "Jazz is the one thing that we have that the world wants. It's a kind of meeting place where one man can feel what another does even if they speak different languages. There's a kind of directness—with no middle man—between the artist and his public."[28]

Bird was able to explore some of the new timbres he had conceived when Norman Granz helped him launch his ensemble of strings. Although the performers on hand were incapable of fully realizing Parker's modern ideas stylistically, Parker recorded some memorable songs with the ensemble. Bird and the ensemble of strings were heard in performances at the Apollo as well as at Carnegie Hall in 1950. His usual working quintet eventually disbanded during this period. He later performed four or five sets one night in 1952, alternating between his regular quintet and his string ensemble, at a benefit dance for Benjamin Davis (an attorney and city council member that had apparently been railroaded by the court) at Harlem's Rockland Palace.

To counterbalance Parker's saxophone sound, Bird asked oboist Mitch Miller (although not an improviser at all) to be the other wind player on the recordings with the strings. Miller also contracted the musicians for Parker's string section, hiring the best players in the NBC Orchestra and other symphony orchestras. Although Bird's recording with strings eventually became his best-selling venture, Parker's fans in the "jazz" community were divided in their impressions of this collaboration. Many were unprepared to hear Parker in such a different musical environment with musicians who did not know how to perform bebop style. Nevertheless, Bird felt this was a highly respectable musical experience, and he did some of his finest playing in the performances with strings.

Parker planned to attend the Academy of Music in Paris to study composition for a few years. After resting for a while, he then wanted to play experimentally with a small group of musicians and to focus his composing toward creating music with "warmth." He was attracted to the admiration, understanding, and respect he found in Paris but realized that the greatest challenges and strongest money market for bebop were in the United States. "You've got to be here for the commercial things and in France for relaxing facilities."

Bird was treated with a bit more respect in America when he returned from Europe. The club Birdland (an elegant club with actual bird cages) was named in his honor. Parker performed there for four years in programs involving the controversial announcer Symphony Sid. Parker's popular 1953 recording of "Cool Blues," performed on a plastic alto saxophone, was made at Birdland.

At the time of the 1949 interview, Parker did not approve of Dizzy Gillespie's move to establish a bebop big band. He felt that "Gillespie's playing [had] changed from being stuck in front of a big band. Anybody's does. He's a fine musician. The leopard coats and the wild hats are just another part of the managers' routines to make him box office. The same thing happened a couple years ago when they stuck his name on some tunes of mine to give him better commercial reputation." Aside from its commercialism, which disconcerted Parker, "that big band [was] a bad thing for Diz. A big band slows anybody down because you don't get a chance to play enough. Diz has an awful lot of ideas when he wants to, but if he stays with the big band he'll forget everything he ever played. He isn't repeating notes yet, but he is repeating patterns."

The new approach to African-American music that evolved as bebop came on the scene was accompanied by a new aesthetic attitude. In comparing some of the musical qualities of bop to cubism, Martha Bayles attempts to isolate some of the modern "jazz" elements:

> Bebop [is] the jazz equivalent of analytic cubism. Bebop's great exemplar, the saxophonist Charlie Parker, was criticized for abandoning the fluid, expressive tone of such predecessors as Benny Carter and Johnny Hodges. Parker's tone is not as harsh and dry as some critics claim, but it is lean and spare— for a reason. Like Picasso and Braque, Parker couldn't have done what he did without first limiting his palette. Here is the poet and jazz critic Philip Larkin's account: "Parker found jazz chugging along in 4/4 time in the tonic and the dominant, and splintered it into a thousand rhythmic and harmonic pieces. Showers of sixteenths, accented on half- and quarter-beats, exhibited a new harmonic fecundity and an originality of phrasing that had scarcely been hinted at before." This is not the gushing of a fan. On the contrary, Larkin dislikes bebop for the same reason many art lovers dislike analytic cubism.

... Then there is the question of the "aura." It is a truism to say
that the Afro-American musician—whether a gospel shouter, a
blues singer, or a jazz soloist—plays a priestly role. This role is
sometimes equated with that of the romantic genius, but they
are different. The genius is exalted as an individual whose inspired utterances may or may not resonate with the group. The
Afro-American musician, by contrast, is elevated chiefly as a
conduit for the expression of communal emotion and experience. In both religious and secular settings, he is obliged to interact with his audience through practices such as call and response, collective movement, and the skilled evocation of
extreme emotional and mental states.

Because these practices can be traced back to tribal Africa,
black cultural separatists often claim that black Americans
make no distinction between the sacred and the secular. Such
claims hardly describe the generations of black folk who have
hotly disputed the type of music that does and does not belong
in church. Yet even so, the cultural separatists have a point.
The music that blacks have traditionally forbidden in church,
notably the blues, is called "Devil's music," a phrase that does
not make it secular so much as spiritually malevolent.[29]

Parker wanted to move in the direction of musical expansion, experimentation and abstraction more rapidly than many of his predecessors. The
roots of his music were firmly planted in the blues and song forms that all
well grounded swing players and composers were required to master. During
the 1940s, his musical environment was much less often the Apollo, Rockland
Palace, the Savoy, or a performance spot within any African-American
neighborhood (like Harlem). Now most bebop pioneers found themselves
downtown in European American neighborhoods where the expression of a
communal musical emotion and a collective sociocultural experience did not
seem as likely to occur.

Certainly the typical young African-American child was not allowed to
stand outside a club on 52nd Street to listen to Parker's music as the young
Parker had done earlier to hear his "jazz" idols and pioneers standing outside
"joints" where they performed. Bebop marked the beginning of a movement
that became increasingly more distanced from younger African-American listeners, essentially due to factors of proximity. It was not so much that the
musical evolution became too complex for African-American taste, but rather
that physical distance separated modern "jazz" from the African-American
neighborhoods (some members of which were beginning to head for the various American suburbs). Separation from the African-American innovators
made it difficult to keep up with evolutionary and revolutionary musical
changes. On the other hand, it was possible for some European-American
students to maintain much closer access to the development of "jazz" after
1950 because of campus performances, college radio broadcasts, and because
the music clubs were now generally situated in European-American social

domains. The social paradox created in the mid-twentieth century had an undeniable effect on Charlie Parker and his musical colleagues. Caught on the cusp between social segregation and an integrated American socioculture, Bird was continually confronted with sociocultural contradictions. Giddins suggests the level of impact this dilemma had on Parker's career.

> [Parker's] appetite for life exhilarated his friends, and made him an easy mark for the parasites and pushers who dogged his steps as relentlessly as his fans. With mobsters like Frank Costello running things, Fifty-second Street was something of a safe house from the Police, though not from such peculiarly American treacheries as white servicemen who taunted black musicians on the stand or in the bars, especially when they were in the company of white women.[30]

Racist and philistine societies are all alike; every artist is unique. The shift in blame from Parker to the mass tethers him to the very prosaicness his art so unequivocally counters. Always one step ahead of the mob, he cut himself down before they could. Still it must be emphasized that as a black man in mid-twentieth century America, Parker suffered more than personal injustices. He also endured a constant debilitating slander against his art. Minority citizens healthily buffered by their own communities do not look to the oppressive majority for a sense of identity. The artist, however, seeks recognition in the community of artists, which defies, or ought to defy, the conventionalism, mediocrity, and pettiness that are inseparable from race and nationalism. In that community, a far worse fate than neglect is acknowledgment followed by expulsion for lack of acceptable pedigree. By all accounts, Parker could not be cowed by the insanity of white supremism. But the frustration he experienced on behalf of his music was lifelong and stifling.

Charlie Parker realized his value as a musician. When he was treated with respect he responded in a way that broke with the self-destructive tendencies he indulged in at times when the press and the general public ignored his musical contributions, or when he was treated with disesteem. After his two triumphant European tours he was so impressed by the love and admiration his fans showed him that he considered moving abroad. When he worked with his string ensemble he always practiced hard, showed up on time, dressed well, and kept his drug usage to a minimum. He was very disappointed when "they took [his] strings away." His heart must have been broken when he was banned from a club originally named in his honor, "Birdland." Racism breeds an embarrassment, pain, and sadness that many people in America refuse to acknowledge. It is the dark side of American society. Despite such denial, artists like Parker are not only forced to stare racist society squarely in the face daily, they have to also endure physical, economic, and emotional burdens of a broader oppression.

Although the path was precipitous, most of today's "jazz" vocabulary is based upon 1940s and 1950s bebop. Parker was always seeking new musical environments. His collaboration with organist Milt Buckner (from which the highly acclaimed 1953 recording of "Groovin' High" was made) occurred before the organ trio became a popular format. The same year Bird worked with the vanguard vocal trio Lambert, Hendricks, and Ross in a recording of "Old Folks" featuring Charlie Parker with orchestra and chorus. The concert called "The Greatest Concert Ever" placed Bird back with his early associates Dizzy, Bud Powell, Charles Mingus, and Max Roach at Massey Hall (in Toronto) later the same year.

Charlie Parker's death was not announced until two days after he passed away at the home of Baroness Pannonica "Nica" de Koenigswarter while watching the Tommy Dorsey Show on May 12, 1955. The exact cause of death was undetermined. The phrase "Bird Lives" that began to appear throughout America in the wake of his death has become a portentous edict.

Misfortune, Drugs, and Alcohol Enter the Bop Scene

Parker's drug habit is often given as much attention as his musical development and artistic contribution. He was a sensitive person who was introduced to drugs at a highly impressionable age. Parker was drawn deeper into that ominous direction as a number of personal tragedies continued to haunt his path in life.

Bird admired the playing of Johnny Hodges (1907–70) and Jimmy Dorsey (1904–57). He eventually found a musical mentor in Kansas City in alto saxophonist Buster Smith (1904–91). Smith was admired by his peers for his ability to double-up on the changes.[31] His bluesy influence registered heavily on the impressionable younger saxophonist. Parker was eventually able to join Smith's band (the Deans of Swing) after a year of music study. The elder musician became very close to Parker. One of the closest friends Parker probably ever had, trombonist Robert Simpson, was also a member of Smith's band. "To say that Charlie admired [Simpson] is perhaps too mild," Parker's neighbor Lawrence Keyes remembers, "Charlie worshipped him and was in his company a great deal."

When Simpson died from a heart ailment at the age of twenty-one, Parker (who was not yet sixteen years old) was inconsolable and soon developed an appetite for Benzedrine inhalers and alcohol.[32] When Bird was in an automobile accident in which one passenger was killed and Parker ended up with several of his ribs broken, he began to use even harder drugs. The blow that would eventually prove fatal to Parker came in 1954 when his daughter, Pree, died of a congenital heart condition before her third birthday. Parker's mode of escapism into the realm of intoxication is as representative of the times, of American society, and of the circumstances he inherited as it is a reflection of his personal vulnerability. Many of Bird's "jazz" contemporaries were also hypersensitive and thus unable to live for much more than a quarter of a century in America under the existing conditions during the 1940s. Drugs were not generally the cause of death for most young "jazz" masters. They left an indelible mark on the evolution of African-American music nonetheless.

Guitarist Charlie Christian (1916–42) died of tuberculosis at the age of twenty-six. Listening to Christian's performances on tunes such as "Rose

Room" (recorded in 1939 with the Benny Goodman Sextet), we hear an innovative and mature approach to the guitar. We also hear a vast difference in recording quality of records made by Benny Goodman as compared to those made by Fletcher Henderson, Art Tatum, Charlie Parker, and other African-American artists recording during this era. Fats Navarro's (1923–50) mastery of bebop trumpet is evident in the beautifully constructed solos he performed on tunes such as "Our Delight" (recorded in 1948 when he was twenty-four). Bassist Jimmy Blanton (1918–42), the first bass soloist to create lines that contained more than embellishments of harmonic arpeggiations, also died prematurely, of tuberculosis.

The association between alcohol and drugs dates back to Storyville roots, where African-American society generally considered "jazz" the "devil's music" because it was performed in "dens of crime, sex, and drugs." Narcotics did shorten the lives of Charlie Parker, Fats Navarro, Stan Getz, Chet Baker, Billie Holiday, and many other musicians, but it was never as pervasive as sometimes thought. It is noteworthy that African-American musicians were less involved with drugs when they performed for African-American communities (even during the Storyville days) than they were once the music began to migrate into European-American venues (downtown in New York City, for instance). Duke Ellington, Jimmy Lunceford, Mary Lou Williams, Fletcher Henderson, Count Basie, Bennie Moten, Lil Hardin, Louis Armstrong, Chick Webb, and their associate musicians (who were young musicians during the 1930s) seem to have kept problems associated with substance abuse to a minimum within their musical organizations.

During the swing era, greater degrees of segregation existed between "Blacks" and "Whites" in America, and there was less drug abuse reported. When the transition to integration placed musicians in new social settings, drug dependency insulated them to some degree from the wrath of the European-American general public and its brusque police force. Synchronic changes invaded the world of the bebop musician and, concomitantly, American society at large. When European-American "pushers" (drug suppliers) began to approach African-American musicians after World War II, narcotics and the "jazz" scene began to mix in unprecedented proportions. Cabaret cards became performance licenses that essentially governed whether a musician remained gainfully employed in their profession. The War Department ban on records and the National Federation of Musicians strike managed to severely reduce a major economic medium for musicians and limited the commercial transmission of artistic ideas. The environment for music was thus altered dramatically. Ortiz M. Walton discusses some social changes:

> Certainly, the invention of heroin cannot be attributed to Jazz or, more specifically, to bop musicians. The same holds true for its manufacture and distribution. Nor, one can be sure, were a few black bebop artists the only members of society who sometimes partook of the drug between the early Forties and mid-Fifties. Yet to judge by the number of arrests, convictions and widespread publicity given to bop musicians for alleged possession of "horse," as it was called, one would conclude that the

above statements were true. For practically all of the outstanding players of bop were arrested during this period, some,
like Sonny Rollins and Gene Ammons, receiving long jail terms.
When narcotics could not be found, they were either planted by
policemen or other charges were preferred. For example, Miles
Davis was incarcerated for nonsupport, having to serve over a
year's time at the notorious Sing Sing prison in New York. Billie Holiday, though not a part of the bop movement was hound-
ed from one city to the next, detectives even breaking down her
hotel-room door during a Philadelphia engagement in the early
Fifties. Detectives somehow always managed to find what they
were looking for in such operations, and the media, particularly
newspapers and magazines, embellished the stories with mor-
bid details. However, one circumstance that the media never
discussed was the wholesale dissemination of opiates into black
communities during and following World War Two, the Korean
War and the present war in Vietnam.[33]

Billie Holiday discusses the effects of narcotics and the police on her
career in a 1947 interview for *Down Beat* magazine. On June 4, 1947, Billie
Holiday's career was interrupted when she was arrested on charges of possessing heroin in her Attucks hotel room.

I'm not offering an alibi, I'm not singing the blues. Things
weren't easy. There were a lot of things I didn't have when I
was a kid. My mother died 18 months ago, the only relative I
had in the world. I guess I flipped out, run through over
$100,000 since then.

. . . But I was trying to go straight. It just seems as though I
have a jinx over me. I was with Count Basie when things were
really rough, then I had a fight with John Hammond and got
fired. I stuck with Artie Shaw through the southern road tour,
we got back to New York, and they had to let me go. It's been
one thing after another.

Now it looks finished. I'm through—at least for a while. After
all this is over, maybe I'll go to Europe, perhaps Paris, and try
to start all over. Sure, I know about Gene Krupa—but don't
forget he's white and I'm a Negro. I've got two strikes against
me and don't you forget it.

I'm proud of those two strikes. . . . I'm proud I'm a Negro. And
you know the funniest thing: the people that are going to be the
hardest on me will be my own race. Look what they did to Billy
Eckstine for three weeks in two of the big Negro papers—and
you know that was a frame-up.

You know, I just spent $3,000 of my own money taking the cure for three weeks. Maybe I was a fool to do it. It put me on record. They may have suspected before, but they were never sure of it. Now the federal people tell me they may send me away for another cure—and they never tell you how long it will be.

Just when things were going to be so big and I was trying so hard to straighten myself out. Funny, isn't it. This year I made a picture, my records were really selling, it was going to be my time.

I've made a lot of enemies, too. Singing that "Strange Fruit" hasn't helped any, you know. I was doing it at the Earle [in Philadelphia] 'til they made me stop. Tonight they're already talking about me. When I did "The Man I Love" [at Club 18 in New York], I heard some woman say, "Hear he's in the jug downtown."

The insistence to which Holiday referred regarding singing the song "Strange Fruit" came after she "stuck with Artie Shaw through the southern road tour" despite having to hide on the bus to avoid being seen by Ku Klux Klan members on a rampage. With the exception of Holiday, the members of the band with which she was touring through the South consisted of European-American men entirely. Racist southerners wouldn't have approved of this type of musical integration. This would have undoubtedly been especially dangerous considering the opprobrious circumstances described in Holiday's song.

"Strange Fruit" was a response to Holiday's witnessing dead bodies of African-American men "hanging from the poplar trees" and to the "smell of burning flesh" that filled the air as she traveled through the nightmare she experienced while trying to share her music with America. A significant portion of European and European-American society (then and now) often refuses to listen to the cries of its tormented victims, whether they be Native American, African-American, Jewish, female, or other. It is perhaps easier to deny that socially embarrassing or horrendous historical events took place at all, or to dismiss them as irrelevant, if they are considered too savage or unconscionable. In Holiday's case she was forced to quit singing her song.

Photos of the Jewish holocaust remind us that atrocities actually took place in Europe in the middle of the twentieth century. We have seen many such photos and films recently in the American media. Nevertheless, America has always refused to publicize its photographs of twentieth-century lynching, mutilations, burning, bombings, rapes, and bizarre medical experiments involving African-Americans. Billie Holiday, John Coltrane ("Alabama"), Don Byron ("Tuskegee Experiments"), Rahsaan Roland Kirk ("The Inflated Tear"), Charles Mingus ("Remember Rockefeller at Attica"), and other African-American artists have been brave enough to suffer the consequences one often pays in America when holding up a mirror to American society. Holiday concludes her article by saying, "Don't forget, though. I just want to be straight with people, not have their sympathy."[34]

For some reason "jazz" historians have not often been straightforward about ways in which the majority culture has treated its African-American innovators. There were countless instances of assaults inflicted upon the African-American musicians who moved downtown during the 1940s to perform. It is through the words of the artists themselves that we are reminded of events of a deplorable nature. In the video "Celebrating Bird: The Triumph of Charlie Parker," Dizzy Gillespie discusses a time when a European-American man (who had been throwing pennies on stage while he was performing with Bird) approached him from behind and hits him over the head with a bottle producing a severe laceration. Miles Davis recounts in detail another racist imbroglio (that took place in the following decade) in his autobiography:

> I had just finished doing an Armed Forces Day broadcast, you know, Voice of America and all that bullshit. I had just walked this pretty white girl named Judy out to get a cab. She got in the cab, and I'm standing there in front of Birdland wringing wet because it's a hot, steaming, muggy night in August. This white policeman comes up to me and tells me to move on. At the time I was doing a lot of boxing and so I thought to myself, I ought to hit this motherfucker because I knew what he was doing. But instead I said, "Move on, for what? I'm working downstairs. That's my name up there, Miles Davis," and I pointed to my name on the marquee all up in lights.
>
> He said, "I don't care where you work, I said move on! If you don't move on I'm going to arrest you."
>
> I just looked at his face real straight and hard, and I didn't move. Then he said, "You're under arrest!" He reached for his handcuffs, but he was stepping back. Now, boxers had told me that if a guy's going to hit you, if you walk *toward* him you can see what's happening. I saw the way he was handling himself that the policeman was an ex-fighter. So I kind of leaned in closer because I wasn't going to give him no distance so he could hit me on the head. He stumbled, and all his stuff fell on the sidewalk, and I thought to myself, Oh, shit, they're going to think that I fucked with him or something. I'm waiting for him to put the handcuffs on, because all his stuff is on the ground and shit. Then I move closer so he won't be able to fuck me up. A crowd had gathered all of a sudden from out of nowhere, and this white detective runs in and BAM! hits me on the head. I never saw him coming. Blood was running down the khaki suit I had on. Then I remembered Dorothy Kilgallen coming outside with this horrible look on her face—I had known Dorothy for years and I used to date her good friend, Jean Bock—and say-

ing, "Miles, what's happened?" I couldn't say nothing. Illinois Jacquet was there, too.

It was almost a race riot, so the police got scared and hurried up and got my ass out of there and took me to the 54th Precinct where they took pictures of me bleeding and shit. So, I'm sitting there, madder than a motherfucker, right? And they're saying to me in this station, "So you're the wiseguy, huh?" Then they'd bump up against me, you know, try to get me mad so they could probably knock me upside my head again. I'm just sitting there, taking it all in, watching every move they make.

I look up on the wall and see they were advertising voyages for officers to take to Germany, like a tour. And this is about fourteen years after the war. And they're going to learn police shit. It's advertised in the brochure; they'll probably teach them how to be meaner and shit, do to niggers over here what the Nazis did to the Jews over there. I couldn't believe that shit in there and they're supposed to be protecting us. I ain't done nothing but help a woman friend of mine get a cab and she happened to be white and the white boy who was the policeman didn't like seeing a nigger doing that.[35]

Bop Brass Instrumentalists

Dizzy Gillespie

John Birks "Dizzy" Gillespie was the trumpet virtuoso who emerged during the 1940s presenting a style and level of control over his instrument that remains unmatched. Gillespie was a colossal modern "jazz" innovator who wielded a strong and positive influence over his fellow "jazz" musicians. His career, spanning more than five decades, stands as a paragon of unparalleled trumpet mastery.

Supporting Dizzy's trumpet legacy is a large repertoire of original compositions, the stylistic incorporation of Afro-Cuban musical influences in many of his performances, and of an array of top quality combo and big band recordings featuring some of the best-known musicians in the business. As one of the top two "bebop educators" (Charlie Parker being the other), Gillespie helped to create and introduce the new vocabulary of bop phrases and concepts. He was also instrumental in expanding the implied functions of harmonic paradigms in modern "jazz." Unlike Parker, Dizzy Gillespie functioned more communicatively as a traditional teacher of the new innovative style. Generally speaking, Parker's approach to his new brand of music had to be learned strictly through listening to his music.

Gillespie was born on October 21, 1917, in Cheraw, South Carolina. Trombone was the instrument he studied first at age fourteen before switching to trumpet the following year. His formal training was minimal during this early period, but he practiced and developed his natural musical abilities. This effort eventually resulted in a scholarship to study theory and harmony at North Carolina's Laurinburg Institute, a boarding school for "black" students. When the Gillespie family moved to Philadelphia in 1935 one of the premier trumpet players of the day, Roy Eldridge (1911–89), became his chief influence. After arriving in New York (in 1937) Gillespie joined the Teddy Hill Band. Hill's band folded two years later, and Dizzy began touring with the Cab Calloway Orchestra.

Before Gillespie's association with Calloway ended abruptly in 1941, he made important musical progress as an improviser and as a composer/arranger. The greatest significance of this period came when Gillespie met Charlie Parker on a road trip through Kansas City. The friends would meet again in 1942 as members of Earl Hines' orchestra, a band that promulgated the emergence of bop vocabulary. A portion of the significance of the Earl Hines Big Band was its nurturing the careers of artists such as Billy Eckstine and Sarah Vaughan, who would later become highly influential mentors in their own rights.

When the new experimental music was founded by Gillespie and Charlie Parker in the early forties, Dizzy was decked out with horn-rimmed glasses, wore a beret, and grew a goatee. This style of appearance caused both fellow musicians and fans of bebop to emulate his lead. His stage presence was much more extroverted and entertaining than Parker's presentation. Gillespie seemed more concerned with the impression he made on employers and his fans than Parker. Those who were close to Dizzy appreciated his gift for humor. Coltrane said, "I don't make a habit of wishing for what I don't have, but I often wish I had a lighter nature. Dizzy has that beautiful gift."[36]

Although Dizzy Gillespie was more conforming and practical (economically and socially speaking), musically he remained Bird's only equal in bebop. This combination of qualities facilitated his rise to the status of an international figure generating widespread interest in "jazz," while Parker's reputation grew more slowly. Dizzy's style was rooted in his own musical vision and ideas; nevertheless, he admitted his debt to Parker on numerous occasions. In a 1989 interview (with Gene Lees) Gillespie states, "[Parker's] style . . . was perfect for our music. I was playing like Roy Eldridge at the time [early 1940s]. In about a month's time [after meeting Bird] I was playing like Charlie Parker. From then on—maybe adding a little here and there."[37]

Bop experiments were further expanded during the early 1940s period when Gillespie and Parker joined pianist-composer Thelonious Monk and drummer Kenny Clarke to jam at after-hours clubs in Harlem, including Minton's Playhouse and Clark Monroe's Uptown House. Monk advised musicians, "Don't play what the public wants, you play what you want and let the public pick up on what you are doing—even if it does take them fifteen or twenty years." Eventually, with this philosophical premise in mind, they collectively laid the foundation for modern "jazz." Gillespie tells us why the new liberated style was so tightly organized:

I go for freedom, but freedom without organization is chaos. I want to put freedom into music the way I conceive it. It is free, but it's organized freedom. You've got to take memory from the universe. Man will never organize anything as well as nature can. It's perpetual, but so many things are happening that you can always discover something else in nature.[38]

In 1943 Billy Eckstine took a large and influential contingent of the band with him when he left Hines to form a big band that became one of the most celebrated large ensembles in modern "jazz" history. Gillespie, Parker, Sarah Vaughan, and other innovators were among those who had defected from Hines' band to join Eckstine. Art Blakey was the drummer who propelled Eckstine's band in an exciting new direction. Eckstine later fronted several other big bands whose popularity was largely due to the vocal talents of Sarah Vaughan.

The era of the pre-bop big band was interrupted, however, when the union ban on recording was initiated. Many professional bands, including the Hines and the Eckstine bands, were forced to fold.

Gillespie and Parker finally collaborated in a combo setting for the Guild-Musicraft studio session that include celebrated recordings of "Groovin' High," "Hot House," and "Salt Peanuts."[39] Although the small combo was in its heyday during bebop (in the mid-1940s), there were also a few innovative big bands after the union ban. Dizzy Gillespie organized a band in 1945 that failed to last a year but was later reorganized in July 1946. Dizzy's new band's impetuous and angular style didn't fit into the common notions of dance orchestral music.

Gillespie's band, nevertheless, made a memorable recording titled "Things To Come," which had torrid tempos and wreaked havoc upon big band conventions established by swing. The leader's popularity soared as the public began to take notice of bop, enabling Dizzy to organize bebop big bands from 1946 to 1950. Within this instrumental framework Dizzy and Cuban drummer Chano Pozo (1915–48) introduced Afro-Cuban rhythms into new charts that lead to pioneering compositions, establishing what later became known as Latin "jazz." Conga drummer Mongo Santamaria (1922–2003) said in an interview for *Down Beat* magazine (April 21, 1977): "Dizzy Gillespie had a lot to do with the popularity of the conga. He introduced Chano Pozo in his band and started to develop things like 'Manteca,' 'Tin Tin Deo' and others. You can't say how great the Gillespie/Pozo relationship was. The importance is blurred a little. You accept the conga now, but it was only bongos and timbales at one time."

The bebop big bands Gillespie led were some of the only successful ones of the bebop era. Gillespie did not mind the term bebop for the music he played. In an interview with John Wilson he said: "Bop is a part of jazz, and jazz music is to dance to. The trouble with bop as it's played now is that people can't dance to it. They don't hear those four beats. We'll never get across to a wide audience until they can dance to it. They're not particular about whether you're playing flatted fifths or a ruptured 129th as long as they can dance."

Gillespie, while highly involved in musical experimentation, felt it important to keep his music accessible to the average person. A portion of the influence that enabled him to maintain roots in the community was his awareness of African-American church music. Musicians benefit from the fact that in the African-American socioculture religious and secular worlds usually overlap. Musical seeds of information, learned in church or at a jam session, are further enhanced by sounds of street vendors, casual conversations, and beat-boxes on the streets of the African-American community. People whistling on the street and children jumping rope outdoors all reinforce communal musical messages, gradually transforming their meanings and perpetuating their development. Dizzy Gillespie said, "Like most black musicians, much of my early inspiration, especially with rhythm and harmonies, came from the church."[40]

The wide range of dynamics and emotional contrasts that can be found within the interchange between pastor, choir, and congregation in many African-American churches inspires people in ways seldom encountered in other aspects of American life. Drummer Max Roach explains that any young performer in church is judged primarily upon "their ability to stir the congregation's feelings" and by "their technical proficiency." The "spiritual feeling" that results from such inspirational performances is described by Don Pate.

> The spirit would also be something that would be transmitted by the minister if he was an eloquent speaker. He could summon it with his message. Often times, it would also be the choir or the soloist in the choir, and occasionally, when the organ player or piano player would be hot, it was like having Ray Charles in church. To me, that's where the spirituality comes in. If the music has spirit, you can feel it. If it's without feeling or meaning, deep inner meaning, then it's spiritless.[41]

The street songs, rhythms, and other musical patterns found in daily life, therefore, are combined and intensified within African-American churches that foster such potent spiritual environments. Concerning the contents of his big band book Diz said, "We'll use the same harmonics, but with a beat, so that people can understand where the beat is. We'll use a lot of things which are in the book now, but we will cut them and splice them together like you would a movie so as to leave out the variation in beat. . . . As long as they say it's a great band, I don't care if they say it's bop or what."[42]

Waning economic support forced Dizzy to break up his band in 1950. He was able to build another working big band for his first State Department tour overseas several years later. This ensemble stayed together from 1956 to 1958. It was not until 1991, when he formed his critically acclaimed fifteen-piece United Nation Orchestra, that Gillespie was able to revisit this particular style with his own large ensemble. After the 1950s, the majority of Gillespie's brilliant trumpet work was showcased primarily in small-group studio dates. His influence on a superb line of trumpet players includes Fats Navarro, Clifford Brown, Woody Shaw, Jon Faddis, and Wynton Marsalis.

Thelonious Monk once said that "every sound influenced Diz. He had that kind of mind, you know? And he influenced everything too."[43]

Along with Dizzy Gillespie, Theodore "Fats" Navarro (1923–50) was influenced by Parker's and Gillespie's new style and eventually becoming one of the most lyrical trumpeters in bebop. He possessed a musical style that incorporated an expressive vibrato supporting a clear and precise instrumental technique. His distinctive soloing approach was often similar to Parker's in formal construction. He replaced Gillespie in Eckstine's band in 1945 and recorded from that time until his death. Billy Eckstine talks about Navarro's performance when he replaced Gillespie in his band: "I got Fats to come by and talk it over, and about two weeks after that he took Dizzy's chair, and take it from me, he came *right* in . . . Great as Diz is, . . . Fats played the book and you would hardly know that Diz had left the band. 'Fat Girl' played Dizzy's solos, not note for note, but his ideas on Dizzy's parts and the feeling was the same and there was just as much swing."[44]

The majority of his colleagues agree that, given ample time and the proper situation in which to develop, there would have been no limits to Navarro's musical achievements. Most of his recordings were as a sideman with Coleman Hawkins, Bud Powell, Tadd Dameron, Kenny Clark, and other notable musicians. Benny Goodman hired Fats for a brief period during the clarinetist's curt flirtation with bop. He would not hire Navarro on a steady basis, however. Joe Newman, in the liner notes to the album *The Fabulous Fats Navarro*, is quoted as saying: "He had everything a trumpet player needs, soul, a good lip, continuity and a good sound (one of those big butter sounds). A guy with as much as he had to work with couldn't have failed if he had remained level-headed." Carmen McRae thought: "He was sort of a cherub, big fat jaws and a big stomach, and he was so young, in his early twenties." Leonard Feather summed up Navarro's brief career this way: "In a context where causes and effects became misty and blurred, it was impossible to know which evil force had moved first in taking Fats from the scene, tuberculosis or narcotics addiction or racial discrimination or artistic frustration, or a witch's brew of all these and more. All we knew was that the trumpet player from Key West, Florida, was dead at the age of twenty-six."[45]

Melba Doretta Liston

Melba Doretta Liston (b. 1926 in Kansas City, Missouri, d. April, 1999), the legendary trombonist and arranger, has been playing with the greatest names in "jazz" since the bebop era. As a trombonist, Liston was most active in Los Angeles and New York City during the 1940s and 1950s. She was raised in Los Angeles from age eleven, and began playing trombone in the Lincoln Theater pit orchestra there at age sixteen. Her professional performing and recording affiliations included bands and orchestras led by Gerald Wilson (b. 1919), Randy Weston (b. 1926), Count Basie, Dexter Gordon (1923–90), Dizzy Gillespie, and Quincy Jones (b. 1933). She toured with Billie Holiday in 1949 and with Dizzy Gillespie in the Near East and Latin America in 1956–57. In 1959 Liston toured Europe with the Quincy

Jones Orchestra, and she was also involved in acting and playing trombone in the Harold Arlen–Johnny Mercer musical, *Free and Easy*.[46]

A 1977 *Ebony Magazine* article reviews the contributions made by this artist, who for years was one of the West Coast's most sought-after musicians: "To the serious fan of Afro-American music, the name Melba Liston immediately recalls the image of a young talented trombonist and composer who, from the mid '40s to the late '50s, was one of the few female musicians to make a significant impact on the jazz world."[47]

Liston was a frontwoman with the Chick Webb band from 1942 to 1944. After working as a member of the Gerald Wilson band between 1944 and 1947, she joined the Count Basie band (1948–49). Her potential as a trombone soloist was clear following her 1947 recording with Dexter Gordon ("Mischievous Lady"). Dizzy Gillespie asked her to bring one of her arrangements to her first rehearsal with his band in 1950. Liston recalls, "And of course they got about two measures and fell out, and got all confused and stuff. And Dizzy said, 'Now who's the bitch?'"[48] The impression she made was indelible. She led her own all-women quintet in New York and Bermuda in 1958 and began working as a freelance arranger. Liston wrote many arrangements for television commercials, vocalists, and musicians such as Randy Weston, Mary Lou Williams, Johnny Griffin, and Milt Jackson.

Liston led an innovative New York–based ensemble in the early 1980s, until she became ill. In May 1993 she was inducted into the Pioneers Hall of Fame at the Intentional Women's Brass Conference (at Washington University in St. Louis, Missouri). Instrumental arrangements and compositions by Liston, that are available in compilations and anthologies including *Christmas Eve*, *Blue Melba*, and many others. On the albums *Randy Weston: The Spirit of Our Ancestors* (Antilles, 1992) and *Volcano Blues* (Antilles, 1993) Liston provides the musical arrangements. Melba and pianist Randy Weston had recently worked as co-leaders. She also performed on the recording "Jazz Club: Trombone," and had several important early collaborations with Mary Lou Williams.

Howard McGhee and Others

Howard McGhee (1918–87), who began studying music on clarinet, was later fascinated by the trumpet playing of both Louis Armstrong and Roy Eldridge. When he started playing bebop, trumpeter Doc Cheatham said he thought he was crazy. Although his background was in swing, McGhee was one of the early pioneers of bop and became one of its chief exponents.

When McGhee left school and moved to California, he worked as a tenor saxophone player with several bands. He began switching to trumpet in 1935 while a member of Art Bronson's band. The following four years were spent touring as a trumpet player. His woodwind experience was applied to his rapidly developing trumpet style, forging an unusually supple approach that allowed him to crowd an inordinate number of notes into any harmonic structure. McGhee's professional break came when he joined Andy Kirk's Clouds of Joy in 1942. Kirk's band was established in 1929 and had such distinguished alumni as Mary Lou Williams and Don Byas (1912–72). Kirk was generous in featuring his players. When McGhee recorded with Kirk later that year, Kirk debuted some of the trumpeter's arrangements, gave him the spotlight, and titled the recording "McGhee Special."

Although this debut recording with Kirk preserved his pre-bop style for posterity, his engagements after 1945 began to display McGhee's bebop style (following his brief stint with Coleman Hawkins). Fats Navarro, who played in Kirk's band while McGhee was the featured soloist, spoke of McGhee's dazzling technique and melodic inventiveness and concluded that "he was *the* influence."[49] His musical contributions serve as an important bridge between pre-bop and bebop styles. His work as leader during the 1940s produced groups containing sidemen such as Charlie Parker, Milt Jackson, Charles Mingus, and James Moody. He continued to develop his bop style in the company of pianist Duke Jordan, bassist Percy Heath, drummer Philly Joe Jones, saxophonist Shahib Shihab, and other adventurous players during the 1950s.

Miles Davis (1926–91) began playing trumpet at age thirteen, and later studied briefly at Julliard. Davis played with the combos of Charlie Parker and Coleman Hawkins early in his career. Parker took an interest in Miles and hired him for performances such as his 1948 Three Deuces date with Duke Jordan on piano, Tommy Potter on bass, and Max Roach on drums. Parker, in turn, played on some of the recording sessions led by the young trumpeter. Miles Davis' 1947 Savoy session (on which Parker played tenor saxophone) was one such occasion. Davis' sound was characterized by a more delicate tone on trumpet than most other boppers. Davis carried the lessons learned from bebop in the 1940s into the Cool style he chose for himself during the 1950s. His style continually evolved over the course of a career that spanned half a century.

Clark Terry (b. 1920) developed his reputation as a member of the Charlie Barnet band (1947), the Count Basie ensemble (1948–51), and the Duke Ellington orchestra. His high-register trumpet passages reveal Gillespie's influence, yet his personalized style remained distinct from other bop trumpeters. His rich tone quality was used to great advantage when he began doubling on flugelhorn in the 1950s.

In addition to recording sessions with small combos, trumpeter Kenny Dorham (1924–72) had been a member of both the Billy Eckstine and Dizzy Gillespie big bands in 1946. He later replaced Miles Davis in Parker's quintet in 1948. His mature sound is heard on 1950s recordings with Max Roach, Thelonious Monk, Horace Silver, and Art Blakey. In 1949 Red Rodney (1927–94) replaced Dorham in the Parker quintet. Rodney came through the European-American big band school (playing with Woody Herman and Claude Thornhill). He soon realized the difference between the type of musical experience gained in Herman's band and the more demanding requirements of bebop. Herman ran his band like a drill sergeant, with much of the music written out and little room for self-expression within the sections of the band. Parker music demanded virtuosity, a personal style, and spontaneity. Between bouts with drugs over the years, Rodney continued to make comebacks to play into the 1990s.

Bebop Pianists

Earl "Bud" Powell

Earl "Bud" Powell (1924–66) held the most fertile imagination among bop pianists. His inventive approach to the piano, coupled with an extraordinary musical drive, a superb sense of structure, and substantial melodic resources, made his contribution to bebop very close in importance to those of Charlie Parker and Dizzy Gillespie. Pianist William "Red" Garland discusses his early musical encounter with Powell:

> When I got to New York, I ran into the tenor player Eddie "Lockjaw" Davis, and I asked him where all the good piano players were. He told me Bud Powell was about the baddest cat in town. "Who's Bud Powell?" I asked him. "Don't worry, you're going to find out," he told me. Well, one night I was working at Minton's with Max Roach, and I looked over toward the door, and in walked Bud. I could hardly play because of everything I had heard about him. I froze. Bud came over and started forcing me off the bench. "Let me play," he kept saying to me. "Let me play." Max was yelling to me, "No! Get him away. Keep him away from the piano." Max was afraid he was crazy or something and was going to ruin the gig. I got up anyway. I figured if Bud wanted it that bad, I wasn't going to stand in his way. Well, he sat down at the piano and scared me to death—he played so much piano! I told Max, "I quit! Give him the job!" See, Bud took my cool.
>
> But a few days later I went over to Bud's house, and he showed me some things. In fact, I came back, day after day to learn from him, and we became buddies. He was really friendly to me, and the greatest influence on me of any pianist, except for Art Tatum. I still don't believe Art Tatum was real.[50]

The same sensitive and delicate artistic constitution that enabled Powell to reach his level of musicianship and creativity led to personal difficulties that tortured his professional and personal life. Some of his misfortune seemed imposed by external forces. After Thelonious Monk was arrested in 1948 for possession of a joint of marijuana (causing his cabaret card to be revoked for a month), he and Powell were apparently setup by police for a subsequent arrest. Later, after receiving head injuries during a racially motivated assault, and following his arrest for drug trafficking for selling a joint of marijuana to a female undercover agent who implored him to do so,[51] Powell spent lengthy periods in mental hospitals and would have to struggle with drug abuse and addiction. These problems made it impossible for him to play at all on many occasions. Eventually the physical and emotional burdens would claim his life. His genius, however, was apparent to his peers and audiences throughout the world during his career. When he was in control of his life, as Lou Levy observes, his performances were incredible:

> One night in Paris, in '58 or '59 . . . Ray Brown and Herb Ellis and I went down to the Blue Note. Bud was playing there with a French rhythm section. . . . He got up at the piano, and proceeded to play like you never heard anyone play before. No one ever heard better choruses than we heard that night. Ray Brown said, "Man, I worked with him on Fifty-second Street, I worked with him with Bird, he never played better than this." He was playing "The Best Thing for You" at a tempo you wouldn't believe. That thing is a roller coaster of [chord] changes . . . and he did it like a loop-the-loop, chorus after chorus, relentless, with such strength. . . . He never ran out of gas. It was a night that I'll never forget! . . . [That] night . . . was the greatest jazz performance I have been lucky enough to hear.[52]

Thelonious Monk

Thelonious Monk (1917–82) had tutored Powell when the latter pianist was a teen. Monk's composition "In Walked Bud" is a tribute to his musical comrade. In turn Powell premiered Monk's "'Round Midnight" on a recording with Cootie Williams. Monk was an important innovator, pianist, and composer during the bebop period. As a composer, he contributed numerous tunes to the bop repertoire that challenged the conventional concept of standard blues and song forms. His roots were in the early stride styles, but his personalized sparse style and eclectic rhythmic sense set him apart from other soloists. Monk enjoyed placing rhythmic accents in unexpected locations, and his harmonic approach weakened or dissolved the bond between functional harmony and "jazz." He did not feel his dissonances were obliged to behave in any kind of prescribed manner (according to any particular musical "rule"), and his frequent employment of augmented, diminished, and whole-tone motives and passages allowed him to further suspend or obscure an implied tonic.

Monk played at Harlem rent parties during his early teens before later leading a trio at a neighborhood bar around 1934. He studied briefly at the Juilliard School before performing regularly with the Keg Purnell quartet in 1939. Monk worked with Kenny Clarke at Minton's and at Kelly's Stables from 1940-42. He also performed with Lucky Millinder, Coleman Hawkins, Kermit Scott, Dizzy Gillespie, Cootie Williams, and other artists in the early 1940s.

Monk began recording with his own group in 1947 and performed with that ensemble at Minton's, the Royal Roost, and at the Village Vanguard. A few years after appearing at the Paris Jazz Festival he assembled a quartet for the 5 Spot Café with John Coltrane, Shadow Wilson (who replaced Philly Joe Jones), and Wilbur Ware. His later collaborators included Johnny Griffin, Charlie Rouse, Roy Haynes, and other prominent musicians.

334 Karlton E. Hester

Those who understood his music admired Monk for his considerable individuality. He was particularly effective in the construction of fresh melodic lines that peaked the interest of both boppers and post-boppers. He worked alone or led a trio or small combo until 1959, when he started to work with orchestras at his Town Hall Concert. His playing sometimes had a stark, somber quality to it. He employed a subtle use of dynamics that are often as unpredictable as the other surprising ingredients of his performances. Monk's angular rhythmic sense coupled with his terse, balanced, and perfectly structured abstract melodies created a musical environment unlike that of any of his peers. He played with Dizzy Gillespie, Charlie Parker, and other important innovators of bebop and maintained his progress within subsequent stylistic movements as well. Although he contributed to the harmonic language of bebop, Monk favored motivic improvisation and influenced Coltrane and other innovators in that regard. Monk's beautiful and unconventional approach to composition has spurred renewed interest in his music since his death.

Women Bop Pianists

Women pianists were less visible publicly during bop than in previous decades; nevertheless, they continued to make their contributions to the musical evolution. Margaret "Countess" Johnson (1919–39) established an impressive reputation in Kansas City during the 1930s as a pianist with the bands of Harlan Leonard and Andy Kirk (substituting for Mary Lou Williams with Kirk's band). During the bebop era vocalist Sarah Vaughan (1924–90) performed four-hand piano pieces with Earl "Fatha" Hines in 1943 and 1945. Pianist Vivian Glasby played at the Rhumboogie in Chicago with The Fletcher Henderson Band for an engagement. Maurita Gordon substituted with Sidney Bechet's New Orleans Footwarmers in Washington, D.C., for a 1947 concert. Another African-American woman pianist who lead her own "jazz" trios was Camille Howard. The Howard Trio appeared regularly in the D.C. area as well as throughout the East Coast during the 1940s.[53] Perhaps because of the particular set of social and musical circumstances in which bop was born, few women instrumentalists or vocalists became intimately involved with the bebop movement, however.

Bebop involved a systematic approach to musical style that was capable of assimilating and transforming other musical languages. Ragtime had possessed a similar ability to transform available African and European musical resources. Ragtime was based upon a syncopated rhythmic structure that could change the meaning of any song brought into its fold. Bebop not only distorted, augmented, and enhanced preexisting rhythmic configurations and succeeded in expanding harmonic melodic structure, it also uncompromisingly opposed established industry formulas such as those exercised by Tin Pan Alley musicians. A battle against the trite products of the tunesmiths began in the 1920s and found an important modern ally in the midst of beboppers. Traditional approaches to familiar standards were revolutionized in the hands of Parker, Gillespie, and other innovators. Songs such as

"What is This Thing Called Love?" became "Hot House" and "How High the Moon" was the harmonic basis for Parker's composition, "Ornithology." Mary Lou Williams felt that "jazz is created in the mind, felt in the heart and heard through the fingertips."[54] In 1954, she described the bebop era:

> My reason for feeling bop is the "next era" music is that it came about spontaneously in the same way as our blues and classic jazz, or any other music that a race of people produces. And I contend that bop is the only real modern jazz, despite the contentions of the copyists of Stravinsky, Hindemith, and Schoenberg. The swing era produced smooth eighth notes, which many of our theoreticians are still playing. The phrasing and timing of bop puts it in a different category altogether. The American Negro musician of today is born to this new phrasing, just as in the past he was born to the rhythm and phrasing of ragtime or boogie and naturally played those styles of music.
>
> Bop has become a powerful and, I believe, permanent influence on our native music. The guys who originated it were as gifted as the creative musicians of the thirties and the eras that came before. I have known older musicians discourage them, speak badly of the music. Perhaps these older players feared for themselves and their positions. If so, they were being ridiculous. If some of them were to add a few modern changes here and there in their own work, it might revive their inspiration and help them avoid the danger of artistic stagnation. The sooner the older musicians and fans accept the new music the better it will be for everyone concerned with jazz.[55]

Other Bop Era Pianists

Dorothy Donegan

At age seventeen Dorothy Donegan (1924–98) was the pianist with the Bob Tinsley Band in Chicago. Daughter of a guitar-playing mother, Donegan began studying music at age five. She went on to study at Chicago Musical College (studying with master pianist Rudolph Ganz) and continued advanced studies in piano at the University of Southern California in the early 1950s, after establishing her reputation nationally as a virtuoso pianist. In time she gained the title "Queen of the Eighty-Eights." Through the years Donegan earned other labels for her powerful style: "the wild one," "the triumphantly unfettered," and "the shoulder-shaking, finger-popping, hip-slapping lioness of piano rooms."[56] An advertisement for one of her 1959 Capitol Records releases read, "She jumps, she wiggles, she bounds and pounds and scowls and growls." Writers always qualified such descriptions, however: she was "wild but polished," the "possessor of enormous technical skill," and "one of the great contemporary jazz pianists—she's brilliant, ridiculously talented; for all of the arm-flinging antics, Dorothy can really play."[57]

Dorothy Donegan (Photo by Lee Friedlander).

Although Donegan was initially trained in the European "serious music" repertoire, she also had several years of experience as a church organist. She developed an acting career that includes appearances in the motion picture *Sensations of 1945* and the Broadway play *Star Time* (1945). Donegan has a number of recordings on the Continental, Decca, Victor, Jubilee, Roulette, and Capitol labels. She headlined the brilliant cast of the first all-"Black" show appearing at Hollywood's famous Tom Breneman Cafe in 1949. Donegan broke the house attendance record at New York City's Embers (an East Side sanctuary for "jazz" pianists) in 1956. She performed regularly at Chicago's London House and in New York City at Jimmy Weston's place, and the Dorothy Donegan Trio (piano, bass, and drums) appeared at the Newport Jazz Festival in 1979. Her trio gave an impressive performance at New York City's Carnegie Hall.[58] In 1978 "jazz" historian Frank Driggs wrote: "Dorothy Donegan may have the best pair of hands in the business and can play any style well. She is often frustrating for a hard-core jazz fancier, since she will play some brilliant passages and then upstage that with some very show-biz stuff for the squares in any club."[59]

In 1978 Chicago Mayor Michael Bilandic proclaimed her birthday "Dorothy Donegan Day in Chicago." Donegan lived and performed in Europe for a number of years. Throughout her career she continued to dazzle and intrigue her audiences with her innovative piano virtuosity. She was a master of boogie-woogie, the blues, contemporary "jazz," and various styles of the European piano repertoire.

Lennie Tristano

Lennie Tristano (1919–78) was a blind, conservatory-trained pianist who was deeply impressed by the styles of Hines and Tatum. After 1946 his energies were directed toward experimenting with combinations of metrical organization and tempos as a leader and teacher in New York. He worked with young developing musicians including Lee Konitz, Warne Marsh, Arnold Fishkin, and Billy Bauer. His work with these students focused on a style that tended to dilute characteristic bebop accents, style of syncopation, and variable phrasing, producing a music that was technically challenging but much less expressive than bop. Nevertheless, his musical associates were fine musicians with somewhat individualized approaches.

Tristano's music had a positive influence on cool "jazz" style. In 1949 he became one of the earliest "jazz" musicians to explore a free-form, collectively improvised atonal approach. While conducting a recording session for Capitol, he instructed his sidemen to begin playing without any predetermined chord structure, melody, tonal center, or form. For example, on "Intuition" and "Digression" (Affinity AFF149), the piano, bass, guitar, and both saxophonists all play independently improvised lines. They achieve a moderate degree of dialogue in the sense that one performer's line provides the melodic or rhythmic content and motivation for another performer to explore and expand upon. Tristano occasionally mimics some of the lines offered by saxophonists Lee Konitz and Warne Marsh. The lack of a drummer on these two pieces allows the performers more freedom in shifting the tempo or applying rubato to obscure the implied metrical pulse. Tristano's experimentation foreshadowed other free "jazz" styles that would take root in the 1950s.

Tristano's experiments had no significant impact upon the majority of innovators and performers in the African-American "jazz" community. His approach to free "jazz" was a concept that never caught on significantly in America. The music that has experienced greater success has an emotional content, striking rhythms or timbres, or other intriguing musical elements that enable the listener to get a grip on what they are hearing. Tristano's music was not as dynamic as later free "jazz" experiments. Capitol (a label Tristano was affiliated with) failed to release the aleatory recordings for several years. Many people in America are conditioned to a small set of definitions of melody, harmony, rhythm, and form through contact with a narrow set of musical experiences in educational institutions and the hyperconservative general media. This makes it difficult for the average person to possess the readiness to accept more abstract approaches, ideas, elements, and structures of music and sound production.

Women Vocalists and Instrumentalists during the 1940s

Sarah Vaughan

Sarah Vaughan (1924–90) began studying piano at age seven. She became a church vocal soloist and organist by the time she was twelve years old. While attending the Newark Arts High School as a pianist she began to sing informally at parties. Vaughan recalls in an interview that "while I was playing piano in the school band, I learned to take music apart and analyze the notes and put it back together again. By doing this, I learned to sing differently from all the other singers."[60]

In 1943 she performed her rendition of "Body and Soul" on the stage of Harlem's Apollo Theater. Sarah Vaughan's splendid voice and expert musicianship would soon thrill audiences and influence future singers for decades. Her parents preferred a career in church or concert music for Sarah, but Vaughan was interested in the "jazz" she was hearing. She recalls that by the early forties "I thought Bird and Diz were the end." "At that time I was singing more off key than on. I think their playing influenced my singing. Horns always influenced me more than voices . . . as soon as I hear an arrangement, I get ideas, kind of like blowing a horn. I guess I never sing a tune the same way twice."[61] Linda Dahl describes this early phase of Vaughan's career:

> Both Ella Fitzgerald and Billy Eckstine, then singing with Earl Hines, came to Vaughan's aid after her Apollo appearance. Fitzgerald cautioned her to be careful about agents and managers, and Eckstine recommended that Hines hire her as co-vocalist for his big band. Within weeks Sarah Vaughan was working with Hines as vocalist and second pianist, alongside many of her player idols. Her lovely voice, supple and true in pitch, immediately pleased her fellow musicians, and her instinctive harmonic sense dovetailed with the explorations of the new crop of instrumentalists soon to be called bop players. With her willingness to dare improvisatory feats, she was quickly hailed as the vocal counterpart of these innovators. A superb addition to the Hines band, she went with Eckstine when he left Hines to form his own modern jazz big band. She then sang with bassist John Kirby's popular group. By 1946 she had established herself as a solo artist, working up from intermission pianist and singer at Cafe Society Downtown to headliner of that and other New York clubs.[62]

In Eckstine's band Sarah Vaughan had the ability to transform everyday songs into magical moments. She made her tone and vibratos expressive and flexible like a wind or bowed string instrument. Vaughan's debut recording for Continental Records in 1944 received good reviews, and by 1947 she had a number of popular tunes recorded. Her version of "The Lord's Prayer" on Musicraft, which displayed her roots in "Black" religious music, received the distinguished praise of the premiere vocalist Marian Anderson. Her phrasing, intonation, range, and inventive powers blossomed quickly. By the fifties she was a major attraction worldwide and had a recording contract with Columbia Records. Her lower register deepened and its timbre enriched as Vaughan's voice matured. With the addition of a beautifully lyrical middle register and clear upper (head) register, her vocal range became increasingly more impressive. Dahl says, "Through years of strenuous work under conditions that would fell an opera diva, Vaughan's singing has only gotten better, more extended in range and less prodigal in technique." She continues:

> One can only wonder as to the still-unexplored possibilities of this marvelous voice. In 1947 Vaughan mentioned that she wanted to do a concert and a recording of spirituals, and she has often expressed the wish that someone would write an opera for her. In recent years she has added Brazilian music to her repertoire. Her interpretations of many standards endure: wonderful versions of "You're Blase," "If You Could See Me Now," "I Cover the Waterfront," "Body and Soul," "Tenderly," "Everything I Have Is Yours," "I'll Remember April," "Easy Living," "I Remember Clifford," "Here's That Rainy Day," "Misty," "Don't Blame Me" and more.[63]

Sarah Vaughan was a member of a small set of outstanding practitioners of the art of scat vocalizing that also included Ella Fitzgerald, Betty Carter, Sheila Jordan, and Anita O'Day. In the spirit of the African-American tradition, scat vocalists (like their instrumental counterparts) take musical risks to stretch their range of musical elements and excite an audience. Of course the ability to scat alone does not qualify a "jazz" singer as an exceptional musician. Rather, because it places all musicians—vocalists and instrumentalists—within a similar musical arena of improvisation, each performer is judged according to a related standard of the innovative "jazz" tradition. Like an efficient wind or string instrumentalist, vocalists of Vaughan's caliber can work in any musical context and inspire the musicians with whom they perform. Scat singing requires the abandonment of a dependency on the melody and text. Instead the artist explores her vocal virtuosity within a realm of nonprescribed limitations. Sarah Vaughan was such an artist.

Carmen McRae

Carmen McRae (1920–94) was a contemporary of Sarah Vaughan who also worked with a trio that functioned as her creative springboard. Born in Brooklyn, New York, in 1922, McRae studied piano and music at an early age and won a scholarship for advanced piano study. As a teenager McRae studied Billie Holiday's style. Lady Day eventually recorded "Dream of Life," one of McRae's compositions, in 1939. McRae returned the tribute later in her career when she dedicated an album of songs associated with Holiday, her early idol. What McRae seemed to appreciate most was Holiday's mastery of the ability to make dramatic statements with any style of lyric. Billie Holiday did not scat but was constantly inventing along a poetic, resilient, and infinite path of musical expression. After high school McRae worked as a government clerical worker in Washington, D.C. By 1943 she had returned to her musical career in New York playing piano and singing in clubs while continuing to hold down a "day gig." She was finally persuaded to get involved in her musical career full time.

Besides the inspiration supplied by Billie Holiday early in McRae's career, she was drawn toward the nascent modern "jazz" scene. She married innovative drummer Kenny Clarke and appeared with the bands of Benny Carter, Count Basie, and Mercer Ellington in the late forties. She moved to Chicago during this time and worked there consistently until the early fifties, when she returned to New York. In 1954 McRae won the "new star" vocalist award in *Down Beat* and subsequently dropped the piano to focus on singing. McRae believed in caressing the details concealed within the text of a song.

Carmen McRae recorded pop tunes as well as "jazz" standards, and earned a reputation for skillful interpretations with the recording of songs such as "For Once in My Life," "Alfie," "Guess Who I Saw Today," and "I'm Always Drunk in San Francisco." She said, "No matter what song I sing the lyrics have to be meaningful and believable—unless, of course, you're doing up-tempo tunes. Then nobody listens to the words. They're too busy keeping time to the rhythm."[64] McRae considered Ella Fitzgerald "the epitome of jazz feeling and the popular song welded together. With her, the transition from 'jazz' to the commercial context wasn't only smooth, it was artistic."[65] She might have been speaking of herself, for McRae too melds "jazz" feeling with the popular repertoire, and makes a persuasive art of it.

Pauline Braddy (Williams)

Pauline Braddy (Williams) was the original drummer with the International Sweethearts of Rhythm when the band was formed at the Piney Woods Country Life School. She left the band in the early fifties and worked in small combos until the late sixties. Braddy eventually moved to Washington, D.C.

There were few female drummers serving as professional models during the 1940s. Braddy remembers the women with Spitalny and D'Artega, "but I didn't know them. I didn't even meet them. There was nobody to look up to." Among the male drummers, Pauline enjoyed hearing Big Sid Catlett, Jo Jones, Ben Thigpen, Gene Krupa, and many others. "I just wanted to play. I never thought that there wasn't many girls that played." Braddy met with typical prejudices against women throughout her career.

In our time, by seeing girl bands, I think that kind of motivated a lot of the kids. They would play hooky from school to come in the theater, and they would have to turn the lights on and put all the kids out, and every little girl either wanted to play drums or piano or trumpet. We had quite a few girl musicians after a while. But now you don't see any girls much. In some places, they [the schools] go back to the roots of jazz, but you ask a kid around here, they don't even know a band from the thirties. . . . I think it helps to hear about the first girl this and the first woman to play piano and the first one that they let do so-and-so, because it's always been hard.

One reason for the Sweethearts' great success was that they presented and maintained a professional level of musicianship, an attractive image, and a strict code of discipline. Braddy said:

We laugh at [the rules] now, but I think they were great for that time. You couldn't go out with a guy if he didn't have on a shirt and tie and jacket. You couldn't dance with one if they didn't have on a tie. People dressed up then. When you hit New York and Washington and Chicago and L.A., you dressed up if you went downstairs to get a pack of cigarettes. You dressed because everybody was watching. We had seven different gowns . . . seven different pairs of slippers that went with those gowns, and you weren't seen on the stage unless you were just so. It was bad in those days for girls if you weren't just so, and we had all those rules and things, and Mrs. Jones would chaperone us, so it was protection. And it was good for us. Mrs. Jones would have died if she saw something in the paper that she didn't know about. She would have had a fit.[66]

Mary Osborne

Mary Osborne was inspired by Charlie Christian and eventually became another pioneer of the electric "jazz" guitar. Osborne toured with a trio of women musicians led by Winifred McDonald, that soon gained the attention of the music industry. Osborne said, "I think that if we had continued, we would have probably been one of the biggest groups in the country."[67] The trio later joined Buddy Rogers performing "jazz" and popular music. Later all three women musicians were married. Osborne became very active in the "jazz" scene after moving to New York. She remembered her early encounters in the Big Apple:

The first year I was in New York they used to have jam sessions on the off-nights on Fifty-second Street and at the Village Vanguard. They would pay certain musicians and pick a leader. What this did was encourage everybody in town to come and sit in at the club. Like the first time I ever played at Kelly's Stables was at a jam session. And one night they had maybe four or five trumpet players up there—Roy Eldridge, Dizzy Gillespie, you name 'em and they would be there sittin' in. There'd be twenty-five guys up there playing! And there I am, sitting in, playing! That's why I'm so glad I was around then. That kind of thing could never happen again. And I felt completely at home in that environment, because that's what I'd been doing all my life.[68]

Osborne performed and recorded with Russ Morgan, Joe Venuti, Mary Lou Williams, Ethel Waters, Coleman Hawkins, and other well-known musicians. Her own trio was heard regularly at clubs on Fifty-second Street until 1949. "We were at Kelly's Stables for a year, and we had every musician, every act or band leader that came into New York ending up coming to Fifty-second Street; we must have performed for everyone. Then I played a lot at the Hickory House, across the street, and that was first rate. Every jazz musician played at the Hickory House."[69]

During the period between 1952 and 1963 Osborne performed regularly on a New York radio show hosted by Jack Serling. This exposure made the public aware of her talent. Nevertheless, during the early 1960s Osborne soon got frustrated with the predictability of her music in this situation.

I got bored playing with my playing and with music in general. I was living a very full life, so it didn't have to do with being stagnant. But I'd listen to the playbacks from the show, and we'd do all these nice, tough little things, and I'd hear myself playing just nice, perfect. In fact, somebody said to me, "Don't you ever play a wrong note?" I said, "Well, I *should*." Not to be afraid to try a new thing, that's what it was. And I thought, "I know exactly what's going to happen there. But I'm better than that."[70]

Osborne studied Spanish guitar with Alberto Valdez-Blaine in 1962 and brought elements of the right-hand fingering and articulation back to her "jazz" and pop music. Before the guitarist died in the early 1990s, she once said (regarding her career), in an interview with Linda Dahl,

It's the preparation that a person has to do for anything like music, dancing, acting. The time spent is not always financially rewarding for a long time, and maybe never. If you've got a wife or husband that's doing the same thing, they understand. You know, it's hard to say, "Look, I'm not going to pay any attention to my children today" or "The house needs cleaning but I have to practice now." . . . I used to think, "What's the big deal about a woman musician?" I know so many women who are musicians. When the attitude came along *later*—"Gee, you don't *look* like a musician"—well what are musicians supposed to look like? It took me a long time to know that anybody would think this way, because I never did. But I never got jobs because I was a girl. I never kept them because I was a girl. Everything I accomplished was because this was the business I was in and this was what I was—a musician.

"Progressive Jazz"

Progressive "jazz" was a mid-1940s development involving the big band style and sometimes using expanded orchestration, nontraditional harmonic changes, and occasional experiments with other atypical musical elements. This musical style usually implied concert performance rather than dance music. It was offered to a segment of European-American society as an alternative to the hard-driving improvisation of Bebop during the 1940s and early 1950s. It was also an attempt to expand the boundaries of big band music by creating innovative orchestral augmentations, expanding the traditional instrumentation established during the swing era.

Stan Kenton, Boyd Raeburn, and Earl Spencer were the main leaders involved in this movement. Stanley "Stan" Newcomb Kenton (1912–79) was a pianist, arranger, and West Coast "Cool jazz" band leader who carried the big band sound to huge university audiences. Kenton attempted to keep the band renewed through experiments in modernity beginning in the mid-forties. His most significant arrangers have been Pete Rugolo, Bob Graettinger, and Bill Holman. No particular soloist stands out among the talents who have passed through the Kenton band, but perhaps the most significant have been Kai Winding, Milt Bernhart (trombones), Shorty Rogers (trumpet), Art Pepper, Bud Shank, Lee Konitz, Lennie Neihaus (altos), Bob Cooper, Bill Perkins (tenors), Laurindo Almeida (guitar), and Shelly Manne (drums). Unlike the bebop combo where soloists were spotlighted, the primary emphasis in Kenton's bands remained on the ensemble arrangements.

Kenton created a distinct band style that was generally non-swinging concert music with rich harmonies and simple counterpoint. His band was known for its loud performances with glossy trombone timbres and a high-soaring trumpet section. The Kenton style became a tributary of the Third Stream movement. His interest in combining "jazz" and European "classical" music produced scores often requiring French horns, tubas, strings, or Latin-American instruments. Most of his arrangements were elaborate orchestrations with less emphasis directed toward spontaneity. Kenton's style did have a large following among the university "jazz" population as well as off campus.

The "Progressive Jazz" movement was affected by the bebop conceptualization of the musician as an artist rather than an entertainer. Yet it attempted to offer a musical alternative to bop, creating a new school of "jazz" for more conservative listeners interested in a tamer, more "traditional," and non-Afrocentric image of "jazz." It shared its anti-bop sentiment with the cool "jazz" genre that would soon emerge on the West Coast. Both "schools" involved musical styles that were technically less demanding (in terms of instrumental virtuosity) and generally more conservative than bebop. Both progressive "jazz" and cool "jazz" initially appealed to the segment of the "jazz" population who refused to keep pace with the music Bird and Gillespie were producing.

Summary

Isaac Goldberg explores influences early African-American music had on American culture from the time of the spirituals and plantation songs to the minstrel show. Goldberg concludes that without African-American music there would have been no Tin Pan Alley.[71] Bop clearly moved "jazz" back toward an African-American musical paradigm. In his book *Music: Black, White and Blue*, author Ortiz M. Walton discusses elements of the power contained within this brand of modern musical advantage:

> Through the use of ingenious coding techniques having evolved from New Orleans "head arrangements," entire songs could be reduced to a few inches of space, with only chord symbols and the melody or head. This format largely replaced the customary "long hand" sheet music, or written-out arrangements, which had evolved from the days of the big bands. For the white bands, arrangements had been a necessity on two counts. First, reading from arrangements precluded the need for improvisation, an artistic mode virtually intrinsic to Afro-American music culture. Second, elaborate, expensive arrangements resulted in white competitors gaining ascendancy in the industry during the Twenties. They were combined with large personnel, elaborate costumes and music stands, managers, band boys and valets, the effect of which was to seriously disadvantage Afro-American musicians without the financial wherewithal to compete against such "show biz" models. In New York during this era a successful Afro-American orchestra on the order of Vincent Lopez or Paul Whiteman was an exception.

The advantage accorded by the shorthand code system so frequently employed during the bop era was the creation of a musical language that could be understood by both those who could read music as well as those who played by "ear." Although piano music had employed chord symbols before, they had been intended mainly for guitar, and were spread over a considerably greater space. Each measure with its appropriate chord symbols contained not only the melody, but harmony and written-out bass and lyrics. Instead of having to use the somewhat unwieldy sheet music version of a composition, two basic types of coding systems were employed.

> . . . Inasmuch as "standards" (those compositions having greatest popularity during a particular era) were required knowledge of the professional Jazz musician, it was an easy step to

their modified usage in the bop aggregation. This situation allowed for a maximum interchange of players, as in the days of New Orleans Jazz. Jazz players could now, more or less, with a minimum of encumbrance, base their performance on a common store of already available material.[72]

A great percentage of innovative African-American music remains spiritually based music concomitantly concerned with evolving new modes of artistic expression. Human expression cannot be expected to conform to (or be limited by) an audience's set of expectations. The esoteric few who genuinely loved bebop during the 1940s share some traits with the small group of nineteenth-century abolitionists and freedom fighters who ignored the habits and expectations of the majority culture to think as individuals. Human expression manifests as highly unusual artistic manifestations because each individual being is indeed unique. In society, nevertheless, many individuals historically tend to follow the crowd. Bebop artists were not conformists. But another important question remains unanswered. "Why are women becoming increasingly more invisible in the music as the modern 'jazz' evolution marches on?" Linda Dahl says that the "jazz" band leaders during the era of the 1940s

> . . . were silent on the subject of hiring women—perhaps wisely so. Their classical counterparts have been more outspoken. In 1946 Sir Thomas Beecham, the English conductor who founded the London and Royal Philharmonics, asserted that, "women in symphony orchestras constitute a disturbing element. If the ladies are ill-favored, the men do not want to play next to them, and if they are well-favored, the men can't."[73] Three decades later, in 1976, Zubin Mehta, then conductor of the Los Angeles Philharmonic, caused a flurry of protest when he explained that he didn't think women should be in orchestra because "they become men. Men treat them as equals; they even change their pants in front of them. I think it's terrible."[74] The attitude of Sir George Solti comes as something of an oasis in this storm of prejudice. "Players of either sex are good, bad, or mediocre," he wrote. "The argument that women players make a different or inferior sound is just not true. . . . I defy anyone to differentiate between 'male sound' and 'female sound.'"[75] Solti's opinion is emphatically not shared by big-band leader and "jazz" drummer Buddy Rich, who once barked, "I would never hire a chick for my band." And he, along with many other "jazz" band leaders, never did.[76]

Notes

[1] Watson was lecturing for my class at Binghamton University where I was a visiting professor in the spring of 1995. He also gave a concert there later that evening.

[2] T. S. Monk is a former funk and R&B drummer who now plays "jazz."

[3] Al Hunter, Jr., *Philadelphia Daily News*, December 26, 1996 (Features).

[4] Albert Murray, *The Blue Devil of Nada: A Contemporary American Approach to Aesthetic Statement* (New York: Pantheon Books, 1996), p. 134.

[5] *Celebrating Bird: The Triumph of Charlie Parker*, Sony Video, 1987. Based on the book by Gary Giddins (published by William Morrow) of the same title.

[6] Ali A. Mazrui, *The Africans: A Triple Heritage* (Boston: Little, Brown, 1986), pp. 29–30.

[7] Samuel Charters, *The Roots of the Blues: An African Search* (London: Quartet Books, 1982), p. 119.

[8] Ibid., p. 120.

[9] Ibid., pp. 120–21.

[10] "The Concurrence" from a private *Master Monograph* of the Rosicrucian Order. Rosicrucian Park, San Jose, Calif., 95191.

[11] K. Welsh-Asante, *African Culture: Rhythm of Unity* (Wesport, Conn.: Greenwood, 1985).

[12] Molefi Kete Asante, "The Principal Issues in Afrocentric Inquiry," in *African Intellectual Heritage: A Book of Sources*, ed. Molefi Kete Assante and Abu S. Abarry (Philadelphia: Temple University Press, 1996), p. 258.

[13] George Fitzhugh, *Cannibals All! or, Slaves Without Masters*, ed. Woodward, C. Vann. (Cambridge: Belknap, 1982), *Commentary*.

[14] *Down Beat,* June 18, 1952.

[15] Milt Hinton, David G. Berger, and Holly Maxson, *OverTime* (1991).

[16] Dizzy Gillespie, *American Way 21*, September 15, 1990.

[17] James Lincoln Collier, *Jazz: The American Theme Song* (New York: Oxford University Press, 1993), pp. 212–14.

[18] Gary Giddins, *Celebrating Bird: The Triumph of Charlie Parker* (New York: William Morrow, 1987), p. 58.

[19] Dizzy talks about Bird in the documentary video *Celebrating Bird: The Triumph of Charlie Parker*, Sony Video, 1987.

[20] Benny Green, *The Reluctant Art: Five Stories in the Growth of Jazz* (New York: Da Capo, 1990), pp. 182–83.

[21] Michael Levin and John S. Wilson, "No Bop Roots in Jazz: Parker, Charlie." *Down Beat* 61, no. 2 (February 1994): 24–26; originally September 9, 1949.

[22] *The Reluctant Art: Five Stories in the Growth of Jazz.*

[23] Giddins, *Celebrating Bird,* p. 10.

[24] Owens' ideas about formulaic construction seem closely allied to those Barry Kernfeld and other writers who rely heavily upon the term "formulaic" in their research. See Barry Kernfeld, "Adderley, Coltrane, and Davis at the Twilight of Bebop: The Search for Melodic Coherence (1958–59)" (Ph.D. dissertation, Cornell University, 1981).

[25] Thomas Owens, *Bebop: The Music and Its Players* (New York: Oxford University Press, 1995), p. 30.

[26] Kernfeld uses the term "unbearable"in his dissertation to describe Coltrane's use of a motive on one of his recordings.

[27] Ibid.

[28] Gillespie in the *San Francisco Chronicle*, January 27, 1957.

[29] Martha Bayles, *Hole in Our Soul* (New York, The Free Press, 1994), pp. 89–93.

[30] Giddins, *Celebrating Bird*, p. 19.

[31] Doubling-up is the ability to play twice as fast as the prevailing tempo.

[32] Giddins, *Celebrating Bird,* pp. 39–40.

[33] Ortiz M. Walton, *Music: Black White & Blue*, p. 98.

[34] Billie Holiday, "Don't Blame Show Biz!" *Down Beat* 61, no. 2 (February 1994): 22–23.

[35] Miles Davis with Quincy Troupe, *Miles: The Autobiography* (New York: Simon and Schuster, 1989), pp. 238–39.

[36] Bill Crow, *Jazz Anecdotes,* 1990.

[37] Gene Lees, "Waiting for Dizzy, Parts I and II," *Jazzletter* 8 (August and September 1989).

[38] Art Taylor, *Notes and Tones.*

[39] Reissued on Gillespie's Prestige album *In the Beginning.* 1973.

[40] Paul F. Berliner, *Thinking Jazz: The Infinite Art of Improvisation* (Chicago: University of Chicago Press, 1994), p. 29.

[41] Ibid.

[42] John S. Wilson, "Bird Wrong; Bop Must Get A Beat: Diz," *Down Beat* 61, no. 2 (February 1994): 27; originally October 7, 1949.

[43] Monk in *Down Beat*, April 21, 1966.

[44] Leonard Feather, liner notes to *The Fabulous Fats Navarro*, LP—Blue Note Records, GXK 8061.

[45] Ibid.

[46] D. Antoinette Handy, *Black Women in American Bands and Orchestras*, p. 136.

[47] "What Happened to Melba Liston?" *Ebony Magazine*, June 1977, p. 122.

[48] Ian Carr, Digby Fairweather, and Brian Priestly, *Jazz: The Rough Guide* (London: Rough Guides Ltd., 1995), p. 390.

[49] Chris Albertson, liner notes to *Howard McGhee: That Bop Thing*, LP—Bethlehem BCP-6039.

[50] Len Lyons, *The Great Jazz Pianists* (New York: Da Capo, 1983), pp. 146–47.

[51] Laurent De Wilde, *Monk*, trans. Jonathan Dickinson (New York: Marlowe, 1997), p. 206.

[52] As quoted in Owens, *Bebop*, p. 145.

[53] Handy, *Black Women in American Bands and Orchestras*, p. 162.

[54] Robert Gottlieb, ed., *Reading Jazz* (New York: Pantheon Books, 1996), p. 116.

[55] Ibid.

[56] Handy, *Black Women in American Bands and Orchestras*, pp. 184–85.

[57] "Wild but Polished," *Time*, November 3, 1958, p. 78.

[58] Ibid.

[59] Liner notes, *Women in Jazz: Pianists*, Stash, ST-112.

[60] Sarah Vaughan, interview by Barbara Gardner, *Down Beat,* March 2, 1961.

[61] Sarah Vaughan, interview by Don Gold, *Down Beat,* May 30, 1957.

[62] Linda Dahl, *Stormy Weather*, pp. 140–41.

[63] Ibid., pp. 140–42.

[64] Ibid., pp. 142–43.

[65] Quoted in Sammy Mitchell, "The Magic of Carmen McRae," *Down Beat*, December 12, 1968.

[66] Sally Plackson, *Jazzwomen* (London: Pluto, 1982), pp. 134–37.

[67] *Stormy Weather*, p. 262.

[68] Ibid.

[69] Ibid.

[70] Ibid.

[71] Isaac Goldberg, *Tin Pan Alley* (New York: John Day, 1930), p. 32.

[72] Ortiz M. Walton, *Music: Black, White & Blue*, pp. 98–106.

[73] As cited in *Stormy Weather*, pp. 47–48; "A Critical Briton Has a Gentle 'Go' at Us," *New York Times Magazine,* July 14, 1946. A rebuttal by conductor Hans Kindler of Washington, D.C., included the following statement: "The women in the orchestras I have . . . conducted, not only in my own National Symphony Orchestra, but recently in Mexico City, Guatemala, Panama, Chile, Peru and Canada as well, proved themselves to be not only fully equal to the men, but to be sometimes more imaginative and always especially cooperative" (*New York Times,* October 20, 1946).

[74] Quoted in *Newsweek*, March 8, 1976. The feminist Women Musicians Collective subsequently picketed concerts of the Los Angeles Philharmonic.

[75] As cited in *Stormy Weather*, pp. 47–48. Letter to the editor, *London Times*, June 22, 1975. Solti had a distinguished predecessor in Leopold Stokowski, who said in 1916, "An in-

comprehensible blunder is being made in our exclusion of women from symphony orchestras. . . . When I think of women as I see them in the musical world, what they are capable of doing, their fine spirit, excellent technic [sic], I realize what a splendid power we are letting go to waste in this country and in other countries, too" (quoted in Frederique Petrides, "Women in Orchestras," *The Etude,* July 1938).

[76] *Stormy Weather*, pp. 47–48.

IX
Innovators Emerging Between 1950 and 1960

My cheeks started bulging out. I didn't get any physical pain from it, but all of a sudden, I looked like a frog whenever I played. I hadn't always played like that. . . . It was technically incorrect for playing with a symphony orchestra; but for what I wanted, it was perfectly correct.

—Dizzy Gillespie

Continued Resistance to African-American Freedom

Although art often reflects the environment in which it resides, it can also provide a social pabulum enabling people to deflect controversial, embarrassing, or uncomfortable conditions. On the surface, "cool jazz" and other musical styles that evolved during the 1950s were less volatile than bebop. Nonetheless, the "strange fruit" Billie Holiday sang about continued to be a reality with which African Americans had to deal. The death of Emmett Till in 1955 reminded us that imperious, sanguineous, and pandemoniac behavior was still very much a part of the American way of life.

Emmett Till was a fourteen-year-old African-American boy from Chicago who was unaccustomed to the racist apartheid practiced in the deep South when he visited his uncle Mose Wright (a preacher) in Money, Mississippi. Emmett had graduated from an integrated school where he felt comfortable with friends of all races.

While on vacation in Mississippi one Sunday in August, while Wright delivered his sermon from the pulpit, Emmett slipped away with his young cousins from church and drove down the road to a grocery store that catered primarily to an African-American clientele. Emmett was dressed in dress slacks, wore a tie, and was a handsome young man. A twenty-one-year-old European-American woman named Carolyn Bryant, who was working as a clerk in the store, later testified that Emmett whistled at her. Mose said his sons told him that Emmett merely told the woman that she was pretty.[1]

Regardless of the exact nature of the verbal exchange that day, Carolyn's husband (Roy Bryant) and his friend, J. W. Moses, forcefully abducted Emmett from the Wright's home later that week and told him, "Boy, you ain't never goin' to see the sun come up again."[2] The men then took Till at gunpoint to a barn in nearby Sunflower County and proceeded to bludgeon the boy with heavy clubs for an extended period of time before tying his dead, distorted body to a cotton gin exhaust fan (weighing almost a hundred pounds) and submerging him in the Tallahatchie River. When a seventeen-year-old fisherman discovered Emmett Till and the local authorities recovered the body, his head was no longer recognizable as human.

Bryant and Milam then ordered the Wrights to bury young Bo (Emmett) three hours after the body was found, telling them, "Don't let the sun go down and that body is out of the ground." He had not even been embalmed. Mrs. Wright shipped the body to Till's mother in Chicago instead. He was the third African-American boy to be murdered in the area within three months. Mamie Till, Bo's mother, refused to allow the undertaker to alter the young Till's appearance for the funeral. She wanted the world to see what had been done to her only son. Reportedly hundreds of thousands of people marched past the open casket in Chicago at A. A. Rayner & Sons Funeral Home.

The trial began Monday, September 19, in Sumner, Mississippi. A surprise witness, Willie Reed was brought forth. He was an eighteen-year-old boy who had heard Till's screams and had positively identified Milam. The Leflore County sheriff, George Smith, testified that one of the defendants admitted abducting Till. Mose Wright also identified the alleged murderers, yet the all-European-American jury found both Bryant and Milam innocent after only an hour and seven minutes. One juror said, "If we hadn't stopped to drink pop, it wouldn't have taken that long."[3] Later, the entire Sumner County bar admitted that sufficient evidence had been presented to convict the pair. Jurors also later confessed that all members of the panel knew the pair was guilty. The African-American community was outraged. The American Jewish Committee sent a seven-page memo from its Paris office to New York stating, "Europe's reaction to the trial and the verdict in Sumner, Mississippi, was swift, violent and universal. There was total and unqualified condemnation of the court proceedings, of the weakness of the prosecution, the behavior of the jury and the judge, and at the verdict for acquittal."[4]

Changes

Many musicians in the late 1940s and early 1950s tailored new styles for themselves that served to express their ideas within the limits of their own technique, temperament, and personal musical aspirations. Miles Davis began moving in his own direction and found a slower, cooler "jazz" more natural for his particular brand of genius to develop. Parker remained a part of his musical world, but Miles was then in control of his own musical destiny. In his autobiography, Miles gives the reader a glimpse of this transition.

> Nineteen fifty-three began all right with me making a record for Prestige with Sonny Rollins (who had gotten out of jail), Bird (who appeared on the album as "Charlie Chan"), Walter Bishop, Percy Heath, and Philly Joe Jones on drums (who I was hanging with a lot at the time). Bird had an exclusive contract with Mercury (I think he had left Verve by then), so he had to use a pseudonym on record. Bird had given up shooting heroin because since Red Rodney had been busted and sent back to prison at Lexington, Bird thought the police were

watching him. In place of his normal big dosages of heroine, now he was drinking an enormous amount of alcohol. I remember him drinking a quart of vodka at the rehearsal, so by the time the engineer was running the tape for the session, Bird was fucked up out of his mind.

It was like having *two* leaders at the session. Bird treated me like I was his son, or a member of *his* band. But this was *my* date and so I had to get him straight. It was difficult, because he was always on my back about one thing or another. I got so angry with him that I told him off, told him that I had never done that to him on one of his recording sessions. Told him that I had always been professional on his shit. And do you know what that motherfucker said to me? He told me some shit like, "All right, Lily Pons . . . to produce beauty, we must suffer pain—from the oyster comes the pearl." He said that to me in that fucked-up, fake British accent. Then, the motherfucker fell asleep. I got so mad all over again that I started fucking up. Ira Gitler, who was producing the record for Bob Weinstock, came out of the booth and told me *I* wasn't playing shit. At this point, I was so fed up that I started packing up my horn to leave when Bird said to me, "Miles, what are you doing?" So I told him what Ira had said, and Bird said, "Ah, come on Miles, let's play some music." And so we played some real good stuff after that.[5]

The idea of a "producer" in innovative African-American music is an interesting phenomenon. During most of the time producers have been associated with "Black" music, they have rarely been knowledgeable about the music they are "producing"; they merely have access to the money needed to cover the costs involved in a recording session. Stravinsky, Bernstein, or Cage never had producers calling the shots in their recording sessions. In a racist society where African Americans are systematically ostracized from the American economic infrastructure, the "plantation" and carpetbagger mentalities inherited from the slave and reconstruction eras persists in the formation of the numerous "middleman" occupations that traditionally leech off the labor of creative African-American musicians. Because their positions go unchallenged (because musicians need work and have few alternatives beyond the modern "plantation store"), people like Ira Gitler become very arrogant and deluded in regards to their professional relevance to the music created. The music evolves regardless of whether Gitler is involved, but the musical direction would be severely altered if Miles and Bird had actually left the session.

Hard bop produced a sound that was more aggressive, darker, simpler melodically, and slower paced harmonically than bebop. The drums are more freely expressive. The hard bop pianist places even greater emphasis on the right hand than bop pianists do. On the West Coast, music became more reserved, less experimental, and more mellow; "cool" rather than "hot" in musical disposition. The social environment in America during that period included the baby boom and an intensified emphasis on structure and social conformity. It was generally a more conservative (and male-dominated) decade than the 1940s. Women gradually disappeared from the workforce in post–World War II years and disappeared from the big bands with whom they played during the 1930s and 1940s. The film *Rosie the Riveter* and other documentaries covering women's roles in American society during those eras clearly portray the social tendencies. Such documentation addressed the styles and forms of propaganda that persuaded American society that women should be confined to the home, taking care of their family's domestic responsibilities. *Rosie the Riveter* also sheds light on the economic elements that served as the catalyst for this movement toward sexist indoctrination.

Art forms are not constantly stable but, rather, are continuously evolving, changing, and reflecting the world in which they exist. The essence of spontaneous art forms is missed when too much attention is focused strictly on analyzing chord progressions or searching for formulaic devices. In focusing exclusively on such an approach, other crucial factors involving personal expression and intuitiveness are eliminated. Miles talks about Bird's approach to music:

> Bird would play the melody he wanted. The other musicians had to remember what he played. He was real spontaneous, went on his instinct. He didn't conform to Western ways of musical group interplay by organizing everything. Bird was a great improviser and that's where he thought great music came from and what great musicians were about. His concept was "fuck what's written down." Play what you know and play that well and everything will come together—just the opposite of Western concept of notated music.[6]

Miles and Bird were the members of the first generation of African-American innovators to develop their music largely outside the African-American cultural milieu. When "jazz" moved downtown into a sometimes, hostile setting out of financial necessity, more impersonal presentation styles or terse aspects of the music emerged, displaying levels of musical and social defiance as a result. The confidence and independence that bebop produced enabled modern musicians to withstand negative consequences of their sociocultural transition.

Harlem produced a phenomenal array of cultural manifestations despite economic disadvantages. In the typical urban American setting, an area like Harlem is economically destined to be a slum where cheap labor is exploited when needed by the more affluent citizens in an area, then discarded after the labor is deemed no longer necessary. Slums are not supposed to produce art forms that influence and modify the entire world. Although it has struggled against shortages of money, security, and political respect, early twentieth-century Harlem has always successfully resisted becoming a slum. Instead it became a community that fostered powerful twentieth-century music, culture, and political thought that influenced social behavior throughout the globe. The Apollo, the Harlem Globetrotters, Marcus Garvey, and other names wielded influence far beyond the United States borders.

European composers began to abandon functional tonality near the end of the nineteenth century. From Richard Wagner's *Prelude to Tristan and Isolde* (1859) (where the listener's awareness of a single nuclear tonal center is reoriented) to more radical adjustments made by the composers of the second Viennese School (Anton von Webern, Alban Berg, and Arnold Schoenberg), efforts aimed toward migrating further from tonal concepts were explored. One method involved devising systems (twelve-tone and serial composition) where no one tone within a set of tones serves as a gravitational tonic.

In the early 1950s, George Russell, Buddy Collette, Gunther Schuller, Jimmy Giuffre, and others used serial techniques in their "jazz" compositions. The Modern Jazz Quartet began to compose and perform music that incorporated instruments such as flutes, cellos, violins, and other instruments usually associated with European chamber music in some of their pioneering work. Gunther Schuller coined the term "third stream jazz" to describe the stylistic movement launched by the Modern Jazz Quartet that fused elements of European "classical" music and "jazz." The quartet (featuring pianist John Lewis [b. 1920], vibraphonist Milt Jackson [1923–1999], bassist Percy Heath [b. 1923], and drummer Kenny Clarke [1914–85] was formed from members of the Dizzy Gillespie Big Band. They moved from Gillespie's big band bebop style to a more restrained and subtle sound associated with "cool jazz" of the 1950s. Of all the musicians who followed the third stream "jazz" line of innovation, the Modern Jazz Quartet came closest to moving beyond a fusion of styles, while still managing to sound less circumspect and self-conscious than most other Third Stream experiments. Other innovators (John Coltrane, for instance) realized that the blues and other modern forms of African-American music had always been styles that "used all twelve tones," but preferred organizing their musical systems in a more intuitive compositional manner.

Mal Waldron developed a style that merged the Silver and Monk approaches to hard bop with his own lyricism. Many hard bop players came to New York from Philadelphia and Detroit.

Among the important hard bop innovators were Sonny Rollins (tenor sax), John Coltrane (tenor/soprano sax), Horace Silver (piano), Cannonball Adderley (alto sax), Art Blakey (drums), Clifford Brown (trumpet), and Wes Montgomery (guitar).

Miles Davis and "Cool Jazz"

Miles Davis began performing professionally during the summer of 1944 while still a teenager in his hometown of St. Louis. When the Billy Eckstine band came to town with Charlie Parker, Gene Ammons, Lucky Thompson, Art Blakey, and other illustrious members, Miles had the good fortune to substitute for one of it's ailing trumpet players. When he later arrived in New York City he replaced Dizzy Gillespie in a band he and Charlie Parker shared. He eventually developed a midrange style that was technically less demanding than Gillespie's, but served as a catalyzing nexus for some of the most innovative music and musicians of the second half of the twentieth century.

Miles Davis (Photo courtesy of HRP Library).

Davis attended casual sessions in Gil Evan's basement apartment where he collaborated with Evans, John Lewis, Gerry Mulligan, and others to produce music at a slower tempo with relaxed solos that were technically much more accessible for most musicians than bebop. Although the era of "cool jazz" eventually began to take root on the West Coast and with a specific set of players (including Lennie Tristano and Lee Konitz), the term was most probably coined when Miles organized his historic session, in collaboration with Gil Evans and Gerry Mulligan, to produce the album *Birth of the Cool* (1949–50). The orchestration of "cool jazz" was sometimes different from that of bebop because it occasionally used an augmented instrumentation that included the tuba and French horn, producing unusual timbres. It stood apart from the big band sound because there were generally no homogenous sections.

The main advocates of the "cool" movement were Miles Davis, Stan Getz, Lee Konitz, and Gerry Mulligan. With Miles, the early "quasi-modal" experiments ("Milestones," "So What!," "Flamenco Sketches") were subjected to a gradual process of development into a mature experimental style such as that heard on the album *Nefertiti*, in free fission experiments like *Pangaea*; and even on fusion albums like *TuTu*.

Some "cool" musicians were influenced by Lennie Tristano and Claude Thornhill. The movement along that stylistic line flourished primarily on the West Coast, where several important groups of European-American musicians congregated in Los Angeles. Some "cool jazz" musicians used bop as its principal structure. Much of the resulting music often adopted a more transparent, Lester Young–influenced style, while conspicuously avoiding obvious characteristics of Charlie Parker's style. Emphasis was often directed toward arranging and composing and less on individual virtuosity. Some talented artists of the "West Coast" style eventually redirected their interest in innovative "jazz" experimentation toward more lucrative commercial "jazz" (Buddy Collette, Quincy Jones, and Oliver Nelson were involved in music for television and film, for example). Film scores also provided a creative outlet and attracted many capable "jazz" musicians on the West Coast because it provided steady and comfortable income. This was a practical move that was useful in popularizing the "cool jazz" movement.

"Deception" (recorded March 9, 1950) was composed and arranged by Davis. The instrumentation for the date included Davis (trumpet), J. J. Johnson (trombone), Gunther Schuller (French horn), John Barber (tuba), Lee Konitz (alto saxophone), G. Mulligan (baritone saxophone), Al McKibbon (bass), Max Roach (drums), and Kenny Hagood (vocals). Miles, Evans, and Mulligan explored a mixture of styles, all of which focused upon seeking freedom and new approaches to conceptual unity. The discovery of a new musical sensitivity within the Miles Davis Nonet marked the beginning of a series of experiments with timbre and orchestration for the iconoclastic trumpeter.

Over the next few decades Davis led a series of innovative groups which included many illustrious young innovators of the "jazz" world. His remarkable sextet in 1957 introduced John Coltrane to a broader audience. Later collaborations with Gil Evans produced such albums as *Porgy and Bess* and *Sketches of Spain*, expanding the *Birth of the Cool* idea into a full orchestral setting. Davis' 1959 album *Kind of Blue* was the recording that popularized quasi-modal improvisation in the 1960s, but later in his career he incorporated electronic music, mixing elements of rock, funk, salsa, blues, and "quasi-modal jazz" into his works. His vanguard performances and recordings as leader of experimental groups set the style for subsequent fusion and "jazz"-rock styled experiments. Miles' music attracted young prodigious "jazz" musicians who were willing to explore new musical territories. *Sketches of Spain* and *Flamenco Sketches*, both based upon Latin-American themes, were excursions involving movement away from restrictive changes. Miles and Gil Evans both realized that African-American and Latin American music merged well (just as Dizzy Gillespie realized).

Davis was well grounded in the bebop style, and later led highly successful groups in the hard bop tradition. In his next phase, Miles Davis evolved a compositional approach that allowed the improviser greater freedom to focus on improvised melodies. Compared to the harmonic frameworks of his original "cool" and hard bop tunes, the number of chord changes were reduced drastically in the subsequent styles. Shifting the emphasis toward melody rather than chord changes was related to the compositional approach Ornette Coleman had introduced earlier. Now, Davis and his sidemen like Coleman began to realize that greater coherence between themes, phrases, and motives could be achieved in this more vertically oriented free fashion.

Beginning with the album *Kind of Blue*, Miles began to break the limitations of modern compositions by breaking with the harmonic progression. The term "modal jazz" was applied to this approach, although the musicians rarely confined themselves to the notes of a particular mode. On "So What," Davis stays the closest to the Dorian mode in his cohesive melodic improvisation, which interjects only a few contradictory embellishments to this set of pitches. John Coltrane, in contrast, stretches the "modal" framework suggested by the pitch sets established by the bass melody. The term "modal" does adequately identify the emphasis Davis placed on his horizontal approach to improvisation and composition. The ensemble from this period, often called Miles' Classic Sextet (which included Cannonball Adderley on alto sax, Paul Chambers on bass, and James Cobb on drums and combined the trumpet of Miles Davis with the tenor sax of Coltrane) stretched the suggested modal areas rhythmically and melodically.

In compositions like "So What" Davis and his ensemble demonstrate a "quasi-modal" approach through a relatively static harmonic underpinning involving only a couple of chord changes over a thirty-two-measure cycle. The formal framework is the same as that of the popular song (AABA) but substitutes a single "quasi-modal" pitch set for the usual type of harmonic progression that might accompany each eight-measure phrase. Cannonball Adderley and John Coltrane, who were members of the Davis ensemble during the beginning of the trumpeter's "quasi-modal" experiments, continued to expand along that horizontal direction throughout remainder of their careers. Davis used fewer notes than he played in bebop, caressing the details of individual notes, rhythms, and phrases. This stood out as much as the new compositional process did during a musical period when other musicians were still striving to achieve technical prowess through the fast-paced technical virtuosity and elemental derivatives of bebop.

The length of the composition and its formal structure also eventually became relatively free of preconception in Miles' new approach. Each player had some degree of control over the length of time spent on each harmonic area of the musical construct. In the composition "Flamenco Sketches," Davis signals a new mode by falling silent and letting the bassist lead into the next tonal "modal" area. When aiming to advance to the next modal area, Coltrane signaled this by increasing the number of notes per beat and intensifying the rhythmic and dynamic strata. Adderley begins to embellish the "modal" notes in his melody just before leading the rhythm section into the next "mode."

The seeds for free "jazz" did not begin with "quasi-modal jazz," or with the experiments of Ornette Coleman or Lennie Tristano. It was instead a cumulative evolutionary and revolutionary process that dated back to the dawn of "jazz." This gradual process included the innovations of drummer Zutty Singleton, one of the earliest precursors of varied meters. The innovations in bass playing initiated by Jimmy Blanton and Leroy ("Slam") Stewart freed the bass from a functional role that set the course for the modern requirements of a freer style of bass playing. Thus, the bass became the foundation for spontaneous composition and improvisation. The enormous experimental progression of early pianists included Earl Hines, Teddy Wilson, Art Tatum, Thelonious Monk, and Bud Powell, all of who contributed to the evolutionary movement away from the stride piano style.

The 1950s musical explorations involved a continued expansion upon the modern "jazz" language. Parker developed his solos on compositions such as "Embraceable You" (recorded October 28, 1947) from motives he developed systematically throughout his improvisation, providing organic coherence. Before bebop, Coleman Hawkins, often regarded as primarily a vertical improviser (he outlines chord changes in shaping his solo), demonstrated how lyrical a harmonic approach could become in his classic recording of "Body and Soul." John Lewis and the other members of the Modern Jazz Quartet placed heavy restraints upon their music and combined African-American approaches with European styles to produce what has been called Third Stream or "classical jazz." Dave Brubeck emphasized meter while he, like the Modern Jazz Quartet, diminished the intensity and vitality of the music bebop unleashed. The search for freedom had always remained at the root of the "jazz" tradition, and "jazz" continued to move in an evolutionary fashion in the 1950s.

There were other "cool jazz" and post-bop directions taken during the 1950s. Claude Thornhill, sometimes referred to as the father of the "cool" style big band, influenced Stan Kenton. Kenton became one of the most renowned big band "jazz" arrangers due to his work on college campuses across America. Marian McPartland and Billy Taylor also spread the word about "jazz" to mass America over the next few decades as their musical messages were broadcasted over the radio. From the early 1940s, the Nat King Cole Trio moved from humble beginnings in small nightclubs in Hollywood and New York City to become an international success. Nathaniel Adams "Nat King" Cole (1917–65) was also a featured actor and performer in film, television, and radio. Between 1956 and 1957 he was the only African American in the country hosting his own variety show on network television.[7]

Although Lennie Tristano modeled his personal approach after Art Tatum's piano style, Tristano's music lacked the rhythmic drive and sophistication of bop innovators. In many ways Tristano's melodies were more predictable and less abstract than bebop, yet he avoided the musical complacency to which many "cool" tunes seemed to succumb. Tristano demonstrated yet another fresh and original set of ideas that were carried over into the 1950s.

The success of the "cool" style of Miles Davis, the Dave Brubeck Quartet, the Modern Jazz Quartet, and others during the 1950s might be due to the fact that "cool jazz" involved more easy listening than bebop. Perhaps many people enjoyed it because it did not challenge their ears to the degree bop did. Nevertheless, the music of Miles Davis from this period provides the perfect archetypes for both "cool" and "modal" stylistic approaches during the 1950s. Miles continued to explore new musical forms and revolt against conventional and conservative ideas. Innovative African-American music has always been progressive. Wayne Shorter once described Miles in unusual terms:

To sum up Miles, I like to call him right now an original Batman. He was a crusader for justice and for value. He'd be Miles
Dewey Davis III by day, the son of Dr. Davis, and at night in
the nightclubs he's in lizard skin suits with dark shades and
he's doing his Batman—fighting for truth and justice. But
Batman had to be a dual personality too, like he knew the
criminal mind. So Miles, whatever he did that was not criminal
but like short-tempered or he cursed everybody out, and when
he was younger he'd hit somebody, or like they say Miles
treated some woman really bad, or something like that. . . . I
would say that Bruce Wayne, the guy that played Batman, he
was capable of doing that too, that's why he was such a good
Batman.[8]

Miles Davis indeed introduced the definitive cool style to the world,
but his career encompassed a much broader range of innovative directions.
After his sextet featuring, Coltrane and Cannonball Adderley separated,
Davis formed another incredible ensemble (this time a quintet) with Wayne
Shorter, Tony Williams, Herbie Hancock, and Ron Carter during the 1960s.
He later experimented with "jazz"/rock/fusion at the beginning of the 1970s
before retreating into a self-imposed exile in 1975. By the 1980s Miles was
again experimenting on the "jazz" scene. He never ceased seeking new sounds
and directions.

Louis Jordan and Sonny Rollins

Louis Jordan was a world-renowned alto saxophonist, vocalist, and
bandleader born in Brinkley, Arkansas, on July 8, 1908. After moving to New
York City, he eventually joined forces with drummer Chick Webb's band.
Jordan gained prominence in the world of rhythm-and-blues in the Big Apple.
Webb featured Jordan as both a vocalist and saxophone soloist between 1936
and 1938.

The "jump band" was a small swing band that developed between the
late 1930s and early 1950s. It generally featured two or three soloists in front
of a swinging rhythm section. It was appealing to the African-American cabaret audiences because it retained the sexual and nuptial humor of the music
from old "Black" vaudeville shows.

In 1938 Jordan ventured out to form his own "jump band," playing and
recording with many of the giants of the music industry, such as Bing Crosby
(1944), Ella Fitzgerald (1945 and 1949), Louis Armstrong (1950), and various
other artists. During these years his combo enjoyed a steady rise to national
and international fame. His combo, known as the "Timpani Five," released
many successful singles in the forties such as "Knock Me a Kiss," "Gonna
Move to the Outskirts of Town," and "Choo Choo Ch' Boogie" (which sold over
a million copies). Jordan broke into show business with his unique combination of visual showmanship, superb musicianship, a strong accent on humor,
and a delightfully original and rhythmic vocal style. Jordan's vocal technique
often incorporated an alternation between head and chest voice ("falsetto

break") related to styles found in vocal music in various regions of Africa, south of the Sahara. He organized a big band for a tour in the fall of 1951 and occasionally augmented his combo for theater dates, but Jordan was primarily a small combo performer by preference. Though Louis Jordan's music remained closer to "jazz," he is generally considered to be the progenitor of rhythm-and-blues.

Louis Jordan performing with the student ensembles (Karlton E. Hester, Director) at Eisenhower High School in 1973 (Photo courtesy of HRP Library).

Louis Jordan (right) with Karlton E. Hester (left) and Eisenhower High School student Debbie Reynolds in 1973 (Photo courtesy of HRP Library).

Theodore Walter Rollins is a "jazz" improviser and composer of significant skill who has always generated a powerful and ascetic tenor saxophone style that seems closely related to his personal lifestyle. Sonny Rollins was born in New York in 1930. Both his brother and sister played musical instruments, and Sonny started his musical studies on piano. He took up the saxophone after being influenced by the sound of Louis Jordan.

In addition to Jordan's hard-swinging influence on Rollins, the younger saxophonist was also fortunate enough to live in the same neighborhood with Coleman Hawkins, Thelonious Monk, and Bud Powell. Hawkins and Monk befriended Rollins and showed him things about bebop music. Of course, Sonny Rollins also came under the spell of Charlie Parker. He recorded his first record for the Capital label, *St. Louis Blues*, in 1948 with Babs Gonzales.

The following year he went into the studio with Bud Powell and Fats Navarro. In 1950 he joined drummer Ike Day in Chicago, an infrequently recorded musician who Rollins considers one of the greatest drummers of all time.[9] Miles Davis, who already developed a considerable reputation at the time, heard the tenor saxophonist in a club in Harlem one night after Rollins returned to New York. Their first recordings together were released on the Prestige record label in 1951. By the end of that year Rollins recorded his first album as a leader. He did not record again with Miles over the next couple years, but performed on recording sessions with Thelonious Monk, Charlie Parker (on tenor), and the Modern Jazz Quartet.

Rollins made important recordings with Miles Davis in 1954. His composition "Oleo," recorded during this period, became a "jazz" standard. After this productive musical phase, and during the height of a battle between critics over whether he or Coltrane was the "best" tenor player of the day, Rollins took the first of many long sabbaticals from public performance. It is interesting that *Down Beat* and other magazines continue to debate the "value" of musicians with their "Readers Polls" and "Critics' Polls" but have never considered the perspectives of the musicians themselves important enough to warrant the founding of a "Musicians' Poll." This neglect is quite an instructive barometer in calculating the levels of arrogance, disrespect, and delusion that Miles, Coltrane, Rollins, and other professional artists encountered in a racist society. Many artists suffer at the hand of the critic, regardless of race, but the levels of pompousness and irrationality found in early literature devoted to African-American music can be startling and embarrassing.

Rollins used the mid-1950s to kick his heroine addiction and returned to the scene in 1955 joining the Clifford Brown–Max Roach Quintet (replacing tenor saxophonist Harold Land, who returned to California). Rollins said, "Clifford was a profound influence on my personal life. He showed me that it was possible to live a good clean life, and still be a good jazz musician."[10] Rollins was playing better than ever in the Brown-Roach ensemble, but then Clifford Brown was killed, on June 26, 1956, in an automobile accident. Donald Byrd briefly took over the trumpet position and was followed by Kenny Dorham. Parker died the year before, and Max Roach left the group the following year. Rollins still managed to record some of the work for which he is best known, such as *Misterioso* (with Thelonious Monk) and his own *Saxophone Colossus* (with pianist Tommy Flanagan and bassist Doug Watkins).

In 1957 Rollins recorded *Way Out West* with Max Roach in a pianoless setting. Ray Brown was on bass and Shelly Manne was the drummer. Rollins' willingness to take a popular song of any kind as an improvisational vehicle has become his trademark. In expressing his feelings about music he said:

> I think eventually that there won't be jazz any more or classical music, but one big music, in which everyone can play what he feels. What they call the third stream is a beginning at that, but the writers haven't left these people alone to work their problems out for themselves. They aren't ready to be analyzed yet. Of course, the real beginning of that attempt is Duke Ellington. Monk is an extension of Duke, I think, and Duke is the unsung giant of American music. I spoke to someone recently who had seen Ellington and Duke said that he had heard some of my records and liked the way I played. Can you imagine how I felt about Ellington saying something like that? I've recorded as many of his songs as I could. Perhaps he heard one of those.[11]

John Coltrane and Other New Approaches to Spontaneous Composition

With the conceptual and technical consolidation of the approaches of Lester Young and Coleman Hawkins with the influence Charlie Parker, the stage was set for a new order of saxophone evolution in the fifties. Dexter Gordon combined elements of Hawkins, Young, and Parker; while Sonny Stitt combined Young and Parker influences to create a synergistic style that served as one of the forerunners of hard bop. It was John Coltrane and Sonny Rollins, however, who ushered in the most influential and distinctive proto-types for "jazz" tenor saxophone after the Young-Hawkins-Parker tradition.

Rollins followed Young's influence more closely. His style emphasized melodic and thematic improvisation, but also involved a big, full sound (characteristic of Hawkins) and an impelling rhythmically driven melodic approach (a Parker trait). Coltrane seem to take more cues from Hawkins. From the beginning of his career, Trane was inclined to employ a systematic and sophisticated harmonic approach (as did Hawkins). His tone quality was centered and had an almost brittle edge that produced a timbre close to the sound quality of the alto sax (which was related to the sound Young and Parker produced). Coltrane's employed a more impetuous rhythmic freedom, involving uneven grouping of notes (a tendency found in works of both Parker and Young).

Both the Rollins and Coltrane style involved many gradual modifications. Initial influences attributed to Young and Hawkins were blurred at times before resurfacing periodically during their various stylistic periods of development. Coltrane was also instrumental in the resurgence of the soprano saxophone. Coltrane's long progression of musical achievements are heard on over a hundred LP and CD recordings and include pivotal performances such as *Kind of Blue* (with Miles Davis), his own *Giant Steps*, *A Love Supreme*, and *Selflessness* later in his career. Rollins' skills and inventiveness are displayed in the albums *Strode Rode*, *Saxophone Colossus*, and *The Freedom Suite*. A few of the musicians displaying the influence of both Rollins and Coltrane are Dexter Gordon, Charlie Rouse, Joe Farrell, Jimmy Heath, Johnny Griffin, George Coleman, Benny Golson, Joe Henderson, Sam Rivers, Yusef Lateef, Wayne Shorter, Frank Foster, David Murray, Branford Marsalis, and Pharoah Sanders.

Charlie Parker innovations also found counterparts in the late fifties and early sixties in the work of Ornette Coleman and Eric Dolphy. Coleman revolutionized the approach to small group improvisation while challenging the tonal and harmonic regularities of the hard bop and "cool" schools of "jazz." Coleman is credited with the founding of the "Free Jazz" school. Dolphy pushed the borderlines of harmony and tonal textures, while bringing the bass clarinet and flute to new heights in the modern "jazz" milieu. Along with the pioneering work of flutists such as Wayman Carver, Buddy Collette, and Herbie Mann, Dolphy's work on flute was paramount in the evolution of the flute into a genuine "jazz" instrument.

A synthesis of the styles generated by the new saxophone dynasty (Coltrane-Rollins-Coleman) set the musical agenda for the primary approaches in "jazz" extant until the end of the twentieth century. Musicians such as Julius Hemphill, Dewey Redman, Branford Marsalis, Oliver Lake, Joshua Redman, Bobby Watson, David Murray, and Arthur Blythe can trace their approaches back to these three saxophonists. But the single most influential saxophonist after Charlie Parker was John Coltrane.

John William Coltrane was born in Hamlet, North Carolina, on the equinox, September 23, 1926. His mother, Alice Blair, and his father, John R. Coltrane, were both minister's children and amateur musicians.

When Coltrane was twelve, he began studying the E-flat alto horn (a brass wind instrument) with Reverend Steele, who formed a community band. He later changed to the clarinet. His mother soon bought him a used alto saxophone for his birthday. "Jazz" composer/performer Benny Golson recalls Coltrane's "exquisite sound" around that time as "even bigger than Johnny Hodges's."[12] In addition to Hodges, it was Lester Young and Coleman Hawkins who made the biggest impression on the young Coltrane.

"Any time you play your horn, it helps you," Coltrane said regarding his stay with Earl Bostic in 1952. His move to the group led by Johnny Hodges in 1953 was a more productive one. "We played honest music in this band," he recalled, "it was my education to the older generation."[13]

Following his productive musical association with Bostic, Coltrane continued to develop a sound knowledge of earlier "jazz" forms. He performed with the Dizzy Gillespie Big Band and was among the few carefully selected sidemen asked to play with Gillespie's new combo when the big band broke up at the end of 1950. Gillespie's ensemble included vibraphonist Milt Jackson, alto saxophonist Jimmy Heath, bassist Percy Heath, drummer Specs Wright, and Fred Strong on conga drums.

In September 1955 Sonny Rollins disappeared from the "jazz" scene "like he said he would," and Miles could not track him down. In trying to find a replacement for him, Davis tried John Gilmore (who was playing with Sun Ra at the time) but he didn't fit Miles' needs. Philly Joe Jones recommended Coltrane, with whom both Miles and Rollins had performed at the Audubon a few years prior. Miles felt that Sonny had "blown him [Coltrane] away that night," so Miles was not extremely excited about Coltrane as a prospect. Much to his surprise, however, Coltrane "had gotten a lot better" in the interim.[14]

Miles and Coltrane did not get along at first. Frustrated, Coltrane left for home only to accept another invitation to rejoin Davis' band later the same year. While Miles produced some of his best work with pianist Red Garland, bassist Paul Chambers, drummer Philly Joe Jones, and later, alto saxophonist Julian "Cannonball" Adderley, it was Coltrane who most radically shaped his style. Gradually Coltrane's style became more confident and progressively more assertive, while his now distinguished full tone acquired a hard resilient sound. Some "jazz" historians feel that the period of "Cannonball" Adderley's association with Miles and Coltrane marked Davis' creative peak.[15]

Although Miles and Coltrane utilized contrasting musical approaches to performance, they shared important general mutual aspirations and worked along similar lines to achieve their objectives. During his bebop days, Davis' technique was criticized as suspect; perhaps due to this criticism,

Miles always tended to incorporate a high level of simplicity into his post-bop stylistic approaches. The severance of his solos from standard bop and hard bop chord changes upon which earlier songs were built facilitated his aims, and this initiated the transition into "quasi-modal" and other musical explorations Davis later codified. While Coltrane, on the other hand, continued to emphasize the harmonic functions and potentialities of a given composition, he too began to focus his improvisation upon scales and horizontal dimensions. The resulting "quasi-modal" approach to improvisation was the most significant innovation to occur in "jazz" since bebop. Miles recognized Coltrane's value to this line of development and appreciated fully the gravity of this historic encounter: "The group I had with Coltrane made me and him a legend . . . put me on the map in the music world, with all those great albums we made for Prestige and later Columbia Records. . . . [It] made all of us stars."[16]

John Coltrane at the *Newport Jazz Festival* in 1960.
(Photo by William Claxton. Courtesy of Demont Photo Management).

Musicians who played in the big bands of the 1930s and 1940s were typically showcased only when they were considered advanced enough to take feature solos. Jam sessions were established so musicians could have more informal solo time to display or ameliorate their improvisational skills. Performers were also invited to sit in with groups in the clubs for a similar pedagogical purpose. The need to increase solo time was one of many factors that caused established bebop directions. As the recording industry eventually replaced the 78rpm record with 33 1/3 LP recordings, "jazz" musicians could then play longer solos without having to worry about more restricted time constraints.

Unlike the bebop era, hard bop produced a large number of excellent tenor saxophone players. Just as the trumpet had been the predominant force in early "jazz," Sonny Rollins and John Coltrane made the tenor sax a dominant hard bop force. Their radical stylistic characteristics influenced rhythm sections as well as front-line "jazz" instrumentalists. The late fifties found Rollins employing themes with bi-tonal implications, where the piano was omitted to provide maximum freedom of improvisational interpretation of the harmonic structures. Coltrane's approach was equally exploratory as he continued to discover material that served as a springboard for a significant portion of his later development.

Although tremendous musical growth was achieved, Coltrane was not sufficiently satisfied. He recorded the album *Mating Call* with Tadd Dameron on November 30, 1956, and a third album with Paul Chambers, in addition to his work with Davis. After performing with Miles throughout 1955 and 1956, Coltrane decided to return home to "woodshed" and to resolve personal problems. He managed to quit his drug habit during this break.

Upon returning to New York, Coltrane joined Thelonious Monk and his highly innovative quartet. This proved to be a challenge that would permanently alter Coltrane's approach to music, as his recordings made in 1957 demonstrate. As Coltrane affirms, his conceptual, technical, and creative authority increased dramatically during his collaboration with Monk.

> In 1955, I joined Miles on a regular basis and worked with him 'til the middle of 1957. I went with Thelonious Monk for the remainder of that year.
>
> Working with Monk brought me close to a musical architect of the highest order. I felt I learned from him in every way— through the senses, theoretically, technically. I would talk to Monk about musical problems, and he would sit at the piano and show me the answers just by playing them. I could watch him play and find out the things I wanted to know. Also, I could see a lot of things that I didn't know about at all.
>
> Monk was one of the first to show me how to make two or three notes at one time on tenor. (John Glenn, a tenor man in Philly, also showed me how to do this. He can play a triad and move notes inside it—like passing tones!) It's done by false fingering and adjusting your lip. If everything goes right, you can get tri-

ads. Monk just looked at my horn and "felt" the mechanics of
what had to be done to get this effect.

I think Monk is one of the true greats of all time. He's a real
musical thinker—there're not many like him. I feel myself fortunate to have had the opportunity to work with him. If a guy
needs a little spark, a boost, he can just be around Monk, and
Monk will give it to him.[17]

In contrast to Miles's quintet, Monk's music was more difficult conceptually and based upon densely constructed chords that were innovative, exciting,
and in defiance of traditional song form and blues formats to which Coltrane had
grown accustomed. Even Monk's approach to performance presentation was
iconoclastic. After ending a piano solo, the leader would often leave his piano
bench for more than a half hour, leaving Coltrane to solo alone as Monk ventured out on an uninhibited spiraling and lurching dance to the music. Of course
Monk's repertoire also contained some pieces that adhered to traditional song
form and blues formats, such as "Ruby, My Dear" (song form), "Straight, No
Chaser" (blues), and others.

As Coltrane expanded his harmonic conception in Monk's band, he
also gained independence from restrictions imposed by chords dictated by the
keyboard and traditional stratified functions of the rhythm section. He began
to explore the principles of multiphonics on the tenor saxophone. "[Monk] also
got me into the habit of playing long solos on his pieces, playing the same
piece for a long time to find new conceptions for solos. It got so I would go as
far as possible on one phrase until I ran out of ideas. The harmonies got to be
an obsession for me. Sometimes I'd think I was making music through the
wrong end of a magnifying glass."[18]

Coltrane's music from his late stylistic periods often had religious titles: "A Love Supreme," "Ascension," "Om," "Crescent," "The Father and the
Son, and the Holy Ghost," "Ogunde," "Meditations," "Amen," "Ascent," and
others. His thinking, much as that of Sun Ra, also focused on cosmic principals and outer space: "Infinity," "Interstellar Space," "Sun Ship," "Cosmos,"
"Out of This World," etc.

Coltrane influenced his musical colleague Cannonball Adderley, and
Adderly affected Coltrane's thinking. Adderley developed a personal modern
style even before joining Miles and Coltrane in the Classic Miles Davis Sextet. Independently of the direction Parker carved out, Adderley developed a
virtuoso musical language of his own, grounded in a soulful saxophone style
that grew from his association with Miles and Trane. While not the revolutionary artist Coltrane ended up becoming, Cannonball was one of the first
altoists since Parker to carve out an independent personal style that retained
the technical and expressive qualities of bop, but with the knowledge of a
newer generation directed along a slightly different path. While admitting
that Benny Carter was another important influence, Adderley apparently
worked out his style without falling under the spell of Parker.[19] While most
musicians seem to understand the value of Adderley's musical contribution,
he has generally been underrated by the listening public.

Ornette Coleman

Ornette Coleman was born in Fort Worth, Texas, in 1930. He bought his first alto saxophone at fourteen after being inspired by his cousin, James Jordan, who was a saxophonist. Unable to afford lessons, he taught himself music from a piano book. The anomalies formed through this self instruction would eventually lead Coleman into a quandary. Taking his own approach to music later got him fired, beat up, and thrown out of places in which he performed.

Ornette was chased out of Natchez, Mississippi, because the local police did not like his skin color, long hair, and beard. After finding work in a rhythm-and-blues band in New Orleans with Clarence Samuels, he was invited to meet some men in Baton Rouge. The trip was a pusillanimous and brutal trap in which Coleman lost several teeth and his tenor saxophone. The local crowd apparently didn't like the attention "their" women gave traveling musicians. Coleman's next job was on a tour to California with Pee Wee Crayton. By the time the band reached Los Angeles Crayton was paying Ornette *not* to perform. The saxophonist returned to Texas. Coleman never forgot the racism he encountered in those early days: "Because of being a Negro, I've been in certain places and had certain kinds of sadness that would never bother you, that you could never conceive. Do you think some sadness surpasses a reason why you don't have to be sad?"

Coleman mentioned one European-American man who said to him, "I got enough money to burn a wet elephant but I ain't gonna give it away," and offered Coleman three dollars a performance, which began at 9 PM and ended at 1 AM. Coleman said:

> I thought that as long as they were white, they all had the same thing in common, to control and rule you.... During intermission, I'd have to go in the back and sit down like I was a porter. One night a drunken woman came right up in front of me and raised her dress over her head, and I was frightened ... people in Texas, they're so wealthy, it's still like slavery. You had to be a servant. You had to be something to somebody to make some money.... The Texan thought I was just a mixed up, complexed Negro.[20]

Coleman left Texas to return to California, where he was married. He worked odd jobs as a stock clerk and elevator operator, while continuing to study theory on his own. Trumpeter Don Cherry and bassist Don Payne heard Coleman at a session in Los Angeles and were impressed with his music. They suggested he take his material to Lester Koenig, owner of the Contemporary record label in Los Angeles. Coleman's collaboration with Koenig resulted in his successful debut recordings with that label. Koenig's interest in Coleman's music thus launched the career that would have a tremendous impact on music in the second half of the twentieth century. Coleman became the harbinger of the direction music would take when he made his vision clear in 1958: "Music will be a lot freer. The pattern for a tune, for instance, will be forgotten and the tune itself will be the pattern."[21] Two albums were recorded for Contemporary Records. The first, *The Music of Ornette Coleman: Something Else* (Contemporary S7551, 1958), featured Coleman on alto saxophone, Don Cherry on trumpet, Walter Norris on piano, Don Payne on bass, and Billy Higgins on drums. The second album Coleman recorded before leaving Los Angeles bound for New York was *The New Music of Ornette Coleman: Tomorrow is the Question*, featuring Ornette, Cherry, Red Mitchell and Percy Heath alternating on bass, and Shelly Mann on drums.

Ornette Coleman in Hollywood in 1959.
(Photograph by William Claxton. Courtesy of Demont Photo Management).

Percy Heath, bassist for the Modern Jazz Quartet, heard Coleman one night and later brought his fellow band member (and pianist) John Lewis to hear him. Upon John Lewis's recommendation, Nesuhi Ertegun recorded the first Ornette Coleman records for the Atlantic record label and paid for his scholarship to the Lenox School of Music. Coleman used the advance payment against his royalties for those two albums to move to New York. His harmolodic approach to spontaneous composition was beginning to take shape when Coleman appeared at the Five Spot Cafe in 1959 for his first extended engagement. His group now consisted of Don Cherry (trumpet), Charlie Haden (bass), and Billy Higgins (drums).

Many of his compositions have programmatic titles. Though his debut at New York City's Five Spot Cafe was essentially triumphant, Coleman's skills and concepts were not yet fully matured. Detractors ridiculed him, accusing him of lacking a basic knowledge of harmony. Others raved about his revolutionary sound. Critics did not like his plastic alto, the same kind Charlie Parker had played earlier. Coleman wanted a new Selmer alto saxophone but only had enough money for either a used Selmer or a new plastic alto. Coleman liked the sound of the plastic horn and bought it.

Coleman's experimentation with collective improvisation involved a significant advancement in liberating the melody from preset chord changes. Many hard bop performers aligned their melodic improvisations closely to preset chord structures, while Coleman devised a conceptual methodology that allowed musicians more autonomy. This freedom applied whether an artist was constructing solo improvisations or playing accompaniment.

Cecil Taylor

Although Cecil Taylor always attracted an esoteric audience of fans and curious spectators, this clientele was often not of the type or size that club owners desired. It was neither conducive to selling drinks nor creating the typical bar room ambiance (ripe for conversation, sexual advances, etc.) because Taylor's audience generally listened and didn't want to be disturbed. His was not background music. Taylor's music filled a musical void. He suggests: "The thing that makes jazz so interesting is that each man is his own academy. . . . If he's really going to be persuasive, he learns about other academies, but the idea is that he must have that special thing. And sometimes you don't even know what it is."[22]

If developing a unique and individual voice within a rich tradition of musical innovation and experimentation is adequate criteria for "jazz," then Cecil Taylor is one of those few artists summarily qualified as a unique "jazz" innovator. "You need everything you can get," Duke Ellington once said. "You need the conservatory with an ear to what's happening in the streets."[23] In the 1970 publication of the book *Jazz People* by Valerie Wilmer, the author describes Taylor as "a genius whose work is the jazz, or black, equivalent of straight composers like Bartok."

Whether or not we are inclined to accept maladroit comparisons of artists, clearly Taylor has chosen to view the world strictly through his own eyes. Among initiated innovators of African-American music, it is understood that uncompromising artistic approaches inevitably lead to the creation of unparalleled artistic expression. Anything from Taylor's discography (that spans five decades) demonstrates that he has always maintained his own musical personality, and his music is grounded in solid preparation.

From the beginning of his career, musicians knew that they had to find new ways of thinking about music when performing with Taylor. Drummer Sunny Murray remembered the difficult time he had adjusting to the music Taylor and saxophonist Jimmy Lyons were playing when he worked with them in Europe. He said, "With Cecil, I had to originate a complete new direction on the drums because he was playing different then; he wasn't playing so rhythmically."[24] Preconceived notions about musical style and performance are innocuous in the realm of exploration that Taylor visits.

Cecil Taylor (Photo by Judy Sneed).

Born in Long Island City in 1929, Cecil Taylor's uncle interested him at an early age in stride pianists like Fats Waller. His mother grew up with Sonny Greer (one of Duke Ellington's drummers), but Taylor's influences were wide-ranging. Cecil graduated from the New England Conservatory of Music in Boston before returning to New York. He attempted to launch a career at a time when work for pianists in clubs was scarce. Wilmer mentions the bitter irony that the roughest of Taylor's difficult times landed him in a restaurant as a dishwasher where his own records were played regularly along with those of Ornette Coleman and John Coltrane's.

Adroit practicing quickly led Taylor out of this dire situation into the controversial role of an uncompromising pianist, experimentalist, and composer who, along with Ornette Coleman, Albert Ayler (1936–70), and other innovators, split the international "jazz" community evenly between (1) those who recognized the significance of innovative artists' contributions to the evolution of American musical tradition and (2) those who insisted upon clinging to well-worn standards of days long past. As with most things of authentic quality and lasting value, however, each of the African-American innovators eventually received just recognition. Ayler did not live long enough to witness the benefit of the eventual appreciation for his musical contribution, but both Taylor and Coleman received the prestigious MacArthur "Genius" Award for their work and have continually expanding audiences for their music.

Record companies had little confidence in Cecil Taylor's music during the 1950s, nonetheless. One of Taylor's recordings with John Coltrane made for the United Artists label during 1958 was not released with his name attached, but instead bore the title *Coltrane Time* (October 13, 1958). Coltrane was well established on the Milestones label at the time and had enjoyed a motivating stint with Thelonious Monk at Five Spot. This was only the third record date for Taylor after a decade of harsh criticism. Despite the misleading attribution, the album stands as an important document for both Cecil Taylor and John Coltrane. The Taylor/Coltrane collaboration proved that six months before Ornette Coleman's first recording session the prevailing musical rules were broken and new standards being set in "jazz."

Cecil Taylor did not get his first steady engagement at the Five Spot in New York until 1957 following his first album recording, *Jazz Advance*. His music in the fifties conflicted sharply with previous "jazz" dialects and traditions. It was dismissed (along with the music of Coltrane and Coleman) as "anti-jazz." It was not music that contained the particular variety of "swing" to which people had become accustomed before the 1950s. A more elastic musical force, that was more difficult to pin down, propelled Taylor's music. Ekkehard Jost attempts to describe the "energy" that often served as a foundation for phases of Taylor's compositions in his book *Free Jazz*.

> As time went on, Taylor compensated the "stagnating" motion (also found in Brubeck's music) by a kind of playing whose dynamic impetus arose not from off-beat phrasing but from combining the parameters of time, intensity and pitch, this term is frequently misused as a meaningless catchword for anything that suggests "power." Let's look closer at this term. Energy is not the equivalent to intensity (measured in decibels) as some of my jazz practitioner countrymen, champions of a misunderstood freedom in jazz, often assume. Energy is, more than anything else, a variable of time. It creates motion or results from motion; it means a process in which the dynamic level is just over *one* variable, and by no means a constant. We need not continue analogies to physics here. Suffice it to say that the kinetic impulses emanating from Cecil Taylor's music are based on the rise and fall of energy.[25]

The most salient elements of a musician's compositional process is often best described by the artist who creates it. Cecil Taylor's unique method of describing his music prepares the listener for hearing it. In the liner notes to his album *Unit Structures* (recorded May 19, 1966), Taylor chooses to describe his composition "Anacrusis to Plain" in this metaphorical fashion: "Joint energy disposal in parts of singular feedings. A recharge; group chain reaction. Acceleration result succession of multiple time compression areas. Sliding elision/beat here is physical commitment to earth force. Rude insistence of tough meeting at vertical centers. Time strata thru panels joined sequence a continuum (movements) across nerve centers. Total immersion."

Listening to the music the composer describes is the only way to understand his description of it. In the same set of composer's notes he comments on "Swing":

> The way—cleansed pearl—many nights passed in isolation darkly what works similar effort. The point of view not to be considered—finally an area of action is created logic in adjustment-end material accumulation dottering fidelity to family breeding class/unaccountable time unseen action resultant produce: overlay reaction 2nd murmurs shape/hunger satiated on plain of absolute; self universal compass/language of silent kings-embodiment-ancestral region hero's plain, a "Gilgamesh" to wine lilacs mania on either side. As high relief fancied time or magic struck winds to play and enscribe tzuringas moan-to meaning; hariecha we propagate/foreign images converge upon consciousness: mind converses/with additional reason the mind color gives/overruled political chatisement moments appeased to survive (in)/life of choice within esthetic curve. Creative energy force = swing motor reaction exchange/fused pulse expands measured activity relating series of events.

Taylor forces the listener to understand that music is not about a simple description that makes the audience feel comfortable. Music is about many things. Spontaneous composition often involves many layers of thought and emotional expression. Musical inspiration or purpose could never be as prosaic as many program notes generally suggest.

Cecil Taylor's approach to performance is often interdisciplinary and has often included dance and poetry with music. A collaborative performance was presented at an outdoor concert presented by the Guggenheim Museum in New York on September 17, 1994, with Taylor on piano and featured dancer/choreographer Min Tanaka (with whom Cecil has worked for over ten years). More recently, the press for his landmark performance at Lincoln Center enthusiastically acclaimed the virtuoso pianist. Cecil Taylor's mastery of his own musical domain and dialect has now been witnessed throughout the world for several decades, and much of his solo and ensemble music is preserved on scores of record albums. A few performances can be viewed on video recordings as well.

Sun Ra

Sun Ra was a visionary composer who realized that discipline, creativity and unity formed the foundation over which freedom is constructed. He realized that any group or ensemble must have a designated leader regardless of the degree of freedom the music involved. His musicians performed and expressed their ideas within the context of Sun Ra's philosophical focus, aesthetic values, artistic conceptions, and with the leader's sense of compositional proportion well in mind. The consequence of Sun Ra's brand of stewardship was the production of musical performances devoid of self-centered expression and egoistic competition between individual artists.

Many younger musicians who came through the Arkestra could perhaps not conform to such conditions for long, but the seasoned veterans who remained with Sun Ra throughout their careers understood the social, political, spiritual, and musical implications involved in Sun Ra's philosophical approach. African retentions within American culture are found in African-American religious practices and magical beliefs.[26] Sun Ra continued to combine metaphysical forces with his cosmic brand of innovative music.

Sun Ra, one of the most individual composer/pianists in twentieth-century America and leader of the first "free" big band on planet earth, was born in Birmingham, Alabama, in 1914. He admits to having used the names Sonny Lee and Herman Sonny Blount at times. When asked about his date of birth he replies, "Actually I don't have an age." When pressed he continues, "Well, really around 1055 or so, I didn't just arrive on this planet you know. I have been around for quite some time. I'm not of any generation, because if I was, I couldn't play the music I am playing."[27] As a follower of numerology and astrology, he refers to his astrological sign, Gemini, in the month of May, but resisted being pinned down to a specific day because of "controversial aspects" involved. "I arrived on this planet on a very important day, it's been pinpointed by wisemen, astrologers as a very important date. I arrived at the exact moment of a very controversial arrival so that's the only reason I don't talk about it. . . . It was controversial because, well, it's the way the stars were set at that moment. In a position where a spiritual being can arrive at that particular point" (Rusch 1978 b:4).

Eddie Gale - former trumpeter with Sun Ra, Cecil Taylor, and others (Photo by Georgette Gale).

Sun Ra's music was always experimental and had a unique ecumenical core. Electronics were incorporated into his Arkestra before any other "jazz" musicians began to experiment with them. Sun Ra's music is unique because of its diversity and the emphasis placed upon sound, traditional or otherwise. He said "I remember things—images and scenes and feelings. I never felt like I was part of this planet. I felt that all this was a dream, that it wasn't real. And suffering. . . . I just couldn't connect."[28] He continues: "I came from somewhere else, but it [the Creator's voice] reached me through the maze and dullness of human existence. It could still reach me because I am pure and sincere. . . . I came from somewhere else, where I was part of something that is so wonderful that there are no words to express it."

Sun Ra recalled keeping the protection and education he received from the creator secret from his parents, who owned a restaurant business. In elementary school he studied solfeggio and his mother bought him a piano when he was around eight years old. Violinist William Gray, a friend, would bring European "classical" music and church music for him to read. Sun Ra said he could perform this music effortlessly because "I could hear so I could read." Most musicians in the Western world approach music in the opposite fashion, with reading being the supreme priority and initial element in the sequence of learning. Sun Ra's understanding of the connection between spontaneous composition and prayer were apparent at an early age. "Everyday I composed something for the Creator. I first started around eleven years old and that's what I was playing. I wouldn't even play for my family. I played just for the Creator."[29]

As a child he listened to Fletcher Henderson records at home and attended theaters regularly with his parents. He also went to blues concerts featuring Bessie Smith, Mamie Smith, Butterbeans, and others. When he was fifteen another friend, trumpeter Bill Martin, encouraged Sun Ra to begin to arrange music, thus motivating him to transcribe "Yeah Man," by Horace Henderson, from a Fletcher Henderson record. This became the first arrangement for his new band composed of fellow students. At this time Sun Ra was also performing professionally with John Tuggle "Fess" Whatley, his band director, while still attending junior high school. His sight-reading skills made him a pianist in demand, playing for both "exclusively White" gatherings and African-American social clubs around Birmingham. Sun Ra was proud of the fact that he was the only student in Whatley's band, which was otherwise comprised of teachers.

Sun Ra's band director arranged a tour that took them from Florida to Chicago. He joined the musicians' union on December 15, 1934, and performed during the Christmas season, (under the name "Sonny Blount") with this band at Chicago's Savoy Ballroom. Later, "Herman S. Blount" was awarded a scholarship to the State Agricultural and Mechanical Institute for Negroes in Normal, Alabama (currently Alabama A & M University) in September, 1935. He was attracted to the teacher's training course because "in that you majored in everything." According to interviews he gave later, Sun Ra left college "as a result of an extra-terrestrial experience." "They said they needed somebody of my kind, my kind of mind and spirit. . . . They were from Saturn, I presume. . . . But I was aware of one being. It always stood on my left-hand side. I really couldn't turn my head fully to see. I could just see the image."[30]

Sun Ra's compositions dating back to the mid-1950s demonstrate both his broad traditional roots and his free "jazz" style. He was a charismatic, knowledgeable, and demanding leader who sought band members who were well disciplined, open-minded and humble. Nightclub owners often complained when his band showed up in "red Egyptian fezzes."[31] The fact that people were listening so intensely that they forgot to buy drinks didn't please these owners either. John Gilmore and Art Hoyle were playing with Sun Ra's quintet at this time. Hoyle talks about a job in Chicago on North Broadway Street during this period. "I heard Sun Ra play some of his most astonishing piano on that job. . . . Because of the less structured situation, he played more, and really played some outstanding things. . . . I was shocked that he could play like that. I had never heard him play in those kinds of veins . . . on regular standard tunes."[32]

The band performed five nights a week (and an afternoon every week); nevertheless, an intensive rehearsal schedule (five hours daily) was still maintained. Sun Ra focused on technical details during these rehearsal sessions: dynamics, articulation, stylistic interpretation, and the like.

Sun Ra always encouraged his musicians to experiment. The bassist Richard Evans (another band member) recalls Sun Ra's musical control over his ensemble: "He was a good programmer of people. He would actually control you, but make you think you were doing it yourself." Music was worked out both by ear and through notation. Evans once asked Sun Ra "Well, what are the chord changes?" He replied, "Whatever you want them to be." At the end of the process Evans realized, "This man is bringing stuff out in me that I didn't know I had."[33] Trombonist Julian Priester, in regards to his early days with Sun Ra, adds:

> He'd set up only the slightest thing going with the band and then he'd suddenly be pointing to me to solo. And I'd get up but I wouldn't know what was going on! I wouldn't know where I was in terms of a harmonic framework, I'd just have to listen to what was going on in back of me with the band—which was liable to be just about anything—and I'd have to work from that. I'd have to measure things instantly and start playing. . . . What he was doing was teaching me to be free. . . . It was a lot of knowledge.[34]

Saturn records was established around the end of 1956 by a group of Sun Ra followers who issued the earliest recorded LP's and 45 rpm's. *Super-Sonic Jazz* was the first issue. The details regarding many Saturn recordings are purposely obscure. In 1957 Sun Ra enclosed a small book of notes with one of his earliest albums, *Jazz by Sun Ra, Vol. 1.* Sun Ra took the time to explain the purpose of his music on this first recording. (This album has been reissued as *Sun Song* on the Delmark label: DD-411.) He wrote:

The Aim of My Composition:

> All of my compositions are meant to depict happiness combined
> with beauty in a free manner. Happiness, as well as *pleasure*
> and *beauty*, has many degrees of existence; *my aim is to express*
> *these degrees in sounds, which can be understood by the entire*
> *world.* All of my music is tested for effect. By effect I mean
> mental impression. The mental impression I intend to convey is
> that of being alive, vitally alive. The real aim of this music is to
> co-ordinate the minds of peoples into an intelligent reach for a
> better world, and an intelligent approach to the living future.
> By peoples I mean all of the people of different nations who are
> living today.

Performance opportunities began to decline around 1960, the year the
Arkestra accepted an engagement at a nightclub in Montreal. "I left Chicago
when a friend of mine said he felt I should because the people weren't listening."[35] They eventually moved on to Quebec City before returning to Chicago
at the end of the year. John Gilmore, Marshall, Pat Patrick, and Ronnie
Boykins moved to New York with Sun Ra soon after their return to Chicago.
Ornette Coleman and Cecil Taylor had arrived a year earlier. The band did
not appear publicly in New York during 1961 but continued to rehearse and
record. Sun Ra's Arkestra was hired for its first performances in New York in
1963. Gene Harris hired the ensemble to perform at The Playhouse at 131
MacDougal Street in Greenwich Village, where Ferrell ("Pharoah") Sanders
was working as a waiter.

Sun Ra added to the musical controversy started by Taylor and Coleman, and soon influential musicians like Coltrane and Dolphy joined this
evolution in the direction of free experimentation. The atmosphere was often
hostile, and the musicians were ostracized from many mainstream musical
venues. John Gilmore was among the most loyal of Sun Ra's band members.
He was offered a position in Miles Davis' ensemble and other prestigious
bands, but remained with Sun Ra despite his towering status on tenor saxophone. There were times of frustration, however, as Gilmore remembers:

> It was getting kind of frustrating. I'd been walking around New
> York, and I wasn't working anywhere, and half the cats were
> out there playing my ideas. I said, what is this? Here I am not
> working, and they're stealing my ideas. . . . So Lee Morgan
> knew me and recommended me to Art Blakey. I was just frus-
> trated at the time, and I had to make some kind of move. I
> couldn't see myself getting myself anything anywhere. All I
> could see was these cats imitating me, and I didn't have a
> quarter in my pocket.[36]

Some of the musicians Gilmore mentioned having had a indelible influence on are Sonny Rollins, Charles Lloyd, Pharoah Sanders, Roland Kirk,
and John Coltrane. Coltrane confirms that Gilmore had a strong influence

during the early 1960s when he was, yet again, modifying his approach to music.

During 1964-65, Gilmore was with the edition of the Jazz Messengers that included Curtis Fuller on trombone, John Hicks on piano, Gary Bartz on alto saxophone, trumpeter Lee Morgan, and Art Blakey on drums. He continued to live in the Arkestra's house with Sun Ra and the other members. Pharoah Sanders replaced him whenever he was on the road with Blakey. John Gilmore was present on March 28, 1965, for the benefit concert for the Black Arts Repertory Theater/School when the Impulse album *The New Wave In Jazz* was recorded. John Coltrane, Archie Shepp, Albert Ayler, Grachan Moncur III, Charles Tolliver, Sun Ra, and Betty Carter were recorded on that date. According to LeRoi Jones, Sun Ra and Betty Carter were omitted from the eventual release due to undisclosed reasons that were apparently known only by the a & r (artist and repertoire) man for the date. Later in his career, John Gilmore also worked and recorded with Babatunde Olatunji, Freddie Hubbard, McCoy Tyner, Paul Bley, Andrew Hill, Elmo Hope, and Chick Corea.

Gilmore was sixty-three when he died on August 20, 1995. He was a pioneer who helped define the fierce, screaming sound of the avant-garde saxophone. He defined his style as "playing rhythmically and melodically at the same time."[37] Gilmore also played bass clarinet and drums with Sun Ra. He was the ensemble's most outstanding soloist and took charge of the Arkestra after the leader's death in 1993.

Sun Ra had a measurable impact on the AACM (Association for the Advancement of Creative Musicians) during its early years of development. There is a related philosophical underpinning that can be discerned in the theatrical presentation of the Art Ensemble of Chicago (members of whom were associated with the AACM), an attitude involving unbridled experimentation with strong elements of traditional African-American history and culture. Sun Ra sums up the function of his music by saying: "I'm actually painting pictures of infinity with my music, and that's why a lot of people can't understand it. And when I say so, a lot of people don't believe me. But if they would listen to this and to other types of music, they'll find that this has something else in it, something from another world."[38]

Charles Mingus

Charles Mingus was a modern "jazz" musician who felt his particular brand of music should be unrestricted yet disciplined melodically, rhythmically, harmonically, and formally. He was one of the most celebrated composer-arrangers of the modern "jazz" era. He was a bassist and bandleader of extraordinary power and enduring musical influence. Mingus and his musical associates studied the experiments of other genres and traditions and applied them to their own natural approach to spontaneous composition. His music was not always cheerful or entertaining in ways that much earlier "jazz" forms were; instead he explored a wide range of moods and emotions in his various "workshops."

Mingus was born in Nogales, Arizona, in 1922 and grew up in Los Angeles. He studied piano, trombone, cello, and solfeggio[39] by the time he was sixteen. Mingus' ambitions were directed toward developing his skill on cello in the European "classical" tradition, but those aspirations waned when he learned that "Black" cellists had no future in symphony orchestras during this time. He then switched to bass and continued to advance his musical knowledge. Mingus participated in the sanctified settings of the Pentecostal and Holiness churches, began studying the works of nineteenth-century European composers, and performed in big band "jazz" settings. He also studied bass for five years with H. Rheinschagen of the New York Philharmonic.

Mingus' professional career began in the early forties. He performed with Louis Armstrong for two years, spent another two years with Lionel Hampton, and performed in bands led by Duke Ellington, Kid Ory, Red Norvo, Charlie Parker, Billy Taylor, Art Tatum, Stan Getz, Bud Powell, and other great musicians. By the early fifties he had founded his own recording label (Debut Records), becoming one of the early pioneers of such efforts among "jazz" musicians. In 1951 Mingus recorded his first album on that label while celebrating his thirty-ninth birthday. Three other "jazz" musicians founded their independent record labels the same year: Dizzy Gillespie (Dee Gee), Lennie Tristano (Jazz Records), and Woody Herman (Mars).[40] One of Debut's most important releases was *Jazz at Massey Hall*, a live recording of a Canadian concert in Toronto's Massey Hall in 1953. This date featured Charlie Parker, Dizzy Gillespie, Bud Powell, Max Roach, and Mingus in a performance that reunited Parker and Gillespie for the first time in many years.

Mingus organized his first workshop during 1954 and continued to explore related experimental formats until his death in January 1979. A sample of Mingus' work during the 1950s is preserved on his album for the Jazztone Society label entitled *Jazz Experiment with Charles Mingus and his Modernists* (originally released in 1955). John LaPorta plays alto saxophone and clarinet; Teo Macero is featured on tenor saxophone; Quincy Jones is heard on trumpet; Jack Wiley plays cello; and the drummer for the session is Clem DeRosa. Mingus is both pianist and bassist on the date. "What Is This Thing Called Love" and other compositions on this album contain music that, like the composer, is rarely static. Colorful counterpoint and timbre are combined to create interesting moods within the context of structured freedom. Both the loose form (which allows such freedom) and the general propensity toward uninhibited swinging became trademarks of Mingus' performances and compositional style. This feature remains constant in both Mingus' small group settings and his extended orchestral works of the sixties and seventies. In each such musical situation, the listener may perceive a balance of musical emotion with ample room for intellectual exploration.

Mingus developed his varied, and frequently complex, compositions with a succession of ensembles, each called the Charles Mingus Jazz Workshop. Mingus' workshops were experimental "conservatories" for prodigiously endowed artists such as Eric Dolphy, Rahsaan Roland Kirk, Clifford Jordan, George Adams, Dannie Richmond, Hamiet Bluiett, Yusef Lateef, John Handy, Jackie McLean, Booker Ervin, Ricky Ford, and Don Pullen. The workshops exemplify Mingus' eclecticism and his willingness to explore new modes and styles of artistic communication. His respect for the process of musical gene-sis gained him the admiration of musicians, but perhaps cost him varying de-grees of popularity among those audiences he was forced to admonish (usu-ally for making noise) during his performances. His temper was not always spent on his audiences, however, as authors Wayne Ernstice and Paul Rubin point out:

> Dubbed "the university of Mingus" by his sidemen, the work-shop provided an intense and exacting training ground, charac-terized by long hours of rehearsal and punctuated by the fre-quent eruptions of Mingus' volcanic personality. As a bandleader, Mingus was notoriously short-tempered with sloppy or superfi-cial playing. During rehearsals, and even on-stage, he was known to stop a number in midstream to chastise a band mem-ber; he commonly warned, "Respect the melody" and "Play in tune." Sometimes in concert he would order his musicians to start a piece all over again.[41]

Mingus was at the height of his musical development during the early part of the 1960s and then fell into obscurity. His 1959 recording of his bit-terly comical and highly polemic composition *Original Faubus Fables*, and his disagreement with Columbia Records over the sales figures for his record-ings, left the company unable to renew their contract with him. The lyrics for his composition did not sit well with some listeners or industry executives:

> Oh Lord, don't let them shoot us
> Oh Lord, don't let them stab us
> Oh Lord, don't let them tar and feather us
> Oh Lord, no more swastikas!
> Oh Lord, no more Ku Klux Klan!
>
> Name me someone ridiculous
> [response] Governor Faubus
> Why is he sick and ridiculous?
> [response] He won't permit integrated schools
> Then he's a fool
> Boo! Nazi Fascist supremacists/Boo! Ku Klux Klan!
>
> Name me a handful that's ridiculous
> Faubus, Rockefeller, Eisenhower
> Why are they so sick and ridiculous?
> Two, four, six, eight
> They brain wash and teach you to hate.

Other Charles Mingus small-group recordings were collected under the title *Pithecanthropus Erectus* in the fifties (Atlantic Records 1956–61). In the mid-1950s and early 1960s, Mingus introduced a number of innovative compositional and improvisational techniques involving structured freedom in which the employment of functional tonality is noticeably minimal. His

1960 recording of "What Love" (from *Stormy Weather*) is an extended composition in which the other instruments drop out well into the development of the piece, leaving Mingus and bass clarinetist Eric Dolphy to begin a collectively improvised dialogue in which both instruments come close to duplicating the inflections of impassioned speech. Mingus' free counterpoint with Dolphy's improvised melodies involves an extension of bass technique beyond all traditional functions exercised before his time.

Mingus departed the United States on a European tour in 1964 in which he visited Scandinavia, Germany, Belgium, and France. The tour featured one of his most exciting workshops. Musicians in his ensemble included Johnny Coles (b. 1926, trumpet), Eric Dolphy (flute, bass clarinet, and alto saxophone), Clifford Jordan (1931–93, tenor saxophone), Jaki Byard (1922–1999, piano), Dannie Richmond (1935–88, drums), and Mingus on double bass. By the conclusion of the tour, Dolphy was offered solo gigs in Paris and began to travel around Europe to Holland, Sweden, and Berlin on his own. Dolphy died alone in his hotel room on June 29, 1964, nine days after his thirty-sixth birthday. He was planning to marry Joyce Mordecai from New York within a few weeks. When Dolphy was admitted into the hospital, European medical personnel assumed he was a "jazz" musician on drugs and failed to treat his diabetes. Dolphy never used drugs. An autopsy revealed his extremely high sugar levels.[42]

Charles Mingus was grief stricken and dropped everything to attend the funeral in Los Angeles on July 9. Dolphy had managed to record his most intriguing bass-clarinet solos on that final tour, where he evolves the art of "vocalizing" instrumental "jazz" in some of the most unusual, evocative, expressively coherent, and animated musical discussion on record. The exchanges are at once confidential raillery and the impassioned yearning of friends separated by an indomitable force. The passion involved is of a type uncommon in Western music. These musical "discussions" are preserved on recordings of the April 26, 1964, concert at Wuppertal Town Hall, West Faubus, and on the Enja recording *Mingus in Europe*, volume 1.[43] When audiences for "jazz" gradually decreased during the 1960s, Charles Mingus fell into obscurity and did not record for several years (between 1966 and 1970). Mingus lived a reclusive existence during this period but returned during the 1970s with some of his best-recorded works for large instrumental ensembles in the "jazz" repertoire.

In his autobiography, *Beneath the Underdog* (first published in 1971), Mingus presents a poignant indictment of racial discrimination, as well as frank (and often revealing) descriptions of his excursions into his own musical mind and personal affairs. It provides an extraordinary glance into the lives of both artists and their fans in frank language and with meritorious clarity.

As cited previously, the hard bop style that prevailed as the dominant "jazz" tendency from the mid-1950s into the following decade emphasized melodic lines that conform to chord structures, a particular kind swing feeling, and the use of a twelve-bar or thirty-two-bar form. Drummers remained timekeepers. Mingus, along with Ornette Coleman, Cecil Taylor, and other music innovators, was among the first musicians to challenge these restrictive conventions beginning in the mid-fifties.

Eric Dolphy (Image by Ramsess).

As a composer, Mingus experimented with variable tempi, alternating meters, polyrhythms, utilized rubato, ametrical structures, and experimented with free collective improvisation. His elevated stature as a composer and bandleader often overshadows his significant contribution as a bassist. As one of the founders of modern bass playing, Mingus extended the range of the instrument from the traditions established by Walter Page, Jimmy Blanton, Slam Stewart, and Oscar Pettiford into the present era.

Two "Jazz" Harpists in the 1950s

Dorothy Ashby

Composer Dorothy Ashby (1932–1986), an accomplished pianist, was self-taught on the harp. She began playing in Detroit in the early fifties, the beginning of what she refers to as the "golden years" of "jazz" in that city. Ashby created a style on the harp that was unprecedented in its authenticity and supple versatility. Traditionally an awkward instrument in music because of its chromatic limitations, the harp would seem an unlikely candidate for "jazz," where one rarely finds music that is simply diatonic. The harp's strings are arranged diatonically and chromatic changes require the movement of one or more of seven pedals, each of which has three notched positions. Ashby overcame this limitation and developed a lyrical and rhythmic voice on the harp that has been equated with the guitar playing of Wes Montgomery.[44] Her father, Wiley Thompson, was a "jazz" guitarist. Her husband is also a musician and composer. Ashby says,

> I played the things that I heard and played along with my father, who taught me more about harmony and melodic construction than I learned in all my years of high school, college, and private study, and sacrificed more time and money than the family could afford for my musical training and instruments . . .
>
> When musicians would come to rehearse with my father, I would get a chance to chord along with the adults, and they thought that was a big thing. I thought it was quite wonderful, too, because I was so young at the time. And from there, I guess my interest was always primarily jazz. My father had perhaps other aspirations for me. He didn't want me to wind up in clubs and suffer the hard times so many of them encountered. The excellence with which they played had nothing to do with the bucks they made.
>
> When I changed to harp, I just tried to transfer the things that I had heard and the things that I wanted to do as a jazz player to the harp. Nobody had ever told me these things shouldn't be done, or were not usually done on the harp, because I didn't hear it any other way. The only thing I was interested in doing was playing jazz on the harp.[45]

The Dorothy Ashby Trio toured (with her husband, the band's drummer) throughout the sixties. By the end of the decade Ashby became increasingly involved with writing and presenting musicals that dealt with African-American concerns. Her husband established an African-American theater company (the Ashby Players of Detroit), and Dorothy wrote scores and lyrics and performed with the events. In the early seventies the Ashbys moved to

California, where Dorothy established herself firmly in the Los Angeles studio scene.

Dorothy Ashby was not the first harpist to play "jazz." Caspar Reardon is considered to be the first "jazz" harpist, and Adele Girard was the first woman to play the harp in "jazz." The distinguishing quality that Ashby's harp playing brings to "jazz" are described by Ira Gitler in the liner notes to Ashby's 1961 album *Soft Winds* (Jazzland Records): "Her feeling for time and ability to construct melodic guitar-like lines mark her as the most accomplished modern jazz harpist." After the release of her album *The Fantastic Jazz Harp of Dorothy Ashby* in 1962, Ashby was given *Down Beat's* Critic's and Reader's Awards as best harpist. A reviewer of the music said, "This isn't just novelty, though that is what you expect. The harp has a clean jazz voice with a resonance and syncopation that turn familiar jazz phrasing inside out."[46] Few recognized the inherent difficulties and unique power and skill involved in creating the music that Ashby executed so flawlessly and effortlessly. She remains relatively unrewarded for her innovative contribution. Because the number of professional harpists performing authentic "jazz" was and is negligible, "people don't know what you're doing," she says. "Nobody else knows enough to know that nobody else is doing it."[47]

Corky Hale

It was not until Corky Hale (harp/piano/organ/flute/piccolo/cello) heard Dorothy Ashby performing in a Detroit club in the early fifties that she realized that there was another harpist exploring "jazz." Hale's primary instrument is the piano. "It's very frustrating to me," she admits, "very frustrating, in that people mostly think of me as a harpist and mainly call upon me because I do something on the harp." "Dorothy is very wonderful," Hale thinks. "I don't want to say that Dorothy and I are the only jazz harpists, but Dorothy and I are the only ones that can go in with a group, sit down, and improvise a tune like a piano player."

In the fifties, Hale was working in the recording studios, clubs, and TV in Hollywood when her career began. She appeared with various all-woman bands and appeared on the 1954 recording session *Cats vs. Chicks*. She performed with Ray Anthony, Harry James, Freddy Martin, Dave Rose, and others. Leonard Feather said in *The Encyclopedia of Jazz*, (in response to her 1954 album with vocalist Kitty White) that she had an "exceptionally modern approach to the harp."

Hale spoke of the brief period she spent with Ada Leonard and Ina Ray Hutton: "Ada was terribly sophisticated, and boy, I was scared to death of her. And, of course, Phil Spitalny called and asked me to go on the road with his all-girl band. I didn't join Phil, and I didn't last very long with Ada or Ina."[48] In a Hal Holly profile titled "Corky, the All-Girl Harpist, Won't Talk on Gal Bands" (*Down Beat*, June 4, 1952, p. 4), Hale discusses her experiences with the all-woman bands. Corky, who considered herself a "sort of well-bred little Jewish girl from northern Illinois" at the beginning of her career, said:

It's like this. . . . If a girl is a good musician she doesn't want to work in an all-girl band because it implies she is working in it because she is a girl. A girl doesn't feel successful as a musician unless she can work with guys—just like one of them. She wants to feel she's been hired not because she's a girl but because she can play the job.

I've always been in a man's world. I've always been in a man's job. Along with that, strangely enough, I always did all those womanly things. After work, at two in the morning, it was very common for maybe sixteen, seventeen guys in the band to come to my apartment and I would cook up an enormous breakfast.

Art Blakey

Art Blakey (1919–1990) (drummer and band leader) made it clear that drums were very expressive and versatile instruments. Like Gene Krupa, Blakey was instrumental in liberating the drums from a purely time-keeping role to that of a front-line instrument. Blakey, originally a pianist, never studied drums formally, but he absorbed the "jazz" drumming tradition by listening and studying the music of Baby Dodds, Big Sid Catlett, Chick Webb, Kenny Clarke, and other great musicians. In 1939 he played in Fletcher Henderson's orchestra, then joined pianist Mary Lou Williams's first big band. In a career that spanned half a century, Blakey's performance and recording credits also include appearances with Errol Garner, Charlie Parker, Dizzy Gillespie, Bud Powell, Thelonious Monk, Miles Davis, and the Billy Eckstine Orchestra.

After 1944 Blakey remained an integral part of Billy Eckstine's big band until it broke up in 1947. He visited Africa during the forties, spending several months in Nigeria and Ghana. He worked constantly when he returned to the United States with Lucky Millinder, Buddy DeFranco, and other bandleaders. He also led his own small combos. Art Blakey's Jazz Messengers later became one of the most important "schools" in modern "jazz."

The earlier African-American "jazz school" involved on-the-job training in the oral/aural tradition with a person who had mastered the evolutionary styles. The master musician (and designated teacher) usually acquired his or her knowledge through a similar process. The Jazz Messengers were the epitome of such a process in modern "jazz," just as the Ellington, Basie, and Eckstine bands had been in earlier eras.

The Jazz Messengers were a series of ensembles that trained young musicians for more than four decades. In Blakey's bands, players learned the meaning of communal balance, precision, style, musicianship, and individual expression. Messengers were trained to bring joy and excitement to an audience through their improvisational and ensemble performance skills. Alumni from Art Blakey's Jazz Messengers include (on trumpet) Clifford Brown, Lee Morgan, Kenny Dorham, Donald Byrd, Freddie Hubbard, Wynton Marsalis, and Terence Blanchard; (on piano) Horace Silver, Bobby Timmons, Ray Bryant, and Joanne Brackeen; (on reeds) Jackie McLean, Hank Mobley,

Johnny Griffin, Benny Golson, Wayne Shorter, and Billy Harper; and (on trombone) Julian Priester and Curtis Fuller. Other recent "graduates" include the Harper Brothers, Branford Marsalis, and many other "Young Lions."

Born in Pittsburgh, Blakey's impact on "jazz" drumming is as notable as his contributions as a leader. Despite his explosive presence and emotional range on the drums, Blakey considered himself first and foremost an accompanist for his ensembles. He understood the power and importance of the drum: "The drums, they can move mountains, tell messages, everything! Whatever the drum says, you got to do it man. They're the pulse of everything. If the pulse isn't there, it's dead. That's my concept of playing drums. If people are out there, I'm going to get them. That's what happens in Africa and other societies. The rhythms make music meaningful. Listen to Stravinsky's *Firebird Suite*. See how militant he is with the drums? It tears you up."[49]

Phineas Newborn

Pianist Phineas Newborn (1931–1989) was born in Whiteville, Tennessee. His father was a bandleader in Memphis, so Phineas learned to play tenor saxophone, French horn, trumpet, baritone horn, vibraphone, and other instruments by the time he was a teen. Calvin Newborn, his brother, can be heard on guitar on many of Phineas' recordings.

When he emerged on the scene in the 1950s, Newborn's piano technique was often ranked with that of Art Tatum and Oscar Peterson by colleagues, fans, and critics. While Bud Powell was considered the driving force on piano during the bebop era, Newborn etched out a piano style "so unique as to make any attempt at copying it seem almost cliché."[50] His career often oscillated between highly productive periods of excellent recordings and periods of self-imposed obscurity. The world in which he was forced to perform involved too much pressure and too many negative experiences for a humble, introspective, and extremely sensitive artist. Pianist James Williams recalls, "I think I actually heard Junior play in person before I heard his recordings. When I heard him and went to the record store the next day, they didn't have any of his albums. I ordered every record they had listed in the category. I didn't know which ones were considered to be the classics . . . but I figured anyone who plays with that kind of emotional depth and expressiveness, anytime they touch the piano it is going to be something worth hearing."[51]

Critics who knew little about Newborn's personal life speculated that he "went into a decline as a consequence of emotional illness." Contrary to comments such as these, as expressed by Leonard Feather in *The Encyclopedia of Jazz in the Sixties*, Newborn spoke of a different reason for his obscurity and reticence. In a radio interview on National Public Radio in the early 1980s (after insisting that his name should be pronounced like the word "finest"—with a long *i*), Newborn told of an incident that took place at a club in the South after his performance one evening. He had just finished playing when an attractive European-American woman in a red dress approached him and said some friends wanted to talk to him outside. He followed her out and was assaulted and beaten savagely by a gang of European-American men until he was unconscious. When he got out of the hospital he went to his mother's house and didn't touch the piano again for a long period. His mother gradually coaxed him into playing again, but it was never to be the same.

Summary

The lyrics of blues singers were usually personal commentaries about intimate topics spoken to a close second party or shared with the general listeners ("Baby Please Don't Go," "I'm Wild About You Baby," "Lightnin' Don't Feel Well," etc.). In the swing era some of the intimacy of the personal song was retained, but vocals with slightly more general commentaries also became common ("Moonlight in Vermont," "That's the Stuff You Gotta Watch," "When a Woman Loves a Man," etc.). A similar degree of change can be measured from listening to the way individual notes are caressed and savored by the swing soloist (Lester Young, for instance), while the bebop player treated notes more as a multitude of distant stars organized into magnificent galactic systems by triumphant strokes of a wise, but impersonal, magician's musical wand.

It may be that bebop was more distanced, inaccessible and curt in musical demeanor partly due to the diminished word usage in connection with that style. Swing lyrics often had an original set of lyrics, even if the songs eventually became best known as instrumental arrangements. The instrumental players usually knew the words to the songs they interpreted, and they worked closely with vocalists in the communal big band settings. Rather than working within the structure of traditional ensembles and exploring its traditional language, bebop pioneers preferred the combo and created a new musical system. This approach involved casting old melodies away and using functional harmony in revolutionary ways to expand the medium to new extremes. Instrumentalists during the 1940s needed to reform the concept of "jazz" for themselves.

Emphasis was on virtuosity and a complete technical knowledge of the conventional functions of music. This set of esoteric knowledge transmitted orally and aurally, deprived musicians on the fringe of the culture access to methods of decoding the new modern "jazz" language. Consequently, the number of bop innovators is far lower than both the number of names commonly associated with swing and other earlier periods. The list of hard bop musicians who emerged during the 1950s, form a larger set of practitioners. Even those few bebop musicians who learned the language thoroughly could not all develop the level of fluency and virtuosity that Parker, Gillespie, or Bud Powell produced, thus a yet smaller inner circle of hyper-esoteric bop innovators stood elevated far beyond their peers.

Despite the early stereotypes that relocated all "jazz" to either the secular domain or, worse, to the realm of "the devil's music," many innovators began to dedicate a portion of their music to sacred domains. Duke Ellington's concerts of sacred music began on September 16, 1965, at Grace Cathedral Church of San Francisco. The second concert occurred on January 19, 1968, in New York at the Cathedral of St. John the Divine, while the final performance was at Westminister Abbey in London on October 24, 1973. In 1957 the Ward singers were persuaded to bring their gospel singing to the Newport Jazz Festival to demonstrate the aesthetic affinity between African-American sacred and secular musical traditions. After Mahalia Jackson sang at the same festival the following year, gospel music annually took its place next to "jazz" and blues at the festival.

Mary Lou Williams wrote three "jazz" masses. Her hymn, "St. Martin de Porres" (Black Christ of the Andes) as well as two other smaller sacred works ("Anima Christi" and "Praise the Lord") are samples of her interest in and dedication to spiritual music. An ordained Catholic priest named Clarence Rivers (b. 1931) is credited with introducing "jazz" and other African-American music into the Catholic religious services. David Baker (b. 1931) has written music for Catholic and Lutheran services including *The Beatitudes* for chorus, narrator, dancers, and symphony orchestra, and *A Modern Jazz Oratorio*.[52]

Negative stereotypes of African-American "jazz" musicians and sociopathic behavior continued nonetheless. Norman Mailer, in his 1957 essay "The White Negro," suggested the complex notion that the attitudes of the "hipster" and "philosophical psychopath," found during the 1950s within the European-American population, was an infatuation with the "Negro" that stemmed from a protest against European Americans' fear of integration. Mailer also felt this rebellion against mainstream America was also somehow due to "White" anxiety over the sexual superiority of African-American males. Mailer's mythological theories were closely related to myths that "motivated the lynching and castration of thousands (maybe millions) of black men since the first slave was delivered to Virginia in 1619."[53] Nelson George discusses the effect of Mailers delusions further:

> Yet in perpetuating the romance of blackness, supporting the notion that black jazzmen, for example, were in touch with some primal, sexual energy, Mailer was guilty of stereotyping blacks as the rednecks and social mainstreamers his white Negroes opposed. While liberals hailed and debated Mailer's provocative rhetoric, many working-class white teens were already living out the ideas Mailer articulated, infatuated as they were with black style and culture. But Mailer saw jazz as the crucial element in this new modern white personality; he had no real idea of what most Negroes, or their white teenage fans, were recording or buying.

> If Mailer had done a little more homework, he might have cited first the white R&B deejays, and then a kid named Elvis Aaron Presley. Elvis had been recording professionally for three years by the time "The White Negro" was published, and it may be that Mailer's musings were at least in part inspired by the white public's perception of this country boy. Elvis' immersion in black culture, both the blues and gospel, was as deep as his white Mississippi background would allow. Aside from the music he heard on black radio (Memphis' WDIA and Nashville's

WLAC were favorites), Elvis also utilized now obscure bits of
black culture to create the style look so integral to his mystique. Even before he'd made his first record, Elvis was wearing
one of black America's favorite products, Royal Crown Pomade
hair grease, used by hepcats to create the shiny, slick hair-
styles of the day. The famous rockabilly cut, a style also
sported by more flamboyant hipsters, was clearly his interpretation of the black "process," where blacks had their hair
straightened and curled into curious shapes. Some charge that
the process hairstyle was a black attempt to look white. So, in a
typical pop music example of cross-cultural collision, there was
Elvis adapting black styles from blacks adapting white looks.[54]

At the end of the twentieth century, are contemporary art forms dominated by the notion that what will sell determines what will be presented?
How can such cycle be broken if music that is considered too abstract or experimental is never heard by general audiences—live or otherwise? Musical
styles are as different or conforming as the individual personalities of the
people in the societies from which they emerge. If people have an opportunity
to hear a cross-section of music, then there will always be an audience for an
infinite variety of musical styles—past and present.

Notes

[1] George E. Curry, "Killed for Whistling at a White Woman," *Emerge Newsmagazine*,
August 1995, pp. 24–32.

[2] Ibid., p. 30.

[3] Ibid., p. 32.

[4] As cited in ibid.

[5] Miles Davis with Quincy Troupe, *Miles: The Autobiography* (New York: Simon and
Schuster, 1989), p. 161.

[6] Ibid. p. 89.

[7] William Barlow and Cheryl Finley, *From Swing to Soul: An Illustrated History of African American Popular Music from 1930 to 1960* (Washington, D.C.: Elliot and Clark Publishing, 1994), pp. 113–14.

[8] Krystian Brodacki, "The Original Batman: Wayne Shorter Remembers Miles Davis,"
Jazz Forum, January 1992, p. 28.

[9] Joe Goldberg, *Jazz Masters of the Fifties*, p. 91.

[10] Ibid. p. 94.

[11] As quoted in ibid., p. 105.

[12] J. C. Thomas, *Chasin the Trane* (Garden City, New York: Doubleday, 1975), pp. 34–
35.

[13] Ira Gitler, "Trane on the Track," *Down Beat*, October 16, 1958, p. 16.

[14] Davis, *Miles*, pp. 194–95.

[15] Mark Gridley, *Jazz Styles: History and Analysis*, 2d ed. (Englewood Cliffs, N.J.:
Prentice Hall, 1985), p. 213.

[16] Ibid., p. 147.

[17] "Coltrane On Coltrane," p. 17.

[18] *Chasin' the Trane*, p. 90.

[19] According to the liner notes on this LP—"*Portrait of Cannonbal*" on Riverside.

[20] Goldberg, *Jazz Masters of the Fifties*, p. 233.

[21] Liner notes to *The Music of Ornette Coleman: Something Else*, Contemporary S7551
(1958).

[22] Introduction to article on Taylor in Valerie Wilmer, *Jazz People*.

[23] Valerie Wilmer, *As Serious as Your Life: The Story of the New Jazz* (London: Serpent's Tail, 1992), p. 52.

[24] Ibid. p. 161.

[25] Ekkehard Jost, *Free Jazz* (Graz, Austria: Universal Edition, 1974), pp. 69–70.

[26] Joseph E. Holloway, ed., *Africanisms in American Culture* (Bloomington: Indiana University Press, 1991), p. 99.

[27] Phil Schaap, *Sun Ra: The Sequel*, WKCR Program Guide, WKCR Radio, Columbia University, New York, March 1989, V(6), p. 28.

[28] Ira Steingroot, "Sun Ra's Magic Kingdom," *Reality Hackers*, Winter 1988, p. 50.

[29] Phil Schaap, "An Interview with Sun Ra," WKCR Program Guide, WKCR Radio, Columbia University, New York, March 1989, V(5), p. 26.

[30] Allan S. Chase, "Sun Ra: Musical Change and Musical Meaning in the Life and Work of a Jazz Composer" (Unpublished thesis, Tufts University, 1992), p. 48.

[31] Graham Lock, "Big John's Special," *Wire*, no. 82/83 (December 1990/January 1991): 22.

[32] Chase, "Sun Ra."

[33] Ibid., p. 91.

[34] Eugene Chadbourne, "Wandering Spirit Song, Pepo's Interview," *Coda*, December 1974, pp. 4–5.

[35] Ibid., p. 151.

[36] John DiLiberto, "John Gilmore: Three Decades in the Sun's Shadow," *Downbeat*, May 1984, p. 28.

[37] *Allegro: Associated Musicians of Greater New York,* Local 802, A.F. of M., October 1995.

[38] Wilmer, *As Serious as Your Life,* p. 74.

[39] The musical science of pitch and key relationships.

[40] Brian Priestley, *Mingus: A Critical Biography* (New York: Da Capo, 1983), p. 46.

[41] *Jazz Spoken Here*, pp. 213–15.

[42] Ibid.

[43] The flute and bass duet on a theme by Eric called "Starting" is a classic recording.

[44] Orrin Keepnews made the comparison in complimenting Ashby on her playing.

[45] Sally Placksin, *Jazz Women* (London: Pluto Press, 1985), pp. 239–40.

[46] Robert Ostermann, "Records in Review," *The National Observer*, undated clipping, courtesy Dorothy Ashby.

[47] *Jazz Women*, p. 239.

[48] Ibid., pp. 243–46.

[49] Liner notes to *Art Blakey and the Jazz Messengers: In My Prime*, vol. 1, Muse Records TI-301 (1979).

[50] Mitchell Seidel, "Truth, Justice and the Blues," *Down Beat*, March 1994.

[51] Ibid., p. 26.

[52] Southern, *The Music of Black Americans*, p. 491.

[53] Nelson George, *The Death of Rhythm* (New York: Pantheon, 1988), pp. 107–8

[54] Ibid., p. 61–62.

X
Innovators Emerging Between 1960 and 1970

The cooler or more intellectual forms mean reversion back to
the original African. It's like modern painting and sculpture.
The same thing with bop—Charlie Parker, Dizzy Gillespie and
those people—that was in the direction of Africa.

—Duke Ellington

Evolution of Innovative Music for 1960s Audiences

By 1960 African Americans had become a highly unique people. Separated from their homeland for a long period of time, the connecting elements
binding African Americans to Africa had grossly diminished. They were generally not accepted as first-class citizens in America. Nevertheless, there
were some unexpected advantages to this alienation. Taking advantage of
unprecedented musical freedom, African-American innovators drew upon
their African heritage freely, unbound by Old World traditions. European
music could be exploited in similar fashion. The lack of a single binding tradition encouraged a cultural, social, and aesthetic freedom that few other people in the world enjoyed. As marginalized people, African Americans were free
to create new celebrations, social customs, dialects, and modes of musical expression. Evolution, invention, and experimentation became survival traits.
The evolution of "jazz" reflects such tendencies.

The distancing of the innovative forms of "jazz" music from the African-American mainstream community that occurred at the dawn of modern
"jazz" was not necessarily a consequence of artistic experimentation becoming
too extreme. The experimental proclivities present during the 1960s reflected
the changes that occurred in the broader world. Many experimental musicians, as well as other African-American citizens involved in the "Black
Pride" movement, were interested in the perpetuation of both African and African-American music and cultural traditions. More African Americans traveled to the African continent and embarked upon careful studies of African
culture and history. Through musical experimentation, musicians began to
demonstrate the inherent compatibility that exists between various forms of
African and African-American musical forms. Nigerian master drummer Babatunde Olatunji worked with a number of master "jazz" musicians in New
York. Sun Ra's concerts displayed a synthesis of various concepts while reflecting the natural evolution of many African-American styles. Sun Ra also
demonstrated that music from several stylistic eras can be merged. Randy

Weston, Dollar Brand, and other musicians contributed to this evolving notion as well.[1]

One set of reasons African-American "jazz" musicians inadvertently distanced themselves from their old audiences after the swing era was the location of performance venues. When bebop musicians emerged on 52nd Street in New York, they performed for a new integrated audience. This new setting was primarily composed of European-American patrons. Modern "jazz" musicians generally performed outside the African-American community after "jazz" moved downtown from Harlem. At the same time, the innovative artists during the 1960s continued to evolve farther from European and popular musical structures, aesthetics, and limitations.

When bebop and hard bebop musicians mastered the required skills, they were highly cognizant of the caliber and value of their music. An artist gained respect in the African-American community for his or her personalized artistic contribution as well as for the technical mastery of a particular musical style. Disappointments came when "Black" artists realized that the broader American society would remain unappreciative of their music regardless of its artistic merit.

Listening to some of the live recordings of performances such as Charlie Parker's "Embraceable You" (*Bird at St. Nick's*),[2] where an apathetic, rude, and noisy drinking crowd is often much louder than the music being performed, gives the listener a clue as to the typical situation with which musicians were confronted during bebop.

In contrast, listening to Betty Carter's live performance of "By the Bend of the River" (at a birthday party at the Village Vanguard) or "Ego" on her first album *Betty Carter* (Bet-Car MK 1001) displays an eager and responsive African-American audience. The audience is actively engaging Carter's music in a communal fashion. Another supportive audience can be heard on performances in Japan of John Coltrane's "Meditation Part I" from *Live in Japan.* Coltrane's album has an excited audience that rivals the enthusiasm of an audience at a rock concert in America. Sun Ra's "For the Sunrise" from his album *Live in Montreux* also displays an extremely enthusiastic European crowd of a type that would be atypical for his Arkestra's performances in the United States during the time in which the performance was recorded.

The club experiences that Charlie Parker, Miles Davis, John Coltrane, Charles Mingus, and other African-American artists ordinarily endured not only produced a frustrating or debilitating situation for African-American artists, but also restricted the range of musical elements that could be explored. Bass solos were often completely lost during live bebop performances, so it was difficult for Parker to pursue his interest in strings in settings in which he typically performed. Musicians were obliged to perform at particular levels of amplitude, and in a dynamic fashion aggressive enough to rise above the general noise level of a nightclub. This, of course was a restrictive adaptation.

Movement away from the big-band format challenged the modern "jazz" artist in ways related to those ragtime pianists confronted during the early period of their development. Back then, musicians were required to produce a sound on the piano that retained all the salient features of the brass bands and other small ensembles that were heard in the barrelhouse environments. Later, "jig bands" and "jig piano" led to the "syncopated songs" that eventually became ragtime in the late nineteenth century.

The modern artists were becoming more self-consciously aware of their musical work. In modern "jazz" individual musical efforts were more exposed than they had been during the era of the big swing bands. Solos became longer, and music was documented for posterity more frequently. Modern "jazz" performance venues became distanced from Kansas City-styled jam sessions. In typical Kansas City sessions, mistakes could often be made and corrected without being preserved in a fixed document where performers and listeners could always find indelible historical reminders of their every musical move. Innovators gradually adapted to the demands imposed and knew they did not need large orchestras, fancy costumes, and stage layouts, or any other expensive tools and equipment to produce meaningful music. Coltrane and Parker needed only a quartet. Yet, as author Valerie Wilmer asserts, the music continued to evolve rapidly.

> Black music has never stood still. One theory to explain the need for this constant change is that it occurs from necessity, that the protagonists are forced to invent new techniques and systems in order to stay one step ahead of white imitators and codifiers. Possibly the musicians of the past were not blessed with an acute political consciousness (hardly surprising in view of their position in society—"entertainers" playing in brothels and bar-rooms); perhaps it is true to say that until Charlie Parker came along none of them referred to their music as art, but in the "sixties" and "seventies" the "different drummer" that Black musicians heard was as often motivated by nationalist considerations as by the aesthetic desire to play something new.[3]

Randy Weston, Betty Carter, Charles Mingus, Horace Silver, Dizzy Gillespie, Sun Ra, and other African-American "jazz" artists attempted to establish their own record labels for several decades, only to find that the real problem lay in breaking into the mainstream distribution networks. Their early record labels paved the way for later artist-owned independent publishing and record companies such as Charles Tolliver's Strata East, Andrew White's Andrew's Music, Wendell Harrison's Wenha, and many others. In an interview conducted by drummer and author Art Taylor, composer-pianist Randy Weston responds inexorably unequivocally to Taylor's question, "Do you think musicians should produce their concerts and records?"

> I believe the musician of today and of the future has to own everything. He should own his own nightclub, even if it's no bigger than a small room. He should either have his own record company or be able to record his own material and lease it to record companies. I am convinced that it's the only step for us to take now. Considering our experience and how artists are ex-

ploited, particularly black artists, we must forget about working
for other people.[4]

**Randy Weston performing at the 2003 _Global African Music & Arts
Festival/Symposium_ at UC Santa Cruz** (Photos by Sarah Blade/Precious
Memories).

Weston's roster of the musicians working with him on the Roulette label was quite impressive. It included

> Clark Terry, Richard Williams, Freddie Hubbard, Benny Bailey. We had only two trombones: Jimmy Cleveland and Quinton Jackson. Julius Watkins was on French horn. Cecil Payne, Yusef Lateef, Budd Johnson, Gigi Gryce, and Jerome Richardson were in the reed section. Les Spann was on guitar. Max Roach, G. T. Hogan, Charlie Persip, Armando Peraza, Candido Camaro, and Olatunji were the drummers. Ron Carter and George Duvivier played the bass.

Melba Liston conducted her own arrangements on this session and used the Swahili language to demonstrate the beauty of African language and to show "how the African language is also part of the African rhythms." The album was recorded in early 1960. Weston continues:

> It came out during a time when we could see things going down. It was not as bad as it is now, but we could feel it happening. We wanted this to be a symbolic gesture by Afro-Americans, to show our pride that some of the countries in Africa were getting their freedom. So the album was called *Uhuru Africa*. *Uhuru* means "freedom" in Swahili.

> This particular album was packaged and put together in 1961. At the time it was a bit unpopular, especially with white people—even white people who were friendly to me. They would hear it once and they wouldn't hear it anymore. Especially the first part, where you have the poem. The other problem was with Roulette Records. They wanted to make some sort of a deal where I would be giving them power over my music. They promised to do a big promotion on me, but I have learned one lesson: Never sell a song. Never give the rights of a song. I don't care how sad you think it is. Never sell a tune! I refused, and therefore the album got buried. There was no publicity put behind it. So because of that and because of the message on the record, it was hard to find.[5]

Weston discussed the gradual erosion of economic power and stability among African-American musicians from the beginning of the "jazz" era:

> In the twenties and the thirties, black artists had a lot of power. They had a lot of strength. They had a hotel in the neighborhood of Sixth Avenue around Fiftieth or Fifty-first Street. It was called the Clef Club. The Clef Club was worth a million dollars. It was a place for black entertainers. Black entertainers and musicians were organized. If you were hungry, if you were a musician or an artist and you came to New York

and you didn't have a place to go and didn't have anything to eat, you could go there.

Our ancestors in this business used to give their own vaudeville shows, because segregation was so rough in those days that they had to do a lot of things on their own. And that's how powerful an organization they had. But when they started to build the Sixth Avenue subway, they tore it down. Harlem started to happen, and everybody got split up. So what happened is this: The old timers let us down, and the reason is because they didn't keep records. It's very hard to find. I've got a book on the history of our people in show business in this country. It's just unbelievable what was happening in the twenties and thirties. But the old people let us down by not having enough written data on this material. A lot of us grew up playing the music not knowing its history, not knowing how the old people used to work together, support one another and feature each other. And we got away from it more and more. The white man took over more and more, and now he's also pushing his artists. See, in those days we didn't have to worry about that too much."[6]

Horace Silver formed his own Silveto label for a number of personal reasons. He suspected that Blue Note was phasing out "jazz" and also wanted to be free to release his spiritual records. Silver said:

I was playing the Keystone Korner in San Francisco, and got the newspaper to read a review on our performance. On the other side of the page there was a review on this book *How to Make and Sell Your Own Records*. I sent for the book and that's what turned me on to saying maybe I should put my money where my mouth is.

I had a couple of offers from labels. I said to myself, "If I'm gonna do straight-ahead, it's okay, but if I want to do this metaphysical thing, they're gonna fight me on it, knock me down, I won't be able to do it. So why don't I just go ahead and start my own label, so I can do my spiritual thing?"

That's why I started the Silveto label. About eight years ago. [mid-1980s] I wasn't thinking about another label. I was just thinking about doing what I wanted to do without fighting anybody. After I had made at least three albums for the Silveto label, I thought, "Why not start another label, the Emerald label, for straight-ahead?" Instead of losing fans who didn't want to go this way. With what I'm doing they can have both.[7]

By the 1960s musicians and other artists were ready to move away from European-American business constraints and regain control of their social, political, and expressive domains. For many musicians this meant a move back to their African heritage.

Restructuring Musical Approaches

Saxophonist Archie Shepp stresses the importance of the oral tradition and its cultural transformation in the twentieth century in his forward to Ben Sidran's book *Black Talk*.[8] Shepp makes clear that the process through which "jazz" (or most African-American music) is passed on through generations differs from educational methods traditionally employed with other forms of music. What is taught orally and aurally isn't necessarily notes or technique exclusively, but includes more esoteric information involving the inherent spirit and other affective aspects of music. The emotional feelings that inspire or overcome musicians or listeners are intangible.

As experimental musicians began to define themselves stylistically during the 1960s, they rejected labels previously forced upon their music. It was clear that terms like "jazz" and "classical" were political labels in America.

During the 1960s, modern "jazz" music began a poignant expansion beyond the traditional set of musical elements particularly associated with instrumental "jazz" styles. This movement involved modifications to conventional approaches to syncopation, stylized "swing" feel, and others that previously served as technical elements and parameters used by mainstream musical society to describe "jazz." Titles of compositions such as Coltrane's "Meditation" and "A Love Supreme" provide conceptual clues to the basis of some new approaches modern innovators explored. "Jazz" musicians traveled worldwide and absorbed from all the cultures with which they came in contact. Musicians from abroad were also making their new homes in America, bringing rich cultural information with them. (Mongo Santamaria, Ali Akbar Khan, Ravi Shankar, Babatunde Olatunji, Miriam Makeba, and Hugh Masakela are a few examples.)

Through a new cross-fertilization musical, philosophical and conceptual seeds were planted in fertile artistic soil. A greater number of "jazz" musicians emerged with conservatory and other institutional training during the modern "jazz" era (Miles at the Juilliard School of Music in New York City, Coltrane at the Ornstein School of Music in Philadelphia, Cecil Taylor at the New England Conservatory in Boston, and Ornette Coleman and Don Cherry at the Lenox School of Jazz in western Massachusetts—where John Lewis was director). The integrated multicultural aesthetic and spiritual base that resulted enabled artists to separate, recombine, classify, assimilate, and apply a vast amount of knowledge to their artistic approaches in fissionable manners. New idiosyncratic laws and principles merged with an ecumenical understanding of music, which each artist adapted to their individual goals and aspirations.

The integration of spiritual concerns with artistic thinking provided a level of insulation for themselves and their art that the consumption of drugs had not provided during earlier periods. The synergy of these new conceptions now limited the systematic destructive potential of certain malicious influences (typically associated with the "jazz" environment).

As African-Americans adopted the slogan "black is beautiful" during the 1960s, their music was relabeled "black classical music," "great black music" (the Art Ensemble of Chicago's slogan), "black jazz," and the like.[9] The new terms of identification were a proactive movement toward reclaiming all aspects of their art form, as African Americans expressed their dissatisfaction with centuries of discrimination and exploitation at the hands of the dominant society. The Pan-African nationalism that reemerged during the 1960s permeated African-American culture generally; music was not an exception.

As young Americans explored alternative lifestyles in defiance of the conservative values promoted in the 1950s, many African-American innovators liberated themselves from musical limitations that impeded creative expression. As new languages evolved, it appears that some European-American critics embarked on a mission involving sustained condescending assaults aimed at the "demystification," systematization, and denial of "jazz's" spirituality through labeling the music of some innovators of the era "angry," "anti-jazz," "nihilistic," etc.

The 1960s liberation movement produced music that was not packaged for conventional radio formats (three- to five-minute songs, etc.). Recording artists produced LPs with expansive and continuous compositions (filling one or more sides of an album) in both rock and "jazz" genres. Listeners took time to give these recordings a thorough listening. Music that evolved during this period contained a broader range of individualized approaches than any other music in twentieth-century America. Many genres of music in America engaged this era of experimentation. Since most experiments were absorbed by a significant portion of the younger Americans' subculture (who were beginning to obtain a sense of communal participation), the lack of a mature sociocultural foundation led to instability. Consequently, principles learned were quickly abandoned once youths within the majority culture cut their hair and headed off in the direction of yuppie individualism during the 1970s.

The easily identifiable styles of artists who reached maturity during the 1960s, such as John Coltrane, Jimi Hendrix, Cecil Taylor, Aretha Franklin, Albert Ayler, Carlos Santana, Janis Joplin, and Sun Ra, set the standards for many of the experimental approaches used today. Much of the postmodern and poststructural music that caught on in the 1980s (the lower east side of New York City artistic crowd is an example) have clear prototypes in music of the sixties and early seventies.

The 1960s innovator often created musical manifestations that involved a method of communication that transcended the limitations of words. Raahsan Roland Kirk's composition "Inflated Tear" tells the story of a southern physician who caused his blindness by prescribing the wrong eye drops when his mother took him in for treatment of an eye infection when he was very young.[10] Coltrane's "Alabama" was written in response to the bombing of a Sunday school class at an African-American church by European-American supremacists, which resulted in the death of three young girls. Jimi Hendrix's version of the "Star Spangled Banner" performed live at the Woodstock Festival (among other places) during the sixties conveyed more than the original words could have ever transmitted. Miles Davis' album *Nefertiti* was an affirmation of his pride in the African tradition and beauty. It was recognition of the importance of African-American music that helped Davis decide to leave Juilliard at the beginning of his career:

> I was learning more from hanging out, so I just got bored with school after a while. Plus, they were so fucking white-oriented and so racist. Shit, I could learn more in one session at Minton's than it would take me two years to learn at Juilliard. At Juilliard, after it was all over, all I was going to know was a bunch of white styles; nothing new. And I was just getting mad and embarrassed with their prejudice and shit.
>
> I remember one day being in a music history class and a white woman was the teacher. She was up in front of the class saying that the reason black folk played the blues was because they were poor and had to pick cotton. So they were sad and that's where the blues comes from, their sadness. My hand went up in a flash and I stood up and said, "I'm from East St. Louis and my father is rich, he's a dentist, and I play the blues. My father didn't never pick no cotton and I didn't wake up this morning sad and start playing the blues. There's more to it than that." Well, the bitch turned green and didn't say nothing after that. Man, she was teaching that shit from out of a book written by someone who didn't know what the fuck he was talking about. That's the kind of shit that was happening at Juilliard and after a while I got tired of it.[11]

As audiences absorbed a wider cross-section of the world around them through engaging a wider range of styles and artistic ideas (including the music of non-Western cultures), vocabularies began to make the crossover. This melding of styles resulted in the creation of new "fusionary" and "fissionary" approaches. In the former, the individual musical components involved remain fairly distinct. In the latter, elements are first broken down deductively to expose their fundamental constituents and then recombined into new formations that produce unique qualities and conceptual approaches.

John Coltrane, for instance, studied a wide assortment of musical styles but did not merely imitate or fuse together musical ideas in his compositions. His understanding of the basic principles of blues, twelve-tone composition, microtones, harmonics, quasi-modal composition, and principles from certain non-Western musical traditions launched an evolution toward a personal language. Coltrane evolved through more distinct styles than most other "jazz" masters (Ellington and Miles, of course, did likewise), embracing rhythm and blues, bebop, hard bop, quasi-modal, avant-garde, and other musical forms that are difficult to label (such as those involved in the compositions "Giant Steps, A Love Supreme, Ascension, Interstellar Space," etc.). Joe Goldberg mentions that Coltrane had expressed an interest in twelve-tone music; but when asked about the seeming impossibility of improvising serially he replied, "Damn the rules, it's the feeling that counts. You play all twelve notes in your solo anyway."[12]

Artistic Expression or Entertainment?

Bebop introduced an immutable dilemma for many artists. Do performing musicians focus solely within themselves (individually or with the ensemble onstage), or should the primary concern be satisfying the audience? In the African-American community the answer had been clear; a musician plays for both. Once the music moved into a more unfamiliar (and often hostile) European-American community, some African-American musicians directed a significant proportion of their attention to fellow musicians and their individual musical goals rather than to their new audiences (which may have appeared hostile or indifferent to their musical presence). Focusing musical attention on the circle of musicians became a subtle feature of a significant portion of the innovative musical experiments of the 1960s.

Music and art of the sixties often caused audiences, who expected to be entertained in a particular or prescribed fashion, to reconsider their positions. The new musical presentation did not always blend well with stylized descriptions to which some critics had grown accustomed. Words like "swing" and "jazz" would have to be reevaluated, replaced, or redefined. The act of reducing music to descriptive terms poses metalinguistic problems impossible to surmount. The relationship between words and other sociocultural phenomena can often be direct, but the indirect nature of instrumental music often conveys abstract yet more intimate meanings.

Titles and descriptive programs sometimes offer narrow sets of possible musical meanings in order to make listeners more comfortable with their subjective interpretations. Without such aids, however, critics may freely project their own ignorance, fears, fantasies, etc. onto the void formed when they feel alienated from unfamiliar music.

Author James Lincoln Collier, for instance, foolishly wonders whether Coltrane had an "oral fixation" that caused him to devote so much time to practicing his saxophone.[13] Readers are less likely to read such insulting comments about European-American composers, whether virtuosos or journeymen. Few have accused writers like Collier of having anal fixations for spending so much time sitting at a typewriter, for instance. Everyone celebrated as artistic geniuses throughout Western history accomplished mastery over their discipline through spending exorbitant amounts of time enraptured and intrigued by their chosen course of study. Judging by some of Coltrane's expressed comments regarding his passion for music, it is more reasonable to conclude that he may have been spiritually and artistically inspired to express himself so incessantly.[14]

We have not yet perfected a metalanguage that allows us to discuss sounds and their spectrums of organization effectively. This limitation becomes increasingly more complex with unfamiliar music. Some spectators tend to blame the art for not conforming to their personal expectations, limitations, aesthetic preferences, and individual temperaments, whether or not they are familiar with the sociocultural traditions, stylistic contexts or particular artistic idioms. Descriptions such as too loud, too fast, too abstract, too many things going on at once, too intense, etc. are obviously all subjective observations.

African-American music that began to receive a series of stigmata during the 1960s (free "jazz," new thing, avant-garde, etc.) was a combination of at least several fundamental convergences: it initiated a new movement toward trans-African musical values; it included a liberated and ecumenical approach to all elements of music making; and it sought new forms of expression. African-American musical styles now embraced more aleatory forms of music (where the composer introduces an element of chance or unpredictability, expressing possibility rather than necessity) and relied less on the tendency of functional harmony to assume that all chord combinations of a key area are variants of the tonic, dominant, or subdominant chords. This new music not only involved changing and abandoning key centers but also expanded timbral notions to include a variety of untempered forms of pitch collections. The musical "cry," the growled "bent" tone, and other expressive factors of traditional African music became increasingly pronounced.

In the exploration of quasi-modality,[15] introduced by Miles Davis and others during the 1950s and expanded during the 1960s, the range of musical possibilities extended further horizontally. Modes were in fashions more akin to usage in traditional African styles, such as that of the Hausa-speaking Muslims in Nigeria. The scale specifications for various praise songs involve flexible approaches to modes such as the ascending configuration E-G-A-B-C-D-E-[F]-G-A.

Ornette Coleman, Eric Dolphy, Albert Ayler, Cecil Taylor, Sun Ra, and other innovators were among those involved in the expansion beyond quasi-modality. With freer approaches to "jazz," traditional forms and patterns were replaced by still more liberated criteria. There are at least four common musical elements that can be discerned in free "jazz": (1) tone color often functions as a structural element, (2) a greater emphasis is (once again) placed on collective improvisation, (3) liberation from traditional roles involves not only the solo functions but applies equally to traditional roles of accompaniment, and (4) all traditional musical rules and elements are open to question, redefinition, and revision.

Free "jazz" covered a large number of musical approaches and sounds. Ornette Coleman (often depicted with his white plastic saxophone) was one of the leading contributors to early free "jazz." In an interview for *Down Beat* magazine, Coleman talks about some of the ways he attempted to expand musical horizons between the 1960s and the 1980s:

> When I had my place on Prince Street, I wanted to not worry about categories, and have people playing all kinds of music, regardless of instrument—it could be a kazoo, or a violin, anything. In the Western world, there's only a few instruments that people adopt to a lead, like the saxophone or guitar. You can't have a person with a Jew's harp be the leader of a band. But why not? It's just another sound.

When you see an African person taking a little handmade instrument and blowing your mind, you know the bassoon is not the only instrument that can have new properties to it.

Basically, all the music in the Western world that's tempered is played on the same notes; the solfeggio system is still used today to get people to say, "Well, you're too flat or you're too sharp, you can sing or you can't." Imagine what it was before they had that.... Everyone was concerned about how they felt.... To me, lots of intellectual things have eliminated the naturalness in human beings. And it has really castrated lots of the pureness of people's hearts.

What I want to do is to make the *coloring* the melodies. Not to *color* the melody, but make the melody the actual statement itself. We do that in Prime Time. That's what it is.

In Prime Time the melody can be the bass line, the modulation line, the melody, or the second or third part. In fact that's how I see harmolodics.[16]

During the early and mid-1960s, as Cecil Taylor, John Coltrane, and Albert Ayler began to assert their influence upon the development of "jazz" in New York City, Coltrane's music seemed to generate the greatest degree of controversy. Coltrane mastered blues, rhythm and blues, quasi-modal, and hard bop styles, and his influence was becoming widespread. Coltrane's music transcended ideological boundaries to a greater degree than the music of Taylor, Coleman, and Charles Mingus managed before him.

Of course, not all music in the 1960s was experimental. Musical styles from the past continued to stay alive and sometimes thrive (blues, ragtime, Dixieland, boogie woogie, rhythm and blues, swing, bebop, hard bop, cool, etc.). After the swing era, two distinct concepts of music making clearly emerged and diverged. Duke Ellington, Mary Lou Williams, Art Tatum, and others who emerged from the swing era created forms of music that were not necessarily dance based. The jump bands led by Louis Jordan and others retained a particular connection with the African-American dancing community that later inspired Cannonball Adderley, Horace Silver, and other artists to create a "funky" brand of "jazz." Their intent was to perform African-American music that would be easily accessible for those seeking groove-oriented styles that retained an ethnically identifiable rhythmic pulsation. Adderley and others were not swayed by those accusing them of engaging musical forms that were geared to entertain rather than crafted to appeal more to the intellect.

A stylistic tendency toward African themes also emerged during the swing era (Ellington's "Caravan" and other "jungle music," for instance). This direction gained momentum during the forties (Dizzy Gillespie's "Night in Tunisia," for example) and then found highly fertile soil during the fifties and sixties (Yusef Lateef's "Mahaba'" Coltrane's "African Brass," Miles' "Nefertiti," etc.).

Betty Carter

Betty Carter (1929–1998) masterfully fused artistry, showmanship, exuberance, and surprise into each of her performances. Willard Jenkins describes her this way:

> A fan's remembrance of Betty Carter begins onstage. For although she made numerous successful and eminently swinging recordings, Betty Carter was most assuredly a creature of the living stage. Her presence, colorfully gowned and tastefully coifed, was not of the regal, untouchable variety, but more an earthy forbearance—a hip African-American earth mother of the first magnitude. She kept all eyes riveted on her every move; twisting, turning, pivoting, she moved her body to the rhythm in a sort of calisthenic of swing that was peerless.[17]

Born Lillie Mae Jones, Carter studied piano before beginning her professional career as a singer in 1946. She sat in with Dizzy Gillespie's big band and with Charlie Parker's quintet before touring with Lionel Hampton as Lorraine Carter from 1948 until 1951. Billie Holiday and Sarah Vaughan inspired her unique stylistic approach. Her powerful compositions and arrangements underscored Carter's vocal agility, much akin to that of Sarah Vaughan and Ella Fitzgerald. Her songs, filled with unpredictable shifts in moods and dynamics, transported listeners on amazing voyages to exciting musical regions. She was one of the select few artists who pressed impressive albums on her own label (Bet-Car Records).

She moved between scat singing and lyrics with remarkable clarity with her own exciting and highly varied arrangements. She formed her own record company, Bet-Car Records, when she came out of a self-imposed retirement to raise her children (until 1969). She introduced many young pianists, bassists and drummers to the international "jazz" community as members of her trios. Pianist Cyrus Chestnut worked with Carter between 1991–93. He felt that, "Betty was one of the major mentors in my development. She really encouraged me to try to find something new; she refused to let me just go on automatic pilot. She always wanted the musicians to be sensitive and get all the love the music had."[18]

Carter was an innovative composer and vocalist whose musical insurrections stand out as prominently as those of Charlie Parker, Thelonious Monk, John Coltrane, and Miles Davis. Her consistent ability to find young and gifted musicians made the Betty Carter School perhaps as significant as that of Art Blakey, from which many of today's young masters graduated. Carter's audiences enjoyed the high level of showmanship as riveting as any of the greatest artists of the twentieth century.

During the early 1960s Carter toured, after recording with Ray Charles, Japan (1963) and Europe (1964). She then retired to raise her children before resuming her performance career in 1969. During the 1970s many considered her music too radical, but audiences soon caught up to Carter's experimental nature.

Alice Coltrane

Alice Coltrane was born Alice Farrow in Detroit, Michigan, on August 27, 1937. She came from a musical family that included her bassist brother, Ernie Farrow. After formal studies in Detroit, she formed her own trio. Bud Powell heavily influenced her after her journey to Europe in 1960. Soon she became the successor to Terry Pollard as vibraphonist with The Terry Gibbs Quartet.

Alice met John Coltrane in 1963. They were soon married and had three children. She replaced McCoy Tyner in Coltrane's quartet in 1966 and continued to perform and promote her husband's music after his death. Alice Coltrane played piano and vibraphone early in her career, but following the death of her husband she extended her talent to include the organ, harp, tamboura, and percussion in live and recorded sessions. In his biography on John Coltrane, "jazz" scholar Bill Cole remarked: "If for no other reason, bringing Alice into the band would have been appropriate at this time, if only because of the need to promote more women players. Unquestionably, there has been tremendous male chauvinism in 'jazz' and too often women have been treated as mere sex objects or exploited as Billy Holiday was by members of the orchestra. But there is certainly more to Alice Coltrane than just her symbolic value in the band."[19]

During the final years of her husband's life musical spiritualism and mysticism became the nucleus of both Alice's and John's philosophical thinking. Alice credited her husband with having taught her "to explore . . . to play thoroughly and completely," and said, "I would like to play music according to ideals set forth by John and continue to let a cosmic principle, or the aspect of spirituality, be the underlying reality behind the music as he did."[20]

Eric Dolphy and the "Jazz" Critics

John Coltrane's first recording for the Impulse record label (*Africa/Brass*)[21] featured arrangements by Eric Dolphy, based upon compositional ideas on which Coltrane and Tyner collaborated. The session utilized an unusual instrumentation: trumpet, four French horns, alto saxophone, baritone saxophone, two euphoniums, two basses, piano, drums, tuba, and Coltrane on soprano and tenor saxophones. Dolphy said, "John thought of this sound, he wanted brass, he wanted baritone horns, he wanted that mellow sound and power."[22] Coltrane listened to many African records for rhythmic inspiration and for a general musical direction. He seemed pleased with the results that were obtained and commented, "I had a sound that I wanted to hear. . . . And what resulted was about it."[23]

Alto saxophonist, bass clarinetist, and flutist Eric Dolphy, like Coltrane, continued to maintain ties between his (hard bop) roots and the more radical degrees of musical experimentation he engaged. The contribution Dolphy made to the polyrhythmic fabric while a member of Coltrane's ensemble is particularly robust, piquant, and diametrical in approach. His solo on "My Favorite Things" in the Burrill Crohn film *John Coltrane: The Coltrane Legacy* provides a clear example of his musical contribution. In that performance,

Dolphy breaks away from the overwhelming predominance of triplets to create a contrasting new and independent layer of melodic and polyrhythmic tension. Similarly, the melodic lines Coltrane improvised added unusually elongated phrase dimensions. The longer rhythmic cycle provided yet another level of polyrhythmic tension to the manifold musical mosaic extant on that performance.

While Coltrane's stylistic development evolved gradually from traditional hard bop to a freer musical approach in a highly systematic and methodical fashion, Dolphy continued to oscillate between opposing stylistic poles. He participated as co-leader in the 1960 *Free Jazz* recording with Ornette Coleman. The next year Dolphy recorded with Oliver Nelson and Booker Little in sessions that were decisively hard-bop oriented. Dolphy's influence on Coltrane served as a catalyst that yielded far-reaching consequences in directing the tenor saxophonist's music toward "free jazz."[24]

Coltrane and Dolphy were friends for many years. During Dolphy's numerous visits to Coltrane's home they often practiced together, eventually realizing their mutual ideas about music. They agreed that there should be a somewhat divaricated quality to their music in order to move away from limitations of conventional constructs and closer to the abstract perfection of nature.[25] Coltrane felt that Dolphy's presence in the band opened up new possibilities along such lines. "Eric and I have been talking music for quite a few years, since about 1954. We've been close for quite a while. We watched music . . . discussed what was being done down through the years, because we love music. . . . Since he's been in the band, he's been a broadening effect on us. There are a lot of things we try that we never tried before."[26]

To Dolphy, exemplifying an attitude related to that of Ornette Coleman's, tempered intonation in "jazz" was of secondary interest. While Coltrane expanded the humanlike quality of his sound with harmonics and multiphonics, Dolphy augmented the timbre of his individual voice with an extraordinarily natural and limpid sound that often avoided restricting musical fixation upon precisely definable pitches. Just as Coltrane's spontaneous compositional vocabulary assimilated the various aspects of the entire range of his career into a unified vocabulary, Dolphy too integrated the variegated musical elements involved in his highly unusual sonic language, creating a style that reflected the natural qualities of the human voice. The strikingly human quality of Dolphy's sound exceeded attempts by other artists to accomplish a similar effect.

Dolphy's disdain for traditional approaches to sound production brought about the same degree of skepticism that critics had attached earlier to Lester Young's music. Young broke with the standard conventions established by Ben Webster and Coleman Hawkins by altering pitches with substitute fingerings. Young also took a linear rather than arpeggiated approach in his melodic conception. To the astonishment of critics, Dolphy admitted that bird songs inspired the conceptual basis for his flute playing.[27]

The longest trip the Coltrane group made was its European tour in 1961. While in Germany, bassist Reggie Workman recalls, Coltrane remarked that he had dreamed (back in 1957) of the band he now led, so he felt that this group had been coming into fruition for quite a while.[28] Shortly after this tour, Eric Dolphy joined the ensemble, and then, Workman says, "we began to deal with another dimension in the music."[29] In live performances Coltrane's solos became longer when Dolphy was in the ensemble. Both men liked to play extended solos and had the techniques, stamina, and the powerful imagination needed to do so convincingly. The fact that they were inspired by each other's musical contributions was the catalyst.

Once connected to the labels conjured up by journalists, such as the "New Thing," Dolphy and Coltrane were at once praised and damned by the press. In a November 23, 1961 *Down Beat* article, associate editor John Tynan became the first critic to take a strong position against these two musicians.

> At Hollywood's Renaissance club, I listened to a horrifying demonstration of what appears to be a growing anti-jazz trend exemplified by these foremost proponents of what is termed avant garde music. I heard a good rhythm section . . . go to waste behind nihilistic exercises of the two horns. . . . Coltrane and Dolphy seem intent on deliberately destroying [swing]. . . . They seem bent on pursuing an anarchistic course in their music that can but be termed anti-jazz.[30]

Although such opinions have damaged the careers and economic status of many innovative "jazz" musicians throughout the century, the claims are generally amateurish, nebulous, perfidious, and clearly devoid of real musical substance. The content of this brand of writing rests upon unsubstantiated and highly subjective lay opinions. This led Cecil Taylor to express a sentiment shared by many of his musical colleagues when he disclosed his general contempt for critics in a 1963 *Village Voice* interview. "Critics are sustained by our vitality. From afar, the uninformed egos ever growing arbitrarily attempt to give absolutes."[31]

Critics rarely assume more meaningful and appropriate positions, restricting their comments to technical, sociocultural or historical aspects of music they are qualified to evaluate. Furthermore, as Frank Kofsky points out, not only are these writers usually lacking in musical, sociological, or historical credentials, but most do not derive the major portion of their income from criticism. Often they are dependent for their livelihoods on other unrelated employment sources. Even the more fortunate few end up writing liner notes for record jackets or preparing advertising copies for the record industry. Consequently, the most basic prerequisite of artistic criticism, that which demands that the critic be free to arrive at his or her verdicts without being subtly or overtly coerced by the conflicting interests of political lobbies or influences, is often preempted by self-serving media politics. Despite such inadequacies, many critics wield influential pens that alter the thinking of a sector of the public at large. One manifestation of this influence is the annual *Down Beat* International Jazz Critics Poll each year.[32] An equally unqualified and improper body of people (controlling a significant economic factor in the business of "jazz" production) rarely brandishes similar influence in any other American or European art forms outside of "jazz" (movie critics may be an exception). Critics and readers polls for symphonic organizations do not exist.

Admittedly, all art experiences some level of political control, but the added onerous burden of residual "slave owner" or "plantation" mentality exasperates the problem with African-American music. The effects of powerful artistic innovation have gradually transformed this situation over time, nonetheless.

> Audiences haven't changed much. They say Dizzy and Bird had to face a lot of hostility; but they had their good audiences too. Eventually, the listeners move right along with the musicians.

> Jazz is so much a music of individuality that every new artist with any originality effects a change in the overall scene. Lester Young represented as great a change, in his time, as some of the things that are happening now. So did Bird.[33]

Paradoxically, "jazz" writers, who have demonstrated an affinity for experimental music, are often labeled "the radical critic-polemicist."[34] Those who apparently fail to acknowledge or understand the unfortunate interchange that occurs between African-American "jazz" and European-American racism misjudge such writers. Kofsky writes:

> I believe that the editorial staff of *Down Beat* is thoroughly ingrained with the precepts of white supremacy—so much so, indeed, that they are an integral part of the magazine's frame of reference which can be taken for granted without conditional reiteration. That is why black nationalism, as well as other forms of radicalism, which threatens to disrupt the status quo, are anathema to its editors, why they are at such pains to discredit all radical ideologies.[35]

The social and journalistic condition to which Kofsky refers is apparently still in evidence today. Radano feels that "at times the polemic of the white radical critic equaled or surpassed that of (Leroy) Jones . . . unquestionably the most hostile was Frank Kofsky." It is painfully revealing when the rare situation occurs where a European-American "jazz" critic shares an "unpopular" perspective with African-American artists regarding revolutionary African-American music. Taking such a position remains threatening, socially unacceptable, and newsworthy in the world of American "jazz" literature even at the close of the twentieth century. Unfortunately, interracial agreement rarely occurs in America, so Kofsky's several-decades-old position still stands as a severely polemic notion.

Pointless cavil certainly affected the careers of Dolphy, Coltrane, and many other artists. Coltrane was delighted with Dolphy's playing and admired the fact that "Eric's into everything."

> He just came in and sat in with us for about three nights and everybody enjoyed it, because his presence added some fire to the band. He and I have known each other a long time, and I guess you'd say we were students of the jazz scene. . . . We'd

exchange ideas and so we just decided to go ahead and see if we could do something within this group. Eric is really gifted and I feel he's going to produce something inspired, but although we've been talking about music for years, I don't know where he's going, and I don't know where *I'm* going. He's interested in trying to progress, however, and so am I, so we have quite a bit in common.[36]

Heavy critical protests led Coltrane's record company advisors to eventually convince him to ask Dolphy to leave his ensemble.[37] Although these advisors have not been identified by name in any of the sources I have found, it is certain that the decision made was heavily influenced by responses to Coltrane's and Dolphy's music in the press.[38] Here we come upon a poignant example of the negative influence of opprobrious press on the music of two African-American innovators. Some people felt that if Coltrane had been able to keep his ensemble with Dolphy intact, it could have turned out to be "one of the most interesting in jazz."[39]

In March 1962, Dolphy left Coltrane's ensemble as a regular member and formed his own group. Although he had worked and recorded regularly with Coltrane, surprisingly few of the recording sessions in which Dolphy participated were ever released; and of those commercially issued recordings on which Dolphy performed, his solos were often edited out.[40]

In an effort to clarify issues and hyperbole surrounding their musical conceptions at the time, Coltrane and Dolphy agreed to an interview with critic Don DeMichael in an article that was printed in *Down Beat* on April 21, 1962.[41] The musicians merely stated the obvious in that interview: basically each said they just wanted to make beautiful innovative music.

Eric Dolphy was one of the motivating forces behind the musical idea for the construction of Coltrane's composition "India." He introduced Coltrane to certain aspects of Indian music and the nucleus of "India," emanated from Coltrane's association with Dolphy. This composition frequently employs bass ostinato and pedal note patterns to provide underpinning for free-flowing improvisation on winds and drums. It also directs emphasis toward the lead melody (played in similar motion by Coltrane and Dolphy at the interval of a fourth apart) or soloist. Ekwueme examined the use of pedal notes in Ibo music and found that they added emphases to the words of choral music. "Pedal notes are used usually, but not always, when more than two parts are involved. The two upper parts follow the shape of the tune (and the intonation of the words) in parallel or similar motion. The lowest part can, therefore, afford to dispense with the limitations of speech inflection in its melodic line, and simply repeat a basic drone while other parts indicate the meaning of the words in their own melodic movement."[42]

These Afrocentric ostinato and pedal note patterns, as well as other related musical devices, provide both tonal and rhythmic orientation despite the unpredictability of the soloists and percussion. It was similarly applied in traditional African instrumental ensembles, where the ostinato provided temporal orientation within polyrhythmic frameworks. With African music, for instance, Ekwueme finds ostinati to be useful organizers. "Accompaniment patterns are useful delimiters. When an instrument (or hand clapping) repeats the same pattern over and over in a piece of music, the duration of one such pattern is probably the best 'bar line' delimiter that one may use, especially in measuring temporal durations, in the form of the music. These patterns common in African music, have been called by different names, such as *clap patterns*, *bell pattern*, or simply, *standard pattern.*"[43]

Coltrane created the thematic materials, but Dolphy investigated Indian music long before settling in New York. Eric explored a range of references to exotic scalar configurations over the quasi-modal framework. At the end of his association with Coltrane, Dolphy's performances on this and other recordings show his focused and matured compositional awareness and his control over the technical devices with which he continued to experiment. Earlier in his career, some musical devices sounded more tentative. Dolphy's understanding of formal structure within an improvisational context was also advanced through this synergistic association. Dolphy, Coltrane, Cecil Taylor, Ornette Coleman, and other innovators relied upon symmetrical patterns to provide musical coherence to their work when other tonal devices were abandoned. Call-and-response patterns and the use of refrains in Afrocentric music are related expressions of symmetry. The use of symmetry was also of paramount importance in African music. Ekwueme observed that Africans felt a need to express the duality they found so frequently in nature.

> Many Ibos will not accept gifts that do not come in pairs, and will reject such offers with the statement that they have not been nursed with milk from only one breast. Where there is lack of proportion, balance, or equality, therefore, there is an error in concept or an accident in the execution of the form.

> . . . The idea of symmetry in nature has probably been overworked, especially as there are many asymmetrical things in nature. Yet it must be borne in mind that the Ibo, like his fellow African, is much closer to nature than his counterpart in the western world. He accepts nature and natural forces without attempting to discover empirical justification for their existence. He subsists in and by nature. His ethics and philosophies are dependent on the forces of nature, and his art comes from it. Symmetry is therefore sought after in all artistic endeavors—music, dance, drama, literature, sculpture, painting, textiles, etc. In choral music . . . symmetry is not limited to the form of the songs; it is present in the scales from which the tunes are themselves constructed.[44]

Dolphy enjoyed the reception he received in Copenhagen and other places in Europe, so he eventually settled there. He was able to secure recorded broadcasts and concerts of his music as a leader in Europe. The *Berlin Concerts* and *Stockholm Sessions* are albums issued posthumously (on the Enja label) that document Dolphy's stellar performances on some of these occasions (despite the inferior rhythm sections on the dates comprised of freelance musicians picked up in Europe).

Dolphy's cadenza-like (unaccompanied) approach to Billie Holiday's composition "God Bless the Child" demonstrates the unchallenged level of virtuosity he obtained on bass clarinet. His ability to make any composition his own through personal interpretations of standards is also revealed in his performances of Holiday's composition. Other compositions such as "Spiritual" represent a big leap forward in his development, leading toward the definitive Dolphy seminal *Out To Lunch*. Dolphy's music, and the music of other 1960s innovators, reflect an important connection between the African-American "jazz" movement of the time and the creative expression of various other revolutionary artists (such as author James Baldwin). Many artists were seeking truth and meaning through their work during this salubrious period of artistic development. Artists often found powerful expression through liberated art forms as they attempted to create new identities for themselves and for their musical traditions. These sincere and uninhibited individuals left interesting records of the period.

Albert Ayler

Albert Ayler (1936–70) was one of the younger musicians who influenced John Coltrane during his late periods of development. Ayler was fascinated with the sound of the saxophone and felt that "you really have to play your instrument to escape from notes to sound."[45] Essentially a melodist with a distinctive vibrato and instantly recognizable tone, Ayler created an approach to "jazz" that was unprecedented.

The works of Charlie Parker significantly affected Ayler. His haunts, shouts, and whines on his instrument created an emotional and vibrant music that used melody as both a motivating force and continuity factor at the root of his free improvisations. This musical freedom was contained within clearly organized structures, episodes of contrapuntal interaction, and was often sustained through motivic developments. His emotional intensity was counterbalanced by the gentleness that could be found in "Saints" and in certain other compositions. He explored the dirge like genres of music akin to that Ornette Coleman often engaged. Ayler used this particular conceptual approach to explore variations in expressive timbres. This basic principle was applied to his composition "Witches and Devils" and others. Ayler felt that

> When there is chaos, which is now [December 18, 1966], only a relatively few people can listen to the music that tells of what will be. You see, everyone is screaming "Freedom" now, but mentally, most are under a great strain. But now the truth is marching in, as it once marched back in New Orleans. And that truth is that there must be peace and joy on Earth. I believe music can help bring that truth into being because music *is* the universal language. That's why it can be such a force.[46]

Coltrane was a musician that Ayler admired, and Ayler wrote his composition "For Coltrane" after the summer when Coltrane died (1967). Ayler said, "John was like a visitor to this planet. He came in peace and he left in peace; but during his time here, he kept trying to reach new levels of awareness, of peace, of spirituality. That's why I regard the music he played as sacred music—John was getting closer and closer to the Creator."[47]

Ayler's compositions insisted that the listener adopt new attitudes for the absorption of music. When Nat Hentoff asked his brother Don Ayler (who played trumpet with Albert) how one should listen to his music, Don told him one way *not* to listen was "to focus on the notes and stuff like that. Instead try to move your imagination toward the sound. It's a matter of following the sound." Albert added, "You have to relate sound to sound inside it. You have to try to listen to everything together." Don concluded, "The pitches, the colors, you have to watch them move."[48] Albert Ayler called the overwhelming vitality of his music spiritual energy that was "purely music of love. While it comes from meditation, it has nothing to do with mysticism. It tries to help bring about new approaches to living for everyone."

Ayler says his composition "Our Prayer" "has its own very distinctive thing to say. It's a prayer to the Creator, a song about the spiritual principles of the universe." Albert Ayler's career was cut short when he was murdered and his body thrown into a river in New York City in 1970. Donald Ayler went into seclusion. They both came in peace and left in peace.

Ayler's intense musical message contained swirling figures with a voicelike timbre. He stretched the upper register of the tenor saxophone and based his melodies on European classical and folk rhythms that lacked the conventional swing feeling. His compositions loosely allude to preset harmonic structures and rhythmic motives. He was among the earliest innovators to improvise without conventional preset chord progressions.

The Association for the Advancement of Creative Musicians

In 1961 Muhal Richard Abrams (b. 1930) formed the Experimental Band, which would later evolve into the Association for the Advancement of Creative Musicians. He later became the AACM's president. Abrams explored new ideas with bassist and multi-instrumentalist Donald Garrett and other musicians for an extended period of time. By 1963 the Experimental Band eventually expanded to include Joseph Jarman (b. 1937), alto saxophone; Fred Berry, trumpet; Henry Threadgill (b. 1944), woodwinds; Gene Dinwiddie, Kalaparusha, and Maurice McIntyre (b. 1936), tenor saxophones; Lester Lashley, trombone; Charles Clark and Donald Garrett, basses; Jack De-Johnette (b. 1942) and Steve McCall (1933–89), drums; and numerous other musicians. Abrams wrote in what he classified as a chromatic style, while Mitchell's compositional area was polytonal and Jarman's approach involved serialized musical experiments.[49]

Pianists Abrams and Jodie Christian, drummer Steve McCall, and trumpeter Phil Cohran formed the AACM in May 1965. Its original members were from several groups that appeared around Chicago. Their goals involved (1) creating a situation where a brand of music of their own choice could be produced, and (2) maintaining self-reliance and control over their music. John Johnson handled most of the administrative responsibilities. Minimal dues were collected from members to cover operational expenses and concerts were presented around town. Members from other parts of the country became interested in the organization and, if nominated by a member, they joined after being told what was expected of them. Lester Bowie (1941–1999), who had been a member of the Black Artist Group (BAG), came to Chicago with drummers Phillip Wilson and Leonard Smith from St. Louis. Trumpeter Leo Smith came from Mississippi.

Leo Smith later worked with Anthony Braxton (woodwinds; b. 1945) and Leroy Jenkins (violin; b. 1932) during a period when the trumpeter evolved closer to the idea of "total creativity." Braxton felt that the creative impulse had become so suppressed that the distance between the innovative artist and audiences continued to grow wider every year. He began spending more of his time in Europe with musicians like guitarist Derek Bailey (1930), who he felt were immersed in developing their own musical worlds.

The seriousness and gravity of the music eventually attracted more innovative musicians (who heard the concerts and rehearsals) into its broadening ranks. As Roscoe Mitchell (woodwinds; b. 1940) explains, "I was cool; I took dope; I smoked pot; etc. I did not *care* for the life I had been given. In having the chance to work with the Experimental Band with Richard and the other musicians there, I found the first something with meaning/reason for doing. That band and people there was the *most* important thing that ever happened to me."[50]

Many others soon to be prominent innovators studied and digested Muhal Richard Abrams's concepts, including Anthony Braxton and Leo Smith. Smith said, "I only play when there is an opportunity for you to explore yourself, when each occasion would bring to those people and myself a complete challenge. And when I say 'challenge,' I don't mean some reference in the back past, but like challenge *right now*, where we are right now—because it is the future."

The Emergence of the Art Ensemble of Chicago

The Art Ensemble of Chicago was one of the most unusual groups to emerge in "jazz." The Art Ensemble of Chicago left Chicago for France in June 1969 and performed at festivals and clubs and gave concerts all over the European continent. Drummer Don Moye (b. 1946), joined the Art Ensemble of Chicago in Paris. The ensemble recorded a wide range of albums during that period and demonstrated their ability to move between blues and other traditional African-American musical norms en route to a highly personal free style. Jerome Cooper (b. 1946) also played with the Art Ensemble of Chicago. He and Leroy Jenkins were also members of the Revolutionary Ensemble.

Lester Bowie, the son of a music teacher and trumpeter, was born in Frederick, Maryland. He began to play the trumpet at age five and developed an eclectic performance style that incorporates the St. Louis half-valve trademark, gut bucket and heraldic trumpet playing. He also experimented with a wide variety of other techniques that span the history of twentieth-century trumpet. He worked as a traveling musician with Jackie Wilson, Joe Tex, Little Milton, and other rhythm-and-blues-oriented bands, while occasionally sitting in with musicians such as James Clay and David "Fathead" Newman (b. 1933). His long association with Julius Hemphill (1940–95), Oliver Lake (b. 1944), Phillip Wilson, and other innovative musicians date back to bebop sessions in St. Louis. Eventually, he became music director for singer and pianist Fontella Bass, who later became his wife. Bowie felt that "if you get a job playing rock-and-roll, you can maybe be a little hip on it, but you're still basically dealing with the idiom. With bebop and free jazz, the boundaries are defined. But with Mitchell there was no limitation about what you could deal from."[51]

Born in 1937, double bassist Malachi Favors was the oldest member of the original quartet that became known as the Art Ensemble of Chicago. He was the son of a preacher in Lexington, Mississippi, who was drawn toward the bass as a teen. In addition to being a unifying musical force in the ensemble, he also branches out from the bass to balafon, banjo, zither, voice, and an assortment of small percussion instruments.

Joseph Jarman (b. 1937), as poet and philosopher, became the spokesperson for the Art Ensemble of Chicago. He had joined forces with Phillip Wilson in 1961 while attending Wilson Junior College, where Jarman wrote stream-of-consciousness-style compositions for words and music that rejected the established musical norms.

The distance between any two opposing poles of phenomena is actually a force that contributes to the definition of the instances at either end of a central void or nucleus. Silence too is such a force. Some musicians realize that this seemingly empty space contributes as much to a musical statement as the notes that surround it. The relationship between space and silence can be methodically controlled to yield profound results. Thelonius Monk and Randy Weston (b. 1926) are spontaneous composers who bring high degrees of meaning to the silences between their sonic events. Along with an understanding of the use of flexible rhythmic placement over a metronomic pulse, both Monk and Weston derive dramatic effects through unpredictable rhythmic augmentation, diminution, and hypermetrical time maneuvers that transform would-be musical simplicity into rich and surprising artistic occurrences.

The inherent strength and beauty of a melody or motive allows it to undergo various transformations and to enjoy a long life within musical situations that demand that continuity be maintained over extraordinary lengths of time. Once established during a musical exposition, working with familiar elements of these types enable the creative composer to transmute an incomplete or abstracted version of the central ideas into an unlimited set of metaphorical possibilities. The constant references to, or embellishments of, the original melodies or motives provides powerful composers like Monk flexible structures for the creation of well balanced musical abstractions.

Whether musical variations and permutations be subtle or profound, various degrees of tension and release are provided as the music finds new ways to breathe that are no longer determined by simple cadences, phrase structures, and binary or ternary formal devices. The music becomes fresh and personal, not only because an individual harmonic and melodic vocabulary has been formulated, but also because musical choices have been enhanced by spontaneously evolving sets of spatial relationships. As a creative artist expands the voids that form the silent centers between sonic events, new territory is excavated that demands exploration. Seemingly empty space can begin to take on personal dimensions and features of its own that form influential mental constructs. The silences can create moods, rhythms, and attitudes that make us apprehensive, curious, pensive, or excited while anticipating approaching sonic events.

The Art Ensemble of Chicago was one of the first groups to place an extremely heavy degree of emphasis on silence in "jazz." When we realize that silence can become penetratingly animated, it eventually becomes apparent that music contains more than length, width, and depth. It contains immeasurable subconscious elements that register strongly upon our senses but remain difficult to define empirically. These elements, both on our initial and subsequent contacts with certain music, fill our imaginations with images and messages that confirm the presence of countless subtle dimensions, the presence of which our minds, bodies, and emotions cannot deny.

Dewey Redman, Art Davis, and the New York Scene

Dewey Redman, a multi-reed specialist, was born in Fort Worth, Texas in 1931. He began studying music as a clarinetist. After attending Prairie View A&M College, he studied the nuances of swing band playing, and admired the work of Johnny Hodges, Earl Bostic, and Charlie Parker. Redman joined the army for a while, then taught full-time in Bastrop, Texas, while occasionally sitting in on alto saxophone with local bands. When he switched to tenor saxophone, Dexter Gordon, Gene Ammons, and Stan Getz became his main influences. He discusses his musical past in a 1992 interview for *Down Beat* magazine.[52] Eventually, "at age 29 I decided to go to New York. And I told myself if I didn't make it in five years, I'd go back to Texas. It didn't work out like that. I've been trying ever since." Dewey Redman later found a stable situation in Ornette Coleman's band. Redman said,

> I've always been into Ornette's music—I knew him when he first started playing. When I got to New York he was in a hiatus, but he had a loft on Prince Street and he'd say, "Well, you're here, so. . . ." He'd write out a tune, and I'd go over it; then he'd write out another tune, and I'd go over that. . . . When Ornette came out of his hiatus, the first gig I had was with him and Denardo [Coleman's son, then a twelve-year-old drummer] and [bassist] David Izenzon. Later [Ed] Blackwell came into the band and Charlie [Haden].
>
> . . . Ornette is a genius, and I consider myself having gone to the University of Ornette because I learned so much—about space, phrasing; how not to be caught up in conventional things, but to appreciate them too. . . . Like changes: changes are *okay*, but I'm not to be limited by them. And not to be limited in my scope.

My technique isn't always what I want it to be, and my sidemen might sometimes play too loud. But it's a strange thing,
man: sometimes when you think you've played your ass off,
people look at you like you're crazy. And then sometimes when
you played the worst solo ever, people say, "Wow! What a great
solo that was!"

To play a little avant-garde—or avant-bop—then a little bebop,
and a little blues, musette, this here, that there; to make it all
come out clean, that's very difficult to do. Some musicians dab-
ble in it, say their multi-directional; but I try to make each one
distinct and clear.[53]

Like Ornette Coleman, Redman passed on his musical knowledge to
his son Joshua. Joshua Redman (b. 1969) graduated summa cum laude from
Harvard and was accepted into Yale (and contemplated a law degree) before
turning to music as a profession.

Musical life in New York is not predictable. For those who are ready
for the challenge musically, there can be endless opportunities to perform,
record, and tour with the best musicians in the world. There are also spells of
inactivity that can prove to be financially difficult and discouraging. With African-American music, there are no musical institutions designated to provide stability for professional artists. During the 1960s, virtually all studio
jobs, teaching positions, positions with symphony orchestras, or any other
stable jobs for professional musicians went to European or European-American men.

By 1969, the year that Arthur Davis (b. 1934) and Earl Madison
brought suit against Leonard Bernstein and the New York Philharmonic Orchestra, there had been a dramatic 200 percent leap in the number of professional African-American musicians engaged in the major symphony orchestras. Generally speaking, this usually meant that orchestras now hired two
African-American musicians instead of one. With the New York Philharmonic
this represented approximately 0.3 percent of the total (525) men and women
employed. Since 1965 significant numbers of federal tax dollars, of which African-American citizens often pay a disproportionate share, have been allo-
cated for American symphony orchestras.

In 1969, $20 million were allocated to the National Endowment for the
Arts and Humanities by the federal government. By 1972 allocations increased to an appropriation of $60 million devoted to these causes. A sizable
proportion of these funds continue to be targeted for American symphony orchestras. Other private foundations, whose tax-exempt status is made possible by philanthropic grants to nonprofit organizations such as symphonic organizations, provide sizable contributions toward the maintenance of musical
institutions that were almost exclusively "European only" cultural establishments.[54] Author Ortiz M. Walton discusses the Davis/Madison case:

For Arthur Davis, who had auditioned for the New York Philharmonic on four occasions, and Earl Madison, who had three
times auditioned, the outcome could hardly be termed just. The

ruling by the New York Commission on Human Rights, after fifteen months of hearings, found the Philharmonic both guilty and not guilty. [After consultation with attorneys representing Mr. Madison and Mr. Bernstein, the latter's name was dropped from Mr. Madison's complaint.] The Philharmonic was found not guilty of the main charge of discrimination against the two black players in terms of permanent hiring. A guilty-of-discrimination verdict was handed down regarding the hiring of substitute and extra players, a procedure, which unlike permanent hiring, did not require auditions.[55]

Art Davis had been featured two or three times a week on the Merv Griffin television show before the hearings began on his case with the New York Philharmonic. After the legal proceedings began he lost his job. Walton continues:

In the music business, things such as reprisals have a curious way of happening to people who dare to speak the truth. We have seen what happened to Scott Joplin when he demanded royalties instead of outright, once-only payment for his masterpieces. He never sold any more music, and was unable to successfully stage a production of this opera, *Treemonisha*. This procedure is aptly enough called blacklisting. Of course, like other forms of discrimination, particularly those which affect the individual performer, the charge is difficult to prove, inasmuch as these actions are covertly accomplished. Erroll Garner, who had contractual disputes with Columbia Records in the early sixties, has rarely been heard of since. Charles Mingus, who dared to vilify in his music such figures as the former governor of Arkansas, Orville Faubus, suffered a similar fate. Word somehow gets around to those non-Blacks who are in charge of the music industry, and shortly a personal boycott results.

The New York Philharmonic is composed, like other major symphonies, of wealthy and powerful interest groups. Their concern with the arts may be most often viewed as supportive to other roles they play in society, politely masking racism under the facade of culture. This veneer, in addition to a fanatical devotion to the tenets of Western European ideas and civilization, assists in the determination and maintenance of the status quo. When an uppity "nigger" comes along to test these notions, and to assist in the redetermination of culture and values, he will then be pushed, forced out of the business.

The most striking statistic to emerge from the evidence presented was that during the 1960's the respondent [personnel manager Joseph De Angelis] hired at least 277 substitutes or extras who played a total of 1773 weeks during that period. Of these musicians, *one* was black and he played for one week. Interestingly enough, the concerts performed during the week this black musician played included a musical work dedicated to the memories of Dr. Martin Luther King, Jr., and Robert Kennedy. Despite general agreement that this black flutist acquitted himself well, he has not been invited by the respondent to return, although white flutists have since been engaged as substitutes.[56]

The *New York Times* reported on November 18, 1970, that cellist Earl Madison and bassist Arthur Davis offered to play against each member of the New York Philharmonic orchestra cello and bass sections if screens were provided to preserve anonymity. Madison said, "We have nothing to lose. They have nothing. They say they are the greatest, so let them prove it." The New York Philharmonic remained intransigent on the issue of screening players during auditions.[57]

Amina Claudine Myers

Composer Amina Claudine Myers (b. 1942) is also a pianist, organist, and vocalist. She was born in Blackwell, Arkansas, on March 21, 1942. Myers began playing and singing as early as age four and began formal lessons at age seven. She served as pianist and organist for both school and church choirs throughout high school. While enrolled at Philander Smith College she was concert choir pianist and, for two years, student director.

In the mid-1960s Myers played organ with The Gerald Donavan Trio and became one of the few female composers affiliated with the Association for the Advancement of Creative Musicians (AACM). She established meaningful contacts during that phase of her development and began touring the country with saxophonist Sonny Stitt in 1970.

Myers soon began a two-year musical association with tenor saxophonist Gene Ammon's Quartet, worked with the AACM Big Band, played with the Vanguard Ensemble led by drummer Ajaramu (Gerald Donovan), performed in Muhal Richard Abrams's piano trio, and played duets with Joseph Jarman. After moving to New York she went on a tour of Europe with Lester Bowie.

In 1977 Myers premiered her musical *I Dream* in Chicago, which received a repeat performance in 1978 in New York City. She has performed solo concerts at numerous universities throughout America and took part in the "Big Apple" Jazz Women band of New York City that gave a highly acclaimed performance at the Kansas City Women's Jazz Festival, in 1979 ("Salute to Women in Jazz"). In addition to recordings made with various gospel groups, Myers has worked and recorded with Little Milton, Lester Bowie, Fontella Bass, Kalaparusha, Henry Threadgill, and her own groups.

Pharaoh Sanders

Pharaoh Sanders was born in 1940 in Little Rock, Arkansas. Sanders was always interested in art and initially wanted to be a painter or commercial artist. He later became fascinated with the music of Coltrane, Dolphy, Ornette Coleman, Rollins, and other African-American innovators. Allowing musicians to recount aspects of their careers can be insightful. An examination of Sanders's career (from his own perspective) provides a glimpse of the West Coast music scene, the musical camaraderie that existed at the time, and the struggle involved in coming east during the 1960s. In an article in *Jazz Change* Sanders recalled:

> My grandfather was a school teacher; he taught music and mathematics. My mother and her sisters used to sing in clubs and teach piano. For myself, I started playing drums in the high school band. Then I played tuba and baritone horn, clarinet and flute. In 1959, I started playing tenor saxophone, still in the school band. At the same time I was listening to Jimmy Cannon, my band teacher, who played jazz. Richard Boone, the Count Basie trombone player—he's from Little Rock too. He would sometimes sit in with the concert band.

> In my own playing I was more or less into rhythm and blues. I liked Earl Bostic a lot. When I finished high school in 1959, I was supposed to take either a music or an art scholarship. I didn't want to stay in Little Rock so I left for the West Coast. I went to Oakland Junior College for a couple of years, and then moved over to San Francisco. I majored in art. But I was getting some rock n' roll gigs playing tenor. I also played alto, flute, clarinet, and baritone whenever possible, but I had fallen in love with the tenor.

> On those blues jobs, I played mostly by ear, but I had some private lessons in Oakland which taught me about harmonics. By this time I was listening to Sonny Rollins, who was a big influence at first; John Coltrane, who was a later big influence; and Ornette Coleman, Eric Dolphy, Booker Ervin, Hank Mobley and Horace Silver's group. I loved Benny Golson on *Moanin'* with Art Blakey.

> When I heard Coltrane's *Blue Train* LP, I really didn't know what he was doing. I had never heard anybody play tenor like that before, with that range. Most of the guys played just in the middle register. When I first heard Ornette's music I liked it— *really*, it was something! It seemed so natural, as if he weren't limiting himself, as if he wanted to let himself just go to the music. I remember talking to Ornette in 'Frisco. I don't know whether he remembers me from then.

By that time I had begun to try to play that way myself. Sonny Simmons, and a lot of people I was playing with in Oakland at the time, were playing a lot freer. They had been playing that way before I came to California. They heard me and invited me to come down and play sometime. I was kind of skeptical about it because up to that point all I had been playing was rhythm and blues. What they played had a good feeling, but I was wondering, what are they doing? Were they crazy? But it felt good. So, I just fell in with it too. Later, I started playing jazz more conventionally and studying the basics—getting my chords and my scales.

Actually I have never had a jazz gig of my own long enough to see what I can really do on conventional tunes. I would like to get one for at least six nights a week so I could try to express myself fully "inside" and see both sides of it. I still take different kinds of jobs. I play rock n' roll for dances, usually in Brooklyn. It's a big help financially, and my profession is music, so it's my business to be able to play any kind of music.

Once when John Coltrane came out to San Francisco, he was asking around about mouthpieces. So I told him that I had a bunch of mouthpieces, and that he could try them. I also said I would take him around to the different places in town if he wanted to try some more. I never thought he'd take me up on it, of course—he was a giant to me then. But he showed up one morning, saying, "Are you ready, man?" I was really shook up! At the time, my own horn was in the repair shop and he offered to pay the bill so I could get it out. All day long we went around to pawn shops and more pawn shops, trying out different mouthpieces.

Sanders drove across the country with a couple of musician friends in 1962. It took awhile to get established in New York once he arrived.

I slept in the subway—the police didn't bother me—or in tenement halls under the stairs. And I pawned my instrument.

I think my first gig in New York was one in a coffee house in the Village called the Speakeasy, with C Sharp and Billy Higgins. . . . We made $8 a night. The job lasted almost a year. I used to live on wheat germ, peanut butter and bread—I still carry a jar of wheat germ in my instrument case. It's good food. I began seeing a lot of Billy Higgins. We would play together, talk, eat; might be together all day long. If he wasn't playing on his drums he would play on the table, or glasses with spoons or whatever else he found.

I took some other jobs. Once I was a combination cook, waiter and counter-man, and all I got was what I ate. Then I caught on that I should be paid, and I split. I was trying to survive, and it is harder to survive in New York than in Oakland or San Francisco. If I wasn't thinking about trying to survive, I was thinking about music. I didn't think much about commercial art by this time.

A friend of mine who lived in Brooklyn, someone I had known in San Francisco, invited me to stay at his place. That's where I met Don Cherry, and we began rehearsing and playing together. We got one job at Pratt Institute in Brooklyn. There was an exhibition of student art work and they wanted some of our kind of music along with it. I had to get my horn out of hock for that one, and the other guys in the group helped me by putting up the money.

When I play, I try to adjust myself to the group, and I don't think much about whether the music is conventional or not. If the others go "outside," play "free," I go out there too. If I tried to play too differently from the rest of the group, it seems to me I would be taking the other musicians' energy away from them. I still want to play my own way. But I wouldn't want to play with anybody that I couldn't be pleased with the way I play. Anyway, Don Cherry seemed to like what I was doing. I was getting different sounds out of the horn then. For my part, I was just trying to express myself. Whatever came out of the instrument just came out, as if I had no choice.

Naturally, you have elements of music and musical skills to work with, but once you've got those down, I think you should go after feelings. If you try to be too intellectual about it, the music becomes too mechanical. It seems that for me, the more I play "inside," inside the chords and the tune, the more I want to play "outside," and free. But also the more I play "outside" the more I want to play "inside" too. I'm trying to get a balance in my music. A lot of cats play "out" to start with. But if I, myself, start off playing "inside" and then let the spirit take over, wherever it goes, it seems better to me. I'm not trying to do anything that is over somebody's head. My aim is to *give* people something. When I give them something they can give me something, the energy to continue.

Sanders had the good fortune to sit in with Coltrane's quartet at the Half Note in New York.

We had become pretty close and had been talking a lot. He would call me and we would talk about religion and about life. He was also concerned about what he wanted to do next in his music, about where he was headed. We got pretty close and sometimes he would say, "Come on down and play something with me tonight," almost as though we were continuing the conversation. So I would just come down and start playing.

By that time, I thought of him not just as a great musician but also as a wise man. But I was still a little self-conscious and wasn't sure what to do with him musically. I thought maybe I was playing too long, and on some numbers, I wouldn't play at all. And sometimes I would start to pack up my horn. But he would tell me not to. Anyway, I'd never play as long as he did because, you know, he might play for an hour on one tune.

Sanders was never asked officially to become a member of Coltrane's group but played with Coltrane whenever he was asked to.

He (Coltrane) might say, "I have a job down in Washington for a week. How about coming on down with me?" Or, he'd say he had a record date coming up and would I like to play on it too.

Always, it was like a communication through music, like he knew some things that I wanted to know that he could express musically, and that I maybe had some things to contribute too. It's hard to talk about it, except in spiritual or religious terms, actually. Still, he had a lot of things on his mind musically. He wanted to decide what he should turn to next, and he needed time to find out. He was a perfectionist, and he wanted to grow, always. Whatever he did, he wanted it to come from inside himself, and he did not want to hold anything back, or hide anything he found there. Good or bad, it had to be expressed. Once he asked me what I thought he should do next, what he should work on—how could he create something different. I told him maybe he should try to better some of the things he had already done, go back and try again on older tunes. I don't really know if that was any help to him; I don't know whether that was what he was looking for or not.

In regards to Pharoah's own playing he says, "In a group, I like to play with anyone who really wants to play, who really wants to put out the energy. If the players don't put out the energy it takes away my own."[58]

Archie Shepp

Archie Shepp, a saxophonist influenced by Ornette Coleman born in 1937 in Fort Lauderdale, Florida, completed his B.A. in dramatic literature at Goddard College in 1959. He intended to become a playwright when he moved to New York. He joined forces with Cecil Taylor instead, and, after playing alto saxophone in local dance bands around the city, met John Coltrane, who greatly influenced Shepp's approach to music. Shepp eventually formed a quartet with trumpeter Bill Dixon (b. 1925), which later became the New York Contemporary Five (including Don Cherry and John Tchicai). With the aid of John Coltrane's recommendation, he recorded the album *Four For Trane* for Impulse Records in 1964. Shepp became an influential figure within the avant-garde music scene in the late 1960s. He collaborated with Bobby Hutcherson (b. 1941), Roswell Rudd (b. 1935), Grachan Moncur III (b. 1937), Beaver Harris (1936–91), and other experimental artists. Shepp is also an educator. After gains made through the efforts of the Civil Rights movement were beginning to take effect, the American university was gradually becoming a potential system of patronage for a few African-American artists.

Shepp began to lead his own groups beginning in the mid-sixties. Roswell Rudd, Beaver Harris, Bobby Hutcherson, and Grachan Moncur III were featured in his ensembles. From 1969 to 1974 he served on the faculty of the black studies program at the State University of New York (SUNY) and in 1974 accepted a faculty position at the University of Massachusetts. He was eventually promoted to associate professor. Shepp credits Duke Ellington, Max Roach, and Charlie Mingus as his chief musical influences because they fused music with sociopolitical opinions. His political views were also shaped by Langston Hughes, Richard Wright, Ralph Ellison, and other writers.[59]

Shepp articulately voiced anger and resentment toward the oppressive tendencies of the dominant society. His messages permeated all levels of his artistic utterances throughout the 1960s, chiding racial policies that discriminated against African-American musicians. He characterizes the economic situation for African-American innovators: "Music for a nigger *is* a hobby! White folks make a lot of money playing black music. A nigger will never make a dime; if he makes a dime, he's lucky. But that's good, because this country is giving up less and less. I'm opposed to what I see, and I'll go on record as being opposed to what I see being done to my people!"[60]

Author David Such argues, "Shepp also posits causal relationships between jazz and certain political and social attitudes."[61] Shepp states clearly that he feels African-American "jazz" is, "self-expression. . . . And a certain quality of human dignity despite all obstacles. Despite the enslavement of the black man and then his oppression. And each of the great players has had so distinctive, so individual a voice. There is only one Bird, one Ben Webster, one Cootie Williams."[62]

Many European Americans, including David Such, consider Shepp's views racist. When commenting on the oppression they encounter and witness in America, African-American musicians have always been criticized flippantly by the majority society.

It was two centuries after the first institutions of higher education were opened in America (in 1636) that an African-American obtained a diploma from a college or university in the United States.[63] As "Black" studies departments began springing up throughout America, a small number of African-American musicians gradually found positions on university faculties. Some, like Bill Dixon, who had taught art history at the university level, found academic life suitable. Dixon found an academic home at Bennington, Vermont.[64]

In 1970 Cecil Taylor joined the University of Madison, Wisconsin. He moved to Antioch College in Yellow Springs, Ohio, when the atmosphere became less accommodating in Madison after a considerable number of his students there failed his course. He was able to establish the members of his performing ensemble as artists-in-residence for a fruitful two-year period at Antioch. Both Jimmy Lyons and Andrew Cyrille benefited from the temporary economic stability and artistic growth the college position provided. Taylor had always experienced difficulty in getting musicians to play his music. Within a university he could develop his compositional ideas and have them played by ensembles that rehearsed regularly.

Of all the universities in the United States that have offered "jazz" courses and performance programs, relatively few have hired educators from the enormous pool of established African-American "jazz" masters. Charlie Parker, John Coltrane, and Miles Davis were never offered tenured positions on university music faculties. Many members of symphony orchestras (who often lack advanced degrees) are frequently employed on university faculties as professors. Since the early 1970s, nonetheless, Donald Byrd, Jackie Byard, John Handy, Yusef Lateef, Art Davis, David Baker, George Russell, Ron Carter, Andrew Hill, Max Roach, Milford Graves, Buddy Collette, Nathan Davis, Jackie McLean, Ken McIntyre, Charles Tolliver, and Clifford Thornton are among the African-American artists who have taught for various periods of times at American universities.

In the 1970s Shepp became a tenured professor in the African-American Music Department in Amherst. He realizes that African-American music has remained a reflector of changing times. In an interview with Charles Gans in the *Jazz Forum* (February 1985), Shepp offered an explanation as to why there are fewer African-American innovators extant at the end of the twentieth century.

> Today people pay money to see a show much like in the '20s and '30s. The music that surfaced in the '40s after the war—so-called bebop music with the small quartets, the virtuosic combinations culminating in John Coltrane—has become perhaps out of step with the times. Young people don't seek to emulate that kind of music anymore. They may try to play like a particular virtuoso. Many saxophone players today try to emulate John's (Coltrane's) music almost note for note regardless of what idiom they play in. But that style of music—so-called "jazz" music—is rapidly disappearing.

> When a music loses its history and its connection to its tradition, it is very hard pressed to stay alive. . . . I mean you don't find many young black people playing that kind of music or the blues—a few but not many. And with so-called "jazz" music, I think relatively few black youngsters are coming into the tradition, so eventually it will lose its innovative aspect. . . .

> This is perhaps the only music created in the Western world that kept pace with technological innovation. When you hear

reggae and those types of music, they are very influenced by African-American blues from the United States. It's the beat that really gives the samba and those kinds of music their specific identities. Many of those rhythms can be found in Africa. They haven't been changed that much.

When we talk about Baby Dodds and Cozy (Cole), Roy (Haynes) and Max (Roach), you are talking about different drummers. But when we talk about the drum set, I think it is an ingenious invention. The American Negro player exchanged the African chorus for the trap set, where one man does what three men used to do in Africa. In Africa the ilya ilyu, kere kere and gudu gudu form a drum choir. But Max Roach with the tom tom, snare and high hat does that same thing . . .

The interesting thing is that people don't play it anymore, at least black people don't. I think that's a sad commentary on the ultimate meaning of that music, because it was made by black people and now it is being neglected and relinquished by black people. That's why it no longer has life.

. . . I would suspect that most people don't think of black people in the United States as having created any culture at all. But that's quite an error, and I think our music is an example of that. It's so distinct and different—and not only so-called "jazz" music . . . Negro music is quite easily identified.

Shepp was well aware of the economic realities that engulf even the most stalwart musicians. He feels that some of the most prominent innovators in "jazz" began to allow economic concerns too strongly affect their artistic judgment.

What perhaps is more negative is that a very strong figure like Miles Davis is trying to play like Michael Jackson too. . . . All of Miles' group—Herbie (Hancock), Wayne (Shorter) and all the cats—are playing something else. I think we should make some kind of statement about this music—that it is worth something and is valid—because even the people who created it are no longer playing it. In fact, they speak rather despairingly of it.

The thing about it is that it's less of a commentary on him than on America. Somehow he was discouraged from being the genius that he's always been, and money was the root of it. According to this book by Clive Davis, the former head of Arista, there was a big shakeup at Columbia when Miles decided that he would not be a jazz musician anymore. He hadn't played for a long time and was supposed to have come and asked for a raise. They told him, "But, gee, Miles, we can't give you a raise, in fact we were thinking of giving you a cut in salary, because jazz doesn't sell the way other kinds of music sell." And Miles reportedly said, "Well, fuck it, I don't play no more jazz then. If it don't sell why play it."

. . . But Blacks who created it are too caught up in the day to day efforts of survival to continue to innovate in this music and therefore it will not last, because this music grows out of a whole cultural matrix, and particularly the Afro-Christian church.[65]

Alcohol and heroin took their toll on many great artists during the 1950s.[66] Money and peace of mind may have become the new lures from the 1970s onward. "Cross-over" musicians from the latter era have included Sony Criss, Yusef Lateef, Don Pullen, Don Cherry, and Sonny Rollins. Usually artists see such ventures as temporary ones allowing them to access a wider audience and to gain capital to finance more creative projects in the future. Whether this process ever in fact reaches the suggested goals still remains to be seen.

EVIL

Looks like what drives me crazy
Don't have no effect on you—
But I'm gonna keep on at it
Till it drives you crazy, too.

—Langston Hughes

Joanne Brackeen

Pianist-composer Joanne Brackeen, born in California in 1938, was largely self-taught as a child. By the time she was a teenager she won a scholarship to the Los Angeles Conservatory of Music, but left the school after just three days, explaining that she "wasn't interested in the classical training it offered." She instead began sitting in at local clubs, where she was able "to learn from such top jazzmen as saxophonists Dexter Gordon and Harold Land." She continued to study and copy the solos of Charlie Parker, Bud Powell, and John Coltrane. Linda Dahl considers Brackeen's playing "informed by a passionate, relentlessly exploratory harmonic approach and ceaseless rhythmic complexity, and her high level of technical expertise is matched by her intense concentration."[67]

Joanne married saxophonist Charles Brackeen in 1960 and left the professional scene for a while (they have since separated). "When I got married, making sure my children had a mother during their younger years was what mattered most to me. [She has four children born close together in time.] I still played and wrote music, and that was enough. It wasn't until we moved to New York in 1965 that I began to appear in public again."[68] By 1969 Joanne secured a job with Art Blakey and the Jazz Messengers and remained as pianist with the band until 1972. She remained the only woman to play with the Messengers for a significant period of time. "I heard Blakey's group in a club. The piano player was just sitting there, but he wasn't playing. He didn't know where they were in the tune. So I went up on the bandstand and started playing. After I finished I thought it was pretty strange for me to do this, but that must have been how I got the job."[69]

Brackeen played with saxophonist Joe Henderson's group from 1972 to 1975 and then joined saxophonist Stan Getz until 1977. She left at that point to begin a career as a solo performer committed to playing her own unique compositions. She moved from California to New York. Since arriving on the East Coast, Joanne has recorded frequently as a leader and has received numerous awards. Her manager Helen Kean observes, "It's hard to believe those delicate arms and hands can get that strength out of the piano, and she has the kind of courage to do *her* material. The real heavyweights in the music compliment her for this. They say, 'Yes, that's what you *must* do. We need something new, we need variety, we need to be excited by something.'"[70]

Her views on the position of women in "jazz" are close to the attitude expressed earlier by Mary Lou Williams, who also insisted that she had to work with musicians best suited for the job. "If I want a bass player, I want a player at Eddie Gomez's level. What woman can I call?" Brackeen asks.

> If a woman wants to be fine and bother to develop the music ... it has to be at the same level that men have taken it to. She can't come fifty years later and be fifty years behind—and let me tell you that they *are*—most of them are. You'll hear them playing the notes but you will not hear the feeling, the flow, the maturity, the spirituality, the thing that you hear from the man. It's not because they're women, it's because they haven't developed. . . . They may think that because they have a little of it, they can see further than they can and they actually think they're great, and they are *good*, some of them are very good, but there's no Charlie Parker on the saxophone, there's no Art Blakey on the drums, there's no Stan Getz on the saxophone.[71]

Charles Tolliver

Down Beat Magazine voted Charles Tolliver (trumpetist, flugelhornist, and composer) Critics' Choice for the trumpet in 1968. After beginning his professional career with Jackie McLean (making his Blue Note debut with the saxophonist in 1964), he performed with such renowned artists as Roy Hanyes, Horace Silver, McCoy Tyner, Sonny Rollins, Booker Ervin, The Gerald Wilson Orchestra, Oliver Nelson, Roy Ayers, Art Blakey and the Jazz Messengers, Max Roach, and many others.

Tolliver formed the quartet Music Inc. in 1969, which gained international recognition for its innovative approach. His tour with this ensemble has taken him to festivals, concerts, radio and television stations throughout the world.

Toshiko Akiyoshi

Toshiko Akiyoshi was born in Manchuria in 1929. She and her three sisters studied ballet, Japanese traditional dancing, and piano when they were young. Toshiko said, "I dropped the dancing and the ballet right away, but I loved the piano. But it was all classical music. I didn't know a thing about jazz, and in fact, didn't like it at all."[72] Akiyoshi was eventually exposed to "jazz" as a teenager when it and other Western music flooded her native Japan during with the American Occupation after World War II. Manchuria became a battleground for contending Japanese, Soviet, and Chinese forces during the thirties and throughout World War II. The Akiyoshi family returned to Japan in 1947 as the Chinese Communists were consolidating their control over Manchuria.[73]

Postwar Japan was a good place for studying "jazz" through recordings, and pianist Teddy Wilson and other musicians influenced Toshiko. She worked in Tokyo as a dance-band accompanist, and she recalls these early experiences: "I didn't know the chord names or anything." Nevertheless, by 1952 she was leading her own band and working steadily. Akiyoshi recorded an album for Norman Granz in Tokyo (1953) and eventually won a full scholarship to study at the Berklee College of Music in Boston with the aid of recommendations from Oscar Peterson and other artists. After moving to America in 1956, Toshiko remembers she "dealt with both racial and sexual prejudice. I played clubs and TV wearing a kimono, because people were amazed to see an Oriental woman playing jazz."[74]

Toshiko married saxophonist Charlie Mariano in 1959. She worked in New York and Japan in a small group context, often with bassist Charles Mingus. Akiyoshi's compositional style is firmly rooted in her Asian identity. This quality gave her music a distinctive rhythmic and melodic style. "I came to think that being Japanese was not a negative aspect [in the "jazz" world]. Rather it was a positive aspect in that I could draw something from my own culture and perhaps return to the jazz tradition something that might make it a little bit richer than before."[75] Akiyoshi has always avoided performing pop charts of any kind and has always maintained a big-band book of almost exclusively her own compositions. She was the first Asian and the first woman to win numerous *Down Beat* polls. Most of her fame and notoriety would come in subsequent decades.

Akiyoshi debuted as composer and leader at Town Hall in New York in a concert that included original solo, trio and big-band compositions in 1967. She then began to set the foundation for her future orchestra, which would begin to mature during the following decade. In 1969 she married saxophonist-flutist Lew Tabackin and formed a quartet with him (having divorced saxophonist Charlie Mariano, with whom she had a daughter). When Tabackin was called to Los Angeles to work in the *Tonight Show* band, the couple began organizing a "jazz" ensemble.

There was "a tremendous amount of skepticism about a Japanese woman writing for a jazz band in Los Angeles."[76] Akiyoshi discussed the difficulty she encountered in several interviews:

Toshiko Akiyoshi (Photo courtesy of HRP Library).

Being female I think you have a little difficulty because you're taking a man's job. Maybe now it's much better than before. . . . When we formed the band it was a new experience for the musicians to rehearse under a woman. I had to think that aspect through very carefully. I think that emotionally a man still has a hard time taking orders from a woman.[77]

. . . Competition wasn't as tough [in Japan] as in the United States, so I could rise to the top quicker. . . . There was less female competition in Japan. Whenever women competed in a man's world in the United States, they didn't succeed. Those that did, became separated from the mainstream and wound up as piano players in the more sophisticated, high class clubs, such as the East Side Club or the Hickory House in New York. A few, such as Marian McPartland, did succeed.[78]

"Traditional Jazz" Continues

Throughout the sixties, the big bands of Stan Kenton (1912–79), Woody Herman (1913–87), Maynard Ferguson (b. 1928), and other musicians continued to advance the stylistic forms initiated by swing during the thirties. The big bands of this era focused on inflexible "tight" arrangements and powerful dynamics rather than on individual soloists and innovative approaches to improvisation. Herman, who was never an exceptional clarinetist, recruited young men into his "Thundering Herd" who were good section players. Kenton, who started out as a cocktail pianist, had been forced to disband his organization during the 1940s. The 1960s witnessed the Kenton organization embarking upon a new era with a brass dominated band, subtitled the Mellophonium Band because he added four mellophones to the five trumpets and four trombones that rounded off his brass section. Maynard Ferguson continued to base his approach upon his ability to play in the extreme upper register of the trumpet for extended periods of time. In terms of instrumentation, trumpeter Don Ellis (1934–78) had the most unusual big band of the period. He experimented with complex meters and later incorporated electrified string quartets, synthesizers, and made other exotic augmentations to achieve his unique ensemble sound.

1960s Music Outside African-American Culture

Related evolution had taken place elsewhere in the African Diaspora. The roots of reggae music are also fixed in slavery. A rich mixture of African peoples and variegated cultures survived after the abolition of slavery in Jamaica (1838), and can be heard today in rural Jamaica. Elements of the musical traditions and cultures of the Ibos, Yoruba, Noko, Sabo, Nago, as well those of African people from the Gold Coast (Mandingos, Coromantee, Hausa, etc.) are among the influences still present in the songs, dances, and rhythms of the region. Jamaican music such as *kumina* (a ritual involving neo-African song, dance, worship, and animal sacrifice), *etu, pocomania, gumbe, buru,* and *tambu* retain many traditional African characteristics. Mento, a music related to calypso music of Trinidad, became the most common music in Jamaica until the early 1950s.

Reggae was an outgrowth of the influence of American rhythm and blues by way of several regional musical forms. Local itinerant deejays ("sound system men") played Jamaican rhythm and blues music and eventually the term "ska" was coined for the new dance created for the music. Thus reggae was born during the national insecurity that took place in Jamaica following its independence from Great Britain in 1962. "Ska" was replaced by a dance music involving a smaller instrumentation called "rock steady." Reggae emerged from "rock steady" around 1968.

Artists involved in twentieth-century European-American art music were also busy redefining musical traditions during the sixties. Composer John Cage documented some ideas he developed and expanded during the era of the 1960s in his book *Silence.*[79] Some of his perspectives on modern music are voiced in his commentaries and rhetorical questions found within this document:

> If words are sounds, are they musical or are they just noises?
> If sounds are noises but not words, are they meaningful?
>
> We know, don't we, everybody else's religion, mythology, and philosophy and metaphysics backwards and forwards, so what need would we have for one of our own if we had one, but we don't, do we?
> But music, do we have any music?
> Would it be better to just drop music too?
> Then what would we have?
> Jazz?
> What's left?
>
> Debussy said quite some time ago, "Any sounds in any combination and in any succession are henceforth free to be used in a musical continuity."
> Why, if everything is possible, do we concern ourselves with history (in other words with a sense of what is necessary to be done at a particular time? . . . In order to thicken the plot?
>
> What is the nature of an experimental action? It is simply an action the outcome of which is not foreseen. It is therefore very useful if one has decided that sounds are to come into their own, rather than being exploited to express sentiments or ideas of order.
>
> . . . one is no longer concerned with tonality or atonality, Schoenberg or Stravinsky (the twelve tones or the twelve expressed as seven plus five), nor with consonance and dissonance, but rather with Edgar Varese who fathered forth noise into twentieth-century music.[80]

Summary: The American Society That 1960s Music Reflected

The music created during this decade reflected a colorful and influential American transition that left an indelible mark on world society. Much of the music of the 1960s concerned itself with eliminating barriers standing in the way of free expression. There was a tendency toward viewing creative evolution as a natural state of being that did not necessarily depend upon conspicuous music knowledge, conventions, and obligatory displays of technical efficiency. For the liberated artist, the world of conceptions expanded without the approval of those who traditionally took it upon themselves to measure (and dictate the value of) artistic expression according to preconceived Western standards.

The seeds of the unprecedented social and political changes of the 1960s era in the United States were sown during the 1950s. The *Brown vs. the Topeka Board of Education* case made the separate but equal doctrine invalid in American education in 1954. A year later, Rosa Parks was arrested for refusing to give up her seat to a "white" man on a bus in Montgomery, Alabama. In 1957, Dr. Martin Luther King organized the Southern Christian Leadership Conference. In 1958 "A Raisin in the Sun" became the first play by an African-American woman produced on Broadway.

During the 1960s, as African-Americans struggled to organize politically and gain equality in America, undercover government agencies made plans to infiltrate and disrupt "black" organizations. Their efforts were directed at fostering chaos among political groups and preventing individual leaders from emerging within the "black militant" community. In 1960 the first student protests involved sit-ins at "whites only" lunch counters at North Carolina A&T University (Greensboro, North Carolina). Wilma Rudolph won gold medals at the Rome Olympics in the 100-meter run, the 200-meter run, and in the 400-meter relay that year. It was also the time John F. Kennedy was elected President of the United States. Two African-American musicians, Ella Fitzgerald and Count Basie, were awarded Grammy Awards for the first time.

America broke off diplomatic ties with Cuba in 1961. That year African-American and European-American "liberals" from the Freedom Riders (a loosely organized group whose mission was to test and demand integration in the South) had men and women members of their organization attacked and beaten by "White" citizens in Anniston and Birmingham, Alabama.

In 1962 three thousand federal troops were ordered to protect James Meredith and suppress riots as he struggled to enter the University of Mississippi. The following year European-American citizens and police attacked and beat civil rights demonstrators and leaders in Birmingham, Alabama, culminating in the arrest of Dr. Martin Luther King, Jr. More than 250,000 people marched on Washington and heard King's "I Have a Dream" speech. The same year (1963), Medgar Evers was assassinated. President John F. Kennedy was also assassinated in Dallas, Texas, that year, and W. E. B. DuBois died in Ghana.

The Civil Rights Act of 1964 was passed during the year Dr. King received the Nobel Prize for Peace. Violence soon struck again in 1965 when Malcolm X (b. 1925) was assassinated in Harlem. Violence erupted in the form of uprisings in Watts (a section of Los Angeles). Thirty-five people died as a consequence of the riots and four thousand citizens were arrested. The Ku Klux Klan shootings continued in Selma, Alabama, after Dr. King led four thousand marchers there to present a "Negro" petition.

In 1966, Huey Newton and Bobby Seale established the Black Panther Party in Oakland, California, and the Student Nonviolent Coordinating Committee elected Stokely Carmichael its leader. Also that year, a Massachusetts Republican, Edward Brooke, became the first African-American elected to the Senate since the Reconstruction era, and Mrs. Indira Gandhi (Nehru's daughter) became Prime Minister of India. Maulana Karenga founded an American organization on the basis of Kawaida principles in 1966 as well; it was the first human rights organization to recognize the need for cultural reconstruction of the African-American people.[81]

The National Organization for Women (NOW) was also formed in 1966. Their focus would soon turn toward legislative and judicial reforms to check discrimination against women in education and employment. NOW also became involved with issues such as women in the media, child care, discrimination in consumer finance, and, after hesitation and debate, eventually affirmed that abortion was a women's rights issue.

In 1967 Thurgood Marshall became the first African-American appointed to the Supreme Court in the United States, and Shirley Chisholm became the first African-American female member of the House of Representatives.

The year 1968 was the unfortunate time of the assassination of Dr. Martin Luther King in a Memphis, Tennessee, hotel. James Earl Ray was arrested in London and extradited to the United States to stand trial for King's murder. The Chicago police rioted against citizens in the city's park during the 1968 Democratic National Convention. While on their uncontrollable rampage, police clubbed innocent bystanders to the ground, tear-gassed women and children at point blank range, and systematically assaulted the varied mixture of peace activists, clergy, academics, long-haired hippies, and other victims while they chanted, "the whole world is watching." Student rioting also broke out in Paris that year.

In 1969 James Earl Ray was sentenced to ninety-nine years in prison for murder. The final year of this proactive decade, students at Cornell University seized the Willard Straight Hall student center. The purpose of their actions was to protest the harassment of African-American females at Cornell and the burning of a cross by European-American students on campus.

Communal living during the 1960s meant that individuals within a group could break with standard social regiments. Many people graduating from high school chose to travel, to put a band together, to "just hang out," or to adopt some other unconventional lifestyle. The extra time these alternative lifestyles provided enabled people to read longer books for pleasure, engage in longer casual conversations (often about philosophical concerns, social conditions, war, and politics), indulge in more "mind-expanding" drugs (marijuana, LSD, hashish, psilocybin, and other psychedelics), and listen to longer musical compositions. Although history has often focused upon the drug culture that was highly conspicuous during the 1960s, it was also a decade involving the awakening of a new sense of social responsibility.

By the end of this revolutionary decade it was clear that a capitalist society could not afford to tolerate loss of control to such a degree. When students protesting against the Vietnam War at Kent State University in Ohio were fired upon in 1970 by the American National Guard (killing four people), this culminating display of destructive force initiated a new age of intolerance and a durable, hyperconservative attitude in American politics and culture. Finally, most European American hippies reconsidered their "liberal" political philosophies, activist postures, and moral awakenings, virtually terminating the 1960s social revolution for the mainstream American youth culture.

Lynching of African-American sociopolitical prisoners continues in America under the high-tech guise of legal action. Out of a total of 3,817 executions between 1930 and 1969, more than fifty percent (2066) involved African-American citizens. Angela Davis described how Marie Hill got on death row in a North Carolina prison.

> Sister Hill was arrested in October, 1968 in South Carolina, and at the age of 15 charged with the murder of a white grocery store proprietor in Rocky Mount, North Carolina. The unfolding of events in the aftermath of the arrest is a classic study in the transformation of the law-enforcement-judicial network into a tool of terror against Blacks.
>
> She was coerced into signing a confession, without having received the advice of an attorney, a confession she later repudiated, saying, "I had no choice." Ill-informed of her right to resist extradition, she was speedily transported to North Carolina. Intensive in-custody interrogation—inherently coercive—with no accompanying attempt to apprise her of her right to remain silent led her to break down once again. This throng of white policemen even tricked her into waiving a preliminary hearing.
>
> A week had already passed before she was permitted to speak to her parents or even confer with her attorney.
>
> On December 17, 1968, she was brought to trial. The prosecution had no evidence of her guilt save her own confession, which she vigorously repudiated on the witness stand. The state could not even offer proof that she had been present at the scene of the killing, and although the prosecution referred to objects touched by the perpetrator of the crime, no fingerprints were produced.
>
> After two days, Marie Hill, then 15 years of age, was found guilty of first-degree murder and was sentenced to die.
>
> In their appeal to the U.S. Supreme Court, her lawyers have stated: "Such a penalty—not law, but Terror—is the instrument of totalitarian government. It is a cruel and unusual punishment, forbidden by the Eighth Amendment."[82]

Emmett Till was lynched outside the law, Marie Hill was being lynched under the color of law.

Notes

[1] Listen to the album by Randy Weston/Melba Liston, *The Spirit of Our Ancestors* (1991).

[2] Recorded in 1950 — JWS-500; reissued as OJC 041.

[3] Valerie Wilmer, *As Serious as Your Life: The Story of the New Jazz* (New York: Serpent Tail, 1992), p. 30.

[4] Arthur Taylor, *Notes and Tones: Musician-to-Musician Interviews* (New York: Da Capo, 1993), p. 20.

[5] Ibid., pp. 22–23.

[6] Ibid., pp. 24–25.

[7] Gene Lees, *Cats of Any Color: Jazz Black and White* (New York: Oxford University Press, 1994), p. 30.

[8] New York: Da Capo, 1981.

[9] Listen to the album *Reese and the Smooth Ones: Reese Part 1* by the Art Ensemble of Chicago, recorded August 12, 1969, and explore the expressed perspective on "Is jazz . . . as we know it . . . dead?"

[10] The physicain purposely caused Kirk's blindness, according to trumpeter Lester Bowie who tells the story on the video "The Leaders In Paris."

[11] *Miles: The Autobiography*, p. 59.

[12] Joe Goldberg, *Jazz Masters of the Fifties* (New York: Da Capo, 1965), p. 210.

[13] James Lincoln Collier, *The Making of Jazz: A Comprehensive History* (New York: Dell Publishing Co., 1979), p. 490.

[14] See the liner notes to Coltrane's album *A Love Supreme*, for instance.

[15] Use of harmonic and melodic formations based on the church modes, a medieval system of eight scales each using the white keys of a C-major scale; a reaction against classical harmony.

[16] Ornette Coleman, "The Color of Music," *Down Beat* 61, no. 2 (February 1994); originally issued December 1982. Harmolodics is the term coined by Coleman to describe his approach.

[17] Willard Jenkins, *Down Beat*, December 1998, p. 67.

[18] Ibid. p. 68.

[19] Bill Cole, *John Coltrane,* p. 192.

[20] "Alice Coltrane Interviewed by Pauline Rivelli," in *Black Genius*, p. 122.

[21] Recorded June 7, 1961.

[22] From the liner notes to the album *Africa/Brass*.

[23] Ibid.

[24] Ekkehard Jost, *Free Jazz*, p. 27.

[25] Bill Cole, *John Coltrane*, p. 134.

[26] Don DeMicheal, "John Coltrane and Eric Dolphy Answer the Critics," in *Down Beat*, April 12, 1962, pp. 20–23.

[27] Ibid., p. 28.

[28] From the liner notes of the album *Coltrane Legacy*, comments by Coltrane.

[29] Ibid., Workman's remarks.

[30] Bill Cole, *John Coltrane*, p. 148.

[31] A. B. Spellman, *Four Lives in the Bebop Business*, (New York, Limelight Editions, 1985), p. 30.

[32] Frank Kofsky, *Black Nationalism*, pp. 71–76.

[33] Leonard Feather, "Coltrane Shaping Musical Revolt," *New York Post (Jazz Beat)*, October 18, 1964.

[34] Ronald Radano in the *Annual Review of Jazz Studies*, 1985.

[35] Quoted in *"Jazz Avant-Garde (with Eric Dolphy)"* (Tunbridge Wells, England: Costello, 1989), pp. 76–77.

[36] "Conversation with Coltrane," p. 7.

[37] Goldberg, *Jazz Masters of the Fifties*, p. 205.

[38] Ibid. Goldberg's observation is echoed by Vladimir Simosko and Barry Tepperman in their biography, *Eric Dolphy: A Musical Biography and Discography* (New York: Da Capo, 1971), pp. 62–63.

[39] Simosko and Tepperman, *Eric Dolphy*, p. 62.

[40] Ibid., pp. 63–67.

[41] Karlton Hester, "The Melodic and Polyrhythmic Developments of John Coltrane's Spontaneous Composition in a Racist Society," (Lewiston, NY: Mellon Press, 1997).

[42] Lazarus Edward Nnanyelu Ekweume, "Ibo Music—Its Theory and Practice." (New Haven, CT: Yale University Press, 1972), p. 225.

[43] Ibid., pp. 69–70.

[44] Ibid., pp. 112–13.

[45] Liner notes to his album *Witches and Devils*, Arista Records (1975).

[46] Liner notes to *Albert Ayler in Greenwich Village*, Impulse A-9155.

[47] Ibid.

[48] Ibid.

[49] Wilmer, *As Serious as Your Life*, p. 117.

[50] Ibid., p. 116.

[51] Ibid., p. 121

[52] Howard Mandel, "Cringe of the Lone Wolf: Dewey Redman," *Down Beat*, February 1992.

[53] Ibid., pp. 22–24.

[54] Ortiz M. Walton, *Music: Black, White and Blue*, pp. 129–37.

[55] Ibid.

[56] Nat Hentoff, "Un-chic Racism at the Philharmonic," *The Village Voice*, December 17, 1970, p. 30.

[57] Providing a screen so judges are forced to be impartial to the musician's auditioning.

[58] As quoted in Martin T. Williams, *Jazz Changes,* (New York: Oxford University Press, 1992), pp. 121–26.

[59] David Such, *Avant-Garde Jazz Musicians* (Iowa City: University of Iowa Press, 1992), pp. 25–26.

[60] Baker, Belt, and Hudson, *The Black Composer Speaks*, p. 300.

[61] *Avant-Garde Jazz Musicians,* pp. 25–26.

[62] Rivelli and Levin, *Giants*, p. 119.

[63] Robert Bruce Slater, "The Blacks Who First Entered the World of White Higher Education," *Journal of Blacks in Higher Education* 4 (Summer 1994): 47.

[64] Wilmer, *As Serious as Your Life,* p. 241.

[65] Charles J. Gans, "Archie Shepp: In the Tradition," *Jazz Forum: The Magazine of the International Jazz Federation* 93 (February 1985): 37.

[66] According to the *San Francisco Sunday Examiner and Chronicle,* July 24, 1977, p. 41.

[67] Linda Dahl, *Stormy Weather*, pp. 70–72.

[68] Quoted in George Nelson, "Joanne Brackeen, Pianist for a New Era," *Down Beat*, July 1980.

[69] Quoted by Amy Duncan, *Baltimore Sun*, May 25, 1980.

[70] Interview by Linda Dahl, June 1981.

[71] Quoted by Don Nelson, *Jazz Times*, April–May 1981.

[72] Quoted in Takashi Oka, "Japanese Jazz Artist Perfects Skills in U.S.," *Christian Science Monitor*, October 12, 1956.

[73] *Stormy Weather*, pp.165–67.

[74] Quoted in Leonard Feather, "Toshiko Akiyoshi: The Leader of the Band," *Ms.*, November 1978.

[75] Quoted in Charles Gans, "T.A.L.T. Conference: A Conversation with Toshiko Akiyoshi and Lew Tabackin," *Jazz Forum*, February 1980.

[76] Peter Rothbart, "Toshiko Akiyoshi," *Down Beat*, August 1980.

[77] Quoted in Gans, "T.A.L.T. Conference."

[78] Quoted in Rothbart, "Toshiko Akiyoshi."

[79] Cambridge: M.I.T. Press, 1971.

[80] John Cage, *Silence* (Cambridge: M.I.T. Press, 1971).

[81] *Historical and Cultural Atlas of African Americans*, p. 188.

    [82] Angela Davis et. al., *If They Come in the Morning: Voices of Resistance* (New York: New American Library, 1971), pp. 104–5.

XI
Innovators Emerging Between 1970 and 1980

> The life of man is a self-evolving circle, which, from a ring imperceptibly small, rushes on all sides outwards to new and larger circles, and that without end. The extent to which this generation of circles, wheel without wheel, will go, depends on the force and truth of the individual soul. For it is the inert effort of each thought, having formed itself into a circular wave of circumstance, as, for instance, an empire, rules of an art, a local usage, a religious rite, to heap itself upon that ridge, and to solidify and hem in the life. But if the soul is quick and strong, it bursts over that boundary on all sides, and expands another orbit on the great deep, which also runs up into a high wave, with attempt again to stop and to bind. But the heart refuses to be imprisoned; in its first and narrowest pulses, it already tends outward with a vast force, and to immense and innumerable expansions.
>
> —Ralph Waldo Emerson, "Circles"

Changes Around the World

During the 1970s America once again declared the death of "jazz." According to earlier self-proclaimed pundits of "jazz" history, the music had died before at the end of the swing era when bebop was in its nascence.

In 1971 George Jackson, author of *Soledad Brother*, was killed at San Quentin Prison in San Francisco and Angela Davis was acquitted of all murder and conspiracy charges. In her book, *If They Come in the Morning: Voices of Resistance* (written while still a political prisoner in America), Davis says, "As a consequence of the racism securely interwoven in the capitalist fabric of this society, Black people have become more thoroughly acquainted with America's jails and prisons than any other group of people in this country. Few of us, indeed, have been able to escape some form of contact—direct or indirect—with these institutions at some point in our lives."[1]

In 1974 the cost of food, fuel, and other goods soared as worldwide inflation (heightened by boosts in oil prices) slowed economic growth to near zero in most industrialized countries. ABC television adapted Alex Haley's book *Roots* in 1977. The series drew the largest television audience of any program in history.

In 1978 a military junta seized power in Afghanistan as violence swept Nicaragua. Muhammad Ali lost the "crown," only to regain his world heavyweight title from Leon Spinks, becoming the first person to win the heavyweight championship three times. In 1979 Franklin Thomas became the first African American to head a major foundation when he was named president of the Ford Foundation, and the Nobel Prize for Economics went to Arthur Lewis, an African American.

Spiritual "Jazz" and New Musical Settings

Duke Ellington, Mary Lou Williams, and other early twentieth-century innovators established a connection between religion and music through their compositions. During the sixties Coltrane, Albert Ayler, Pharaoh Sanders, Mingus, and others were among the expanding communities of African-American musicians who labeled many of their compositions with sacred music titles. "Jazz" always maintained a connection with spiritual music on both technical and emotional levels. For those pianists and vocalists who began their musical careers in the church, this connection was particularly difficult to avoid. Since the majority of African-American children attended churches during the first half of the century (where music making was a communal experience), most musicians who lived in those communities shared a common knowledge base of African-American spirituals and sacred music. Michael J. Budds outlines the long tradition of religious connections with African-American music in his book *Jazz in the Sixties: The Expansion of Musical Resources and Techniques.*

> Although there has always been a close family relationship among spirituals, gospel music, the blues, and jazz in musical terms, the latter two have evolved and prospered in the realm of secular life. The blues and jazz sprang from the rituals of Friday and Saturday nights; spirituals and gospel soared from the ceremonies of Sunday morning. During the sixties such arbitrary restrictions between sacred and secular were disregarded as leading jazz musicians reevaluated the role of music in their own lives. Many discovered a vital connection between their spiritual beliefs and their musical activities and deliberately set out to bring these two important aspects of their lives into closer harmony. It is not too far-fetched to propose that some jazz musicians began to perform as preachers, with the music taking the place of sermons. Others were content to bear witness to their faith by the nature of their lifestyles and the attitudes reflected in their music. The more noticeable, perhaps, were those who embarked on a spiritual journey into non-Western religious thought and came to perceive their own performances as a form of meditation. In effect, by employing their music to express personal religious convictions, these individuals expanded the jazz tradition in purpose and content.[2]

Many instrumentalists and vocalists began broadening and transforming established musical norms and conventions as the "loft jazz" era of the 1970s created new performance possibilities. The levels of experimentation generated by the AACM and BAG, and other organizations that promoted the development of innovative art forms in the late 1960s, were advanced by a new experimental venue that enabled independent musicians to maintain greater control over their artistic directions.

While most club owners preferred hiring established musicians who played styles of music that their clientele theoretically preferred, the "loft jazz" scene generally provided open formats in which a variety of stylistic or conceptual approaches could be tested. A direct line to audiences bolstered the confidence and productivity of experimental musicians, dancers, poets, and visual artists who presented works in "loft jazz" settings during this era during the early 1970s.

Some of the most important and striking stylistic changes in "jazz" took place in alternative performance spaces that eventually drew fairly large and responsive audiences who preferred hearing challenging new music in unpretentious and relaxed settings. Unlike music presented in typical concert halls and commercially oriented clubs, many alternative venues seemed the quintessential contemporary environment. The alternative music scene inherited the task of educating, cultivating, and enriching their audiences, many of whom may have experienced experimental or abstract art forms for the first time. A sampling of the diverse spectrum of musical styles presented during this brief era was preserved on the limited issue five-record set *Wildflowers (1–5): The New York Loft Jazz Sessions*. Recorded live in 1977, *Wildflower* was produced by Alan Douglas and Michael Cuscuna in association with Sam Rivers. Sam Rivers is an innovative saxophonist (and flutist) who played with Miles Davis briefly and continued to develop a highly personal and unique spontaneous compositional approach during the 1970s. Over sixty musicians performed on the twenty-two performances that were released.

Changing Attitudes in Europe

A serious exodus of African-American musicians to Europe began in 1969 when the BYG record label initiated the Actuel Festival of Jazz, Rock and New Music. Rock groups such as Pink Floyd and Frank Zappa were headliners originally signed, but the festival invited "jazz" musicians if they paid their own way overseas. Upon arrival in Europe, there were often possibilities for "jazz" musicians to record. BYG released a series of albums immediately after the festival. Only a small proportion of the money collected from the sale of those recordings went to the performing artists, however.[3]

While some "jazz" innovators gained a nominal degree of exposure and recognition at home and abroad, their music was not always well received. Performances of Afrocentric experimental music rarely made huge profits for the artists involved.

Andrew Cyrille (b. 1939) was touring Europe with Cecil Taylor during that time and recorded a solo percussion album *(What About?)* that displayed an original approach to drumming. He had little success with this particular recording in America. John Hammond at Columbia records said, "The computer is not interested in creative drumming, it's interested in making money."

He also assured Cyrille that no other company would be interested in his material either.[4]

There was originally a festival planned for Les Halles in Paris. Trouble with earlier festivals there in 1968 made local business establishments reluctant to allow another such episode so soon afterward, so the plan was denied. The festival took place in Amougies, Belgium, nevertheless, inside a huge tent. Over 75,000 people witnessed the concerts. Joseph Jarman, Sirone, Archie Shepp, Steve Lacy, Sunny Murray, Don Cherry, Leroy Jenkins, Grachan Moncur III, Frank Wright (tenor saxophone), Noah Howard (saxophone), Ray Draper, Earl Freeman, and others participated. Veteran drummer Philly Joe Jones (1923–85) performed with Shepp, Moncur, Freeman, South African musicians Johnny Dyani (bass), and Louis Moholo (drums). Frank Zappa sat in with this ensemble as well.

Experimental music proved completely accessible to the new breed of young European audiences. At the Ann Arbor Jazz and Blues Festival two years later, promoters avoided using the term "jazz," and the experimental music presented was generally accessible. As a consequence, audiences drawn to the familiar names of rock and blues artists adapted favorably to the new musical approaches presented by the innovators of the day.

In time, European audiences grew less receptive to African-American "jazz" musicians, as Britain and Germany became nationalistic in their "jazz" preferences, favoring local (European) adaptations of African-American styles to the music of the originators. For a slightly longer period, France preferred to hear African-Americans perform Afrocentric music.

French presenters generally provided appropriate performance conditions and fairly good earnings, while French fans remained enthusiastic. Many musicians adopted Paris as a home base and were able to gain enough business leverage to negotiate favorable contracts, enhance their performance resumes, and were granted a temporary break from the bleak New York scene. The Art Ensemble of Chicago had the means and foresight to buy property in the Paris suburbs where they could work and live. Nevertheless, only on rare occasions was an African-American group able to sustain a comfortable life as musicians in Europe after 1975. The Frank Wright Quartet was a notable exception. Wright's group included Bobby Few and Alan Silva, and Muhammad Ali (Rashied Ali's brother) was the drummer.[5]

For a while, Europeans considered the African-American musician an exotic and artistic revolutionary, on display for reasons that often had little to do with music. Although most African-American innovators did not perceive of themselves as merely entertainers, much of the audience, apparently attending purely for the novelty of the occasion, wanted entertainment much as that imported during the era of the early black-faced minstrels.

Connecting Fusion, Miles Davis, and Jimi Hendrix

Miles Davis was at the forefront of another musical movement when he began his experiments with electronics during the late 1960s. His 1969 album titled *Bitches Brew* maintained a shift of focus toward the rhythm section and continued to incorporate fewer chord structures. Woodwind specialist Benny Maupin (b. 1946) recalls:

> Miles was in top form, and the condition of his life was so high that we each responded to his non-verbal communication. He never really stated what he really wanted with words. Through his actions it was clear to me that everything he wanted from each of us should be based on trusting our intuition and the courage to move from one note to the next with total confidence in each other and the music.[6]

Miles based a large portion of his musical unfoldings upon bass ostinati and other short rhythmic bass patterns. The form of the album relies upon medleys, presenting musical "environments" rather than standard improvisational formats. In the twenty-first century *Bitches Brew,* the album that shocked a significant segment of the musical world, remains in vogue and remains one the most unorthodox departures from the "jazz" mainstream. Drummer Jack DeJohnette (b. 1942) sums up the recording date:

> Miles assembled an experiment with musicians he liked. He wrote a few sketches, but the idea was to get the spontaneity down. It wasn't a stop-and-start recording. It was Miles conducting an orchestra in real time. He was like a painter changing the canvas by conducting his group.[7]

A variety of electronic instruments provided environmental textures and colorful arrays of evocative timbres, while keyboardists take surprisingly few solos on *Bitches Brew*. Davis continued to incorporate electronics on both the *Live Evil* (1970) and *On the Corner* (1972) albums, while also beginning to experiment with multiple drummers.

Miles incorporated electronics into various styles throughout the seventies. This drew sharp criticism. Larry Birnbaum asserts in his article "Metal Steps To Heaven" that "back in the days of platform shoes, blow-out Afros, and blaxploitation flicks, Miles Davis—to the disgust of jazz critics, former colleagues, and lifetime fans alike—plunged headlong into funk."[8] Despite claims that Miles sold out, the albums from this period actually sold few copies and missed the young African-American audience for which they were allegedly targeted.

Recordings from two live sets at Osaka Festival Hall in Japan (February 1, 1975) were released by Japanese CBS/Sony on double LPs. Aghartha, the matinee performance, was the only recording of the performances issued in the United States, however. The recording produced some of Miles's most unconventional and least accessible music of his career. His compositions, laced with thick polyphonic textures, involved ametrical percussion coloration that typical 1970s American audiences found difficult to digest. Some critics attacked it with vacuous terms (such as those associated with certain of Ellington's works such as the bigoted label "jungle music," for instance). Miles simply felt his new approach was "a deep African-American groove."[9] Guitarist Reggie Lucas, an AACM member, provided a Hendrix-inspired ambiance, while veteran Al Foster established a strong rhythm foundation. Michael Henderson was the bassist, and James "Mtume" Foreman (Jimmy Heath's son), supplied additional percussion. Sonny Fortune, on temporary leave from McCoy Tyner's ensemble, was the woodwind specialist in this electrifying performance. Typically, Miles directed the ensemble through the spontaneous moods of each movement with his trumpet statements.

Davis was attracted to the electronic music produced by African-American musicians who generated huge popular followings during the 1960s and early 1970s. Miles talked about his musical and personal association with Jimi Hendrix in his autobiography:

> The music I was really listening to in 1968 was James Brown, the great guitar player Jimi Hendrix, and a new group who had just come out with the hit record, *Dance to the Music*, Sly and the Family Stone, led by Sly Stewart, from San Francisco. The shit he was doing was badder than a motherfucker, had all kinds of funky shit up in it. But it was Jimi Hendrix that I first got onto when Betty Mabry [Miles' wife at the time] turned me on to him.

> I first met Jimi when his manager called up and wanted me to introduce him to the way I was playing and putting my music together. Jimi liked what I had done on *Kind of Blue* and some other stuff and wanted to add more jazz elements to what he was doing. He liked the way Coltrane played with all those sheets of sound, and he played the guitar in a similar way. Plus, he said he had heard the guitar voicing that I used in the way I played the trumpet. So we started getting together. Betty really liked this music—and later, I found out, she liked him physically too—and so he started to come around.

> He was a real nice guy, quiet but intense, and was nothing like people thought he was. He was just the opposite of the wild and crazy image he presented on the stage. When we started getting together and talking about music, I found out that he couldn't read music. Betty had a party for him sometime in 1969 at my house on West 77th. I couldn't be there because I had to be in the studio that night recording, so I left some music for him to read and then we'd talk about it later. (Some people wrote some shit that I didn't come to the party for him because I didn't like having a party for a man in my house. That's a lot of bullshit.)

> When I called back home from the studio to speak to Jimi about the music I had left him, I found out he didn't read music. There are a lot of great musicians who don't read music—black and white—that I have known and respected and played with. So I didn't think less of Jimi because of that. Jimi was just a great, natural musician—self-taught. He would pick up

things from whatever he was around, and he picked up things quick. Once he heard it he really had it down. We would be talking, and I would be telling him technical shit like, "Jimi, you know, when you play the diminished chord. . . ." I would see this lost look come into his face and I would say, "Okay, okay, I forgot." I would just play it for him on the piano or on the horn, and he would get it faster than a motherfucker. He had a natural ear for hearing music. So I'd play different shit for him, show him that way. Or I'd play him a record of mine or Trane's and explain to him what we were doing. Then he started incorporating things I told him into his albums. It was great. He influenced me, and I influenced him, and that's the way great music is always made. Everybody showing everybody else something and then moving on from there.

But Jimi was also close to hillbilly, country music played by them mountain white people. That's why he had those two English guys in his band, because a lot of white English musicians liked that American hillbilly music. The best he sounded to me was when he had Buddy Miles on drums and Billy Cox on bass. Jimi was playing that Indian kind of shit, or he'd play those funny little melodies he doubles up on his guitar. I love it when he doubled up shit like that. He used to play 6/8 all the time when he was with them white English guys and that's what made him sound like a hillbilly to me. Just that concept he was doing with that. But when he started playing with Buddy and Billy in the Band of Gypsies, I think he brought what he was doing all the way out. But the record companies and white people liked him better when he had the white guys in his band. Just like a lot of white people like to talk about me when I was doing the nonet thing—the *Birth of the Cool* thing, or when I did those other albums with Gil Evans or Bill Evans because they always like to see white people up in black shit, so that they can say they had something to do with it. But Jimi came from the blues, like me. We understood each other right away because of that. Both him and Sly were great natural musicians; they played what they heard.[10]

Hendrix, while appreciated by many African musicians, did not gain the wide acceptance in the African-American community that Sly Stone enjoyed. In *The Death of Rhythm and Blues*, author Nelson George discusses possible reasons for this phenomenon:

Hendrix used blues and R&B as his building blocks, and Sly Stone worked from gospel and soul. Hendrix was rejected, while Sly was viewed, before the drug days, as a hero.

The difference was that Hendrix drew from a style blacks had already disposed of; Sly shrewdly stayed just a few steps ahead of the crowd. Both were children of the R&B world. Hendrix had been sideman for numerous R&B bands after leaving Seattle in his teens, including the Isley Brothers. Sly, baptized as Sylvester Stewart, was reared in a roof-raising, sanctified church and worked as a popular deejay on several Bay Area stations. And both Sly and Jimi rebelled against the narrowmindedness in which they grew up. It is not coincidental that they blossomed in environments removed from the traditions of black America, Hendrix in London and Sly in "free-love" San Francisco, where they each plunged into the hippie life-styles of those two countercultural centers, emerging in black-based sound drenched in flower-powered rhetoric that had little in common with the soul consciousness of James Brown or Aretha.

After a prolonged sabbatical following this period, Miles made a successful comeback in 1981. Other experimental material was introduced fifteen years later during the emergence of a 1990 funk-metal movement.

Jazz-Funk Fusion

Virtuoso pianist and composer Herbie Hancock (b. 1940) thoroughly absorbed the new experimental formulas he encountered while performing with Miles Davis, and he displayed this influence on his album *Crossings* in 1972. This direction continued as Hancock evolved toward a heavily funk influenced style on subsequent albums: *Headhunters* (1973), *Sextant* (1973), and *Thrust* (1974).

The electronic hues Hancock produced on Arp Synthesizers, Fender Rhodes electronic piano, Echoplex, Hohner D-6 Clavinet, and other new instruments were exciting and impressive. His jazz-funk albums set new standards for the genre in the early 1970s. The electric bass was now an established instrument in the jazz-fusion idiom. Bassist Paul Jackson, who played on several of Hancock's early fusion albums, helped to codify the new virtuoso bass vocabulary. Scott La Faro used the two-finger plucking style that allowed the modern electric bassist greater intricacy and speed on the instrument, creating melodic flexibility, grace, and rhythmic fluidity in the low register of new electric ensembles. Jackson too used multiple fingers to gain speed, but grounded his style in an understanding of complex funky rhythms.

Stanley Clark (b. 1951) is another electric bass guitarist to emerge during the 1970s. Clark worked with Pharoah Sanders, Getz, Gordon, Blakey, Gil Evans, Horace Silver (b. 1928), Joe Henderson (1937-2001) and Chick Corea (b. 1941). He was a founding member of Corea's group Return to Forever. His early influences include Charles Mingus, Paul Chambers, Ron Carter, Jimi Hendrix, and James Brown. His approach to the electric bass involves precisely executed rapid bass lines, slap bass technique, and a powerfully articulated attack to his melodic and syncopated phrasing.

Pianist Ramsey Lewis, traditionally a hard-bop-style pianist, collaborated with the popular ensemble Earth, Wind & Fire in 1974 to produce a "cross-over" album titled *Sun Goddess*. Another interesting "cross-over" album from the early part of the seventies was vocalist Flora Purim's Brazilian-influenced *Butterfly Dreams* (1973).

Jazz-Rock Fusion

The Don Ellis jazz-rock fusion big band recording *Electric Bath* (Columbia—CS 9585) employs multiple and complex time signatures in its compositions. Ellis' augmented big band (with strings, sitar, woodwind doubles, etc.) also explored systematic experiments with pitch that produced interesting results. (Ellis played a quarter-tone trumpet.)

Chick Corea's first influence was Horace Silver. His father, a trumpet player, led his own groups, and started Chick on piano at age four. After transcribing Silver's solos, Corea studied the music of Bud Powell and Bill Evans. His introduction to Latin music arrived before Chick graduated from high school in 1959. He attended the Juilliard School of Music before realizing two months later that the training he wanted was best obtained playing with New York's Latin-jazz groups. He performed with Mongo Santamaria, Willie Bobo, Herbie Mann, Blue Mitchell, and Stan Getz before recording his first solo album, *Tones for Joan's Bones* (later retitled *Inner Space*). The Latin rhythms and melodies recorded during the seventies on albums like *Light as a Feather* (Polydor PD 5525) and the jazz-rock oriented *Musicmagic* won him a popular following.

Saxophonist Wayne Shorter (b. 1933), pianist Joe Zawinul (b. 1932), and bassist Miroslav Vitous (b. 1947) formed the nucleus of the jazz-rock group Weather Report, which began to evolve in 1971. Shorter and Zawinul incorporated many of the musical lessons introduced by Miles Davis while they were associated with the trumpeter's band into their new ensemble. Weather Report explored novel approaches to collective improvisation through fusing rock-and-roll elements with emancipated rhythmic and metrical approaches. Weather Report placed emphasis upon electroacoustic timbres, a mixture of interesting textures, and on the employment of simple structural and formal conceptions.

As one of jazz-rock's longest lasting groups, Weather Report produced *Sweetnighter* (1973), *Mysterious Traveler* (1974), *Black Market* (1976), and a number of experimental albums during the 1970s. The distinction between soloist and accompaniment was blurred intentionally as conventional instrumentation mixed with electronic ambiance. Both bassists with the group, Miroslav Vitous and Jaco Pastorius (1951–87), continued to advance the virtuosic techniques introduced and developed by Paul Jackson, Scott Lafaro (1936–61), and other bassists operating earlier in the 1970s. Electric bass virtuosity began to flourish as the requirements of the new fusion music demanded expanded flexibility, speed, and diversity of styles.

Donald Byrd

Donald Byrd (b. 1932), a "jazz" pioneer, innovator and scholar, came through the hard bop school of the 1950s before establishing another type of fusion in the seventies with his highly successful group, the Blackbyrds. He grew up in Detroit and was educated at Wayne University, the Manhattan School of Music, and Columbia University. He also studied composition with Nadia Boulanger in France. Byrd, one of the first teenage trumpet wizards, is hailed historically as one of the most creative and influential musicians of all time. In the 1950's, his career flourished in the realm of bebop and hardbop. At the age of 23, his collaboration with Art Blakey and The Jazz Messengers was only the beginning, as he later went on to work with jazz giants including Max Roach, Sonny Rollins, Charlie Parker, Thelonious Monk, Coleman Hawkins, Lionel Hampton, John Coltrane and Herbie Hancock, among others. In the late fifties, he began recording on the legendary Blue Note label. His artistry on that label is exemplified by the classic album *Black Byrd*, which became the largest selling album in the history of Blue Note.

Then, through phenomenal hits like "Rock Creek Park," "Happy Music," "Blackbyrds Theme," "Places and Spaces," and "Do It Fluid," Dr. Byrd became a living legend. The jazz fusion movement of the early 70's, which enjoyed success in both mainstream as well as purist circles, thus established Dr. Byrd as a pioneer of a new sound. With over 60 albums to his credit, his range in style and his ever-expanding spiritual strength continue to reach far beyond the traditional jazz scene.

In addition to being a major force as an artist, Dr. Byrd has also been a seminal figure at the forefront of jazz education. He has helped bring to fruition jazz programs at institutions such as Rutgers University, Howard University, North Carolina Central University, Oberlin College and Queens College. His ability to thus embrace jazz on all levels has captured the hearts and minds of whole generations since he started his career. Recently, his work with Guru's *Jazzmatazz* project introduced him to a younger audience whose jazz inheritance was gained through hip-hop's breaks and samples. Not only did the *Jazzmatazz* project fuse two musical genres, it is in essence generations coming together. Dr. Byrd is a creative force in many different disciplines. He has started his own line of Bb cornet and trumpet, The Blackbyrd. For 1991 alone, he toured in Japan and around the world for Phillip Morris; appeared on The McCreary Report and BET's Noon Day Live; participated in the Louis Armstrong House Committee, the Louis Armstrong Archive Committee, the Dizzy Gillespie Committee and the music panel at the Black Congressional Caucus; lectured at the Brooklyn Academy of Music and the All Faith Church in Berkeley, CA; and raised $50,000 for the Girls and Boys Club of Central Newark, NJ. Currently, he is archiving original African-American art with a collection of over 100 pieces.

Byrd remains a frequently recorded artist,[11] with more than fifty albums to his credit, and he has often been criticized for embracing popular formulas to gain that success. In a 1990 interview with Leonard Feather,[12] Dr. Byrd explains his perspective on the music business.

Byrd begins by responding to Brazilian musician Mayuto's argument that the profit motive was severely affecting the quality of music and that producers (and not great composers) have become a powerful force in shaping the listening public's tastes. Byrd's reaction was simply to state that times have changed. Musicians who have adapted with the times are themselves producers and know the ways of business.

> It's just a lack of understanding and education on the part of the artist. When I was in law school, I learned the rules of the game. . . . Mayuto should stay within the scope of his understanding, and that's music.
>
> He [Mayuto] worked with me, but we never really sat down and really talked the way I've talked with men like Freddie Hubbard. I spent one whole day talking strictly business with Hubbard. Mayuto only knew me as a musician. Similarly, during the last conversation I had with John Coltrane before he died, he never got into any of those mystical, ethereal things he was identified with; we dealt with whether or not he could get back certain copyrights.
>
> It would be like denying the existence of people like James Brown. . . . I've never in my life been as impressed by a musician as I have been by James Brown. . . . People like James Brown and Berry Gordy are much more meaningful to me, in my life, than a lot of so called historical jazz figures. They have done more for black people.
>
> This is not a racial issue. The same thing is happening to white musicians who are being put in the position where they have to compromise. . . . If they are, it's because they've been emulating the black musicians.
>
> . . . I think that which sells the best *is* best.[13]

Beyond the knee jerk reaction that Byrd's comments may invoke from some readers, there is an important perspective being delivered. Byrd apparently feels that eschewing the "starving artist" image is important for musicians' advancement in a capitalist society. He also realizes that most people, given the opportunity to think for themselves, are intelligent enough to appreciate beautiful music. The music of Bach, Mozart, Beethoven, and other European innovators remains popular among many people today, although the artists themselves had more than their share of struggles with the audiences of their times. Innovators do not choose to be unappreciated "starving artists." Therefore, if we calculate ticket or record sales by centuries instead of months, then Byrd's points become crystal clear.

Dr. Donald Byrd as guest speaker (top) and guest artist (bottom) with the Cornell University Lab Ensembles as part of the annual *Cornell University "Jazz" Festival* **series (Karlton E. Hester, Director)** (Photos courtesy of HRP Library).

Dr. Donald Byrd performing at the 2003 *Global African Music & Arts Festival/Symposium at UC Santa Cruz* **(Karlton E. Hester, Artistic Director)** (Photo by William P. Johnson).

Today, after initiating "jazz" programs at Howard University, Oberlin, and elsewhere, Byrd is active as a teacher, art collector, historian, music theorist, and remains an influential innovator. Other current projects involve developing compositional and pedagogical approaches that combine music, art and math in new ways.

The Crossroads of Stylistic Evolution

Historians generally divide the evolution of "jazz" into distinct periods by isolating distinctive elements of style and tracing origins and innovations through the most dominant musicians of each era. There was little attempt to evaluate "jazz" seriously, objectively, or in a scholarly manner before World War II. The bias against African-American music maintained by many writers was obvious from the scarcity and inferior quality of "jazz" documentation. A general lack of knowledge and diminished respect for a sociocultural subject has always produced inaccurate reporting (take the history of women in the Western world before 1950, for instance), and this was often the case with African-American music. After the Second World War, a greater effort was made to examine African-American music more empirically. Unfortunately, references often used to substantiate research still failed to involve primary subjects, the African-American musicians who produce the music, and rarely involved total transposition of the music examined.

Total transcription places all notes performed on a musical occasion on a fixed score. Such a process enables theorists to make meaningful studies of the interactive nature of "jazz." Thorough study requires an advanced knowledge of Afrocentric music theory and requires a significant investment of time. Most transcriptions of "jazz," unfortunately, include only curt efforts involving the examination of small portions of an improvised melody isolated from its musical context. Chord symbols are traditionally written above the melody on the lead sheets. The chord symbols alone have limited meaning since serious practitioners never play chords as reflected by written symbols. Limiting the investigation to superficial dimensions allowed almost anyone an opportunity to become an instant "jazz" analyst. Like the "emperor's new clothes," these methods usually stand unchallenged, resulting in an unfortunate perpetuation of the status quo.

Where a person studied, how many performances they have attended, or the size of the record collection they own has less validity to non-Western cultures than an individual's knowledge of the given culture. Many cultures (including African-American "jazz" culture) measure knowledge according to an individual's performance proficiency or other tangible criteria. Ward states: "A collective 'us,' whether a reference to Westerners, white males, or ethnomusicologists, is no more valid than a collective 'them,' which lumps people with different abilities and levels of knowledge about tradition and culture."[14] This fact was a poignant one in the early "black" and "white" minstrel tradition in the United States, where grossly distorted perspectives about "us" and "them" were held by minstrels of all colors. The distance between "us" and "them" must first be reduced if meaningful analysis of African-American music is to emerge from within the majority culture.

Although musicians still perform all substyles of "jazz," historians tend to present an individual era as though its rise, peak, and decline follow predictably before the subsequent cycle begins. The careers of Ellington, Miles, Coltrane, and others tell us otherwise. The evolutionary development of "jazz," from early New Orleans styles to bebop cannot be restricted to stylistic differences that serve to simplify historical reporting.

Not only do bebop and hard bop share many common elemental features, but seemingly diametrically opposed styles such as "free jazz," swing, and New Orleans "jazz" also maintain essential similarities. All of these styles involve blues-based foundations that share sustained intensity, syncopation, complex rhythms, improvisation, and other characteristics rooted in an African-American dialect. Innovators of each new era generally acknowledge a connection to Afrocentric tradition, and often perform and record tributes to past eras. Many "jazz" styles borrow from a repertoire of standard compositions and share a common approach to fundamental harmonic orientation and melodic phrasing. There is much to be learned through the examination of differences; but there is an equal amount to be learned from considering similarities and retentions.

More Conceptual Expansion

Charles Mingus Reemerges during the 1970s

Mingus was a recluse from 1966 to 1970, falling into temporary obscurity, playing no music publicly, and producing no recordings. He emerged early in the 1970s, formed a new band, and released several memorable large-ensemble and small-group records. His big band performances in New York City on September 23 and November 28, 1971, included compositions (some of which were arranged by Sy Oliver) that were eventually released on an album entitled *Charles Mingus: Let My Children Hear Music.*[15] A concert billed as "Charles Mingus and Friends" in 1972 was another project involving a large ensemble on which Mingus collaborated with Sy Oliver.

The 1977 release of the album *Three or Four Shades of Blues,*[16] Mingus's best-selling record ever, fully revived his career. Mingus uses three electric guitarists on the album, which sold over fifty thousand copies. Shortly after his remarkable comeback, Mingus was diagnosed as having amyotrophic lateral sclerosis (Lou Gehrig's disease). By 1978 he was unable to play the bass, but he continued to compose for large ensembles. On several dates, his new works were recorded while Mingus led the musicians from his wheelchair (including the session that produced the album *Me, Myself an Eye*). Some of these recordings were released posthumously, and other extensive compositions were also performed after his death.

His wife, Sue Mingus, selected Gunther Schuller to edit and prepare the manuscript for a concert of Mingus's *Epitaph,* written for an assembly of thirty musicians and never performed during the composer's lifetime. That Mingus was not able to gain support for a performance of this piece—which Schuller accomplished—is conspicuous evidence of the American racism he encountered while trying to produce his own music after being "blacklisted" following his recording of his composition "Fables of Faubus." Mingus was not known for either a lack of motivation or inadequate business competence. It is perhaps due to frustrating sociocultural obstacles that account for the resignation reflected in Mingus's notes for *Epitaph,* where he simply said that he "wrote it for [his] tombstone." He apparently realized that his composition would never be performed during his lifetime. Mingus' multimovement *magnum opus* (composed intermittently between 1940 and 1962) was recorded at Avery Fischer Hall in 1989.

Mingus attempted to produce his own large-scale works once before in 1962 for an ill-fated concert at Town Hall in New York City. The date for the concert was originally set for November 15, 1962, then United Artists advanced the date forward five weeks earlier to October 12. The inconsiderate rescheduling placed Mingus in a position where outside arrangers had to be hired to try to rush to complete his music by the new deadline. This was the first of a series of inconsiderate circumstances and unfortunate events. Gunther Schuller discusses other experiences that occurred at the performance of the work:

> The first series of tragedies occurred when Mingus, out of strain and frustration, swung-out at his long-time friend, trom-

bonist Jimmy Knepper, who had been assisting with the preparation of the score. With scant rehearsal time Mingus assembled his musicians at Town Hall where two copyists were seated with the orchestra on stage, preparing instrumental parts from the newly finished score while the musicians played! The recording engineers were unable to provide playback monitors on stage or even to see the musicians, and thus communication was almost non-existent. Furthermore, when Mingus discovered the promoters had advertised the event as a concert and not as an open recording session with its stops and starts, he encouraged customers to demand their money back.

The full realization of his music was thwarted not only by a lack of rehearsal but by the fact that he had to act as composer, contractor, conductor, bassist/soloist, consultant, advisor, and virtually, director and producer. Mingus persevered until midnight when the unionized stagehands began to close down the hall. One musician, Clark Terry, broke into Ellington's "In A Mellow Tone," and as the weary artists sought release through a jam session on a familiar theme, the stagehands brought down the curtain. What came out of the Town Hall recording issued by United Artists is fragmentary and disparate. Titles were mislabeled, splicing and editing was done without Mingus' knowledge, and little of the two hours of recorded music appeared on the album. And if this wasn't enough, Mingus found himself in court on two counts: one to bring suit against United Artists for more than $18,000 in copying costs and, later, to answer assault charges made by Knepper.

Although trouble frequently plagued Mingus, the fiasco at Town Hall and the drama of his eviction in 1966 [captured on film by Tom Reichman] illuminated in a dark way the strength and sensitivity of one of America's greatest composers.[17]

Experimental music-making with the controversial bassist/composer was dubbed by his sidemen "the University of Mingus." His workshops (which took place either in closed rehearsals or live performances) involved long rehearsals where sloppy playing and attitudes were forced to confront the composer's wrath. If Mingus felt the playing lacked musicality and sincerity at any point during the "workshop," he had no qualms about stopping a composition midstream to chastise an individual musician or the entire ensemble, reminding them that they should always treat music (melody in particular) with "respect."

Anthony Braxton

Woodwind multi-instrumentalist and composer Anthony Braxton (b. 1945) has remained a major figure in contemporary instrumental music since the mid-seventies. He contributed to the body of experimental music produced by members of the Association for the Advancement of Creative Musicians (AACM), and still continues to resist categorization. His unique contributions as a composer distinguish him in the evolution of African-American music, particularly of the 1970s. Braxton's interest in exploring unconventional approaches to timbre, formal construction, and other compositional elements is expansive. His technical proficiency on woodwinds extends to a variety of rarely seen horns including such instruments as the sopranino and contrabass saxophones.

Braxton's recognition as a composer, whose works form a bridge between contemporary African-American "jazz" and European "classical" avant-garde idioms, is becoming increasingly more widespread. He has received a Guggenheim Fellowship and a National Endowment for the Arts grant for composition. The range of his work extends from solo performances to scores for multiple orchestras. Between those poles Braxton creates music for an array of small and large "jazz" ensembles, as well as unusual compositions for various other settings. He has also written film soundtracks, pieces for dance companies (including Merce Cunningham's) and has received chamber orchestra commissions.

Braxton studied harmony and composition at the Chicago School of Music and pursued graduate work in philosophy at Roosevelt University. His first love was European "classical" music, but the influence of cool-style saxophonists Paul Desmond, Lee Konitz, and Warne Marsh inspired his interest in "jazz." Upon receiving a discharge from the army in 1966, following a two-year tour of duty in Korea, Braxton joined the AACM. The experimental AACM workshop offered a conducive environment for Braxton's conceptual explorations of new synergetic musical resources related to the vanguard styles of both "free-jazz" players like Ornette Coleman, and the music of musicians such as John Cage, Karlheinz Stockhausen, and other European and European-American vanguard composers.

In 1967 Braxton, trumpeter Leo Smith, and violinist Leroy Jenkins formed the Creative Construction Company and recorded Braxton's debut album with those fellow AACM musicians later that year: *Three Compositions of New Jazz* (Delmark Records, 1967). During the following year, Braxton began to document his groundbreaking solo performances with his recording *Anthony Braxton, For Alto* (Delmark Records, 1968), which featured Braxton on unaccompanied alto sax. The critical acclaim for both releases created little financial profit for Braxton, a typical economic situation in the free "jazz" subculture. During this period Braxton often earned his living through engaging in hustling chess games on the street.[18]

Braxton became associated with the European electronic music scene shortly after he and many of his AACM peers moved to Europe (in 1969). He performed with the Italian improvising ensemble Musica Elettronica Viva in 1970. Avant-garde musicians during the 1970s expected to find a more sympathetic audience for their music abroad. It was during that period that Braxton joined pianist Chick Corea, bassist Dave Holland, and drummer Barry Altschul to form the short-lived group Circle. The musical empathy and improvisational inventiveness of Circle was documented on a recording of a live performance in Paris.[19] After Circle disbanded in 1971, a recording date the following year with the Dave Holland Quartet involved the multi-instrumentalist on an album entitled *Conference of the Birds* (that featured Braxton on reeds and flute).[20]

Braxton found that the delayed impact of his album *For Alto* eventually increased the demand for him as a solo performer in Europe. Braxton's burgeoning reputation at the time was reflected in the estimation of him as "the greatest living alto saxophonist," according to Coda, Canada's premier "jazz" magazine.[21] His African-American peers, who certainly knew better than to make such deluded claims, did not share this inflated enthusiasm for his playing. Braxton's music included more elements of European musical approaches to the saxophone than did most African-American altoists. His command of the instrument, and his inventiveness as a spontaneous and pre-meditative composer, certainly did not surpass contributions of Coleman Hawkins, Lester Young, Charlie Parker, John Coltrane, Cannonball Adderley, Ornette Coleman, or countless other innovative African-American saxophonists.

Braxton moved to New York in 1974 and recorded with his former AACM and Circle colleagues. He also found work with other musicians in small-combo settings (duets, trios, and quartets). These efforts produced several unusual albums including *Anthony Braxton, New York, Fall 1974* (for quartet on Arista Records, 1975); *Anthony Braxton, Five Pieces* (for quartet on Arista Records, 1975); *Anthony Braxton, Duets with Richard Abrams* (Arista Records, 1976); *Anthony Braxton, for Trio* (Arista Records, 1978). Braxton began to compose records for large ensembles during this phase of his career, and he created an early masterwork, *Anthony Braxton, Creative Orchestra Music* (Arista Records, 1976). His compositional imagination became intensified during the next two years. He toured Europe with his own experimental ensemble in 1978 and released a three-record set that documents a huge aggregation of 160 musicians organized into four orchestras performing on-stage at Oberlin College in Ohio (*Anthony Braxton, For Four Orchestras*, Arista Records, 1978).

Braxton's concern seems directed toward constructing new musical and structural paradigms. His music often involves pulse track structures:

> The term pulse track refers to the horizontal placement of given factors in the forward space of the music, horizontal variables that define how the space is conceived in the same sense as vertical harmony does, except here we're dealing with conceptual areas that I've generated in my own music, areas that in this context have to do with the nature of event-forming and construction dynamics. And these horizontal variables establish a dialogue, on the first level between the individual and the process, then the individual and the other players; then later the individual and the composite group consciousness.[22]

The World Saxophone Quartet

The World Saxophone Quartet was formed in St. Louis in 1977 by three saxophonists from the Black Artists Group who became prominent during the 1970s and a younger Bay Area born saxophonist. Oliver Lake (b. 1942), Julius Hemphill (1940–95), and Hamiet Bluiett (b. 1940) were the members of BAG who founded the WSQ with saxophonist David Murray (b. 1955). Their complementary styles are demonstrated in numerous recordings of live and studio performances. The range of influence includes elements as diverse as Ornette Coleman, the Art Ensemble of Chicago, and Albert Ayler, on the one hand, with Duke Ellington, Igor Stravinsky, and Charles Mingus on the other. Their music incorporates humor, world music, traditional African-American music, and a diverse spectrum of sources.

The longevity of the World Saxophone Quartet's (over twenty years) was interrupted in April 1995, when Hemphill died. Multi-reedist John Purcell joined the quartet as a performer, producer, and saxophone consultant. Purcell has worked with Tito Puente, Dizzy Gillespie, Stevie Wonder, and others. In an article for *Down Beat* magazine, Bluiett attributed the staying power of the quartet to a strategy against the tendency of the American music industry to divide and conquer African-American artists: "We have managed to stay together by not trying to stay together. This was my formula because I know this industry. If you try to stay together, it will pull you apart. By pursuing our own careers, we somehow kept coming back together, and it was just a matter of making ourselves available for the various concert and recording dates. But we also like playing together. And furthermore, we are not just a group, we are a non-profit business, and no decision is made unless we all agree."[23]

Joe Henderson

Joe Henderson first came into prominence in a group he co-led with trumpeter Kenny Dorham (1924–72) between 1962 and 1963. He later made classic recordings with Horace Silver (b. 1928) and organized the Jazz Communicators with trumpeter Freddie Hubbard (b. 1938). He played a televised concert with Herbie Hancock, Ron Carter, and Tony Williams in 1985 and recorded his highly acclaimed recordings live at the Village Vanguard around that time.

Favorable things finally began to happen for Henderson during the early 1990s, as the general public finally began to realize what all "jazz" musicians had always known: Joe was one of the most powerful tenor players to emerge from the 1960s. He absorbed from all the great tenor players that came before him but emerged with his own distinctive melodic style. He is one of the contemporary masters.

Joe Henderson rehearsing with the Cornell University Lab Ensembles for a performance as part of the annual *Cornell University "Jazz" Festival* in 1993 (Karlton E. Hester, Director) (Photo courtesy of HRP Library).

Joe Henderson as guest artist at the annual *Cornell University "Jazz" Festival* in 1993 (Karlton E. Hester, Director) (Photo courtesy of HRP Library).

McCoy Tyner

Pianist McCoy Tyner, perhaps best known in connection with the Coltrane ensembles, was the driving force in front of his own varied groups by the early seventies. He transfers his powerful piano solo style to big band scores on occasion, but, Tyner says, "I do big band dates in Europe from time to time, but only a couple of times here in the States. It's expensive and I don't want to be on the road constantly."[24]

Tyner's mother, a pianist, encouraged and instructed young McCoy. Bud and Richie Powell were his main influences, and Tyner soon led his own teenage "jazz" band in his native Philadelphia. McCoy always followed his devout Muslim religious beliefs closely, and adopted the name Sulaimon Saud around that time. Tyner always used his original name when he performed, however.

In 1959 Tyner played with the Jazztet, a group co-led by Art Farmer and Benny Golson. He then joined the Coltrane sextet for five years (1960–65). His album with Joe Henderson, Ron Carter, and Elvin Jones that followed the period with Coltrane is one of the important recordings to come out of the late sixties. When asked about the Coltrane influence on his playing McCoy replied:

We can never recapture anything, because it [the world] is always changing. It's always different. People leave the planet but their styles remain here. They're here in spirit. What I'm saying is that to try and duplicate anything doesn't make sense. That's the reason why when I left John, Jimmy [Garrison] and Elvin [Jones] were ready to leave, and they said, "Let's play as a trio." I said, "No," because it's like a tree, your roots are there but you branch off. What I'm doing is like an extension of what I did with them. It's 1995, and I'm still drawing strength from those roots. . . . John is always present. Like Charlie Parker, he's there, and that's good.[25]

The pianist was also influenced by Monk and Art Tatum. He has, in turn, influenced the younger generations of pianists. McCoy says, "I try to listen to music from many different countries: Africa, India, from the Arabic world, European classical music . . . all kinds of music are interconnected."[26] Tyner made a number of impressive recordings during the 1970s. He participated in an all-star tour in 1978 with Sonny Rollins, Ron Carter, and Al Foster. He later made a film as a solo pianist in 1985 when Blue note relaunched its label. He continues to experiment with modern Afrocentric music at the piano. In 1996 he remarked: "I take a particular interest in African culture because it's in me and it's reflected in a lot of my songs."[27]

Instrumental Style Continues to Evolve

The saxophone continued to remain among the most dominant "jazz" instruments, exerting a wide-ranging influence during the seventies. Yet the trumpet, piano, bass, trombone, flute, and other instruments began to make impressive strides as well. A careful examination of American trumpet history shows we can trace an uninterrupted and powerful line through the styles of King Oliver, Louis Armstrong, Roy Eldridge, Dizzy Gillespie, Miles Davis, and Lester Bowie. Each of these innovators acknowledged the importance of past traditions, but contributed a salubrious personal style that produced a votary of followers.

When a new mainstream style reasserted itself during hard bop, Horace Silver, Randy Weston, Tommy Flanagan, Elmo Hope, Herbie Nichols, Mal Waldron, and other pianists emerged from that movement. Ramsey Lewis, Wynton Kelly, Ray Bryant, Andrew Hill, and others created an eclectic piano style that revitalized an interest in blues, gospel, and other soulful African-American music, while often incorporating elements of European impressionism, Latin styles, and other elements drawn from around the world. Pianists McCoy Tyner, Herbie Hancock, Milt Buckner, and Bill Evans had popularized the use of quartal harmony making its usage increasingly more common.

The interval of the fourth was a favorite of other musicians (during the 1950s) who introduced quartal dyads and triads as supporting chord structures or as extensions of chromatic harmony. Later, compositions like Hancock's "Maiden Voyage" experimented with combinations of quartal harmony, harmonics, and polytonality. Interestingly, as Kubik notes, the !Kung of Southeastern Angola and other Africans employ a related harmonic approach.

> Tonal systems based on the use of harmonies over two fundamentals [Hancock uses four fundamentals in "Maiden Voyage"] . . . frequently encountered in areas where the musical bow is known, particularly the mouth-bow in its varieties. These fundamentals are yielded either by two segments of the string when it is divided by means of a brace or noose on an unbraced bow when the string may be stopped with a finger or a stick and thus shortened to obtain the higher note. . . .

> The tonal system of the !Kung of Southeastern Angola is tetratonic with frequent pentatonic extensions. My surprise finding, however, while doing research in the area of Kwitu-Kwanavale in 1965, was that the !Kung tetratonic system manifests itself in three different phenotypes with different intervals, depending on the width of the basic interval to which the music bow is tuned. . . . Unaccompanied vocal music is totally in line with the bow harmonics, and a song stands in any of the three phenotypes, unless of course, it is pentatonic.[28]

Hard bop musicians and other stylists also became interested in making modern "jazz" more appealing to African-American audiences during the mid-fifties and mid-sixties.

Since the dawn of modern "jazz," saxophonists consistently excelled as the most influential innovators of each eras beginning around 1940. The innovations of Charlie Parker that marked the beginning of the modern "jazz" era were honed into new approaches during the late fifties and early sixties by Ornette Coleman, Eric Dolphy, Sonny Stitt, Cannonball Adderly, and other saxophonists. Coleman restructured small-group "jazz." His "harmolodic" revolution defied most of the tonal and harmonic conventions established by the hard bop and cool styles. Coleman was instrumental in the creation of what became known as free "jazz." With Dolphy's approach, saxophone style was again modified, expanding harmonic, melodic, timbre, and other expressive borderlines while introducing the bass clarinet as a new lead instrument. Dolphy was also instrumental in liberating the role of the flute in "jazz."

The synthesis of styles developed by Sonny Rollins, John Coltrane, Eric Dolphy, and Ornette Coleman became the new extension of the saxophone legacy established by Ben Webster, Coleman Hawkins, Lester Young, and Charlie Parker. Many saxophonists of the seventies and eighties (such as Julius Hemphill, Dewey Redman, Branford Marsalis, Oliver Lake, Sam Rivers, Yusef Lateef, Joe Henderson, David Murray and Arthur Blythe) can trace their musical approach back to that stylistic "school." The hard bop approach that developed between 1955 and 1965 branched out into two distinct styles: those players who continued to be guided by preset chord changes, and those who moved away from prescribed forms, melodies, and harmonies.

In the seventies an additional type of "jazz" saxophone style emerged. "Jazz" saxophone style was influenced by popular styles of the day and, in turn, influence styles of popular music. The music that resulted was labeled "jazz"-fusion and "jazz"-funk, but this line of influence extends back to the rhythm-and-blues style of the late forties and fifties (produced by musicians such as Illinois Jacquet, Flip Phillips, Earl Bostic, and others). Their lineage continued into the sixties, affecting the musical directions of David Fathead Newman, Cannonball Adderley, Hank Crawford, Tina Brooks, King Curtis, Gene Ammons, Grover Washington, Jr., and Stanley Turrentine. Grover Washington Jr. (1943–99) developed an influential lyrical saxophone sound (particularly on soprano) that eventually became the primary prototype for a much more watered-down and popular smooth-"jazz" saxophone sound.

Other saxophonists developed styles that, while not as influential as the more dominant innovators, were clearly outside the mainstream sound. Among these personal styles are the Texas tenors Booker Ervin and Jimmy Tyler; soprano saxophonist Steve Lacy; saxophonists Joseph Jarman, Albert Ayler, and Roscoe Mitchell; and multi-instrumentalists Anthony Braxton and Rahsaan Roland Kirk. These musicians' distinctive approaches have less clearly defined links to the two adjacent saxophone dynasties mentioned above.

The general temperament of the African-American community was reflected in the styles of many musicians during the sixties. The nature of this movement contributed to redefining African-American sociocultural and personal identity, as well as to reshaping modes of artistic expression. The music of the seventies, on the other hand, began to become more assimilated into mainstream American culture and world musical styles, as the social environment briefly became somewhat neutralized. Perhaps several totalitarian shows of force during the early 1970s caused activists (of all colors) to rush to the barber shops across America to shed their Afros and long straight hair. The show of military force at Kent State and then the militarized police aggression in Los Angeles that mercilessly crushed the Symbionese Liberation Army (on national television) were two such incidents. The systematic infiltration and disruption of the Black Panther Party was a related and effectively orchestrated conspiracy. The youth cultures of the 1960s began grooming themselves for radically more conservative lifestyles in America of the 1970s.

The Evolution of the Flute

When Samuel Mordecai writes about the Richmond, Virginia, of the "bygone days" in 1860, he makes it clear that the flute was already an instrument used at American dances. He mentions a famous "Negro fiddler Sy Gilliat" and a "Negro flautist London Brigs" in connection with performances at state balls where they "dressed in a courtly fashion." Mordecai says, "To the music of Gilliat's fiddle and London Brigs' flute all sorts of capers were cut.... Sometimes a 'congo' was danced and when the music grew fast and furious, a jig would wind up the evening."[29]

The low audibility of the flute made it difficult for the instrument to be heard in the noisy environments in which early "jazz" musicians performed. Like the double bass and guitar, the flute would eventually enjoy greater popularity when amplification of musical sounds became more refined. Nevertheless, the flute has always had a place in the "jazz" evolution. There were certainly early flute players who failed to gain historical recognition. A flute and piccolo specialist in Chicago named Flutes Morton (1900–62) performed at the Sunset Cafe in the middle of the Roaring Twenties. Norvel E. Morton lived in Chicago for many years and worked regularly with violinist (and multi-instrumentalist) Erskine Tate (1895–1978) and pianist Dave Peyton (1885–1956). In 1932 Morton was a member of the Eddie King band and was with Reuben Reeves's group between 1933 and 1934. He also performed briefly with Louis Armstrong, Earl Hines, and Noble Sissle.

Although the clarinet was the preferred woodwind double of most swing era saxophonists (because of its greater amplitude), the flute found a place in some big bands. One of the first solo flutists to be featured on a "jazz" recording was Wayman Carver (1905–67). He is the earliest master of "jazz" flute. Carver produced not only a beautiful tone, displayed an impressive technique, and improvised superbly on that traditionally delicate woodwind instrument, but he also demonstrated an equally impressive control and imagination on the clarinet and saxophones. He began to study the flute seriously at age fourteen and was soon performing with Elmer Snowden's band (1931–32). Carver worked with Benny Carter (b. 1907) for a couple of years and was featured on a recording session in New York with bassist Spike Hughes (1908–87) that produced "Sweet Sue Just You."

Carver gained his greatest exposure from 1934 to 1940 while a member of master drummer Chick Webb's band featuring Ella Fitzgerald. He was also proved to be an interesting arranger, contributing renditions of "Down Home Rag," "My Heart Belongs to Daddy," and other arrangements in Webb's book. Chauncey Haughton often performed duets with Carver on Gershwin's "I Got Rhythm," Harry White's "Congo," and other diminutive swing-style arrangements for a quintet (formed on the band-within-band principle) from Webb's big band format.

In the early 1950s Yusef Lateef (b. 1920) began to use flute, oboe, and a wide range of other wind instruments from around the world. William Evans (Lateef's name before he embraced Islam in the late 1940s) moved from Detroit to New York in 1946. He soon found work as a tenor saxophonist with Lucky Millinder, Roy Eldridge, and Hot Lips Page before joining Dizzy Gillespie for a year. The exotic compositions Lateef introduced affected the music of John Coltrane and other musicians during the 1960s.

Almost all of the early flute innovators doubled on the saxophone. James Moody (b. 1925) began on the alto saxophone before taking up the tenor the following year. During the 1940s he worked with Dizzy Gillespie, Miles Davis, Tadd Dameron, and Max Roach. Moody was based in Paris from 1948 to 1952 and began to play the flute when he returned to the United States in the mid-1950s.

Eric Dolphy (1928–64) not only created a new role for the flute in "jazz" but was also one of the first vanguard multi-instrumentalists to master all of his instruments convincingly. Dolphy studied with another brilliant Los

Angeles–born multi-instrumentalist, Buddy Collette (b. William Marcel in 1921). Collette was a founding member of the Chico Hamilton quintet. In the late 1950s, Buddy Collette's Swinging Shepherds recorded ground-breaking flute quartets (for piccolo, flute, alto flute, and bass flute) with flutists Bud Shank, Paul Horn, and Harry Klee. Collette continued to work with Monk, Dizzy Gillespie, Benny Carter, and others, but soon focused on freelance studio performance and teaching. His ability to maintain a beautiful tone on flute while switching from one instrument to another with utmost ease places Collette in a special class of multi-instrumentalists. Flutist James Newton (b. 1953) studied with Collette, but his style is firmly grounded in Dolphy's musical approach.

Other tenor players who made important contributions to the development of the flute during the 1950s and early 1960s were Frank Wess (b. 1922), Harold Land (b. 1928), Sam Rivers (b. 1930), and Herbie Mann (b. 1930). Wess and Mann began to popularize the "jazz" flute during the mid-1950s. It was Rahsaan Roland Kirk (1936–77), though, who moved furthest away from the idiomatic "jazz" flute approach that was heavily influenced by the prevailing saxophone styles. Kirk's extended flute technique was broad enough to incorporate virtually all twentieth-century devices.

James Spaulding (b. 1937), Art Webb, Lloyd McNeill, and other flutists would follow in the tradition of the earlier flutists. Hubert Laws (b. 1939) put his tenor saxophone aside after working with Mongo Santamaria (b. 1922) and dedicated full energy to moving the flute and piccolo playing to new levels of technical mastery. Although flutists Bobbi Humphrey and Kent Jordan chose to express their musical ideas in fusion and popular styles, both were heavily influenced by Laws.

Hubert Laws' elevated flute technique to a new level of control and virtuosity. His style involved the exploitation of an expanded array of the inherent qualities of the flute. He also introduced his audiences to the piccolo and the alto and bass flutes during his numerous concerts. He studied at the Juilliard School of Music and used this knowledge to engage the innovative improvisational style of 1970s fusion. He was born in Texas, the birthplace of many other innovative "jazz" flutists (including Leo Wright, James Clay, Prince Lasha, John Carter, and the author).

Laws performs both Afrocentric "jazz" and Eurocentric "classical" influenced works with supreme authority. Laws contributed music to the repertoire of 1970s "jazz"/classical fusion that would continually gain in popularity throughout the decade. His albums *Afro-Classic* (1970) and *The Rite of Spring* (1971) are the earliest of his albums that display an ability to move between baroque, impressionistic, pop, and early-twentieth-century European styles while maintaining stylistic connection with the African-American music tradition.

Although the role of the "jazz" flute is relatively marginal, few orchestral woodwinds or strings have enjoyed the influential status assigned to the saxophone in "jazz" history. Nonetheless, the more subtle sound of the violin has remained attached to the evolution of "jazz." Ray Nance, Stuff Smith, Stephane Grappelli, Joe Venuti, Billy Bang, Michael White, Noel Pointer, Jean-Luc Ponty, and Regina Carter are just a few of the notable musicians who demonstrated the powerful capabilities of the "jazz" violin. Just as all instruments are potentially virtuoso instruments, so each one is capable of "jazz" expression.

Buddy Collette performing as guest artist at Eisenhower High School in 1974 (Photo courtesy of HRP Library).

Buddy Collette and Karlton E. Hester (then director of ensembles) at Eisenhower High School (Photo courtesy of HRP Library).

Buddy Collette at Eisenhower High School
(Photo courtesy of HRP Library).

Yusef Lateef and Karlton E. Hester at the annual conference of the
***International Association for Jazz Education* in Toronto, January**
2003 (Photos by William P. Johnson).

Classical – "Jazz" Fusion and Other New Approaches

"Classical" is a general term that can be equally applied to the music
of any culture, including "jazz." The music called "jazz," on the other hand,
has its primary traditional roots in innovation and experimentation, and it
generally involves an evolutionary process requiring continual artistic revolution. In the past, innovative "jazz" musicians have been less concerned with
the perpetuation of tradition than with each finding their own unique voice.
Dorothy Donegan, Hubert Laws, and Wynton Marsalis are only a few of a
growing number of African-American musicians who consciously direct their
musical attention toward building bridges between "classic" African-American and European music.

Cleo Lane is a remarkable vocal recitalist who was living in London
when the influence of "jazz" found her. For Lane, this period of discovery (in
the 1970s) led to the creation of a fresh vocal approach. Lane's unusually impressive vocal range supported a stylistic approach capable of winning almost
immediate popularity. Her 1973 album *I Am a Song* exemplifies a cross-
section of Lane's early style. Lane's music on that recording involved yet another example of fresh ways of fusing European musical aesthetics with African-American musical styles.

The various roles of women musicians during the seventies were not
restricted to vocalists. Sharon Freeman was playing concerts and studio sessions in the late 1970s. Sharon Freeman was equally adept on the French
horn and piano after graduating from New York City's High School of Music
and Art and later the Manhattan School of Music (with a Bachelor of Music

in Theory and French Horn). She eventually worked with the Gil Evans Orchestra, Sam Rivers' Harlem Ensemble, Charles Mingus' Big Band, Kenny Dorham Quintet, New York Jazz Repertory Company, Jazz Composers' Orchestra Association, McCoy Tyner's Big Band, the French Horn Ensemble (of which she was organizer/leader), and with Carla Bley.

Composer/pianist Carla Bley (b. 1938) composed and performed her own unique brand of experimental music and founded a record distribution company (New Music Distribution Company). Although women instrumentalists were poorly promoted during this period, they continued to create music in a variety of settings. Paula Hampton emerged as a dynamic New York City drummer during the seventies. She appeared regularly with The Jazz Sisters. Hampton was also a featured drummer at the "Salute to Women in Jazz" (in New York City) in 1978. Hampton performed with the Universal Jazz Coalition's "Big Apple" Jazz Women Ensemble in New York, and was a guest artist at the Kansas City Women's Jazz Festival in 1979.

During the 1970s, saxophonist Oliver Lake (b. 1942) contributed to the innovative evolution of the fissionary variety of spontaneous composition. He and other innovators, unable to find recording companies in America who were eager to embrace their music, began recording abroad for Black Saint records and other European labels. The ideas for compositions on his 1976 album *Holding Together* introduce fresh approaches to musical organization.

As an increasing number of 1970s college music students began to study "jazz" and European music simultaneously, the ivory tower that traditionally elevated European "art music" above all other world music was often forced to justify its lofty claims. Today, examining music strictly in terms of the notes and empirical theories involved makes the justification for Eurocentric musical snobbery an impossible case to prove.

Since the 1970s, African-American musicians began to receive increasingly more institutional support for their innovative work. Ornette Coleman, Cecil Taylor, Charles Mingus, Charlie Haden, James Newton, David Murray, and George Russell have received Guggenheim Foundation Fellowships. Taylor, Coleman, Steve Lacy, Anthony Braxton, and George Lewis are among those who have received MacArthur grants. Billy Harper, Grachan Moncur III, the JCOA, Kenny Durham, and Lee Konitz were among the early recipients of the National Endowment for the Arts (NEA) "jazz" composition grants. Ed Blackwell and other artists received awards from the NEA for producing method books.[30] Despite significant changes in funding policy for the arts in the United States, the support provided by American corporate agencies and educational institutions for African-American music has remained disproportionately low.

Artistic barriers such as social conditioning, arrogance, and lack of exposure to new music prevent many people from understanding that most world music contains beauty, knowledge, inspiration, and sophistication that can benefit all listeners. Author Alain Danielou offers an interesting perspective on attitudes regarding the eminence of European music:

> Modern Western music was able to develop its polyphonic system only by deliberately sacrificing the greater part of its possibilities and breaking the ties which connected it with other

musical systems. Formerly, all the musical systems were near to each other and, in spite of differences, could generally be understood from one country to another; this can clearly be seen in the success that the musicians who came with the Turkish Empress had in China, in that of some Negro musicians in the Mussalman [sic] world during the first centuries of Islam, or that of the Gypsies in Europe. But since the middle ages, there has been, in the West, a tendency to accept those simplifications of the theory which had already been rejected everywhere else as being incompatible with a refined form of Art. Therefore, when, in the words of M. Amédée, 'Guido d'Arezzo (990–1040), having reduced everything to the diatonic, and given the last blow to the quarter-tones inherited from the Greek melody, directs our scale toward temperament and facilitates the progress of polyphony. D'Arezzo, in reality, only gives a blow to all popular forms of music whose very complex modal and rhythmic forms will place to an official art, heavy and simplified.[31]

There is little difference between solitary or simultaneous occurrences of tones in a planned system and those forming related harmonies spontaneously during improvised music. Sound is sound whether read from a sheet of music or produced spontaneously. There can be elements of predictability and surprise, tension and release, or joy and sadness in any artistic expression. The involvement of inspiration, musical knowledge and technical virtuosity are inherent in music from all over the world.

Even as educators across the country seek answers to the problems involved in educating today's morally, economically, and emotionally neglected children, they apparently fail to recognize the importance of artistic creativity in the nurturing and shaping of young minds, bodies, and spirits. If an appreciation of the arts is not a high priority in education, society will eventually devolve toward a point of creative impotence.

Santeria and Musical Freedom

By the 1960s Santeria had made its way to New York City, bringing with its rituals the music of the bata drum. Many of the "free" players were eager to incorporate these new rhythmic sounds into their musical universe, bringing the evolution of African-American music full circle—back (so to speak) to its point of origin (African music).

The origins of Santeria can be traced back to the traditional religion of the Yoruba people of West Africa. Its system of beliefs and rituals emerged in Cuba in the 1940s before making its way to neighborhoods in New York City, where many Cuban, Puerto Rican, and Dominican (Dominican Republican) people resided. John Amira and Steven Cornelius describe interesting aspects of this religion in *The Music of Santeria: Traditional Rhythms of the Bata Drums.*

Traditional Yoruba religion is constructed upon a hierarchical, pantheistic system of thought which stretches from Almighty God in the most rarefied heaven to man on earth. Man can fulfill his destiny by avoiding the wrath of gods, and actually improve his lot through proper veneration and sacrifice to them.

Olorun is The Deity, God Almighty, and is generally considered to be responsible for the creation of the universe. Olorun is an austere and remote God who by representing all things, all possibilities, is beyond human comprehension. Therefore, practitioners direct their entreaties to the orichas, deities who, positioned directly below Olorun, are both relatively fathomable and accessible. Each oricha embodies various aspects from the totality of Olorun. These aspects are personified from natural features (rivers, oceans, mountains) or from elemental forces acting within nature (wind, lightening, disease). Through these associations, each oricha is believed to govern specific aspects of the universe. What evolves from these conceptions are layers of religious belief which reveal multiple notions of, and means to, the sacrifice.

Religious practitioners use music and various types of prayer to communicate with and praise the orichas. In turn, the orichas mediate between man and God Almighty. Direct contact with the orichas is sometimes achieved through spirit possession. This is an important aspect of worship in some areas of West Africa and central to New World music ritual.[32]

In addition to the musical associations "jazz" musicians had with bata drummers and other people practicing African-based religions, many African-American "jazz" musicians were impressed with other forms of worship. Dizzy Gillespie spoke to Art Taylor of the difference that his new faith made in his life. Gillespie was a follower of the Baha'i faith, which means "follower of Baha'ullah" (Baha'ullah means "glory of God" in Persian):[33] "Since I became a Baha'i, which is my religious faith, I've been much more aware of unity. Because the Baha'is are destined to bring unity to the world: unity of religion, of races, of finance, of everything. I'm looking at it like this: if you have a group, the group is like a painting, a masterpiece. Each one of the instruments represents a specific color, and the diversity of colors makes it beautiful. You've got five pieces, and none of them sound alike, but they must have unity."[34]

While an audience for the innovative forms of "jazz" was gradually developing downtown in New York City as well as in other urban areas, audiences did not include large proportions of African-American listeners. Appreciation for an art form is enhanced through formal and casual education that is a by-product of direct and continued exposure to artistic experiences. Young African Americans remained less likely to frequent lofts located in European-American neighborhoods. Just as the proportion of African-American listeners declined when the musicians left the Harlem nightclubs and theaters in New York to perform downtown on 52nd Street and other areas (especially during the bebop era), a related trend continued to distance contemporary African-American innovators from young people in African-American neighborhoods. While this trend continued for decades in America, a significant number of young Europeans and European Americans became better exposed to the newer approaches to "jazz" that were emerging than young African-American adults and (especially) children. Thus, as "jazz" became less Afrocentric, socioculturally speaking, it lost its potency and its relevance to young African Americans.

With innovative artists now cordoned off and isolated from their indigenous communities, European Americans began increasing their control over African-American music. In an attempt to build an independent, self-contained, self-defined and viable community infrastructure, pianist Horace Tapscott (1934–99) formed the Pan-Afrikan Peoples Arkestra and organized the associated activist artistic community organization the Union of God's Musicians and Artists (UGMAA) around 1959. It was difficult to sustain such noble efforts. The trend towards Eurocentric controls over Afrocentric music even angered some of the more amiable and broad-minded musicians. Dizzy Gillespie revealed his feelings regarding these developments to Art Taylor. Taylor opens the line of discussion by asking Dizzy, "What do you think about the word jazz?" Gillespie responds:

> It's no longer fashionable to say Negro, which is what the white man named us. If we want to call it jazz, we'll make them call it that. It's our music, whatever we want to call it. I don't know who made up the word *jazz*. The blacks might have named it jazz themselves, but I don't know much about it. It's a misnomer only when it is identified with white musicians. On a television program someone was asked to say who was known as the king of jazz. The answer was supposed to be Paul Whiteman. That's a misnomer, because he couldn't be the king of our music.

> Take Stan Kenton, for instance: a big phony, really, because he had a big band at the same time I did. People used to walk up to me and think they were saying something nice, like: "I like you and Stan Kenton." I'd be looking at them like this, and I'd question their taste. History will either off you or make you valid. History has wiped Stan Kenton out completely. They thought he was a master, they thought he was greater than Duke Ellington, and that motherfucker couldn't even keep time. I went on a tour with him as a soloist, and when I came on, he left and you didn't see him no more. On the next show he'd come and do his thing in the front, then he would announce me and leave, and the band played my music better than they played his. I found a deeper respect from all his musicians, because all of them came up from my school. Everyone in his band came up under us, not under Stan Kenton. So they recognized the fact, and when I walked on the bandstand, there

were twenty smiles. You should see what they looked like when he was playing. It made me feel good.

Anyway, our documentation is so strong now with all our records that they can't get it. I think the idea now is for blacks to write about the history of our music. It's time for that, because whites have been doing it all the time. It's time for us to do it ourselves and tell it like it is. The whites have a whitewash look at our music. Naturally they're going to try to ooze off as much as they can to the whites, but they can't, because we're documented in records, and the truth will stand. History will tell you what it is about.[35]

One thing Gillespie failed to anticipate was that European Americans could take a major portion of the documentation off the market shelves as records in one format (LPs) and reissue this information at will on CDs. Today, only a relatively small sampling of the works of Gillespie, Tatum, Parker, Coltrane, Miles, Donegan, Williams, or any other African-American "jazz" master has been released, although CDs have been widely available on the market for over a decade. Record companies are not as concerned about making all the historically significant documents (formerly released on vinyl) available to the public as they are developing market strategies that will insure them a steady flow of capital. Before the change of format from LP to CD occurred, a much larger proportion of artists' works was available in most large "jazz" record stores as both regular issues or cut-outs. The types of recordings by "jazz" artists sold in record stores were altered during the music industry's transition from analog to digital recordings. This essentially became a European-American businessman's editing project that arbitrarily filtered through the history of African-American music. As a consequence, yet another revision of African-American history occurred. In many record stores across the United States, the recordings of European-American musicians have replaced many of the recordings of African-American "jazz" progenitors.

The intensified and perpetual tendencies of revisionists to control "jazz" and redesign its history have haunted African-American musicians throughout the twentieth century. Thumbing through any of the numerous current "jazz" periodicals exposes related revisionist trends in "jazz." Because the majority of America lacks a basic education in the history of African-American music, they are not aware of its many innovators (Herbie Nichols, Horace Tapscott, Sam Rivers, Ted Curson, etc.). Therefore, it is difficult for most Americans to realize what important musical documents are currently out of print. In a September 1998 *Down Beat* interview titled "Take Back the Music," the innovative saxophonist Gary Bartz discusses his disgust "with the quality of music recorded by top artists who allow major labels to exercise control over the final product."

Record labels feel like part of their job is to bother the musicians. They think they have a better idea of how to sell the music. I have the best idea: Stay out of the studio and sell the music. Don't tell me to put a young trumpet player on my album when I have a great trumpet player with me already. If I did put a young trumpet player on the album, they still aren't going to sell the record, so what's the deal? They want you to further their cause. They want me to build up a young trumpet player when I'm trying to make music—which is all I'm interested in.[36]

There is an additional sociocultural disposition that complicates this problem. Historically, the majority of European Americans found it difficult to acknowledge the contribution African-American citizens made to American society as inventors, political leaders, inventors, innovators, and spiritual messengers. As a consequence, the European-American "jazz" musician serves as a more "digestible" image for many Americans, thus enabling them to partake in an African-American art form without acknowledging its source. Unfortunately, if African-American musicians finally gain recognition for their greatness (currently Miles, Monk, Mingus, Dolphy, Coltrane, etc.), their physical images are vigorously displayed on posters, T-shirts, calendars, and in other ways that celebrate their exemplary accomplishments only posthumously. African-American artists are often appreciated by the music industry only for the profit they yield, and profit can be made posthumously. When asked why record labels don't sell records, Bartz evaluates the situation this way:

It's counterproductive for them because they couldn't get a tax write-off in the first year or two after the record comes out. Now, they know when they make the record it's never going to lose money. If it takes 200 years, that record will make its money back. Unfortunately, the musicians don't last quite that long. Musicians have a high mortality rate and die at a very young age, so the record companies have their cake and eat it, too. That's why they don't sell the music. They know if the musician passes away, their recordings become very valuable.[37]

A Historical Summary

From West African musical roots two distinct but related lines of secular music traditions evolved in North America. We will call one a "jazz" tradition and the other a blues tradition. The seeds for the African-American "jazz" evolution originally began to take shape around 1502, when the first slaves arrived in America. The definitive aspects of these traditions culminated in the innovative African-American music of the 1970s.

The blues tradition was an offspring of African-American work songs, field hollers, and protests songs, whereas sacred folk spirituals, which began to appear at the end of the seventeenth century, were influenced by game songs and social songs. The folk spiritual became formalized by the middle of the eighteenth century, when arranged spirituals were heard throughout the country. Traveling musicians like the Luca Family and others sang a brand of spirituals performed around the world a few years later by the Fisk Jubilee Singers.

The influence of spiritual music, songs of both oppression and joy, eventually led to the rural blues around 1880. At about the same time syncopated dance music, which can also be traced back to the 1600s, gradually gave rise to ragtime. The melodies and harmonies of both the spirituals and syncopated dance music were influenced by the European hymns, concert music, and the marches with which it came in contact. African and African-American music, in turn, affected European and European-American music during these early periods of stylistic development.

Around 1890 African-American sacred music produced a folk gospel (gospel hymn) containing elements of rural blues, ragtime, and New Orleans "jazz" (which was a by-product of ragtime). This early "jazz" also contained rural blues elements and, in turn, had an effect on the Vaudeville blues that, along with boogie woogie, was a direct descendant of the early blues and barrelhouse piano. Blues and boogie woogie forms evolved during the birth of the gospel hymn around the turn of the century.

By the 1920s New Orleans "jazz" had made the initial transition into the early big bands, many of which were to emerge as swing bands of the 1930s. Many of the 1930s swing bands retained aspects of stride and boogie woogie styles. By the subsequent decade, however, a new bebop style was born that would mark the birth of modern "jazz." Hard bop and cool styles followed bebop during the 1950s.

The gospel hymn evolved into traditional gospel by 1930, and traces of vaudeville blues exist in the new gospel music. Later, along with soul and rhythm and blues, this sacred style would influence secular civil rights songs during the early 1960s. Traditional gospel not only produced the gospel quartets that became popular around the 1940s but was an important part of the cross-genre pollination that took place between rhythm and blues and urban blues during that period. Other gospel groups emerged later during the 1940s. The new gospel groups' stylistic influence eventually made its way into the work of hard bop musicians like Cannonball Adderley, Horace Silver, and others.

By the 1950s there were African-American gospel choirs of various sizes throughout America. This time it was soul music (born a decade later) that became the secular cross-fertilization partner. By the time Contemporary Gospel entered the picture in the early 1970s, sacred African-American music was enjoying additional influences of both funk and "jazz" fusion.

The urban blues qualities of the 1930s, retained in 1940s rhythm and blues, became the foundation for rock and roll in the early 1950s. Rhythm and blues and urban blues adapted musical elements from the swing bands of the 1930s (by way of the jump bands). Urban blues and R&B eventually merged with certain soul music elements the following decade. Soul, "jazz," funk, disco, and other Afrocentric music inherited these traits. Funk music, with its broad range of power, its popularity, and its ability to sway general audiences, was in this sense the precursor of the "jazz" fusion and rap styles that emerged in subsequent decades. A listener can detect a related influence in other African-American music of the next decade such as techno funk, house music, and go-go.

While cool "jazz" failed to produce an offspring, hard bop figured prominently in the production of both soul "jazz" in the 1960s and "jazz" fusion in the 1970s. A more innovative third by-product of bebop was the experimental music labeled avant-garde that revolutionized the music scene during the 1960s.[38] Many observers have commented on the flexible nature of the "jazz" evolution.

> Hard bop and bebop are sometimes considered separately, which illustrates that the differentiation of styles constitutes no more than drawing arbitrary lines at given points along a continuum. The same also applies to labeling performers. It would be a great disservice to Lester Young if one were to label him strictly as a big band saxophonist, since he continually sought to broaden his style of musical performance throughout his career. For example, Young performed in the small group settings of the 1930s; on occasion, he also performed with bebop musicians.

> Because the above model for the development of jazz mainly attributes stylistic change to purely musical considerations, it also overlooks certain cognitive components of behavior. For example, the processes of composing and performing music involve a countless number of decisions that performers make on both the conscious and unconscious levels. Leonard Meyer summarizes: "What remains constant from style to style are not scales, modes, harmonies, or manners of performance, but the psychology of human mental processes—the ways in which the mind, operating within the context of culturally established norms, selects and organizes the stimuli that are presented to it."[39]

> Such processes operate in situations when jazz musicians assimilate different musical styles. In other words, as jazz musicians come into contact with other styles of musical performance, they may borrow certain features and adapt these to fit their own styles of musical performance. Since the 1940s, jazz musicians increasingly began to look to non-Western music as sources for new ideas. For example, Charlie Parker and Dizzy Gillespie incorporated into their music African-influenced rhythms from Cuba such as the mambo. Furthermore, in the 1950s, Bud Shank and Oscar Peterson recorded tunes using the Brazilian samba rhythm.

> The practice of assimilation plays a central role throughout the development of the African-American folk music continuum as well. In the 1700s, for example, African slaves brought to the New World lived amidst the pressures of the dominant European culture. Unable to fully sustain their African musical traditions under these conditions, they began to borrow and adapt

features from the music of the dominant culture. In fact, some
African slaves became skilled in playing European dance tunes
on Western instruments.[40]

Furthermore David Such asserts, "aural-oral modes of perception are
also important factors of stylistic change in the jazz continuum." It is a set of
modes of communication, similar to that which traditional African societies
established for the perpetuation and documentation of knowledge, that enabled African Americans to overcome the limitations of oppression and establish sociocultural convergence on multiple levels. It forged a positive force
that became "jazz." The transmission of musical information through this
system of oral/aural knowledge enabled saxophonist Marion Brown and others to absorb and then modify Ornette Coleman's "free jazz." It is readily apparent in Thelonious Monk's influence on pianist Andrew Hill and others.
When Eddie Jefferson performed lyrical versions of "Billie's Bounce" and
"Parker's Mood," he was acknowledging the musical sources of those classics
while continuing along his personal line of evolutionary "jazz," which requires
each artist to contribute something uniquely their own to the tradition. The
aural/oral tradition produces unique stylistic qualities and musical expectations that mark Joe Henderson, Stanley Turrentine, and Yusef Lateef as
standout tenor saxophonists. Such concludes:

> These, too, are rooted in African culture, in which ideas and
> knowledge are communicated using mainly non-written forms
> such as speech. In improvised jazz, the aural-oral mode en-
> courages the direct expression of the performer's inner emo-
> tions and creative impulses through musical sound. To ensure
> the vitality of this process, jazz tends to incorporate highly
> flexible and relatively noncomplex rules governing perform-
> ance. This is precisely what enables musicians like Eric Dolphy
> to extract sounds from the environment and transform them
> during a musical performance. Saxophonist Ornette Coleman
> comments, "Regardless of race or nationality, if you are not try-
> ing to compare your values with those of other people, but are
> interested in expressing musically something that you have in
> your mind and not trying to get anyone's approval—then jazz
> seems to be the most honest and freest form of taking the op-
> portunity to see if you can express something."[41] Along these
> lines drummer Elvin Jones adds, "A solo can take any form the
> artist chooses; he can use any form he wants within the frame-
> work of the composition. It goes back to getting away from the
> rigidity that jazz had to face when it was primarily dance mu-
> sic."[42] Jones' comments also suggest that when the rules grow
> too complex or too staid and fresh expression is inhibited, some
> musicians may seek alternative ways to organize improvisa-
> tion.[43]

Although Herbie Hancock and other musicians exploring "jazz" fusion
during the 1970s relied on traditional African-American dance orientation in

their new stylistic approaches, other musicians made metrical, formal, and conceptual modifications that continued to expand the range of elemental possibilities. The music explored by avant-garde experimenters on the forefront of African-American music was on the verge of becoming truly ecumenical.

Race has always mattered in America and the consequences of racism are far reaching. Racism has always affected the way many Americans think and feel about certain music. Bigotry has limited the growth and development of music in America. How much greater contribution could African-American musicians such as Louis Armstrong, Duke Ellington, Art Tatum, Charlie Parker, Charles Mingus, John Coltrane, and countless other innovators have made in their musical quests with institutional support and respect equivalent to that given the composers of European dodecaphonic music? What would the range of possibilities for rap music be if the music and creative arts programs had not been abducted from inner city school programs? Had "jazz" remained a function of the African-American community, how might the music have affected the development of knowledge, self-esteem, and creative imaginations of young people who are now desperately seeking positive African-American role models?

Notes

[1] Angela Davis et. al., *If They Come in the Morning: Voices of Resistance* (New York: New American Library, 1971), p. 143.

[2] Michael J. Budds, *Jazz in the Sixties: The Expansion of Musical Resources and Techniques* (Iowa City: University of Iowa Press, 1990), p. 127.

[3] Valerie Wilmer, *As Serious as Your Life: The Story of the New Jazz* (London: Serpent's Tail, 1992), p. 250.

[4] Ibid., p. 229.

[5] Wilmer, *As Serious as Your Life,* p. 252.

[6] Down Beat, December 1999, p. 34.

[7] Ibid.

[8] Larry Birnbaum, "Metal Steps to Heaven" *Village Voice*, August 24, 1990, p. 78.

[9] As he suggested in his autobiography.

[10] *Miles*, pp. 292–93.

[11] Selected Donald Byrd Albums: *Off to the Races* (Blue Note BLP-4007); *Fuego* (Blue Note BST-84026); *Caricatures Blue Note* BN-LA-633-G; *A City Called Heaven* with Joe Henderson and Bobby Hutcherson (Landmark LCD-1530-2); *John Coltrane—Black Pearls* (Prestige-7316); *John Coltrane—The Believer* (Prestige-7292); *John Coltrane—The Last Trane* (Prestige-7378); *Art Blakey Big Band* (Bethlehem-6027); *Red Garland—High Pressure* (Prestige 7130); *Red Garland—Dig It* (Prestige 7229); *Sonny Clark—Sonny's Crib* (Blue Note 1576); *Paul Chambers—Whims of Change* (Blue Note 1534).

[12] As cited in Leonard Feather, *The Passion for Jazz* (Da Capo, New York: 1990).

[13] Feather, *Passion for Jazz*, pp. 100–105.

[14] W. E. F. Ward, "Music in the Gold Coast," *Gold Coast Review* 3 (July–December 1927): pp. 222, 223. As cited in Kofi Agawu, "Representing African Music," *Critical Inquiry* 18 (1992): 260.

[15] Columbia 31039.

[16] Atlantic Records, 1977.

[17] Gunther Schuller, liner notes in *Mingus: Epitaph,* CBS Records (1990).

[18] *Jazz Spoken Here*, pp. 49–50.

[19] ECM Records, 1971.

[20] ECM Records, 1972.

[21] Ibid.

[22] Graham Lock, *Forces in Motion: The Music and Thoughts of Anthony Braxton* (New York: Da Capo, 1988), p 196.

[23] *Down Beat*, September 1996, pp. 23–24.

[24] *Down Beat*, January 1996, p. 20.

[25] Ibid., p. 18.

[26] Ian Carr, Digby Fairweather, and Brian Priestley, *Jazz: The Rough Guide* (London: Rough Guide, 1995), p. 654.

[27] *Down Beat,* January 1996, p. 20.

[28] Gerhard Kubik, *Africa and the Blues* (Jackson, MS: University Press of Mississippi, 1999).

[29] Marshall Stearns and Jean Stearns, *Jazz Dance: The Story of American Vernacular Dance* (New York: Da Capo, 1994), pp. 21–22.

[30] Wilmer, *As Serious as Your Life.*

[31] Alain Danielou, *Introduction to the Study of Musical Scales* (New Delhi: Oriental Books Reprint Corp., 1979).

[32] John Amira and Steven Cornelius, *The Music of Santeria: Traditional Rhythms of the Bata Drums* (Crown Points, Ind.: White Cliffs Media, 1992), pp. 5–6.

[33] Arthur Taylor, *Notes and Tones: Musician-to-Musician Interviews* (New York: Da Capo, 1993), p. 124.

[34] Ibid., p. 123.

[35] Ibid., pp. 126–27.

[36] *Down Beat*, September 1998, p. 24.

[37] Ibid.

[38] Joseph E. Holloway, ed., *Africanisms in American Culture* (Bloomington: Indiana University Press, 1991).

[39] Meyer, *Music*, p. 7, as cited in *Avant-Garde Jazz Musicians*, pp. 31–33.

[40] Such, *Avant-Garde Jazz Musicians*, pp. 31–33.

[41] Morgenstern, "Ornette Coleman," p. 17.

[42] Rivelli and Levin, *Giants*, p. 54.

[43] Such, *Avant-Garde Jazz Musicians*, pp. 31–33.

XII
Innovators Emerging Between 1980 and 2000

Facts do not cease to exist because they are ignored.

—Aldous Huxley

African-American Music in American Marketplace

African music developed for thousands of years before the European slave trade. Once abducted from their indigenous continent and isolated as a community in America, Africans developed music, dance, and other art forms over hundreds of years in an environment that remained independent of European socioculture. Thus African-American music can only be as integrated as are African-American communities. These communities stand less divided as America approaches the end of the twentieth century, but a sociocultural hiatus remains a part of American life.

Music throughout time reflects sociopolitical trends. During the 1970s, African-American music moved gradually from fusion forms to the more solid retrospective styles of the following two decades. Whereas African-American innovators were previously members of a progressive vanguard, young musicians now looked to the past for the lion share of their ideas. Due to a decline in music education in America, and a consequent decline in music appreciation and knowledge, the majority of the African-American and European-American communities began championing similar artistic values. The most popular kinds of "jazz" were those that resembled styles created decades earlier. Without an emphasis on invention and musical exploration, African-American "jazz" musicians began playing a conservative style. This was a break for executives in a Eurocentric "jazz" industry, which never wants to take chances on "products" that have not proven themselves. Record companies focused on packaging the types of fashionable youthful images previously exploited in rock and roll.

Rap and other young styles reasserted degrees of innovation and resourcefulness during the 1980s, but because of the unfortunate separation between young people in the African-American communities and senior Afrocentric innovators, these styles reflected a lack of direct connection to elder progenitors of the "jazz" legacy. The lack of instrumental virtuosity, compositional technique, and technical musical depth within the new American musical styles was largely a consequence of deteriorating American music programs, particularly in inner-city schools.

The African-American music that enjoyed the widest dissemination from the mid-1970s to the present, therefore, was retrospective, simplified, and easily duplicated. Evolutionary progress equivalent to that which extended through ragtime, swing, bebop, hard bop, quasi-modal, free "jazz," etc. failed to surface. Unlike any other music, "jazz" transformed its musical elements dramatically at least once a decade for the first seventy years of the twentieth century. It is inevitable that a momentary reprieve from such an intense era of experimentation and discovery would occur at some point.

The media increased its control over artistic expression and dissemination during the 1980 and 1990s. In an open letter to Black Music Radio and the music industry published in *Emerge* magazine, Bob Law suggests that the media take a greater sense of responsibility. He suggests that "Black music radio has the ear of [the younger] generation," and he asks that these industries "help us reclaim the minds of our young." During "this critical time, when violence and confusion abound," Law feels,

> What is needed is a rebirth of the cultural arts movement—music, literature, images, and film totally committed to the empowerment of the African-American community. We must return to the level of liberating ideas. Artists and political activists must be on the same mission; they must resist the seductions of a weaker moral self while moving to sustain a stronger spiritual and more perfect self. The true role of the artist and activist must go beyond protest to become shapers of the future reality. The Black artist must link his work to the struggle for the liberation of his people. Unfortunately, the best efforts of Black artists seem trapped within a music industry that has always been willing to sacrifice the interest of the artist and community in order to control the profits and flow of ideas.

> Oscar Brown Jr. once told me that we will have to free the music so that the awesome power of the music can free the people. A conscious Black arts movement is what is needed. I have a reasonable request for African American music industry executives: Just as you have found innovative ways to serve your bosses, perhaps you can find some small way to serve your people.[1]

In general, by the end of the twentieth century, recorded "jazz" became over-produced, nostalgic, and replete with what Rob Leurentop called "boardroom concepts" in an effort to popularize the music for greater profits. When Miles Davis responded to a question regarding the term "popular" in a documentary film on Quincy Jones, he said, "Popular! Doesn't that mean White music?" Miles implied that genuine African-American music is not popular unless it is packaged with Eurocentric consumption in mind. Much of the music of the 1980s and '90s was so intended. Younger African-American musicians were led into neo-classic bebop and hardbop styles because the music's popularity was already well established. The cultivation of such qualities of "Black" musicians legitimized the general trends of the majority of European and European American musicians to adopt more retrospective and popular approaches to Afrocentric music. As Eurocentric aesthetics began to dominate "jazz," the most conspicuous results were smooth-"jazz," various forms of fusion, retrospective trends, and other parodies and diluted forms of Afrocentric music. Inevitably, this trend will remain as long as Afrocentric music remains increasing exploited, marginalized or dominated by Eurocentric culture.

The problems that African-American innovators confronted at the beginning of the twentieth century remain as the century draws to an end. Some Americans remain troubled whenever African-American artists insist upon self-determination. The society that fabricated race records, elected a "White" King of Swing and a "White" King of Jazz, and denied that African Americans were the creators of "jazz" has made some economic and social progress. Nonetheless, Law's request comes at a time when *Down Beat* magazine has proclaimed Brian Setzer the "New King of Swing."[2] One disgruntled journalist recently insinuated that those who acknowledge "jazz" as an African-American invention "have falsified the record, indulging in what Plato calls, in the *Republic*, the Noble Lie."[3] Finally, in an article in the *Wall Street Journal* (January 27, 1999), a writer proclaimed that "open admissions . . . has proved as disastrous to education as Coltrane has been to jazz."[4]

The music industry retained a plethora of labels to categorize African Americans. Many African-American innovators and style setters, nevertheless, have preferred the generic term "music" to describe their art. Differences between Eurocentric and Afrocentric sociocultures are reflected in personal aesthetics and musical style. When artists assert that European-American and African-American musicians have distinct sounds that can be recognized, critics often try to trip them up in blindfold tests and such. All such tests prove are that just as a European American can imitate African-American speaking styles (or vice versa), musicians who learn to imitate the style of an innovator may succeed in deceiving some listeners. Experiences of individual musicians in America consistently broaden as the distances between social domains shrink. When racism finally wanes and citizens finally desegregate themselves, it will then be possible to create an American music. Some "jazz" masters feel there is a glimmer of hope on the horizon. When asked about the new recordings made during the 1990s, Randy Weston replied:

> I didn't really listen to new records. I still get up every morning and listen to Art Tatum.

> I'm pleased that finally it looks like the world is recognizing how important Africa is and has been. The music and the culture. People are looking back at history, science and art in Western culture, but so much of all that was already happening first in Africa.[5]

Emphasis Moves from Innovations to Youthful Image

Some claim that Paul Whiteman was a popular artist rather than a "jazz" musician because of low levels of improvisation in his music. American audiences considered Whiteman a "personality" more than an innovative artist. Few people remember Whiteman's instrument. The classification "popular" can be tricky, however. Music of the swing era was very popular. Mozart's *Le Nozze di Figarro* (1786) and other comic operas were popular during the European classical era. Labels of this sort do not necessarily give reliable information regarding musical content.

Charlie Christian, Fats Navarro, Charlie Parker, Miles Davis, and others had established their reputations at an early age. Many of these artists did not live much beyond twenty or thirty years. On June 30, 1982, the Kool Jazz Festival presented a concert of new music performed by seventeen exceptional young musicians. The music was released on the Elektra Musician label (cat. no. 60196-1 R) the following year under the title *The Young Lions*. The following musicians were included:

John Blake—violin
Hamiet Bluiett—baritone saxophone
Ronnie Burrage—drums
Anthony Davis—piano
Paquito D' Rivera—alto saxophone
John Purcell—double/single reeds, flute
Avery Sharpe—electric and acoustic bass
Kevin Eubanks—electric and acoustic guitar
Chico Freeman—tenor saxophone, bass clarinet, flute
Fred Hopkins—double bass
Wynton Marsalis—trumpet
Bobby McFerrin—voice
James Newton—flute
Daniel Ponce—percussion
Craig Harris—trombone
Jay Hoggard—vibraphone
Abdul Wadud—cello

Saxophonist Dave Murray (b. 1955, one of the founding members of the World Saxophone Quartet), bassist Stanley Clarke (b. 1951, who played with Chick Corea and others), pianist Amina Claudine Myers (b. 1942),[6] and countless other Young Lions and Lionesses could have been included in this list. The goals of the project were specific, however. There were no women or European-American "jazz" musicians on the recording. In the liner notes to the album Michael Gibbs (a festival organizer) says, "In the past few years I've been increasingly aware of a fresh optimism in the jazz world, a new acceptance of the music as today's young people discover them for themselves, and a renewed acceptance of it by the older fans as they recognize their need for it." The festival and album were aimed at refuting the notion that "jazz" was dead, as Nesuhi Ertegun reveals:

Self-appointed prophets of gloom have long played a monoto-
nous chorus: jazz is dying, jazz is dead. For decades, generation
after generation has announced the demise of this besieged art-
form. Jazz died with Jelly-Roll [*sic*] Morton, we were told, then
with Bix, then with Pres, then with Bird.

Those great artists created new styles and made enormous contributions, but jazz didn't end with any of them. It even survived Coltrane and Mingus, Ellington and Armstrong.

This album is dedicated to youth and jazz and survival. The
Young Lions know and understand their past. They are aware
of jazz roots; they know all about fusion and rock and Berg and
Cage. They know free and funk, R&B and J.S.B. . . . they have
chosen jazz.

Regardless of whether it was the intention of Ertegun and Bruce
Lundvall (who together initiated the project) to establish emphasis on Young
Lions as a marketing trademark, the youthful image of rock and roll now
transferred to "jazz." Other Young Lions entered the scene in the late 1980s
and early 1990s. Peter Watrous ran an article on some of the younger performers in the *New York Times* on June 16, 1991. His article, titled "The
Youth Movement Puts Jazz Back in JVC," mentions that the younger players
had the advantage of having learned jazz in elementary school, attending
magnet schools, and an increasing number of high schools for the performing
arts.

Roy Hargrove (b. 1969), one of the most heavily promoted trumpet
players to follow Wynton Marsalis, is a gifted Texas-born musician who attended an elementary school that taught "jazz." Marsalis discovered the
younger trumpeter when Hargrove later attended a special arts school. While
at Berklee College of Music, he commuted to New York to perform with
Kenny Barron, Harold Mabern, John Hicks, and other master musicians. Record companies competed for his services after his performance at the Mount
Fuji Festival in Japan, resulting in the release of several new albums.

Marlon Jordan is a year younger than Hargrove and developed his
full-bodied trumpet sound in his hometown, New Orleans. He attended the
prestigious New Orleans Center for the Creative Arts, a magnet school in
that city. He comes from a musical family: his mother plays piano; his sister,
the violin; his father is a saxophonist and teacher; and his brother is a "jazz"
recording artist on flute. He began practicing six or seven hours daily at age
six or seven. He decided to stay in New Orleans, rather than moving to New
York, because he appreciated the supportive environment there. The faculty
at the creative arts school in New Orleans stressed the importance of knowing musical tradition. Jordan said, "I was brought up around serious music,
whether it was John Coltrane or Stravinsky." He attended summer music
programs such as Symphony School of America and Tanglewood regularly.

As the young players benefited tremendously from formal preparation,
they also gained easy access to the music market place because they presented retrospective music that is highly accessible. That they are all attrac-

tive young "stars" is no handicap to music promoters in today's youth oriented culture, where "jazz" musicians can receive a style of promotion and
treatment formerly reserved for rock and roll musicians. Nevertheless, musicians who serve as models for this new generation of musicians, and the more
adventurous and rebellious players from the 1960s and 1970s are effectively
ostracized from the music scene. Jordan is very much aware of this fact: "I
feel sorry for the older musicians; we're in the right place at the right time,
and between promoters and audience the demand for young musicians has
turned into a bit of a freak show. But it makes me feel good, to show America
that young black musicians can be serious and not worry only about the financial rewards."[7]

Guitarist James Whitfield is another young musician who anchors his
music in the bebop tradition. He also attended Berklee College and performed
there regularly with pianist James Williams. Upon George Benson's recommendation, he gained a contract from Warner Brothers, and he joined Jack
McDuff's band.

Terence Blanchard attended the New Orleans Center for the Creative
Arts and studied "classical" piano at an early age. At Rutgers University, he
studied with Kenny Barron and Paul Jeffries before going on the road with
Lionel Hampton in 1982. He and Donald Harrison replaced Wynton and
Branford Marsalis in the Art Blakey band in the early 1980s. Harrison and
Blanchard formed a band in 1986. Harrison has performed on and wrote the
music for some of Spike Lee's films (*Mo' Better Blues* and *Jungle Fever*).

Steve Turre is a trombonist and composer. Art Blakey brought Turre
from San Francisco to New York in 1973 as a Jazz Messenger. Turre performed and recorded with numerous others and led his own experimental ensembles. He is one of the most imaginative and gifted trombone virtuosos of
his generation. Turre expressed his virtuosity as a trombonist in both traditional and avant-garde idioms and has composed music in fresh new ways.
He is one of the world's greatest performers on the conch shells, and he has
recorded the "jazz" classic "All Blues" and many other compositions on that
unusual instrument.

Cellist, composer, and improviser Akua Dixon Turre plays in Quartette Indigo. The ensemble (which includes her sister, Gayle) has recorded on
Carmen McRae albums and for Dizzy Gillespie's music for the film, *Winter in
Lisbon*. Quartette Indigo also provided music for James Blood Ulmer's album
for guitar and string quartet. Dixon arranges or composes most of the quartet's music. She worked with the Neo-Bass Ensemble, performed on the
soundtrack for Spike Lee's *School Daze*, and played on Turre's albums *Right
There*, *Fire and Ice*, and others. In the late 1980s she received a Rockefeller
grant to compose her work the *Opera of Marie Laveau*, presented at the
Henry Street Settlement House Playhouse. Dixon also sang on Archie
Shepp's album *Attica Blues Big Band* in the late 1970s.

Bassist Christian McBride was another successful "young lion." At the
end of the twentieth century he made the following comments:

> The whole "young lions" hype which, unfortunately, I was a
> part of, peaked in the early 1990s. I say "unfortunately" be-
> cause the hype was so strong, I don't think any musician from

that "movement" will ever be looked upon by certain people as serious musicians. We'll be looked at as puppets for the record companies and managers, or People magazine-type personalities. Record companies, of course, jumped on the hype to sell some records, and they did . . . for a while.

After the young lion hype died down, the focus was put on what's known as "concept" records (i.e., X plays the music of Y; X plays love songs; X plays music for driving to. Fortunately, there have been some concept records that have been wonderful, but I believe that when a record company tries to FORCE a "vibe" on a record, rather than letting the music flow on its own power, we will hear some very untrue CDs. Which, in my opinion, flooded the market in the '90s.[8]

Families of Musicians

Wynton Marsalis (b. 1961), one of the leading trumpeters today, was trained in the European classical tradition and repertoire. Louis Armstrong and Miles Davis also influenced Marsalis. Trumpeter Charles Tolliver points out that Marsalis's approach to the trumpet is also clearly related to that of trumpeter Al Hirt. His adroit musicianship, aided by a recording contract with Columbia Records early in his career, propelled Marsalis into the forefront of the Young Lions movement in the 1980s. Whereas other African-American artists had demonstrated deft skill in both African-American and European art music (Arthur Davis, Hubert Laws, Dorothy Donegan, Branford Marsalis, and Keith Jarrett, among others), Marsalis has proved to be more controversial, largely due to his high profile and outspoken disposition.

Wynton Marsalis comes from a musical family. His father is a "jazz" pianist of note. Branford Marsalis (b. 1960), a Tonight Show band leader for several seasons, has become one of the leading saxophonists today. His style crosses traditional "jazz" boundaries into rap and other popular music. He studied with the distinguished New Orleans clarinetist Alvin Batiste at Southern University, and with Frank Foster and Barry Harris while attending the Berklee College of Music in Boston.

Wynton's brother Branford joined the Art Blakey band after the drummer heard him when he visited Wynton in New York. He later worked with Clark Terry and others. In addition to his skill as a "jazz" performer, Branford demonstrated superb command of the soprano saxophone and twentieth-century European repertoire on his 1986 recording *Branford Marsalis: Romances for Saxophone.* Delfeayo Marsalis is a fine trombonist while another brother, Jason, plays the drums. As with Joshua Redman (son of Dewey Redman), drummer Denardo Coleman (Ornette Coleman's son), drummer T. S. Monk (Thelonious Monk's son), and other offspring of professional "jazz" artists, the Marsalis children have benefited from having parents who are professional musicians.

Sharp contrasts between styles and philosophies often exist between family members. In an interview for *Down Beat* magazine with Wynton and

Branford Marsalis from 1982, we find such differences. There is also agreement on fundamental issues. Wynton expresses an aversion to the term "jazz" because "it's now taken on the context of being everything. Anything is jazz. Quincy Jones' shit is jazz; David Sanborn . . . that's not to cut down Quincy or David. I love funk, it's hip. No problem to it. The thing is, if it'll sell records to call the stuff jazz, they'll call it jazz. They call Miles' stuff jazz. That stuff is not jazz, man. Just because somebody played jazz at one time doesn't mean they're still playing it."[9]

Branford agrees on that point. "Cats come up to me and say: 'What do you think of Spyro Gyra?' And I say: 'I don't.' That's not an insult to Spyro Gyra. I just don't like it when people call it jazz when it's not." Wynton: "Music goes forward, Music doesn't go backward. Whatever the cats couldn't play before you, you're supposed to play." Branford: "There's a huge movement for the perpetuation of ignorance in jazz."

Regarding music in the concert halls, Wynton feels it hasn't hurt the music because the club scene was already deteriorating. He also thinks, "one of the biggest problems is that nobody wants to do somebody else's song. Everybody thinks that they can write great tunes, and all the public wants is that it sounds different. Music has to be played before it gets old. The music that Ornette Coleman played, that Miles and Trane played in the '60s, some of the stuff that Mingus and Booker Little and Charlie Rouse and these cats were starting to do . . . that music isn't old because nobody else has ever played it."

Wynton's extensive training in European "classical" music led to a special citation as Outstanding Brass Player from the Berkshire Music School in Tanglewood, and to performances under the baton of Seiji Ozawa, Leonard Bernstein, and other distinguished conductors. He began studies at Juilliard, and was a substitute trumpeter in a Broadway pit orchestra as he began touring with Art Blakey in 1979. "Music has a tradition that you have to understand before you can move to the next step," he says. "But that doesn't mean you have to be a historian."

Currently, many critics and fans consider Wynton Marsalis to be the most influential exponent of "jazz." In 1984 he won Grammy Awards for both a classical recording and a "jazz" recording, performing primarily in the hard bop and bebop idioms. He was awarded the Pulitzer Prize for his opera *Blood on the Fields* in 1997.

Wynton ventured out as featured soloist with his own band after his extraordinary debuts with Art Blakey and Herbie Hancock at the age of twenty-one. At one time he refused to take seriously the music of Cecil Taylor, Anthony Braxton, the Art Ensemble of Chicago, and other more emancipated styles of "jazz." His position has softened a bit with maturity. Taylor has commented that Marsalis is more respectful in person than his earlier comments might have suggested. Nevertheless, his general attitude about "jazz" aligns with those of his close associate, writer Stanley Crouch: "The jazz musician wields power that is neither melodramatic nor obnoxious, achieving individuality through the collective affirmation of the swinging band, now and again meditating on the moment at the piano keyboard and orchestrating the individual consciousness through the paces of blues and swing."[10]

No single individual's set of perspectives can serve as the basis for defining a music as broad and elusive as "jazz." In the March 1997 issue of *Jazz Times*, saxophonist-composer Henry Threadgill contributed a more equitable analysis: "There are those people who are trying to protect [jazz] or say exactly what it is, and they're destroying it, because it grew from the mere fact that it embraced all the things that were available, from the Caribbean, from Spanish music, everything. It was all these things that allowed [jazz] to happen and it has been those types of ideas that have made it progress."

John McDonough presents another aspect of Wynton's philosophy in an article titled "Original Intent Comes to Jazz" (*Wall Street Journal*, July 21, 1992). One of the most interesting things in the article was the conflict between Gunther Schuller and Wynton Marsalis. Marsalis felt that "jazz" musicians have to play notes their own way, while Schuller's desire was to create jazz "repertory" music. Schuller apparently feels that since people today obviously can't hear a band lead by Louis Armstrong, Duke Ellington, or Count Basie, there's nothing wrong with modern bands performing the old classics for the modern audiences. Schuller claims that "just as every symphony has within it the possibility of individual interpretation without altering a note, . . . so does jazz repertory." Marsalis realizes that "jazz" is not the same as European art music, and so do most other African-American musicians and musicologists. It is as absurd to copy a Louis Armstrong recording note for note in performance and insist on calling the results "jazz." It would be equally inappropriate to improvise on a Mozart symphony and call it European "classical" music. As McDonough points out, "It does not surprise Mr. Schuller that some of the fiercest attacks against [Schuller's desire] have come from black musicologists, who complain that it imposes a Eurocentric view on something that is Afrocentric. Their conflict is just one aspect of the overall fight going on now over the history of jazz."

On some level, the difference between Schuller's Eurocentric viewpoint and that of most Afrocentric "jazz" innovators is a cultural one that existed throughout "jazz" history. Ben Sidran concludes:

> Whereas white society in America tends to be *conformist*, black culture is collective, or communal. This is due, partially, to its reliance on music as a socializing agent. Black culture did not need *formal* entertainment the way whites did. Rather, it sought an outlet through which Negroes could more or less entertain themselves. The commercial orientation of whites during the twenties was primarily responsible for the subsequent return to segregated (i.e., black jazz for black audiences) music of the thirties and was a major event in the evolution of a self-consciousness within black culture.[11]

Benny Goodman expressed the prevailing Eurocentric "jazz" aesthetic of his day when he said, "I am such a bug on accuracy in performance, about playing in tune, and want just the proper note values . . . in the written parts, I wanted it to sound as exact as the band could possibly make it."[12] Sidran continues:

Conversely, black musicians, even within the big band context, developed idioms that relied on no written parts. Count Basie's band had up to seventeen men playing harmonically and rhythmically advanced music without any music. The black player, even as he was becoming more involved with harmonic exploration, relied on his ear rather than his ability to read music to find his way through the technical maze. In the midst of an increasingly complex environment, the black musician turned to the free-flowing oral modes; hence, he played "off the beat" to avoid the stagnant feel of Goodman's "on the beat" precision; he used increased vocalization, or tone "impurity," to help break through the passive detachment of big band work and to return the emotional honesty to jazz idioms.[13]

In the debates and opinions regarding the impact the "Young Lions" have had on "jazz" music, the spiritual aspect of modern "jazz" receives little mention. Perhaps a conspicuous emphasis on technical mastery replaced spiritual considerations. An important aspect of the "Young Lions" phenomenon, nevertheless, reminds us that the music of the past is not a series of temporary, disposable fads so shallow that we can quickly move from style to style—forgetting or discarding the value of the previous era in a headlong quest for something "different." The so-called "neoclassical" African-American musician realizes that the blues will neither be fully explored, nor its rich set of potentials depleted, for some time (Perhaps its influence will last as long as the three-hundred-year reign of European tonal harmony). From some perspectives, nonetheless, the problem is that "neoclassicists" fail to maintain the high levels of innovation that supply integral and characteristic ingredients to "jazz" evolution. One could spend a lifetime learning the vocabularies that Tatum, Bird, Ellington, Coltrane, Dolphy, Monk, Miles, etc., left for posterity, however. Critics suggest that many good musicians (during the 1980s) got stuck on the "etudes" left by certain earlier "jazz" masters, while others side-stepped the grueling initiation required of past innovators in a rush to popular exposure and validation.

Dewey Redman (b. 1931) collaborated with his son Joshua (b. 1969) on the elder Redman's album *Dewey Redman Featuring Joshua Redman: African Venus* (Evidence Music, 1994). In the liner notes Redman says, "I would like if I'm not categorized, stylized. Like, if someone heard me and said, 'Oh, that's Dewey Redman,' I don't think I'd like that. What I'd like, in whatever context—it may be symphonic, anything—you'd hear me and say, 'That's a good player.' My ambition is not to be a stylist—I think of myself as a student of music, and I study all kinds in order to project myself and make my music better."

The personnel on the recording include Dewey Redman (tenor, alto sax, musette), Joshua Redman (tenor sax), Charles Eubanks (piano), Anthony Cox (bass), Carl Allen (drums), and Danny Sadownnick (percussion). Dewey spent most of the sixties in the Bay Area, where the community was exploring the new freedoms expressed by Coltrane and Ornette Coleman. He went with Keith Jarrett's quartet during the 1970s, moving stylistically from a period of intense concentration to a more languid lyricism. He finally formed his own ensemble, Old and New Dreams.

Joshua's mostly mainstream tenor playing is muscular, exciting, and precise. Understandably, the younger Redman's has not yet fully developed the level of musical flexibility and freedom found in his father's mature style. Dewey's musical depth is evident, incorporating a variety of styles from straight ahead to liberated approaches.

Chico (Earl) Freeman (b. 1949) is the son of notable tenor saxophonist Von Freeman (b. 1922). Von did not release his own album until 1972, but, as Rahsaan Roland Kirk observed, he had influenced the saxophone in Chicago for over a decade. "How he has been overlooked in jazz is a crime," complained Sonny Stitt.[14] The launching of Chico's career was more fortunate. He studied with Muhal Richard Abrams and Joe Daley, and became an AACM member in 1972. After settling in New York in 1976, he worked with Cecil McBee, Sam Rivers, Elvin Jones, Don Pullen, Sun Ra, and others. He also recorded and toured with his father and with an innovative band called The Leaders.

The Age of the Freelance Musician

The 1980s and 1990s present an era dominated by individual leaders and freelance musicians. There are groups of musicians who have replaced the communal training "camps" established by Ellington, Sun Ra, the Modern Jazz Quartet, the Mingus Jazz Workshop, the Art Ensemble of Chicago, and similar ensembles. The interest of most earlier innovators was geared toward creating artistic environments where musical minds could gather to cultivate mutual vocabularies. The musical styles and languages that manifested through such processes provided models often imitated by younger generations of musicians.

Traditional vocabularies allow those who settle into them the opportunity of becoming "lions" at an earlier age. Just as young musicians become impressive performers of European art music, the same is true in "jazz" once the artistic and technical goals become fixed or standardized. There have been rare instances of teenage virtuosi establishing convincing musical languages and styles. Reproducing traditional styles as and end in itself drastically simplified conceptual problems, though the technical challenge remains tremendous.

Innovators created a musical legacy consisting of expressive innovative forms. New generations must continue to explore the world and the inner self in the pioneering spirit of Duke Ellington, Billie Holiday, Mary Lou Williams, Charlie Parker, Charles Mingus, John Coltrane, Eric Dolphy, Cecil Taylor, Sun Ra, and countless others African-American innovators.

As the Young Lions advance in age, prestige, and wisdom, they continue to provoke controversy. Wynton Marsalis's interest in European music seems to have changed directions as he matured. He apparently lost the need to validate himself to mainstream America in that regard. Perhaps a similar transition will occur within neoclassic "jazz" styles as artists continue along a path toward finding unique voices. As artistic director for the Jazz Department at Lincoln Center, Marsalis has done a fine job elevating the status of "jazz." With Dr. Billy Taylor's Jazz at the Kennedy Center, African-American musicians have for the first time held prominent positions at two of America's prestigious cultural centers. Marsalis' presence has caused many European-American critics to lash out at him for an assortment of reasons. Predictably, an African-American outspoken musician such as Marsalis has left Eurocentric critics in an uproar.

The *NYSO Journal* published an article that asked, "Despite his enormous contributions to jazz over the last 10 years, are Wynton Marsalis' notions of the jazz aesthetic limiting the reach of jazz at Lincoln?"[15] The scope of Marsalis' projects augments and blends into the Lincoln Center's structure, which essentially includes European ballet, opera, and symphonic music. Nonetheless, the editor asks, "Though already one of the most sparkling and exciting trumpeters on the scene, is Roy Hargrove properly equipped to tackle a composing commission at Lincoln Center as he did last September?" He suggests that Phil Woods, Steve Lacy, and others would be more appropriate choices for some of Marsalis' concerts. The article admits that

> There can be no quibble with the execution of Lincoln Center jazz presentations. They are well-rehearsed (significant paid rehearsal time is admirably built into each and every Jazz at Lincoln Center presentation), beautifully staged and sound re-inforced, . . . finely crafted programming, with an overall emphasis on good taste that often elevates the presentations to event status. Marketing materials have been very extensive, advertising is significant and characteristically high-toned, and insightful programs are the rule rather than the exception. The educational program appears to be impeccable. Audiences have been eager, alert, demographically varied, respectful, sizable, and there is ample evidence of repeat ticket buyers.

On the basis of the editor's comments, it seems that the problem is not one of lack of quality but a disappointment that Wynton has not chosen other players and composers for his performances. Other writers (Lincoln Collier, for instance) are less evasive and make it known that they would like to see more European-American musicians on-stage. Marsalis counters that he chooses the best musicians he can get for the concerts, many of whom are European Americans (he generally lists them to refresh memories). Kevin Whitehead took such a high-handed approach to reviewing one of Marsalis' concerts that Wynton decided to respond in print and held no punches.

Whitehead's article claimed that the "Wyntonians" (as he referred to them) failed to "cut it technically."[16] He continued to insult Marsalis and the performers by suggesting, "Patrons paid $35 to listen to on-the-job training, which raises the larger issue of why Jazz at Lincoln Center really exists: to educate the public about and expose it to quality jazz, or to subsidize Wynton's working groups, whose members are heavily featured uptown?"

Readers would have to search long and hard to find similar comments (in print) hurled at European-American musicians of Marsalis' caliber and position. The following excerpts are from Wynton's straightforward and exhaustive reply:

> As one reared in a tradition that greatly respects "playing the dozens," I have often enjoyed the twelve or thirteen years of insults posing as aesthetic insight from some segment of what masquerades as the jazz critical community. Normally, I take the position that nothing below me can hurt me, and nothing above me would, but a recent article by Kevin Whitehead in the Voice's jazz supplement—"It's Jazz, Stupid"—was such a mixture of personal attack, attempted condescension, and disinformation that I have decided, finally, to step down into his arena, where arrogance and ignorance are served up in place of information. This must end. It is not the fact of criticism that disturbs me; criticism can easily lead to enlightenment for the musician and listener. I am disturbed, however, by our neophyte pundit's combination of inaccuracy and disrespect, which proves, under scrutiny, that if he thinks any one is stupid, it must be our audiences, who have enthusiastically supported our efforts for the past seven years with sold-out concerts and standing ovations . . .
>
> My integrity is then impugned by the insinuation that Jazz at Lincoln Center concerts are being used to subsidize my band members. My band members are on my annual payroll. We play about 120 concerts a year. The three or four concerts we play at Lincoln Center have negligible impact on our financial situation. To imply that an old boy system has to be in place for the public to want to hear Marcus Roberts [who won the 1st annual Thelonious Monk competition] or Herlin Riley or Wessel Anderson, is inappropriate and disrespectful.

Marsalis introduces a question that many African-American innovators have often posed privately when confronted with arrogance from Eurocentric critics: "Who has this writer studied with or played with, and what is the source of his authority other than poor editorial decisions?" He continues: "Henceforth, I want to make it clear that I will no longer silently tolerate your willful disrespect of the skills required to play jazz music. I will be responding to inaccuracies in your reporting when I am made aware of it. My intention is not just to expose you for the charlatans that you are, but to supply the public with another opinion."[17]

Wynton Marsalis is a tremendous talent focused on furthering "jazz" tradition. He has gained a great amount of respect from his peers and audiences. He insists that respect be paid to the "jazz" tradition. Regardless of subjective analysis of his style, he has certainly contributed more to the development and perpetuation of African-American music than Whitehead or other self-appointed critics.

Jazz at Lincoln Center has continued to evolve since 1987, when Alina Bloomgarden, Lincoln Center's director of visitor services, started a concert jazz program to take advantage of the vacant concert halls in August. On December 18, 1995, the Lincoln Center Board awarded the institution's "jazz" department equal status with the New York Philharmonic, the Metropolitan Opera, the New York City Ballet, and the other constituents of the complex. Respect has been slow to arrive in America, but "jazz" evolution continues.

Snapshot: Bay Area "Jazz" in the Early 1980s

The distinction often made to separate East Coast "jazz" during the 1940s and '50s from West Coast variety generally determines that the East Coast variety is more experimental and vibrant. The comparison often weighs the accomplishments and styles of musicians in and around Los Angeles and San Francisco against innovative musicians in New York City. During World War II and in the postwar years, the Bay Area flourished for a while, and San Francisco became a hotbed for "jazz." Miles, Coltrane, and most other important artists of the day came through the Bay Area, performing at "jazz" establishments like the Blackhawk, the Hungry I, Jazz Workshop, Jimbo's Bop City, the Island of Jazz, the Matador, and the Keystone Corner. During the late 1970s and early 1980s, the Bay Area was a haven for experimentation involving highly varied, novel, and personal stylistic approaches including multi-ethnic and interdisciplinary presentations.

The Center for World Music at the Fort Mason Cultural Center, a 126-year-old fort that occupies one of the most dramatically beautiful areas on the Bay, is the gateway to the 35,000-acre park called the Golden Gate National Recreation Area on San Francisco's waterfront. Since 1977, Fort Mason has provided performance spaces, exhibitions, workshops, and classes for thousands of people and hundreds of organizations. It became a vibrant arts center, presenting a rich cross-section of various art forms from around the world. New dance presentations, mime, poetry, television and film workshops, feminist theater, children's programs, etc., were a part of Fort Mason's daily schedule of events.

During 1981, for example, Fort Mason presented an array of interesting music and interdisciplinary events. The "Festival of the Sea" was an eclectic presentation featuring the Chinese Instrumental Ensemble, directed by Sek Cheong Siu; Los Travadores, playing Mexican jarocho harp repertoire; and a concert titled "Anglo-Irish Sea Shanties," with Stan Hugill, Jon Bartlett, and Rika Ruebsatt. A North Indian Classical Music Festival with Hariprasad Chaurasia (flute), Malabika Kanan (female vocalist), Zakir Hussain, and others also took place as a part of the festival.

Indian virtuoso Ali Akbar Khan (a virtuoso whose father played over two hundred musical instruments) opened a School of North Indian Music in Marin County during this period. Khan had lived in the Bay Area for thirty years. He performed with his brother-in-law Ravi Shankar, alto saxophonist John Handy, Bola Sete, and violinist L. Subramaniam on numerous occasions. These musicians performed a mixture involving "jazz" and North Indian music in various Fort Mason performance spaces.

Malonga Casquelourd and Fua Dia Congo, Viva Brasil, and Klezmorim (a sextet) were other concerts presented at the center. In 1981 the last of these revived the four-centuries-old East-European Yiddish musical tradition. There was also music of the Middle East with "Jazayer." The Kearny Street Workshop and Fort Mason presented the First Annual Asian Jazz Festival in the Fort Mason Conference Center. The Asian "jazz" concerts featured Russel Baba (flutist/saxophonist) with drummer Eddie Moore; Mark Izu (bass), with clarinetists Paul Yamazaki and Ray Collins; guitarists Makoto Horiuchi and Peter Fuji with bass guitarist Shido. The tendency toward cross-cultural music activity of this period eventually led to a strong "world beat" movement in the Bay Area.

A group of experimental musicians, sometimes referred to as the "Heralds of California's 'third wave'"by the press, also performed frequently at Fort Mason and a variety of other alternative performance spaces throughout the San Francisco Bay Area. The New College of California presented a series of concerts during 1981–82 featuring Andrew Hill, the Rova Saxophone Quartet, Sonny Simmons and Barbara Donald, the Billy Bang/John Lindberg Duo, solo percussion by Eddie Moore, Paul Stevens and the Eulipian Ensemble, Leon Williams and Impact 77, United Front, Karlton Hester and the Contemporary Jazz Art Movement (CJAM), and many other artists. The performance hall in which the concerts occurred was formerly a funeral chapel, but the festival was very much alive. In 1982 (February through April), CJAM produced a series of eight concerts (featuring a host of musicians, dancers, poets, and visual artists) in another festival at San Francisco's Western Addition Cultural Center. A review of one of the festivals presented at the New College printed in *Down Beat* (July 1981) displays some of the diversity of the programming.

> Trumpeter George Sams organized this three-night festival in February at the New College of California in celebration of Black History Month. . . . It was James Newton's first S.F. appearance, and his expressive solo flute quickly entranced his audience. His original compositions were tributes: a lyrical portion of *Dream of Freedom* (for Paul Robeson) and *Toru* (for Japanese composer Toru Takemitsu). Packed with overblown notes, multiphonics, and cascading colors, *Toru* explored the tonal range and spectrum of the flute's possibilities.

> . . . Images of a caravan traveling through the desert were conjured by *Africa 456 According to Herodotus*,[18] Karl Hester's composition for the Contemporary Jazz Art Movement.[19] The group includes some of the Bay area's finest. . . . Percussion, congas, traps, two basses, and piano created a textural rhythmic undercurrent functioning as an open ended drone. Oboe, bassoon, bass flute, clarinet, and English horn added to the Oriental flavor.

> At midnight, pianist Horace Tapscott began his solo set with a sharp, crashing attack, as if to clear the air. An orchestral collage of sound then emerged from his keyboard; a pleasing shock of richness and variation, contrasting themes woven

through several modes, fleeting insights into *Motherless Child*, *Well You Needn't*, and countless other tunes.[20]

Master saxophonists Joe Henderson, John Handy, and Pharaoh Sanders; pianist Ed Kelly and Andrew Hill; violinist Michael White, bassist James Leary, and drummer Eddie Moore were just a sampling of the world-class artists living and performing around the area. Music was everywhere in the San Francisco Bay Area during this period. An organization called Music by the Bay (in cooperation with Bay Area Music and radio station KJAZ) presented "Jazzmo" in September 1981. Funding from the San Francisco Hotel Tax Fund, and assisted by the Hyatt Regency, radio stations KMEL, KMPX, and KBLX, made "Jazzmo" an entire month of concerts. Over forty performances came under the "Jazzmo" umbrella. Performance spaces throughout the region opened their door to the celebration, featuring the Bishop Norman Williams Quintet; Eddie Moore and Creative Force featuring Eddie Henderson, Mary Watkins, Linda Tillery, Alive, Ed Kelly Quintet, Pee Wee Ellis and the Assembly, Pony Poindexter, Idris Ackamoor, Mel Martin and Listen, Oakland Jazz Complex Orchestra, Rasul Siddik and the Now Artet, Russel Baba, CJAM, and Women in Jazz Seminars.

The Contemporary Jazz Art Movement (Karlton E. Hester, Musical Director) (Photo courtesy of HRP Library).

Music was not restricted to usual venues. The Haight Street Theater and the Charles Turner Gallery presented the George Sams Quartet, Night Escape with Abdul Waahid, CJAM, and others. Noe Valley Ministry presented Noe Valley Music. The Theater Guild of San Francisco presented Gamelan Sekar Jaya (music and dance of Bali) with I Wayan Suweca, director and dancer I Nyoman Wenten, and French mime in Eliane Walis's *Imagenes* (with CJAM) at the Victoria Theater on 16th Street at Mission. During Black History Month (February 1982), the Oakland Theater of Dance (directed by Jane Brown) presented Duke Ellington's *Such Sweet Thunder* at the Laney College Theater. *Such Sweet Thunder* is a work composed by Ellington and arranged by Billy Strayhorn in 1957. It is a classic suite of twelve thematic portraits dedicated to the peerless Avon poet.

The mix continued to heat up with a host of other experimental and traditional events. The Metropolitan Art Center (Geary at Van Ness) presented a variety of "jazz" combos as well as other solos, duets, and interesting ensembles. An outdoor series at the Golden Gate Park Band Shell held a Conga Drum Festival featuring Batucaje, Babatunde, Kwaku Dadey, Peraza and Flores Percussion Ensemble, and other guest artists. An African Cultural Festival featuring UC Berkeley musicologist C.K. Ladzekpo, Jose Lorenzo, and O.J. Ekemode, took place at the Oakland Auditorium Theater. The Julia Morgan Center on College Avenue in Berkeley invited Batucaje to join them in a concert of folk and ethnic music. The Intertribal Music House presented an "American Indian Music Festival." The People's Cultural Center on Valencia Street (in the Mission District) created a series of performances involving various duets, trios, and quartets. The Communications Center on Sacramento Street funded by the Friends of the San Francisco Public Library presented a similar series. Kuumbwa Jazz Center in Santa Cruz presented some of the most interesting concerts in the greater Northern California area, featuring artists such as Sonny Simmons and Barbara Donald, the Art Ensemble of Chicago, Sun Ra, Oliver Lake, CJAM, Anthony Braxton, and many others. Dimension Dance Theater presented African-American dance by director and choreographer Debra Vaughan (with co-founder Elendar Barnes).

There were also "jazz" concerts at the Great American Music Hall that featured Betty Carter, Bobby McFerrin, Ed Kelly, Pharoah Sanders, and others. Keystone Korner, on Vallejo St. in North Beach had George Cables, Billy Harper, Freddie Hubbard, Tito Puente, McCoy Tyner, Sheila Jordan, Horace Silver, Arthur Blythe, Toots Thielemans, Brazilian musicians Jose Lorenzo and Airto Moreira, and other familiar names on its schedule. Lorenzo's fifteen-member dance, and music company Batucaje (composed of an international group of performers from Brazil, Nicaragua, the Philippines, etc.) also performed at Fort Mason.

The Kronos Quartet, then a young string ensemble serving as artists in residence at Mills College in Oakland, presented a concert in the Museum of Modern Art's Green Room. McCoy Tyner and Cecil Taylor also performed there.

Because the high level of intensity that characterized that period was not sustained sufficiently, many of the Bay Area's creative artists gradually migrated to New York and abroad. For a moment in the early 1980s, however, the San Francisco Bay Area produced innovative "jazz" and world music in a balanced, interdisciplinary setting. The "joint was jumpin'."

This period inspired a subsequent Asian-American "jazz" scene that continues to evolve. Today's seekers of Afro-Asian synthesis, such as Miya Masaoka (a Japanese American koto player who recently recorded an album of Thelonious Monk's music), violinist Jason Huang and baritone saxophonist Fred Ho (both are Chinese Americans), continue to create innovative "jazz"-influenced music that affirms their own ancestral identities. The Bay Area remains an exciting place for music.

The Contemporary Midwestern "Jazz" Scene

"Jazz" musicians such as bassists Richard Davis (of Madison, Wisconsin) and Don Mayberry (Farmington Hills, Michigan), pianists Pamela Wise, Teddy Harris, and Harold McKinney, trumpeters Marcus Belgrave and Charles Moore, reedman Wendell Harrison, cellist David Baker, and drummer Leonard King, Jr. (all from Detroit, Michigan), are but a few among the growing number of artists developing a thriving scene in the Midwest. The area includes Illinois, Iowa, Indiana, Michigan, Minnesota, Ohio, Wisconsin, and the Dakotas. Arts Midwest and other arts organizations support cultural and educational programs that stimulate "jazz" activities that have evolved into a vital urban force.

During the 1960s Wendell Harrison (b. 1943) lived in New York and performed with the Joe Henderson—Kenny Dorham Big Band, Betty Carter, Charles Tolliver, Jimmy Owens, Art Pepper, with Jack McDuff and others on the "organ grinder circuit" (Harlem, Newark, Patterson). He played the saxophone much of the time, but eventually fell in love with the clarinet. Harrison performed and recorded with his clarinet ensemble (composed of a variety of soprano, alto, and bass clarinets, with rhythm section). His latest recordings are available on his Wenha label.

In the early 1970s the vibrant Detroit club life of earlier days declined with the downward spiral of the city's industrial base. Detroit musicians soon countered, forming informal collectives and developing community-rooted forums for the presentation of their music. Wendell Harrison was an entrepreneur and "cultural activist" who advanced alternatives to the nightclub circuit and conventional music business channels.

Harrison formed an interdisciplinary organization called Tribe. Tribe began as a performing ensemble with Belgrave, Moore, Harrison, bassist Will Austin, and trombonist Phil Ranelin among its members. It eventually emerged to include a highly topical magazine with a focus on "jazz;" an independent record label; an advertising agency; and a graphic design company. Today Harrison and his wife, Pamela Wise, run Rebirth Inc., which has produced concerts featuring Ellis Marsalis, Freddie Hubbard, Jerry Gonzalez, Karlton Hester, Hank Jones, Don Byron, and other artists. Some Rebirth guest artists perform on WDET Radio in Detroit, on the radio show "Destination Out," hosted by Kim Heron.

Geri Allen (b. 1957) is a pianist, teacher, composer, recording, club, and concert artist who is emerging as an innovative force in Detroit. She taught at Howard University before being ranked among the critics' choices in *Down Beat* and winning first place as Talent Deserving Wider Recognition in 1993. After moving to New York, Allen worked with Oliver Lake, Joseph Jarman, Lester Bowie, Betty Carter, Steve Coleman, and a host of other innovators. Her style reflects her interest in the music of Thelonious Monk and Herbie Nichols, but Allen has developed a unique voice of her own. Her recordings reflect her wide range of interest. She was an early member of the M-Base Collective and appeared on three of their recordings. She has also appeared with Ornette Coleman, Ralph Peterson, Dewey Redman, and Wallace Roney. Allen and pianist Hank Jones (another Michigan native) were the subjects of a January 1994 *Down Beat* cover article "Me and Mister Jones" by Howard Mandel.

Wendell Harrison (Photo by Barbara Barefield).

Pamela Wise (Photo courtesy of HRP Library).

Akua Dixon (Photo courtesy of HRP Library).

Adela Dalto (Photo courtesy of HRP Library).

In 1991 Violinist Regina Carter moved to New York from her home-town, Detroit. By 1996 she was performing a series of concerts at Sweet Basil in New York with trombonist Steve Turre's ensemble. Although her first re-cordings were of the smooth-"jazz" variety, her live performances with Turre, and later with pianist Kenny Barron's (b. 1943) group, display Carter's im-peccable musicianship, virtuosity and imagination. While performing Turre's "Blackfoot" (an extremely brisk composition that uses the chords of "Chero-kee") at one of her first New York appearances Carter remembers thinking, "Oh my God, they think I can't play, they probably think the only reason Steve hired me was because I'm a woman!" Soon her audiences knew differ-ently. Her natural lyricism is captivating. Carter says:

> Part of it, I've been told, is an energy that I have when I play,
> even if I'm really nervous or I'm not quite sure how I'm going to
> get back to shore. I had a big band teacher who always said if
> you're going to make a mistake, do it loud and do it with ven-

gence. So I just give it my all. Maybe I can't play as many notes
or as many complicated phrases as other people play, but it
really comes from inside.

While touring with Wynton Marsalis' *Blood on the Fields* production,
Carter's finale brought down the house.[21] Her performances with Wynton
Marsalis and Cassandra Wilson brought highly favorable reviews from the
press, eventually leading to an opportunity to headline her own group at
Sweet Basil. Her music and reputation continues to evolve and she has
signed a contract with Verve Records at a time when many other artists are
being dropped.

Rap and Hip-Hop Culture

Hip-hop culture emerged in Harlem in 1977. Younger Afrocentric musicians began looking for ways around the limitations and trappings of mainstream culture. Denied access to instrumental music programs, mentors, and
musical instruments in inner city schools, African-American youth movements created an innovative music that was not a fusion (like "jazz"-rock,
third-stream "jazz," acid-"jazz," etc.) of musical elements from past traditions.
In the spirit of a long-standing legacy of African-American innovation, young
African-American students would not have their creativity stifled by economic limitations. Using materials at hand (including the human body as
percussion and the rhythmic scratching of LP vinyl records, young musicians
created an innovative personal style of music. The music of Flash, Herc, and
Bambataa (from the Bronx), along with new uptown sounds from Kurtis
Blow, Spoonie G, and The Sugar Hill Gang were distributed by hand on the
streets of New York.

Rap is revolutionary and an original style of music that reflects its urban social environment clearly and efficiently. The Sugar Hill Gang released
the first rap track in 1979. This unknown group, with "zero street credibility,"[22] called "Rapper's Delight" was a historic novelty release recorded in a
small New Jersey studio. It introduced the world to the music that was
emerging from the streets of New York.

The progenitors of rap were able to use independent economical means
to produce a form of self-expression that was so socially powerful that it soon
began to dominate the popular music scene. Equipped with a stack of records,
a stereo mixer, a couple of turntables, and speakers, rap pioneers became the
new "gangsters," frankly reflecting African-American culture through its
poignant blasts of "noise." Equating rap with various "jazz" styles on a purely
technical basis is futile. Hip-hop culture shares roots with "jazz" and other
innovative Afrocentric music, but direct access to that virtuosic musical tradition was denied. Authors Havelock Nelson and Michael A. Gonzales claim:

Without a doubt hip-hop culture can be traced back to the
tribes of Africa, back to James Brown sliding across the stage
at the Apollo, back to the chatter of men-folk inside a barber
shop, and yet, much like Futurism, hip-hop/rap began as an

avant-garde arts movement for the people on the street who were tired of the same-o, same-o.

Although the hip-hop creators paid homage to past musical influences, this new noise was strictly post-modern: constructed (rather than composed) from sounds, bass lines or guitar riffs scratched from existing texts (other records). The noise found on hip-hop tracks could be anything that bounced off the "walls of sound," from cartoon voices to high-pitched screams. As Tisdall and Bozzolla wrote in their book *Futurism*, "Noise did not mean just din and cacophony . . . the wealth of sound in the world ignored by the conventions of music ranged from the primary noises of nature to the roar of life and machines in the modern city."[23]

Rap uses intriguing and simple rhythmic phrases, motives, and innovative textures to support its poetry. Nevertheless, rappers did not have the opportunity to absorb the rich knowledge contained within the caldron of "jazz" styles and traditions from Afrocentric elders. Rap, as the name implies, places greater emphasis on the rhythms and messages contained within modern "street" language in poetry.

Rap artists are generally much less interested in sophisticated melodies, harmonies, textures, and other musical elements explored in other Western music. This aspect of the art form bothers many "jazz" artists. Socially conscious Rap is akin to the spirit of innovative African-American music through its tenacity, potency, and universal influence among the members of its generation. It employs a rich verbal vocabulary that involves double entendre messages and the sustained intensity of other African and African-American music. Just as numerous critics predicted the death of "jazz," reggae, rhythm and blues, and other Afrocentric music, others stated that hip-hop was only a fad that would disappear on as quickly as it emerged. Two decades have passed since the earliest prognostications; L. L. Cool J, Public Enemy, Ice-T, Queen Latifah, KRS-One, Salt-n-Pepa, Heavy D, Grandmaster Flash, and other veteran rap artists are still on the scene.

Between 1900 and the 1950s, the "dozens" (also referred to as the "Dirty Dozens," "Signifying," "Cap," "Bad Talk," etc.) was an elaborate African-American verbal rhyming social game traditionally involving boys insulting each other's relatives (especially their mothers) in twelve censures. The object of the game was to test the opponent's emotional strength. We can trace loose ties to "rap" tradition back to African-American religious sermons, the "dozens," and to The Last Poets (considered by many the progenitors of rap) and other revolutionary bards from the late 1960s and early 1970s. The liner notes to the 1997 Mercury Records release *The Last Poets: Time Has Come* tell the listener, "Muthafuckas ran f'cover:"

Nobody was ready.

Had 'em, scared o' revolution. Scared o' the whyte man's god complex. Scared o' subways. Scared o' each other. Scared o' themselves. And scared o' that totem of onanistic worship—the eagle-clawed *Amerikkan* greenback!

The rhetoric made you mad. The drums made you pop your fingers. And the poetry made you sail on the cushions of a fine hashish high.

Most importantly, they made you think and kept you "correct" on a revolutionary level.

We all connected. 'Cause it was a Black communal thing. Like the good vibes and paper plate of red-peppered potato salad at a neighborhood barbeque. The words and the rhythms were relevant. We joined together around the peace pipe and the drum. And when it came to the rhythm of the drums, the drums said, "check your tired-ass ideology at the door."

Meanwhile, the "hip-hop generation" who've had to grow up without a clue that life can be about something other than non-stop and mostly futile pursuit of that eagle-clawed greenback, has somehow recognized and claimed The Last Poets as the Godfathers of rap. Savvy young rappers have continued to spin 'em on the air.

Problems of breaks in cultural continuity intensified regarding the appreciation of "jazz" in the rap and hip-hop communities, as popular music created wealthy young musicians. When people equate musical value with success, then the "jazz" artist has a harder time convincing younger African-Americans of the intrinsic value and importance of innovative music of the past traditions. Once directly exposed to substantive art of any kind, however, young people develop curiosity, desire to develop better musical skills, and deepen their levels of appreciation for the process of artistic creation. More European-American students study and learn to play "jazz" because of formal exposure to a variety of music before college. African-American students are also more inclined toward music that reflects today's culture and pace. Nelson George thinks this difference in attitude is also due to other cultural factors:

The black audience's consumerism and restlessness burns out and abandons musical styles, whereas white Americans, in the European tradition of supporting forms and style for the sake of tradition, seem to hold styles dear and long after they have ceased to evolve.

The most fanatical students of blues history have all been white. These well-intentioned scholars pick through old recordings, interview obscure guitarists, and tramp through the Mississippi Delta with the determination of an Egyptologist. Yet with the exception of Eric Clapton and maybe Johnny Winter, no white blues guitarist has produced a body of work in any way comparable to that of the black giants. Blacks create and then move on. Whites document and then recycle. In the history of popular music, these truths are self-evident.[24]

Rappers fully realized a fact that has remained a capitalist fiat: profit supersedes racism or any other social motive. The young entrepreneurs who sold early rap records on the streets of New York did not become owners of record companies, distribution networks, and publishing rights to the African-American rap music that later turned unprecedented profit. Sylvia Robinson (Sugarhill Records), Russell Simmons (Def Jam), Andre Harrell (Uptown Enterprises), Luther Campbell (Luke Records), and a few other independent and visionary African-American capitalists were the exceptions. In the tradition of older "jazz" innovators, most rap artists gave their music away to enterprising European-American business people, as Public Enemy's "media assassin," Harry Allen discussed in *The City Sun*.[25]

It's extremely rare to see a European-American male wearing a T-shirt bearing the image of their favorite living African-American musician. A European-American female celebrating such artists is infinitely rarer. The majority culture has not found many opportunities openly to celebrate African-American heroes or heroines. At the end of the twentieth century people are beginning to show greater respect for African-American artists (albeit, in the case of "jazz," more often than not posthumously). Rap is aiding in the integration of the audience for African-American music without sacrificing Afrocentricity. Rap artists are also beginning to cultivate relationships with older "jazz" artists (like the collaboration between Donald Byrd and Guru). This is an important beginning toward the reunification of the African-American community, reuniting generations of music and people after remaining divided and alienated for a half-century. Brief or superficial unions yield shallow results, nonetheless. Big Daddy Kane was asked about his collaboration with jazz musicians and other rappers on a Quincy Jones album in an interview. He said: "That was cool. Me and Quincy talked and he pointed out that what The Last Poets were doing was similar to rap, and he showed the connection. He showed me a picture of his father with a flattop haircut. You know like evolution, everything just turned back around. I thought that it was cool. So the combination was real cool. It's like it was all there, the first generation and the second generation coming together doing the same music."

When pressed further it became apparent that brief collaborations could not produce miracles. It will take more time to produce greater results. Kane said: "Me personally, I'm not into jazz to tell you the truth. So Quincy was sitting there telling me things like they used to call Sarah Vaughn 'Divine Sassy' and she did this. So I'm just taking notes and putting this in rap form."[26]

Contemporary Politics & Labeling African-American Culture

When people attach labels such as gospel, spiritual, blues, "jazz," soul, or rhythm 'n blues to different pieces of music, one might ask: "Why are the various forms of African-American expression categorized as though they were grossly unrelated to each other?" We have a human need to label our environment in easily definable categories to enhance clarity. Important aspects of Afrocentric styles apply mutually to all categories. African-American music shares African roots. Each generation of African-American musicians produces new art forms with noticeable degrees of independence from earlier forms, yet they evolve from related social environments and social constraints (racism and sexism). We can dissect African-American music into distinct styles, but they all developed from a single tradition.

The oppression of African-American artists is not simply a matter of American racism. The hardship that Bach, Mozart, Beethoven, and contemporary European composers endured during their lifetimes is related to the suffering that African-American innovators have encountered. Beethoven's music in particular received many disparaging comments during his lifetime. Some of these descriptions were ridiculous and belittling in ways akin to those critics used to describe African-American innovators. Rellstab, a "romantically inclined and hero-worshipping" fan,[27] was surprised that Beethoven's "face was much smaller than I had pictured it in accordance with the likeness which has forcibly constrained it to an appearance of powerful, genial savagery."[28] The composer's works received adverse criticism on various occasions during his life, but his letter to the music publisher Breitkopf and Haertel of Leipzig (dated April 22, 1801) demonstrates that he soon arrived at conclusions many serious artists can appreciate: "The outcry at first of your critics against me was so humiliating, that when I began to compare myself with others, I could scarcely blame them; I remained quite quiet, and thought they do not understand it. And I had all the more reason for being quite quiet when I saw how men were praised up to the skies who here are held of little account by the better musicians *in loco*, and who here are almost forgotten."

Music today remains affected by racial and sexual politics nonetheless. Such proclivities are motivated by social insecurity, quests for economic dominance, and ignorance. Since interracial unions are as old as the human species, there are no "pure" races. J. A. Rogers told us that:

> A great deal of American color prejudice, too, is mere deceit. . . .
> In private life most of the blatant Negrophobes show no prejudice, and are usually well-liked by the Negroes who know them well. Sometimes such [bigots] go out of the way to aid Negroes, as Cole Blease. The latter, when governor of South Carolina turned out Negro convicts by the thousands saying that they had been put in there unjustly. One of the most violent attackers of the Negro in Congress and on the political stump of his own state had a Negro family. The Negro housekeeper was the real boss of his mansion, and the white wife almost a nonentity.

Of course, no right-thinking individual will admire this type of individual. They are that detestable combination of opportunist and hypocrite.[29]

The transformation of Beethoven's physical image by artists over the years is an interesting footnote. A comparison between early portraits and later ones prompted many Afrocentrists in the 1970s to propose that the composer may have been of mixed African and European heritage. Alessandra Comini, in her book *The Changing Image of Beethoven: A Study in Myth Making*, traces the continuous alterations that visual artists made in representing the composer during and after his lifetime. Comini noted that those who knew Beethoven in his extreme youth tended to all keep an "unswerving line of pure physical description." She mentions that a baker named Gottfried Fischer (c. 1780–1864) was the son of the couple who owned the house in which Beethoven grew up in Bonn. His "quite self-conscious"[30] description of the "former physique of Herr Ludwig van Beethoven" was as follows: "Short and thick-set, broad across the shoulders, short neck, large head, rounded nose, dark-brown complexion; always leaned forward a little in walking. When still a boy they used to call him 'der Spanol' in our house."[31] Joseph Neeson's silhouette of Beethoven, as well Louis Letronne's 1814 pencil drawing, supports the Bonn baker's description.

According to Comini, an engraving based on Letronne's drawing pleased Beethoven the most. We know that he presented copies of it to visitors and friends. Anton Felix Schindler (c. 1795–1864),[32] Beethoven's devoted (and unpaid) secretary and factotum, spoke reverently of the composer when he said: "Of all the famous musical geniuses, perhaps Beethoven had the head with the most distinctive features, starting with the thick mass of hair and continuing with the forehead, eyes, mouth, and chin in harmonious proportions, in which the only dissonance was the rather broad nose."[33]

Whether Beethoven was "Black" (as some Afrocentric scholars assert) is not the important issue. More significantly, history apparently performed remarkable surgery on certain aspects of particular iconography and description over the years to create a certain image of Beethoven. The color of a composer's skin should have no bearing on the appreciation of her or his works. It is true, nevertheless, that any such postulations infuriate Eurocentrists. The levels of complexity increase exponentially when we hang veils to disguise obvious bias. David Theo Goldberg has interesting ideas along these lines:

> The claim that racism is nothing more than ideological is confusing or delimiting in a different way. It misleadingly leaves the deleterious effects of racist practices and institutions to be captured by some other term like racialism or racist discrimination. Alternatively, by insisting that the raison d'etre of the racist ideological structure is to hide some underlying form of economic, social, or political oppression, this widely shared claim refuses to acknowledge, and so leaves unexplained, the fact that racist expressions may at times define and promote rather than merely rationalize social arrangements and insti-

tutions. Sepulveda's characterization of Mexican Indians as fit only for slavery enabled their enslavement to be conceived rather than simply serving to rationalize their exploitation ex post facto. I will undertake to incorporate the distinctions between belief structure, aims, practices, institutions, principles, and effects into a coherent characterization of the concepts of racism.[34]

Critics of Afrocentrism attacked claims that Egypt had significant influence on Greece. Mary Lefkowitz, in the name of "rational thought," attacked the scholarship of George G. M. James (*Stolen Legacy*, 1954), Martin Bernal (*Black Athena*, vols. 1–2, 1987–91), and other scholars who propose that many achievements accredited to Greek civilization actually have roots in Egyptian and other African history. Although authors such as James, Bernal, Ivan Van Sertima (*They Came before Columbus*, 1976), and Chief Musamaali Nangoli (*No More Lies about Africa*, 1988) generally research their subject according to traditional Western protocol, they are often systematically dismissed as "persistently imprecise." According to Lefkowitz, in her article "Afrocentrism Poses a Threat to the Rational Tradition,"[35] "the Afrocentrists, . . . not only are assigning credit to African peoples for achievements that properly belong to the Greeks; in the process they are destroying what is perhaps the greatest legacy of Greek philosophy—rational thought." Interestingly, Lefkowitz does not provide a single footnote. John E. Coleman and other scholars have reacted to Bernal (in particular) and Afrocentricity in equally agitated fashions.[36]

The things they encounter in the world influence everyone. The Egyptians they encountered in Africa must, have influenced Socrates, Herodotus, and other Greeks. Egyptians absorbed cultural elements from foreign people with whom they came in contact. After four hundred years of tonal music in the West, the twentieth century ushered in two new approaches: the blues and twelve-tone music. The blues, based largely upon a flexible approach to pitch and melody, operated in alliance with tendencies of tonal harmony. Despite this blending, its true nature remained somewhat elusive because the blues was not a result of simple music fusion. Each chord of the basic blues is dominant.[37] In its modern guise, the tendencies toward total chromaticism (clearly outlined in typical blues walking bass patterns), reveal basic formulas that supply musicians like Coltrane devices with which to devise their own twelve-tone approach to "jazz."

Rock and roll, a derivative form of blues, was cordoned off from other African-American music to enhance its salability among the majority population. Various forms of the blues include rhythm and blues that emerged in the 1940s, which became rock and roll in the 1950s. Perhaps a more precise and honest division of "jazz," blues, and rock could be Eurocentric American "jazz," blues, and rock and Afrocentric American "jazz," blues, and rock. Such labels better reflect the conditions extant in American society reflected in American music.

Labeling people and the art they express can never be a simple task if labels are to have substantive meaning.

African-Americans have never consisted of a perfectly harmonized and totally communal fabric. There is tremendous variety among all groups and cultures. In some regions of the United States, African Americans have grown up in a culture that was more European American (or even Hispanic) than African-American. Since it is increasingly more possible for people to align themselves with political, social, or cultural positions at will in America, it is difficult to generalize meaningfully about any sector of the population. Although racism creates predictable paradigms, there will fortunately always be a number of exceptions within a democracy. Human nature tells us that it is futile to expect all African Americans, European Americans, Asian Americans, Hispanic Americans, or any other group of intelligent human beings to restrict their tastes to those things produced by their human subgroup.

Recently, some musicians involved in the creation of music in the European tradition have apparently felt slighted as "jazz" and other African-American music has received an increasing degree of attention. Composer George Walker,[38] in an article in the *New York Times* (November 3, 1991) expressed his feelings that "Black composers are left behind again in the rage for black popular music and jazz." Apparently, according to this statement, Walker does not consider Ellington, Mingus, and Joplin as "Black" composers. He continues: "Folk music, of which jazz is a form, has been assimilated and transformed by composers of all periods. Though many Americans, white and black, began with jazz and moved on to concert music, my background did not include jazz. My exposure to classical music and to European folk music came at an early age. I never listened to jazz until I went to college."

Walker possibly found it necessary to classify "jazz" as folk music to separate his approach to music from other African-American music. Most musicians did not "begin" with jazz and then "move on" to concert music, because most formal instruction musicians received in America this century (privately or in school) was music of European tradition. Jelly Roll Morton, Louis Armstrong, Jimmy Lunceford, Charles Mingus, Dorothy Donegan, Miles Davis, and John Coltrane are examples.

Walker, like earlier African-American church members (who considered "jazz" the "devil's music"), prefers either to distance himself from the negative stereotypes assigned to innovative African-American music or to speak disparagingly about music that is not Eurocentric. Martha Bayles, who also considers "jazz" a folk art, touches on this:

> Of course, the vast majority of people who appreciate jazz do so without any fancy ideas about it one way or the other. Most people don't relate to music, especially popular music, on an intellectual level. But that is precisely why the misconceptions I've been talking about are so influential. The public, whose opinion is registered in dollars, not ideas, offers little resistance.

Likewise jazz musicians. Along with most artists, jazz musicians accept whatever intellectual acclaim they can get, whether or not it is based on an accurate assessment of their art. In particular, they endorse the Stalinist view of jazz as a folk art corrupted by commerce—largely because it makes room for racial resentment. Too often there *is* a sharp dividing line between the "folk" artist (black) and the "bourgeois" exploiter (white). And too often the memory lingers of the grinning blackface minstrel, bought and sold for the entertainment of whites. What self-respecting jazz musician wouldn't prefer a more heroic image?[39]

Walker is also contemptuous of the notion that "some jazz performers and promoters are trying to redefine the term classical and enshrine jazz as America's classical music. I do wonder what I have been composing for the last 50 years." Walker composed music based upon the European tradition. It cannot be African-American music merely because of the composer's genetic code. Benny Goodman, Stan Getz, Phil Woods, Bill Evans, and other European-American "jazz" artists created music in the African-American tradition (based upon stylistic considerations). For some, such notions are hard to take.

As the world citizens begin to have common experiences that traverse racial classifications, then, and only then, will music eventually be produced that can reflect a generic American experience. As we approach the end of the century, there are signs that Americans are having more shared experiences throughout society. The characteristics Locke described long ago, although reflecting attitudes typical of passed generations, remain features of innovative African-American music:

The Negro, a musical force, through his own distinct racial characteristics has made an artistic contribution which is racial but not yet national. Rather has the influence of musical stylistic traits termed Negro, spread over many nations wherever the colonies of the New World have become homes of the Negro people. These expressions in melody and rhythm have been a compelling force in American music—tragic and joyful in emotion, pathetic and ludicrous in melody, primitive and barbaric in rhythm. The welding of these expressions has brought about a harmonic effect, which is now influencing thoughtful musicians throughout the world. At present there is evidenced a new movement far from academic, which plays an important technical part in the music of this and other lands.[40]

During the long period involving "slave master mentality" in America, Eurocentric claims and stereotypes about Africans or African-Americans went unchallenged. The slave's job was strictly to provide services for the oppressor without ever questioning a request or challenging an opinion, regardless of how ridiculous or demeaning it may have been. These attitudes apparently remain buried deep within the collective unconsciousness of a large portion of American society. Many who have grown accustomed to the delusions and economic advantages of a diabolical system since manumission, are sometimes reluctant to abandon final vestiges.

Some European Americans become aggravated at continual reminders of the legacy of racism in America. Confronting racism on a daily basis is much more enervating. African-American music innovators have confronted such attitudes and responded with the creation of beautiful music. Walton discusses some of the ways race entered into some of the marketing practices in the San Francisco Bay Area:

> Little choice is left for the consumer and aspiring musician since the centralized industry composed of radio, television and recording companies emphasize to a great extent the same type of material; that is, whatever has been contrived by the taste-makers to be the most salable at that particular time. For example, out of thirteen AM and fifteen FM stations in the San Francisco Bay Area, eleven, or close to 40 percent, are rock stations, playing an average of twenty-five minutes of rock music per half hour. A sampling of Chicago radio stations reveals a similar pattern.

> There is [at the time] only one Jazz station in the Bay Area. All of the disc jockeys are white, except for one who is an Asian American. Programming, with a few exceptions, leans heavily on the big-band genre. The Dorsey Brothers, Glenn Miller or Stan Kenton are more likely to be heard than "Sonny" Rollins, Horace Silver or Coleman Hawkins. When national Afro-American groups play the one or two "big-time" Jazz clubs in the area, there is usually an increase in the frequency of play given to that artist's recordings. Once he or they have gone, the station quickly resumes its previous format. In like fashion, so-called black stations usually exclude Jazz, airtime being given mostly to other Afro-American musics.[41]

Sidran points out in *Black Talk*, "The black musician, in taking the process of cultural definition into his own hands, infuriated a vast number of whites."[42] Should the label "jazz" be dropped? Many artists remain disgusted with the label "jazz." Once attached, labels are difficult to remove. Innovators are criticized for abandoning preconceived notions of "jazz."

Summary: Afrocentric Snapshots of a Shrinking Society

> I come here to make a speech, to tell you the truth. If the truth is anti-American, then blame the truth, don't blame me.
>
> —Malcolm X[43]

Mary Lou Williams died in 1981. African Americans made many advances during the twentieth century, but racism maintained an economic stranglehold on "Black" socioculture. The absence of African-American record companies, distribution networks, conservatories, and publishing houses show clearly that "Black" music also remained a subject of oppression.

By 1983 South Africa had adopted a new constitution giving limited political rights to "Colored" and "Asian" South Africans, but the privileges were not extended to "Blacks." In November 1984, Israel began a secret airlift of Ethiopian Jews (Falashas) from Sudan in what was called "Operation Moses." Bishop Desmond Tutu, general secretary of the South African Council of Churches, was awarded the Nobel Peace Prize. South Africa launched combined land and air raids against alleged A.N.C. stations in Zambia, Botswana, and Zimbabwe in 1986, ending hopes of truce with the A.N.C. just after a withdrawal from Angola the year before. Mike Tyson (at age twenty) became W.B.C. world heavyweight champion after defeating Trevor Berbick. In 1988, South African "Black" workers staged a three-day strike against a new labor legislation.

The 1990s witnessed the dismantling of apartheid in South Africa and Nelson Mandela was elected its first President. At home in the United States, many sociopolitical issues and problems continued to confront American society as racial divisions increased. In 1989 Charles Stuart, a "White" businessman in Boston, murdered his pregnant wife to collect the insurance money. He claimed a "Black" man killed his wife and then shot him, thus sending the racist element in that city on a rampage against African-American men. An African-American male with a police record was falsely accused. It was not until Stuart killed himself in January 1990, as his scheme began to fall apart, that the accused man—and Boston's "Black" community (!)—was exonerated.[44]

The bigotry that surrounded the birth of African-American music still remains in contemporary American society. A tearful Susan Smith later claims that a carjacking occurred where a "demonic" African-American male allegedly abducted her two angelic infant sons in Union, South Carolina. Her plea for the return of these children is the subject of national media. Actually, she had drowned the children in a nearby lake. As an article in *Emerge* magazine observed, "Susan Smith knew the powerful grip the image of the dangerous 'Black' man has on White American's psyche."[45]

Contemporary American media continually portrays African-American males as criminals. The age of violent criminals in America is becoming much younger than ever before, but they are not of a single race or class.

Stray bursts from eleven-year-old Robert Sandifer's semiautomatic gunfire accidentally killed Shavon Dean, a fourteen-year-old bystander. Chicago police found Sandifer's body four days later. The allegation that the incident was an element of gang warfare in the "mean streets" of the African-American ghetto resounded loudly in the media. A concerted effort seems directed toward accumulating evidence that "implicitly declare the problems of the ghettos a manifestation of 'Blacks' pathological attitudes . . . which has nothing to do with mainstream [White] American society."[46]

Elsewhere, on the same day, a thirteen-year-old European-American boy shot and killed his eleven-year old friend in the blue-collar town of High Bridge, New Jersey. Two twelve-year-old boys, Manuel Sanchez and John Duncan, are also arrested for the unrelated murder of a fifty-year-old man in

Wenatchee, Washington. The victim was shot eighteen times because he complained about the boys shooting a gun too close to his home. *Emerge* described another thirteen-year-old boy, Moses Prado, who was charged as an adult on four counts of murder in connection with a grocery store bombing in which four people died in the Bronx. Fourteen-year-old Eric Smith of Bath, New York, was tried and convicted as an adult for strangling and bludgeoning a four-year-old boy. Gerald McCra III, a fifteen-year-old boy, stood accused of murdering his parents and his eleven-year-old sister because he was not allowed to have his girlfriend spend the night. Because none of these boys were African-American there was no media frenzy.

> These are people who, because the assertion of "inferiority" is dressed in pseudo-scientific garb, would pretend that it is not what it really is: The declaration by those of one ethnic group that another ethnic group is "inferior" and therefore has no right to exist except by the super group's permission. They would pretend that *The Bell Curve*—the thesis of which could be posed only in a climate of rising intolerance—is not a declaration of war.

> These are people well-skilled in the art of evading moral responsibility. They are the spiritual descendants of those who rationalized the traffic in chattel slavery, who turned a blind eye to the declinations of Native-Americans and who declared that at least Hitler made the trains run on time while claiming not to know about the human cargo and deadly destinations.[47]

During the early 1990s, Michael Jordan, Mike Tyson, and Michael Jackson all met ill-fated destinies that are pounced upon by the media. The "trial of the century" finds O. J. Simpson innocent of murder in 1995, but the press apparently continued to assume Simpson was guilty. It was one of a few instances in American history where a jury of her/his peers tried an African-American defendant, yet the majority culture suggested that "Black" people are not capable of trying each other fairly as a result of the Simpson verdict. Track sensation Michael Johnson won Olympic gold in both the 200-meter and 400-meter sprints to make his mark in sports history. Nonetheless, Johnson was not considered to have enormous money making potential (from product endorsements) because the television industry concluded he "doesn't smile enough."

In South Africa, Bishop Desmond Tutu continues to head the Truth Council that grants amnesty to those who confess of atrocities committed under apartheid. As a consequence Africans have heard how their young relatives were "blown to smithereens" or burned alive on a pyre of old tires and wood while their murderers picnicked,[48] much as their American counterparts had done earlier in the United States.

The assassination of Martin Luther King, Malcolm X, along with those claiming the lives of John and Robert Kennedy, signaled the beginning of a quarter-century of ultra-conservative sociopolitical dominance in America. In earlier African-American communities, such as Harlem, drugs were largely confined to musicians and their associates. Now drugs began their malignant infestation, consuming unprecedented numbers of people of all ages in inner city neighborhoods. Conditions eventually became so severe, and suspicions ran so high, that a representative from the CIA attended a town meeting in Los Angeles in the fall of 1996 to defend the agency against claims that the CIA planted drugs in African-American neighborhoods allegedly to destabilize them.

Is the recent appreciation of retrospective Afrocentric music evidence of a natural tendency to reclaim the past before embracing the uncertainties of a complex future? Should we expect retrospection in large dosages as a jam-packed millennium comes to an end? Courtney Pine (b. 1964), a young multi-reedman and composer who makes no compromises, summed things up this way in the liner notes to his album *Courtney Pine: Underground* (Antilles, 1997):

> I truly believe that jazz music should reflect the social climate of the current times. It does this by being influenced by the part, which enables the user (the musician) to see the future with a clear insight. Sometimes external influences, i.e., critics or negative entities, do not, due to the lack of research, understand the mix of certain elements, and will run down a concept because it does not fit into their vision of a jazz artist. I have been fortunate enough to have met enough people (and critics) around the world that have expressed their understanding of this mixture of the traditional (blues, bebop, soul, jazz, avant-garde, etc.) and modern day musical communication (hip-hop, drum and bass, acid jazz, trip-hop, etc.) forms of music. This record is for you as I watched you become at one with the music (whilst on stage), you inspired me to piece this record together. Some may say that I am playing for the audience. What about musical content? Have I lost the battle between backbeat and swing? Well, I have never had a desire to climb that lonely staircase up into that ivory tower . . . there is nothing that we jazz warriors can do to change your minds (c'est la vie) but this will not stop me on my quest to find like-minded warriors, swing as hard, long and purposeful as possible.

So how can we produce a unified genre of music in the United States? America today wants to claim "jazz" as America's classical music. If this desire becomes strong enough to eliminate the racism that results in segregated American sociocultures, and if it manages to bring a fragmented society together, then we can expect to produce a strong, vibrant, and unified American music in the next millennium. A truly unified culture cannot tolerate government leadership that tolerates or contributes to economic and social inequities, that plants drugs and nuclear waste in "minority" neighborhoods that incarcerates the majority of young African-American males as political prisoners, or that limits employment and educational opportunities for underprivileged youth. The long-standing Western imperialist tradition of confiscating art, land, and knowledge from around the world and claiming ownership of them cannot continue to happen.

Guest speakers and performers of the 2003 *Global African Music & Arts Festival/Symposium at UC Santa Cruz* **(Karlton E. Hester, Artistic Director)***:* **(back) bassist Larry Ridley, trombonist Nelson Harrison, flutist/saxophonist/composer Karlton E. Hester, guitarist Pascal Bokar Thiam, Trumpeter William P. Johnson, visual artist Carl E. Lewis; (front) saxophonist Carl Atkins, Reggae musician Ras Midas, trumpeter Donald Byrd, and pianist Freddie Redd** (Photo by Sarah Blade/Precious Memories).

African-American "jazz," admired, celebrated, and analyzed for the abundance of musical joy, direction, and knowledge it yields, is also a part of the African-American musical legacy chronicling the cultural, psychological, emotional, spiritual, and intellectual history of Africans in the "New World." The music's evolutionary path stands as a reminder of the strength, knowledge, wisdom, durability, and genius of a sector of the American population said to have contributed little to American culture.

Above: Nelson Harrison and Donald Byrd performing with Hesterian Musicism at the 2003 *Global African Music & Arts Festival/Symposium* (Photos by Sarah Blade/Precious Memories).

Notes

[1] *Emerge*, January 1999, pp. 70–72.

[2] Ed Enright, *Down Beat*, February 1999, pp. 20–26.

[3] Richard M. Sudhalter, *New York Times,* January 3, 1999.

[4] John McDonough, *Wall Street Journal*, January 27, 1999.

[5] *Down Beat*, January 2000, p. 35.

[6] Listen to *Jumping in the Sugarbowl* (1984) and other Myers albums from this period.

[7] Peter Watrous, *The New York Times*, June 16, 1991, p. 22.

[8] *Down Beat*, January 2000, p. 33.

[9] A. James Liska, "A Common Understanding: Wynton and Branford Marsalis," *Down Beat* 61, no. 2 (February 1994); originally issued December 1982.

[10] As cited in *NYSO Journal* 5, no.1: 1 (a National Jazz Service Organization publication).

[11] Ben Sidran, *Black Talk* (New York: Da Capo, 1981), p. 76.

[12] Benny Goodman and Irving Kolodin, *The Kingdom of Swing*, p. 241.

[13] Sidran, *Black Talk*, p. 90.

[14] Liner notes in *Fathers and Sons*, Columbia Records FC37972 (1982).

[15] "Editorial commentary: Jazz at Lincoln Center," *NYSO Journal* 4, no. 4.

[16] Kevin Whitehead, *Village Voice*, November 23, 1993, jazz supplement.

[17] Wynton Marsalis, "Wynton Speaks: 'Who Actually Is Stupid,'" *NYSO Journal* 5, no. 1.

[18] The actual title is *Africa, According to Herodotus—456 B.C.*

[19] Karlton Hester organized the Contemporary Jazz Art Movement (CJAM) in 1978. Many of the members of the Contemporary Jazz Art Movement also led their own groups.

[20] *Down Beat*, July 1981, p. 56.

[21] John Janowiak, *Down Beat*, June 1999, p. 22.

[22] Havelock Nelson and Michael A. Gonzales, *Bring the Noise: A Guide to Rap Music and Hip-Hop Culture* (New York: Harmony Books, 1991), p. xix.

[23] Ibid., p. xviii.

[24] Nelson George, *The Death of Rhythm and Blues* (New York: Pantheon Books, 1988), p. 108.

[25] Nelson and Gonzales, *Bring the Noise*, p. xx.

[26] Joseph D. Eure and James G. Spady, eds., *Nation Conscious Rap* (New York: PC International, 1991), p. 29.

[27] Rellstab first met the composer in person in 1825 when Beethoven was internationally acclaimed.

[28] Alessandra Comini, *The Changing Image of Beethoven: A Study in Myth Making*, p. 22.

[29] J. A. Rogers, *Sex and Race* (St. Petersburg, Fla.: Helga M. Rogers, 1972), 3:85.

[30] Fischer knew that he was describing a famous man.

[31] Comini, *Changing Image of Beethoven*, p. 30.

[32] Schindler became Beethoven's first major biographer.

[33] Comini, *Changing Image of Beethoven*, p. 27.

[34] Goldberg, *Racist Culture* (Oxford: Blackwell, 1994), p. 95.

[35] *Chronicle of Higher Education*, May 6, 1992.

[36] Coleman wrote an article, "Did Egypt Shape the Glory That Was Greece?" that takes a position similar to that of Lefkowitz.

[37] A major or minor tonic is never established in accordance with Western tonal harmony in authentic blue forms.

[38] Walker is African American.

[39] Martha Bayles, *Hole in Our Soul: The Loss of Beauty and Meaning in American Popular Music* (New York: Free Press 1994), p. 85.

[40] Alain Locke, preface to *The Negro and His Music* (Port Washington, N.Y.: Kennikat, 1968).

[41] *Music: Black, White, and Blue*, p. 137.

[42] Sidran, *Black Talk*, p. 97.

[43] As cited in *Emerge: Black America's News Magazine*, February 1995.

[44] Ibid., p. 60.

[45] Ibid., p. 62.

[46] Ibid.

[47] Ibid., p. 64.

[48] From a radio broadcast of live confessions on National Public Radio, December 12, 1996.

Index

A

52nd Street, 318, 392
AACM, 377, 411, 417, 439, 441, 453, 454, 487
Abubakari, 62
Abusir, 16
Acholi, 22, 23
Acid-jazz, 498
Adams, George, 378
Adams, John, 65
Adderley, Cannonball, 167, 315, 353, 356, 358, 363, 366, 388, 402, 454, 459, 460, 472
Africa
    Equatorial, 46
    South, xxxix, 10, 31, 37, 40, 43, 121, 440, 508, 509
    Sub-Sahara, 14, 28, 37, 38, 40, 42, 44, 46
    Sub-Sahara, 22, 41
African musicians, xxiv, 10, 20, 37, 38, 44, 46, 147, 293, 440, 443
African Sea, 62, 295, 346
Agako, 33
Agawu, Kofi, 47, 475
Agwara, 23
Akako, 33
Akiyoshi, Toshiko, 427
Alabama
    Birmingham, 134, 373, 374, 431
    Normal, 374
Ali, Muhammad, 437, 440
Ali, Rashied, 315, 440
Alkaita, 32
Allen, Carl, 486
Allen, Geri, 494
Al-Omari, 62
Amaaloolu, 45
American Revolution, 72, 74, 75, 77, 81, 111
Amistad, 65, 79
Ammons, Albert, 187
Ammons, Gene, 263, 308, 322, 353, 414, 460
Angola, 32, 459, 508
Ankole, 42
Annang, 28
Antiphony, 38, 60
Apollo, 5, 226, 250, 251, 267, 308, 316, 318, 338, 352, 498
Arabia, 32, 40, 49, 51, 294
    Arab, 5, 20, 21, 22, 32, 50, 65, 294
    Arabic, 20, 25, 65, 75, 458

Arada, 63
Aristotle, 4
Arizona, 378
    Nogales, 378
Armstrong, Lil Hardin, 174, 186, 202, 221, 252, 253, 254
Armstrong, Louis, xxx, xxxi, xxxv, 128, 133, 138, 150, 152, 153, 160, 171, 172, 174, 180, 183, 185, 186, 199, 202, 205, 213, 214, 216, 217, 218, 219, 221, 222, 223, 224, 227, 239, 240, 244, 253, 258, 260, 261, 263, 265, 274, 278, 280, 310, 321, 330, 358, 378, 446, 458, 461, 475, 483, 485, 505
Arrangement, 374
Art Ensemble of Chicago, xxiii, xxviii, 377, 398, 412, 413, 414, 434, 440, 455, 484, 487, 493
Aryanists, 4
Asante, Molefi Kete, 4, 79, 346
Ashby, Dorothy, 382, 383
Asiento, 64
Atlantic Ocean, 62
Attucks, Crispus, 81
Auen, 31, 156
Austin, Lovie, 133, 213, 252, 253
Austin, Will, 494
Australia, 13
Awoka, 27
Ayler, Albert, 113, 370, 377, 398, 401, 402, 410, 411, 438, 455, 460
Ayler, Donald, 411
Aztec, 58

B

BaBenzele, 27
Babinga, 27
BaBira, 25
BAG, 412, 439, 455
Bagandou, 24
Bahia, 63
Bailey, Benny, 395
Baker, Chet, 321
Baker, David, xxx, 387, 423, 494
Bakweri, 25
Balese, 25, 27
BaLese, 25
Baloo, 46
Bambara, 44
Bambari, 24
Bambataa, 498
Bamileke, 25
Bamoun, 25

BaNdaka, 25
Bangbetu, 25
Bangia, 33
Bantu, xxiii, 6, 23, 25, 31, 36
Banzie, 25
Baritone horn, 144, 385, 404, 418
Barnet, Charlie, 224, 237, 331
Baroque, 72, 79
Barrett, Emma, 174, 253, 287
Barron, Kenny, 481, 482, 497
Bartz, Gary, 377, 470
Basie, Count, xxvii, xxxi, xxxv, 160, 187,
    188, 189, 190, 206, 219, 223, 234, 235,
    236, 243, 245, 247, 248, 250, 260, 261,
    262, 266, 269, 281, 284, 287, 292, 306,
    321, 322, 329, 330, 331, 340, 384, 418,
    431, 485, 486
Basongye, 44
Bass, xxix, 34, 142, 157, 158, 159, 161, 164,
    355, 356, 361, 362, 368, 369, 377, 378,
    380, 381, 392, 395, 402, 404, 408, 410,
    411, 413, 417, 426, 441, 443, 444, 445,
    451, 458, 459, 461, 462, 480, 486, 491,
    494, 499, 504, 510
    Acoustic, 480
    Electric, 163, 164, 444
Bassa, 28, 40
Bassoon, 194, 402, 491
Batiste, Alvin, 483
Batouques, 28
Batucaje, 493
Bayles, Martha, 198, 240, 317, 346, 505,
    513
Bebey, Francis, 10, 54, 121, 154
Bebop, xxii, xxiii, xxxvi, 79, 116, 123, 135,
    158, 161, 162, 163, 187, 188, 189, 190,
    191, 192, 223, 236, 243, 255, 256, 258,
    260, 261, 262, 291, 292, 293, 296, 297,
    298, 299, 300, 301, 302, 303, 304, 305,
    306, 307, 308, 309, 310, 312, 315, 316,
    317, 318, 319, 321, 325, 326, 327, 329,
    330, 331, 332, 333, 334, 335, 337, 343,
    345, 349, 351, 352, 353, 354, 355, 356,
    357, 360, 363, 365, 385, 386, 392, 399,
    402, 413, 415, 423, 437, 446, 450, 469,
    472, 473, 478, 482, 484, 510
Bechet, Sidney, xxxi, 125, 164, 177, 179,
    180, 181, 222, 243, 260, 272, 273, 334
Beethoven, Ludwig van, xxxvii, 310, 311,
    312, 447, 502, 503, 513
Beiderbecke, Bix, 174, 204, 222, 481
Belgium, 380, 440
Belgrave, Marcus, 494
Benin, 5, 53, 114
Berklee College of Music, 427, 481, 483
Berlin, 71, 79, 139, 140, 269, 274, 279, 380,
    409
Berlin, Ira, 71, 79

Bernal, Martin, 504
Bernstein, Leonard, 415, 484
Berry, Chu, 229, 263
Besmer, Fremont, 64
Beti, 25
Big Daddy Kane, 501
Bigu, 8
Bishop, Walter, 350
Black Music Radio, 478
Blackwell, Ed, 466
Blake, Eubie, 182
Blakey, Art, 44, 191, 259, 286, 327, 331,
    353, 376, 377, 384, 403, 418, 425, 426,
    446, 475, 482, 483, 484
Blanchard, Terence, 384, 482
Blanton, Jimmy, 161, 230, 321, 356, 381
Bley, Carla, 466
Bley, Paul, 377
Blount, Herman, 373
Blow, Kurtis, 498
Blue Note, 333, 396, 426, 446, 475
Blues, xx, xxi, xxii, xxiii, xxvi, xxvii, xxxii,
    xxxvi, xxxvii, 36, 39, 61, 67, 71, 72, 77,
    83, 84, 85, 86, 88, 91, 92, 94, 96, 102,
    105, 107, 118, 121, 122, 123, 124, 126,
    127, 129, 130, 131, 132, 133, 134, 135,
    136, 137, 147, 148, 152, 162, 164, 168,
    169, 170, 171, 172, 173, 174, 175, 177,
    178, 179, 181, 183, 185, 186, 188, 191,
    201, 202, 206, 210, 211, 214, 234, 236,
    245, 263, 266, 273, 279, 283, 291, 295,
    302, 303, 305, 308, 312, 313, 314, 318,
    322, 333, 335, 337, 353, 355, 358, 359,
    366, 367, 374, 386, 387, 399, 402, 412,
    415, 418, 419, 423, 424, 429, 438, 440,
    443, 450, 458, 460, 471, 472, 484, 486,
    499, 500, 502, 504, 510
Bluiett, Hamiett, 455
Blythe, Arthur, 363, 459, 493
Bolden, Buddy, xxxi, 148, 149, 180, 215,
    244
Bompili, 43
Boogie woogie, 159, 168, 186, 205, 402, 472
Bossa Nova, 63
Bostic, Earl, 263, 363, 414, 418, 460
Boston, 54, 72, 81, 106, 127, 145, 153, 219,
    252, 346, 370, 397, 427, 483, 508
Boston Massacre, 81
Bowie, Lester, 223, 412, 417, 434, 458, 495
Boykins, Ronnie, 376
Brackeen, Charles, 425
Braddy Williams, Pauline, 340
Brand, Dollar, 392
Braud, Wellman, 160
Braxton, Anthony, xxx, 270, 412, 452, 453,
    454, 460, 466, 484, 493
Brazil, 63, 66, 156, 157, 493
    Bahia, 63

Brazilian, 63, 127, 156, 339, 445, 446, 473, 493
Britain
British, 54, 63, 65, 66, 71, 79, 100, 105, 157, 230, 291, 303, 351
Broonzy, Big Bill, 91
Brown, Clifford, 328, 353, 361, 384
Brown, James, 442, 444, 447, 498
Brown, Marion, 474
Brown, Oscar, 478
Brown, Ray, 162, 268, 333, 361
Brubeck, David, 316, 357
Bryant, Ray, 384, 458
Bugisu, 42
Bugunda, 23
Bullroarer, 8, 9, 42
Bulungi, 23
Burial, 111, 147, 149
Bushmen, 31, 156
Butterbeans, 175, 374
Butzer, Karl, 16
Bwansi, 23
bwola, 23
Bwola, 23
Byard, Jaki, 118, 184, 380
Byas, Don, 262, 331
Byrd, Donald, 361, 384, 423, 446, 475, 501
Byron, Don, xxxii, 323, 494

C

Cables, George, 493
Cairo museum, 16
California
Oakland, 418, 419, 420, 431, 492, 493
San Francisco, xxv, 54, 79, 237, 259, 340, 346, 386, 396, 418, 419, 420, 437, 442, 444, 482, 490, 491, 492, 493, 494, 507
Call and response, 89
Calloway, Cab, 174, 194, 209, 223, 230, 239, 247, 258, 274, 301, 326
Cameroun, 25, 27
Campbell, Luther, 501
Caribbean, xxix, 62, 63, 64, 127, 214, 485
Carter, Benny, xxx, 181, 227, 248, 263, 282, 317, 340, 366, 461, 462
Carter, Betty, 339, 377, 392, 393, 403, 493, 494, 495
Carter, John, 462
Carter, Regina, 462, 497
Carter, Ron, 163, 358, 395, 423, 444, 455, 457, 458
Carver, Wayman, 267, 362, 461
Catlett, Big Sid, 340, 384
Celestin, Papa, 174, 253
Cello, 163, 378, 383, 417

Census, 77
Central African Republic, 24, 25
Chambers, Paul, 163, 356, 363, 365, 444, 475
Chambers, William, 69
Chant, 30, 67, 74, 114
Chari, 24
Charleston, The, 184
Charlie Parker, xxx, xxxv, xxxvii, 167, 293, 300, 302, 306, 307, 308, 309, 311, 312, 313, 315, 316, 317, 319, 320, 324, 326, 333, 338, 344, 346, 350, 351, 352, 392, 407, 422, 481, 486
Chechen Itza, 62
Cherry, Don, 367, 369, 397, 420, 422, 425, 440
Chesapeake Bay, 71
Chicago, xxxv, 102, 104, 117, 118, 134, 138, 146, 150, 152, 154, 159, 160, 170, 173, 175, 183, 186, 187, 189, 194, 202, 203, 204, 213, 220, 221, 222, 228, 236, 239, 240, 247, 249, 252, 254, 334, 335, 337, 340, 341, 349, 350, 360, 374, 375, 376, 377, 398, 411, 412, 413, 414, 417, 432, 434, 440, 453, 455, 461, 484, 487, 493, 507, 508
Chikona, 10
China, xxxix, 50, 62, 157, 467
Chord, xxii, xxiii, xxv, 39, 59, 79, 84, 125, 126, 135, 136, 141, 142, 144, 148, 160, 163, 171, 181, 183, 185, 186, 187, 188, 189, 190, 191, 192, 210, 211, 217, 234, 255, 257, 260, 261, 269, 275, 285, 300, 301, 302, 304, 305, 306, 310, 312, 333, 337, 344, 352, 355, 356, 357, 364, 366, 369, 375, 380, 382, 401, 411, 419, 420, 427, 441, 443, 450, 458, 459, 497, 504
Christian, Charlie, 190, 281, 284, 285, 286, 320, 341, 480
Christianity, xxi, 23, 60, 61, 64, 84, 105, 106, 113, 122, 192
Church, xx, 14, 15, 16, 18, 60, 61, 63, 64, 69, 70, 71, 72, 75, 78, 85, 86, 95, 99, 105, 106, 107, 108, 109, 110, 111, 112, 113, 114, 115, 134, 153, 173, 179, 186, 192, 193, 201, 205, 215, 252, 272, 304, 318, 328, 336, 338, 349, 374, 378, 386, 398, 417, 425, 434, 438, 444, 446, 505, 508
CIA, 510
Cinqué, 65
Civil War, xx, 60, 74, 79, 86, 89, 91, 92, 98, 148, 179, 201, 208, 298
Clapton, Eric, 500
Clarinet, 17, 133, 148, 152, 179, 180, 182, 183, 187, 194, 202, 217, 225, 231, 249, 273, 287, 305, 330, 362, 363, 377, 378, 380, 410, 418, 459, 461, 480, 491, 494
Clark, Charles, 411

Clarke, Kenny, 326, 333, 340, 353, 384

Clarke, Stanley, 480

Clayton, Buck, 265

Clef Club, 142, 143, 395

Cole, Nat King, 357

Coleman, Denardo, 483

Coleman, Ornette, xxviii, xxx, 113, 123,
    162, 356, 362, 367, 368, 370, 371, 376,
    380, 388, 397, 401, 405, 409, 410, 414,
    415, 418, 421, 434, 453, 454, 455, 459,
    466, 474, 483, 484, 486, 495

Coleman, Steve, 495

Coles, Johnny, 380

Collette, Buddy, 262, 353, 355, 362, 423,
    462

Collier, James Lincoln, 280, 287, 346, 400,
    434

Collins, Ray, 491

Coltrane, Alice, 404, 434

Coltrane, John, xxviii, xxx, xxxv, xxxvi,
    xxxviii, 113, 128, 163, 181, 263, 270,
    292, 302, 303, 310, 323, 326, 333, 334,
    346, 353, 355, 356, 358, 361, 362, 363,
    365, 366, 370, 371, 376, 377, 388, 392,
    393, 397, 398, 399, 400, 402, 403, 404,
    405, 406, 407, 408, 409, 410, 418, 419,
    420, 421, 422, 423, 425, 434, 438, 442,
    446, 447, 450, 454, 457, 459, 461, 470,
    471, 475, 479, 481, 486, 487, 490, 504,
    505

Columbia Records, 265, 339, 364, 379, 416,
    483, 513

Composition, 362, 376

Congo, 14, 17, 22, 23, 25, 27, 40, 43, 44, 57,
    86, 104, 111, 113, 114, 126, 127, 200,
    201, 461, 490
  Basongye, 44
  Congolese, 23, 71, 75, 105

Congo Square, 43, 86, 104, 111, 113, 200,
    201

Connecticut
  New Haven, 73
  Saybrook, 73

Cool J., L. L., 499

Cooper, Jerome, 412

Corea, Chick, 377, 444, 445, 453, 480

Cortes, 58

Counterpoint
  Imitative, 70

Cox, Anthony, 486

Cox, Ida, 170, 172, 173

Creole, 68, 104, 114, 148, 149, 152, 153,
    174, 186, 200, 221, 227, 231, 244, 253,
    269, 271, 287

Crouch, Stanley, 484

Cuba, 66, 112, 134, 157, 431, 467, 473

Curson, Ted, 470

Cyrille, Andrew, 423, 439

D

da Gama, Vasco, 62

Dahl, Linda, 10, 54, 194, 246, 266, 287,
    338, 342, 345, 425

Dahomey, 10, 27, 61, 66, 114

Daluka, 32

Dance, xix, xx, xxii, xxvii, xxxvii, xxxix, 2,
    3, 6, 10, 11, 12, 15, 17, 18, 23, 25, 33, 35,
    38, 39, 43, 47, 48, 58, 62, 63, 64, 67, 72,
    73, 74, 86, 89, 90, 92, 95, 96, 98, 100,
    102, 103, 104, 112, 125, 126, 127, 134,
    136, 137, 140, 142, 145, 146, 147, 156,
    160, 164, 171, 173, 180, 201, 203, 204,
    207, 213, 214, 223, 224, 226, 236, 237,
    239, 246, 249, 274, 275, 280, 282, 292,
    301, 304, 316, 327, 341, 343, 366, 372,
    402, 409, 421, 427, 429, 453, 472, 474,
    477, 490, 493
  Tribal, 28

Darfuk, 32

Davis, Arthur, 414, 415, 416, 417, 423, 483

Davis, Miles, xxii, xxviii, xxix, xxxi, 128,
    158, 163, 172, 181, 191, 219, 223, 285,
    291, 292, 308, 322, 324, 331, 350, 353,
    354, 355, 356, 357, 358, 360, 361, 362,
    366, 376, 384, 388, 392, 399, 401, 403,
    423, 424, 439, 440, 441, 444, 445, 458,
    461, 478, 480, 483, 505

Davis, Richard, 118, 494

Davis, Tiny, 251

Davis, Wild Bill, 180

Dee Gee, 378

Def Jam, 501

DeFranco, Buddy, 384

DeJohnette, Jack, 411, 441

Delaware, 77, 106

Delmark, 375, 453

Der, 28

Descartes, René, 73

Desmond, Paul, 262, 316, 357, 453

Detroit, 282, 299, 353, 382, 383, 404, 446,
    461, 494, 497

Dhuramoolan, 8

Diaspora, 1, 58, 82, 208, 315, 429

Diaz, Bartholomew, 62

Diaz, Bernal, 58

Dingi-dingi, 23

Diop, Cheikh Anta, 65

Dixon, Akua, 482

Dixon, Bill, 422

Dobeit, 32

Dodds, Baby, 152, 153, 157, 384, 424

Dodds, Johnny, 152, 153, 179, 202, 213,
    217

Dolphy, Eric, 162, 163, 362, 376, 378, 380, 401, 404, 405, 406, 407, 408, 409, 410, 418, 434, 459, 461, 471, 474, 486, 487

Donaldson, Lou, 315

Donegan, Dorothy, 188, 189, 251, 335, 337, 465, 483, 505

Dorham, Kenny, 331, 361, 384, 455, 466, 494

Dorsey, Jimmy, 224, 274, 320

Dorsey, Tommy, 224, 233, 248, 258, 320

Down Beat, 183, 189, 243, 281, 287, 309, 316, 322, 327, 340, 346, 361, 383, 388, 401, 406, 407, 408, 414, 426, 427, 434, 455, 470, 475, 479, 483, 491, 495, 513

Drone, 38, 163, 408, 491

Drum, xxi, 8, 10, 11, 12, 16, 17, 23, 24, 25, 27, 28, 32, 33, 34, 37, 41, 42, 43, 44, 54, 59, 60, 63, 64, 65, 71, 73, 77, 83, 86, 87, 92, 102, 105, 112, 113, 114, 115, 128, 142, 143, 147, 148, 149, 152, 153, 154, 156, 157, 158, 159, 161, 164, 178, 186, 200, 202, 225, 228, 235, 281, 305, 306, 308, 313, 331, 336, 341, 343, 350, 351, 353, 355, 356, 363, 368, 369, 370, 377, 380, 384, 385, 404, 408, 411, 412, 418, 419, 424, 426, 443, 467, 483, 486, 493, 500, 510

Barrel, 16

Bompili, 43

Congas, 491

Daluka, 32

Ingoma, 24

Maitu, 27

Membranophone, 43

Mona, 27

Motopae, 27

ngoma, 43

Zlet, 28

Du Bois, W. E. B., 49

Dutch, 71, 156

Duvivier, George, 197, 395

E

East Africa, 11, 22, 23, 37

Eckstine, Billy, 223, 308, 322, 326, 327, 329, 331, 338, 353, 384

Economics, xxviii, xxxii, xxxiv, xxxv, xxxix, 11, 12, 13, 47, 58, 63, 64, 67, 78, 89, 91, 92, 94, 97, 99, 102, 104, 142, 150, 167, 168, 173, 208, 212, 213, 236, 238, 292, 293, 301, 307, 319, 321, 328, 351, 352, 395, 406, 422, 423, 424, 437, 453, 498, 502, 503, 507, 510

Efik, 28

Egypt, xx, xxxviii, 4, 5, 6, 16, 17, 18, 22, 37, 47, 49, 54, 84, 109, 178, 294, 296, 504, 513

Abydos, 4

Edfu, 4

Egyptians, 4, 16, 17, 18, 32, 40, 47, 49, 115, 294, 296, 375, 504

Esna, 4

Kom Ombo, 4

Philae, 4

Upper, 16

Egyptian

MUSIC, 16

Ejagham, 28

Ekoi, 28

Ekpo, 28

Eldridge, Roy, 229, 326, 330, 342, 458, 461

Election Day, 71, 73

Elektra Musician, 480

Elima, 26

Ellington, Duke, xxv, xxvi, xxvii, xxix, xxxi, xxxv, xxxvi, xxxvii, 94, 95, 105, 128, 152, 154, 160, 161, 162, 176, 183, 184, 187, 188, 189, 191, 194, 199, 205, 209, 210, 217, 219, 223, 224, 228, 229, 230, 231, 233, 236, 239, 243, 245, 247, 248, 256, 257, 259, 262, 269, 270, 271, 272, 273, 274, 275, 276, 280, 281, 287, 292, 302, 308, 310, 321, 331, 340, 361, 369, 370, 378, 384, 386, 391, 399, 402, 422, 438, 441, 450, 452, 455, 469, 475, 481, 485, 486, 487, 493, 505

Ellis, Don, 163, 223, 429, 445

Emerge magazine, 388, 478, 508, 509, 513

Emhab, 17

English horn, 491

Enja, 380, 409

Ernstice, Wayne, 379

Ertegun, Nesuhi, 368, 480

Ervin, Booker, 378, 418, 426, 460

Ethiopia

Ethiopians, 4, 18, 19, 54, 99, 109, 238, 508

Ethnomusicology, 47

Eubanks, Charles, 486

Eubanks, Kevin, 286

Europe, James Reese, 142, 143, 144, 210, 307

Europeans, xix, xx, xxi, xxii, xxiii, xxvii, xxviii, xxxi, xxxii, xxxiii, xxxiv, xxxv, xxxvii, xxxviii, xxxix, 1, 2, 3, 4, 5, 6, 7, 8, 10, 11, 12, 13, 14, 21, 28, 31, 34, 36, 37, 39, 46, 47, 48, 52, 53, 57, 58, 59, 60, 61, 62, 63, 64, 65, 66, 67, 68, 69, 70, 71, 72, 73, 74, 75, 76, 77, 78, 81, 82, 83, 85, 86, 88, 89, 91, 92, 95, 96, 97, 98, 99, 100, 101, 102, 103, 104, 105, 106, 107, 108, 109, 110, 111, 112, 114, 115, 117, 118,

121, 122, 123, 124, 125, 126, 127, 128,
129, 130, 133, 135, 136, 137, 138, 139,
140, 141, 142, 144, 145, 146, 147, 148,
149, 150, 151, 154, 156, 157, 163, 167,
170, 173, 174, 176, 179, 180, 188, 192,
198, 199, 201, 202, 203, 208, 209, 211,
212, 213, 214, 218, 219, 222, 224, 232,
233, 236, 237, 239, 254, 255, 256, 269,
272, 273, 274, 276, 277, 278, 279, 280,
281, 284, 292, 293, 294, 295, 296, 297,
300, 303, 304, 307, 308, 311, 318, 319,
323, 331, 334, 336, 337, 343, 349, 350,
353, 355, 357, 367, 374, 378, 380, 385,
387, 391, 392, 396, 398, 400, 405, 406,
407, 411, 412, 415, 416, 422, 429, 431,
432, 440, 447, 453, 454, 458, 462, 465,
466, 468, 469, 470, 471, 472, 473, 475,
477, 479, 480, 483, 484, 485, 486, 487,
488, 491, 500, 501, 502, 503, 505, 506,
507, 508
Evans, Bill, xxxvi, 192, 443, 445, 458, 506
Evans, Gil, 223, 354, 355, 443, 444, 466
Exploitation, 1, xxviii, xxxvi, xxxvii, 1, 7,
57, 67, 130, 167, 170, 173, 179, 191, 212,
231, 232, 238, 294, 398, 462, 504

F

Farmer, Art, 457
Favors, Malachi, 413
Feather, Leonard, 240, 293, 329, 383, 385,
434, 446, 475
Ferguson, Maynard, 429
Few, Robert Bobby, 440
Fiddle, 31, 40, 64, 71, 73, 102, 125, 156,
169, 281, 460
Field hollers, xxii, 61, 76, 85, 179, 214, 471
Field song, 67
Finas, 45
Fitzgerald, Ella, 129, 267, 269, 283, 305,
338, 339, 340, 358, 403, 431, 461
Fitzhugh, George, 68, 298, 346
Flash, 498, 499
Florida, 131, 168, 174, 175, 207, 329, 374,
421
Floyd, Samuel, 77, 122, 164
Flugelhorn, 225, 331
Flute, 5, 10, 17, 39, 42, 43, 312, 353, 460,
462
    Alto, 462
    Bass, 462, 491
Fok, 25
Folk music, 505
Ford, Ricky, 378
Form, xix, xxi, xxii, xxiii, xxv, xxvi, xxvii,
xxix, xxxiii, xxxiv, xxxv, xxxvii, xxxix, 3,
6, 7, 12, 18, 22, 25, 30, 32, 34, 38, 39, 40,

42, 43, 44, 45, 48, 58, 59, 60, 61, 62, 65,
67, 73, 76, 78, 82, 83, 85, 86, 87, 88, 91,
94, 95, 97, 98, 100, 102, 103, 105, 106,
107, 112, 113, 114, 116, 118, 122, 123,
124, 126, 127, 128, 129, 130, 134, 136,
137, 139, 140, 144, 146, 147, 150, 152,
156, 158, 167, 168, 170, 171, 178, 179,
181, 182, 185, 187, 197, 200, 201, 202,
209, 210, 211, 217, 220, 223, 224, 237,
238, 243, 246, 247, 249, 256, 271, 272,
273, 274, 275, 277, 278, 279, 283, 284,
292, 295, 296, 298, 300, 305, 308, 310,
315, 318, 327, 333, 337, 338, 352, 353,
357, 358, 363, 366, 377, 378, 380, 386,
388, 391, 397, 398, 399, 401, 402, 406,
407, 409, 410, 414, 416, 424, 429, 431,
437, 438, 439, 441, 453, 459, 467, 468,
471, 472, 474, 477, 479, 481, 487, 490,
498, 499, 500, 501, 502, 503, 504, 505,
510, 513
Fusion, xxii, 67, 79, 164, 286, 353, 355,
358, 444, 445, 446, 460, 462, 472,
473, 474, 477, 479, 481, 498, 504
Foroolu, 45, 46
Fortune, Sonny, 442
Foster, Al, 442, 458
Foster, Frank, 362, 483
Foster, George Pops, 160, 161, 281
France, 69, 78, 127, 145, 198, 213, 272,
278, 280, 281, 317, 380, 412, 440, 446
    French, xxxii, 5, 66, 75, 76, 103, 104,
    126, 143, 144, 146, 147, 153, 157,
    164, 199, 201, 220, 272, 278, 303,
    333, 343, 354, 355, 385, 395, 404,
    440, 465, 493
Freeman, Bud, 204, 261
Freeman, Chico, 440
Freeman, Sharon, 465
Freemen, 77, 111
Fula, 25, 74
Fuller, Curtis, 377, 385
Funy, 33
Fusion, xxii, 67, 79, 164, 286, 353, 355,
358, 440, 444, 445, 446, 460, 462, 465,
472, 473, 474, 477, 479, 481, 498, 504

G

Gagaku, 44
Galien, 32
Gambia, xxxix, 27
Ganda, 22, 23
Garland, Red, 363, 475
Garner, Erroll, 191, 416
Garrett, Donald Rafael, 411
Garrison, Jimmy, 163
Garuri, 33

Genocide, xxxi, 58

Georgia, xx, 59, 71, 76, 77, 124, 131, 150, 152, 168, 221, 225, 252, 254, 257, 262, 267

Savannah, 76, 110, 152, 221

Germany, xxxi, 78, 157, 198, 280, 325, 380, 405, 440

Getz, Stan, 181, 199, 262, 321, 354, 378, 414, 426, 445, 506

Gewel, 77

Ghana, 5, 11, 27, 34, 39, 50, 51, 384, 431

Gibbs, Terry, 404

Gillespie, Dizzy, xxviii, 128, 156, 161, 162, 189, 190, 223, 259, 268, 285, 293, 297, 298, 300, 301, 305, 307, 308, 317, 324, 325, 326, 327, 328, 329, 330, 331, 332, 333, 334, 342, 346, 349, 353, 355, 363, 378, 384, 391, 393, 402, 403, 446, 455, 458, 461, 462, 468, 469, 473, 482

Gilmore, John, 363, 375, 376, 377

Girard, Adele, 383

Gitler, Ira, 351, 383, 388

Glasby, Vivian, 334

Gomez, Edgar, 426

Gonzales, Babs, 360

Gonzales, Michael A., 498, 513

Gonzalez, Jerry, 494

Goodman
Benny, xxxv, 234, 281, 479

Goodman, Benny, xxxv, 161, 172, 187, 199, 204, 224, 228, 229, 245, 258, 265, 274, 281, 285, 321, 329, 485, 506, 513

Gordon, Dexter, xxx, 162, 263, 329, 330, 362, 414, 425

Gordon, Maurita, 334

Gospel, xx, xxv, 86, 110, 116, 122, 134, 162, 168, 318, 387, 417, 438, 443, 458, 472, 502

Gottschalk, Louis, 69, 127

Grandmaster Flash, 499

Graves, Milford, 423

Gray, Wardell, 162, 262

Gray, William, 374

Great Britain, 5, 69, 70, 71, 74, 75, 78, 83, 85, 105, 126, 155, 273, 280, 295, 345, 429, 443, 491

Grebo, 28

Greece, xxxviii, 4, 5, 6, 22, 39, 49, 51, 54, 467, 504, 513

Green, Bennie, 163, 269

Greenwich Village, 376

Greer, Sonny, 184, 370

Griffin, Johnny, 330, 333, 362, 385

Grimes, Tiny, 256

Griot, xxxix, 21, 46, 107, 121, 293, 295

Gryce, Gigi, 395

Guinea, xx, 14, 22, 27, 35, 43, 72, 121

Guitar, xxix, 40, 91, 94, 122, 130, 133, 149, 153, 154, 163, 164, 169, 178, 187, 191, 202, 215, 225, 235, 283, 284, 285, 286, 305, 321, 337, 341, 342, 343, 344, 353, 382, 383, 385, 395, 401, 442, 443, 461, 480, 482, 499

Gumuz, 33

Guru, 446, 501

H

Haden, Charlie, 369, 466

Haiti, xxiii, 60, 61, 62, 66, 75, 104, 112, 113, 114, 115, 157

Limbe, 75

Hale, Corky, 383

Haley, Alex, 68, 437

Hamilton, Chico, 163, 462

Hampton, Lionel, 164, 281, 378, 403, 446, 482

Hancock, Herbie, 163, 358, 424, 444, 446, 455, 458, 459, 474, 484

Hand clapping, 33, 43, 60, 408

Handy, John, 378, 423, 490, 492

Handy, William Christopher, 96, 104, 131, 134, 135, 143, 182, 206, 210

Hargrove, Roy, 481, 488

Harlem, xxvi, xxvii, 92, 93, 94, 118, 141, 172, 177, 178, 183, 184, 192, 205, 206, 207, 208, 209, 223, 224, 230, 231, 240, 251, 252, 257, 267, 268, 271, 285, 301, 316, 318, 326, 333, 338, 352, 360, 392, 396, 431, 466, 468, 494, 498, 509

Harlem Renaissance, xxvi, 192, 207, 208, 209, 240, 271

Harmony, xxi, xxxviii, 5, 28, 48, 59, 82, 83, 85, 89, 108, 109, 122, 126, 135, 136, 137, 139, 141, 144, 147, 148, 159, 161, 163, 171, 182, 183, 189, 190, 191, 210, 211, 226, 256, 260, 261, 269, 283, 286, 294, 298, 300, 302, 303, 305, 310, 326, 328, 333, 337, 343, 344, 362, 366, 369, 382, 386, 401, 434, 438, 453, 454, 458, 459, 467, 472, 473, 486, 499, 504, 513

Harp, 6, 11, 17, 25, 40, 44, 46, 54, 77, 122, 154, 178, 382, 383, 401, 404, 490

Harper, Billy, 385, 466, 493

Harrell, Andre, 501

Harris, Barry, 483

Harris, Beaver, 422

Harris, Eddie, xxx

Harris, Gene, 191, 376

Harris, Teddy, 494

Harrison, Donald, 482

Harrison, Wendell, 393, 494

Hassies, 33

Hausa, 28, 30, 37, 42, 64, 74, 401, 429

Hawkins, Coleman, 150, 177, 181, 190, 197, 199, 207, 227, 228, 229, 234, 256, 259, 260, 261, 262, 282, 283, 308, 310, 329, 331, 333, 342, 357, 360, 362, 363, 405, 446, 454, 459, 507
Heath, Jimmy, 362, 363, 442
Heath, Percy, 331, 350, 353, 363, 368
Heavy D, 499
Hemiola, 43, 44, 182
Hemphill, Julius, 67, 363, 413, 455, 459
Henderson, Eddie, 492
Henderson, Fletcher, xxxi, 171, 174, 177, 205, 207, 223, 224, 227, 228, 229, 233, 234, 244, 245, 252, 260, 261, 262, 274, 282, 321, 334, 374, 384
Henderson, Horace, 374
Henderson, Joe, 362, 426, 444, 455, 457, 459, 474, 475, 492
Hendrix, Jimi, 285, 286, 398, 440, 442, 444
Herc, 498
Herman, Woody, 162, 224, 263, 331, 378, 429
Herodotus, 4, 491, 504, 513
Heron, Kim, 494
Hester, Karlton, 491, 492, 493, 494, 513
Higgins, Billy, 368, 369, 419
Hill Teddy, 245, 326
Hill, Andrew, 377, 423, 458, 474, 491, 492
Hindewhu, 27
Hindu drumming, 44
Hines, Earl, 184, 185, 188, 213, 223, 258, 274, 306, 308, 326, 338, 357, 461
Hip-hop, 498, 499, 500, 510
Hirt, Al, 483
Hispaniola, 61, 64
Ho, Fred, 494
Hodges, Johnny, 181, 262, 263, 281, 317, 320, 363, 414
Holiday, Billie, 84, 129, 162, 170, 234, 262, 264, 265, 266, 267, 281, 321, 322, 323, 329, 340, 346, 349, 403, 410, 487
Holland, Dave, 453
Homophony, 70
Honduras, 62
Hope, Elmo, 377, 458
Horne, Lena, 209, 239
Howard University, 272, 446, 449, 495
Howard, Noah, 440
Huang, Jason, 494
Hubbard, Freddie, 377, 384, 395, 447, 455, 493, 494
Humphrey, Bobbi, 462
Hutcherson, Bobby, 422, 475
Hymnody, 61

I

Ibibio, 28
Ice-T, 499
Idiophone, 11, 114
Ijala, 30
Illinois, 263, 325, 383, 460, 494
    Chicago, xxxv, 102, 104, 117, 118, 134, 138, 146, 150, 152, 154, 159, 160, 170, 173, 175, 183, 186, 187, 189, 194, 202, 203, 204, 213, 220, 221, 222, 228, 236, 239, 240, 247, 249, 252, 254, 334, 335, 337, 340, 341, 349, 350, 360, 374, 375, 376, 377, 398, 411, 412, 413, 414, 417, 432, 434, 440, 453, 455, 461, 484, 487, 493, 507, 508
Indentured servant, 69
Indian Ocean, 22, 62
Indiana, 79, 118, 282, 300, 494
Ingoma, 24
Instrument
    Bass, xxix, 34, 142, 157, 158, 159, 161, 164, 392, 404, 411, 413, 417, 482, 491
    Congas, 491
    Drum, 17, 23, 64, 65, 112, 467
    Fiddle, 40, 64, 71, 73
Instruments
    A-lal, 16
    Alkaita, 32
    Alto Saxophone, 263, 281, 308, 313, 317, 355, 363, 367, 368, 369, 377, 378, 380, 404, 411, 414, 421, 461, 480
    Awoka, 27
    Baloo, 46
    Bangia, 33
    Baritone horn, 144, 385, 404, 418
    Bassoon, 194, 402, 491
    Cello, 163, 378, 383, 417
    Clarinet, 17, 133, 148, 152, 179, 180, 182, 183, 187, 194, 202, 217, 225, 231, 249, 273, 287, 305, 330, 362, 363, 377, 378, 380, 410, 418, 459, 461, 480, 491, 494
    Daluka, 32
    Drum, xxi, 10, 11, 12, 16, 17, 23, 24, 25, 27, 28, 32, 33, 34, 37, 41, 42, 43, 44, 54, 59, 60, 63, 64, 71, 73, 83, 86, 92, 105, 113, 114, 142, 148, 149, 152, 153, 154, 156, 157, 158, 161, 164, 178, 200, 202, 225, 228, 235, 281, 308, 331, 336, 341, 343, 350, 351, 353, 355, 356, 363, 368, 369, 370, 377, 380, 384, 385, 404, 408, 411, 412, 418, 419, 426, 443, 483, 486, 493, 500
    English horn, 491

Fiddle, 31, 72, 73, 102, 125, 156, 169, 281, 460
Flugelhorn, 225, 331
Flute, 5, 10, 17, 39, 42, 43, 312, 353, 460, 462
Fok, 25
Guitar, xxix, 40, 91, 94, 122, 130, 133, 149, 153, 154, 163, 164, 169, 178, 187, 191, 202, 215, 225, 235, 283, 284, 285, 286, 305, 321, 337, 341, 342, 343, 344, 353, 382, 383, 385, 395, 401, 442, 443, 461, 480, 482, 499
Harp, 6, 11, 17, 25, 40, 44, 46, 54, 77, 122, 154, 178, 382, 383, 401, 404, 490
Hindewhu, 27
idiophone, 11, 114
Ingoma, 24
Kettledrum, 43
Kooraa, 46
Lute, 12, 17, 21, 40, 44, 46, 178, 194, 380, 383, 480
Maitu, 27
Mangaze, 27
Manza, 24
Membranophone, 43
Mona, 27
Motopae, 27
Mvet, 25, 46
Ngoma, 43
Nyungu, 42
Oboe, 144, 194, 461
Organ, xxii, 127, 154, 205, 206, 207, 244, 286, 320, 328, 383, 404, 417, 473, 494
Penah, 33
Rebec, 32
Sanza, 14, 24, 25, 31, 41
Saxophone, 154, 180, 181, 187, 225, 226, 260, 261, 262, 263, 281, 300, 308, 313, 315, 316, 317, 330, 331, 355, 358, 360, 362, 363, 365, 366, 367, 368, 369, 376, 377, 378, 380, 385, 400, 401, 404, 410, 411, 414, 418, 421, 423, 426, 440, 454, 455, 458, 459, 460, 461, 462, 480, 483, 487, 494
Trumpet, 10, 16, 17, 42, 153, 222, 224, 225, 233, 259, 429
Vibraphone, 191, 385, 404, 480
Violin, 68, 92, 101, 133, 149, 154, 158, 162, 252, 262, 374, 401, 412, 453, 461, 462, 480, 481, 490, 492, 494, 497
Xylophone, 11, 24, 37, 42, 46
Zlet, 28
Iowa, 222, 475, 494
Italy, 6, 9, 12, 72, 198, 291, 453
Venice, 12
Ituri, 25
Ivory Coast, 27, 35

Izenzon, David, 414

J

Jackson, Andrew, 81
Jackson, John G., 46
Jackson, Mahalia, 387
Jackson, Michael, 424, 509
Jackson, Milt, 330, 331, 353, 363
Jacquet, Illinois, 263, 325, 460
Jali, 46, 83, 295
Jalis, 45
Jaliyaa, 45
Jamaica, 60, 66, 115, 157, 193, 429
James, George G. M., 504
James, Harry, 224, 281, 383
Jamestown, 74
Japan, 392, 403, 427, 428, 441, 446, 481
Jarman, Joseph, 411, 413, 417, 440, 460, 495
Jarrett, Keith, 483, 486
Jazz at Lincoln Center, 488, 489, 513
Jazz Records, 378
Jefferson, Blind Lemon, 129, 133, 169
Jefferson, Eddie, 474
Jefferson, Hilton, 263
Jewish, xxxi, xxxii, 58, 109, 193, 231, 232, 280, 323, 350, 383
Jews, xxxi, xxxix, 58, 109, 232, 325, 508
Jim Crow, 98, 115, 116, 137, 176, 218, 308
John Hicks, 377, 481
Johnson, Budd, 262, 395
Johnson, Frank, 69, 100, 101
Johnson, J. J., 355
Johnson, James P., 183
Johnson, Michael, 509
Jones, Elvin, 44, 118, 158, 314, 315, 457, 474, 487
Jones, Hank, 494, 495
Jones, Jo, 308, 340
Jones, Philly Joe, 331, 333, 350, 363, 440
Jones, Quincy, 329, 355, 378, 478, 484, 501
Joplin, Janis, 398
Joplin, Scott, xxxi, xxxv, 103, 138, 140, 141, 182, 189, 205, 416
Jordan, Clifford, 378, 380
Jordan, Duke, 331
Jordan, Kent, 462
Jordan, Louis, xxxvii, 170, 185, 267, 283, 358, 359, 360, 402
Jordan, Marlon, 481
Jordan, Michael, 509
Jordan, Sheila, 339, 493
Jordan, Winthrop, 69
juba, 87, 88
Juba, 1, 87, 88, 92, 127
Julliard, 331

K

Kalahari Desert, 31
Kanem-Bornu, 5
Kansas
    Kansas City, 141, 146, 150, 170, 206,
        213, 223, 234, 235, 257, 259, 261,
        308, 320, 326, 329, 334, 393, 417, 466
Kansas City, 141, 146, 150, 170, 206, 213,
    223, 234, 235, 257, 259, 261, 308, 320,
    326, 329, 334, 393, 417, 466
Karamojang, 23
Karankeolu, 45
Kelly, Ed, 492, 493
Kenton, Stan, 223, 224, 343, 357, 429, 469,
    507
Kenya, xxiii, 22, 39
Kettledrum, 43
Keyboard, 126, 183, 185, 187, 190, 191,
    235, 254, 256, 284, 286, 366, 484, 491
Keystone Korner, 396, 493
Khan, Ali Akbar, 397, 490
Khoisans, 6
Khufu, 6
Kiga, 23
Kija, 42
King of Swing, xxxv, 234, 281, 479
King Oliver, 152, 153, 157, 159, 180, 186,
    213, 215, 217, 221, 222, 238, 244, 458
King, Leonard, 494
King, Martin Luther, 417, 431, 432, 509
Kírári, 64
Kirby, John, 158, 160, 338
Kirk, Andy, 187, 248, 257, 258, 259, 283,
    330, 334
Kirk, Rahsaan Roland, 84, 118, 323, 376,
    378, 398, 460, 462, 487
Kitosi, 42
KJAZ, 492
KMEL, 492
KMPX, 492
Konitz, Lee, 181, 262, 337, 343, 354, 355,
    453, 466
Kool Jazz Festival, 480
Kooraa, 46
Kordufan, 32
Kpelle, 28
Kralin, 28
Kronos Quartet, 493
KRS-One, 499
Kru, 28
Krupa, Gene, 158, 224, 281, 322, 340, 384
Kufo, 25
Kujur, 33
Kush, 16, 18, 49

L

L'Ouverture, Toussaint, 75, 76
La Rocca, Dominick James, 222
Labor, 6, 7, 57, 58, 60, 63, 64, 67, 69, 71,
    76, 81, 86, 91, 92, 93, 99, 112, 208, 218,
    238, 291, 309, 351, 352, 508
Ladnier, Tommy, 133
Lake Chad, 27, 52, 74
Lake, Oliver, 67, 363, 413, 455, 459, 466,
    493, 495
Lali, 25
LaPorta, John, 378
Laraka oraka, 23
Last Poets, The, 499, 500, 501
Lateef, Yusef, 362, 378, 395, 402, 423, 425,
    459, 461, 474
Latin America, 63, 114, 193, 202, 313, 329,
    343, 355
Laws, Hubert, 462, 465, 483
Leclerc, 75
Lee, Sonny, 373
Lefkowitz, 4, 504, 513
Lewis, John, 127, 353, 354, 357, 368, 397
Lewis, Ramsey, 444, 458
Liberia, 27, 28, 40
Libya, 16, 32
    Desert, 16, 32
Lincoln Center, 372, 488, 489, 513
Linda music, 24
Lining out, 61
Liston, Melba, 330, 395, 434
Little, Booker, 405, 484
Lloyd, Charles, 376
Locke, Alaine, 58, 79
Long Island, 72, 370
Lorenzo, Jose, 493
Lowa, 28
Luke Records, 501
Lunceford, Jimmy, 223, 233, 245, 321, 505
Lundquist, Barbara Reeder, 46
Lundvall, Bruce, 481
Lute, 12, 17, 21, 40, 44, 46, 178, 194, 380,
    383, 480
Lyons, Jimmy, 370, 423

M

Mabern, Harold, 481
Macero, Teo, 378
Macumban, 63
Mahass, 32
Maiden Voyage, 458, 459
Mailer, Norman, 387
Maitu, 27
Makanda, xxviii, 97, 167, 423
Makandal, 75

Makeba, Mariam, 397

Mali, 5, 11, 27, 51

Mandel, Howard, 495

Mandela, Nelson, 508

Mandingo, 51, 62

Mandinka, xxxix, 45

Mangaze, 27

Manhattan, 71, 72, 163, 198, 231, 240, 446, 465

Mann, Herbie, 362, 445, 462

Mansa Musa, Emperor, 62

Manumission, 75, 77, 507

Manza, 24

Marable, Fate, 157, 220

Mardom, 33

Maroons, 65, 71, 75

Marriage, xxxiv, 18, 28, 33, 45, 57, 68, 69, 70, 107, 168, 187, 268, 315

Mars, 378

Marsalis, Branford, 286, 362, 363, 385, 459, 482, 483, 484, 513

Marsalis, Delfeayo, 483

Marsalis, Ellis, 494

Marsalis, Wynton, 152, 222, 328, 384, 465, 481, 483, 484, 485, 487, 488, 489, 498, 513

Marsh, Warne, 337, 453

Martin, Bill, 374

Maryland, 69, 71, 412

Masakela, Hugh, 397

Massachusetts, 71, 167, 252, 397, 422, 431
    Boston, 54, 72, 81, 106, 127, 145, 153, 219, 252, 346, 370, 397, 427, 483, 508

Matriarch, 12, 200

Mauretania, 27

Mayberry, Don, 494

Mbanza, 23

M-Base Collective, 495

Mbgwana, 25

Mbuti, 27

McBee, Cecil, 487

McBride, Christian, 482

McCall, Steve, 411

McDuff, Jack, 286, 482, 494

McFerrin, Bobby, 493

McGhee, Howard, 330

McIntyre, Ken, xxviii, 97, 167, 423

McKinney, Harold, 103, 194, 494

McLean, Jackie, 315, 378, 384, 423, 426

McPartland, Jimmy, 204

McPartland, Marian, 251, 357, 428

McRae, Carmen, 266, 329, 339, 340, 482

McShann, Jay, 223, 308

Mélange, 68, 104, 201

Melisma, 27

Melody, xxi, xxiv, xxix, 2, 21, 32, 34, 39, 40, 41, 59, 60, 79, 82, 83, 88, 89, 91, 95, 102, 109, 112, 118, 134, 135, 136, 137, 139, 140, 141, 142, 144, 148, 150, 155, 161, 163, 164, 170, 177, 182, 183, 185, 189, 190, 191, 201, 202, 206, 211, 217, 226, 233, 246, 255, 256, 260, 261, 264, 268, 270, 272, 280, 286, 287, 295, 296, 297, 298, 300, 302, 305, 306, 310, 311, 312, 334, 337, 339, 344, 352, 355, 356, 357, 369, 379, 380, 386, 402, 408, 410, 411, 413, 443, 445, 450, 452, 459, 467, 472, 499, 504, 506

Melting pot, 68

Menats, 17

Mendou, 25

Merewetiks, 32

Meter, 313

Metronism, 43

Mexico, 62, 66, 82, 134, 178, 184, 249, 490, 504
    Chichen Itza, 62
    La Venta, 62

Mezquitas, 58

Michigan
    Detroit, 282, 299, 353, 382, 383, 404, 446, 461, 494, 497

Microtone, 82, 399

Middle Passage, 64, 74, 75, 102, 114

Miley, Bubber, 177, 230

Miller, Glenn, 224, 226, 233, 236, 507

Millinder, Lucky, 178, 213, 333, 384, 461

Mills College, 493

Mingus Jazz Workshop, 378, 487

Mingus, Charles, xxxi, 162, 270, 320, 323, 331, 377, 378, 379, 380, 392, 393, 402, 416, 422, 427, 444, 451, 455, 466, 475, 487, 505

Minnesota, 494

Minstrel show, 89, 95, 98, 99, 102, 126, 131, 132, 137, 138, 179, 214, 344

Miscegenation, 63, 70

Mississippi, 101, 102, 125, 129, 168, 171, 185, 200, 201, 204, 206, 213, 220, 237, 249, 349, 350, 367, 387, 412, 413, 431, 500
    Delta, 200, 201, 213, 249, 500

Mitchell, Roscoe, 412, 460

Mobley, Hank, 262, 384, 418

Modern Jazz Quartet, 353, 357, 360, 368, 487

Molasses, 64

Molimo, 26

Mona, 27

Monk, T. S., 292, 346, 483

Monk, Thelonius, xxxv, 164, 188, 189, 190, 191, 260, 285, 292, 300, 305, 326, 329, 331, 332, 333, 334, 346, 353, 357, 360, 361, 365, 366, 371, 384, 403, 413, 446, 458, 462, 471, 474, 483, 486, 489, 494, 495

Montgomery, Wes, 285, 286, 353, 382
Moody, James, 262, 331, 461
Moore, Charles, 494
Moors, 5, 6, 54, 58, 62
Moreira, Airto, 156, 493
Morgan, Lee, 376, 377, 384
Morton, Jelly Roll, xxxi, xxxv, 136, 149, 150, 152, 159, 181, 182, 183, 214, 216, 217, 225, 244, 505
Moshembe da, 33
Mosque, 58
Moten, Bennie, 223, 234, 250, 261, 321
Motopae, 27
Mount Fuji Festival, 481
Moye, Don, 412
Mozart, Wolfgang Amadeus, xxxvii, 5, 273, 310, 312, 447, 480, 485, 502
Mulligan, Gerry, 262, 354
Murray, David, 362, 363, 455, 459, 466, 480
Music
  EGYPTIAN, 16
Muslim, 64, 74, 79, 401, 457
Myers, Amina Claudine, 417, 480

N

Nankasa, 23
Napoleon, 75
National Public Radio, 385
Native American, xxi, xxxii, xxxiii, xxxvi, 58, 62, 66, 67, 69, 71, 76, 82, 110, 115, 199, 218, 232, 323, 509
Navarro, Fats, 321, 328, 329, 331, 360, 480
Nboemboe, 25
Negro, xxiv, xxx, xxxiii, 49, 58, 68, 69, 70, 76, 77, 79, 84, 86, 88, 92, 96, 98, 102, 107, 108, 109, 110, 111, 116, 118, 122, 126, 127, 128, 137, 142, 143, 144, 145, 157, 174, 177, 193, 194, 200, 207, 208, 231, 238, 240, 244, 270, 272, 274, 275, 276, 277, 322, 335, 367, 387, 424, 431, 460, 467, 469, 502, 506, 513
Nelson, Havelock, 498, 513
Nelson, Oliver, 355, 405, 426
Neolithic era, 16
Netherlands, 69, 71
  Dutch, 71, 156
New England, 61, 64, 73, 78, 105, 127, 154, 370, 397
New Jersey, 72, 167, 234, 248, 498, 508
New Orleans, xxxv, 63, 68, 76, 79, 86, 99, 104, 111, 127, 131, 146, 147, 148, 149, 150, 152, 153, 157, 158, 159, 164, 170, 173, 174, 175, 176, 180, 181, 182, 183, 186, 187, 194, 199, 200, 201, 202, 203, 204, 213, 214, 215, 216, 217, 220, 221, 222, 225, 226, 227, 235, 238, 239, 240, 244, 253, 267, 281, 287, 301, 305, 306, 307, 334, 344, 345, 367, 410, 450, 472, 481, 482, 483
New World, xx, xxiii, xxxiii, 3, 48, 58, 60, 62, 63, 65, 66, 67, 74, 75, 82, 112, 127, 200, 206, 208, 283, 468, 473, 506, 511
New York, xxvii, 54, 71, 79, 92, 94, 98, 100, 101, 103, 106, 108, 109, 118, 126, 134, 138, 142, 143, 145, 146, 150, 154, 155, 163, 164, 167, 168, 169, 171, 174, 175, 177, 184, 187, 189, 193, 194, 197, 202, 204, 205, 206, 207, 208, 213, 221, 222, 223, 226, 227, 228, 230, 234, 235, 236, 239, 240, 248, 250, 251, 252, 254, 256, 259, 266, 267, 270, 272, 279, 287, 298, 299, 301, 308, 321, 322, 323, 326, 329, 330, 332, 336, 337, 338, 339, 341, 342, 344, 346, 350, 353, 357, 358, 360, 365, 368, 369, 370, 371, 372, 376, 378, 380, 386, 388, 391, 392, 395, 397, 398, 402, 409, 411, 414, 415, 416, 417, 419, 420, 421, 422, 425, 426, 427, 428, 434, 439, 440, 445, 451, 454, 461, 465, 466, 467, 468, 475, 481, 482, 483, 487, 490, 493, 494, 495, 497, 498, 501, 505, 509, 513
  Greenwich Village, 376
  Harlem, xxvi, xxvii, 92, 93, 94, 118, 141, 172, 177, 178, 183, 184, 192, 205, 206, 207, 208, 209, 223, 224, 230, 231, 240, 251, 252, 257, 267, 268, 271, 285, 301, 316, 318, 326, 333, 338, 352, 360, 392, 396, 431, 466, 468, 494, 498, 509
  Long Island, 72, 370
  Manhattan, 71, 72, 163, 198, 231, 240, 446, 465
  New York City, xxvii, 92, 94, 98, 100, 101, 103, 126, 143, 154, 169, 175, 187, 198, 205, 208, 222, 223, 226, 234, 239, 254, 259, 299, 308, 321, 329, 336, 353, 357, 358, 369, 397, 398, 402, 411, 417, 451, 465, 466, 467, 468, 490
New York City, xxvii, 92, 94, 98, 100, 101, 103, 126, 143, 154, 169, 175, 187, 198, 205, 208, 222, 223, 226, 234, 239, 254, 259, 299, 308, 321, 329, 336, 353, 357, 358, 369, 397, 398, 402, 411, 417, 451, 465, 466, 467, 468, 490
Newborn, Phineas, 189, 385
Newman, Joe, 329
Newton, James, 462, 466, 491
Nicaragua, 437, 493
Nichols, Herbie, 458, 470, 495
Nichols, Red, 274
Niger, 23, 27, 43, 51

Nigeria, 11, 27, 28, 30, 32, 34, 37, 42, 53, 63, 64, 114, 384, 401
Nigerian
   Nigerian, 28, 34, 391
Nile River, 32
Nketia, J. H. Kwabena, 11, 82, 118
Nkole, 42
Nkumbi, 26
North America, 28, 43, 58, 71, 74, 79, 104, 137, 156, 471
North Dakota, 167, 494
Norvo, Red, 161, 378
Nubia, 5, 16, 18, 32, 49, 50
   Nubians, 16, 18, 32, 50
Numoolu, 45
Nyungu, 42

O

O'Day, Anita, 339
Oakland, 418, 419, 420, 431, 492, 493
Oboe, 144, 194, 461
Octoroon, 68
Ohio, 93, 101, 167, 254, 423, 432, 454, 494
Olatunji, Babatunde, 156, 377, 391, 395, 397
Oliver, Joe, 150, 152, 153, 157, 159, 180, 186, 213, 215, 217, 220, 221, 222, 238, 244, 253, 254, 458
Olmstead, F. L., 68, 79
Olorun, 468
Onomatopoetic repetition, 27
Oppression, xxi, xxviii, xxxiv, 7, 13, 15, 58, 60, 77, 96, 97, 107, 109, 116, 125, 140, 173, 319, 422, 472, 474, 502, 503, 508
Organ, xxii, 127, 154, 205, 206, 207, 244, 286, 320, 328, 383, 404, 417, 473, 494
Ory, Kid, 133, 220, 378
Osborne, Mary, 341
Ostinato, 38
Oubangui, 24
Ovamboland, 31
Owens, Jimmy, 494
Ozawa, Seiji, 484

P

Page, Oran Hot Lips, 461
Page, Walter, 160, 281, 381
Palaeolithic, 18
Pan-Afrikan Peoples Arkestra, 469
Panama, 62, 141
Pappenheimers, 78
Parallel fifth, 27
Parker, Charlie, xxviii, xxx, xxxv, xxxvii, 67, 156, 162, 167, 199, 261, 263, 293, 297, 298, 299, 300, 302, 305, 306, 307, 308, 309, 310, 311, 312, 313, 315, 316, 317, 319, 320, 321, 324, 325, 326, 331, 332, 333, 334, 338, 344, 346, 350, 351, 352, 353, 355, 360, 362, 363, 369, 378, 384, 391, 392, 393, 403, 407, 410, 414, 422, 423, 425, 426, 446, 454, 458, 459, 473, 475, 480, 481, 486, 487
Parker, Leo, 308
Patriarchy, 12
Payne, Cecil, 395
Penah, 33
Pennsylvania, 71, 107, 167, 169
   Philadelphia, 1, 72, 85, 101, 106, 107, 108, 299, 322, 323, 326, 346, 353, 397, 457
Pentecost Sunday, 71
Pepper, Art, 315, 343, 494
Pergolesi, Giovanni Battista, 72
Persip, Charlie, 395
Peterson, Oscar, 162, 189, 191, 269, 385, 427, 473
Peterson, Ralph, 495
Pettiford, Oscar, 162, 381
Philadelphia, 1, 72, 85, 101, 106, 107, 108, 299, 322, 323, 326, 346, 353, 397, 457
Philippines, 493
Piano, xxii, 14, 25, 39, 78, 81, 85, 91, 94, 98, 101, 102, 103, 116, 127, 131, 133, 136, 138, 139, 142, 148, 149, 150, 152, 153, 154, 158, 160, 161, 170, 171, 173, 177, 179, 181, 182, 183, 184, 185, 186, 187, 188, 189, 190, 191, 202, 205, 206, 210, 214, 215, 216, 217, 222, 225, 227, 228, 229, 234, 235, 236, 238, 244, 248, 252, 253, 254, 255, 256, 257, 262, 270, 281, 284, 285, 286, 305, 308, 328, 331, 332, 333, 334, 335, 337, 338, 339, 341, 344, 353, 357, 360, 365, 366, 367, 368, 372, 374, 375, 377, 378, 380, 383, 384, 385, 386, 392, 403, 404, 417, 418, 426, 427, 428, 443, 444, 445, 457, 458, 465, 472, 481, 482, 484, 486, 491
Pinkster, 71, 72
   Day, 71
Pitch, 112
Plantation, xxxvii, 7, 58, 59, 65, 68, 69, 71, 73, 75, 76, 78, 83, 84, 87, 89, 91, 92, 93, 98, 99, 102, 107, 111, 126, 137, 156, 204, 213, 314, 344, 351, 407
Plato, 91, 479
Play song, 26, 73, 74, 212
Polyphony, xxix, 27, 36, 38, 39, 41, 60, 67, 121, 152, 181, 183, 187, 202, 217, 243, 305, 441, 466
Polyrhythm, xxii, 41, 43, 44, 45, 59, 60, 63, 70, 116, 128, 135, 158, 297, 313, 314, 315, 381
   African, xxi, xxx, 59, 313, 315

Port Elizabeth, 31
Portugal, 23, 28, 31, 32, 63, 66, 157
Powell, Bud, 185, 188, 189, 190, 255, 300,
    305, 306, 320, 329, 332, 357, 360, 378,
    384, 385, 386, 404, 425, 445
Predynastic era, 16
Psalmody, 61
Public Enemy, xx, 499, 501
Puente, Tito, 455, 493
Pulitzer Prize, 484
Pullen, Don, 378, 425, 487
Purcell, John, 455
Pygmy, 14, 22, 25, 26, 27
    BaBenzele, 27
    Babinga, 27
    Mbuti, 27

Q

Quakers, 77, 101, 107, 111
Quebec, Ike, 263
Queen Latifah, 499

R

Ra, Sun, xxiii, xxx, xxxv, xxxvi, 162, 228,
    229, 363, 366, 372, 373, 374, 375, 376,
    377, 391, 392, 393, 398, 401, 487, 493
Racism, 1, xxxiv, xxxv, xxxvii, xxxviii,
    xxxix, 4, 12, 13, 47, 97, 105, 124, 140,
    199, 204, 232, 251, 278, 279, 282, 293,
    298, 304, 308, 319, 367, 407, 416, 437,
    451, 475, 479, 501, 502, 503, 505, 507,
    510
Ragtime, xxii, xxxv, xxxvi, 79, 89, 92, 95,
    96, 98, 100, 102, 103, 105, 116, 118, 121,
    124, 126, 129, 137, 138, 139, 140, 141,
    142, 143, 145, 146, 148, 150, 155, 158,
    159, 168, 179, 181, 182, 183, 184, 185,
    186, 189, 193, 201, 203, 204, 205, 210,
    211, 214, 234, 238, 278, 279, 291, 313,
    334, 335, 392, 402, 472, 478
Rainey, Gertrude, 129, 130, 131, 132, 133,
    164, 170, 171, 175, 179, 210
Ranelin, Phil, 494
Rap, xx, xxii, 91, 472, 475, 477, 483, 498,
    499, 500, 501, 513
Reardon, Caspar, 383
Rebec, 32
Rebirth Inc., 494
Red Hot Peppers, 183
Redman, Dewey, 363, 414, 459, 483, 486,
    495
Redman, Don, 133, 207, 223, 227, 274, 282
Redman, Joshua, 363, 415, 483, 486
Reinhardt, Django, 280, 285

Religion, xx, xxi, xxv, xxxiii, 3, 5, 7, 11, 12,
    13, 15, 17, 20, 21, 26, 36, 37, 48, 57, 58,
    60, 61, 63, 64, 68, 71, 72, 74, 75, 77, 79,
    86, 90, 96, 104, 105, 106, 107, 108, 109,
    110, 112, 113, 114, 115, 146, 156, 172,
    179, 188, 192, 200, 201, 258, 259, 310,
    314, 318, 328, 339, 366, 373, 387, 420,
    421, 430, 437, 438, 457, 467, 468, 499
    Catholic, 18, 63, 64, 75, 112, 113, 115,
        157, 168, 188, 199, 200, 387
    Christianity, xxi, 23, 60, 61, 64, 84, 105,
        106, 113, 122, 192
    Lutheran, 387
    Pentecost, 71, 72, 114, 192, 378
    Protestant, xx, 14, 63, 105, 106, 108,
        112, 199, 214
    Roman Catholic Church, 64, 113, 115
Renaissance, 12, 70, 79, 192, 207, 208, 209,
    240, 271, 406
Revolution, 72, 74, 75, 105, 111, 237, 298
Rhythm, xxi, xxii, xxv, xxvi, xxviii, xxxvii,
    2, 7, 8, 11, 21, 22, 23, 28, 33, 34, 37, 41,
    42, 43, 48, 60, 64, 70, 73, 83, 87, 88, 89,
    90, 93, 102, 103, 104, 107, 111, 112, 114,
    121, 122, 130, 136, 137, 138, 141, 142,
    143, 147, 148, 150, 156, 158, 159, 160,
    161, 162, 163, 167, 170, 182, 183, 185,
    187, 189, 201, 202, 204, 210, 211, 213,
    217, 222, 224, 226, 234, 235, 236, 237,
    247, 249, 250, 251, 252, 254, 256, 257,
    261, 263, 269, 270, 278, 285, 286, 287,
    296, 298, 302, 304, 305, 306, 312, 313,
    315, 327, 328, 333, 335, 337, 340, 346,
    356, 358, 359, 365, 366, 367, 385, 395,
    399, 402, 403, 406, 409, 411, 412, 414,
    418, 419, 424, 429, 440, 442, 443, 444,
    445, 450, 460, 461, 467, 472, 473, 494,
    499, 500, 502, 504, 506, 513
Rich, Buddy, 345
Richardson, Jerome, 395
Richmond, Dannie, 378, 380
Rivers, Sam, 362, 439, 459, 462, 466, 470,
    487
Roach, Max, 44, 158, 314, 315, 320, 328,
    331, 332, 355, 361, 378, 395, 422, 423,
    424, 426, 446, 461
Robinson, Sylvia, 501
Rock, xxxviii, 164, 168, 178, 236, 259, 285,
    297, 355, 358, 392, 398, 413, 418, 419,
    429, 440, 445, 472, 477, 481, 482, 498,
    504, 507
Rock and roll, xxxvii, 236, 285, 472, 477,
    481, 482, 504
Rogers, Milton Shorty, 343
Rolfe, John, 74
Rollins, Sonny, 67, 262, 322, 350, 353, 358,
    360, 362, 363, 365, 376, 418, 425, 426,
    446, 458, 459

Roney, Wallace, 495
Roulette Records, 395
Rouse, Charlie, 333, 362, 484
Ruanda, 36, 37, 40, 44
Rubin, Paul, 379
Rublowsky, John, 10
Rudd, Roswell Hopkins, 422
Rugolo, Pete, 343
Rum, 64
Running Wild, *184*
Rushing, Jimmy, 236
Russell, George, xxx, 353, 423, 466

S

Sachs, Curt, 16, 54
Sadownnick, Danny, 486
Sahara, xxii, 5, 6, 14, 32, 359
Saint John's Parish, 59
Saint-Domingue, 75, 76
Salt-n-Pepa, 499
Samba, 63
San Francisco, xxv, 54, 79, 237, 259, 340,
    346, 386, 396, 418, 419, 420, 437, 442,
    444, 482, 490, 491, 492, 493, 494, 507
Sanborn, David, 484
Sanders, Pharoah, 270, 362, 376, 377, 444,
    493
Sangha, 27
Santamaria, Mongo, 156, 315, 327, 397,
    445, 462
Santana, Carlos, 398
Santeria, 112, 467
Sanza, 14, 24, 25, 31, 41
Saturn Records, 375
Savannah, 76, 110, 152, 221
Savoy Ballroom, 89, 268, 308, 374
Saxophone, 154, 180, 181, 187, 194, 225,
    226, 252, 259, 260, 261, 262, 263, 281,
    300, 308, 313, 315, 316, 317, 330, 331,
    353, 355, 356, 358, 360, 362, 363, 365,
    366, 367, 368, 369, 376, 377, 378, 380,
    385, 400, 401, 404, 410, 411, 414, 418,
    421, 423, 426, 440, 453, 454, 455, 458,
    459, 460, 461, 462, 480, 483, 486, 487,
    494
  Alto, 187, 194, 233, 263, 281, 292, 308,
      313, 315, 317, 320, 353, 355, 356,
      358, 362, 363, 367, 368, 369, 377,
      378, 380, 404, 411, 414, 421, 453,
      454, 461, 480, 486, 490
  Baritone, 308, 355, 404, 480
  Soprano, 180, 181, 362, 483
  Tenor, 154, 227, 233, 248, 251, 259, 260,
      261, 262, 263, 281, 283, 330, 331,
      353, 356, 360, 361, 362, 365, 366,
      367, 376, 378, 380, 385, 404, 405,
      411, 414, 417, 418, 440, 461, 462,
      474, 480, 486, 487
Scale, xxii, xxiii, xxiv, xxv, xxxi, 37, 39, 59,
    73, 85, 134, 135, 250, 251, 260, 293, 302,
    303, 305, 310, 312, 364, 401, 409, 419,
    434, 451, 467, 473
Scandinavia, 380
Schoenberg, Arnold, 28, 139, 293, 335, 353,
    430
Schuller, Gunther, 217, 229, 240, 353, 355,
    451, 475, 485
Scott, James, 141
Sebei, 42
Senegal, 27, 65, 66, 74, 103, 157
Senufo, 44
Sertima, Ivan Van, 62, 504
Setzer, Brian, 479
Sexism, 1, xxxiv, xxxvi, xxxviii, xxxix, 9,
    12, 13, 47, 57, 154, 502
Shaigai, 32
Shank, Bud, 315, 343, 462, 473
Shankar, Ravi, 397, 490
Shaw, Artie, 224, 246, 266, 322, 323
Shearing, George, 189, 191
Shepp, Archie, 377, 397, 421, 440, 482
Shilluka, 33
Shorter, Wayne, 163, 357, 358, 362, 385,
    388, 445
Shouts, 74
Siddik, Rasul, 492
Sidran, Ben, 397, 485, 513
Sierra Leone, 27
Silver, Horace, 191, 331, 353, 384, 393,
    396, 402, 418, 426, 444, 445, 455, 458,
    472, 493, 507
Silveto, 396
Simmons, Huey Sonny, 121, 419, 491, 493
Simmons, Russell, 501
Sims, Zoot, 262
Singing, xxi, xxii, xxiii, xxiv, xxxvii, 6, 10,
    12, 17, 18, 21, 22, 27, 31, 32, 33, 35, 37,
    38, 39, 42, 44, 45, 46, 49, 60, 61, 62, 63,
    64, 67, 70, 71, 73, 77, 78, 83, 85, 87, 89,
    91, 93, 95, 96, 97, 98, 101, 105, 107, 108,
    109, 113, 122, 125, 126, 131, 132, 134,
    135, 136, 137, 142, 147, 149, 155, 161,
    162, 169, 170, 171, 172, 174, 177, 178,
    186, 200, 204, 214, 217, 234, 238, 249,
    253, 263, 265, 267, 268, 286, 295, 296,
    322, 323, 338, 339, 340, 349, 387, 402,
    403, 417, 418, 471, 482
Singleton, Zutty, 168, 281, 356
Sirone (Norris Jones), 440
Slave
  Mentality, xxviii, 4
Slavery, xx, xxix, xxxiii, xxxvii, xxxix, 4, 6,
    21, 27, 43, 57, 58, 59, 61, 63, 67, 68, 69,
    77, 81, 82, 84, 87, 91, 101, 110, 112, 124,

126, 167, 201, 208, 232, 237, 314, 367, 429, 504, 509
Breakers, 64
European, 7, 65
Owner, 60, 63, 68, 70, 71, 75, 78, 314, 407
Runaway, 75, 76
Slave
    trade, xx, 3, 6, 10, 13, 25, 27, 46, 48, 62, 63, 64, 65, 67, 69, 70, 477
Slave era, xx, xxi, xxxiv, xxxviii, xxxix, 1, 3, 14, 15, 34, 49, 57, 60, 63, 64, 77, 78
Slaves, xxviii, 3, 21, 28, 43, 59, 61, 63, 73, 76, 79, 82, 85, 87, 89, 92, 115, 156, 225, 346
Systems, 7, 65, 71
Smith, Bessie, 129, 131, 132, 133, 135, 164, 170, 171, 172, 174, 175, 186, 194, 227, 234, 239, 263, 264, 265, 267, 374
Smith, Joe, 172, 177
Smith, Leo, 412, 453
Smith, Mamie, 133, 170, 177, 374
Smith, Willie, 177, 181, 233, 263
Smith, Willie "The Lion," 183, 184
Snow, Valaida, 252
Social conflict, 57
Sogo, 22
Somalia, 22
Song of praise, 37, 67
Songhay, 5, 51
South
    Lower, 75
South Africa, xxxix, 10, 31, 37, 40, 43, 121, 440, 508, 509
    Venda, 10, 37
South America, xxxviii, 62, 156
South Carolina
    Charlestown, 59, 76, 77, 93, 325, 433, 502, 508
    Stono, 59
    Union, 508
South Dakota, 167, 494
Southern University, 483
Southern, Eileen, 67, 79, 95, 108, 238
Spain, 58
    Spanish, 58, 63, 64, 66, 75, 104, 146, 157, 199, 342, 485
Spanier, Muggsy, 213
Spann, Les, 395
Spaulding, James, 462
Spiritual, xix, xx, xxi, xxii, xxiii, xxv, xxix, xxxii, xxxix, 3, 7, 8, 9, 21, 26, 60, 61, 67, 71, 72, 74, 75, 84, 86, 89, 91, 95, 96, 104, 105, 107, 108, 109, 112, 113, 114, 115, 116, 118, 121, 122, 123, 127, 129, 135, 137, 149, 156, 168, 179, 200, 204, 214, 225, 258, 259, 270, 280, 311, 314, 328,

339, 344, 373, 387, 396, 397, 411, 421, 438, 446, 471, 472, 478, 486, 502, 509, 511
Spoonie G, 498
Sprechstimme, 28, 138
Spyro Gyra, 484
St. Cyr, Johnny, 183
St. John the Divine, Cathedral of, 386
Stanley Pool, 23
Stewart, Rex, 282
Stewart, Slam, 161, 191, 256, 381
Stitt, Sonny, 163, 262, 315, 362, 417, 459, 487
Storyville, 104, 146, 147, 148, 215, 216, 220, 321
Strabo, 4
Strata East, 393
Stravinsky, Igor, 118, 140, 141, 278, 279, 293, 302, 303, 316, 335, 351, 385, 430, 455, 481
Strayhorn, Billy, 94, 230, 493
Such, David, 48, 422, 474
Sudan, 14, 22, 25, 28, 32, 33, 37, 508
    NORTHERN, 32
    WESTERN, 32
Sugar cane, 64
Sugar Hill Gang, The, 498
Sugarhill Records, 501
Sumer, 16
Swahili, 395
Sweden, 380
Sweet Basil, 497, 498
Swing, xxii, 83, 150, 157, 160, 178, 204, 222, 223, 224, 234, 236, 244, 245, 246, 275, 281, 287, 320, 372, 386, 388, 479, 513
Switzerland, 78
Syncopation, xxi, 11, 43, 45, 60, 83, 94, 116, 125, 126, 128, 135, 140, 141, 159, 181, 182, 184, 249, 278, 313, 315, 337, 383, 397, 450
Táké, 64

T

Tanglewood, 481, 484
Tanzania, 22
Tapscott, Horace, 469, 470, 491
Tate, Buddy, 262
Tatum, Art, xxxi, xxxvi, 161, 184, 185, 187, 188, 189, 190, 192, 199, 244, 254, 255, 256, 257, 300, 305, 306, 308, 321, 332, 337, 357, 378, 385, 402, 458, 470, 475, 479, 486
Taureg, 11
Taylor, Arthur, 393, 434, 468, 469

Taylor, Cecil, xxx, xxxv, 162, 270, 310, 369, 370, 371, 372, 376, 380, 397, 398, 401, 402, 406, 409, 421, 423, 439, 466, 484, 487, 493

Taylor, Dr. Billy, 250, 357, 378, 488

Tchicai, John, 422

Teagarden, Jack, 172, 199

Temple at Kawa, 17

Temple of Warriors, 62

Tennessee
Whiteville, 385

Terry, Clark, 331, 395, 452, 483

Thielemans, Toots, 493

Third-stream jazz, 498

Thompson, Lucky, 181, 262, 353

Thompson, Wiley, 382

Thornton, Clifford, 423

Threadgill, Henry, 411, 417, 485

Till, Emmett, 349, 350, 433

Timmons, Bobby, 384

Tirro, Frank, 10, 54, 124, 164

Tizol, Juan, 230

Togo, 27, 61

Tolliver, Charles, 377, 393, 423, 426, 483, 494

Torture, 64, 78

Tribal Music, 12

Tribe, 494

Trinidad, 60, 66, 115, 157, 193, 429

Trobiand Islands, 13

Trombone, 104, 144, 148, 149, 152, 153, 159, 160, 183, 202, 215, 217, 220, 221, 226, 230, 231, 248, 308, 329, 330, 343, 355, 377, 378, 385, 411, 418, 458, 480, 482

Trumbauer, Frank, 261

Trumpet, 92, 100, 149, 153, 154, 174, 175, 176, 180, 181, 183, 185, 202, 214, 215, 217, 218, 221, 226, 230, 231, 244, 248, 249, 251, 252, 259, 260, 281, 301, 306, 308, 321, 325, 328, 329, 330, 331, 341, 342, 343, 353, 355, 356, 361, 365, 368, 369, 378, 380, 384, 385, 404, 411, 412, 426, 429, 442, 445, 446, 458, 470, 481, 483

Tubman, Harriet, 77, 94

Tucker, St. George, 77

Turner, Nat, 72, 270

Turre, Steve, 482, 497

Turrentine, Stanley, 460, 474

Tusi, 23

Tutankhamen, 16

Tutu, Bishop Desmond, xxxix, 508, 509

Tyner, McCoy, 223, 377, 404, 426, 442, 457, 458, 466, 493

Tyson, Mike, 508, 509

U

Uganda, 11, 22

Ulmer, James Blood, 482

Underground Railroad, 61, 77, 84, 94

United States, xx, xxxi, xxxiii, 1, 61, 66, 67, 70, 74, 75, 76, 79, 88, 92, 99, 118, 137, 143, 156, 157, 162, 164, 169, 176, 177, 188, 193, 197, 202, 206, 208, 213, 223, 237, 247, 251, 280, 281, 291, 295, 299, 308, 317, 352, 380, 384, 392, 422, 423, 424, 428, 431, 432, 441, 450, 461, 466, 470, 505, 508, 509, 510

Upper Volta, 27, 44

Uptown Enterprises, 501

V

Vai, 28

Vaudeville, 100, 137, 472

Vaughan, Sarah, 308, 326, 327, 334, 338, 339, 403

Ventura, Charlie, 262

Verve Records, 498

Vibraphone, 191, 385, 404, 480

Violin, 68, 92, 101, 133, 149, 154, 158, 162, 252, 262, 374, 401, 412, 453, 461, 462, 480, 481, 490, 492, 494, 497

Virginia, 59, 69, 77, 93, 110, 111, 154, 173, 250, 267, 387, 460

Vivaldi, Antonio, 72

Vocalists, 9, 11, 38, 46, 84, 85, 86, 127, 129, 131, 170, 171, 173, 174, 175, 185, 224, 233, 251, 263, 264, 281, 283, 296, 330, 334, 338, 339, 340, 358, 383, 386, 403, 417, 438, 445, 465, 490

Vodun, 63, 114, 200

Voice, xxxix, 3, 39, 60, 61, 64, 77, 81, 83, 84, 85, 86, 99, 128, 129, 130, 133, 135, 154, 159, 163, 164, 171, 172, 179, 200, 231, 248, 266, 269, 283, 285, 295, 296, 302, 338, 339, 358, 369, 374, 382, 383, 405, 413, 422, 465, 495

Voodoo, xxiii, 63, 72, 74, 75, 90, 104, 111, 112, 113, 114, 115, 127, 130, 156, 170, 200, 201, 203, 240

W

Walker, George, 505

Wall Street Journal, 479, 485, 513

Waller, Fats, xxvi, xxxi, 183, 184, 188, 190, 199, 205, 206, 211, 219, 235, 239, 240, 244, 246, 248, 256, 300, 370

Ward, W. E. F., 48, 475

Washington, Grover, 460

Watisu, 23, 33, 37

Watkins, Julius, 395

Watrous, Peter, 481, 513

WDET, 494

Webb, Chick, 158, 228, 267, 268, 283, 321, 330, 358, 384, 461

Webster, Ben, 228, 230, 262, 263, 300, 405, 422, 459

West India, 75, 76, 113, 193, 200

Weston, Randy, 329, 330, 392, 393, 413, 434, 458, 479

White, Andrew, xxx, 393

Whitehead, Kevin, 488, 489, 513

Whiteman, Paul, xxxv, 199, 222, 223, 224, 228, 233, 237, 238, 274, 281, 344, 469, 480

Williams, Bishop Norman, 492

Williams, Cootie, 281, 333, 422

Williams, Mary Lou, xxxv, 184, 187, 188, 257, 258, 259, 270, 282, 308, 321, 330, 331, 334, 335, 342, 384, 387, 402, 426, 438, 487, 507

Williams, Richard, 395

Williams, Tony, 163, 358, 455

Wilmer, Valerie, 369, 393, 434, 475

Wilson, Cassandra, 498

Wilson, Gerald, 233, 329, 330, 426

Wilson, Phillip, 412, 413

Wilson, Teddy, 265, 266, 281, 283, 357, 427

Winding, Kai, 343

Winter, Johnny, 501

Wisconsin, 167, 423, 494

Wise, Pamela, xxxii, 494

Witchcraft, xxiii, 33, 46, 77, 78, 115, 232, 329

Women, xxiv, xxix, xxxiii, xxxiv, xxxvi, xxxix, 8, 9, 10, 11, 12, 13, 16, 17, 20, 21, 22, 25, 35, 43, 45, 57, 61, 68, 69, 70, 76, 78, 81, 84, 85, 86, 88, 92, 94, 100, 101, 102, 103, 112, 114, 117, 121, 126, 131, 132, 133, 136, 139, 146, 153, 154, 167, 169, 170, 172, 173, 174, 178, 179, 186, 197, 200, 201, 232, 237, 243, 246, 247, 249, 250, 251, 252, 253, 258, 259, 263, 264, 266, 298, 306, 319, 323, 325, 334, 340, 341, 342, 345, 349, 352, 358, 367, 383, 385, 399, 404, 415, 426, 427, 428, 431, 432, 449, 465, 466, 480, 497

African, 9, 10, 86

Daughters, 21, 50, 52, 68, 79, 253, 320, 335, 427, 431

Negro, 68

Sexism, 1, xxxiv, xxxvi, xxxviii, xxxix, 9, 12, 13, 47, 57, 154, 502

Witchcraft, 77, 78

Woods, Phil, 315, 488, 506

Work song, xxiii, 36, 37, 60, 61, 67, 71, 73, 74, 84, 86, 89, 93, 129, 156, 225, 471

World Saxophone Quartet, 455, 480

Wright, Frank, 440

X

X, Malcolm, 1, 431, 507, 509

Xylophone, 11, 24, 37, 42, 46

  Manza, 24

  Sanza, 14, 24, 25, 31, 41

Y

Yale College, 73

Yale Collegiate School, 73

Yoruba, 28, 30, 34, 63, 67, 114, 157, 429, 467, 468

Young, Lester, 129, 181, 228, 234, 259, 260, 261, 262, 265, 267, 281, 307, 308, 355, 362, 363, 386, 405, 407, 454, 459, 473

Z

Zaire, 23

Zambezi River, 62

Zimbabwe, 41, 508

Zlet, 28